Children's
Literature
Review

Guide to Gale Literary Criticism Series

When you need to review criticism of literary works, these are the Gale series to use:

If the author's death date is: **You should turn to:**

After Dec. 31, 1959
(or author is still living)

CONTEMPORARY LITERARY CRITICISM

for example: Jorge Luis Borges, Anthony Burgess,
William Faulkner, Mary Gordon,
Ernest Hemingway, Iris Murdoch

1900 through 1959

TWENTIETH-CENTURY LITERARY CRITICISM

for example: Willa Cather, F. Scott Fitzgerald,
Henry James, Mark Twain, Virginia Woolf

1800 through 1899

NINETEENTH-CENTURY LITERATURE CRITICISM

for example: Fedor Dostoevski, Nathaniel Hawthorne,
George Sand, William Wordsworth

1400 through 1799

LITERATURE CRITICISM FROM 1400 TO 1800
(excluding Shakespeare)

for example: Anne Bradstreet, Daniel Defoe,
Alexander Pope, François Rabelais,
Jonathan Swift, Phillis Wheatley

SHAKESPEAREAN CRITICISM

Shakespeare's plays and poetry

Antiquity through 1399

CLASSICAL AND MEDIEVAL LITERATURE CRITICISM

for example: Dante, Homer, Plato, Sophocles, Vergil,
the Beowulf Poet

Gale also publishes related criticism series:

CHILDREN'S LITERATURE REVIEW

This series covers authors of all eras who have written for
the preschool through high school audience.

SHORT STORY CRITICISM

This series covers the major short fiction writers of all nationalities
and periods of literary history.

ISSN 0362-4145

volume 19

Children's Literature Review

Excerpts from Reviews,
Criticism, and Commentary
on Books for Children
and Young People

Gerard J. Senick
Editor

Sharon R. Gunton
Associate Editor

 *Gale Research Inc.*

DETROIT • NEW YORK • FORT LAUDERDALE • LONDON

STAFF

Gerard J. Senick, *Editor*

Sharon R. Gunton, *Associate Editor*

Susan Miller Harig, Melissa Reiff Hug, Motoko Fujishiro Huthwaite, *Assistant Editors*

Jeanne A. Gough, *Permissions & Production Manager*
Linda M. Pugliese, *Production Supervisor*
Jennifer E. Gale, Suzanne Powers, Maureen A. Puhl, Lee Ann Welsh, *Editorial Associates*
Donna Craft, Christine A. Galbraith, David G. Oblender, Linda M. Ross, *Editorial Assistants*

Victoria B. Cariappa, *Research Supervisor*
Karen D. Kaus, Eric Priehs, Maureen Richards, Mary D. Wise, *Editorial Associates*
H. Nelson Fields, Rogene M. Fisher, Judy L. Gale, Jill M. Ohorodnik, Filomena Sgambati, *Editorial Assistants*

Sandra C. Davis, *Permissions Supervisor (Text)*
H. Diane Cooper, Kathy Grell, Josephine M. Keene, Kimberly F. Smilay, *Permissions Associates*
Maria Franklin, Lisa M. Lantz, Camille P. Robinson, Shalice Shah, Denise M. Singleton, *Permissions Assistants*

Patricia A. Seefelt, *Permissions Supervisor (Pictures)*
Margaret A. Chamberlain, *Permissions Associate*
Pamela A. Hayes, Lillian Quickley, *Permissions Assistants*

Mary Beth Trimper, *Production Manager*
Evi Seoud, *Assistant Production Manager*

Arthur Chartow, *Art Director*
C. J. Jonik, *Keyliner*

Laura Bryant, *Production Supervisor*
Louise Gagné, *Internal Production Associate*
Michelle M. Stepherson, *Data Entry Associate*
Kelly L. Krust, Sharana Wier, *Internal Production Assistants*

Library of Congress Catalog Card Number 76-643301
ISBN 0-8103-2779-1
ISSN 0362-4145

Printed in the United States of America

Contents

Preface

As children's literature has evolved into both a respected branch of creative writing and a successful industry, literary criticism has documented and influenced each stage of its growth. Critics have recorded the literary development of individual authors as well as the trends and controversies that resulted from changes in values and attitudes, especially as they concerned children. While defining a philosophy of children's literature, critics developed a scholarship that balances an appreciation of children and an awareness of their needs with standards for literary quality much like those required by critics of adult literature. *Children's Literature Review (CLR)* is designed to provide a permanent, accessible record of this ongoing scholarship. Those responsible for bringing children and books together can now make informed choices when selecting reading materials for the young.

Scope of the Series

Each volume of *CLR* contains excerpts from published criticism on the works of authors and illustrators who create books for children from preschool through high school. The author list for each volume is international in scope and represents the variety of genres covered by children's literature—picture books, fiction, nonfiction, poetry, folklore, and drama. The works of approximately twenty authors of all eras are represented in each volume. Although earlier volumes of *CLR* emphasized critical material published after 1960, successive volumes have expanded their coverage to encompass criticism written before 1960. Since many of the authors included in *CLR* are living and continue to write, it is necessary to update their entries periodically. Thus, future volumes will supplement the entries of selected authors covered in earlier volumes as well as include criticism on the works of authors new to the series.

Organization of the Book

An author section consists of the following elements: author heading, author portrait, author introduction, excerpts of criticism (each followed by a bibliographical citation), and illustrations, when available.

- The **author heading** consists of the author's full name followed by birth and death dates. The portion of the name outside the parentheses denotes the form under which the author is most frequently published. If the majority of the author's works for children were written under a pseudonym, the pseudonym will be listed in the author heading and the real name given on the first line of the author introduction. Also located at the beginning of the introduction are any other pseudonyms used by the author in writing for children and any name variations, including transliterated forms for authors whose languages use nonroman alphabets. Uncertainty as to a birth or death date is indicated by question marks.

- An **author portrait** is included when available.

- The **author introduction** contains information designed to introduce an author to *CLR* users by presenting an overview of the author's themes and styles, occasional biographical facts that relate to the author's literary career or critical responses to the author's works, and information about major awards and prizes the author has received. Where applicable, introductions conclude with references to additional entries in biographical and critical reference series published by Gale Research Inc. These sources include past volumes of *CLR* as well as *Authors & Artists for Young Adults, Contemporary Authors, Contemporary Literary Criticism, Dictionary of Literary Biography, Nineteenth-Century Literature Criticism, Short Story Criticism, Something about the Author, Something about the Author Autobiography Series, Twentieth-Century Literary Criticism,* and *Yesterday's Authors of Books for Children.*

- **Criticism** is located in three sections: **author's commentary** and **general commentary** (when available) and within individual **title entries,** which are preceded by **title entry headings.** Criticism is arranged chronologically within each section. Titles by authors being profiled are highlighted in boldface type within the text for easier access by readers.

The **author's commentary** presents background material written by the author or by an interviewer. This commentary may cover a specific work or several works. Author's commentary on more than one work appears after the author introduction, while commentary on an individual book follows the title entry heading.

The **general commentary** consists of critical excerpts that consider more than one work by the author or illustrator being profiled. General commentary is preceded by the critic's name in boldface type or, in the case of unsigned criticism, by the title of the journal. Occasionally, *CLR* features entries that emphasize general criticism on the overall career of an author or illustrator. When appropriate, a selection of reviews is included to supplement the general commentary.

Title entry headings precede the criticism on a title and cite publication information on the work being reviewed. Title headings list the title of the work as it appeared in its country of origin; titles in languages using nonroman alphabets are transliterated. If the original title is in a language other than English, the title of the first English-language translation follows in brackets. The first available publication date of each work is listed in parentheses following the title. Differing U.S. and British titles of works originally published in English follow the publication date within the parentheses.

Title entries consist of critical excerpts on the author's individual works, arranged chronologically by publication date. The entries generally contain two to six reviews per title, depending on the stature of the book and the amount of criticism it has generated. The editors select titles that reflect the entire scope of the author's literary contribution, covering each genre and subject. An effort is made to reprint criticism that represents the full range of each title's reception—from the year of its initial publication to current assessments. Thus, the reader is provided with a record of the author's critical history. Publication information (such as publisher names and book prices) and parenthetical numerical references (such as footnotes or page and line references to specific editions of works) have been deleted at the editor's discretion to provide smoother reading of the text.

Entries on authors who are also illustrators will occasionally feature commentary on selected works illustrated but not written by the author being profiled. These works are strongly associated with the illustrator and have received critical acclaim for their art. By including critical comment on works of this type, the editors wish to provide a more complete representation of the author's total career. Criticism on these works has been chosen to stress artistic, rather than literary, contributions. Title entry headings for works illustrated by the author being profiled are arranged chronologically within the entry by date of publication and include notes identifying the author of the illustrated work. In order to provide easier access for users, all titles illustrated by the subject of the entry will be boldfaced.

CLR also includes entries on prominent illustrators who have contributed to the field of children's literature. These entries are designed to represent the development of the illustrator as an artist rather than as a literary stylist. The illustrator's section is organized like that of an author, with two exceptions: the introduction presents an overview of the illustrator's styles and techniques rather than outlining his or her literary background, and the commentary written by the illustrator on his or her works is called illustrator's commentary rather than author's commentary. Title entry headings are followed by explanatory notes identifying the author of the illustrated work. All titles of books containing illustrations by the artist being profiled as well as individual illustrations from these books are highlighted in boldface type.

- Selected excerpts are preceded by **explanatory notes,** which provide information on the critic or work of criticism to enhance the reader's understanding of the excerpt.

- A complete **bibliographical citation** designed to facilitate the location of the original book or article follows each piece of criticism.

- Numerous **illustrations** are featured in *CLR*. For entries on illustrators, an effort has been made to include illustrations that reflect the characteristics discussed in the criticism. Entries on major authors who do not illustrate their own works may also include photographs and other illustrative material pertinent to the authors' careers.

Other Features

- An **acknowledgments,** which immediately follows the preface, lists the sources from which material has been reprinted in the volume. It does not, however, list every book or periodical consulted for the volume.

- The **cumulative index to authors** lists authors who have appeared in *CLR* and includes cross-references to *Authors & Artists for Young Adults, Contemporary Authors, Contemporary Literary Criticism, Dictionary of Literary Biography, Nineteenth-Century Literature Criticism, Short Story Criticism, Something about the Author, Something about the Author Autobiography Series, Twentieth-Century Literary Criticism,* and *Yesterday's Authors of Books for Children.*

- The **cumulative nationality index** lists authors alphabetically under their respective nationalities. Author names are followed by the volume number(s) in which they appear. Authors who have changed citizenship or whose current citizenship is not reflected in biographical sources appear under both their original nationality and that of their current residence.

- The **cumulative title index** lists titles covered in *CLR* followed by the volume and page number where criticism begins.

Suggestions Are Welcome

In response to various suggestions, several features have been added to *CLR* since the series began, including author entries on retellers of traditional literature as well as those who have been the first to record oral tales and other folklore; entries on prominent illustrators featuring commentary on their styles and techniques; entries on authors whose works are considered controversial or have been challenged; occasional entries devoted to criticism on a single work by a major author; explanatory notes that provide information on the critic or work of criticism to enhance the usefulness of the excerpt; more extensive illustrative material, such as holographs of manuscript pages and photographs of people and places pertinent to the authors' careers; a cumulative nationality index for easy access to authors by nationality; and occasional guest essays written specifically for *CLR* by prominent critics on subjects of their choice.

Readers who wish to suggest authors to appear in future volumes, or who have other suggestions, are cordially invited to write the editor or to call our toll-free number: 1-800-347-GALE.

Acknowledgments

The editors wish to thank the copyright holders of the excerpted criticism included in this volume, the permissions managers of many book and magazine publishing companies for assisting us in securing reprint rights, and Anthony Bogucki for assistance with copyright research. We are also grateful to the staffs of the Detroit Public Library, the Library of Congress, the University of Detroit Library, the University of Michigan Library, and the Wayne State University Library for making their resources available to us. Following is a list of the copyright holders who have granted us permission to reprint material in this volume of *CLR*. Every effort has been made to trace copyright, but if omissions have been made, please let us know.

COPYRIGHTED EXCERPTS IN *CLR*, VOLUME 19, WERE REPRINTED FROM THE FOLLOWING PERIODICALS:

ALAN Review, v. 11, Winter, 1984. Reprinted by permission of the publisher.—*Appraisal: Children's Science Books,* v. 7, Fall, 1974; v. 9, Winter, 1976; v. 9, Fall, 1976; v. 10, Spring, 1977; v. 10, Fall, 1977; v. 12, Spring, 1979; v. 12, Winter, 1979; v. 13, Spring, 1980; v. 13, Winter, 1980. Copyright © 1974, 1976, 1977, 1979, 1980 by the Children's Science Book Review Committee. All reprinted by permission of the publisher.—*Appraisal: Science Books for Young People,* v. 14, Spring, 1981; v. 15, Winter, 1982; Fall, 1982; v. 16, Winter, 1983; v. 16, Fall, 1983; v. 17, Fall, 1984; v. 18, Spring, 1985; v. 18, Autumn, 1985; v. 19, Winter, 1986; v. 19, Summer, 1986; v. 20, Winter, 1987; v. 20, Fall, 1987; v. 21, Spring, 1988. Copyright © 1981, 1982, 1983, 1984, 1985, 1986, 1987, 1988 by the Children's Science Book Review Committee.—*Best Sellers,* v. 25, August 15, 1965. Copyright 1965, by the University of Scranton. Reprinted by permission of the publisher./ v. 37, October, 1977; v. 38, April, 1978; v. 40, November, 1980; v. 42, June, 1982; v. 45, July, 1985; v. 45, September, 1985; v. 45, January, 1986; v. 46, June, 1986. Copyright © 1977, 1978, 1980, 1982, 1985, 1986 by Helen Dwight Reid Educational Foundation. All reprinted by permission of the publisher.—*The Black Scholar,* v. 13, Summer, 1982. Copyright 1982 by *The Black Scholar.* Reprinted by permission of the publisher.—*The Book Report: The Journal for Junior and Senior High School Librarians,* v. 2, January-February, 1984. © copyright 1984 by Linworth Publishing, Inc. Reprinted by permission of the publisher.—*Book Week—New York Herald Tribune,* November 13, 1966. © 1966, *The Washington Post.* Reprinted by permission of the publisher.—*Book Week—The Sunday Herald Tribune,* September 29, 1963; November 1, 1964; November 21, 1965. © 1963, 1964, 1965, *The Washington Post.* All reprinted by permission of the publisher.—*Book Week—Chicago Tribune,* November 5, 1967 for "Doctor of the Year" by Digby Whitman. © 1967 Postrib Corp. Reprinted by permission of the author.—*Booklist,* v. 73, October 1, 1976; v. 73, October 15, 1976; v. 73, November 1, 1976; v. 73, February 1, 1977; v. 73, April 15, 1977; v. 74, April 1, 1978; v. 75, October 15, 1978; v. 75, December 1, 1978; v. 76, May 1, 1980; v. 78, November 15, 1981; v. 78, December 1, 1981; v. 78, January 1, 1982; v. 78, June 15, 1982; v. 79, October 1, 1982; v. 80, October 15, 1983; v. 80, June 1, 1984; v. 81, November 1, 1984; v. 81, December 1, 1984; v. 81, April 1, 1985; v. 81, June 15, 1985; v. 82, October 1, 1985; v. 82, January 15, 1986; v. 82, February 15, 1986; v. 82, April 15, 1986; v. 84, February 1, 1988; v. 84, April 1, 1988. Copyright © 1976, 1977, 1978, 1980, 1981, 1982, 1983, 1984, 1985, 1986, 1988 by the American Library Association. All reprinted by permission of the publisher.—*The Bookman,* London, v. LXVII, December, 1924.—*Books,* New York, November 12, 1961; November 11, 1962. © 1961, 1962 I.H.T. Corporation. Both reprinted by permission of the publisher.—*Books for Keeps,* n. 44, May, 1987. © School Bookshop Association 1987. Reprinted by permission of the publisher.—*Books for Young People,* v. 1, December, 1987. All rights reserved. Reprinted by permission of the publisher.—*Books for Your Children,* v. 20, Spring, 1985; v. 23, Spring, 1988. © *Books for Your Children* 1985, 1988. Both reprinted by permission of the publisher.—*Books in Canada,* v. 8, December, 1979 for "Small Wonders" by Mary Ainslie Smith; v. 10, October, 1981 for a review of "Jonathan Cleaned Up—Then He Heard a Sound" by Mary Ainslie Smith; v. 11, August-September, 1982 for a review of "The Boy in the Drawer" by Mary Ainslie Smith. All reprinted by permission of the author.—*Books: Journal of the National Book League,* Winter, 1970 for "Writers and Writing" by Joan Aiken. Copyright © 1970 John Aiken Enterprises Ltd. Reprinted by permission of Brandt & Brandt Literary Agents, Inc.—*British Book News,* Autumn, 1980; March, 1986. © *British Book News,* 1980, 1986. Both courtesy of *British Book News.*—*British Book News Children's Books,* March, 1986; December, 1987. © The British Council, 1986, 1987. All reprinted by permission of the publisher.—*Bulletin of the Center for Children's Books,* v. XVI, May, 1963; v. XVIII, February, 1965; v. 24, December, 1970; v. 25, April, 1972; v. 25, May, 1972; v. 27, April, 1974; v. 28, May, 1975; v. 31, October, 1977; v. 31, February, 1978; v. 32, February, 1979; v. 33, July-August, 1980; v. 34, September, 1980; v. 34, November, 1980; v. 35, September, 1981; v. 36, July-August, 1983; v. 37, December, 1983; v. 37, June, 1984; v. 38, February, 1985; v. 39, September, 1985; v. 39, October, 1985; v. 39, November, 1985; v. 39, March, 1986; v. 39, April, 1986; v. 39, May, 1986; v. 40, June, 1987; v. 40, July-August, 1987; v. 41, December, 1987; v. 41, January, 1988; v. 41, April, 1988; v. 41, May, 1988. Copyright © 1963, 1965, 1970, 1972, 1974, 1975, 1977, 1978, 1979, 1980, 1981, 1983, 1984, 1985, 1986, 1987, 1988 by The University of Chicago. All reprinted by permission of The University of Chicago Press.—*Canadian Children's Literature,* n. 26, 1982 for a review of "The Paper Bag Princess" and others by Joan McGrath; n. 30, 1983 for "Munschkinland Revisited" by

Children's
Literature
Review

Joan (Delano) Aiken

1924-

English author of fiction, picture books, and short stories; poet; dramatist; and reteller.

Aiken is a versatile, well-respected author who has written in nearly every genre of children's literature. Despite its diversity, all of her work is characterized by vivid characterization, evocative imagery, and fantastic happenings. Her shorter books for preschool and elementary-grade children feature special animals and their humorous antics; notable examples are Aiken's "Mortimer" tales, originally written for the BBC television program "Jackanory." These stories tell of a small but competent girl and her mischievous pet raven who subject their family to outrageous predicaments resulting from his devilry. Aiken's short stories, written for the early elementary grades and up, portray a realistic, contemporary world imbued with disquieting supernatural and fantasy elements. Ranging from the humorous to the horrific, these stories are noted for their striking originality. Aiken is, however, probably best known for her longer fiction, read mainly by readers from nine to thirteen years of age. Often compared to the works of Charles Dickens for their melodramatic plots and memorable characters, these books take place in an imaginary past and, like the best picaresque novels, are packed with adventure and heroic exploits. In her series featuring the resourceful London street urchin Dido Twite, for instance, Aiken devises her own version of early nineteenth-century England, where a fictitious Stuart king reigns over a country beset by constant threats, including Hanoverian rebels determined to assassinate him. While embroiled in such challenging situations, Aiken's protagonists—feisty, intelligent children—face unspeakably evil adult opponents; despite the odds, nonetheless, good wins out. As Aiken has said of her writing: "On the whole, my books are concerned with children tackling the problem of an adult world in which things have gone wrong; I suppose this is a kind of exposition of a feeling that things in the real world have gone badly wrong, and our only hope is that our children will be able to put them right."

Aiken received the Lewis Carroll Shelf Award in 1965 for *The Wolves of Willoughby Chase,* the Guardian Award in 1969 for *The Whispering Mountain,* which was also designated a Carnegie Medal honor book in 1968, and the Edgar Allan Poe Award in 1972 for *Night Fall.*

(See also *CLR,* Vol. 1; *Contemporary Literary Criticism,* Vol. 35; *Something about the Author,* Vols. 2, 30; *Something about the Author Autobiography Series,* Vol. 1; *Contemporary Authors New Revision Series,* Vol. 4; and *Contemporary Authors,* Vols. 9-12, rev. ed.)

AUTHOR'S COMMENTARY

[*The following excerpt originally appeared as "Purely for Love" in the Winter 1970 issue of* Books: Journal of the National Book League.]

I for one feel strongly that the ideal writer for children should do something else most of the time. Writing for children should not be a full-time job. Let me repeat that because it is probably the most important thing I have to say here: writing for children should not be a full-time job. . . . [That's one] thing Dickens, Masefield, de la Mare, Lewis Carroll, Ruskin, Kipling, Hans Andersen and William Blake had in common—children's writing was a sideline with them. (If indeed they were really writing for children at any time?) They had plenty of other professional interests. Which meant, first, that their writing was enriched by their other activities, knowledge, background—that it had plenty of depth; second, that they wrote, when they did write for children, purely for love. And that is the way children's writing should be done; it should not be done for any other reason. (p. 146)

Another reason why children's writers should have some other, predominant occupation, is simply because children have a greater respect for them if they do. Children, bless their good sound sense, are naturally suspicious of adults who devote themselves to nothing but children. For one thing, such adults are too boringly familiar—there aren't any mysteries about them. Don't you remember how at school the teachers who disappeared to their own pursuits after school were respected and how the ones who were always at hand doing things with the children as if they had nothing

1

else to do, no better way of occupying themselves were despised? . . .

When I was a child, one of my greatest pleasures was listening to my elder brother play the piano. He was a lot older and he played pretty well. But the point was that he was playing for his benefit, not for mine. Part of my pleasure was the feeling that it was a free gift, that my brother and I were independent of one another. Another part was the understanding that some of the music was beyond my scope, which intensified my enjoyment of the easier bits. If my brother had said, "I'll play for you now, choose what you'd like," I would have been not only embarrassed and nonplussed, but also horribly constricted by such a gesture, it would have completely changed the whole experience. I think the essence of the very best children's literature is this understanding that it is a free gift—no, not a gift, a treasure trove—tossed out casually from the richness of a much larger store. Of course there are exceptions to this generalisation—I can think of several fine children's writers now at work who do nothing else at *present*—but my feeling is that they have the capacity to, and probably will do something else in due course. (p. 147)

The notion of any restraints or controls at all over writers is a horrifying one, I'm glad to think. And yet on the other side of the Iron Curtain such controls are in force. And in the field of children's literature, both in this country and America, I have come across educators who made fairly plain their feeling that some children's writers are a bunch of tiresome anarchists who could perfectly well be a bit more helpful if they chose, in the way of incorporating educational material and acceptable ethics into their writing. As if they were a kind of hot-drink vending machine and you had only to press the right knob to produce an appropriately flavoured bit of nourishment. I do not agree with this point of view. I do not think it is possible to exercise any control over what a creative artist produces, without the risk of wrecking the product. . . .

I would not dream of making suggestions to other writers as to what they should write. But I do have strong views as to the kind of intentions one should *not* have when setting out to write anything for children. Childhood is so desperately short, and becoming shorter all the time: they are reading adult novels at 14. . . . Furthermore, children have so little reading-time, compared with adults, and that is growing less—there's school, there's bedtime, all the extracurricular activities they have now. I am not decrying adventure playgrounds and drama groups and play classes and organised camp holidays, I think they are splendid—even television has its points—but all this means a loss of reading-time, and *that* means that when they do read, it is really a wicked shame if they waste any time at all reading what I am going to group under the heading of Filboid Studge. *Filboid Studge,* if you recall, was the title of a short story by Saki about a breakfast food which was so dull and tasteless that it sold extremely well because everybody believed that it *must* be good for them. (p. 149)

It is lucky that at least children have a strong natural resistance to phoney morality. They can see through the adult with some moral axe to grind almost before he opens his mouth—the smaller the child, the sharper the instinct. I suppose it's the same kind of ESP that one finds in animals—the telepathy that transmits to one's cat exactly which page of the Sunday paper one wishes to read so that he can go and sit on it. Small children have this to a marked degree. You have only to say, "Eat your nice spinach" for a negative reaction

to be triggered off. You don't even have to add "because it's good for you." They pick that up out of the atmosphere. They sense at once when we want them to do something because it suits *us.* (pp. 149-50)

On account of this tough natural resistance, I'm not bothered about hypocritical moral messages. . . . [The following quotation from *Jane Eyre*] is a beautiful example of the calm and ruthless logic with which children bypass any bit of moral teaching they are not going to concern themselves with.

> "What must you do to avoid going to hell?"
> "I must keep in good health and not die."

It's an example of lateral thinking, anticipating Edward de Bono by one hundred and twenty years.

Unfortunately, as children grow older, this faculty becomes blunted because of education. So much of education consists of having inexplicable things done at one for obscure reasons, that it's no wonder the victims presently almost cease to resist. I can see that some education is necessary, just as the wheel is necessary. We have to learn to get into gear with the rest of the world. But it is remarkable how little education one *can* get along on. (p. 150)

It is a dangerous thing to decry education. But I feel there's something wrong with our whole attitude to it. The trouble is, we have taken away the role of children in the adult world. Instead of being with their parents, learning how: helping on the farm, blowing the forge fire, making flint arrowheads with the grownups, as would be natural, they are all shoved off together into a corner. And what happens then? We have to find them something to do to keep them out of mischief. I think too much—far, far too much—of education is still fundamentally just this: something cooked up to keep children out of their parents' hair till they are grown. I don't see how you can learn to have a spontaneous, creative, intelligent, sensitive reaction to the world when for your first six or twelve or eighteen years there is such a lot of this element of hypocrisy in how you are treated. And the worst of it is that this element is not only present in education, but in reading-matter too.

There's a whole range of it—from *The Awfully Sudden Death of Martha G—*, through *A Hundred and One Things to Do on a Wet Saturday and Not Plague Daddy,* and *Sue Jones Has a Super Time as Student Nurse,* to the novels, some of them quite good, intended to show teenagers how to adjust to the colour problem and keep calm through parents' divorce and the death of poor Fido. I even saw in a publisher's catalogue a series of situation books for *under-sixes.* I suppose they serve some purpose. But just the same I count them as Filboid Studge. And how insulting they are! Adults are not expected to buy books called *Mrs. Sue Jones—Alcoholic's Wife,* or *A Hundred and One Ways to Lose Your Job and Keep Calm.* Maybe some adults would be better adjusted if they did. It's true people will swallow things wrapped in this form of fictional jam. They will swallow it because they have been conditioned to it all their lives, because from the first primer their reading has become more and more impure—I'm not using impure in the sense of obscene, but in the sense of being written with a concealed purpose. In that same publisher's catalogue, advertising a series of basic vocabulary classics aimed at backward readers, the blurb said that in secondary schools a surprising number of children read nothing for pleasure except comics. Can you wonder, if the poor things have had nothing but situation books handed out to them?

If you are bombarded with Filboid Studge, either you go on strike, or you become dulled, you cease to recognise propaganda when you hear it. I'm sure if children's reading were kept unadulterated, they would be quicker and clearer-minded as adults, more confident in making judgements for themselves.

I can see an objection coming up here—some of the greatest and best known children's books have a moral message. C. S. Lewis and George MacDonald: the Christian religion. Kipling: How to maintain the British Empire. Arthur Ransome: How to get along without parents just the same as if they were there. They had a moral message mostly because they were rooted in the nineteenth century when moral messages came naturally; everybody wore them like bustles. As we get farther and farther away from the nineteenth century the moral message has become more cautious and oblique, though it is still often there. Don't mistake me—I'm not opposed to a moral if it is truly felt—you can't have life without opinions, you can't have behaviour without character. I just don't like tongue-in-cheek stuff. Konrad Lorenz said somewhere that our intuitive judgements of people are partly based on their linguistic habits which is an interesting idea and I'm sure it is true. I certainly find it true in myself and not only on an intuitive level: from someone who uses sloppy secondhand phrases I would expect sloppy inconsiderate behaviour, whereas a person who uses vigorous, thoughtful, individual language will apply the same care to his behaviour—and this applies with double force to the written word. What I mean is that the author of a really well written book needn't worry about inserting some synthetic moral message—it will *be* there, embodied in the whole structure of the book. (pp. 150-52)

Really good writing for children should come out with the force of Niagara, it ought to be concentrated; it needs to have everything that is in adult writing squeezed into a smaller compass. I mean that both literally and metaphorically: in a form adapted to children's capacities, and at shorter length, because of this shortage of reading-time. But the emotional range ought to be the same, if not greater; children's emotions are just as powerful as those of adults, and more compressed, since children have less means of expressing themselves, and less capacity for self-analysis. The Victorians really had a point with all those deathbed scenes. (p. 152)

[There] is another thing a children's story ought to do, I suppose, put things in perspective; if you think about it, a story is the first step towards abstract thought. It is placing yourself on one side and looking at events from a distance; in psychological terms, mixing primary mental process—dream-imagery, wish-fulfilling fantasy—with secondary process—verbalisation, adaptation to reality, logic. A story is like a *roux* in cookery: by the chemical process of rubbing fat into dry flour you can persuade it to mix with a liquid. So by means of a story you can combine dream with reality and make something nourishing. I think this mixing dream with reality, far from confusing children, helps them to define the areas of both.

I said something in my talk at Exeter last year which I would like to repeat here: it is about the texture of children's books. Children read in a totally different way from adults. It's a newer activity for them. To begin with they have to be wooed and kept involved. And then, when they are involved, reading isn't just a relaxation for them, something to be done after work. It's a real activity. . . . Children's reading-matter is going to be subjected to all sorts of strains and tensions, it needs to be able to stand up to this at every point. Children read the same book over and over, or just make for the bits they like best, or read the book backwards; there's a psychological explanation for all this re-reading, apparently it fulfills a need for security, a need to make sure the story is still there. (Or you could just call it love, of course.) And children may read very slowly or very fast; they gulp down books or chew them, they believe passionately in the characters and identify with them, they really participate. In order to stand up to all this wear and tear a book need almost be tested in a wind-tunnel before being launched. Furthermore, if it is going to be read and re-read, by the same child, over a span of perhaps ten years—my children certainly did this—it needs to have something new to offer at each re-reading. It is impossible to predict what a child's mind will seize on at any stage. . . . A lot of children will miss humour in a story at first reading while they concentrate on the plot. Richness of language, symbolism, character—all these emerge at later readings. Conversely anything poor or meretricious or cheap may be missed while attention is held by the excitement of the story, but sticks out like a sore thumb on a later reading. Reading aloud, of course, is the ultimate test—an absolutely basic one for a children's book. . . . (pp. 152-53)

Another factor which I think is of tremendous importance in this enrichment of texture is a sense of mystery and things left unexplained—references that are not followed up, incidents and behaviour that have to be puzzled over, language that is going to stretch the reader's mind and vocabulary. (p. 153)

[It] is not surprising [children] are fascinated by mysteries. An immense proportion of the world they live in, after all, must be mysterious to them, since they are expected to take most adult behaviour on trust, without explanations—not only adult behaviour but anything else that adults themselves can't explain or haven't time to account for. And there's no doubt that children do love mysteries; they are poets, too; they have a natural affinity for the crazy logic of magic. And they like open endings that they can keep in mind and ponder.

Since children's reading needs richness and mystery, and a sense of intense pleasure, and dedication, and powerful emotion, and an intricate story, and fine language, and humour—it is plain that only one lot of people are competent to write for children. They, of course, are poets—or at least people with the mental make-up of poets: writers who can condense experience and make it meaningful by the use of symbols. . . .

I've said that I don't think children ought to be filled with Filboid Studge. And that the best children's writers should be mostly otherwise occupied, and should be poets. And I've ruminated a bit about what should be written or not be written. But—except insofar as what I've said may have been a conscious summing-up of unconscious processes—I can't claim to practise what I preach. There's a relevant fairy tale, which crops up in many folklores, so it must be a pretty basic message, the one about the helpful pixies. I expect you remember it. Mysterious little helpers do the farmwife's work for her every night—spin the flax, collect the eggs, make the butter, and so forth; but when she watches and discovers who is helping her and, to reward them, makes all tiny suits of clothes, they put on the clothes, they are pleased, to be sure, and dance all about, but that's the end of them; they disappear and never return. That tale is a powerful warning against too much tinkering about with one's subterranean creative processes. I can't claim to write according to any of the lofty ideals I've put forward. But I said nobody should write for children unless it is with the whole heart. And I can claim to do that. (p. 154)

Joan Aiken, "Writers and Writing," in Children and Literature: Views and Reviews, *edited by Virginia Haviland, Scott, Foresman and Company, 1973, pp. 131-68.*

GENERAL COMMENTARY

JOHN ROWE TOWNSEND

Joan Aiken is one of the liveliest and most exuberant of today's writers for children. She is also one of the hardest to assess, for she has few points of resemblance to anyone else. She is an original, a writer who has marked out a special territory of her own.

For children at least, her appeal is primarily as a storyteller of great pace and resource. But she is a storyteller whose invention is peculiarly uninhibited; her plots are so wild and whirling, her disregard for probability so outrageous as to be highly enjoyable to some tastes while much less acceptable to others. At the same time, she is a humorist of individual flavour; and humour, too, is notoriously a matter of taste. If therefore, as I do, one responds wholeheartedly to her work, the response tends to be personal and spontaneous, appreciative rather than critical, and not easily susceptible to analysis.

Up to 1970, Miss Aiken has written—in addition to books for adults—four novels for children and four collections of short stories. The novels are all based on a single curious premise: that the Hanoverian succession to the throne of England never happened. (p. 17)

The first three novels—***The Wolves of Willoughby Chase, Black Hearts in Battersea,*** and ***Night Birds on Nantucket***—are loosely linked together and have characters in common. . . . The fourth book, ***The Whispering Mountain,*** stands somewhat apart. . . . (p. 18)

These are stories of eye-defeating speed and complexity which carry the reader breathlessly onward from page to page. There is no time to stop and consider probabilities; and indeed any writer of a rapid-action adventure story, even without the open licence which Joan Aiken has written for herself, faces less exacting standards of probability than does the realistic novelist. The two kinds of book run in different gears, and episodes are acceptable in one that would be quite unconvincing in the other. Yet a price must be paid for the high-speed storyteller's freedom of action, and it is in the portrayal of character. Character development in depth is a process of slow unfolding; the tempo is not the same. Miss Aiken commonly draws her characters with a few swift strokes; sometimes hardly draws them at all. When Miss Slighcarp, the newly-arrived governess in ***The Wolves of Willoughby Chase,*** snatches up a heavy marble hairbrush and strikes a savage blow at the maid who innocently picked up her private papers, we immediately know all we need to know about her. Both she and her brother—who appears in ***Night Birds on Nantucket***—are double-dyed villains, and that is that.

Joan Aiken is, in fact, a caricaturist and a mimic. She catches a likeness and presents it in exaggerated form so that it is

clear and recognizable—in the way in which a cartoonist's figures are clear and recognizable—by the exploitation of a salient feature. Because she works in words, the salient feature is usually a way of speech. Again and again her minor characters are defined by their idiosyncrasies of language. (pp. 18-19)

With Miss Aiken's gift for mimicry and caricature goes a tendency to burlesque. It would be misleading to describe her novels as parodies of earlier fiction, but there are elements of parody in them nonetheless. ***The Wolves of Willoughby Chase*** and ***Black Hearts in Battersea*** can be seen in one light as comic Victorian melodramas. ***Night Birds on Nantucket*** has in it something of a light, and light-hearted, skit on *Moby Dick,* for one of its main characters, Captain Casket, is the strange, sad skipper of a New Bedford whaler, obsessed with the pursuit of the pink whale Rosie. And ***The Whispering Mountain*** looks suspiciously like a send-up of all those children's stories in which elaborate riddles from the past are ingeniously unravelled.

There is a high Dickensian colour about the first two books which reminds one that Dickens, too, was, among other things, a mimic and a caricaturist. Although Joan Aiken does not for a moment attempt to be a writer of comparable weight, it seems clear that Dickens has been a major source of inspiration. Possibly he is master and victim at once, since much of his work could be described as Victorian melodrama and is part of the material she seems to be parodying. . . . It is a curious literary relationship. (p. 20)

Joan Aiken is, I think, essentially a lightweight writer; and there is nothing wrong with that. Lightweights of quality are scarce. She is something more than a 'mere' entertainer, for the sheer imaginative stretch of her work must in itself have some liberating effect; the child who reads these novels must experience some widening of its own imaginative range. But I can see no moral or psychological complexities in her books; nor do they try to convey any view of life more subtle than that of the ordinary decent person. Good is good and bad is bad, and there is never any doubt which is which. And, reassuringly, good always triumphs in the end.

I cannot find any clear line of development in the first three novels, though there are differences of flavour. ***The Wolves of Willoughby Chase*** has a deliberate artlessness which the later books seem less concerned to maintain. ***Black Hearts in Battersea*** is the funniest of the books, and has some of the most splendid incidental details. . . . ***Night Birds on Nantucket*** seems slightly less satisfactory, perhaps because Miss Aiken, in spite of her American and Canadian ancestry, is a very English writer, and her work does not quite transplant successfully. (pp. 21-2)

The Whispering Mountain takes the proliferation of character and action as far, one would think, as it can go. It is so crowded that even an attentive reader forgets who all the people are and cannot grasp all that is happening. It is a feast; but possibly enough would have been as good. I feel that Miss Aiken will have to thin down the mixture a little. (p. 22)

Where extravagance is of the essence, it is hard to draw the line beyond which a writer is to be regarded as *too* extravagant. To say that Joan Aiken often develops an idea or situation beyond reasonable limits, makes her characters behave absurdly, and indulges in wild excesses of word-play is not necessarily to make an adverse criticism. It could be retorted that these are exactly the things she sets out to do and that make her work what it is. And if the snaffle and the curb are not much in evidence, at least there is no doubt about the presence of the horse. Energy, speed, inventiveness, a gift for mimicry, a total command over words and, not least, a reckless audacity: it all adds up to a formidable array of qualities, and indicates why Joan Aiken can get away with ventures that the majority of sensible authors would never even attempt. (pp. 22-3)

John Rowe Townsend, "Joan Aiken," in his A Sense of Story: Essays on Contemporary Writers for Children, *J. B. Lippincott Company, 1971, pp. 17-27.*

MARY CADOGAN AND PATRICIA CRAIG

Restraint is the last quality which has guided the composition of Joan Aiken's "unhistorical" adventure stories, but these have an exuberance, a pantomimic largeness which is . . . effective. There is nothing original about her plots, but she has brought to bear on them a sensibility which *is* original, if only because of its ability to assimilate, re-channel, enliven, send up, make good use of elements and conventions already traditional. She has effected a fusion of Gothic with Baroque, set off by a manneristic flair for detail, both idiomatic and ornamental. Her books have reputable antecedents in *Uncle Silas*, the novels of Thomas Love Peacock, Dickens, the Brothers Grimm, *Treasure Island* and John Masefield's "Kay Harker" stories. But Joan Aiken's Nightmare Abbeys are all her own, her "Midnight Folk" are given an unexpected location—they are *Nights Birds on Nantucket*, "Hanoverian" plotters, whose drastic design is to fire a gun across the Atlantic which will slaughter the English king Jamie III at St James's Palace.

Joan Aiken has created, for her own purposes, a period in English history which never existed: the time is around 1832, but she has placed a Stuart king on the throne, infested the countryside with wolves and disgruntled Hanoverians, and erected a castle, a folly along the lines of the Brighton Pavilion, in Battersea Park. This device has a great economy: events which take place in an imaginary era obviously are not governed by restrictions of plausibility, either social or temperamental. The period's non-existence serves mainly to emphasize that the stories are not meant to be pegged to the ground, their purpose is to take off as stylishly as possible. In a time that never happened anything *can* happen: wild dashes by air balloon; encounters with flirtatious pink whales; rides to London on an elephant named Rachel.

In the first book, *The Wolves of Willoughby Chase*, the Gothic mood predominates. . . . The principal girls in this story, Bonnie and Sylvia, are spirited but uninspired. Things happen to them, they have to deal with wolves and wicked governesses and suffer awful privations in an orphanage, but their characters are not developed, they lack the sheer perverse charm of the back-chatting urchin Dido Twite, whose appearance (in *Black Hearts in Battersea*) is unheralded by the conventional build-up for a heroine. Dido "was a shrewish-looking little creature of perhaps eight or nine, with sharp eyes of a pale washed-out blue and no eyebrows or eyelashes to speak of. Her straw-coloured hair was stringy and sticky with jam and she wore a dirty satin dress two sizes too small for her." She is, however, an archetypal scene-stealer, but the author *has* built up qualities in her which make for an expansion of this rôle. She is emphatically not a cute or beaming child in the Shirley Temple tradition. She is forthright, scornful, tough; knowing in the usual way of a London street-child; completely "modern" in her lack of emotional encum-

brances. She has no use for her relatives, just as they have none for her. She is resourceful, intolerant of any kind of dithering, and prone to encounter and get the better of a whole cast of villains, including a spidery West Indies witch and a sinister "Mr Mystery". Miss Slighcarp, the awful governess of *The Wolves of Willoughby Chase*, turns up again in *Night Birds on Nantucket;* she is passing herself off as the timid Pen's Aunt Tribulation, and sits up in bed exactly in the manner of Red Riding Hood's wolf. Pen (short for Dutiful Penitence), befriended by Dido on board a whaling ship, is a slender-reed type of person who needs the irrepressible, sensible Dido to prop her up.

Joan Aiken's one failure is with Simon, the central figure of *Black Hearts in Battersea.* Simon has a whole pastoral tradition behind him, which to some extent has had a flattening effect. He is a type of rustic, noble-natured boy who has made a success of bringing himself up in a wood, living on chestnuts, who turns out to be a prince—or at least the Duke of Battersea. With Simon there is a slackening of the author's controlling amusement; she almost presents him seriously. She has given him no quirks of temperament, no interesting rough edges. He is an amalgam of Dick Whittington, a babe in the wood who survived (his sister survived too, as it turns out) and Oliver Twist. He sets out for London with a donkey and a kitten, to study art at Dr Furneaux's Academy in Chelsea, and is embroiled at once in a situation of Hanoverian intrigue. He is, however, played off the stage by Dido Twite, whose heart he has won, incidentally, by providing her with a new dress, a replacement for the dirty satin one, "two sizes too small". The new dress serves its purpose, is ruined in a shipwreck, and Dido takes to dressing like a sailor boy. By now her character has evolved sufficiently to fit this costume. She and Simon lose sight of one another for a couple of years, but are reunited up a Cuckoo tree—a scene, however, which is left to the reader's imagination.

The richness of the books is underlined by their dramatic contrasts. There is opulence on the one hand and squalor on the other, and the characters are subjected to the most extreme experience of each. *Midnight is a Place* has its Midnight Court, a vast, stately, gentleman's residence set in a park, from which its hero, the boy Lucas Bell, goes out to work in the sewers of Blastburn. There is of course a comic sense, an unseriousness, which informs even the most horrific of Joan Aiken's events: horror is all on an extravagant level, which makes it less threatening, though it continues to stimulate. The books have a fairground kind of grotesqueness which is forceful and decorative. The fantasy which these stories contain is in no sense personal or nostalgically retrogressive; they are fanciful in a way that is formal, lucid and objective. (pp. 357-60)

Mary Cadogan and Patricia Craig, " 'Time Present and Time Past . . .'," in their You're a Brick, Angela! A New Look at Girls' Fiction from 1839-1975, *Victor Gollancz Ltd., 1976, pp. 355-72.*

SHEILA A. EGOFF

One aspect of light fantasy explored by writers for children is that of comic melodrama. Joan Aiken is one of the most original in her interlinking series of fantastical histories set in a time that never was, a British never-never land, rampant with wolves and melodramatic villains in the reign of the imaginary King James III at the beginning of the nineteenth century. The tone of her *The Wolves of Willoughby Chase*,

Aiken with her mother, brothers, and sisters, 1935. From left, sister Jane, mother Jessie, Aiken, and brothers John and David.

Black Hearts in Battersea, Night Birds on Nantucket, and **The Cuckoo Tree** is humorously gothic and Dickensian, and the wildly improbable, outrageous plots read like tongue-in-cheek parodies of crypto-Victorian melodrama and high adventure.

Aiken has a flair for bright, crisp dialogue, and the pungencies of musical dialect; she writes with an affection for the profound and nonsensical power of words, taking delight in the witty interaction of language, dialogue, and character. There is a striking sense of childlike play inherent in her plots; they are rambunctious, rollicking, fast paced to the point of a frantic race, and form magnificent stages for the courageous derring-do of her various insouciant child protagonists. Aiken deliberately makes use of stock characters, themes, and plots from British and American eighteenth- and nineteenth-century adult novels in a witty salute to the classics, with a nod to the adult reader's appreciation of parody and as well to the child reader's love of drama and humor. (pp. 120-21)

Sheila A. Egoff, "The New Fantasy," in her Thursday's Child: Trends and Patterns in Contemporary Children's Literature, *American Library Association, 1981, pp. 80-129.*

DAVID REES

Joan Aiken is an immensely prolific author. She has written a wealth of books for children—plays, verse, collections of short stories, a dozen full-length stories—as well as many novels for adults. The gusto and enormous energy of her work is only equalled among contemporary children's writers by Leon Garfield, and, like him, she can be called, rather loosely, a historical novelist. Her methods and intentions, however, are very different from his—or, indeed, anyone else's. She is the one author, more than any other, who is able to make a virtue of improbability; the wilder, the more absurd her invention becomes, the better the result. With the exception of **Go Saddle the Sea,** her straightforward, realistic novels are not as successful as the sequence of books that begins with **The Wolves of Willoughby Chase,** which are set in an imaginary, fantastic period of the nineteenth century that bears little resemblance to the real Victorian era; indeed, Queen Victoria in these stories never existed. This sequence of books displays all her gifts at their most beguiling: magnificent plots that are often so lavish in their ingenuity that first-rate ideas can get tossed aside in an almost spendthrift way; a delightful sense of humour; and an increasingly sure ear for language that manifests itself in parody and the dialects, vocabulary, and speech rhythms of various periods of history.

This latter ability is not conspicuous in **The Wolves of Willoughby Chase** itself. The dialogue here often sounds wrong, veering uncertainly at times—even in the same sentence—from a pastiche of Victorian English to modern slang; and there are rustic minor characters who are stereotypical and unconvincing. But things show a marked improvement in **Black Hearts in Battersea** with the homespun pronouncements of Scottish King James, and in **Night Birds on Nantucket** with the archaic Quaker speech of the Nantucketers. Then from **The Whispering Mountain** onwards there is a riot of extraordinary vocabulary and speech rhythms: Welsh sentence structure, Sussex dialect, Cockney rhyming slang, nineteenth-century criminal slang, nineteenth-century military slang, anachronistic Elizabethan English, and so on, all of it handled very deftly by an author who now knows exactly what she is doing.

Like Leon Garfield, Joan Aiken is influenced by Dickens, but what she takes from him is different from what Garfield borrows. Description of place and the physical appearance of people is in Garfield often Dickensian, as are certain recurrent themes: the quest for financial "great expectations"; the exploitation of the innocent child in a crowded, filthy, urban environment. Only in **Midnight is a Place** does Joan Aiken explore the latter idea; and, with the exception of the opening paragraphs, the snow-bound countryside, and the train journey in **The Wolves of Willoughby Chase,** she spends remarkably little time—in her first six books—describing scenery and weather. (pp. 42-3)

The Dickensian influence is strongest in the scenes in **The Wolves of Willoughby Chase** which occur in Mrs Brisket's school; we are reminded of Wackford Squeer's academy in *Nicholas Nickleby,* or Thomas Gradgrind's in *Hard Times.* But there are few other direct parallels, and by **Night Birds on Nantucket** Joan Aiken seems to have abandoned Dickens as a source of ideas and turned to Melville: this book is, in part, a parody of *Moby Dick:* the gloomy, religious Captain Casket is a comic version of Captain Ahab, and the flirtatious pink whale a send-up of the white monster, old Moby himself. (Even in **The Wolves of Willoughby Chase,** the wicked governess, Miss Slighcarp, is more a parody of Charlotte Bronte than Dickens.) The Dickensian influence, however, continues in Joan Aiken's plot methods, the names of her characters—Gripe, Moleskin, Pelmett, Fringe, Fitzpickwick, Firkin, Gusset, Twite, Luggins, Prigman, etcetera—and, most strikingly, in the marvellously atmospheric openings of her books. (p. 43)

The main strength of *The Wolves of Willoughby Chase* sequence is, as I have said, in the breath-taking improbabilities of the plots . . . [In] *The Stolen Lake,* perhaps the most ingenious and original book of the series, we are in a British excolony, New Cumbria, which is in South America and has peasants who speak Latin, an Inca-like capital city called Bath Regis, man-eating birds, a princess who can ride a leopard, a queen who is over a thousand years old, and, most daring of all, a lake that is actually stolen. (The king of the next-door country removes it when it is frozen; his soldiers cut the ice into blocks and take them away on teams of llamas.) (pp. 44-5)

Usually the characters are done with a few brief strokes, and are either wholly good or wholly bad at first sight. (p. 45)

There is little of the ambiguity that one meets in Stevenson's or Garfield's villains—Long John Silver in *Treasure Island,* for instance, or Solomon Trumpet in *Jack Holborn*—though Dido Twite's father is an exception; and people rarely change sides. (Again, there are a few exceptions, such as Professor Breadno in *Night Birds on Nantucket.*) Occasionally a good person may be ambiguous (Grandfather Hughes in *The Whispering Mountain* is selfish and insensitive, yet essentially honest and virtuous), but for the most part the characters are done in black and white. The minor characters, like the villains, are at their most convincing when they are caricatured. (pp. 45-6)

But when Joan Aiken resorts to stereotypes, the results are not so effective. Lord Malyn in *The Whispering Mountain* contains too many characteristics of the typical stage baddie to be interesting, whereas Miss Slighcarp—a superb caricature—always holds our attention. . . .

As far as the heroes and heroines of these books are concerned, the girls are usually more convincing than the boys. Sylvia, Bonnie, and Dido are sharply differentiated, but Simon, Nate, and Owen are too alike. Simon and Owen, in particular, are too gifted, too cool in a crisis, too mature to seem quite real. They *always* have an answer. This is perhaps not very disturbing as everything and everyone in these stories is outrageous and fantastic, but in the realistic novels it is a problem. *Midnight is a Place* and *Bridle the Wind* have children who think, feel, and act as if they were adults, and who overcome difficulties that seem to suggest their real ages are at least twenty.

The Wolves of Willoughby Chase, Black Hearts in Battersea, and *Night Birds on Nantucket* follow one another in chronological order. The fourth book of the series, however—*The Whispering Mountain*—is concerned with a different set of characters, and takes place at the same time as *Night Birds on Nantucket.* The fifth, *The Cuckoo Tree,* is, chronologically, the finale of the sequence, using characters from all its predecessors to bring matters to a satisfying conclusion. *The Stolen Lake,* the last to be written, is about Dido's adventures between the end of *Night Birds on Nantucket* and the beginning of *The Cuckoo Tree.* (p. 46)

In *The Whispering Mountain* and *The Cuckoo Tree* the narrative is tighter and more complex than in the first three books. The last fifty pages of *The Cuckoo Tree,* which portray the chaos that precedes the coronation of King Richard IV and the final comeuppance of the Hanoverian villains, are unrivalled in the whole sequence for breakneck narrative gusto, imaginative invention, and crazy humour—they are a sheer delight to read. Both books show an increase in weird vocabulary, bizarre dialects, and all kinds of speech oddities. Some critics have objected to this, on the grounds that it creates unnecessary difficulties for the child reader, but the charge doesn't stand up; meaning is invariably clear through what has happened previously in the plot:. . . . (p. 47)

The Stolen Lake has a thoroughly entertaining, complex narrative, and the usual interest in odd words. Joan Aiken is here at the height of her powers; to look back from this point to *The Wolves of Willoughby Chase* is to look from something flawless to a first novel that has, despite its originality and appeal, weaknesses and uncertainties. The plot complexities of *The Stolen Lake* are neatly illustrated by this amusing paragraph:

> It is a considerable shock when somebody you have known (you thought) very well indeed, and have been fond of, proves to be, not only a completely different person from the one you believed to be your friend, but also not to remember you at all. If, on top of that, he turns out to be a king, reborn after thirteen hundred years, the shock is greater still. And if, into the bargain, he is married to one of the wickedest and most horrible people you have ever met, you can hardly help feeling very unhappy about it. Especially if he seems to be showing rather too much interest in a princess who certainly *isn't* his wife.

The linguistic novelties extend to place names, such as the thirteen great volcanoes—Ambage and Arrabe, Ertayne and Elamye, Arryke, Damask, Damyake, Pounce, Pampoyle, Garesse, Caley, Calabe and Catelonde—recall the lines in W. J. Turner's poem, *Romance,* that discuss the magic of names, in this case also South American volcanoes:

> Chimborazo, Cotapaxi,
> They had stolen my soul away.

They also suggest another author who delights in invented worlds and has a gift for place names: Ursula Le Guin. The archipelago of Earthsea that Ursula Le Guin created gave birth to three novels (*A Wizard of Earthsea, The Tombs of Atuan,* and *The Farthest Shore*), but the reader is left with the feeling that it could lead to many more. Similarly, Joan Aiken's imaginary Britain with its Tudor-Stuart kings and its oldest ally, New Cumbria, suggests the possibility of stories yet to come. (pp. 48-9)

Two of Joan Aiken's realistic novels, *Night Fall* and *The Shadow Guests,* have a modern setting; the others—*Midnight is a Place, Go Saddle the Sea,* and *Bridle the Wind*—are set in the nineteenth century. *Night Fall* . . . is essentially a minor work, but it has its virtues. It is both a murder mystery and a romance. The characterization, however, is not very subtle; the murderer and the Cornish locals in particular seem little more than stereotypes. The romantic elements contain some sentimental prose reminiscent of women's magazines: the two men in Meg's life are both somewhat misty, Barbara Cartland-ish creations. But the whodunit narrative is handled well, and the Cornish background is good, too. This is not the picture-postcard Westcountry of Susan Cooper's *Over Sea, Under Stone,* but the real Cornwall of industrial decline and desolate landscapes. . . . (p. 49)

There are also some apt observations on the subject of self-satisfied men patronising women, and the occasional striking image:

> I had come down here to try and dig out memory,
> like a buried splinter; what was the use of turning
> tail at the first twinge of the needle?

As pot-boilers go, many are a lot worse than *Night Fall.*

Cosmo, the central character in *The Shadow Guests,* is another of Joan Aiken's young heroes who has lost a parent and/or sibling: it is almost an obsessive theme in her work. Meg, Dido, Simon and Sophie, Tobit and Cris, Sylvia, Owen, Penitence are all in the same situation. Often these characters have to suffer rejection by the remaining parent or relative; Owen, Meg, Sim, and Dido are examples. Cosmo, in addition, suffers from the knowledge that his family is burdened by a curse that goes back to Roman times: the eldest son always dies young, unmarried, in a fight. As the novel progresses he meets some of the eldest sons from previous ages—a device similar to that used by Lucy Boston in the first three books of the Green Knowe series—and, through learning their history, he comes to terms with the fact that his first-born son may die in the same way. *The Shadow Guests* is one of Joan Aiken's few excursions into the supernatural, and it is not altogether successful. (pp. 49-50)

Cosmo's experiences with the ghosts, however, help him to solve the problems he has with his classmates at school. The best writing in the book depicts boarding-school life: the boredom of routine, and the petty nastiness that is sometimes displayed when children gang up together. (Joan Aiken uses this theme again in *Go Saddle the Sea,* where it is also well handled.) (p. 50)

There are some good perceptions too: that people, for instance, may offer sympathy only because they need it themselves; it can be a "stupid, spongy craving." But *The Shadow Guests* fails because it doesn't really know which slot it belongs to: it is in part a children's story, in part young adult fiction. Cosmo, like other central characters in Joan Aiken's books, thinks and feels too maturely to be convincing. Also, too much of the dialogue, especially when Eunice is speaking, merely exists to impart information.

Midnight is a Place is a more ambitious work than either *Night Fall* or *The Shadow Guests.* It is set in nineteenth-century Blastburn, the hideous industrial town that was first mentioned in *The Wolves of Willoughby Chase,* but none of the characters from that book appears in this one. It is a wholly realistic piece—which is a pity, as many of the audacious ideas Joan Aiken gets away with in the fantasies do not succeed in a straightforward historical novel. Coincidence, for example, improbability, or making the villains totally villainous and the good people entirely good, spoil *Midnight is a Place.* Anna-Marie is absurdly adult for her age, far too knowing; Lady Murgatroyd, living for years in the ice-house undetected, is just not credible. Sir Randolph Grimsby is a cardboard, two-dimensional villain; and the harsh working and living conditions that are forced on Lucas and Anna-Marie leave them remarkably unscathed. (The plight of children in Victorian industrial society is done much better, in contemporary children's fiction, in William Rayner's *Big*

Mister.) Long before the story ends one ceases to care very much about what is going to happen to any of the characters: it's impossible to suspend one's disbelief. The theme and the background details remind one of Leon Garfield, in particular the emphasis on the consequences of chance. . . . (pp. 50-1)

Garfield, however, would have done it all with rather more conviction. On the other hand, there are some good descriptive passages that recall the Dickens of *Hard Times,* even if they lack his savage intensity. (p. 51)

One minor theme that is well-conceived is the Luddite mentality. Peter Dickinson in his first two books, *The Weathermonger* and *Heartsease,* also used this idea, but it is better explored in *Midnight is a Place.*

In contrast, *Go Saddle the Sea,* as an attempt at historical realism, is entirely successful. It is a picaresque novel, told in the first person, and it recalls Cervantes or Fielding in method, though not in content or style: each incident is a little, self-contained episode, often introducing characters who do not reappear elsewhere, the one unifying factor being the narrator, Felix, who is present all the time. This is the structure of *Don Quixote* or *Joseph Andrews.* The setting is early nineteenth-century Spain, and the story is an account of Felix's adventures: he is a cheerful, physical, extrovert boy, half-English and half-Spanish, who runs away from his grandfather's stifling, aristocratic household because he is treated badly. He rides or walks across most of northern Spain to Santander, then sails to England in order to find his English relatives who turn out to be very different—but no more congenial—than the Spaniards he has deserted. En route he meets a gallery of typical Joan Aiken rogues and eccentrics and some pleasant, charitable people who help and befriend him; also an amiable mule and a very amusing talking parrot. Felix, for the most part, is credible and attractive—we care about him, and what may happen to him—even though there are one or two moments when he behaves, or thinks, in a way that is too adult for his years. The main reason why this book succeeds, however, is the deliberately adopted tone of voice of the narration, a simple well-handled pastiche of nineteenth-century vocabulary and sentence structure that never falters at any point. It is an excellent instrument for Joan Aiken's purposes. . . . (pp. 51-2)

Go Saddle the Sea is an exciting adventure story with a well-paced narrative, full of incident, humour, and enjoyable characters.

The sequel, *Bridle the Wind,* in which Felix does the journey in reverse (he has decided his Spanish grandfather is preferable to his English grandfather) is a disappointment. The adopted tone of voice slips—Felix often sounds more like Joan Aiken than himself—and the picaresque method is unfortunately replaced by a conventional plot structure that lacks probability and relies too much on coincidence. Felix and the other main character, Juan, consistently seem older than they really are, and they far too conveniently overhear the conversations of the villains. (This is a sloppy device to short-circuit narrative longueurs that also mars parts of *The Whispering Mountain* and *The Cuckoo Tree.*) The relationship between Felix and Juan is done quite well, but the disclosure at the end that Juan is really a girl (Juana) seems to lack point. . . . The best scenes in the book are the early chapters in the monastery; the monks are credible and human, particularly the mad, sinister abbot who virtually imprisons Felix and Juan because he needs more novices. But the way the second half of the narrative is influenced by supernatural events is a serious fault, as if something from a different genre had strayed into the wrong novel: the "magic" seems like a cheap bag of tricks, another lame device to solve plot problems. There are some good descriptive passages, particularly of the Pyrenees, but the references to local life and culture, which, in *Go Saddle the Sea,* were so naturally introduced and integrated into the story, are here an intrusive digression: the author undoubtedly has a real affection for the Basque people, their music and language, the scenery—but she has much too strong a desire to tell us about it, to teach us history and geography lessons.

Joan Aiken, in "A Thread of Mystery," said she didn't think her books were great literature—they weren't "worth a lot of analysis"—but she wanted to give children the same sort of pleasure she had derived from her own childhood reading. In the fantasies she succeeds admirably in giving us *all* pleasure, children and adults alike; in most of the realistic novels the pleasure is less. Her main achievement is the creation of a world, in *The Wolves of Willoughby Chase* series, that is uniquely odd, hilarious, exuberant, and endlessly imaginative. She is the only writer I can think of whose work is at its best when it is at its most crazily improbable: this is also "a very special kind of talent." (p. 53)

> *David Rees, "The Virtues of Improbability: Joan Aiken," in* Children's literature in education, *Vol. 19, No. 1, Spring, 1988, pp. 42-54.*

THE KINGDOM UNDER THE SEA AND OTHER STORIES (1971)

Joan Aiken has become well known by now as a writer of considerable stature, both for her novels and her short stories. Jan Pienkowski is an artist who rises ever more magnificently to the demands made upon him. Together they have produced, in *The Kingdom under the Sea,* a book of such sheer magic as to make all previous encomiums seem suddenly misapplied. The old superlatives, abraded with misuse, will not do, for they conjure up a picture of what has been seen before and this is a book like nothing that was ever seen before: mysterious, comical, powerful, dramatic, elegiac—simply beautiful.

> *"Grit for the Oyster," in* The Times Literary Supplement, *No. 3640, December 3, 1971, p. 1511.*

It is difficult to find anything wrong with this book, author, artist and publisher all having done a first-rate job. The author retells Russian and Balkan folktales with her usual skill and feeling for language, plainly and yet rhythmically. . . . Perhaps it is greedy to ask for more but some indication of sources would have been useful, though the children will hardly worry about that. The stories themselves are of mermaids and witches, kings and goosegirls, old favourites in new settings and some less known tales and they have been toned down a little for the tender age they are meant for—but not too much.

> *C. Martin, in a review of "The Kingdom Under the Sea," in* The Junior Bookshelf, *Vol. 36, No. 1, February, 1972, p. 28.*

THE SKIN SPINNERS (1976)

A few individual volumes give us confidence that children's poetry of a high order can still be written. The most outstanding new collection, *The Skin Spinners* . . . is the work of a writer better known for her prose. The Skin Spinners of the title are poets, who, like spiders, "make of air and dust and flesh / a subtle and a silver mesh"; and the web of words that Joan Aiken spins in these pages will delight young readers. She has an engaging sense of humor that communicates itself in a variety of verse forms. She can with freshness recapture the magic of old rhymes, and she can write a spirited nonsense poem about a young lady who is loved by a sewing machine and another about a geography teacher whose shadow gets tacked to a map of Spain. In free verse, couplets, quatrains and ballad stanzas, she can be both tender and terrifying. And, above all, her poetry, at its best, has the resonance that is much needed and rarely met with today. (p. 42)

> *William Jay Smith, "Sounds of Wind, Sea and Rain," in* The New York Times Book Review, *May 2, 1976, pp. 23-4, 42.*

A gifted writer has gathered together more than fifty of her poems, varied in meter and form and unified only by the fecundity of her imagination. Joan Aiken's poetry is as multifaceted as her short stories—eerie, dreamlike, impish, whimsical, enigmatic—and always the precise words are summoned to illuminate the idea, to vitalize the image. . . . Ordinary things assume uncanny qualities and become objects of fantasy: motorways, airplanes, seashells, clouds, a sewing machine, trains, and even algebra in a poem called "π **in the Sky**"—

> Who'll solve my problem? asks the moon
> Moving across the sky
> Who'll calculate my radius
> And multiply by π?
> The shining flood of light I pour
> By half a world is shared
> And yet this area, figured out
> Is merely πr^2.

> *Ethel L. Heins, in a review of "The Skin Spinners: Poems," in* The Horn Book Magazine, *Vol. LII, No. 4, August, 1976, p. 416.*

Joan Aiken's *The Skin Spinners* is perhaps not as full of surprises and energy as Hughes' [*Moon-Bells*], but it contains poems less deliberately shocking and more genuinely accessible to their intended audience, while still demanding that listeners use their heads and their hearts to apprehend them. Neither flossy nor patronizing, *Spinners* holds appeal for adults as well as children and makes most recent single-poet collections for the young seem amateurish, dull, and meatless.

Varied in meter, form and length, these multi-mooded poems can be gentle, sly, whimsical, terrifying, or humorous as Aiken describes bad dreams, alligators in New York sewers, and ghosts of children in an old house, and retells an Eskimo legend. She asks us to pity the girl whose hair was turned to crystal because she mocked a wizard and watch where we step on the train platform lest we never return. The poem about the grandmother who talks with her long-dead husband is a perceptive and endearing portrait, while the one where Miss Pallant's shadow gets tacked to the schoolroom map of Spain is just plain funny.

Some poems are clearly fantasy, like that of the boy caught

in his own bad dream. Others are realistic: the speaker recalls specific, concrete detail with a touch of nostalgia. . . . One section is devoted to storysongs, but many other pieces have a music which catches, thrills, and whirls in one's head, like the jingly **"Air on an Escalator"** and the pensive **"John's Song"**. . . . Aiken is especially skillful at investing ordinary, everyday things with new vitality. She sees bridges, algebra, cats, money, and night with fresh images that cling, arouse, and even sometimes comfort and caress. . . . (pp. 7-8)

Some poems are very direct and literal, and a few don't amount to much, are just momentary observations pithily put. But all exhibit scrupulously accurate choice of language for what they are expected to do, the same kind of artistry with words that we have come to appreciate in Aiken's novels and stories. Consider how idea, form, rhyme, rhythm, image, even line length, combine in **"Night Landscape"** to not only create the picture and sensation of a train speeding through the night, but also get into the head of a youthful passenger imagining he is the very scene itself. . . .

The Skin Spinners is a collection where poetic vision and artistic integrity have resulted in poems that will wear well and give pleasure for many readings. It is the pace-setter of our time. (p. 8)

> *Alethea K. Helbig, "The Place of Poetry," in* Children's Literature Association Quarterly, *Vol. 5, No. 3, Fall, 1980, pp. 7-8.*

THE FAR FORESTS: TALES OF ROMANCE, FANTASY, AND SUSPENSE (1977)

What delicious diversion the author provides in this collection. Here are 15 stories from Aiken's soaring imagination, all with unexpected facets and totally believable even though impossible. It's hard to pick a favorite but **"Postman's Knock"** could be it—a mixture of hilarity, pathos and fantasy. Fred becomes a postman to escape the unpredictable results of fame. A shy man, he's stunned to find himself in love with a girl in a tiny village where he is seeking anonymity. Marilynne loves Fred but never recognizes him; she has brought up identical triplet brothers, so everyone looks alike to her. The story of their problems and their resolution is crazy and endearing. Some of the other stories are tragic, others are horrifying, all are excellent and astonishingly original. (pp. 91-2)

> *A review of "The Far Forests: Tales of Romance, Fantasy, and Suspense," in* Publishers Weekly, *Vol. 211, No. 11, March 7, 1977, pp. 91-2.*

A collection of sophisticated, witty tales for mature readers, this has the polished style that's Aiken at her best; it hasn't the exaggeration that is enjoyed by some of her younger readers in books like **Nightbirds on Nantucket** or **The Whispering Mountain** but it has just as much imagination and humor. And a touch of the macabre. And magic, and diversity.

> *Zena Sutherland, in a review of "The Far Forests: Tales of Romance, Fantasy, and Suspense," in* Bulletin of the Center for Children's Books, *Vol. 31, No. 2, October, 1977, p. 25.*

THE FAITHLESS LOLLYBIRD AND OTHER STORIES (1977)

The Lollybird in the title story from Joan Aiken's latest collection is a sort of weaver bird which helps its master, Luke, to create ravishing fabrics and glittering tapestries, but then turns truant, popping up in various capital cities, and amusing itself by weaving sparkling canopies of (for instance) "coloured ribbons and bits of tissue paper, metal foil, orange-peel, tufts of fur from poodles, silvery rings from Coke cans, and long shining strands from the tails of police horses". This story sticks in the mind because of the almost perfect image it offers of Joan Aiken's own art. Her stories seem to be made of whatever comes to hand, every-day details and bits of fairy-tale all mixed up together and woven, with apparently casual ease, into a crazy, sparkling whole. It is an art that shows to best advantage in her long novels, which allow her to demonstrate her gift for deviously complicated plotting to the full, and to cram her fantasy worlds with inventive detail. But these short stories, though one or two of them falter and fall over the edge of nonsense into silliness, are generally steadied, like the novels, by a characteristic matter-of-factness. The collection contains stories about a king who loses part of his backward memory and gains a forward one, of a mini-skirted witch with a nasty taste for poisonous gardening, and of the defection to the West of the Carpathian football team, who live in fear of being sent to the saccharin mines.

The first and last stories in the book sound a different note. Both are about a relationship between an old person and a child. Both end with death, and confront grief. Joan Aiken is a tactful enough storyteller to handle important feelings like this without bruising. There is an optimistic energy about these stories, which is a source of strength in all her narratives.

> *Myra Barrs, "Crazy Collage," in* The Times Literary Supplement, *No. 3931, July 15, 1977, p. 863.*

Joan Aiken is the acknowledged master of that neglected form, the children's short-story. The dozen tales in this collection demonstrate convincingly the scope and variety of her craft. The disciplines imposed by the medium are all benefit; here is none of the prolixity, or the piling of incidents, which mar her full-length novels.

The stories mix in characteristic fashion the wonderful and the ordinary, humour and poetry. . . .

All is done with Miss Aiken's fine professionalism, with economy—although some of the stories are quite long—and with deep respect for the meaning and the beauty of words. A very good collection.

> *M. Crouch, in a review of "The Faithless Lollybird," in* The Junior Bookshelf, *Vol. 41, No. 5, October, 1977, p. 283.*

By a master storyteller, twelve stories and one poem ranging from the wildly imaginative and exuberant to the sad and wistful. . . . Written with lush description and extraordinary imagery, the stories celebrate loyalty, steadfastness, and goodness of heart; an ageless collection as rich as a plum pudding.

> *Ann A. Flowers, in a review of "The Faithless Lollybird," in* The Horn Book Magazine, *Vol. LIV, No. 3, June, 1978, p. 281.*

STREET (1978)

Lovers Hannah and Toomey live on opposite sides of the extraordinarily busy superhighway which divides their tiny village of Street. Because of the tremendous amount of dangerous traffic and the feuding of their families, they have never met. They communicate through sign language until witchcraft causes bulls to come from the forest and trample the unscrupulous and greedy promoter of progress. This Romeo-Juliet farce in two acts, intended for performance by and for children, combines high action, wit, and nimble wordplay to satirize materialism and greed. Although the symbolism of the bulls is obscure, this exuberant blend of the comic and the macabre never lags or fails to engage the emotions and should be fun to produce, participate in, and view.

> *Alethea K. Helbig, in a review of "Street: A Play,"
> in* Children's Book Review Service, *Vol. 6, No. 8,
> March, 1978, p. 74.*

If you want to keep your hands and arms,
And your legs and knees and feet,
Look to the right, look to the left,
. . . *And then: don't cross the street!*

That's the song villagers chant in opening portions of this surreal allegory, and it vocally expresses what's already visually apparent from stage directions: that crossing the street in the town of **Street** is a life-and-death matter, for its only thoroughfare is ruled by rushing trucks that service nearby mines. Moreover, the town's physical division is echoed in hostilities between those who live on the river side and those who live on the forest side of the street. . . . The pace is brisk, the plotting tight, with humor and dramatic tension aplenty. The combination of a contemporary setting with strong currents of myth and magic is imaginative; and Aiken's prefatory suggestions for performance put this in reach of groups with even the most minimal facilities.

> *Denise M. Wilms, in a review of "Street: A Play for
> Children," in* Booklist, *Vol. 74, No. 15, April 1,
> 1978, p. 1251.*

GO SADDLE THE SEA (1978)

Even though the time is as remote as the early nineteenth century and the setting is Spain, the story is told with such intense immediacy that today's readers will quickly lose themselves in the adventures of a young orphan boy running away from an unhappy life with unloving relatives.

No ordinary runaway is young Felix Brooke, however. He is an intelligent, quick-witted, likeable boy determined to find his father's family in England. His series of adventures as he makes his way to the sea through the primitive Spanish countryside borders on the incredible. Yet the details of his exploits are so realistic, the flavor of the era so well captured, and the tension of the story line so aptly managed that the reader believes almost in spite of himself.

In addition to its merit as a good adventure tale enriched by historical and geographic detail, the novel has value also as a study of the timeless aspects of human nature. The psychological maturing of the young hero, his personal commentary on the varied types of people he meets, and his occasional philosophical and religious observations are aspects of the novel which will expand the horizons of the young reader.

*Aiken with her family, living in a reconverted single-decker bus in
Chipstead, Kent, 1952. From left: Aiken, daughter Liz, son John,
and first husband Ron.*

In short, this interesting book is a delightful combination of entertainment and enlightenment for adolescent readers. (pp. 12-13)

> *Diane A. Parente, in a review of "Go Saddle the
> Sea," in* Best Sellers, *Vol. 38, No. 1, April, 1978, pp.
> 12-13.*

Written in a style which recalls *Gulliver's Travels*—including descriptive chapter headings—the picaresque adventures follow one upon another. During a few short weeks Felix prevents the vendetta murder of an innocent man and his afflicted daughter; he witnesses a duel and is accused of the murder of the dead man; he is clapped into prison and escapes in disguise, carrying a parrot; he is nearly sacrificed by a primitive tribe; and he even makes the mistake of booking passage on a ship, the crew of which has been paid by his great-aunt to mutilate him and sell him as a monster for carnivals. The tale is breathless and rollicking, full of derring-do and panache. The good are vindicated, the evil punished; love conquers all. The hero must contend with forbidding mountain ranges and roaring floods, wild storms at sea, kidnappers, murderers, secret police. Of course, all of this is too much for one boy to have accomplished in a lifetime, let alone in the space of a few weeks. Does it really matter? Not at all. Such is the author's genius as a spinner of tales that the adventures are made credible and spellbinding by their sheer audacity.

> *Beryl Beatley, in a review of "Go Saddle the Sea,"
> in* The Horn Book Magazine, *Vol. LIV, No. 2,
> April, 1978, p. 160.*

Here, for once, is a book which turns its back on present-day vogues and goes back joyously and without shame to the great tradition of the "yarn". Miss Aiken complements her unmatchable talent for story-telling with formidable intelligence. Her book provides a shrewd historical comment on

Europe in the aftermath of a great war. It contains a gallery of brilliantly sketched, attractive and never laboured portraits. The first-person narrative and the dialogue are beautifully sustained, fluent, convincing and free of olde-worlde tushery. But it is the tale that matters, a tale in which excitement, leavened with humanity and spiced with humour, is sustained, into which each episode is dovetailed with masterly craftsmanship.

> *Marcus Crouch, "Tales of a Picaro," in* The Times Literary Supplement, *No. 3966, April 7, 1978, p. 376.*

TALE OF A ONE-WAY STREET AND OTHER STORIES (1978)

Joan Aiken's settings, brilliantly matched by Jan Pienkowski's illustrations, are surrealistic in style—that is, they offer an apparently familiar view of a world in which freakishness is in the process of taking over. As always, her stories have a humorous authority in them, as though a moral or philosophical point were just about to be stated. In the title-story, for example, a sharp defence of imagination, Tom Mann the plumber's son defeats the power of bureaucratic habit by walking *up* Narrow Street instead of returning from school by the prescribed back way; he finds himself in a strange world reflecting all the items of a picture he has just done at school, and the accompanying coloured picture has just the right touch of irrationality in colour and shape to match a boy's fancy. In **"The Alarm Cock"** a curious little house of folk-tale style perches on top of a modern tower block; in **"Clean Sheets"** a boy helping his mother finds a memory leaf from a Brazil nut tree and his elders recover lost treasures and pleasures. The tales are crisp, quick-moving and teasing in their witty implications, while the silhouettes and full-colour pictures stir the imagination as the words do, with a particular sharp aesthetic experience. (pp. 3355-56)

> *Margery Fisher, in a review of "Tale of a One-Way Street and Other Stories," in* Growing Point, *Vol. 17, No. 2, July, 1978, pp. 3355-56.*

These eight stories are set in Dreamland: sometimes openly, as when Euan adventures in his flying drum or Tansy walks on the Moon with great-great-grandma Dido, sometimes simply because fantasy land is where Joan Aiken is happiest, so that even her real one-way street contains horses and thrushes which call out instructions. The stories work well because this author seldom forgets to anchor her ingenious fancifulness with a realistic possibility—Euan's birthday presents are confused because Aunt Bertha slits open the envelope in a hurry, and so cuts his birthday letter into four easily muddled pieces, and the dragon overlooks Bridget because she always wears a blue hat and this camouflages her as part of a nearby pool.

> *R. Baines, in a review of "Tale of a One-Way Street," in* The Junior Bookshelf, *Vol. 42, No. 4, August, 1978, p. 189.*

MICE AND MENDELSON (1978)

The setting is once more Midnight Park, but for a collection of bedtime stories, with a background resumé before each for greater security. Joan Aiken's unrivalled matter-of-fact nonsense is united, for even greater humour, with the catchy dia-

logue-rhythms of Yiddish. Despite his obviously Semitic origins, Mr. Mendelson is an Orkney pony, fond of music. His young master, going off to school, suggests to his grandfather the Old Lord that Mr. Mendelson should have a piano, so that his friends Bertha and Gertrude can give him nightly concerts (they are mice, adept at mazurkas and minuets and also, patently, of Jewish extraction). Add the Irish gypsy, Dan Sligo, who sees his own use for the piano, for Mr. Mendelson's watch and young Tim's pouter pigeon, concocts marvellous schemes to steal them, and is—almost always—foiled, and you have a deliciously funny set of stories, one for each night of the week.

> *M. Hobbs, in a review of "Mice and Mendelson," in* The Junior Bookshelf, *Vol. 43, No. 1, February, 1979, p. 23.*

THE SHADOW GUESTS (1980)

It is a mysterious business—the capacity of a real storyteller to enfold the reader: to wrap him up, as it were, in the friendly blanket of a story. When we are young, it is a positively physical experience, producing a general sensation of well-being. Joan Aiken's books always remind me of that young delight. Partly it is feeling that the writer has immense amounts of story in reserve. It is not in her nature to be short of another twist or extra turn. She is aboundingly devoted to our entertainment.

In *The Shadow Guests,* as it happens, I fancy Joan Aiken has been almost over-generous. Cosmo Curtoys (her usual boldness with names) has come to England because his mother and elder brother have disappeared in Australia. It all begins at Heathrow, and much of the first half dozen pages is common airport experience: but notice how it is made to bear upon the (at this point in the story) mysterious condition of the young hero. Cosmo's destination is an old mill house near Oxford, long associated with his family: at the moment lived in by his brilliant and, it is once or twice suggested, unconventionally beautiful cousin Eunice, self-described as Dracula's Aunt, who happens to be a professor of mathematics—and none of your common or garden dull-minded professors, either. Eunice is a sort of glamorous academic tomboy, intelligent, casual: and almost certainly the heroine of some other book on the edge of this one.

There turns out to be a family curse, going back to the seventh century, involving mothers and elder sons. This produces shades from the past, ancient and mostly boyish Curtoyses with whom Cosmo practises battle with net and trident, or horsemanship in preparation for some unnumbered crusade. On top of this there's the quite awful school, Morningquest, where Cosmo is ostracized—partly, it seems, because he claims once to have seen a kangaroo. The headmaster, who may be appalling or not, is actually called Gabbitas. (There is no sign of a Thring.) Throw in some poltergeistery, a phantom coach and horses, and a revenant from the Hellfire Club. At the last moment, admit a witch. . . .

And it is beautiful. It is not, on second thoughts, one of Joan Aiken's best: it contains too many ingredients: it is a sort of anthology of agreeable horrors, supernatural and everyday. But it does provide that blissful brisk blanket. Brisk because, like the best blankets, it does not wholly lull: at times, for example, it is unmoved by the unnatural and ghastly, but appalled by the mundane and unremarkable. In cheerful conflict with a young—but in fact very old—Curtoys who's doomed to lose his life as a gladiator, Cosmo is struck by the thought that net and trident are much to be preferred, as games equipment, to beanbags. The writing is a constant unobtrusive pleasure: crossing ploughed land is "like walking over the back of a whale, high and windy". And underlying this magic stew of a narrative there is a fascinating feeling for the inadequacy of human perceptions: "We're like a little old lady with an ear-trumpet and a crystal set, trying to hear the London Philharmonic which is playing away at top volume in the next room. . . ."

> *Edward Blishen, "Unnatural Causes," in* The Times Literary Supplement, *No. 4018, March 28, 1980, p. 357.*

The Shadow Guests would be a major novel even without the supernatural elements; with them it is uniquely interesting. (p. 183)

What gives the fantasy credibility and distinction is that it is set against a brilliantly drawn contemporary backcloth. . . . The book blends its incompatible ingredients, magic and Mars bars, with consummate skill. The biggest factor in the novel's undoubted success is Cosmo himself, an eminently sensible boy who meets school bullies, ghosts and poltergeists, and a Professor of Mathematics, and adjusts to them all with the same practical thoughtfulness. (p. 184)

> *M. Crouch, in a review of "The Shadow Guests," in* The Junior Bookshelf, *Vol. 44, No. 4, August, 1980, pp. 183-84.*

ARABEL AND MORTIMER (1980)

It needs a very lively imagination to appreciate these fast-moving zany tales, of a surprisingly mature Arabel who, although too young for school, still copes with telephones, table tennis, and calculations, takes solo train journeys, helps to catch thieves, and assists in a rescue in a store. The stories have a swinging style, varied dialogue and originality, making them real "fun" to read or hear. (pp. 235-36)

> *A. Thatcher, in a review of "Arabel and Mortimer," in* The Junior Bookshelf, *Vol. 44, No. 5, October, 1980, pp. 235-36.*

Joan Aiken has a gift for this sort of story and the stories in this collection are perfect for reading aloud to four-year-olds and upwards. The wicked, somewhat evil, but rather endearing raven, Mortimer, rushes from crisis to crisis leaving havoc in his wake. . . . There is a feeling of inspired lunacy about these tales, held in check by good writing and timing.

> *Janet Fisher, in a review of "Arabel and Mortimer," in* The School Librarian, *Vol. 28, No. 4, December, 1980, p. 369.*

Back after seven years, the trouble-oriented pet of sweet little Arabel gets into one jam after another in three hilarious stories in which the author successfully attempts to avoid the believable and combines arrant nonsense with a bland delivery. Very effective, this nonsense, and Aiken throws in Arabel's mother, a rival to Mrs. Malaprop, a series of deliberately stereotyped characters, occasionally speaking deliberately stereotyped dialect ("Och, mairrcy," says the ship's engineer Hamish McTavish) and sundry improbable coincidences. . . .

> *Zena Sutherland, in a review of "Arabel and Mortimer," in* Bulletin of the Center for Children's Books, *Vol. 35, No. 1, September, 1981, p. 2.*

THE STOLEN LAKE (1981)

Joan Aiken's elaborately idiosyncratic historical inventions are extended here in a highly diverting adventure for Dido Twite. On her way back to England, after the affairs described in **Night Birds on Nantucket,** Dido is involved in the mysterious intrigues of Queen Ginevra, who rules a part of South America originally colonised by Romans in the fourth century, and who has appealed to England for help in regaining a lake high in the mountains which, it oddly appears, has been stolen by a neighbouring monarch. As the story unfolds in all its intricacy, with its wild humour, weird characters and wholly plausible details of place and circumstance, the reader has no time to remember that history did not in fact take this course. Nothing seems more likely than that the Queen should lose her land to the romantically obvious claimant or that Dido Twite, that superb Cockney heroine, should play a vital part in the unriddling of a superbly devised extravaganza.

> *Margery Fisher, in a review of "The Stolen Lake," in* Growing Point, *Vol. 20, No. 2, July, 1981, p. 3920.*

Devotees of Joan Aiken will be delighted to learn that **The Stolen Lake** recounts the further adventures of the remarkable Dido Twite who first made her appearance in **Black Hearts in Battersea.** Newcomers can however read this story independently. . . .

The machinations by which the stolen lake is returned, a lost princess rescued, with the help of Dr. Johnson's dictionary, a rightful king restored, and various villains dispatched to suitably horrific ends, make for exciting reading. Dido, a born survivor, enhances her reputation still further, and assuredly we have not heard the last of one of Joan Aiken's most original creations. The characters live—from the liquor-loving Mr Brandywine (the British Agent in New Cumbria, whose fingers are paralysed by a spell), the aloof Captain Hughes, Master of the Thrush in which Dido is a passenger, the too-good-to-be-true Mr Holystone (who turns out to be King Arthur, reborn) to Dido herself. Not to mention Mr Bran, whose magical powers identify him irrevocably as Merlin the magician, though this is never actually mentioned.

None of this author's stories are ever dull. She is one of the most imaginative and consistently entertaining writers—especially for the nine to thirteen age group, or, indeed, any children (or grown-ups for that matter). Her capacity for creating interesting, idiosyncratic characters, strong plots and adventurous situations seems boundless. It is perhaps slightly churlish to suggest that it is in the lack of bounds there lies a weakness. There is almost a superabundance of talent—too much for any one story. The wealth of detail, of literary allusions, of Cockney slang and foreign phrases—not to mention the distinctive Aikenish invention of language—present a difficult hurdle for young readers. The fates and fortunes become at times so outrageous that they can seem absurd.

For example, in **The Stolen Lake** young girls are kidnapped, then sacrificed by being hurled into the lake where they are devoured by piscadores—man-eating fishes—and their skeletons are retrieved and ground into paste which is subsequently eaten by Queen Ginevra in order to maintain her immorality. This fearfully wicked women lives and perishes in a rotating palace, with a fiendish revolving door—and so on. For good measure, the country abounds in Aurocs (cousins of the pterodactyl) and other dreadful, bloodthirsty creatures. The deliberate alteration of history seems not particularly significant, since few children of this age are specially knowledgeable or very concerned as to which monarch follows whom and when.

In her earlier, and arguably most successful book, *The Wolves of Willoughby Chase,* these excesses have been kept in control and a firm control exercised over characters and situations. The reins have been loosened perhaps a little too much in this story; nevertheless it remains an original and splendid entertainment.

> *Brian Baumfield, "Dido Lives," in* The Times Literary Supplement, *No. 4086, July 24, 1981, p. 839.*

Dido has surfaced once again. The adventure Miss Aiken has dished up for the intrepid 12-year-old in *The Stolen Lake* is zanier and more devilishly fiendish than ever.

A genius at mixing history and mythologies from diverse cultures, the author can make her readers believe anything is possible. . . .

Even though Miss Aiken has a penchant for trussing her heroine in gunnysacks and occasionally lapses into repetitiveness, *The Stolen Lake* is a novel that will keep good readers turning pages and less able ones scurrying to the dictionary. And the rare kid who knows Celtic myth, the Bible and Arthurian legend will chuckle even through the most gruesome episodes.

> *Bryna J. Fireside, in a review of "The Stolen Lake," in* The New York Times Book Review, *February 14, 1982, p. 28.*

MORTIMER'S CROSS (1983)

The raven Mortimer has been disrupting the Jones' family life, and that of their neighbours, for some years now, but Joan Aiken's sense of the ridiculous and her witty way with words are as rich and energetic as ever. *Mortimer's Cross* contains three stories of domestic disaster built on the five-act principle of ascending hyperbole suitable for the 'Jackanory' television series. **'The Mystery of Mr. Jones's disappearing Taxi'** makes the most of London streets and buildings; the title-story moves from London to Hereford and introduces a splendid new character, deafly eccentric Great-Aunt Olwen; the Irish setting of **'Mortimer's Portrait on Glass'** juxtaposes with impeccable logic a bog, an iceberg and a dinosaur. Tom Foyle the harbour-master does wonder whether the 'folks at Derrycoughan and Killimore may not be best pleased to have a dinosaur come leaping up the road, and they with no warning or expectation of the occurrence', but there is no question of the pleasurable amusement readers of all ages will derive from these gloriously extravagant sequences of accidents sustained by the lamentably anti-social but lovable raven.

> *Margery Fisher, in a review of "Mortimer's Cross," in* Growing Point, *Vol. 22, No. 4, November, 1983, p. 4153.*

Welcome back, Arabel, and raucous pet raven Mortimer. This not-quite school-aged child will have even sixth graders

in stitches with the situations she and Mortimer get into. The plots of these three episodes zip along as if cushioned on a thin slip of air, never quite touching ground. . . . Aiken knits colorfully eccentric order out of this chaos, and she maneuvers her plots so deftly that, intricate and impossible though they are, readers will speed right through—incredulous but laughing. . . . Good humor is rare, and this is as accessible as it is good. A must for libraries where *Arabel's Raven* or *Arabel and Mortimer* are popular.

> *J. Alison Illsley, in a review of "Mortimer's Cross," in* School Library Journal, *Vol. 31, No. 4, December, 1984, p. 78.*

A trio of stories centered around the unpredictable raven Mortimer, last encountered in *Arabel and Mortimer.* The plots are farcical, with dizzy developments standing or falling on the strength of Aiken's narrative wit and sense of absurdity. In fact, the three tales are not equal in strength. The best is the first, **"The Mystery of Mr. Jones's Disappearing Taxi,"** in which Arabel and Mortimer become entangled in a pop star's kidnapping. **"Mortimer's Cross"** has a bit less agility but is still amusing as it recounts what happens when Arabel's redoubtable Great-Aunt Olwen arrives to help out when Arabel's mother is ill and manages to ship Mortimer off to the wilds. The least effective tale is the last. Here the Jones family's visit to Ireland takes a strange and too-incredible twist with the appearance of an iceberg and a real dinosaur. Add this where Arabel and Mortimer have a following.

> *Denise M. Wilms, in a review of "Mortimer's Cross," in* Booklist, *Vol. 81, No. 15, April 1, 1985, p. 1116.*

BRIDLE THE WIND (1983)

The further adventures of thirteen-year-old Felix Brooke—the hero of *Go Saddle the Sea*—again proceed at a breakneck pace. On his way home from England Felix is shipwrecked on the French coast, where he has a supernatural vision and suffers a case of amnesia. He rouses to find himself a novice in the monastery of St. Just de Seignanx, ruled by the abbot Vespasian, a mad, evil monk. There, Felix rescues the object of his vision, Juan, a miserable Basque boy who was kidnapped by the Mala Gente, a sort of local Mafia. With the aid of the friendly monks, they escape from the monastery, and Felix resolves to restore Juan to his family before he himself returns home. Their subsequent adventures involve the Mala Gente, hairsbreadth escapes, the demonically possessed abbot, and the final powerful exorcism of the evil spirit. But most important is the slowly growing friendship between the two quite different boys. Felix is pious, kindhearted, and thoughtful, impulsive enough to get into trouble and resourceful enough to escape. Juan is proud, poetic, not so strong as Felix and—no surprise to the reader but a stunning shock to Felix—a girl. Only Joan Aiken can carry off such feats of the imagination; the breathtaking story is an outstanding example of the picaresque novel for children, and it should leave readers eager for a third story about Felix. (pp. 714-15)

> *Ann A. Flowers, in a review of "Bridle the Wind," in* The Horn Book Magazine, *Vol. LIX, No. 6, December, 1983, pp. 714-15.*

As in her other works, Ms. Aiken skillfully creates a masterful and rich plot while highlighting the unique characters that come alive on every page through realistic dialogue and sharp nature imgery. Good and evil are clearly delineated here, and readers will thrill at the bizarre and frightening events that ultimately lead to the destruction of evil. The novel in its archetypal and simple beauty will attract readers from age twelve on up. And every reader, male or female, will be in for a lovely surprise at the conclusion of the tale.

> *Marjorie Kaiser, in a review of "Bridle the Wind,"
> in* The ALAN Review, *Vol. 11, No. 2, Winter,
> 1984, p. 25.*

The many hazards and encounters of [the tale] provide excitement enough but a certain air of unreality makes itself felt at times. Miss Aiken's descriptive passages are fine but the narrative itself often reads as part of Crusoe's diary; the prose occasionally sounds like a translation; there seems a certain vagueness over money transactions; but perhaps such criticisms are carping in an adult reader. All in all, the story makes an exciting and substantial read; even so, the surprise at the end is not as convincing as it might have been. (pp. 30-1)

> *A. R. Williams, in a review of "Bridle the Wind,"
> in* The Junior Bookshelf, *Vol. 48, No. 1, February,
> 1984, pp. 30-1.*

FOG HOUNDS, WIND CAT, SEA MICE   (1984)

With what mastery Joan Aiken meets the restrictions and the opportunities of the Early Reader. Flying Carpets, of which this is one, are collections of tales with a folkish flavour to them. Miss Aiken's three stories are all original and contemporary—or at least timeless. Witchcraft and magic exist in a society of radio news and retired bank managers. The stories are nicely varied: one romantic, one comic and one on the borderline of tragedy. Miss Aiken pays her audience and her craft the compliment of taking them quite seriously, and our reaction, whether of laughter or tears, is the more sincere and spontaneous. The restrained and economical style make these ideal material for reading, or telling, aloud. . . .

> *M. Crouch, in a review of "Fog Hounds, Wind Cat,
> Sea Mice," in* The Junior Bookshelf, *Vol. 48, No.
> 6, December, 1984, p. 250.*

[Joan Aiken] is undoubtedly at her creative best when writing about the power and mystique of the elements. She can evoke the smell of the sea into your kitchen, a web of damp clinging fog into your bedroom, or the sweep of the wind through your sweater as you sit in front of a fire reading the story to the kids sprawled around. Children love to be thrilled, and this is the book to do it—especially the first story, which is rather like a *Hounds of the Baskervilles*. So this book is really *"shivers with a happy ending,"* as one youngster put it!

> *Ron Morton, in a review of "Fog Hounds, Wind Cat,
> Sea Mice," in* Books for Your Children, *Vol. 20,
> No. 1, Spring, 1985, p. 16.*

On the cover of this paperback we read that *this masterly collection (is) specially written to bridge the gap between first picture books and longer stories.* The adjective *masterly* comes naturally to mind when one sits down to enjoy a Joan Aiken story and these three are no exception to this expectation. However I regret very much the absence of Jan Pienkowski's usually accompanying illustrations which provide an added dimension for beginning readers. And I doubt whether this paperback format allows young readers to find this volume a suitable bridge between picture books and longer stories: the printed page is rather too crowded and Joan Aiken's prose particularly in **"Fog hounds"** rises to heights of eloquence which only competent upper primary readers would comprehend. With these reservations the three stories are written with her usual imaginative vitality: boundaries between fairy tale and real life are almost imperceptible in her world. Sagacious older sisters just could be witches: animals and highly sensitive humans enjoy an implicit understanding; the forces of nature will bend to favour the innocent in adversity. To sum up, a set of three stories to be treasured by those who love the processes of fairy tale and folklore and the imaginative enchantment to be expected from Joan Aiken.

> *Bernice Eastman, in a review of "Fog Hounds, Wind
> Cat, Sea Mice," in* Reading Time, *Vol. XXXI, No.
> IV, 1987, p. 39.*

UP THE CHIMNEY DOWN AND OTHER STORIES   (1984)

Although the setting of these 11 short stories moves between New York, London and Paris, the real locale is Aiken country where a baker makes cakes for the wind, a rare bird is saved from extinction and a rainbow makes itself comfortable in a small house in a "rather wild part of London." Life is hard in Aiken's world, but greed, a frequent phenomenon, is thwarted and goodness triumphs. . . . Sometimes whimsy takes over and dissipates the impact of a tale, such as the leisurely **"The Dog on the Roof"** and **"Up the Chimney Down"** in which a twin, Clove, rescues her sister Cinnamon from the clutches of an evil and greedy witch. If some stories are more tightly plotted than others, no matter. Aiken's ability to write so that one can see, hear and even taste is consistent and welcome.

> *Amy Kellman, in a review of "Up the Chimney
> Down and Other Stories," in* School Library Journal, *Vol. 32, No. 4, December, 1985, p. 85.*

Joan Aiken is so entertaining a writer that readers may not fully appreciate the craft that is the basis for what seems an effortless, fluid style. Her words are deftly chosen and carefully honed, her humor is under control even when it seems most ebullient, her characters are memorable even when they are not quite believable. And she has that prime requisite of good fantasy writing, a logic-within-illogic that sits firmly on its realistic base. This collection of fantastic stories has variety, wit, momentum in varying degrees, and an appealing combination of the humorous and the eerie.

> *A review of "Up the Chimney Down and Other Stories," in* Bulletin of the Center for Children's Books, *Vol. 39, No. 7, March, 1986, p. 121.*

With her usual flair Joan Aiken has concocted a menu of deliciously extravagant short tales to suit every palate. The moods are as varied as the subjects, ranging from the broad humor of **"The Happiest Sheep in London"** to the haunting, almost mystical tone of **"The Gift Giving."** . . . In each of the eleven tales the author's talent for description creates memorable moments and vivid impressions. Where else but in an Aiken story could one expect to find as neatly phrased a character sketch as this one from **"The Last Chimney Cuckoo"**: "He was a thin sallow prim gray-haired flat-faced softspoken man with a small mouth like a hyphen"? Only the title story borders on the precious. As a group, the tales demonstrate continuing growth without sacrificing the vivacity, pace, and flamboyant imagination which are the hallmarks of Aiken's work.

> *Mary M. Burns, in a review of "Up the Chimney Down and Other Stories," in* The Horn Book Magazine, *Vol. LXII, No. 2, March-April, 1986, p. 205.*

THE LAST SLICE OF RAINBOW AND OTHER STORIES (1985)

Joan Aiken, most imaginative of all modern children's writers, has fashioned another widely varied collection of her own style of fairytale, from gauzy guardians of domestic objects, a traditional kelpy, a sinister stone garden gnome freed at his child-helper's expense, to the mysterious timeless melancholy of a Hans Andersen or Oscar Wilde, with humorous modern magic too. She is, moreover, one of the few writers whose incidental verse is not a let-down.

> *D. A. Young, in a review of "The Last Slice of Rainbow," in* The Junior Bookshelf, *Vol. 50, No. 1, February, 1986, p. 19.*

Joan Aiken's short stories are full of magic—magical elements, magical imagery, magical language and magical atmosphere. They are modern fairy-stories in which time is of no import, where dragons snarl up traffic on airport runways, stone goblins ride tricycles, kelpies and fairies move in and out of children's lives, rainbows can be caught and dreams recaptured. The scope of Joan Aiken's imagination is breathtaking, as each of the nine stories demonstrates. (pp. 14, 27)

The stories are rich in imagery, and fantasy, yet every now and again a sense of the ridiculous peeps through, bringing the reader back to earth. There is also a strong moralizing element, traditionally found in fairy-stories, but here with the special Joan Aiken touch. Who else would think of a pair of legs going off, leaving their owner to get around on his hands or on a skateboard until he can learn to be kind to butterflies, which is what happens to Tod in **'Lost—One Pair of Legs'**? . . . Children of five to nine should have these stories read to them; perhaps some of the richness of words, ideas and imagery in them will spill over into their lives. (p. 27)

> *Linda Yeatman, in a review of "The Last Slice of Rainbow, and Other Stories," in* British Book News Children's Books, *March, 1986, pp. 14, 27.*

Surely not even Margaret Mahy is a more versatile writer than Joan Aiken. Her last book was another selection of comic stories featuring her enterprising and tetchy raven, Mortimer. This new offering, also of short stories, is of a very different kind. These are mock fairy tales but with very little humour in the mockery. The first third of the nine stories consists of delicate fantasies, beautifully done as ever but somewhat lacking in appeal to our robust infants. The tales get tougher as the book progresses, and some of the variations on folktale themes are most ingenious, but I still feel that Miss Aiken is giving them only a part of her formidable powers and that the less attractive part. Clever and well crafted, and in the hands of a skilled adult interpreter highly effective, the book is unlikely to be within the reach of those children who might be attracted by the subject-matter.

> *Marcus Crouch, in a review of "The Last Slice of Rainbow," in* The School Librarian, *Vol. 34, No. 2,*

June, 1986, p. 147.

MORTIMER SAYS NOTHING (1985)

Joan Aiken here presents four more stories of Mortimer the Raven and the Jones family. Fans of Mortimer (who still quotes 'Nevermore' when disgruntled) will not be disappointed. Realistic, down-to-earth characters in crazy situations and ridiculously contrived plots are Joan Aiken's forte and they provide hilarious reading for children over nine. In this book Mortimer wrecks both the preparations for Mrs Brown's lunch party and the aspirations of a German ornithologist; puts spoilt Cousin Annie's equally spoilt Winky Doll in the incinerator and neatly escapes revenge; unwittingly helps to catch a vandal; and, after a week of typically total confusion at the Jones's house, is found dead drunk in the bottom of the jug that should have contained homemade martini mix.

> *Valerie Caless, in a review of "Mortimer Says Nothing," in* British Book News Children's Books, *March, 1986, p. 14.*

Four more stories of Mr and Mrs Jones, their daughter Arabel, and their raven Mortimer. In moments of stress, Mortimer is apt to cry 'Nevermore!' but otherwise behaves like any other old, tetchy, spoilt and self-willed family pet. The Joneses move from one domestic crisis to the next, always on the brink of despair but never quite toppling over, even when Mortimer seems to have been blown up by a juvenile terrorist's bomb. Their everyday adventures which, given the circumstances and the characters, are never quite beyond possi-

Aiken at her desk.

bility, are very funny and are recounted with unfeigned zest. These Jones stories may be the light relief of an important writer, but Joan Aiken does not reserve any of her talents for more serious work. . . . A lovely book for reading aloud and for entrapping those who have decided that reading is not for them.

Marcus Crouch, in a review of "Mortimer Says Nothing," in The School Librarian, Vol. 34, No. 1, March, 1986, p. 40.

DIDO AND PA (1986)

Aiken's tales of Dido Twite are among her rollicking best, and **Dido and Pa** is no exception. Reunited at long last with Simon (whom readers first met in **The Wolves of Willoughby Chase**), Dido has just begun to describe her adventures when her Pa, having decoyed Simon, kidnaps his daughter and returns with her to London. The evil Eisengrim, head of the Hanoverians with whom Mr. Twite has long been involved, is plotting to overthrow King Richard and install his own puppet, a look-alike whom Pa expects Dido to prepare for his role as royal imposter. In an operatic plot filled with shifting scenes and shifty characters, complications are presented, compounded, and finally undone, with nearly all of the right people in the right places at the end. Mr. Twite, however, is absent from the final curtain call; and Dido, although painfully aware that her pa is bad beyond helping, recognizes the worth of his music and knows that without him, her life will lack some of its rich color. Aiken's talent for language and dialogue gives voice to the vigorous London street life she portrays: the children of poverty, the sellers of foodstuffs, the laborers. Building one subplot upon another, she moves from scene to scene with the ease of a skilled dramatist, creating entanglements that, like a cat's cradle, all come neatly together at the end of the tale. Satisfying. (pp. 168-69)

Dudley B. Carlson, in a review of "Dido and Pa," in School Library Journal, Vol. 33, No. 2, October, 1986, pp. 168-69.

Nobody does this sort of thing so well as Joan Aiken. Her skill lies in a buoyancy of invention that keeps the reader in a state of constant happiness. Partly this is a matter of language: much of it drawn, one guesses, from scattered actual dialects. People feel nohowish, and don't so much die as hop the twig. Then there is a general sensation, as to London itself, of blunt modernity alongside a kind of architecture in which Dickens's city is grafted on to Shakespeare's. Heroes and heroines, who abound, are of the different kind: so though we imagine Dido might in the eighth or ninth book become Duchess of Battersea, or even Queen of England, this instalment ends with her digging her elbows into the nearest ribs at the very thought of it. Here and there, a name says all: what more needs to be known about Mr Twite's appalling lady friend than that she is called Lily Bloodvessel?

There are two special triumphs. One is the character of Mr Twite, a villain who raises fleeting ethical issues: subsumed in Dido's thought that perhaps the tunes are what is important, not Pa. An act of major callousness, and even of murder, causes in him only a burst of song:

Oh what a fearful finish
To sink beneath the ice
But let your tears diminish
He's now in Paradise.

Many young readers will boo Mr Twite, while reserving the right, a page or two from the end, to mourn for him.

The second triumph lies in the way the story is underpinned with children: in the street, passing messages vital to the health of the State: everywhere, playing games that reflect on the plot. In the end, what this warm book in this warm series offers, apart from the pleasure of making a mess of history, is the joy of a sort of heroic gossip. A message on which the entire climax depends comes by way of someone's dad—"and his dad told my dad, and my dad told my mum, and my mum told Mrs Watkins, and Mrs Watkins told Peggy Watkins and Peggy Watkins told me".

Edward Blishen, "Hanoverian Hopes," in The Times Literary Supplement, No. 4365, November 28, 1986, p. 1343.

Those who have been following the fortunes of Dido Twite and Simon, Duke of Battersea, through their several books of adventure, starting with **The Wolves of Willoughby Chase,** will be pleased to know that Dido is as fiesty and quick-witted as ever. . . . The plot, as usual, so twists and turns as almost to defy description, but it concerns the efforts of Dido's Pa and his cohorts to overthrow the newly crowned King Richard. The master villain is the Margrave of Nordmarck, the Hanoverian ambassador, who plans to kill all the King's friends and replace the King with a double and so rule the kingdom. There follows such a swirl of adventure, of plots and counterplots, hairsbreadth escapes, slimy henchmen, clever and true-hearted guttersnipes, pathetic street children, and attacks by packs of prowling wolves as only Joan Aiken could manage to gather in one book. In the end the evil Margrave is defeated; Dido's Pa is killed; righteousness triumphs; but Dido refuses to marry Simon. Dido, always an interesting character, has developed considerably—besides being sharp-witted, she has become compassionate and reflective. Although she despises her Pa, an eminently despicable person, she sometimes wonders if his superb music does not somehow make recompense for his evil life. But it's clear this book will be enjoyed more for its headlong pace and excitement than any considerations about realism and character development. There do not seem to be any remaining malefactors to cause trouble—though it is unlikely that this would be any problem at all to Joan Aiken—but it would be very gratifying to have a sequel. (pp. 746-47)

Ann A. Flowers, in a review of "Dido and Pa," in The Horn Book Magazine, Vol. LXII, No. 6, November-December, 1986, pp. 746-47.

PAST EIGHT O'CLOCK (1987)

In each of these eight stories the author takes a well known folk song and weaves it into a story. Straightforward enough at first glance, but what really impresses is the way the weaving is done, so that there are all kinds of levels and subtleties and half-glimpses of something just out of reach. The children I teach, and their teachers, were spellbound when I read **"Pappa's Going to Buy you a Mocking Bird"** in assembly, and the echoes of the story haunted me for the rest of the day. A powerful imagination at work here. . . .

Gerald Haigh, "Folk and Fairy," in The Times Literary Supplement, No. 3685, February 13, 1987, p. 42.

On literary and physical counts alike this must qualify as one of the most distinguished books of 1986. Joan Aiken's eight short stories show her at her most relaxed. The words flow beautifully, making the book essentially one for reading aloud, in class or at bedtime. What gives it its unusual degree of unity is the device of associating each tale with a familiar song or rhyme, and each of these prompts the author to her own memorable and musical verses. More successfully than most, Ms Aiken blends traditional and modern elements in her stories, giving them contemporary relevance without introducing any incongruous notes. And, if all this seems to make the book appear solemn, let me add that warmth and humour pervade every story.

> *M. Crouch, in a review of "Past Eight O'Clock," in* The Junior Bookshelf, *Vol. 51, No. 2, April, 1987, p. 80.*

Eight stories woven around a theme of sleep and dreams incorporate newly worked traditional rhymes and lullabyes into contemporary settings. This sometimes results in a hodgepodge of magic, with the fantastical elements more assumed than developed. Folklore-based figures from Weaselly Winkie to a wicked Kelpie make arbitrary appearances in the world of modern kitchens and television programs. As word play and spoof, the stories work well, but they're not as convincing as some of Aiken's other work.

> *Betsy Hearne, in a review of "Past Eight O'Clock," in* Bulletin of the Center for Children's Books, *Vol. 40, No. 11, July-August, 1987, p. 201.*

A GOOSE ON YOUR GRAVE (1987)

There is much variety in Joan Aiken's new collection of short stories. . . . Far from being "a deadly cocktail—sample it if you dare" as the publisher's blurb would have us believe, this is a generally agreeable anthology of magic, fantasy and humour. Sadly, there are moments when Miss Aiken does not seem to be concentrating as hard as she might. Surely no school forced to make one of its staff redundant would ditch its physicist ("and he's such a good teacher")? Motorways do not have laybys and boys in boarding schools rarely talk about *home*work.

I would guess that the stories are intended for the 9 to 13 age range but some may be just a little outside the average young reader's experience. Grig is an ordinary enough boy except that his father just happens to be our ambassador in Paris and there is a disproportionate number of boys' public school stories. The dialogue in these is not always convincing but the story of the invention which causes everyone to go bald and the boy who invents a "cure" which makes the victims' scalps grow grass is very funny.

> *David Self, "Bite-Size Novels?" in* The Times Educational Supplement, *No. 3701, May 6, 1987, p. 59.*

The unusual and the abnormal subtly season the everyday events unfolded in this collection of short stories. Each story starts firmly rooted in the world we all know from our own experience. It slips almost imperceptibly into the paranormal. A small boy retrieves the spectacles of the victim of a street accident. He visits the Louvre in the care of the au pair who for her part is interested only in meeting her boy friend. As he dons the spectacles a whole new way of seeing opens up before him.

Some of the stories demand careful reading if their full implications are to be realised. A final sentence can be so enigmatical that you are sent scurrying to the first few lines for elucidation. **"The Lame King"** is a positive delight in the manner in which it brings the reader, by a series of hints so slight as to be easily missed, to the realisation that the elderly couple are being taken by their son and daughter-in-law on the final ride to Last House. It is a poignant and penetrating piece.

A real treat for the sophisticated young adult reader.

> *D. A. Young, in a review of "A Goose on Your Grave," in* The Junior Bookshelf, *Vol. 51, No. 4, August, 1987, p. 189.*

This collection from a master storyteller is not so much spine chilling as escapism from the unpleasant facts of existence. How often when life seems unbearable do we wish for something 'out of this world' to change everything? Joan Aiken makes us feel the despair, and then invents such original methods of turning the tables that we are constantly taken by surprise. Time-slips, pink-tinted glasses that reveal people's thoughts and bring paintings to life, travellers from space, all spring from Miss Aiken's fertile brain, with wry twists that make each development unexpected. There is even a ghost story to jerk the heartstrings. Only in the very last story do we feel a cold finger on our spines, and even then the victims appear to deserve their fate. I have always found Joan Aiken's stories particularly suitable for reading aloud, and these promise to be just as popular . . . especially if read with the lights dimmed. (pp. 344-45)

> *Patricia Peacock, in a review of "A Goose on Your Grave," in* The School Librarian, *Vol. 35, No. 4, November, 1987, pp. 344-45.*

THE MOON'S REVENGE (1987)

Joan Aiken has the great gift of imbuing much of her writing with a magical quality and this book is no exception. Seppy, the seventh son of a seventh son, is devoted to his fiddle playing but destined by birth to be a coach-maker. How he realizes his ambition, the part played by the moon and the uncanny spell which it casts upon his young sister Octavia, all add to the richness of this tale. . . . This is a book that could well become a classic to be enjoyed by any age, children and adults alike. It uses language at its best to involve, enrich and lead the reader on and is very highly recommended.

> *Elizabeth J. King, in a review of "The Moon's Revenge," in* British Book News Children's Books, *December, 1987, p. 11.*

Readers will find in this picture book many of the qualities of Aiken's short stories: a period setting; sympathetic characters; an exciting, original plot with more than a touch of magic; and a generous, skilled way with words. . . . Though the slender format may put off older independent readers, this is a book well worth introducing to them, or of course, reading aloud.

> *Carolyn Phelan, in a review of "The Moon's Revenge," in* Booklist, *Vol. 84, No. 11, February 1, 1988, p. 929.*

Seppy, seventh son of a seventh son in a seaport town, is himself seven: this is a clear enough sign that *The Moon's Revenge* is firmly based on tradition although the story comes from Joan Aiken's fertile imagination. . . . With felicitous phrases and small appropriate details the story develops, duplicated [by illustrator Alan Lee] in finely composed scenes in muted colour spread over and round the text, in a properly integrated and elegantly produced book where sea and shore, medieval costume and dramatically presented monster command careful attention. A book to keep, for reading aloud and for quiet private perusal, notable in atmosphere and in the teasing suggestions of a universal philosophical point. (pp. 4940-41)

> *Margery Fisher, in a review of "The Moon's Revenge," in* Growing Point, *Vol. 26, No. 6, March, 1988, pp. 4940-41.*

THE TEETH OF THE GALE　(1988)

After the sea and the wind comes the gale: this is the third of Joan Aiken's novels dealing with the breakneck adventures of a boy called Felix Brooke, in nineteenth-century Spain. Felix is half Spanish and half English, an aristocrat in both countries, and a magnet for excitements of all kinds. . . . Felix, now five years older, is a student of law at Salamanca when *The Teeth of the Gale* begins, and his cherished companion of the Pyrenean adventure, Juana (once known as Juan), is a postulant in a convent. It isn't long before the two, once again, are in the thick of an exotic enterprise: the proposed rescue of three children—or is it two?—from their lunatic father, who is holding them in a ruined castle at the top of a 200-foot crag. In fact, the father turns out not to be insane at all, only a sufferer under the illiberal regime of Ferdinand VII; this—the late 1820s—is a turbulent time for Spain.

Felix, along with Pedro (his friend and an employee on his grandfather's estate), the stolen children's imperious mother, a couple of nuns, coachman, postilions, mules and a lot of baggage, sets off across forested mountain slopes, through remote towns and villages and valleys, beset by blizzards and bears and various kinds of chicanery. A positive little demon of a child—not unlike the young Dido Twite in Aiken's

"James III" sequence of novels—keeps popping up all over the place, greatly to the discomfiture of Don Amador the portly government official in whose charge she appears to be. An episode of poisoning, some dramatic exits, a good deal of ill-doing, an endangered inheritance and some lost gold all come into the story, which is recounted in Aiken's usual boisterous, full-blooded and dashing manner. Once an Aiken plot gets going, there is no let-up at all in animation or intrigue.

> *Patricia Craig, "The Elements of Nature," in* The Times Literary Supplement, *No. 4440, May 6-12, 1988, p. 513.*

Between the years of about eleven and fifteen I devoured literally hundreds of adventure stories . . . I became adept at recognizing the formula, picking up the clues and following the trail. The prediction and recognition was part of the total enjoyment. In this third of Joan Aiken's books about Felix Brooke, grandson of a Spanish nobleman and an English Milord as well, can be found all the hallmarks of the robust, swashbuckling adventure story. There is the quest, the journey, dangers, double dealing, hair-breadth escapes, even the mandatory episode where the hero (and the heroine, too, in this instance) is bound and gagged and only sharp teeth and a knife can effect a rescue.

Where *The Teeth of the Gale* differs from my boyhood reading is in the grace of the prose, the intriguing political background (it is set in Spain in the late 1820s) and the fact that the hero's fellow protagonist is a young nun with whom he has shared previous adventures (before she entered the convent!) and with whom he is in love. This is a marvellous period piece with full bodied stereotypes, mystery, suspense and a completely satisfying dénouement. Readers who enjoyed *Go Saddle the Sea* and *Bridle the Wind* will queue up for this third of the trilogy. (pp. 31-2)

> *Maurice Saxby, in a review of "The Teeth of the Gale," in* Magpies, *Vol. 3, No. 5, November, 1988, pp. 31-2.*

Richard (Tupper) Atwater

1892-1938

Florence (Hasseltine Carroll) Atwater

19??-

American authors of fiction.

The following entry presents criticism of *Mr. Popper's Penguins.*

The Atwaters are well regarded as the creators of *Mr. Popper's Penguins* (1938), a story which has become considered a classic of humorous fiction for children. The tale of a mild house painter with a passionate interest in polar exploration who receives a penguin as a gift, the book, which is filled with absurd adventures, is told with a gravity and seriousness which underscores its fun. Richard Atwater, a translator and columnist who had already published a book for children, *Doris and the Trolls* (1931), was inspired to create *Mr. Popper* after viewing a film on the first expedition to the Anarctic by Admiral Byrd. Although he was excited by his idea for the book, Atwater was dissatisfied with his presentation of the story and abandoned the manuscript of *Mr. Popper* in a desk drawer. After his death, his wife discovered the manuscript and decided to finish it, rewriting the first few chapters and completing the final chapters. Illustrated by Robert Lawson, whose pictures are often thought to match the merriment of the text, *Mr. Popper* is often praised for the charm of its characters, the hilarity of its plot, and the successfulness of its blending of fantasy and reality. *Mr. Popper's Penguins* was named a Newbery Honor Book in 1939.

(See also *Something about the Author,* Vols. 16, 27, 54.)

Here is a find, a book not only funny, but universally funny. Children will cherish it; so will anybody with a love of joy. I read it for the first time on the way to the dentist and for the second time on the way back, and it made both journeys joy rides. Need I say more?

Mr. Popper was a mild and popular painter and decorator. . . .

[His mind] was at the Poles. If a "movie" about these regions came to town, he sat through three shows. He had read every book in the public library about Arctic and Antarctic exploration—preferably the latter because of penguins. Mr. Popper thought penguins must be the funniest and most ingratiating of birds—as indeed they are. One night when he was listening to the broadcast from the Antarctic he heard Admiral Drake say: "Hello, Mamma. Hello, Papa. Hello, Mr. Popper. . . . Watch for a surprise." It seems that the admiral had been so pleased with a letter Mr. Popper had written him about how nice penguins were, that he was sending him one. It came by air express, packed in dry ice, lively, curious and profoundly delighted with its new surroundings.

Can you imagine Captain Cook—the new arrival—beamingly marching up and down the bathtub and tobogganing down its side on his stomach? Or Mr. Popper air-conditioning the electric ice-box for use as a nest? Or trying (by telephone, too) to take out a license for leading a penguin on a leash through the streets? Or leading him (Captain Cook in the lead)?

However, the bird's interest waned: he was fading away. The family wrote to a great aquarium for advice. It also had one penguin who was fading away, and decided that they might as well fade together. Greta arrived. Soon there were ten more penguins.

So the only way to meet their heavy expenses was to put Popper's Penguins on the stage. This is too good to condense. The fun holds out to the last moment and its complete surprise—fun with just a touch, now and then, of something very like pathos in the character of good little Mr. Popper. No wonder everybody in Stillwater liked him: anybody would.

May Lamberton Becker, "Mr. Popper's Penguins," in New York Herald Tribune Books, *September 25, 1938, p. 6.*

A really funny book is always a treat. **Mr. Popper's Penguins,** by Richard and Florence Atwater, with perfect pictures by Robert Lawson that are just as merry as the story, measures up to all the requirements and is guaranteed to make you laugh. We enjoyed it so much we want to share it with all our friends. . . .

[The story of the arrival of the penguins and their] success in making a contract for Popper's Performing Penguins to appear in a chain of theaters operating all over the country is a riot of fun. Don't miss it!

Florence Bethune Sloan, "Fun, Fancy, and Friends in Books," in The Christian Science Monitor, *September 26, 1938, p. 6.*

[The] best part of the extravaganza lies in the adjustment of the first polar visitor to the everyday life of the painter's household, which immediately became anything but humdrum, and this is described with a quiet matter-of-factness only matched by Mr. Popper's, which underscores the incongruity and general daffiness. One penguin, on whom the authors have expended most of their ingenuity, manages to be funnier than twelve, although the account of twelve penguins settling themselves with characteristic dignity into a bus is not to be disregarded. The poker-faced gravity with which the farce is developed will appeal to adults, even though it never quite touches the heights of hilarity, and the situations themselves are enough to make any child chuckle and perhaps hope for word from Admiral Drake.

Ellen Lewis Buell, "Speaking of Popper and His Penguins," in The New York Times Book Review, *October 23, 1938, p. 11.*

[*Mr. Popper's Penguins* is] a book in which a little man who never did live in the flesh becomes permanently and nonsensically alive. . . . Here is a book to read aloud in groups of all ages. There is not an extra or misplaced word in the story. Amusing as it is, and impossible as it all is, under the sway of the author's quiet assurance we are convinced that all did happen as stated. . . . Robert Lawson evidently enjoyed the book, for his pictures fairly dance with the text. . . . Here's a book that is more fun than twenty-five movies. (p. 370)

A review of "Mr. Popper's Penguins," in The Horn Book Magazine, *Vol. XIV, No. 6, December, 1938, pp. 367-70.*

In **Mr. Popper's Penguins** you find a family who depart from all the conventional ways of family life and make it seem reasonable. They leave all the windows in the house open so that their penguins will be comfortably cold; they install a freezing plant in the basement (moving the furnace up to the living-room to make room for it) so that the penguins can raise a family, and when ten beautiful little penguins hatch out, the Poppers proceed to train them for a vaudeville act.

The troupe goes on tour, and everything happens! [Our family] laughed so hard when we first read about it that we had to stop reading to avoid hysterics. Now that we can control ourselves a little, we go over it slowly, dwelling on each episode, and savoring the utterly stupendous absurdity of it. The bit we all love the best is the first penguin's setting up housekeeping in the icebox. What he took in with him is the most extraordinary list of objects I know, and we can never read it without howls of laughter. . . . (pp. 166-67)

Annis Duff, "Some Funny Books," in her "Bequest of Wings": A Family's Pleasures with Books, The Viking Press, 1944, pp. 160-69

After more than forty years this book remains funny and refreshing. Part of the humor arises from the Poppers' matter-of-fact modification of their own lives to provide a suitable environment for the penguins. For example, after Greta arrives, Captain Cook's bachelor quarters in the refrigerator are too small so Mr. Popper decides they will leave the living room door and windows open so that it will be comfortable for the birds there. The authors comment that the Poppers soon were accustomed to sitting around in their overcoats and "Greta and Captain Cook always occupied the chairs nearest the open windows." The book contains many similar ridiculous situations. Robert Lawson's excellent illustrations capture the mood of the text. (p. 71)

Marilyn Leathers Solt, "The Newberry Medal and Honor Books, 1922-1981: 'Mr. Popper's Penguins'," in Newbery and Caldecott Medal and Honor Books: An Annotated Bibliography, *by Linda Kauffman Peterson and Marily Leathers Solt, G. K. Hall & Co., 1982, pp. 70-1.*

Stan(ley) Berenstain
1923-
Jan(ice) Berenstain
19??-

American authors and illustrators of picture books.

As collaborators, the husband and wife team of the Berenstains are the creators of enormously popular early reading books which are filled with slapstick humor and teach children by addressing everyday subjects. Most of these works feature a family of bears—Papa Bear, Mama Bear, Brother Bear, and Sister Bear—who walk children through common experiences like visiting the dentist and dealing with strangers wisely as well as comic adventures like finding a missing dinosaur bone. Each member of the Bear family has a distinct personality and function in the book; as Jan Berenstain has said: "the small ones are alert and smart and learn a lot from the big ones who are very sincere and expert but make a lot of mistakes while trying to impart their vast knowledge to their young." It is for this, in fact, that the Berenstains have been attacked by some critics, who feel that the portrayal of the bumbling, inept Papa Bear is demeaning and unwarranted. Other detractors have raised doubts as to the effectiveness and the artistic merit of the Berenstains' works. However, many observers recognize the easily accessible information and guidance offered by the books and cite their immense readership as an indication that the Berenstains indeed recognize the young child's needs and tastes. While depicting a comfortable, secure family full of affection and concern for

one another, the Berenstains teach children about important issues in a light manner that is characterized by its mirth and optimism.

(See also *Something about the Author,* Vol. 12; *Contemporary Authors New Revision Series,* Vol. 14; and *Contemporary Authors,* Vol. 25-28, rev. ed.)

AUTHORS' COMMENTARY

In our travels around the country in behalf of our eponymous bear books, we have fielded many questions. These range from the straightforwardly curious ("Why do you draw just bears?" Answer: "We don't—we also draw rocks, sunny dirt roads, trees, flowers, rainbows and even, on occasion, people") to the curiously straightforward ("How do you get along being together all the time?" Answer: "Ours is an old-fashioned Mom and Pop operation in which both partners do whatever needs to be done—writing, illustrating, cooking, bottle washing").

We find our work (and our bears) tremendously stimulating and enjoyable and, while we don't always agree on every dot and line, we have managed to harmonize successfully over 34 years of working together as cartoonists-writers and for the past 18 as author-illustrators of children's books. We do have one rule—a sort of unilateral veto—which has helped us over the humps. If one of us strongly objects to some point, project or approach, it is dropped without argument.

Not long ago a child asked us an interesting question, as children so often do: "Is it fun to do the bear books, or is it hard?" Our answer, after pondering a moment, was that it's both—or to coin an evasion: it's hard fun.

One of the more persistent and intriguing questions we have been asked over the years is, "Why don't you put the bears on television?" The answer is that we finally have. After about eight years of trying with various degrees of unsuccess, we managed to make the jump from printed page to glowing tube with an animated special called *The Berenstain Bears' Christmas Tree,* which was shown on NBC in December 1979. (pp. 99-100)

Having operated as a Mom and Pop store for so long, it took us a little while to get used to the collaborative complexities of what is essentially a film enterprise. There were meetings, story conferences, character drawings, color tests, network approvals and—yes—artistic differences. In the case of the latter, all we can remember is one occasion when we over-reacted to a suggestion that Papa wear a bowtie and suit at the Christmas dinner which closes the show. (The very *idea* of Papa even *owning* anything so effete as a bow tie!) . . .

Our second special, a Thanksgiving story called *The Berenstain Bears Meet Bigpaw,* aired last November 20, again with gratifying results. Easter and Valentine's specials are in production. Though our experience in helping to turn our printed page bears into talking, singing and dancing animated bears has been fun (*hard* fun), books remain our first love. With four new titles scheduled for fall publication and more being planned, we are absolutely married to the Berenstain Bears book series.

Television does make an interesting mistress, though. (p. 100)

> Stan Berenstain and Jan Berenstain, "You Can't Animate a Plaid Shirt," in Publishers Weekly, Vol. 219, No. 9, February 27, 1981, pp. 99-100.

GENERAL COMMENTARY

JOYCE HOFFMANN

The Berenstain Bears are the hottest ticket in children's publishing today. Although there are sharp divisions in children's book circles over whether their success is rooted in literary and artistic merit or in clever marketing techniques, the Berenstains' popularity is indisputable.

Among contemporary authors of children's books, probably only the venerable Theodor Seuss Geisel—the Dr. Seuss whose books have sold more than 100 million copies and who was the Berenstains' first editor at Random House—is ahead of them. . . .

"Right now, we could sell almost any book that had the Berenstain Bears in it," says Janet Schulman, editor-in-chief of books for young readers at Random House. She credits their widespread appeal (mainly to youngsters 3 to 7) to the comforting familiarity of the bear adventures and the coziness of the family, saying that the topics make children want to read more. (p. 16)

Not everyone, to be sure, is delighted with the Berenstain Bear books. Certainly there are sharp differences between the way in which the Berenstains see their work and the way their creations are viewed by some critics of children's books.

For example, when asked to explain the success of the Berenstain Bear books, Stan says, "Our world is family humor. I see us in the Peter Rabbit mold, popular, gentle, straightforward and noncontroversial—yet we don't sugar-coat life. We deal with reality. We're basically the only ones dealing with these kinds of problems."

"That's rubbish," says Betsy Hearne, author of *Choosing Books for Children* and co-editor of *Booklist, the American Library Association Journal,* which over the years has refused to review about 20 Berenstain Bear books because, according to Hearne, "they seem openly cluttered, cartoonish, and utterly didactic."

According to Hearne, plenty of children's authors are writing about the same experiences the Berenstains have capitalized upon and are doing it better.

"Harlow Rockwell's books *My Doctor* and *My Dentist* treat [experiences] more sensitively and with finer artwork," Hearne says."The Berenstains have been marketed very well. They wouldn't have this kind of popularity otherwise." On a title-by-title basis, Hearne predicts, the Berenstain Bears books will never wear as well as classics like Maurice Sendak's *Where the Wild Things Are.* (pp. 16, 18)

The criticism of the Berenstain Bear books enrages Stan Berenstain. "When you're commercially successful, the scholarly types are suspicious of you. If you're selling this many books, some people think there has to be something wrong." . . .

Moreover, the Berenstains have their defenders among educators and librarians. Carolyn Field, now retired from the Free Library of Philadelphia where she kept Nancy Drew mysteries off the shelves on grounds that the taxpayers' money could be better spent, did buy the Berenstains' books, and is one of their fans. "The Berenstains cover all the everyday subjects children are interested in," she explains. "They're not great art. Nobody's calling them great literature—but then how much great literature is there today?" . . .

One thing is certain: Kids do like the Berenstain Bear books. They are not just getting them because parents or grandparents think they will like them. The kids are asking for them. As Stan Berenstain puts it, "Kids don't like the bears—they are just crazy about them." (p. 18)

The Berenstains were drawn to children's writing by their own two growing boys. They found it difficult to satisfy the boys' appetites for funny children's stories. "Our kids loved Dr. Seuss," recalls Jan. "But beyond that, there weren't many robust, laugh-out-loud funny children's books. So we decided to do some."

Their publishing success began with *The Big Honey Hunt,* bought by Random House in 1962. At the time, Jan remembers, the most successful children's books seemed to be about bears and bunnies. They settled on bears "because they stand up on their hind legs and they look good in clothes," she explains.

Writers of how-to manuals on children's picture books note that animal characters serve the dual purposes of introducing a child to the creatures of his world as well as standing in for humans as universal personalities that are devoid of any racial stereotypes.

The Berenstain Bears' personalities, the setting, and even some of the clothing created for *Honey Hunt* remain part of the repertoire more than two decades later. That first story is the saga of a maladroit but well-meaning Papa Bear whose efforts to impress a wide-eyed son with his superior wisdom all end in comical disasters.

The original bears were scraggly, unrefined creatures, but even then Mama wore her polka-dot shirred bonnet, Papa was dressed in bib overalls, and they lived in a tree house with a bouncy little cub.

Sister Bear first became part of the bear family in 1974, the year that *The Berenstain Bears' New Baby* was published. From the very beginning, the books' illustrations were characterized by the use of cheerful, primary colors. (pp. 20-1)

A Berenstain Bear book begins with an idea that rattles around in Stan's or Jan's head for weeks or months. Thoughts about future books are most often discussed at breakfast, before they begin their 8- to 10-hour days sketching and painting at their drafting tables.

Some ideas get kicked around for years, like the prospect of having the bear family visit the moon. . . . (p. 22)

The Berenstains look for some universal experience, one that troubles and challenges both parents and children. They search for the critical blend of a title that conveys a sense of tension, and a story line that lends itself to pictures. And, most important, the subject has to interest them.

Random House has been suggesting a "First Time" book about a hospital stay, but Stan says he dislikes the thought of creating a story line requiring his bears to endure pain and suffering. "That just spooks me out," he says. "I just don't want to do it. It chills me."

Still using the characters, setting, and themes that were so successful, the recent books confront some universally frightening experiences and attempt to help children learn how to cope with various stressful situations. "We try to give kids the courage to face what they have to face," Stan explains. "You have to tell kids what to do."

After more than 20 years, the Berenstains pretty much have *carte blanche* with their publishing house. They generate their own ideas and can say "no" to a proposal they dislike.

While both Berenstains agree that children need an understanding of subjects like death and divorce, they say that such topics are inappropriate for Bear Country. To precipitate sad feelings in a popular series might be interpreted as a betrayal, Stan explains. "The context is all wrong. It would be like Bob Hope doing Sophocles."

The Berenstains' themes reflect conventional values. Their world is relentlessly middle-class. Mama and Papa Bear, for example, first left their cubs in the care of a baby-sitter, not to spend a night on the town but rather to attend a municipal meeting. And when Mama goes to work, she won't become a bank president or a counselor at Planned Parenthood. She will instead be running her own quilt shop.

The bears' future "First Time" experiences are likely to focus on subjects like new neighbors, a schoolyard bully, nightmares, and grandparents, says Stan. "The cubs aren't going to get into dope, Sister Bear isn't going to be an unwed mother, and Grizzly Gramps isn't going to die, I can guarantee you that," he adds.

In an age when the media concentrate on the darker side of life, Jan says, their books offer optimism, hope, and a positive picture of family life. (pp. 22, 31)

> *Joyce Hoffmann, "Bear Facts: What the Berenstain Bears Teach America's Kids About Life," in* Chicago Sunday Tribune Magazine of Books, *November 4, 1984, pp. 16-22, 31.*

THE BIG HONEY HUNT (1962)

For beginning independent readers, a bear story written with controlled vocabulary; illustrations are cartoon-like and quite repetitive. The story is slight in concept, rather drawn-out but with some humor. Some pages have poor division of sentences into phrases. Mother Bear sends Dad out for honey, and he explains to Small Bear that they are going to a bee tree rather than to a store. Boasting to the end, Dad makes one mistake after another as they race from tree to tree; they evade an owl, a porcupine, and a family of skunks; they are pursued by a swarm of angry bees and go to the store, Dad explaining that there you can get the best kind of honey.

> *Zena Sutherland, in a review of "The Big Honey Hunt," in* Bulletin of the Center for Children's Books, *Vol. XVI, No. 9, May, 1963, p. 138.*

A Beginner Book about a bear and his son looking for honey. The rather horribly humanised father shows off and is discomfited in front of his son by a bird, a porcupine, a family of skunks and a swarm of enraged bees: he finally buys honey at a booth. 150 words arranged for easy reading: high jinks in a vulgar vein.

> *Margery Fisher, in a review of "The Big Honey Hunt," in* Growing Point, *Vol. 5, No. 8, March, 1967, p. 867.*

THE BIKE LESSON (1964)

The Berenstain Bears first rollicked on to the easy reading scene in *The Big Honey Hunt. The Bike Lesson* is an excellent follow-up—a long rhyme in short words with a broad smile at fathers. Dad Bear gives Small Bear a new bike, but won't relinquish it until he's had a good ride. He claims that he's giving a series of bike-riding lessons but he wheels into a series of disasters until Small Bear has to pump him home on the handle-bars. Four color cartoon illustrations in the Berenstain's well known style.

> *A review of "The Bike Lesson," in* Virginia Kirkus' Service, *Vol. XXXII, No. 16, August 15, 1964, p. 812.*

A book for beginning independent readers; again Papa Bear (as in *The Big Honey Hunt*) gets into trouble while Small Bear remains sensible and calm. . . . Humorous, but the slight theme is over-extended; the illustrations are of comic-strip calibre, and the small value of the story is in the simple

From The Bears' Nature Guide, *written and illustrated by Stan and Jan Berenstain.*

vocabulary and the repetition that will afford reading practice.

> Zena Sutherland, in a review of "The Bike Lesson," in Bulletin of the Center for Children's Books, *Vol. XVIII, No. 6, February, 1965, p. 82.*

FLIPSVILLE. SQUARESVILLE. (1965)

The Berenstains seem to have a feeling for witty comment on the fads and foibles of youngsters and their parents. This is a "turn-over" book, meaning that Flipsville, the adult's guide to Teen-age Behavior begins on side one; Squaresville, the teen-ager's guide to Adult Behavior begins from the other side. The whole contraption is amusing and ought to make a number of people, young and old, smile, chuckle and hoot.

> Stephen J. Laut, in a review of "Flipsville. Squaresville," in Best Sellers, *Vol. 25, No. 10, August 15, 1965, p. 200.*

THE BEARS' PICNIC (1966)

Blandly and grandly ignoring the critics who are demanding dignity for fathers in stories and on TV serials, the Berenstains have made Papa Bear a well-intentioned bumbler in **The Bike Lesson** and **The Big Honey Hunt.** He is as stubborn as Donald Duck, not as ill-tempered and nearly as amusing.

This time, he's choosing a picnic site and each attempt to settle and eat is disastrous until they finally go home to enjoy themselves. This is becoming a universal experience as traffic increases and open land disappears. As usual, the Berenstains' broad color cartoons and simple, rhyming text provide good practice for easy reading and gentle teasing.

> A review of "The Bears' Picnic," in Virginia Kirkus' Service, *Vol. XXXIV, No. 14, July 15, 1966, p. 686.*

The Berenstains' bears are high on my list of good slapstick. The third book is as funny as the others. The bears go on a picnic, and Papa Bear is sure he can find "the perfect picnic spot." After young bear has pointed out the limitations of all of them they find the perfect spot—their own home. (pp. 36-7)

> A review of "The Bears' Picnic," in Saturday Review, *Vol. XLIX, No. 34, August 20, 1966, pp. 36-7.*

THE BEAR SCOUTS (1967)

[A] story in verse with cartoon illustrations. . . . Father Bear is once again portrayed as a bumbling idiot as the bear scouts go camping. Again, the lack of sublety in the humor will limit its staying power.

> Trevelyn Jones, in a review of "The Bear Scouts," in

School Library Journal, *Vol. 14, No. 4, December 15, 1967, p. 88.*

[Devotees] of the Berenstains unable to resist getting *The Bear Scouts* are in for a disappointment. Covering much the same ground as its two predecessors—Father Bear's decidedly shaky advice proving almost self-destructive—it lacks the ring of truth that made *The Bike Lesson* such a favourite. The pictures are as amusing as ever.

A review of "The Bear Scouts," in Children's Book News, *London, Vol. 3, No. 5, September-October, 1968, p. 240.*

THE BEARS' VACATION (1968)

Poor father is still the same oafish idiot he has always been and the same cartoonish color illustrations remain. However, father bear's advice on water safety is sound and will be remembered by young readers who find slapstick humor appealing.

Trevelyn Jones, in a review of "The Bears' Vacation," in School Library Journal, *Vol. 15, No. 3, November, 1968, p. 107.*

The Bears' Vacation . . . comically and ironically tells how to be safe at the beach. Father Bear supplies the rules, Small Bear supplies the rescues, and they both survive. Good holiday lessons for summer, taught with a twist of humor in bright color and cartoon-style drawings.

"You Do It Like This," in The Christian Science Monitor, *November 7, 1968, p. B8.*

INSIDE, OUTSIDE, UPSIDE DOWN (1968)

Inside Outside Upside Down . . . involves a bear and a box. The bear gets in the box, the box is turned upside down accidentally and taken outside. One line is added to the previous one in a cumulative fashion, the refrain being "outside, inside a box, upside down." The repetition will appeal to small children, as will the large, vividly colored, cartooned illustrations. The concepts suggest the need for adult explanation, but on the whole kids should find this great fun.

Trevelyn Jones, in a review of "Inside, Outside, Upside Down," in School Library Journal, *Vol. 15, No. 9, May, 1969, p. 107.*

Inside outside upside down has a story, introducing the young to a few useful prepositions; a bear (or is it a dog?) creeps into a box, is trucked off by a porter and put on a lorry, is precipitated off the lorry as it swerves, and runs home to his tree-house shouting cheerfully 'Mama! Mama! I went to town. Inside, outside, upside down . . .' (you can see by the pictures this is exactly what he did). A child who wants to expand the story a little will find the caricature pictures helpful in their dotty but explicit sequence.

Margery Fisher, in a review of "Inside, Outside, Upside Down," in Growing Point, *Vol. 8, No. 2, July, 1969, p. 1349.*

BEARS ON WHEELS (1969)

Bears on Wheels . . . relies for humor on the somewhat

shaky basis of vicarious enjoyment of tipsy balancing acts and spills: "Four bears on one wheel . . . one on two . . . five on one . . . five on none," and other variations. On the whole, the effect is slapstick and not up to [the Berenstains'] usually clever standard.

Della Thomas, "Counting-Down on the 1-2-3's," in School Library Journal, *Vol. 17, No. 7, March, 1971, p. 97.*

Another counting book with the emphasis on teaching to read with numbers appearing incidentally. As with Dr. Seuss, the treatment is humorous and the counting is more of a surprise for the child as the numbers do not rise in order from 1 to 10. One bear starts off with one wheel, picking friends up on the way, the animals perching unsteadily one on top of the other and swaying perilously until four bears on one wheel, meet one bear on two wheels, and they continue to fall off and on to one, two and three wheels to ring the changes.

Pat Garrett, in a review of "Bears on Wheels," in Children's Book Review, *Vol. I, No. 5, October, 1971, p. vi.*

THE BEARS' CHRISTMAS (1970)

The Bear's Christmas is a pleasant, somewhat unimaginative book, emphasizing the well-used Father-Plays-With-The-Toys theme which traditionally emerges in cartoon form each Christmas. But the unmistakable cartoon style single-handedly carries the day.

Guernsey Le Pelley, "To a Child's Unprejudiced Eye, the Cartoon Is a Fine Art," in The Christian Science Monitor, *November 12, 1970, p. B3.*

A rhyming text, cartoon-type pictures, a theme that's been used before, not without success: Papa Bear, a great show-off, demonstrates his talents with dire results. Here the exhibition is in pursuit of instruction, Small Bear having received new skates, skis, and a sled for Christmas. Papa Bear can't do anything; Small Bear knows how to do everything; the story ends with Papa rolling home as the middle of a huge snowball, trimmed with street decorations he has picked up, inadvertently, en route. Slapstick humor, obvious but with undeniable appeal, and a Christmas setting as assets; father-denigration and a trite format as weaknesses.

Zena Sutherland, in a review of "The Bears' Christmas," in Bulletin of the Center for Children's Books, *Vol. 24, No. 4, December, 1970, p. 54.*

OLD HAT, NEW HAT (1970)

Shopping for a new hat, the Berenstain bear looks at several—flat ones, tall ones, frilly and silly ones, bumpy and lumpy ones. In addition to the slapstick humor, *Old Hat, New Hat* . . . does offer several simple concepts of size and shape. Fine for beginning readers, with very few, easy words to a page and brightly colored, large, undetailed illustrations.

Trevelyn Jones, in a review of "Old Hat, New Hat," in School Library Journal, *Vol. 17, No. 4, December, 1970, p. 68.*

A child who is barely reading will find the first half dozen pages of this book very persuasive, for he need only read one or two words often repeated; then suddenly the pace quick-

The Berenstains in their study.

ens, as the dog looking for a new hat rummages through the shop, complaining "Too beady, too bumpy, too leafy, too lumpy, too twisty, too twirly, too wrinkly, too curly" and so on. The joke is simple and its resolution obvious from the start, and the splendid pile-up of words is well calculated to convince the laziest child that reading can be fun. Any last shadow of doubt will be dispelled by the crazy and really funny pictures.

> *Margery Fisher, in a review of "Old Hat, New Hat,"*
> *in* Growing Point, *Vol. 9, No. 9, April, 1971, p.*
> *1713.*

THE BERENSTAINS' B BOOK   (1971)

Stan and Jan Berenstain have in ***The B Book*** created another zany nonsense collection, illustrated with color enlivened, bold-line cartoons. It's a cumulative tongue-twister involving such unlikely "B" combinations as a brown bear, a blue bull and a "beautiful" baboon (a blonde, by the way, in ballet garb) who became involved with bubbles, bands, baseball teams, baby birds, and a balloon which breaks—Bam! How much this will contribute to basic growth in reading is problematical. It has just as questionable a relevance to children's needs as "the list." But *Sesame* influence is clearly at work here, and the book may indeed provide a head start into phonics (giving Dick and Jane a run for their money).

> *Eleanor C. Trimble, in a review of "The Berenstains'*

B Book," in School Library Journal, *Vol. 18, No. 4, December, 1971, p. 68.*

Cumulation in the text and the nonsense-plot are the appealing elements in a slight book for young children who are ready to read. For most of the story, all words begin with the letter "b" and even at the close there are few others. The drawings, in cartoon style, show "Big brown bear, blue bull, beautiful baboon blowing bubbles biking backward, bump black bug's banana boxes and Billy Bunny's breadbasket . . ." ending with "and that's what broke Baby Bird's balloon." Since Baby Bird has had no part in the story, this adds a note of urgent contrivance to a tale not distinguished for its restraint.

> *Zena Sutherland, in a review of "The Berenstains'*
> *B Book," in* Bulletin of the Center for Children's
> Books, *Vol. 25, No. 9, May, 1972, p. 134.*

BEARS IN THE NIGHT   (1971)

One of a series of books for children just beginning to learn reading, this has lively cartoon-style pictures and a minimum of text, all in prepositional phrases. After their mother has said goodnight and closed the door, a bevy of bear cubs goes out the window, down a tree, over a wall, and so on—off to explore in the night. Frightened by the sudden hoot of an owl, they speedily retrace their steps, the story using the same set of phrases in reverse, ending, " . . . Over the wall, Up the tree . . . In the Window! Back in bed." There's plenty of action, the sort of humor small children enjoy, the appeals of animal characters and reversal of word pattern, and a side benefit: clarification of prepositions.

Zena Sutherland, in a review of "Bears in the Night," in Bulletin of the Center for Children's Books, *Vol. 25, No. 8, April, 1972, p. 117.*

Bears in the Night is a mad cumulative exercise in nothing very much, simple, absorbing and infectious. Writers for this age-group too rarely realise the need for simple ideas of this kind. The result is that a number of enormous, quite beautiful picture-books are tossed aside after a minute because there is nothing in situation or story to interest the child. (p. 762)

John Fuller, "Animal Allsorts," in New Statesman, *Vol. 83, No. 2150, June 2, 1972, pp. 762-63.*

Bears in the Night has the compulsion of absolute simplicity. It is a poem of prepositions. But, sadly, like so many from the Dr Seuss stable, the book is visually undistinguished. Indeed the bears have a completely unbearlike appearance. But at least the pictures faithfully mirror the words. "In bed", it says, and there are the seven bears all in one big bed.

"Strong but Simple," in The Times Literary Supplement, *No. 3672, July 14, 1972, p. 805.*

C IS FOR CLOWN: A CIRCUS OF "C" WORDS (1972)

Beyond the **B Book** to a cacophonous chorus of C's—pyramiding from a single Clown (peering from behind a closed curtain) to "Clarence Clown carrying cats carrying canes and collies carrying clubs." "Can Clarence Clown carry cats carrying canes and collies carrying clubs *and* cows carrying candles *and* Caroline Catfish *and* Clara Canary?" No. Can this corny commercial calamity clarify the confusion of "C" words children cope with daily? No way.

A review of, "C Is for Clown: A Circus of 'C' Words," in Kirkus Reviews, *Vol. XL, No. 17, September 1, 1972, p. 1025.*

C Is for Clown: a Circus of "C" Words is a sequel to **The B Book,** but is less effective. "Can Clarence Clown carry cats carrying canes and collies carrying clubs and cows carrying cakes and candles and Caroline Catfish and Clara Canary?" No. And beginning readers can't read all those words either. Stan and Jan Berenstain build a very slight plot through repetition to the entirely predictable ending. The pictures are colorful but the whole is unsuccessful.

Carol Chatfield, in a review of "C Is for Clown: A Circus of 'C' Words," in School Library Journal, *Vol. 19, No. 4, December, 1972, p. 71.*

THE BEARS' ALMANAC: A YEAR IN BEAR COUNTRY (1973)

First you should know some things about Berenstain bears. Their progenitors are the anthropromorphic animals found in the treasuries of Richard Scarry and others. These bears are unlikely to attain a place in your memory and affection as say, Pooh Bear and Smokey, or Gentle Ben, the British Paddington, Goldilocks' trio—or even Gladly the Crosseyed Bear. As drawn, they are comic and cartoony. If they didn't have a black olive sitting on the end of their snouts, hairy an-

kles and furry hides you'd swear they're really mom and pop, sis and junior in disguise. They act human: sweep and snooze, fly kites, ride bikes, dress up at Halloween, stuff stockings at Christmas, yet they lack distinct personalities. They are message carriers, mediums to teach and instruct as they've already done in a dozen volumes labeled Beginner Books and Bright and Early Books.

Their new **Almanac** is in much the same tradition—a scaled-down gathering of observable phenomena about the holidays, weather and seasons along with labeled pictorial descriptions of associated activities. "Summer brings sun and fun . . . swimming, floating, diving, boating . . . tanning, fanning . . . hot dogs, mustard, frozen custard." As is usual in most Berenstain books father is a bit of a flub, although this time he shares the role with scraggly Great Natural Bear. The serious, scholarly case is presented by Actual Factual Bear who imparts basic facts about snow and sun, thunder and lightning, the wind and the moon. The book is taken notice of here because it is unpretentious, has some modest mirth and instruction. You can live without it of course, but it is a pleasant companion with which to hibernate for brief spells. (pp. 8, 10)

George A. Woods, "The Bears' Almanac," in The New York Times Book Review, *November 25, 1973, pp. 8, 10.*

A romp through the seasons is provided in **The Bears' Almanac: A Year in Bear Country**. . . . Starting in January, each season is described in rhyme, followed by a factual section about natural phenomena which occur during it (snow, thunder and lightning, etc.). The major holidays are mentioned, and each section concludes with a list of the various objects and activities typical of that season. Every page is filled with amusing pictures of the familiar Berenstain bears, which nonreaders as well as readers will find funny. Unfortunately, an error mars this entertaining offering: it states that Thanksgiving falls on the "next-to-last Thursday in November," which, of course, is not always the case. Nevertheless, **The Bears' Almanac** will be popular with primary graders.

A review of "The Bears' Almanac: A Year in Bear Country," in School Library Journal, *Vol. 20, No. 4, December 15, 1973, p. 58.*

Not really an almanac, this oversize book is divided into four parts, and for each of the four seasons, the busy, busy pages describe the weather, seasonal activities, holidays, "Some of the Things" the season brings, and "Actual Facts about . . ." (snow in winter; wind in spring, or rain; sun in summer, and thunder and lightning; the moon in fall). Certainly the book can serve to impress on children the distinguishing features of each season, but the "actual facts about . . ." section seems more disruptive than helpful, especially because the phenomena they describe are not necessarily seasonal. However, the bears dash about merrily, and there's humor in many of the pictures, the animal characters will be found appealing, and there's some text in rhyme as well as some in prose.

Zena Sutherland, in a review of "The Bears' Almanac: A Year in Bear Country," in Bulletin of the Center for Children's Books, *Vol. 27, No. 8, April, 1974, p. 123.*

HE BEAR, SHE BEAR (1974)

He Bear, She Bear . . . is an annoying attempt to demonstrate equal employment opportunity for males and females. He Bear and She Bear jingle their way through a list of things they can do whether they are "he or she"—from racing cars to taming tigers. The lackluster verse ("I see her. She sees me. We see that we are he and she.") has none of the charm of earlier Berenstain Bear books, and the bright and busy illustrations don't lift the story out of the doldrums.

> *Alice Ehlert, in a review of "He Bear, She Bear," in* School Library Journal, *Vol. 21, No. 4, December, 1974, p. 49.*

A small offering for International Woman's Year. 'He', is distinguished by a peaked cap, 'She' by an inane pink ribbon in her hair. Having established the indisputable fact the 'He' cannot be a mother, nor (however much she may wish it) 'She', a father, the book goes on to list all the things that either can be. Compared with the side-splitting humour of so many of the 'Bear' books, this is a dreary come-down.

> *Valerie Alderson, in a review of "He Bear, She Bear," in* Children's Book Review, *Vol. V, No. 2, Summer, 1975, p. 76.*

THE BEAR DETECTIVES: THE CASE OF THE MISSING PUMPKIN (1975)

In joint pursuit of whoever stole farmer Ben's prize pumpkin, bumbling Papa bear follows his hound and his instincts while the young bears are guided by their detective book. When the book finally tells them to follow their noses the mystery is solved: "The pumpkin was pied by Mrs. Ben." The rhyme, the frenetic chase and the slapstick false leads might keep beginners on the trail, but as easy reading sleuths go *The Bear Detectives* have nothing like the class of our favorite, *Nate the Great.*

> *A review of "The Bear Detectives: The Case of the Missing Pumpkin," in* Kirkus Reviews, *Vol. XLIII, No. 20, October 15, 1975, p. 1180.*

What have the Berenstains and Roald Dahl in common? They appeal to children partly because they poke fun at adults from the child's viewpoint. Dad, in the 'Bear' books, always takes command of the situation (remember *The Bike Lesson* and *The Great Honey Hunt*?) but always fails. He never admits to failure and his offspring bear up his illusion. They patronise him! *The Bear Detectives* is the latest addition to the series and should be as popular as the rest. A useful device which makes the text less difficult by increasing redundancy is the use of rhyme. This also tends to increase the books' read-aloud potential, and their length is ideal for tape presentation as 'talking books'.

> *Cliff Moon, in a review of "The Bear Detectives," in* The School Librarian, *Vol. 25, No. 3, September, 1977, p. 237.*

THE BEARS' NATURE GUIDE (1975)

Another winner from the Berenstains whose books, while considered to be overly busy by some critics, are consistently loved by children. As usual, there is lots to see, and the rhyming text blends in perfectly. The bears, equipped with walking sticks, proceed on a very informative, funny, and colorful nature walk. This can be read and re-read, and the illustrations will provide children with something new to see each time.

> *Patricia Bock, in a review of "The Bears' Nature Guide," in* School Library Journal, *Vol. 22, No. 5, January, 1976, p. 35.*

The subtitle of this book, "A Nature Walk Through Bear Country," describes, in general, its contents. The book features the well-known "Berenstain Bears" in colorful and amusing drawings as they travel in nature. The authors attempt to introduce the pre-school child to numerous nature concepts through an illustrated, rhymed story. Children will probably find this book delightful, but, overall, far too many concepts are introduced for so elementary an audience. Parents and teachers could use a few pages at a time to introduce a limited number of concepts as a basis for getting young students to think about some of their own experiences. Beginning readers may have some difficulty in following the placement of the rhymes throughout the pages. The book probably is best suited for reading aloud to pre-readers, since most children beyond this age will probably find the story too cute and babyish.

> *Donald J. Nash, in a review of "The Bears' Nature Guide," in* Science Books & Films, *Vol. XII, No. 1, May, 1976, p. 37.*

This is Nature without Tears, with a vengeance! A gaily-coloured guided tour by Papa Bear, his various mistakes and accidents are viewed tolerantly by Momma and the two cubs. With various other characters, they demonstrate to young readers what nature is: animals, birds, sea-creatures, insects and reptiles, and land and sea. There are frequent recaps and elementary classification, all in Dr. Seuss-like verse, with mnemonic jingles to learn. It works very well, provided you are not too fussy over the mixture of fact and fantasy, and the inevitable inclusion of so many features of American rather than English wildlife. It is all great fun and may indeed prove a useful introduction to nature matters.

> *M. Hobbs, in a review of "The Bears' Nature Guide," in* The Junior Bookshelf, *Vol. 41, No. 6, December, 1977, p. 332.*

THE BERENSTAIN BEARS' COUNTING BOOK (1976)

The *Counting Book* makes a difficult concept even more difficult. Pre-readers would not gain any understanding of this concept, unless they could count or recognize written numbers. Further, a young child would not always know that a blue line separates the consecutive number and thus may be confused by the number of bears on two facing pages. . . . The book's format does have several redeeming features. First, it is compact; children enjoy looking through and holding a book that they can easily manipulate. Second, the book is sturdy, an important factor when purchasing books for the novice learning to appreciate and value books. Third, the cardboard pages make it easy to manipulate by young children developing fine motor skills. Still, I would not recommend this book; durability is not enough when considering a book for young children. (pp. 157-58)

> *Lynn H. Aspey, in a review of "The Berenstain Bears' Counting Book," in* Science Books & Films,

Vol. XII, No. 3, December, 1976, pp. 157-58.

THE BERENSTAIN BEARS' SCIENCE FAIR (1977)

The Berenstain productions are seldom passed up by adults looking for children's gifts. The books are obvious choices, reasonably priced and solid methods of teaching, not to mention amusing. Dizzy cartoons in brash colors show Papa, Mama, Small Bear and Sister at a science fair. The story of their day is told in rhymes that expose bumbling Papa's slim knowledge of scientific facts. That gives experts the chance to deliver authentic information about how a machine works, about the three kinds of matter, about energy, etc. The book is fun and it contains suggestions for projects (some irresistibly nonsensical) that kids will want to adopt or adapt.

A review of "The Berenstain Bears' Science Fair," in Publishers Weekly, *Vol. 212, No. 17, October 24, 1977, p. 76.*

Learning theorists may argue that the tell-tell strategy of this book is not appropriate for the intended audience, especially when dealing with science. However, for those students who have learned to appreciate the Berenstains' other works in children's literature, there is a real value in the book, namely, that the book tries to sell science to youngsters. This reviewer feels that the Berenstains have hit the mark. The book is readable and exciting for youngsters (attested to by this reviewer's sample of 30 primary school age children). In addition, the bottom line of the book (i.e., have your own science fair) might encourage youngsters to do just that.

Howard L. Jones, in a review of "The Berenstain Bears' Science Fair," in Science Books & Films, *Vol. XIV, No. 2, September, 1978, p. 111.*

Provided it is not taken too seriously this is an excellent introduction to science for the very young. They will greatly appreciate the illustrations of the Bear family learning about science, without necessarily understanding the text or the concepts behind the various subjects. The bears start by learning facts about machines and then continue through levers, wedges and wheels on to facts about matter and energy. Each point is delightfully illustrated using members of the Bear family, with Father always managing to get himself in a mess, thereby producing humour in what can be a serious subject.

G. L. Hughes, in a review of "The Berenstain Bears' Science Fair," in The Junior Bookshelf, *Vol. 43, No. 1, February, 1979, p. 24.*

THE BERENSTAIN BEARS AND THE SPOOKY OLD TREE (1978)

The Berenstain Bears and the Spooky Old Tree may fill the gap in Halloween stories accessible to the very young. The bears of the series encounter fairly friendly dangers (it's difficult to make an alligator ferocious in cartoon style)—just enough for a pleasant spinal chill. The illustrations by authors Stan and Jan Berenstain, repetition, and simple word choice will encourage beginning readers.

A review of "The Berenstain Bears and the Spooky Old Tree," in School Library Journal, *Vol. 25, No. 4, December, 1978, p. 65.*

Position words and the shivers combine for an eerie visual treat in **The Berenstain Bears and the Spooky Old Tree.** Kindergartners beg for rereading to savor details of the illustrations.

A review of "The Berenstain Bears and the Spooky

From The Berenstain Bears Learn about Strangers, *written and illustrated by Stan and Jan Berenstain.*

Old Tree," in The Reading Teacher, *Vol. 34, No. 4, October, 1979, p. 94.*

THE BERENSTAIN BEARS AND THE MISSING DINOSAUR BONE   (1980)

A bone is missing from the dinosaur in the Bear Museum and the three cubs and their dog Snuff are determined to find it before opening time. As they prowl around the dark building, they encounter a number of scary figures which turn out to be museum pieces when the lights are turned on. In the end they discover that Snuff has buried the bone and the case is solved. Not a very clever ending, but the colorful drawings by authors Stan and Jan Berenstain and the usual bear antics are always a hot item.

> *Drew Stevenson, in a review of "The Berenstain Bears and the Missing Dinosaur Bone," in* School Library Journal, *Vol. 26, No. 9, May, 1980, p. 84.*

THE BERENSTAIN BEARS' CHRISTMAS TREE   (1980)

The search for **The Berenstain Bears' Christmas Tree** takes Pop and the kids on a trek through the countryside as snow falls and Christmas Eve draws near. Determined to cut down the perfect tree even if doing so leaves other animals homeless, Pop gets into one scrape after another until he realizes that Christmas is a time to be unselfish. It is hard to recommend the book for its intrinsic value. The poetry sometimes clumps along. "Maybe it was / The tiny twig tree, / Or maybe the seeds / That helped Papa see / The other guy's need." The moralizing is heavy-handed. "There was something IMPORTANT / That he was forgetting— / Christmas is for giving! It isn't for getting." But fans of Stan and Jan Berenstain's madcap bears will clamor for this Christmas outing, especially after the TV special on which the book is based is aired again.

> *A review of "The Berenstain Bears' Christmas Tree," in* School Library Journal, *Vol. 27, No. 2, October, 1980, p. 162.*

An oversize flat has a rhyming Christmas story, undersize but equally flat. Here the frenetic bear family is preparing to decorate a tree, getting out all their ornaments and then realizing they have forgotten the tree. Pop and the two children set off to find the perfect tree; each time Pop thinks he's found it, he discovers that it's the home of other creatures. Back they go to buy a tree, as Mom had suggested, but the trees are all sold. However, when they near home, Pop and the children see that all the creatures they've spared have decorated their house with every family ornament, a grateful tribute that—in a sudden excess of sugar frosting—shows the true meaning of Christmas. And the *"real* Christmas Star" fills the sky with a silvery light, and the true Christmas spirit fills the heart of every bear. A mawkish ending to a contrived story written in often-halting rhyme and meter.

> *Zena Sutherland, in a review of "The Berenstain Bears' Christmas Tree," in* Bulletin of the Center for Children's Books, *Vol. 34, No. 3, November, 1980, p. 47.*

THE BERENSTAIN BEARS AND THE SITTER; THE BERENSTAIN BEARS GO TO THE DOCTOR; THE BERENSTAIN BEARS' MOVING DAY; THE BERENSTAIN BEARS VISIT THE DENTIST   (1981)

The dearth of material on these subjects and the popularity of the Berenstain bears push these books into the recommended category. Each story unfolds straightforwardly, with the cubs unenthusiastic about moving, going to the doctor and dentist, or having a baby-sitter. Papa and Mama bear reassure, the event occurs and, of course, turns out much better than anyone anticipated. The treatments are cursory and sometimes contain alarming elements, as in the illustration of a giant hypodermic needle or the dentist's pliers, referred to as "yankers." Rockwell's books on medical visits, *My Dentist* and *My Doctor,* are much superior, but parents often like a choice of source materials in these situations, and this series provides another option.

> *Ilene Cooper, in a review of "The Berenstain Bears and the Sitter" and others, in* Booklist, *Vol. 78, No. 9, January 1, 1982, p. 596.*

There are few books introducing small children to the offices of doctor or dentist that have the appeal that these two "first time" books starring the Berenstain Bears will have! (p. 12)

In spite of the light-hearted approach to the subject, the information gleaned from these books is straightforward and acceptable and can prepare a child adequately for that first dentist or doctor's appointment. (p. 13)

> *Heddie Kent, in a review of "The Berenstain Bears Go to the Doctor" and "The Berenstain Bears Go to the Dentist," in* Appraisal: Science Books for Young People, *Vol. 15, No. 3, Fall, 1982, pp. 12-13.*

With their usual humor and understanding of children's fears, the Berenstains have written and illustrated a new series for some of the important firsts in children's lives. The doctor is a woman bear and her explanations to Brother and Sister are good, but I really didn't like her making an example of Sister Bear when it was time for shots. Perhaps more should have been said about drilling Brother's cavity as this is usually what everyone dreads most. However, these are an adult's picky objections: children are just glad to see more about Berenstain's bears.

> *Elizabeth Monette, in a review of "The Berenstain Bears and the Sitter" and others, in* Children's Book Review Service, *Vol. 10, No. 6, Winter, 1982, p. 51.*

THE BERENSTAIN BEARS AND THE MESSY ROOM (1983)

The latest in the Berenstains' First Books, a series that deals with family situations, is sure to make toddlers smile while they absorb an implied lesson. Brightly colored cartoons of the popular Bear family illustrate the story and prove that everything in Bear Country—on the grounds outside and in their comfortable treehouse—is shipshape, except for the room shared by Brother and Sister. It is a mess because the cubs argue over who should neaten up instead of working together. Mama Bear loses her temper and tosses all her children's possessions into a carton that she intends to throw on the junk pile. When Brother and Sister scream in protest, Papa rushes upon the scene with a proposal for cooperation that soothes hurt feelings and ends the story.

A review of "The Berenstain Bears and the Messy Room," in Publishers Weekly, *Vol. 223, No. 24, June 17, 1983, p. 74.*

Brother and Sister Bear share a very messy room with toys scattered in typical childlike fashion. While they occasionally neaten it up, they spend more and more time " . . . arguing about clean-up chores instead of sharing the job and working as a team" while a grumpy Mama Bear does the real cleaning. They cry and protest when a disgusted Mama begins throwing everything into a large box, calling it all junk. Papa comes to the rescue, designing and building boxes and storage for everything. This is not a story to be shared and enjoyed, chuckled over and discussed between parent and child; rather it is a treatise on how to clean up a shared room in which the bears are merely a vehicle. (pp. 58-9)

Carole B. Kirkpatrick, in a review of "The Berenstain Bears and the Messy Room," in School Library Journal, *Vol. 30, No. 3, November, 1983, pp. 58-9.*

THE BERENSTAIN BEARS AND TOO MUCH JUNK FOOD (1985)

The bears have got into the habit of snacking at the mall and are pudgy and out of shape. Mrs. Bear and Dr. Grizzly set them back on a nutritious path. Almost inescapably preachy, but brightly done.

A review of "The Berenstain Bears and Too Much Junk Food," in The New York Times Book Review, *July 21, 1985, p. 14.*

This book is fun for parents and children to read together. Everyone will love the names of different junk foods, such as "Sweetsie Cola" and "Choco-Chums." The book reminds us of a few bad habits that promote junk food, such as snacking at the movies or while watching television. Mama Bear observes that the cubs are getting chubbier, and they all witness Papa splitting his pants as he reaches for candy that has fallen on the floor. Mama packs all the remaining junk food in the freezer, and the next day they all go shopping for healthy, nourishing foods: whole grain bread and cereal, fresh milk and cheese, and fresh fruits and vegetables. A visit to Dr. Grizzly (a female) turns into an educational slide show on the anatomy and physiology of the nervous sytem, muscles, bones, and digestive tract as well as an explanation of which foods help build and strengthen different parts of the body. Dr. Grizzly says that junk foods just pile on the fat. She also briefly mentions the benefits of exercise as the Bear family leaves her office, and they decide to jog home. Mom has healthy snacks ready now for munching: nuts, raisins, frozen yogurt, and carrot sticks. The family starts a jogging program and competes in a three-mile run. I highly recommend this book as a most enjoyable introduction to good nutrition and exercise.

Ellen R. Paterson, in a review of "The Berenstain Bears and Too Much Junk Food," in Science Books & Films, *Vol. 21, No. 2, November-December, 1985, p. 78.*

THE BERENSTAIN BEARS ON THE MOON (1985)

A delightful tale told in rhyme and supported by captivating color illustrations. In an adventure to the moon and back, the bears and their pooch cope with weightlessness, meteor showers and moon dust. They explore, plant a flag, take notes and collect moon rocks. The Berenstains have once again produced a winner for beginning readers.

Anne Wirkkala, in a review of "The Berenstain Bears on the Moon," in School Library Journal, *Vol. 32, No. 2, October, 1985, p. 148.*

This "Bright & Early Book" is designed for very young children. The authors' goal is to use "humor, rhythm and limited vocabulary to encourage preschoolers to discover the delights of reading for themselves." The story tells of two bears and a puppy that travel to the moon, and it is nicely illustrated and reasonably scientifically sound. It deals with weightlessness and shows the use of pressurized suits on the moon, but the lunar landscape is unfortunately not accurately illustrated. The book also misrepresents a meteor shower as a compact bunching of material. However, as a read-aloud book for youngsters, this book is a delight. Its scientific shortcomings are not serious for the intended audience.

Darrel Hoff, in a review of "The Berenstain Bears on the Moon," in Science Books & Films, *Vol. 21, No. 2, November-December, 1985, p. 70.*

THE BERENSTAIN BEARS LEARN ABOUT STRANGERS (1985)

The 'all American' Berenstain bears may not appeal to everyone but this particular book is worthy of review because it tackles a predicament faced by so many parents—how to teach children to rationalise their reactions to strangers. A balance is achieved by featuring two very different bear cubs. A sister, naturally exuberant and outgoing, who overreacts to her parent's cautions, and brother, more reserved by nature and level-headed in his response to their advice. By comparing the way in which each behaves in everyday situations even children as young as three or four should be able to effect a compromise and so gain reassurance from the book. The reassurance may also extend to adults who are nervous about broaching the subject, or who have done so in the past but are still unsure of its reception.

Coverage is comprehensive. Examples of the potential dangers are lifted from stories in the newspaper and bedtime reading material before being modified by the maxim about rotten apples in a barrel. Yet no mention is made of sexual harrassment until the check-list of precautions on the last page of the book which gives adult readers the chance to include or ignore this aspect of the problem as they see fit. It also ensures the book's suitability for use with the youngest children.

Suki Bond, in a review of "The Berenstain Bears Learn about Strangers," in Books for Your Children, *Vol. 23, No. 1, Spring, 1988, p. 31.*

Paul Berna

1910-

French author of fiction.

The writer of mysteries and adventure stories for middle and upper graders, Berna is often praised for creating works which present familiar plots and character types in a fresh and original manner. He is best known as the author of *A Hundred Million Francs* (1957; U. S. edition as *The Horse without a Head*), the story of a gang of ten shrewd street urchins in a Paris suburb who become involved with the criminals who have stolen the children's three-wheeled headless horse. The youngsters are aided in their sleuthing by a sympathetic police officer, Inspector Sinet, and other adult members of the community. Commended for its vivid atmosphere, exciting plot, humor, vitality, and convincing picture of a classless society of children, *A Hundred Million Francs* was awarded the Grand Prix de Litterature du Salon de l'Enfance in 1955 under its original title *Le Cheval sans Tête*. Many of Berna's subsequent books are structured similarly to *A Hundred Million Francs*. In these works, which are set in suburban Paris as well as in locales such as the French Riviera and the south of France, he characteristically depicts the courage and camaraderie which grows out of crisis in narratives filled with danger and action. Berna has also written several series throughout his career. He followed *A Hundred Million Francs* with two stories about the adventures of his popular gang and their eleven dogs, created three humorous mysteries about young amateur detective Bobby Thieret which also feature Inspector Sinet from *A Hundred Million Francs,* contributed to the science fiction genre with two novels which describe the establishment of a research station on the moon in 1970, and wrote two stories about the exploits of the adventurous and independent Mael family in both France and the South Seas. Several of Berna's books include topical themes, a characteristic which allows him to invest these works with philosophical undertones. Starvation in India, for example, underscores the adventure *A Truckload of Rice* (1968), while the negative effects of war is the basis for *They Didn't Come Back* (1969), a mystery which Berna wrote for his two sons about the legend of a lost band of young patriots who fought for the French Resistance. Berna is usually considered an author whose skill with characterization, ability as a storyteller, and understanding of children makes him an especially well respected contributor to the field of international juvenile literature.

(See also *Something about the Author,* Vol. 15 and *Contemporary Authors,* Vols. 173-76.)

GENERAL COMMENTARY

MARGERY FISHER

These two fine stories [**Threshold of the Stars** and **Continent in the Sky**] tell how Colonel Rey reaches the Moon and how he establishes research bases there. Streets ahead of most English equivalents because hackneyed subjects are livened by attention to character. The greed for gain, the jealousy of

technicians, the precarious courage of a boy in a new world— it is these themes that make Berna's stories so good.

> *Margery Fisher, in a review of "Threshold of the Stars," in* Growing Point, *Vol. 1, No. 9, April, 1963, p. 144.*

A HUNDRED MILLION FRANCS (1957; U.S. edition as *The Horse without a Head*)

[This book] will most certainly be made into a film, because in film parlance, it "has everything"—excitement, adventure, humour, stress, character and above all, life—life in the ten street urchins for whom a headless horse on three wheels can provide a lifetime's enjoyment, and life in the wretched crooks who can only find their enjoyment in stacks of banknotes. The superb illustrations [by Richard Kennedy] make this altogether a delicious book which will take its place in the school library alongside some few others which are always out and never in. (pp. 71-2)

> *Phyllis Hostler, in a review of "A Hundred Million Francs," in* The School Librarian and School Library Review, *Vol. 9, No. 1, March, 1958, pp. 71-2.*

Everything about this book is first-rate: children, story, dogs, setting, grown-ups. The illustrations are witty and brief, and show a part of France and its inhabitants seldom seen by visitors. As for the gang, Inspector Sinet has summed up their qualities when he thinks of one of them, Marion, "an odd sort of girl, not yet 12 and of poor parents, and yet there was something about her that made you think twice. She was worth having on your side." This book will be popular with discriminating readers for a long, long time, and it well deserves to be.

Marjorie Fischer, in a review of "A Hundred Million Francs," in The New York Times Book Review, *November 2, 1958, p. 40.*

The swift pacing of the story, the vivid atmosphere of the Paris slums, and the fascinating delineation of character have won for **The Horse Without a Head** the Grand Prix Litteraire of the Salon de l'Enfance. A book which appeals, both because of the unusual story it tells and because of its conviction that, in any genuine community where members fiercely concern themselves with each other's interests, even the struggle for survival is sweet.

A review of "A Hundred Million Francs," in Virginia Kirkus' Service, *Vol. XXVI, No. 23, December 1, 1958, p. 871.*

[Late] in 1958 came one of the best books of that or any year, **The Horse Without a Head.** Eleven to thirteen-year-old boys and girls should enjoy it as soon as possible. Like two others of our favorites for this age, *Tistou of the Green Thumbs* and *Treasure of Green Knowe,* it is from abroad, . . . but unlike them it is a book for realists, the lovers of true-life stories, of mystery, excitement and danger (real danger—no milk and water variety). It has all the elements children like most, swift action, a loyal group of youngsters, sturdy and self-reliant, surmounting difficulties with skill and determination, a puzzle to unravel and plenty of suspense.

No reader of any age could put it down unfinished after meeting in the first chapter Gaby and Marian's intrepid gang from Poverty lane as they hurtle one by one down a steep hill, mounted on a derelict wooden hobby horse on wheels, risking a "glider landing" by postponing braking until the last possible moment. Soon the headless horse provides more than hot-rod sensations. Sinister thugs show a strange interest in it, steal it and challenge the gang's skill in detective work. With the help of their families and the police, but chiefly by the use of their own shrewd wits plus a remarkable "ride to the rescue" by Marian and her sixty dogs, they solve an amazing crime. An excellent story, well plotted, original, lively, which makes most books for this age group seem like thin gruel.

Margaret Sherwood Libby, in a review of "A Hundred Million Francs," in New York Herald Tribune Book Review, *March 8, 1959, p. 10.*

In this country [England] Paul Berna's reputation stands firmly on the rock of **A Hundred Million Francs.** (I was astonished to discover recently, in conversation with a party of young French children, that his is not a household name in his own country.) **A Hundred Million Francs** is a story in the 'Emil' tradition in that it portrays children going about their own business in an adult world, not divorced from that world—as, for example, Ransome's children are—but living successfully alongside it. Like *Emil,* **A Hundred Million Francs** shows a classless rather than a proletarian society. The children and their parents are certainly all poor but not self-consciously so. Poverty is a part of everyday life like eat-

ing and playing. When the children, and their headless horse, help to solve the mystery of the missing haul from the great train robbery, the promise of reward briefly threatens the independence which their freedom from property gives them. The promise fades, fortunately. The gang would not have survived the assault of affluence. Besides, their parents would never have agreed. As Fernand's father said: 'It wasn't his way of earning money', and the kids had certainly enjoyed 'a couple of million's worth of fun'.

The book, like *Emil* and unlike the mainstream of adventure stories, shows not only a classless but a sexless society, or one in which no sex distinctions operate. Marion is a full member of the gang, earning the right by her forty-mile-an-hour rides on the headless horse and by losing a couple of teeth in the process, and consolidating her position by training her team of dogs for just such a crisis as the affair of the hundred million francs offers.

Kids outwitting a gang of professional crooks is a familiar theme, almost the most outworn of formulae and one which has produced some of the dreariest of all stories. Basically this is the theme of **A Hundred Million Francs,** but with significant variations. The children do not play a lone game; this is a combined operation between children and adults, and the courage and ingenuity of the former are in no way diminished by their calling on their parents and the police for help. The thieves are defeated by their own mean-spiritedness, by the professional skill of Inspector Sinet, and by Marion's love of animals which has given her the finest pack of crook-hunting dogs in France.

The book gives a highly convincing and satisfactory picture of society. Ultimately, however, it is the society of the children which gives Berna's book its unique quality, those Petits Pauvres for whom the street which witnesses their operations is happily named. Not since *Emil* have children been depicted with such spirit and unsentimental affection. Whether playing their break-neck games or hunting criminals, they are always credible, always high-spirited, never wholly serious. (pp. 40-2)

For many children this book must have the quality of a wish-fulfilment, and this is partly the secret of its success. That children can be so self-reliant and have such dangerous fun, hindered not at all by the at-most mild opposition of parents—' "One of these days, I warn you, you'll go and break your neck",' says Madame Douin casually—who are too busy to temper love for their offspring with admonition and restriction. Well-intended grown-ups have sometimes been appalled on reading about the headless horse which takes its riders headlong down the slum streets to the hazard of their limbs and the annoyance of sensitive neighbours, fearing that young readers will wish to emulate the feats of Gaby and Fernand. Children are more sensible. Joyfully suspending disbelief in enjoyment of a superbly told story, they know nevertheless that this, for all its persuasive credibility, is not their world.

Berna never matched the success of **A Hundred Million Francs.** (p. 42)

Marcus Crouch, "High Adventure," in his The Nesbit Tradition: The Children's Novel in England 1945-1970, *Ernest Benn Limited, 1972, pp. 26-47.*

A Hundred Million Francs, though not without its literary defects, is a book which brings a deal of pleasure to many children and is well worth being made available to them. In addition it has for the adult reader a number of interesting aspects, the most intriguing of which has to do with the symbolic relationship between the old toy horse which the children ride down the streets of their village and the gang of children itself. It is this relationship, and its ramifications, which will be discussed here.

There is little difficulty in recognising the horse to be a symbol of the gang itself. At the lowest level of representation the horse functions as the gang's emblem or mascot. More importantly it is seen to be itself the uniting of the gang—it is the one body which makes all the individual members of the gang one body. When the horse is stolen then the gang, too, is lost. That is to say that when the horse is stolen the gang is at a loss and in danger of disintegration. The physical similarities between the gang and the horse also strengthen this notion of a symbolic relationship. The horse, for example is neither impressive nor attractive in appearance and the gang is a motley collection of unprepossessing individuals. (p. 183)

Once we recognise the horse as a symbol of the gang two more parallels can be drawn. The first is relatively minor but the second is of paramount importance to this discussion.

Firstly, both the horse and the gang lasted longer than was expected.

Secondly, and more importantly, both the horse and the gang are headless. It is immediately apparent that the horse lacks a head but this assertion that the gang is headless, or without a leader, is one which requires some justification.

Gaby is the nominal leader of the gang but when we examine the nature of his leadership we find that the situation is not so clear cut. It is not Gaby but Marion who wields most of the power in the gang. This power derives largely from her almost magical control of the dogs which she conjures up as a *deus ex machina* when the gang is physically threatened. Even five adult crooks are no match for Marion. Add to her power over the dogs the fact that as treasurer Marion controls the purse strings of the gang and we have a character strong enough to enforce, as Marion does, her moral decisions on the rest of the gang.

Gaby then is only the nominal, makeshift leader of the gang and when he is knocked from his position by the new-comer, Marion, the gang is left headless. Similarly the horse. . . . . (pp. 183-84)

The claims of two other members of the gang for the role of "head" can be dismissed easily. Fernand, as owner of the horse, wields some power but, in using his power to enrol the too powerful Marion in the gang, he forfeits whatever authority he may have had. Marion, on the other hand, is unacceptable as the head of the gang for symbolic reasons. She removes, but does not replace, the cardboard head and she is seen to represent too clearly the physical or bodily strength of the gang. (The children would probably say she is unacceptable because she is a girl.)

This notion that no child in the gang is the "head" is reinforced in the episode on The Abandoned Factory when the children don enormous carnival masks and stand the horse's head on a poker "like a totem-pole". Clearly here all the children are false heads, the real or true head of the gang being present within the circle only symbolically. In addition there is the hint that there is nothing within the gang itself which

can lead us to its "head". This is derived from the fact that, although the horse's body holds the key (in both senses of the word) to the solution of the robbery, it holds no clue to the whereabouts of its own head.

We could at this stage be satisfied to say that both the horse and the gang are headless, that both function very efficiently without heads, and that the headless horse is an effective symbol of the leaderless gang. There is, however, one fact which forces us to further consideration—*the horse's head is known to exist!*

Let us assume that the physical existence of the horse's head is a reliable symbolic clue and so continue our search for the gang's "head". An examination of the symbol itself, the horse's head, may lead us to that which it symbolises.

What, then, do we know of the horse's head? We learnt of its discovery [by] the rag-and-bone man. . . . He tried to stick the head back on to the horse's body but it wouldn't hold so he kept it and later gave it to Monsieur Douin, Fernand's father. It was taken and hung on a coat hook in the Douin home where it terrified Roublot when he tried to search the house. Later it was taken to the shed of the sawmill (the children's new club room) where it was seen by Inspector Sinet as he watched the masked children from the nearby bushes. After the recovery of the stolen money Fernand took the horse's head into the Magistrate's Court but did not expose it there. Finally Monsieur Douin stuck the head on "with insulating tape reinforced by a good dolop of glue" but it was soon dislodged again in a spectacular crash when Gaby ran into the bottle collector's cart. Gaby, claiming that the horse "doesn't want a head,' kicked it into the long grass off the side of the road. And there, presumably, it is lying still.

Where does an examination of this information lead us? Let us consider one point at a time:

(i) The character we are seeking comes into contact with the gang but can never belong to it. This seems to suggest an adult but the only adults in the book are parents, crooks, policemen, and the odd minor character like the rag-and-bone man. All appear very unlikely but no other characters seem eligible so we must press on.

(ii) The character we are seeking is in the community but not of it. This would eliminate the parents from our list but clearly applies to the other adults, including the rag-and-bone man.

(iii) Roublot is frightened of the character we are seeking. There are a number of possibilities here but from those remaining on our list a policeman would seem the most likely.

(iv) The character we are seeking both looks like a horse and at the same time looks like something else. (Remember that the rag-and-bone man thought at first that the horse's head was a dog.) *There is only one character who fits this description—the policeman (bloodhound?) Sinet.*

> For Inspector Sinet was definitely horse-faced. It was common knowledge, and all policemen pulled his leg about it.

So Inspector Sinet is our man; he is the horse-head we have been seeking all this time. This discovery tends to come as a surprise at first but we should not be taken aback. We have been shown quite clearly, through the symbolism, that the relationship between the gang and its "head" is a very strange and tenuous one so we should have been prepared to expect the unexpected.

In the light of our new knowledge of the importance of Inspector Sinet as the "head" of the gang to the structure of the book as a whole, some additional observations are worth making. For example we can now recognise the relevance of the otherwise puzzling fact that Sinet is the only character in the book to develop.

The connection between the presentation of the horse's head to the children at the time they had lost their horse and their meeting with Sinet because they were lost without their horse is now apparent—in both cases the head has turned up when the body is lost. Similarly the undisclosed presence of the horse's head in the Magistrate's Court now clearly refers to Sinet, whose developing relationship with the gang has not been revealed to the Magistrate.

With our additional knowledge we are also now able to enjoy more the complexity of the episode where Sinet observed the children in their masks. A brief re-examination of this passage should prove rewarding.

Because the horse is missing at the time, the body of the gang is symbolically absent although the members of the gang itself are present. However, each member is wearing a mask, so in that sense there is no *body* present at all, only the false heads of the children and the real head of the horse. The real "head" of the gang is also present in the person of Sinet watching from the bushes. He, of course, does not need to put on a mask as he *is* the head and wears his horse-head permanently. His presence is represented symbolically by the horse's head on the poker although, naturally enough, neither he nor the children realise that this is the case. We cannot blame the Inspector, however, for thinking "he had stepped into another world" and for finding the whole situation "a nightmare".

The final point concerns the conclusion of the book. The casual reader, and presumably the child reader (although we must be careful not to assume anything of what any child does or does not discover in a given book), is provided with a happy ending in which, although the Inspector does not actually join in the children's game, he and the gang go their own ways in a mood of warm, mutual acceptance of each other. For the more attentive reader, however, the ending is less comfortable and more thought provoking. Such a reader can see that the gang, having made use of Inspector Sinet, will now once again reject him forcefully and completely.

> The horse hadn't suffered much, but the smash had taken the head clean off. "Well, it's plain he doesn't want a head!" said Gaby, in a tone that brooked no answer. And with that he booted it as hard as he could, and sent it flying into the grass on the Clos Pecqueux.
> Rather shyly Inspector Sinet came up the rue de la Vache Noire. He kept to the side of the road, for he was rather ashamed to be trespassing on their favourite spot, nor did he like to butt in when they were so obviously enjoying themselves. But his appearance upset no one—on the contrary! 'Hi! Inspector!' called Zidore, pointing to the horse with a polite gesture of invitation. Don't you sometimes want to have a go?' Inspector Sinet closed his eyes, put out his arms, and, a look of horror coming over

his face, made off up the rue des Petits-Pauvres as hard as he could go.

And so the head we have sought and found we must finally leave behind, lying in the deep-rooted weed bed of Inspector Sinet's restrictive adulthood. (pp. 184-86)

> *Ralph E. Norris, "In Search of a Head: A Consideration of One Aspect of Paul Berna's 'A Hundred Million Francs'," in* The Junior Bookshelf, *Vol. 42, No. 4, August, 1978, pp. 183-86.*

THRESHOLD OF THE STARS (1958)

This is the story of a research station in 1970, where a visit to the moon is planned. Here live scientists, pilots and technicians and their families, and it is through the eyes and the minds of the children that we see the exciting manoeuvres and developments that lead to the ultimately successful landing. The author knows his children, and Michael and Jean in particular impress and convince. The vagaries of childhood are here expressed in the classroom and outside and always there is the jostling atmosphere of a crowd of children. There are also glimpses of the adult as his world impinges on the child's, but M. Wurtz, the tutor is a stilted and narrow character whose lessons give an unrealistic air. Surely a curriculum at such a time and in such a place would include more than the geography of the moon. The theme itself is not an uncommon one, but is not an easy one to handle successfully. Here it is dealt with boldly but somewhat ruthlessly. The outlines are true but they are harsh and there is little warmth or feeling. One gets a sense of other worlds here, a glimpse at a likely future, but it is not attractive. The narrative is clear and planned with a single minded thoroughness to the last detail. (pp. 287-88)

> *A review of "Threshold of the Stars," in* The Junior Bookshelf, *Vol. 22, No. 5, November, 1958, pp. 287-88.*

Science fiction closely meshed with factual data in the trend of development in space research. . . . Good adventure, and so well translated [by John Buchanan-Brown] than one never has a sense of the author being a Frenchman. There are a number of characters who have a thoroughly adult quality and the ideas of what the future holds are made credible.

> *A review of "Threshold of the Stars," in* Virginia Kirkus' Service, *Vol. XXVIII, No. 21, November 1, 1960, p. 924.*

CONTINENT IN THE SKY (1959)

This is a sequel to **Threshold of the Stars,** and describes a flight to the moon and the interruption of scientific work there by the intervention of power politics. The story is again told by Michael Jousse, one of those resourceful youngsters who are so useful to writers of adventure stories and who would be so intolerable in real life.

Few books of lasting quality have been written in the form of science-fiction, and of those still fewer have been written about space-travel. . . . [When] writers put on their spacesuits they seem to take off their skill in narrative and characterisation. Not that **Continent in the Sky** is a bad story, but it is a goodish story in spite of, not because of, being about space-travel. The moon is only incidental to the story, which might with minor alterations have been set in almost any difficult terrain. M. Berna, who wrote so brilliantly about Paris and its gamins in *A Hundred Million Francs,* is—can we be surprised?—less at home on the moon, and his narrative and his characterisation never rise above the conventional. A disappointing book. (pp. 214-15)

> *A review of "Continent in the Sky," in* The Junior Bookshelf, *Vol. 23, No. 4, October, 1959, pp. 214-15.*

THE KNIGHTS OF KING MIDAS   (1961)

Another of Paul Berna's epics of French child-gangs, *The Knights of King Midas* has all its author's usual liveliness, but rests on a preposterous premise. Outside the Riviera town of Port-Biou, a settlement of elderly squatters get their shacks burnt down in a forest fire; unless they can raise a million francs to erect improved dwellings within a month, they will be evicted. Some of the local children set about gathering the money by various methods, at prodigious personal cost and sacrifice, and finally achieve it. Such a degree of sustained good-Samaritanism by young children is quite beyond belief, and their series of happy accidents is too good to be true. Granted this, it is an exhilarating story. (p. 716)

> *Roger Gellert, "Small Swede, Neo-Nesbit," in* New Statesman, *Vol. LXI, No. 1573, May 5, 1961, pp. 715-16.*

[In *The Horse without a Head*], a gang of adventurous children kept things humming in a Paris suburb. In this new tale, set in a village on the French Riviera, we meet an equally vital and appealing gang of 11 boys and girls.

The ability of the children to earn money—by selling fish and rare stamps, by winning a prize in a yachting regatta, acting in a film, taking part in a television quiz show, and a myriad other ways—is a marvel of ingenuity. Their earnest dedication to their cause and their obstinacy in the face of almost certain defeat are truly heroic. The goal of 1,000,000 francs and the amounts earned—all figured in francs—will seem stupendous to American readers and their achievements spectacular.

Wonderfully warm, exciting, and funny, *The Knights of King Midas* is head and shoulders above most of the current crop of books. It should not be missed by discerning readers.

> *Polly Goodwin, in a review of "The Knights of King Midas," in* Chicago Sunday Tribune Magazine of Books, *January 14, 1962, p. 12.*

Paul Berna never makes the mistake of letting his characters remain static. In *The Knights of King Midas* he describes a group of children and, as always, makes each one recognisable and *active* in the situation he invents for them. . . . The theme of children making money is familiar enough; Berna's version of it is fresh and entertaining. His description of the regatta, and of the part played by the children in the procession of boats, is as good a piece of narrative as any in his work—or, indeed, in any story of this type. (pp. 520-21)

> *Margery Fisher, in a review of "The Knights of King Midas," in* Growing Point, *Vol. 4, No. 1, May, 1965, pp. 520-21.*

FLOOD WARNING   (1962)

What a master Paul Berna is, and here he has a subject to stretch him. Instead of city crooks he is now dealing with a natural catastrophe and its effect on a closed community.

The flood comes to Chateau-Milon, a small boarding-school in the valley of the Loire. When the waters recede and life returns to normal, some subtle changes have taken place in the school. Everyone has been tried by ordeal by water.

The story of the flood is superbly done, without any extravagance or lofty writing. It is in the portrayal of character that the book excels. This kind of school has been described so often that almost all the possible changes have been rung: the shy master, the bully, the glutton, the malcontent, and so on. They are all here, but instead of being lay figures they are real people, acting not according to literary convention but to their true natures.

Flood Warning is exciting, funny, tremendously readable. It is above all profoundly convincing, the work of a story-teller who is also a first-rate novelist.

> *A review of "Flood Warning," in* The Junior Bookshelf, *Vol. 26, No. 5, November, 1962, p. 256.*

[*Flood Warning*] is a story of a French boarding-school for boys in the Loire valley and too much in the valley by half, for floods are the trouble. . . . It is a St Martin's summer they are having, very warm it is and odd. Then the whirlwind comes, the storm and the rain. At first it is only the tributary that breaks bounds. But dynamiting the Loire banks, hopefully to drain the floods that way, simply lets loose that grand river. How wild and eerie all is now, with the swirling icy element at large and the fog sitting fast upon it. And the incidents of danger are so good, the floods lapping to the upper dormitory, the escape by ladder-bridge to the old tower, the Vicomte paddling the canoe again and again over the pathless water to the highland refuge. M. Sala becomes brave, all the people are slightly altered, but it is the eeriness one remembers, above the good jokes and the courage, the eeriness and the creeping up.

> *Stevie Smith, "Flooded Out," in* New Statesman, *Vol. LXIV, No. 1652, November 9, 1962, p. 658.*

Storms swell the River Loire. The boys and masters in a school have to fight for their lives against a flood. This necessarily bald summary gives no idea at all of the tremendous tension and excitement of the book. But more than that, one feels Paul Berna is in touch with the spirit of the times, is keenly aware of the anxiety of his age. "We are on the knife-edge of disaster; it seems to be typical of the age we live in", says the headmaster.

His characters are not pitting themselves against other men but against the forces of nature, which are dangerous and deadly now, but which will later resume their cooperative unifying character. And it is in this positively-directed drama that the characters develop, learn to make decisions, learn to appreciate one another, learn that they are part of a whole while still remaining individuals. The writing—originally French, which perhaps makes it more dispassionate than a similar English book would be—has a startling feeling of accuracy and authenticity.

> *A review of "Flood Warning," in* The Times Literary Supplement, *No. 3169, November 23, 1962, p.*

902.

THE MYSTERY OF SAINT-SALGUE (1963)

We have come to expect from Paul Berna something out of the ordinary run of children's stories; once again we are not disappointed. His gang of ten youthful eccentrics (the heroes of *A Hundred Million Francs*, now grown up) and their eleven dogs are traveling on holiday to the south of France in a battered Citroen van, affectionately dubbed "Calamity Jane." Inevitably they are sucked into a whirlpool of skulduggery which keeps them dodging a pair of undesirables to the final climax—the discovery of a lost village which is the goal of a group of shady businessmen and two Canadian philanthropists.

The action of the story bounces along, propelled by tantalising clues and a mounting tension which is not slackened until the last chapter. But it is disconcerting to find a writer of Berna's stature using chance overheard conversations, delayed recognition and an unconvincing situation in which "Calamity Jane" stops a large runaway car by nosing her way in front of it at speed—a bumper-to-bumper manoeuvre that would tax the skill of a Stirling Moss.

> *A review of "The Mystery of Saint-Salgue," in* The Junior Bookshelf, *Vol. 27, No. 5, November, 1963, p. 277.*

This complex tale of trickery centres round a village once 'drowned' for a water scheme and now to be raised to life again. It turns out that the gang from Louvigny are closely connected with Saint-Salgue for their parents were evacuated from here to the Paris suburb years before. This seems a somewhat strained pretext for continuing the adventures of the gang but few readers will grudge the author his pretext because he gives us a cunningly fresh view of the children, some of them now almost grown up, but as ebullient as ever and just as ready with their good sense and their humorous attitude to difficulties. A story full of the excitement of action and character.

> *Margery Fisher, in a review of "The Mystery of Saint-Salgue," in* Growing Point, *Vol. 2, No. 7, January, 1964, p. 270.*

The enchanting gang of children who made their debut in the author's *A Hundred Million Francs* make a welcome reappearance. . . . They are soon involved in adventures and mysteries in a profusion which ensures that there is never a dull moment on the journey or a dull page in the book, and there is a fine and satisfying climax. The characters will not make quite the initial impact on readers who first encounter them in this book as they did in the earlier books, which children should be encouraged to read first. Recommended also for top-class juniors.

> *Robert Bell, in a review of "The Mystery of Saint-Salgue," in* The School Librarian and School Library Review, *Vol. 12, No. 1, March, 1964, p. 85.*

THE CLUE OF THE BLACK CAT (1964)

This is a really good story which holds the attention from start to finish. The characters are well defined and I particularly liked the ubiquitous detective, Inspector Sinet, who allows the children to do much of his detecting but is always

there when needed. In this respect Paul Berna scores heavily over lesser writers whose children do everything by themselves, outwitting dangerous and ruthless criminals while all adults have a holiday a long way away. (pp. 302-03)

> *A review of "The Clue of the Black Cat," in* The Junior Bookshelf, *Vol. 28, No. 5, November, 1964, pp. 302-03.*

Inspector Sinet of *A Hundred Million Francs* is once again in charge of a case in Paul Berna's new mystery story *The Clue of the Black Cat*. Once again it is the children of a Paris suburb who help him to solve it. Confidence tricksters persuade M. Thiriet, who is desperate to find a decent home for his wife and four children, to part with all his savings for an apartment which is not theirs to sell. Then they disappear leaving the memory of a mysterious black cat as the only clue to their identity. It is M. Thiriet's son Bobby who remembers the cat and with the help of school friends and an ingenious use of the school magazine for publicity he tracks down the criminals and recovers his father's money. From the mystery angle this is Paul Berna's best work and would rate high among thrillers for adult readers, but the characters are less individual, less memorable than in *The Hundred Million Francs*. Atmosphere and scenes are as vivid as ever. . . .

> *"A Matter of Taste," in* The Times Literary Supplement, *No. 3274, November 26, 1964, p. 1080.*

The Clue of the Black Cat is a cleverly plotted, divertingly written story, with just enough Gallic salt to pique the taste.

The local prefect of police, Inspector Sinet, . . . proves to be a coony fellow, if a little slow on the uptake compared to the kids. There are a few farfetched elements in the plot, but on the whole it washes: the droll wit helps.

> *Taliaferro Boatwright, "Having the Crime of Their Lives," in* New York Herald Tribune, *October 31, 1965, p. 24.*

MAGPIE CORNER (1966)

Paul Berna always convinces me with his children but (as a foreigner, true) I must express doubt about the casual comic-opera policemen in *Magpie Corner,* who take some unorthodox short cuts during their investigations of cigarette smuggling. Investigating on his own is Frederick Langlais, a bright lad whose garage-owning father refuses to talk about his obvious secret worry. Like all Berna's stories, this is a nicely judged mixture of high spirits and provincial exactness, with a splendid climax focussing attention once and for all on the dominant element in the book, the corner of a by-pass in the Saône valley, car numbers and car repairs, and the unceasing noise of traffic. A pretty tall story but immensely enjoyable.

> *Margery Fisher, in a review of "Magpie Corner," in* Growing Point, *Vol. 5, No. 2, July, 1966, p. 739.*

THE SECRET OF THE MISSING BOAT (1966)

Paul Berna anchors the fantasy of his boy-foils-crooks stories, usually, by an adept use of local colour. *The Secret of the Missing Boat* has for background an island off the coast of Brittany, where a young fisher-boy is successfully evading his school teacher on the mainland in order to finish work on a dinghy he has salvaged. Fanch's capabilities as a craftsman being well established from the start, it is easy to believe also in the natural nosiness that leads him, with his friend Lise, to start a private investigation into Beany, the lodger, and his unpleasant friends. The secret, the theft of a pretty remarkable treasure, would be hard to swallow on its own, but supported by details of currents and weather and by youthful chatter it becomes acceptable.

> *Margery Fisher, in a review of "The Secret of the Missing Boat," in* Growing Point, *Vol. 5, No. 9, April, 1967, p. 879.*

Many of the orthodox elements of a children's adventure yarn are here: the slightly off-beat boy-hero with sufficient depth of character to cope with crises, a pair of rather nasty criminals, a "goody" in disguise, an ogre-schoolmaster who turns out to be a staunch ally, and buried treasure.

In the hands of Paul Berna, however, the familiar is given an unusual twist and a convincing reality. Set on the coast of Brittany, **The Secret of the Missing Boat** quickly poses a number of mysterious questions. The suspense never flags; the pace of the story, like young Fanch's newly-salvaged dinghy, fairly zooms along; the climax is skilfully engineered and neatly linked with the opening pages of the story through a minor character. (pp. 115-16)

> *A review of "The Secret of the Missing Boat," in* The Junior Bookshelf, *Vol. 31, No. 2, April, 1967, pp. 115-16.*

THE MULE ON THE MOTORWAY (1967; U.S. edition as *The Mule on the Expressway*)

The hardworking staff of the *Puisay Students' News,* the school magazine which solved the mystery of **The Clue of the Black Cat,** once more take up detective work through its pages. Its subscribers save an apparently worthless mule involved in an accident from the slaughterhouse, only to find a ruthless gang of criminals after it too. This is a lively narrative of industrial espionage in a Paris suburb, with Bobby, the youngest detective, in danger through his intuitive understanding of the animal's plight. The translation, however, with its odd slang and portentous long words sounds alien, in spite of allusions to James Bond and *Private Eye,* and the meaning of the dialogue is often not clear at first reading. Even these obstacles, however, cannot dim the excitement of the mystery.

> *A review of "The Mule on the Motorway," in* The Junior Bookshelf, *Vol. 32, No. 1, February, 1968, p. 44.*

The school magazine and its staff which were introduced in **The Clue of the Black Cat** . . . are again used as the instruments for unravelling a mystery. The story run by the magazine concerns a run-away mule which appears on a motorway. The teenage staff of the magazine, aided by Inspector Sinet, other enjoyable adults and, of course, the many readers of the magazine, begin to disentangle the reasons why the mule was loose on the motorway, and this leads, by fascinating stages, to the discovery of the inevitable crooks and their capture. It is all rather hard to swallow but very entertaining and well written and, as always with this writer, enlivened both by its distinct characterization and highly-flavoured local background.

> *David Churchill, in a review of "The Mule on the*

Motorway," in The School Librarian and School Library Review, *Vol. 16, No. 1, March, 1968, p. 88.*

A TRUCKLOAD OF RICE (1968)

In this story we are still in Paul Berna's favourite Paris suburb, Puisay, and Commissioner Sinet is still at the helm. This time he is after a particularly nasty crook who, disguised as a blind man, steals money destined for famine relief in India. But the boy he steals from is a sticker, and he doesn't rest himself, or leave the police in peace, until his man has been tracked down. There are plenty of leads for the budding detective to follow in this ingenious story, and for those who enjoy Paul Berna's Puisay stories with their local colour and thin, racy plots, this one is up to standard.

> *P. M. Royds, in a review of "A Truckload of Rice," in* Children's Book News, *London, Vol. 4, No. 1, January-February, 1969, p. 23.*

A truckload of rice will find readers at once, for Berna always mixes his elements skilfully. Though I am somewhat late in reviewing this spirited thriller I still feel it would be unfair to outline a plot that depends so much on surprise and on the connexion of apparently irreconcileable subjects. Very plausibly Berna brings together a street collection for a starving Indian village and a free gift of goldfish in certain Puisay shops. The mystery begins when Geoffrey Verdier is robbed of the splendid contribution of a group of schoolboys: it ends after Bobby Thiriet, Berna's amusing amateur sleuth, has pursued clues with his usual insouciant chatter and inspired snooping. Beneath the high spirits of Bobby and his fellows lies a very real indignation at the meanness of this particular confidence trick; the book has a salutary topical point to it.

> *Margery Fisher, in a review of "A Truckload of Rice," in* Growing Point, *Vol. 7, No. 8, March, 1969, p. 1274.*

Geoffrey Verdier is taking his son's splendid collection of 1500frs. to headquarters when the envelope containing three 500 franc notes is stolen from his inside pocket. The mystery is solved as one might expect in an ingenious way.

Paul Berna's books must be in every collection for young readers and this latest . . . merits special attention because it deals with an ever present problem, the starving in Asia, and how one small suburban community reacted to it. (pp. 112-13)

> *A review of "A Truckload of Rice," in* The Junior Bookshelf, *Vol. 33, No. 2, April, 1969, pp. 112-13.*

THEY DIDN'T COME BACK (1969)

Paul Berna has stated that he wrote **They didn't come back** for his own sons. 'I wanted to show them that war is not a game, and that the bitterest reminders of this are the scars which war leaves on the bodies and minds of the survivors'. Berna has always cast his stories in the real world of today; his children may enjoy fictional luck in solving the mysteries they conveniently stumble on but they are children of the urban civilisation we know—matter-of-fact, well aware of wages and family troubles, noisy and nosy. This new story is no exception in its characters but it touches a depth only hinted at in previous books. Berna's setting is a new estate purpose-built for a factory just moved to an empty, mountainous district of Southern France, not far from Vercors, the scene of some of the most heroic *maquis* stands. The legend of a lost band of young patriots, swallowed up by the forest as they fled from German troops in 1944, is resurrected by the local priest, who hopes to lay a personal ghost and to help the new community to set down roots, by persuading the schoolchildren to look for fresh clues to this mystery of twenty-five years before. The mystery *is* cleared up but in an unexpected way which gives the author the chance to make his point bluntly, to show that the years of bitterness were as harsh as the annihilation of the young men. The youngsters concerned in the search—cheerful, ready for the next enterprise—are nevertheless touched by the sombre adventure; we feel (and how seldom we feel this) that adventure has changed them all a little. This is a fine story, based on an actual incident, redolent of hillside and forest, expert and swift in the telling, triumphantly contemporary in a completely mature and un-dogmatic way. (pp. 1417-18)

> *Margery Fisher, in a review of "They Didn't Come Back," in* Growing Point, *Vol. 8, No. 5, November, 1969, pp. 1417-18.*

It is a relief to find that this title and its suggestive jacket do not herald a grim, violent and harrowing tale of military massacre although the mystery which is investigated as it were in retrospect was distressful enough, and had its parallel in fact. Instead, the youngsters of a new industrial settlement on the outskirts of the forest of Chabrières are prompted into using their spare time to some purpose in trying to find out why it was that some hundred *maquisards* disappeared without trace just before the liberation of France somewhere in the forest or its environs. Their detective work, aided and sometimes organised by adults with a vested interest in the discovery (or concealment) of the truth, unveils a number of incidental extraordinarinesses and leads to combination of the younsters' normal 'adventure' activities amid mounting suspense. Perhaps there is just not quite enough room for character development but none of the figures involved remains a mere cipher. Altogether the story makes an informative source for the many younger readers who show a growing interest in the events of the second war and especially in its underground movement, without failing in any way as a stimulating novel.

> *A review of "They Didn't Come Back," in* The Junior Bookshelf, *Vol. 34, No. 1, February, 1970, p. 28.*

Writing with the aim of showing that war is not a game but an experience that scars the bodies and minds of those who survive it, Paul Berna, author of more than a dozen lively and skilful stories, here through children's questions and adults' revelations burrows back to find the truth about an incident that happened in the summer of 1944. . . . This is a serious and a wise book and it is interesting to see the author using his old techniques for a new end. At the finish one of the boys says, 'They've made proper fools of us! There's nothing we can do now . . .' and is only cheered up by thoughts of gaining fame by climbing a mountain, but his friend sits quietly, seeing around him the ghosts of the young men who died for them so many years before. His reward, as for the reader, is increased vision and understanding.

> *David Churchill, in a review of "They Didn't Come Back," in* The School Librarian, *Vol. 18, No. 1,*

March, 1970, p. 76.

MYNA BIRD MYSTERY (1970)

Paul Berna seems lately to have left the insouciant mood of his earlier tales for something more topical and more pungent altogether. *Myna bird mystery* is set in a shanty town adjacent to a building site, housing workers of all nationalities with their families; since they must live near their work the tenants are at the mercy of 'the Mangler', who owns the ground and the derelict property and charges exorbitant rents. A young orphan who calls himself Cady, drifted in from a slum settlement not far away, persuades the local children that they can successfully organise opposition to the Mangler and his gang; they are helped by the mynah bird they pick up and feed, which has caught bits of information about shady deals while travelling in a lorry driven by the Mangler's men. The efforts of the crooks to find the bird are in vain and the children win the day—but less easily than is usual in such stories and in a way that leaves the reader aware of the social implications of the story.

> *Margery Fisher, in a review of "Myna Bird Mystery," in* Growing Point, *Vol. 9, No. 9, April, 1971, p. 1709.*

The essential Frenchness of this book may make it difficult reading for many children. The story has philosophical and social undertones and the unfamiliarity of the names makes it hard to distinguish the individual children. At times the gang speak a middle-class English, possibly due to the translation [by John Buchanan-Brown], but the story vividly portrays a life of abject poverty with no concessions to young readers nor promises of miraculous and instant improvements. All that the children and Cady have achieved at the end is the downfall of the immediate enemy which buys them a little more time; the real changes must come from the community itself. A thoughtful story told with zest and humour, which should appeal to the more mature child in lower secondary forms.

> *Margaret Payne, in a review of "Myna Bird Mystery," in* The School Librarian, *Vol. 19, No. 3, September, 1971, p. 255.*

GABY AND THE NEW MONEY FRAUD (1971)

They are all here, the gang from *Hundred Million Francs,* but of course older Gaby and Ziodore have left school and are working, Marion still has her dogs. . . . [The] gang are involved with counterfeiters of the New Franc through an old red van they buy. However, without giving away the plot, let me say that in spite of Inspector Sinet they do not end up in prison, and that the dogs play a large part in the climax.

The children are common to all countries, and a reader in Hamburg or Birmingham can equally well identify himself with Marion and her friends. Paul Berna is a true storyteller and a realist. His characters, even the hated Madame Macherel who is continually at odds with the gang, are all real people. This is the core of his success, for children detect and reject unconvincing characterisation more quickly than most. Boys and girls of ten to thirteen will enjoy this book. (pp. 234-35)

> *A review of "Gaby and the New Money Fraud," in*

The Junior Bookshelf, *Vol. 35, No. 4, August, 1971, pp. 234-35.*

This is the latest adventure of the gang of children who first came to life in *A Hundred Million Francs.* The children are growing up now and Gaby and Zidore have jobs, but Marion still has her dogs in her mother's garden and the rest of the children have their distinguishing characteristics that make them so easy to identify and remember from the earlier stories. . . . [The gang] do seem to have shed much of their instinct for the dishonesty and mystery around them which helped them solve the mystery of *The Street Musician.* However, all ends happily with the help of the redoubtable Marion. . . .

Sylvia Mogg, in a review of "Gaby and the New Money Fraud," in Children's Book Review, *Vol. I, No. 4, September, 1971, p. 122.*

[*Gaby and the New Money Fraud*] is as topical as the title suggests. . . . As in the old days it is [the older children] who identify the counterfeiters who are using them as a cover and the car-chase that brings events to a fortunate conclusion is handled in Berna's best manner, almost equal to the unforgettable scene with the carnival masks in the first story about this lively gang.

Margery Fisher, in a review of "Gaby and the New Money Fraud," in Growing Point, *Vol. 10, No. 3, September, 1971, p. 1779.*

VAGABONDS OF THE PACIFIC (1973)

I always considered *They Didn't Come Back* proof enough of Paul Berna's possession of the true writer's gift, and his new *Vagabonds of the Pacific* reinforces my opinion. His sea-going family, the Maels, are nice to know: his presentation of the mise-en-scene, the South Sea Islands, intriguing without being fussy, and the sailing exciting without being too technical. The plot is not overcomplicated and, if the denouement savours too much of a dea ex machina, the Maels are such a nice family that one does not begrudge them the happy ending to their adventure and the chance to start a new life in a new world. In the Robinson Crusoe escapist genre it is a first class story for boys with saltwater in their veins and a yearning for the South Seas.

D. A. Young, in a review of "Vagabonds of the Pacific," in The Junior Bookshelf, *Vol. 37, No. 4, August, 1973, p. 263.*

It cannot be denied that Paul Berna is a master craftsman who always tells a good tale. His name on the cover guarantees an absorbing story, whatever the background, and this book is no exception. . . .

It is a good tale, but it lacks the authenticity that generally makes M. Berna's stories that much better. The feeling that the author has experienced the events himself is lacking. There are details of storms at sea, the behaviour of whales, sharks and dolphins, but one gets the impression that these have been gleaned from the author's conversations with Robin Knox-Johnson, who shares the dedication with Governor Grimald who may have provided the background of life in the Pacific islands. Paul Berna's skill enables him to develop characters and embellish events, but one fears he would be unable to answer questions on background, because he has never been there. With most of his books, this would not apply, which is perhaps why it is so obvious here.

Sylvia Mogg, in a review of "Vagabonds of the Pacific," in Children's Book Review, *Vol. III, No. 4, September, 1973, p. 111.*

Pace, and the sense of camaraderie binding together those threatened by crisis, are the outstanding features of Paul Berna's earlier works. His new book is less successful precisely because these qualities are lacking. No other strong points are evident in this story of a family concerned at all costs to preserve their independence to sail the South Seas. Both heroes and villains lack individuality and even the rich smuggler who hires the yacht 'Iris' seems flaccid. The style (or maybe [John Buchanan-Brown's] translation) is conventional, and the language smacks of *Biggles'.* David, the son acting as cabin-boy, has little personality, and his father, with whom we are presumably meant to sympathize, is scarcely attractive.

Perhaps the book's one good feature is the fascination with the sea and its creatures, shared by all members of the family, so they will endure discomfort for the sake of continuing their 'vagabond' life. But the narrative lacks the essentials of any adventure story: I should have been quite content to remain ignorant of the Mael family's ultimate fate.

M. G. Harvey, in a review of "Vagabonds of the Pacific," in The School Librarian, *Vol. 21, No. 3, September, 1973, p. 260.*

THE VAGABONDS ASHORE (1973)

Readers of *Vagabonds of the Pacific* and who liked it will certainly enjoy this sequel, even though the end of chapter seven sees the end of the family's Pacific adventures, and vagabondage is transferred to a contrived escape from a school at Castellane and a complicated hike back to the family at Narbonne. The Pacific episodes, to my mind, are worth all the rest, even if it does take in some sort of son et lumiere event in which the boys David and Geoffrey become involved at the remains of Mirabal, although Geoffrey has to abandon his dream of a faithful childhood sweetheart in the process. One senses the affection with which Paul Berna writes of the countryside of Southern France, and this compensates, as elsewhere in his work, for the slightly forced note of his story manipulation. Like the earlier book, this is good entertainment.

A. R. Williams, in a review of "The Vagabonds Ashore," in The Junior Bookshelf, *Vol. 38, No. 2, April, 1974, p. 104.*

Since *A Hundred Million Francs* was first Englished in 1957, Paul Berna's authentic portraits of children and convincing clearly-told adventure have been consistently popular. *The Vagabonds Ashore* follows and keeps up the standard. Self-sufficient, although a sequel to *Vagabonds of the Pacific,* it condenses much into its short span: enemies, debt, and shipwreck put an inexorable end to the Pacific life of the Mael family, who return to France to start again with nothing. David is the one most to resent their loss of freedom, and yet escape—involving police and soldiers and stowing away on the Narbonne express—leads to a bitter-sweet folk-festival and a farcical court scene, and through these to the hope of recapturing their lost world of freedom and the sea. Focus on character and use of happy coincidence bind the varied and lively scenes together in this swift-paced and episodic story.

C. Stuart Hannabuss, in a review of "The Vagabonds Ashore," in The School Librarian, *Vol. 22, No. 2, June, 1974, p. 174.*

Margery Williams Bianco

1881-1944

(Also wrote as Margery Williams) English author of fiction, nonfiction, picture books, and short stories; reteller; and translator.

Although she wrote successfully in a variety of genres, Bianco is best known as the author of *The Velveteen Rabbit* (1922), the story of a stuffed toy who is transformed into a real bunny because of his owner's affection. Celebrating friendship and loyalty while presenting young readers with the idea that it is when we are loved that we become truly alive, *The Velveteen Rabbit* has become a classic of children's literature as well as a cult book popular with young adults and adults. Bianco is also recognized for writing *Poor Cecco* (1925), the tale of the exploits of a wooden dog and his toy and animal friends which is often lauded as her finest piece of writing. Personal interest in and connections with her subjects are characteristic features of Bianco's works. Her stories of nursery toys, which also include *The Little Wooden Doll* (1925), a work illustrated by her daughter, Pamela Bianco, *The Adventures of Andy* (1927), and *The Skin Horse* (1927), also illustrated by her daughter, were inspired by her family's toys as well as by the ones she had loved as a child. In addition, she based her autobiographical story *Bright Morning* (1942) on the London childhood she shared with her older sister, and wrote informational books about animals and gardening which reflect her own experience. Bianco also created two works, *Winterbound* (1936) and *Other People's Houses* (1939), which are considered precursors of the young adult novel and are praised for the realism they projected during a time when overly sentimental stories were the usual reading fare for young women. Compared to Hans Christian Andersen for her skill as a prose stylist, Bianco is regarded as a writer whose works range from charming and humorous to sophisticated, wise, and beautiful. Although some observers consider her books dated, Bianco continues to receive acclaim for her ability as a storyteller and insight into both children and the animal world.

(See also *Something about the Author,* Vol. 15 and *Contemporary Authors,* Vol. 109.)

AUTHOR'S COMMENTARY

Nothing is easier than to write a story *for* children; few things harder, as any writer knows, than to achieve a story that children will really like. Between the two lies that great mass of literature, often charmingly written, instructive, attractive, containing apparently every element that should appeal to the child mind yet destined, for no reason that its creators can see, to remain nicely kept upon the nursery or library shelves, while the public for whom it is intended thanks us politely and returns to the comic strips.

It isn't that children are not easily pleased. They are the most eager and receptive audience that anyone can have. They are pleased, as any adult knows, by the most absurd and ridiculous things; and being pleased by these things once, they will continue to enjoy them to the end of time—but they are not always pleased by the very thing that we think is going to please them. For this reason, one is inclined to believe that the really successful children's book is just a thing that happens; that it is very rarely the result of deliberate plan or foresight or, if it began that way, that it took, somewhere, a mysterious turn of its own in the making. Just as we might imagine [an] actor, if he were a good actor and his play any sort of real play, becoming so engrossed in it that at a certain point he would forget all efforts to please his audience, would consign it to oblivion, and simply go ahead and do the thing to please himself, only to find perhaps at the end that his audience was for the first time really with him.

Children are extraordinarily quick to detect any effort to engage their attention. They have at times an almost diabolical clairvoyance and skepticism regarding the grown up's intention; they are eternally suspicious and ready to jump the other way. . . . To engage children's interest in anything you have to be keenly interested in that thing yourself; if you are not, if you are merely pretending or playing up to them, they will promptly catch you out.

There are two things the story teller can always count on with some degree of certainty, love of adventure and love of surprise—the kind of surprise that is really an open secret between the inventor and the listener, something which the listener has all the joy of expecting beforehand and can await trustfully, knowing that after whatever suspense or complication it will unfailingly appear, at just the right moment and with all the accumulated dramatic effect. Children love to be taken, as it were, into the writer's confidence. However often the miracle appears, it will never miss fire. (pp. 249-50)

But the surprise must always be a logical one; it must arise out of something indicated beforehand, not merely happen like that, for no reason, out of a clear sky. I think a good many writers for children are apt to forget this, to think that invention may consist of a series of quite unrelated and extravagant incidents, that imagination simply means having anything at all happen at any moment you like; whereas if true invention lies anywhere it lies in making the utmost use of very definitely limited means, and imagination which does not spring from some correlation of ideas is apt to be just about as interesting as delirium. In a world where anything at all can happen, nothing can ever be surprising. In other words, there's no sort of fun about it.

The child mind is far more logical and orderly, far more concerned with the value of realities, than is sometimes supposed. It is concerned with them, in fact, very intensely and stubbornly, and it is ready to preserve and defend them at all cost. The fact that these realities may differ from our own has no bearing on the question. To the child a doll, let us say, may have an existence quite apart from its material one. The laws of that existence are to her quite clear and definite. To the grown up, whose attitude toward the whole thing is that of concession to the child's imagination, these laws do not exist. He cannot see why, if a doll is assumed to do certain things, it cannot do certain others. He will never, for instance, realize the enormity of making a doll stand on its head or fly through the air.

In the world of imagination these same laws hold good; you cannot successfully evade them. Here everything must be on scale, everything preserve its own definite characteristics. You must observe the conventions. It is a game in which the author is expected to play fair. Your ship must not at a certain moment become an airplane; your crocodile's egg cannot, without serious danger, suddenly bring forth an elephant or a fairy princess, though it may hatch as sophisticated and unsaurian a crocodile as you like. If your stage setting is a forest all that happens in it, however fantastic or nonsensical, must be evolved strictly from the materials and possibilities of that forest and from nowhere else. (pp. 250-51)

Children will usually respond immediately to any association of the fantastic with the commonplace. The goblin in the enchanted forest isn't nearly so thrilling as the goblin in the tea kettle, or the little man who lives behind the kitchen cupboard and squeaks whenever the door is opened. What appeals to children is not so much adventure in its wider sense as the possibility of adventure in everyday surroundings and among everyday things—something that might, by a happy chance, conceivably happen in their own lives. (p. 251)

Details loom very important in a child's mind, especially with young children. If there was a supper they want to know exactly what everyone had to eat and how much of it; they insist on knowing whether the baby elephant was so big, or only *so* big. They have in fact a passion for detail and verisimilitude which is not so very far removed in kind from the passion of the confirmed detective story reader—which by the way has nothing to do with mere hunger for the sensational. Not only

is the shape, color, or size of things of such importance to them that they will hold up an exciting narrative in order to have some minor point of this nature determined, definitely and beyond doubt, but they do seem to get a real thrill from facts as facts, apart from any relative value to the story. How else account for the absorption with which they will devour page after page of minutiae which to older minds would appear about as exciting as a trade catalogue. However much detail you put in a story, you can seldom put enough to satisfy a child. . . . As to moralizing, I don't believe children mind it half so much as is frequently supposed.

They have certainly a very clear sense of justice. Things must in the end come out right. They take a healthy pleasure in seeing the wicked punished, or at least frustrated, and they have an equally healthy dislike of unnecessary tragedy, or of having their feelings harrowed merely for the exigencies of the story. It is taking an unfair advantage. They prefer in the main stories about happy people and happy things, and thus they go back in their demand to the original purpose of a story, which after all is to entertain. And I think on the whole they thoroughly despise sentimentality.

It is true that some of the most beautiful stories ever written for children, including the greater number of Hans Andersen's, have been sad stories. But it is the sadness which is inseparable from life, which has to do with growth and change and impermanence, and with the very essence of beauty. These after all are conceptions of the older mind. It is quite possible that to the child, so far as he is aware of them, those things may not be sad at all: they may be quite natural and inevitable, and just as they should be—perhaps his way of looking at them, and not ours, is the right one. Possibly what his mind grasps is really the essential truth. The Little Fir Tree did have a happy time while it lasted, and after all its memories and regrets of lost youth it did ultimately finish in a blaze of light, and that final glory may just as well have been the flame of life as the pyre of death.

There is a very real satisfaction in writing for children. They are both deeply appreciative and highly critical. Before them the author is put on his mettle. They refuse to be side-tracked by any mere exercise of art. All those skilful embroiderings and unessentials, the nice picking of phrases and building up of "atmosphere" which he may fall back upon to cover an awkward gap or to get away with a story which he knows to be fundamentally weak, are perfectly useless; through them all his emptiness will be revealed. To these critics style means very little. They care more for the thing itself than for how it is done, and they are the one audience whom you cannot hoodwink nor deceive. Unless your story is there no ingenious juggling with words is going to save the situation for you. If it is, and it's a good story from their point of view, and if you have once got their confidence, then there is established magically that cooperation which almost amounts to a conspiracy between story teller and audience, by which they will be willing to forgive you almost any shortcoming and bear with you through all vicissitudes to the end.

Invention, sympathy, humor, sentiment—all these count, but the one essential thing the writer must have, to succeed at all, is a real and genuine conviction about his subject, whatever it be. It has got to be real to him. He must believe in it himself, or no one else will. He has got to write it out of sheer enjoyment or not at all. This you may say is true of all art, but it is especially true where an audience of children is concerned.

They are very ready to detect insincerity, and they will have none of it.

Here at least there must be no olympic standing outside one's own creation. The personal element counts above all else, and this is a thing that cannot be faked or simulated successfully with all the art and ingenuity at one's disposal. I believe, if one came to analyze it, that all the most successful children's books, irrespective of subject, were actually written in this spirit of sincerity. (pp. 251-53)

Margery Williams Bianco, "Our Youngest Critics," in The Bookman, *New York, Vol. LVII, No. 3, November, 1925, pp. 249-53.*

GENERAL COMMENTARY

MARCIA DALPHIN

Did you ever let yourself think seriously about wood—just plain wood, as such? . . .

Evidently Margery Williams Bianco feels the appeal of wood, and more especially of the living creature simulated by it. To be sure she did begin her day as a writer of stories for children with *The Velveteen Rabbit,* but she soon deserted the stuffiness of fabric for the wistful angularity of such creations as Cecco, Jensina, and the Little Wooden Doll. There are minor characters executed in other mediums in her stories, of course; there is Bulka, the inimitable rag puppy; and Ida, whose last name was Down, and who was flat and square, dressed in pink satin with a silk cord all round. But the heroes and heroines of the piece are of stanch, steadfast wood. Wood for heroes!

This medium lends itself particularly well to the character of Poor Cecco, the wooden dog, "the cleverest of the toys." His name, it should be said, is evidently a term of accustomed endearment, and does not imply anything essentially grief-stricken about his personality, or any sad fate in store for him. So resourceful is Poor Cecco, so cheerful, so ready for any turn of fortune, that one cannot imagine anything adverse happening to him as he starts away on his travels with Bulka, leaving his world of the toy cupboard. . . .

It is hard to select extracts from *Poor Cecco,* there are so many tempting ones, and it is a crime to tell the story even in outline, because there really is a plot, and a sufficiently interesting one withal to keep children to whom one reads it calling for more. One of the friendliest pleasantest things you ever read is the chapter in which Poor Cecco lets the blind man's little black dog have a holiday, while he attracts pennies to the cup by thumping his half tail on the bridge. "He couldn't wag it sideways, for it wasn't made that way, but he lifted it up and let it drop—bang—just like a door knocker, and that did quite as well."

One may get a good idea of the flavor of the book from the part about the treasure hunt, in which Poor Cecco, unfortunately, lost half his tail.

Children enjoy the ridiculous fun of this sort of thing, and they like, too, the description of Bulka's first sight of a stream of water. . . .

The story is full of drolleries, and there is plenty of action in it. After Jensina enters upon the scene there certainly is no lack of movement. Jensina was a wooden doll who lived on the ash heap in a check gingham apron which she had made herself. . . .

Jensina, like the Mariner, is a person of infinite resource and sagacity, and your confidence in her ability to extricate herself from places of any tightness whatsoever is fully justified. . . .

Poor Cecco is decidedly a book to be put on your holiday gift list. It is abundantly able to stand on its merits as a story.

The Little Wooden Doll represents a much less ambitious attempt on the part of its publishers than *Poor Cecco,* yet just what is lacking in the latter—this quality of lovableness in physical make-up—is found in it. Two things contribute: its size and shape, which is uniform with the other books in the Little Library series, and the illustrations, made by Pamela Bianco, the author's daughter. They were done when the artist was a little girl. . . .

The story is as delicate as the illustrations. We prophesy that again and again children who have learned to love it will call for the story of the little wooden doll who lived neglected in the attic with the mice and the spiders. They will not forget the eventful day when she fell out of the window, nor the gossamer frock the spiders wove for her, and the kind mice who woke up the flowers and borrowed their paints to color her cheeks and her eyes, and the gold coin that the rat bit a hole in and hung round her neck for a locket. They will want to hear again how she came in the end to the little girl in the cottage and how she got her lovely name.

Even more strikingly in *The Little Wooden Doll* than in *Poor Cecco* Mrs. Bianco reminds the reader of Andersen. It is in a trick of cadence or rhythm as much as anything. One would be willing to wager that she is steeped in her Andersen, for the sound of him to an Andersen lover is as unmistakable as that of a person who has, unconsciously or otherwise, molded his style on the King James version. After all, Hans Christian Andersen remains the absolute master of the toy story, and it is the highest possible praise to say of any one writing in that genre that she resembles him.

With all the indubitable charm of Mrs. Bianco's writing, its vividness, the reality of the characterizations, it is a pity that now and then there creeps into the text a note of sophistication, a little playing to the adult gallery. Children do not require it in their books, and even a very little of it will lower the tone of an otherwise charming story. This fault is entirely absent from *The Little Wooden Doll,* but *Poor Cecco* has a touch of it here and there.

Marcia Dalphin, "Hearts of Oak in the Toy Cupboard," in New York Herald Tribune Books, *October 11, 1925, p. 6.*

THE SATURDAY REVIEW OF LITERATURE, NEW YORK

[*The Skin Horse*] relates the tale of a skin horse which had been handed down from one child to another in a family until all were grown up and then sent to a hospital to become the favorite of a very sick little child. The child's dearest wish is that the horse will one day take him on a journey round the world and in the end the animal does turn into a kind of angel-horse and bears the little patient away from his pain. It is all very delicately and sympathetically done and the illustrations [by Pamela Bianco] have exactly caught the delicate, imaginative mood, making a charming whole.

When we turn to [*The Adventures of Andy*], however, we are disappointed. It is a nonsense story about a doll who is rescued from a balcony by an acrobatic aviator and carried through a host of rather disconnected adventures with animals and things similar to the adventures of *Alice in Wonderland*—so similar in atmosphere and style of conversation indeed that one must suspect Mrs. Bianco's subconsciousness of playing her tricks. While there are amusing situations, this book misses the wit and fine character-drawing of the Alice books, and while it may appeal to certain children we think their elders will not back them up.

A review of "The Skin Horse" and "The Adventures of Andy," in The Saturday Review of Literature, *Vol. IV, No. 15, November 15, 1927, p. 290.*

ANNE THAXTER EATON

Margery Bianco's *The Velveteen Rabbit* is a beautifully told story, and William Nicholson's drawings for the book have the same poetry and tenderness as the text, expressing the affection that sensitive and imaginative boys and girls have both for dearly loved toys and for pets. (pp. 101-02)

The Good Friends by Margery Bianco is [a] book with an American country background. The autumn pastures with their stone walls, gray boulders, and dry, rustling sumac bushes, are vividly and unmistakably New England, and so are the terse speech and practical commonsense of Mrs. Green, Mary's grandmother. All children have probably imagined at one time or another that animals could talk with them; thus *The Good Friends* is like a dream come true, for here are the animals, when their owner, "old man Hicks," has to go off to the hospital, trying to stick together, and Mary and her grandmother doing their best to help them. As we read about "Rhoda," the Jersey cow who "had more sense than most if it weren't for her vanity"; Fanny and Billy, the two reliable old horses; Rufus the hound; Mrs. Happy and her kittens; and Rosie, the irrepressible little goat—it seems quite believable that they should keep house by themselves, and the story is told so naturally that we seem to be overhearing real conversations carried on by Mary and her grandmother and the animals. There is no child and hardly an adult who will not be charmed to make the acquaintance of these animals whom Mrs. Bianco has so skillfully characterized and has described in such a fine spirit of light-hearted make-believe. (pp. 103-04)

Anne Thaxter Eaton, "Unicorns and Common Creatures," in her Reading with Children, *The Viking Press, 1940, pp. 97-118.*

ANNE CARROLL MOORE

Since about 1925 the name of Margery Bianco has been associated with a rare quality of criticism and appreciation as well as creative work of unusual character and distinction.

At this time of heightened interest in the interchange of significant books with other countries, I am freshly impressed by the quality and variety of Mrs. Bianco's interests, her skill as a writer and translator, the reliability and richness of her background and, above all, by the wisdom, the humor, the spiritual integrity she brought to the field of children's books after World War I.

In her, as I believe, the *St. Nicholas* of Mary Mapes Dodge might well have found the creative editor so sorely needed at the half-century turn of that lamented magazine. . . . With an inexhaustible store of first-hand knowledge of literature and of art values, of nature, and of human beings at her command, Mrs. Bianco had also the gift of insight which belongs to the editor who knows the real thing at once. An inexorable critic of her own work and that of others, she knew the cost of creating and inspired confidence in the novice.

I have never known so modest a person who was at the same time so assured, so firmly rooted in sound information, common sense and discriminating taste. As an editor, I never questioned any statement of hers. She *knew* where I might have been guessing. As a writer I received confidence and inspiration from her.

Her influence during the period of rich flowering of children's books in the United States was a very potent one on the authors, artists, editors and librarians and booksellers with whom she came into personal contact.

Editors of children's books in publishing houses were just getting on their sea legs and were eagerly scanning the horizon for just such an author. . . . (pp. 3-4)

Read in the order in which [*Winterbound, Other People's Houses, Bright Morning* and *Forward, Commandos!*] appeared, they seemed to take their place as parts of a commentary on everyday living which has continuity, serenity, and the practicality born of imaginative understanding and adventurous spirit.

The Velveteen Rabbit has poignant associations for me personally. An unbound copy of the book was sent to me by Eugene Saxton, then chief editorial adviser to the George H. Doran Company, with this query: "Do you think we could sell 1200 copies if we import the sheets?" "If you don't publish it, I will," was my reply. "It belongs in the true Hans Christian Andersen tradition. Who is Margery Williams and how came William Nicholson to illustrate it?" (p. 7)

I spent the spring and summer of 1921 in a devastated area of northern France and in England, and I paid another short visit to these countries in the fall of 1922. I came back with vivid first-hand impressions of children whose toys and pets and books had been destroyed, and of the apathy of the publishers I met. A notable exception was Mr. Sidney Pawling of Heinemann's, who had fallen in love with the story of *The Velveteen Rabbit;* he believed it to be a classic, and, wishing to give it the very best format he could devise, had persuaded the artist to take it away with him on a holiday. "I felt sure Nicholson couldn't resist it," he said.

The artist confirmed this information when I mustered the courage to go to see him in his studio in Appletree Yard. One had only to spend an hour in that enchanting studio and listen to a flow of refreshing talk to realize that the shabby velveteen rabbit on the chimney piece and the old skin horse who had served as models to some extent, the artist said, had been in his family for years. Imaginative understanding of the past—the reality of children and their interests in his own life, the timeless magic of transformation—held the secret of his pictures. I came away invigorated and with lively impressions of the Bianco family who had spent a holiday in Wales not far from the Nicholsons. I was to hear more of this delightful holiday from Margery Bianco when we met for the first time in the Children's Room behind the Library Lions. I walked out of Appletree Yard with the precious original drawings under my arm along with two copies of *The Velveteen Rabbit* characteristically inscribed by the artist with an identification tag—one for me and one for the Children's Room where the originals were to be shown as part of the holiday exhibition of 1922. (pp. 7-8)

"You can almost see the Velveteen Rabbit changing into a real one," the children said when they saw the pictures. "Read us the story," begged the two who had lingered after the Christmas Story Hour. And so I read from the very book I had just brought back from London. Out of their listening and the conversation that followed was born the idea of putting Nicholas, the mascot who had accompanied me on my travels, into a book.

Years afterward when we had become very good friends, I told Margery Bianco of that reading in the Fifth Avenue window seat of a room which had grown very dear to her. I told her of the child skeptic who regarded Nicholas as "just a wooden boy" and of the other child who had said, "That's because you don't know enough. He's real to me. I suppose that is the way every story begins—somebody has to believe in it and know enough to write it down. You can do it; just get lots of paper and pencils and keep at it until it is done."

"A wise child! That is all there is to writing a story," said Mrs. Bianco. "It is the believing in it and the keeping at it that are important."

Her respect for children and their opinions was one of her strongest characteristics. She agreed with Kenneth Grahame that children have just as much sense as we have; it is only experience they lack, and she treated her own children and grandchildren accordingly. Clear memory of her own childhood and youth made her relations with all children and young people perfectly natural. (pp. 9-10)

[She] wrote in a personal letter to the editor of *The Horn Book*],

> Death should be treated naturally. You don't have to educate children about death. Speak of it as a natural occurrence and they will do the same.
>
> More than ever, I think, children need imaginative literature as an interpretation. Nature does resist discouragement and not only in the young. The impulse is always toward life and the future. Children are taken up with war and the excitement of it, but it doesn't mean to them what it means to us, unless we make it so. Their own imagination, I think, tends to make of it something like a highly exciting game. It is a defense and like all Nature's defenses, wise. Last night I was reading *My Brother's Face* by Mukerji. Do you know that chapter where, speaking of his mother, he describes the extraordinary gentle wisdom with which she used legend and stories to interpret the spiritual problems of life?

All her life Margery Bianco so regarded the fairy tales of Hans Christian Andersen. "Everything has a story to tell," she reminded the readers of *The Horn Book* for May, 1927. "Andersen knew this and made no effort to choose the bright side of things, or even to insure a happy ending unless it happens naturally. He wrote of the world about him and of the things in it as colored by his vision."

And this, as I view her work, is exactly what Margery Bianco herself did. (pp. 11-12)

There can be little doubt that Margery Williams inherited from her father [Robert Williams, a distinguished classical scholar who became a barrister and newspaperman,] not only the desire to write, but also the instinct for form and sound workmanship which distinguished her work. *Bright Morning,* based on incidents of her childhood happily combined with that of an older sister, reveals the scholarly father in warm human relationship to his family in more than one slight incident. The characters in this little book live for the reader in their city and seaside backgrounds as real people. *Bright Morning* has the freshness of a spring morning in London, and it also holds the joys and terrors of the sea for a child who was always to look upon it with wonder. (p. 13)

When she wrote, "I disliked everything I had written before. I wanted to do something different but did not know what it should be," Margery Bianco had had an experience of life that must have been full of possibilities for a writer of her ability. Fifteen years had passed since the publication of her last novel, and she had published nothing during those years save a small book about Paris ([*Paris*], 1910).

As one of a series, "Peeps at Great Cities," published in England by A. & C. Black, this little book with its picture plan of Central Paris and its excellent full-page illustrations in color I have just read for the first time, although it has held a place on public library shelves for years. (p. 14)

It is written from direct observation. A fine selective instinct governs the choice of material, but there is no writing down to children. "Paris reminds one of a big village," says the author, and proceeds to treat it as a place where she is living and enjoying its small shops and street markets no less than its beautiful gardens and palaces. There must have been a general pattern for the "Peeps," but Margery Bianco held Paris rather than an outline before her. The book has life and color in it and holds suggestion for the writer of children's books about other cities and countries.

"It was by a sort of accident that *The Velveteen Rabbit* became the beginning of all the stories I have written since," says Mrs. Bianco. "By thinking about toys and remembering toys, they suddenly became very much alive—Poor Cecco and all the family toys that had been so much a part of our lives; toys I had loved as a little girl—my almost forgotten Tubby who was the rabbit, and old Dobbin the Skin Horse, the toys my children had loved."

I have always felt that the life tenure of *Poor Cecco,* dedicated to Pamela and Cecco, was threatened by the too elaborate format characteristic of a lavish period. Here, as I think, is a novel in miniature, original and true to form, with a well-defined plot which may some day emerge in a dress better suited to its nature.

In *Winterbound* and in *Other People's Houses,* Mrs. Bianco wrote two books for girls which bid fair to outlive most of the career stories of the time in which they were published. "I wrote these books as experiments," she says, "because I have always been interested in everyday stories as long as they were real."

Winterbound is the story of a family faced with a new kind of life in an old house situated in the Connecticut Hills to which they had come to live in order to save money.

It was while making her home in the region of *Winterbound* that Mrs. Bianco also wrote *The Street of Little Shops* (inimitable short stories with interpretive pictures in color [by Grace Paull]), *The Hurdy-Gurdy Man,* so spontaneously illustrated by Robert Lawson, and the lovely *Green Grows the*

Garden for which Grace Paull made effective decorations. These books are an expression of American country and village life and character which we may send to other countries with pride.

Of *Other People's Houses,* Mrs. Bianco wrote to [May] Massee:

> *Other People's Houses* is just a plain story of everyday life. It has no trimmings, almost no plot, and it concerns the experience of a girl who wants to earn her living in a city and is willing to try anything that turns up, domestic jobs included, rather than give in.
>
> All over the country there are girls very much like Dale in this book. They are girls who haven't got college degrees or a chance of getting them and have no special training for careers. They aren't likely to blossom out into successful artists or writers overnight, to discover lost wills hidden in old furniture, to inherit odd pieces of property and convert them into thriving business concerns within a year on no capital, to unravel mysteries, save impossible situations through heroism or meet strangers who turn out to be wealthy long-lost uncles. Just what would they do if they wanted to earn a living, and what sort of a time would they have trying it out?
>
> That was the starting point of the story and I have tried to work it out in the way it very probably would happen. I was trying to get away from the average success story which I never felt is playing fair to the reader.

It is significant and characteristic of Margery Bianco's desire to do something new and different in each of her books that the last one, *Forward, Commandos!,* should be concerned with living boys and their natural interests so closely allied to her own. Its crisp dialogue and real understanding of boy nature give it an immediate appeal and assure it an enduring place among boys' books. Her familiarity with New Jersey woods and the fascinations of a tidal river reach back to the novels of her youth of which I have spoken.

The search for reality and the clear sight of one who has lived very close to Nature in all its aspects are to be found in all of Margery Bianco's writings. Economic conditions might threaten as they did during the years of depression, but the integrity of her art was never deflected from its course.

"I write to please myself," she once said when she was asked to give some account of her method to a group of librarians. It is only by writing that one learns to write. Rejection slips had taught her early to take an objective view of her own efforts.

I have dwelt at length upon Mrs. Bianco's work at this time because I feel it important that her books be kept in print and made more widely known to writers and students of literature for children as well as to children of the postwar world.

"Imagination is only another word for the interpretation of life," Margery Bianco reminds us in her own tribute to de la Mare. "It is through imagination that a child makes his most significant contacts with the world about him, that he learns tolerance, pity, understanding and the love for all created things."

I give back these words in her memory. (pp. 14-18)

Anne Carroll Moore, "Margery Williams Bianco: 1881-1944," in Writing and Criticism: A Book for Margery Bianco, *edited by Anne Carroll Moore and Bertha Mahony Miller, The Horn Book, Inc., 1951, pp. 3-20.*

PAMELA BIANCO

My mother always encouraged us to keep pets. Starting from the [days when we lived in Golder's Green in London, my brother] Cecco and I owned a series of hedgehogs, guinea pigs and rabbits. Usually they came in pairs, Cecco's being named Paul, and mine Virginia. In addition to our pets Cecco and I had little garden plots, and in winter a hyacinth bulb each to watch growing in water. (p. 25)

One night in Golder's Green, long after I had fallen asleep, [our governess] Dorothy woke me up again and handed me a beautiful doll with pale golden hair. It was a present from Uncle Angelo, who had just arrived on a visit from Italy. I was carried downstairs into the sitting room to greet him.

Uncle Angelo was my father's younger brother. He had a delightful sense of humor, and during this visit to Golder's Green, used to join Cecco and myself in many of our games. Later, when we went to live in Italy, Uncle Angelo was to be our constant friend and companion. He survived the First World War, serving in the front line trenches, only to die under tragic circumstances not long after we left Italy.

I named the doll Uncle Angelo gave me Daisy, but somehow I never played with her as I did with Tubby, of whom my mother wrote in *Poor Cecco.* Tubby, half teddy bear, half cat, and her sister Fluffy were my cherished playthings. For them I spent endless hours sewing elaborate dresses. Bulka, who had two reincarnations, belonged to Cecco, and was named after Count Tolstoi's dog. The first two Bulkas were china bulldog banks that broke, but Bulka the third was made of more durable papier-mâché. Later, when he wore out in Turin, my mother re-covered him in gold-colored cloth, and Tubby and Fluffy were re-covered at the same time to match. My mother always treated our toys as though they were just as real to her as they were to us. (pp. 25-6)

Pamela Bianco, "Her Children Long Ago," in Writing and Criticism: A Book for Margery Bianco, *edited by Anne Carroll Moore and Bertha Mahony Miller, The Horn Book, Inc., 1951, pp. 21-34.*

VALENTI ANGELO

It was in 1937 that I made [Margery Williams Bianco's] acquaintance. (p. 35)

As I studied [her] house from across the street one spring day in 1937, I began to ponder on the lives of authors. I did so because from that day on, without my knowledge of it, I too was to become an author.

Carrying the many-times-revised, page-frayed manuscript of my first book, *Nino,* I started across the street. A group of children playing on the doorsteps gave me no notice. They went on with their games. Stepping gingerly among them I reached the door. I stood there a moment as memories of some years passed through my mind. These memories were concerned with Margery Bianco, who through those years had not been totally unknown to me. I became acquainted with her writing through *The Skin Horse,* a small book published in 1927.

It was really through the drawings made for this little book by her gifted daughter, Pamela Bianco, that I first learned of Margery's writing. I fell deeply in love with both the drawings and the story, and as time passed, learned more about this author's work. For in Margery's writing as well as the drawings of Pamela, I discovered a rarity seldom found in literature and pictures made for children in those days. There was something about her work which seemed to fit my nature. It stuck there, and I nourished the thought that some day I might have the good fortune to meet these two people who had aroused in me a desire to look into more books made for children.

It will sound fantastic perhaps to say that one can readily make friends with the work of another, or even to fall completely in love with it. It is nevertheless true, for in my case it was not only a matter of friendship, but a case of love at first sight. And as I touched my finger to the doorbell, I had a sincere feeling that I was about to meet an old acquaintance—a friend whom I had loved through the years in my imagination. One whom I knew I would love from that day on. (pp. 36-7)

There was a graciousness about her I am unable to express here because it is now so deeply rooted in me. Words alone are not sufficient to give vent to my feelings. But this I must say in humble sincerity—whatever it was Margery Bianco possessed and gave abundantly to others is needed desperately among people today.

I had come to Margery Bianco for advice and guidance in the matter of writing. She had already read my story which the publishers had sent to her for editorial work. Now I awaited the verdict. I had never written a book and felt my efforts to be feeble. I knew that a judgment must be passed on the work by someone with more knowledge and experience in grammar, composition, punctuation, and so on than I had. My two years of schooling had not been sufficient to give me the confidence needed in the matter of English.

I knew I had a story to tell, but I had no faith in my manner of telling. So good fortune led me to the home of Margery Bianco. It is strange how much one leans on others, when actually, as sooner or later one realizes, the strongest support comes not from the outside but from within oneself.

Margery Bianco pointedly told me as much during that afternoon visit, and for that lesson I was deeply grateful. It was a visit which I can relive vividly, because on that day I learned that in order to be a writer one must have a great deal of patience and understanding, particularly with oneself. Margery made everything seem clear and simple in the most natural way I have ever known. "Be yourself," she would say. (pp. 38-9)

As she spoke she convinced me that the faults in my book were largely grammatical. That the important thing was the play, the story. The sincerity. "You have had something to say—to impart to others. You have said your say in the only way you know. What more?" (p. 40)

As we spoke about children, parents, and stories written for children, a warmth of feeling enveloped the room. I knew and felt in the presence of Margery Bianco that here was a person—an ageless person—who not only loved youth, with all its minor idiosyncrasies but also had a great faculty for understanding it. (p. 41)

As the afternoon wore on I learned that Margery Bianco's philosophy was a simple one, easy to understand, earthy and wholesome, imbued with a sensitive view of life and the world as a whole. Her personality at no time seemed to deviate from the simplicity and honesty of thought which was, during those trying years of depression and struggle, being imperiled by the many "isms" and supposedly new styles in every mode of life, and especially in that of the art of writing. Later on when I read *Other People's Houses, Winterbound,* and others of her books, I found in them that same philosophy. One of understanding of the meaning of life, and of what constitutes the highest good. To find this trend of thought in books for children is something for which we all should be grateful. In their deep-felt excursions into a life now threatened by upheaval and unrest, these stories have a power to make the young reader live and glory in the living.

Many writers, I learned later, follow the leader or whoever happens to be dominant at the moment, thereby neglecting a duty to their art and to themselves. This was never true of Margery Bianco.

The knowledge and understanding of the nature of things she expressed in her work enriched the lives of others. Her insight into the animal world was uncanny, as proved by the books *All About Pets, More About Animals,* and *The Good Friends.* She possessed a sense of humor devoid of the burdensome drollery which so many clever authors have exercised in order to gain attention. (pp. 41-2)

When I left Margery Bianco's house that day, I knew that I had learned many things. I also felt that I had renewed an old acquaintance. To me it seemed, even long after that visit, that in this world there is no such thing as meeting and parting in friendship. The visits that followed were many. The years that followed made richer the friendship between us. The thread of friendship—of delicate fiber and easily severed—seemed to grow stronger. I feel honored to have been among her many friends.

Margery Bianco will always be alive to me, and to all her friends. No person who has left to the world of literature for children such wisdom and sympathy and love of Nature will ever die. Her work should not go unnoticed in time to come. There is a great need for her kind of writing today, for her work is reaching for some lost dignity in life, and in reaching helps to bring it back. (pp. 42-3)

Valenti Angelo, "A Living Friendship," in Writing and Criticism: A Book for Margery Bianco, *edited by Anne Carroll Moore and Bertha Mahony Miller, The Horn Book, Inc., 1951, pp. 35-43.*

RUTH HILL VIGUERS

[Margery Bianco] had vivid memories of the toys she had loved as a child, and this thinking about toys and remembering toys suddenly brought them to life. In two sensitive stories, *The Velveteen Rabbit,* which introduced the English portrait painter, William Nicholson, to the field of children's books, and *The Skin Horse,* which her own daughter Pamela illustrated, she revealed not only a memory of well loved toys, but a deep understanding of children's feelings toward their toys. She continued to write with enchantment of dolls and toys—two stories were long adventures of nursery friends, *The Adventures of Andy* and *Poor Cecco,* and the third an unpretentious little book, *The Little Wooden Doll.* This last, with illustrations by Pamela Bianco, has been much loved, and perhaps its long life may be attributed to the fact that in its exquisite simplicity it is completely childlike, is entirely lacking in sophistication as are the best loved toys themselves, which go with a child in all his play and accompany him to bed. (p. 473)

[*Winterbound* and *Other People's Houses*] have complete reality; the things that happen to Dale, who had to make her own living and took any job available, have happened to many girls, and the four young people who face their first winter in the country with new responsibilities for the comfort and happiness of their home have many kin in real life. (p. 555)

> *Ruth Hill Viguers, "Modern Fancy," and "Experiences to Share," in* A Critical History of Children's Literature *by Cornelia Meigs and others, edited by Cornelia Meigs, Macmillan Publishing Company, 1953, pp. 467-81; 539-60.*

JON C. STOTT

Although one of [Margery Williams Bianco's] books, *Winterbound,* was awarded a Newbery Honor Medal, they are seldom read now. They are told with the author's customary charm, good humor, and sympathy; however, too many of the objects and ideas are dated.

Margery Bianco's stories of nursery toys have been favorably compared to Collodi's *Pinocchio*, Rachel Field's *Hitty, Her First Hundred Years*, and A. A. Milne's Winnie-the-Pooh stories. . . . The vividness of these stories arises from the fact that she told them from the toys' point of view.

The first of the toy series, *The Velveteen Rabbit,* has become a minor children's classic. Early in the story, the title hero learns from the wise skin horse that "when a child loves you for a long, long, time, not just to play with you, but REALLY loves you, then you become Real." At the end of the story, because of a boy's affection, it is transformed into a living rabbit. *The Little Wooden Doll* deals with a toy's greatest fear, being abandoned, and its greatest need: "Deep in every doll's heart there is a longing to be loved by a child." Like Andersen's "The Steadfast Tin Soldier," *Poor Cecco,* considered by many critics to be Bianco's finest children's novel, treats the secret life of toys when human beings are absent. (p. 34)

Children in the early elementary grades who still treat their stuffed animals as living beings will particularly enjoy *The Velveteen Rabbit.* In the middle elementary grades children can see that what applies to the rabbit applies to people, who also need love to be completely alive. (p. 35)

> *Jon C. Stott, "Margery Williams Bianco," in his* Children's Literature from A to Z: A Guide for Parents and Teachers, *McGraw-Hill Book Company, 1984, pp. 34-5.*

THE VELVETEEN RABBIT; OR, HOW TOYS BECOME REAL (1922)

[*My Roads to Childhood was originally published in 1939.*]

The rarest of books is an acceptable Christmas story, and *The Velveteen Rabbit* . . . is destined to live in the remembrance of every child and grown-up who follows the adventures of the Velveteen Rabbit from his first appearing in a Christmas stocking until he is turned into a real bunny by the Nursery

Magic Fairy. The story is told with simplicity and direct appeal to a child's heart. (p. 137)

> *Anne Carroll Moore, "Who Is Writing for Children?" in her* My Roads to Childhood: Views and Reviews of Children's Books, *The Horn Book, Inc., 1961, pp. 135-41.*

[*Teabag and the Bears*] is Margaret J. Baker's fifth book about the Shoeshop Bears, a crew who, in contrast to Paddington, are all models of responsible behaviour and selfless devotion to duty. When, during their seaside holiday, first one and then another of them gets lost, their primary concern is always to shield their young owner from distress. They all seem too consciously good to be genuine bears and the fantastic side of the book, perhaps because it is presented as absolutely commonplace, seems whimsical and contrived. . . .

[*The Velveteen Rabbit*] contains very similar impossibilities, but, by presenting them quite frankly as the outcome of magic, makes them easier to digest. Its preoccupations, too, are the same as those of Margaret Baker's book but because we are shown plainly the boy's fierce need and love for the toy rabbit, its own devotion seems inevitable. The story may be too sentimental for modern adult taste, but it is hard to imagine it offending a five or six-year-old, who will probably be deeply moved by the account of the child-toy relationship, and at the same time greatly intrigued by the book's invitation to examine different definitions of reality.

> *"Teddy Bears' Picnic," in* The Times Literary Supplement, *No. 3589, December 11, 1970, p. 1458.*

It seems that *The velveteen rabbit* has become a cult in the United States and that the book has even been quoted in sermons. This seems to me almost as odd as the fact that student politics in that country were for a time based on hobbitry. It seems a pity to weigh down this perspicuous little tale with ponderous moral comment. I would guess the author had no thought of doing more than make her own child happy when she explained how a toy rabbit became real because after suffering neglect it was taken back into favour and truly loved. This, goodness me, is a child's bedtime story, not a sermon. Its style is playful, a little naive, its story slender indeed beside the masterly thrills of *Poor Cecco,* and the much-praised lithographs by William Nicholson are not entirely appealing examples of a style that has somehow remained frozen in its period of nearly half a century ago. I hardly think the book merits such an expensive revival.

> *Margery Fisher, in a review of "The Velveteen Rabbit," in* Growing Point, *Vol. 9, No. 7, January, 1971, p. 1657.*

What can the humble reviewer say of a book that has received the benediction of the Flower Children, and in which—to quote the editor of *Woman's Own*—there is hidden 'a deeper, more significant meaning than you might at first expect'? The metaphysics appear to flow from the author's propensity to spell real with a capital R (sure sign for post-Kantian idealists that something significant is about to happen), but the story itself is altogether less imposing, moving from an opening that has something of the sharpness of Andersen about it to a conclusion, refulgent with the sentiment of the Sussex school of children's literature (nightlights in the nursery, fairies in the garden and Martin Pippin in all the daisy fields).

Because it so admirably represents the approach to children's books that was prevalent in 1922 *The Velveteen Rabbit* is well worth republication, and ordinary children (along with the Flower variety) may well still wrap themselves happily round the sugar at its centre. Nor should anyone carp at the pleasure of seeing once more William Nicholson's perfect illustrations. . . . Artistry of this order can do more for the Reality of velveteen rabbits than all the Nursery Magic Fairies between Peasmarsh and Fittleworth. (pp. 17-18)

> *B. W. A., in a review of "The Velveteen Rabbit or How Toys Become Real," in* Children's Book Review, *Vol. 1, No. 1, February, 1971, pp. 17-18.*

Since [the Velveteen Rabbit] is a passive hero, lying about after the fashion of stuffed animals, waiting for someone to pick him up, carry him, cuddle him, the longevity of the book must lie in its message not in its call to adventure. Like *E.T.* and the story of Tinker Bell over which E.T. cried, **The Velveteen Rabbit** is a fable of the animating power of love. "When a child . . . REALLY loves you," the Skin Horse tells VR, as I shall call him, "then you become Real." The Boy does love him and the toy does become real, to the Boy at least, but there is a second step in which VR becomes a bona fide rabbit. After sharing the Boy's bed while he has scarlet fever, VR is discarded as a health hazard. He cries a real tear that sprouts into a flower and disgorges a Fairy who saves him from the auto-da-fé and turns him into a genuine rabbit.

Now, I may be "a Bear of Very Little Brain," but the second step has always baffled me. I do not mind that the Fairy, who professes to look after beloved toys no longer needed, has not turned the Skin Horse into a real horse, or that, while first-step reality "lasts for always," being a real rabbit involves mortality. The problem for me is that the final transformation is brought about not by love but by self-pity. . . .

One can see its appeal for illustrators. Although there are not many dramatic scenes, there are occasions for drawing Christmas ornaments, toys of all kinds, medicine bottles, flora and fauna; if the central events are a bit static, the backgrounds can keep busy. One can see its appeal to publishers as well. There is an apparently growing audience, and the story is out of copyright in this country. . . .

But, when it comes to rabbits, I will stick with Peter. He has more gumption.

> *Gerald Weales, in a review of "The Velveteen Rabbit," in* The New York Times Book Review, *April 3, 1983, p. 13.*

POOR CECCO: THE WONDERFUL STORY OF A WONDERFUL WOODEN DOG WHO WAS THE JOLLIEST TOY IN THE HOUSE UNTIL HE WENT OUT TO EXPLORE THE WORLD (1925)

AUTHOR'S COMMENTARY

It is hard to remember beginnings when they seem so far away, but I think that I first began writing stories when I was about nine, soon after my family came to America for the first time. Up till then, I had spent most of my life in London. I had read many stories about America in *St. Nicholas* magazine, which we always had at home, and it was wonderful to be really there, especially since we went to live in the country, as I had always wanted to do. I felt so inspired by it all that first winter, I remember, that I wrote a poem. It was a horrid little poem, but someone got it printed for me in the local

paper. When I saw it, I felt so shy I burst into tears. So that finished poems!

Stories seemed better, and I wrote reams with a pencil and pad, mostly sitting on the landing at the head of the stairs, with my back to the wall. To this day I prefer writing with my back to the wall! My stories all had grown-up characters, and I always wanted them to be about exciting places like the Amazon or the Wild West. But after a few chapters, which began like a house afire, I would find I had used up everything that I knew about those places and would have to stop. Those stories must have been rather like young tadpoles, all head and no body! Still I had a lot of fun with them.

It was years before I learned to try and write about the things I did know, more or less. Maybe I'm not quite cured yet. As our family always seemed to move about a great deal, my schooling was rather irregular, but I made up for that by reading. It suited me just as well. Particularly anything about animals or travels. As I grew older, I wrote all the time, mostly grown-up tales, many of them pretty bad, but some that people liked well enough to publish. In between I wrote some stories for children, and it happened this way. A London firm that published Christmas books used to send me pictures, colored pictures of nice fat little girls or puppies or dolls, and would say: "Write a thousand-word story in which we can use these pictures." Well, I would sit and stare at the pictures, and hate them, but think: "Somewhere there is a story for this. All I have to do is to find it." And sooner or later I did. I didn't like working that way, but it was really very good training.

Then for years I kept writing other things, and the next stories for young people were written only after my own children were beginning to grow up. Among the family toys—only we didn't think of them as toys—were three in particular: Poor Cecco, Tubby, and Bulka. They were all exactly as they are in my book, **Poor Cecco.** They had their own language, and they used to talk it. Bulka was forever getting his feelings hurt, and then he cried like a five-finger exercise. It almost drove one crazy. Tubby would feel neglected and retire to Tubbyland. At least she disappeared for days at a stretch and wrote me letters, dated from Tubbyland and printed in big capitals, which I found under my pillow in the morning. Even though I suspected that Tubbyland was really somewhere behind the sofa pillows, I had to pretend that I believed her. Poor Cecco was splendid at finding anything that was lost, like rings or a thimble, and would present them to one the next day on a plate, very proudly. So when I came to write a story about the toys, knowing them all so well, it was the easiest book I ever wrote in my life.

Poor Cecco sent his picture for the artist who made the drawings [Arthur Rackham]. They are exactly like him. He is twenty-five years old now, but as spry as ever. He hopes you will like this story about him and his friends. (pp. 21-2)

> *Margery Williams Bianco, "Poor Cecco Was a Member of Our Family," in* Writing Books for Boys and Girls, *edited by Helen Ferris, Doubleday & Company, Inc., 1952, pp. 21-2.*

[For] the children who have welcomed the return of **The Velveteen Rabbit** every Christmas and Easter since 1922, no disappointment lurks inside the covers of **Poor Cecco.** . . .

There is color, flavor, sophistication, yet a child's delight, in Margery Williams Bianco's story. . . .

The book is dedicated to Pamela and Cecco, to whom it belongs by every natural and inherited right; but it will be claimed by all who have not thrown their toys away. . . . [The] look and the feel of garden and countryside as well as the nursery is in the story and the personalities of living animals are no less real than are those of the toys. (p. 180)

It is [the] sure sense of the personalities of her characters, whether toys or living creatures, and her complete grasp of dramatic requirements that give Mrs. Bianco's work an assured high place among children's stories. (p. 181)

> *Anne Carroll Moore, in a review of "Poor Cecco,"
> in* The Bookman, *New York, Vol. LXII, No. 2, October, 1925, pp. 180-81.*

This is a delightfully quaint story for children, all about a wooden dog. . . . His adventures, and those of his companions, are told in an easy, entertaining style, and with a sympathetic touch that makes us grow quite fond of the various members of the little household to which Poor Cecco belongs. . . . ***Poor Cecco*** is a gift-book that would be welcome in any stocking this Christmas.

> *A review of "Poor Cecco," in* The Bookman, *London, Vol. LXIX, No. 411, December, 1925, p. 160.*

Winnie-the-Pooh and *The House at Pooh Corner* have picked up much of the soft atmosphere of children's writings in the 'twenties. There is at least one toy story of the period which has conspicuously avoided this, a book which should never have been allowed to go out of print. ***Poor Cecco*** . . . is something on its own, full of character, full of incident, delivered straight from child to child, as it were, with no middleman. Cecco, the wooden dog, with his conscientious, rather laborious care for the other inmates of the toy-cupboard; lonely, home-loving Jensina; Tubby and Bulka, the two sentimental, rather witless plush dogs; the wax dolls, Gladys and Virginia, with their snobbish idiom; and the rascally cat, Murrum; they are all as real and exciting as their adventures. The story, told in a vivid style, is perfectly adjusted to a child's world. (pp. 38-9)

> *Margery Fisher, "There and Back by Tricycle," in her* Intent Upon Reading: A Critical Appraisal of Modern Fiction for Children, *Brockhampton Press, 1961, pp. 36-49*

A toy acquires character through action and the conviction of the creator who takes readers seriously, doesn't talk down or subject them to a kind of bifocal awareness that suggests that the author is talking to adults over the reader's shoulder. There is none of that here; the prose is quite demanding at times for the youngest, but none the worse for that. . . .

All young children should come to know ***Poor Cecco*** well.

> *Elizabeth Grey, in a review of "Poor Cecco," in* The School Librarian, *Vol. 22, No. 1, March, 1974, p. 97.*

THE APPLE TREE (1926)

[***The Apple Tree***] is a wistful haunting tale that Mrs. Bianco tells of the little brother and sister who, watching longingly for Easter's coming, under the old dead apple tree, entertain

unaware a stranger there. Once again, as in her ***Little Wooden Doll***, Mrs. Bianco's style reminds us strongly of Andersen's. Slight as it it, the book possesses two outstanding qualities—a simplicity of treatment well suited to the delicate theme of the story, and a homeliness of incident which, while it relates the story strongly to everyday life, brings out all the more clearly its spiritual values.

> *Anne Carroll Moore, "The Three Owls," in* New York Herald Tribune Books, *April 4, 1926, p. 6.*

THE ADVENTURES OF ANDY (1927)

The adventures of Andy are all pleasant, at least for the reader, for Andy is a wooden doll, and so nothing very painful can happen to her. Moreover, the style in which the tale is written is so merry that her few harrowing experiences will make even sensitive and softhearted children laugh. It is a delicious work, with many touches of delicate humor throughout. It ripples along in a sunny stream of seemingly artless but actually artful prattle, a mixture of fun, fancy and poetry.

> *Peggy Bacon, in a review of "The Adventures of Andy," in* The New Republic, *Vol. LII, No. 676, November 16, 1927, p. 367.*

THE SKIN HORSE (1927)

This slender book seems to us about perfect. The brief, pathetic tale relates the love of a sick child for an ancient toy, and how their mutual wish came true on Christmas Eve. Scattered throughout this seasonable fantasy, which is recounted with fluent grace, weave Pamela Bianco's lovely drawings. . . . There are no flaws that we can see in this artful little volume.

> *Peggy Bacon, in a review of, "The Skin Horse," in* The New Republic, *Vol. LII, No. 676, November 16, 1927, p. 365.*

ALL ABOUT PETS (1929)

[***All About Pets***] should be in every family where there are animal loving children. It will teach them the sane, intelligent care of their pets, how to feed them, to house them, to train them to be well-behaved animals, and incidentally to reflect the character of their masters. . . . It is quite evident that Mrs. Bianco writes out of her own experience, so practical are her suggestions.

> *A review of "All about Pets," in* The Catholic World, *Vol. CXXX, No. 777, December, 1929, p. 80.*

All About Pets will suit the most scientific supervisor of youth; which is not meant to be so damning as it sounds. For it is a good little book, and belongs in all families where pets happen. Only it should be bound with blank pages, for the scribbling of additional notes and reminiscences. I read the chapter on cats to a roomful of people, plus one small yellow kitten, and could hardly finish because of the flood of comment it elicited. We voted that a real person wrote that book and one who knew what she was talking about. ***All about Pets*** is not as encyclopedic as its title suggests, but it will stand the challenge of Audrey: "Is it honest in word and deed? Is it a *true* thing?" And that, after all, properly understood, is not a bad slogan.

> *Elizabeth Woodbridge, in a review of "All about Pets," in* The Saturday Review of Literature, *Vol. VI, No. 21, December 14, 1929, p. 575.*

Animals—mice, rats, dogs, cats, rabbits, guinea pigs, birds and goldfish—enter this volume to show what they are like as pets, how they should be treated, and what weaknesses and good points they may possess. It is written sanely and practically but with a refreshing style throughout and a humorous, friendly approach that makes it most desirable. One is quietly amused to learn of the keen auditory sense of the guinea pig, and of the meticulous ablutions performed by rats, while the author refutes the popular idea that cats have nine lives and shows the fallacy of such a belief.

> *A review of "All about Pets," in* The New York Times Book Review, *December 15, 1929, p. 12.*

A STREET OF LITTLE SHOPS (1932)

Imaginative children make from books a hidden world, where they can retire and wander to their hearts' content. . . . **The Street of Little Shops** will take its place among the most charming of these byways. From the first tale of the only quarrel Mr. A. and Mr. P. ever had, through the sad disaster that befell, when Mr. Murdle's large heart was removed from the peg among his very miscellaneous stock to the last, every story is a delight and the older reader can hardly wait to share them with a friend, who may be anywhere from 6 to 10, or, indeed, considerably older. Mrs. Bianco knows children. She writes in a key of perfect make-believe that has the logic of true nonsense. Here are the details children love and the manner that never breaks faith with child readers by turning to the adult audience.

> *Anne T. Eaton, in a review of "A Street of Little Shops," in* The New York Times Book Review, *October 23, 1932, p. 13.*

A busy little street with pink and green and yellow shops on both sides, seven of them and a story in each, as all shops have stories, only these are droll, demure, and sometimes curiously moving; this is the pattern of Mrs. Bianco's new book. The brightest patch in the pattern seems to me "Mr. Murdle's Large Heart," about the shop that keeps all those foolish little things that other stores forget, one where children loved to come and cats sort of accumulated, perhaps because the proprietor had a Large Heart. . . .

Whatever Mrs. Bianco writes, some one is bound to bring up **The Velveteen Rabbit.** It is something to say of a story that it even reminds one in spirit some times of the kind and tender classic she put into children's literature, and these little stories do have that touch.

> *May Lamberton Becker, "Tales for Little Children," in* New York Herald Tribune Books, *November 13, 1932, p. 8.*

For sheer fun and charm we nominate Margery Williams Bianco's **Street of Little Shops** a book of stories about the stores of a small town that would have warmed the cockles of Hans Andersen's heart and yet is American enough to satisfy even Carl Sandburg himself. Here one may find intimate revelations concerning the private lives and doings of such

nationally known characters as "Mr. A. and Mr. P," "The Cigar Store Indian," and others. Our special favorite is about the old-fashioned lady milliner, who, despairing at the popularity of tailored hats, turned her skill to trimming hats for horses.

> *Rachel Field, "The Gossip Shop," in* The Saturday Review of Literature, *Vol. IX, No. 18, November 19, 1932, p. 256.*

THE HURDY-GURDY MAN (1933)

Vanished from most towns now is the hurdy-gurdy man with his monkey, and it is almost as a legendary hero that he appears in Margery Bianco's wise little tale. . . . **The Hurdy-Gurdy Man** has given Robert Lawson his best opportunity for drawings and designs of a spontaneity all too rare in an illustrated story. This charming little book is for younger children than **The Street of Little Shops.** (p. 9)

> *Anne Carroll Moore, "What Keeps a Child's Book Alive for Years," in* New York Herald Tribune Books, *November 12, 1933, pp. 8-9.*

There is no better story-teller than Mrs. Bianco, for she enters thoroughly into the events she describes, and her characters, whether they are a "Velveteen Rabbit," a "Skin Horse" or a broken wooden doll, are conceived with so much imagination that they continue to have a real existence for us even after the book is closed. **The Hurdy-Gurdy Man,** one of the finest of this year's books for children, is no exception to the rule.

The reader has a pleasant feeling that if he set out he, too, might find this quaint and charming little village, so much too neat that it was necessary for the hurdy-gurdy man, with his gayety and common sense, to come to show the inhabitants that if they would enjoy life, kindliness and fun and understanding are equally as essential as thrift and tidiness. The hurdy-gurdy man's monkey plays an important part, and so do Tommy Meeks and Miss Gay, who lived in the only houses in town that were shabby and out of repair, but who had gardens full of flowers and a friendly welcome for strangers. The baker, the policeman, the Mayor and the school teacher were a very different lot, but after the hurdy-gurdy man played his third and final tune, a strange change of heart came to them all and the tale ends with the whole town happily enjoying the gayest kind of a picnic.

It would be hard to find a book in which text and illustrations are more perfectly in accord. The exquisite black-and-white drawings give us the feeling that [Robert] Lawson must have crossed the border into the land of make-believe and made his pictures of scenes and people on the spot. (pp. 11, 20)

> *Anne T. Eaton, in a review of "The Hurdy-Gurdy Man," in* The New York Times Book Review, *November 12, 1933, pp. 11, 20.*

MORE ABOUT ANIMALS (1934)

Mrs. Bianco's **All About Pets** is the most satisfactory and appealing book on the subject for the younger children, and in **More About Animals** she has provided a delightful companion volume. There is a spontaneity in these chapters and a humor that will prove irresistible to animal lovers of any age. The author writes of what she has seen and experienced just as she might tell it to some small neighbor who sits listening with breathless interest. Mrs. Bianco enjoys pets herself, and along with the accuracy of her description she shows a sympathetic understanding of what pleases and interests a child. Buster, the dog who adopted the kind of family he felt he could enjoy; Trotty, the Scotch terrier, and Mrs. Woodchuck, who scolded him for his curiosity; Zinia, the mother cat that tried to look after the human baby as well as her own; Spiky, the little hedgehog, that went to sleep in such unaccountable places that he was once thrown out with the rubbish and once carried away in an overcoat pocket, will delight child readers. In the account of Lunar moths and other insects and in the chapter called "A Queer Night," with its strange procession of spiders, there is a quality that suggests the old folk tales.

> *Anne T. Eaton, in a review of "More about Animals," in* The New York Times Book Review, *April 15, 1934, p. 12.*

Intimate and loved friends—eccentric neighbors—strange mixtures of principles and whims just like human beings—that is what animals are, and the naturalness with which Mrs. Bianco depicts them is one of the book's greatest charms. Apparently, all her pets are gifted with decided individualities. How else can one account for a horse that would not remain long with any one owner because of his passion for travel, a dog that feigned politely to be spending the night under his own bungalow when he was secretly slumbering in a neighbor's bedroom, or a cat that on hearing a baby's long drawn cry, dropped a fat, dead mouse into its cradle?

There are fourteen brief stories very vivid, very succinct, each bringing the child reader remarkably close to wild or tame animal as the case may be—dog, cat, crow, skunk, woodchuck, hedgehog. . . .

The high water mark of animal psychology in the book is in "The Cat Who Watched for the Mailman." . . .

Petless children big or little, will want to possess some live creature after reading these adventures. . . .

> *Laura Benet, in a review of "More about Animals," in* New York Herald Tribune Books, *May 6, 1934, p. 9.*

THE GOOD FRIENDS (1934)

Here is a book about which one may be wholeheartedly enthusiastic, for any one is to be pitied who does not enjoy the flighty goat Rosie, Rhoda, the cow who liked curtains, the old horses, Fannie and Billy, and the other animals who make up the company of "good friends." Though Mr. Hicks is forced to desert these animals of his, Mary and Mrs. Green solve the problem of their board and bait and keep them from falling into the hands of the "Society" man. The pictures [by Grace Paull] are as humorous and entertaining as the story. (pp. 296-97)

> *A review of "The Good Friends," in* The Horn Book Magazine, *Vol. X, No. 5, September, 1934, pp. 296-97.*

Margery Bianco never tells a story like any one else, and when she tells an animal story all the chances are in favor of its turning out a book so different it falls pleasantly out of all classifications. But who cares if this delightful tale about animals is so, or only ought to be so, or whether a goat can talk

as entertainingly as this one does, or whether the Society man really did find a horse in the china closet? . . .

Old Man Hicks has to go to the hospital, and the disposal of a large family of quite inexpensive animals becomes a problem preying on the minds of his young neighbor Mary and her grandmother, Mrs. Green. None of the animals is exactly beautiful, the old dog is not even so very healthy, but they are all chock full of personality. . . . [To] make a lovely story short, Mary and her grandmother take all the animals and keep house for them: Rhoda the cow, Fanny and Billy the old horses and Rufus the old hound, the resourceful Mrs. Happy and her kittens, Rosie the goat, who takes a vacation and brings back two goatlets—it is a large and sensible family, and its conversation is unexcelled. Any one who has gone to more trouble for a pet than he fears his human friends would think justifiable will chuckle over the family cares of the Greens and, as for children, they have the right attitude to animals' rights, and it agrees with Mary's.

> *"North, South and Everywhere," in* New York Herald Tribune Books, *November 11, 1934, p. 12.*

All children have probably imagined at one time or another that animals could talk with them, and nothing is more fascinating to boys and girls than the animals they see on a farm. Thus *The Good Friends* is like a dream come true, for here are the animals, left behind when "old man Hicks" has to go off to the hospital, trying to stick together and Mary and her grandmother doing their best to help them. . . . As we read about them in Mrs. Bianco's book it never seems anything but natural that they should keep house themselves without breaking up the family, and the story is told so naturally that we seem to be overhearing real conversations carried on by Mary and her grandmother and the animals. (p. 10)

This is a thoroughly American book; the Autumn pastures with their stone walls, gray boulders and dry, rustling sumach bushes, are vividly and unmistakably New England, and so is the terse speech and practical common sense of Mrs. Green, Mary's grandmother. There is no child and hardly an adult who will not be charmed to make the acquaintance of these animals that Mrs. Bianco has so amazingly well characterized and has described with such delightful sympathy. Of them all, perhaps, Rosie, the irrepressible little goat, is the most appealing, and in spite of her mischief, even Mrs. Green must needs succumb to Rosie's endearing charm. (p. 16)

> *Anne T. Eaton, in a review of "The Good Friends," in* The New York Times Book Review, *November 11, 1934, pp. 10, 16.*

TALES FROM A FINNISH TUPA (with James Cloyd Bowman, 1936; British edition as *Tales from a Finnish Fireside*)

[Tales from a Finnish Tupa *was reissued in England in 1975 as* Tales from a Finnish Fireside.]

The motifs of the stories in *Tales from a Finnish fireside* are familiar in other countries in the Western world. "Jurma and the Sea God", for example, is a variant of the Bluebeard story, and the title of "The girl who sought her nine brothers" speaks for itself. Though there is a certain impression of northern remoteness in the stories, their chief mark of geographical distinctiveness is in the frequent use of magic words of enchantment and transformation—in "The Mouse Bride", for example, in which the prosaic craft of weaving is illuminated by incantation. As well as folk tales of the expected kind, the book also contains drolls, like the grouped anecdotes about "The Wise Men of Holmolay" which are in a well-known tradition, and there are a few animal fables that seem equally widespread. The style of the re-telling is smooth and civilised . . . The book . . . has an air of sober dignity about it which perhaps points to those older readers who still enjoy tales of magic.

> *Margery Fisher, in a review of "Tales from a Finnish Fireside," in* Growing Point, *Vol. 14, No. 4, October, 1975, pp. 2717.*

GREEN GROWS THE GARDEN (1936)

Some part of the practically certain success of Mrs. Bianco's gardening book for ten-year-olds up will be due to her admirable habit of talking to children, not as if she were their age, but as if they were hers. This is something to which an intelligent child invariably responds, and as most intelligent children either have a garden or wish they could have one, the book has its readers with it from the first.

It does not give formal directions for making and keeping a garden, but talks informally, as keen gardeners always do talk when they meet. These amusing and inspiriting chapters are really exchanges of experience, the exchange coming as the reader involuntarily pauses to put in his word. It would be hard to find a book for children this year so hard for any one to read through altogether to one's self; the urge to cry "Listen to this," is far too strong. Yet these cheerful and apparently unguided reminiscences have no mere chatter in them at all. Everything is good gardening advice from the ground up (or down), in what amounts to chronological order. She starts her flowers from seeds. . . . She follows the flower garden through the summer, makes a rock garden, a herb garden and a vegetable patch, shows how to coax wild flowers to settle in a camp garden, and takes plants indoors for winter windows. Over at the back are a couple of chapters on gardens remembered from an English childhood. The suggestions are not only sound, but in a curiously impromptu sort of tone, most inspiring. . . .

The whole book has true amateur spirit, using the word in its almost forgotten original beauty. For Mrs. Bianco writes as one who gardens for pure love of it, and such love always gives itself not only to the work but to the help of others who love the work. It will be difficult for a child to retrieve this book from any middle-aged beginner who lays hold of it.

> *May Lamberton Becker, in a review of "Green Grows the Garden," in* New York Herald Tribune Books, *April 12, 1936, p. 9.*

It is now the season to invite a garden, any kind of a garden, into one's life; and a charming and highly practical invitation is extended in this book, itself like a pot of fresh, deep loam in which to make flowers and herbs sprout at an amazing rate. Mrs. Bianco has reasoning ideas on cottage gardens and small patches of bloom and those heavily disappointing things—rock gardens! Her words on "Herb Gardens" are intriguingly poetic, and you will find a "Dish Garden" to be small things of the wood arranged microscopically in a dish. But the author being English born, is perhaps at her best in two fragrant chapters called "In an English Garden" and "Some English Wild Flowers."

> *"Cottage Gardens," in* The Commonweal, *Vol. XXIV, No. 2, May 8, 1936, p. 56.*

WINTERBOUND (1936)

Mark this down if you are looking for a story of young folks in the teens willing to work hard to keep the home going.

The four city-bred children of the Ellis family looked forward to a winter on their newly acquired old house in Connecticut as a sort of winter picnic in the society of their efficient, ebullient mother. Their scientist father had been offered an unexpected chance to join an expedition; that meant everybody's turning to, so he could take it. The cottage being seven miles from a railroad and having for modern conveniences but a zinc tub in the kitchen and a telephone only heightened the fun. But when an imperative call from New Mexico took Mother to spend the winter there, when the hastily chosen substitute housekeeper proved to be a monument of inefficiency, when the cold set really in and the pretty fireplace had to be blocked by a stove the size of a baby hippo, when housekeeping money acted as it does in the hands of young and hopeful housekeepers, it did take resilience and bounding good humor to get through. . . .

Mrs. Bianco's apparently effortless style is partly responsible for the easy flow of the story; she writes as if thinking aloud, but with far more direction than most of us use in thinking, and her talk is always alive and jolly.

> *May Lamberton Becker, in a review of "Winterbound," in* New York Herald Tribune Books, *October 25, 1936, p. 10.*

Winterbound is a story for girls of two other girls who spend a long, snowy Winter in [a] country home. . . .

Mrs. Bianco writes with a pleasing simplicity and directness. These young people, Kay, the artist, eager to catch on paper the riot of October color she saw from her window; Garry, with her talents for using tools and making plants grow, are such girls as we might meet and know; the New England country is drawn from life. The story of the sisters' pluck and perseverance and of Garry's resourcefulness in meeting unexpected situations, is one that will appeal to readers in their teens from the very fact that the tale is so well within the bounds of possibility and because it gives the impression that the author has lived through some of the experiences described.

> *Anne T. Eaton, in a review of "Winterbound," in* The New York Times Book Review, *November 1, 1936, p. 10.*

Interest centers in the characters, but there is sufficient action to keep the story moving. The setting of the small house in the country is important and well done. The reader visualizes the interior through the eyes of Kay, who does much to make it comfortable and attractive. The exterior surroundings are seen through the eyes of his sister Garry, the skillful gardener. This story has reality and is a contrast to the sentimental, extremely unrealistic adult novels girls commonly turned to before books such as this were written. (p. 64)

> *Marilyn Leathers Solt, "The Newbery Medal and Honor Books, 1922-1981," in* Newbery and Caldecott Medal and Honor Books: An Annotated Bibliography, *by Linda Kauffman Peterson and Marilyn Leathers Solt, G. K. Hall & Co., 1982, pp. 11-226.*

[*Winterbound* is a] domestic novel set on a Connecticut farm in the 1930s. . . . Characters are well differentiated, and there are some amusing moments, but the novelty of two young women coping alone seems so dated that the novel is of interest mostly as social history. (pp. 571-72)

> *Alethea K. Helbig and Agnes Regan Perkins, in a review of "Winterbound," in their* Dictionary of American Children's Fiction, 1859-1959: Books of Recognized Merit, *Greenwood Press, 1985, pp. 571-72.*

RUFUS, THE FOX: ADAPTED FROM THE FRENCH OF SAMIVEL (1937)

An amusing French tale . . . makes exciting book history, and will delight parents as well as third and fourth grade readers. The machinations of our wily friend the fox were never more intriguing, nor were the just deserts of the villain wolf more gratifying. . . . This is a charming book for a child to own. It will be a welcome addition to any picture book collection.

> *Carolyn E. Smith, in a review of "Rufus the Fox," in* Library Journal, *Vol. 62, November 15, 1937, p. 881.*

OTHER PEOPLE'S HOUSES (1939)

This book is so sensible girls will need it and so sympathetic they will want it.

When Dale's father died, her mother . . . retired with her younger daughter to Baltimore to help her elder sister run a tearoom, Dale, with no particular training, stayed on in New York, where she had been so fortunate as to get a job. It soon appeared that the fortune was not so good. As companion of a Park Avenue authoress she had nothing to do that was worth doing: it was parasitic work likely to cease at a moment's notice. When it did, Dale found another as mother's helper with a terror of employment agencies, stood it a month and was glad to take care of a young couple's house where a new baby is just back from hospital. There she was happy, hopeful and helpful. Then she was governess in a family living in "a tight, secure little world of their own where nothing mattered and nothing and nobody outside it had any importance, when all they cared about was to have a good time and where there would always be some one to do the work and straighten up after them." In intervals she lived at a boarding house her old friend, Dick, found for her, and in the end she is bringing her mother from Baltimore to help her run one in the town where Dick is to have his own business. They will marry. She will not live in other people's houses any more.

This is told without rancor or setting of class against class, poor against rich. But girls should note the differences between what Dick calls "the phony jobs"—easy money, leading nowhere—and those that involve thinking things out and planning ahead. Too many sentimental stories have been based on parasitic types of employment. Mrs. Bianco's story is good entertainment: It is about lively people, whether idle or working, and is all the better for its sympathy with the urge of young folks for a place of their own. But because it faces the fact that people with different incomes may live in different worlds and come no nearer because they are tempo-

rarily under the same roof, a girl just growing up may find in it light on the path of her career, wherever that may lead.

> *"Young Folks at Work," in* New York Herald Tribune Books, *November 12, 1939, p. 16.*

One of the best things about *Other People's Houses* is its way of meeting the exact situation in which many girls find themselves, without training, yet obliged to earn their living. While Dale Forrest is a normal girl with a liking for clothes and good times she shows courage in facing realities, meeting her limitations by a willingness to accept even distasteful opportunities and get a laugh out of them. A thread of romance in her story will appeal to many girls and her pluck will win their respect.

> *Alice M. Jordan, in a review of "Other People's Houses," in* The Horn Book Magazine, *Vol. XV, No. 6, November-December, 1939, p. 384.*

Other People's Houses is a story for girls of a type which is all too rarely found. In this tale . . ., there is none of the artificial atmosphere and over-vivacity which too often characterize the story of a girl who faces the world on her own. Dale is a normal average girl, with no unusual gifts, but she has pluck and a sense of humor, interest in people, a determination to try anything, domestic jobs included, rather than give in, and her job-hunting experiences in New York City make good reading. Probability is never strained and Dale's romance has the natural, humorous touch which characterizes the book.

Other People's Houses, a city story, is a companion piece to Mrs. Bianco's *Winterbound,* a story of a girl life with a country background, and in this second tale the author handles her characters with an even surer hand. She explains that she herself has always been interested in everyday stories so long as they were real. It is this real quality in her own books which girls from 12 to 15 detect, a quality which pleases and satisfies them, and one which makes those interested in providing good reading for young people very grateful to Mrs. Bianco.

> *Anne T. Eaton, in a review of "Other People's Houses," in* The New York Times Book Review, *January 14, 1940, p. 12.*

FRANZI AND GIZI (with Gisella Loeffler, 1941)

Two qualities make this one of the gayest, prettiest picture books of the year for little children [the illustrations are by Gisella Loeffler]: the natural charm of unspoiled childhood, and the traditional folk-art of Hungary. One plays into the other's hands: the story is of two fat little chubs, babes in the wood without any wicked uncle, told not only in words but with the naive symbolism, brilliant colors and familiar forms of a national decorative scheme that old as it is manages always to look as if it had been invented yesterday for the special pleasure of some little child.

The sun wakes Gizi under featherbeds, that, and Franzi tickling her with a feather. They pack up the sausages Franzi loves, feed a barnyard full of animals, and set off into the forest with Meck Meck the goat. Anyone whose spirits need a lift should open the book to the colored plate with the caption: "Such a happy life! Hei-lee, Hei-lo! Singing and dancing!" Gizi is so fat you'd think she couldn't get her feet off the ground, but dance she does. They eat strawberries: Franzi restrains her from eating toadstools too. They fight like little wildcats and make up like little cherubs. They talk about Easter and whether it is nice as Christmas: I think not, with such a Santa as the one they are thinking of. Then they come home hand in hand. The story is not sentimental; there is too much food in it for that: Margery Bianco can speak like a little child. . . .

A review of "Franzi and Gizi," in New York Herald Tribune Books, *November 2, 1941, p. 14.*

BRIGHT MORNING (1942)

Any eight-year-old girl will read this story over and over, but do not let her enjoy it alone. Read it to her first; she will repeat the process for herself more than once, or just borrow it some day when you feel you must "get out of all this" or fly apart. Children's books can offer brief sanctuary for driven adult nerves when they are about the good life such as you yourself led in an earlier day, or as you wished you could. Mrs. Bianco, who is blest with the gift of remembering childhood, creates a little Victorian family world a world where children were happy, not from what they had, but from the delight they took in it. It is a world so many Americans remember that the English differences only give spice to the sweetness of memory.

It was on a drab, rainy afternoon that I first read about Chris (eight) and Emmie (five) and their busy, eager adventures when sweeps still swept chimneys and went in procession on May Day; when the monkey or the organ was magic and the paroquet that chose your "fortune" was mystery; when accidentally locking yourself into the bathroom was a strategic problem for the family. It is a merry story, told with the faint breath of homesickness that children will not notice but that grownups will share.

May Lamberton Becker, "In Countries Overseas," in New York Herald Tribune Books, *November 15, 1942, p. 22.*

As a prism catches the light and separates it into colors delicately gay and clear, so in *Bright Morning* Mrs. Bianco has captured the quality of early childhood, when sensation is keen and every experience intensely personal and absorbing. . . .

Chris and Emmie are natural and entertaining, often mischievous and occasionally downright naughty, though it was not with intention that Emmie locked herself in the bathroom and had to be rescued by means of the window.

There is a sedate charm and humor as well in the quiet round of life of this Victorian family, and not only does Mrs. Bianco succeed in giving the very essence of childhood at the end of the nineteenth century but of London itself in the springtime, when everywhere sparrows were chirping and the air smelled of soot and gravel, when there were daisies and yellow daffodils in the park and old men were selling bunches of flowers, or when the rain ran down in steady trickles against the window panes, is brought before the reader vividly and with nostalgic charm.

While recognizing Chris and Emmie as children like themselves, 8 to 11 year olds of today will enjoy the book's fresh unhackneyed setting and quiet humor. This little volume with its charmingly simple and appropriate format brings to children not only pleasure but a widened horizon through its effortless presentation of an earlier day.

Anne T. Eaton, "A Victorian Family," in The New York Times Book Review, *December 20, 1942, p. 7.*

It states on the dust jacket that Miss Bianco writes from her own experiences as a child in Victorian London, and there is no doubt that she has remembered what it is like to be a child and live in a child's world. Chris and Emmie, two little girls in the days when children wore buttoned boots and learnt lessons by rote from a governess, are charming and real. Nothing very exciting happens in their story, yet the small everyday happenings are important and hold attention. . . .

This attractive and quaint picture of early childhood should appeal to children of about eight or nine.

A review of "Bright Morning," in The Junior Bookshelf, *Vol. 9, No. 3, November, 1945, p. 93.*

PENNY AND THE WHITE HORSE (with Marjory Collison, 1942)

On the end papers of this charming combination of story and four-color drawings, the ancestry of the merry-go-round is traced to the carrousel, the mock joust that took the place of the tournament, and the little swords with which riders on our wooden horses used to reach for rings take their place as distant relatives of lances in days of old. But the carrousel on which little Penny loved to ride stood in a modern park, so modern indeed that it found the old horses in their faded paint had grown too shabby for their surroundings. Not for little Penny however; she had one nickel a week to spend on one ride and the only question she had ever had was which splendid steed to choose. Now that was settled; she always took the beautiful white one.

Until the old outfit was sold, and the white horse went off in a cart to a new owner. Nothing could comfort Penny. But one day she hears "A penny a ride!" in a poor, crowded street. There was one of those touching little merry-go-rounds in a cart, such as a man turns by hand, around which stood very little people with pennies in their hands. There was Penny's dear white horse, lovely as ever. His paint was chipped, but no more than that of a beloved doll. He still wanted her to ride him—and now she knew that every summer he would come back and she could ride him for ever and ever.

So in these dreamy yet realistic scenes, with the merry-go-round swirling across the wide pages and the smiles of happy children shining, Penny puts a great dream upon the page. For it is the dreamlike quality of happiness in childhood that as long as it goes on it goes on for ever and ever.

May Lamberton Becker, "All Sorts of Little Stories," in New York Herald Tribune Books, *November 15, 1942, p. 30.*

Children who find fun and magic in a merry-go-round, as most of them do, will enjoy Margery Bianco's and Marjory Colleson's picture story book, which tells in genuinely childlike fashion of a little girl named Penny. . . .

This simple little story is told with charm and understanding and the lovely drawings with their softly blended colors seem to combine the green and gold of Springtime with the lightheartedness of childhood, and the gayety and romance which the merry-go-round has brought to many generations of children.

Anne T. Eaton, "The Wooden Horse," in The New York Times Book Review, *January 31, 1943, p. 10.*

FORWARD, COMMANDOS! (1944)

Commandos have surely been a boon to boys. From my window overlooking a park I can see, at any hour, units of from six to a dozen in number and from six to twelve years in age, storming heights and squirming through bushes of Morningside to surprise and surround "Them." All over our country such bands operate in back lots, and any one of them would receive this book with rapture. For it deals, hand to hand, with such exploits carried on by Red, Jimmy, Kit, Fatty and Banty in small town raids, unmarred by girls save for one superior sister who tries to keep Mother informed on their deeds, and is not encouraged. . . .

Naturally the boys get into trouble near home. How could they know that in crawling with blackened faces through a barbed wire entanglement, they would bring down a washline full of wet clothes? "Heaven knows there's the pine woods and the whole of River County to play anything you want to in," says Mrs. Mills, who has lived through pirates and Superman and is getting a trifle edgy. So they take to the woods and practically all of River County, New Jersey—and do things whizz!

A story with the play-spirit of boys at the restless, exuberant, ingenious time of life centering at ten, it will be read and re-read by such boys, and makes perfect reading aloud. Do not tell these small boys that we have just lost dear Margery Bianco. For they have not. They never will. She joins their company for keeps in this book, as she did that of little children long ago in **The Velveteen Rabbit.**

May Lamberton Becker, in a review of "Forward, Commandos!" in New York Herald Tribune Weekly Book Review, *October 1, 1944, p. 6.*

Margery Bianco has caught that timeless thing, the spirit of boyhood, and with skill and complete understanding, has given it today's dress. Basically, the boys are the same as they were when Thomas Bailey Aldrich wrote *The Story of a Bad Boy.* Fatty Hick's flair for making money hasn't reached here the advanced stage of Doc Macnooder in *Tennessee Shad,* but it is promising. What boy, of any age, wouldn't refuse to pick blueberries by the hour—unless, of course, he got twenty-five cents a quart for them? There is a certain lack of robustness of plot here that may prevent boys of twelve or over from finding the story themselves; but it has so much that is familiar to them and its attitude will seem so right to them—they may adopt it, as they did *Penrod,* as one of "their" books.

Elizabeth B. Spring, in a review of "Forward, Commandos!" in The Saturday Review of Literature, *Vol. XXVII, No. 46, November 11, 1944, p. 32.*

In Captain Red and his cohorts boys of 8 to 12 will surely recognize themselves and the gang on the block. Mrs. Bianco's ambition to write a story for boys has been amply justified here. In our deep regret for the loss of that understanding heart and humorous wisdom which gave us some of our most beloved children's books of this generation we can, nevertheless, be glad that she left us this one, as true in spirit as any she ever wrote.

Ellen Lewis Buell, in a review of "Forward, Commandos!" in The New York Times Book Review, *January 28, 1945, p. 16.*

Anthony (Edward Tudor) Browne

1946-

English author and illustrator of picture books and reteller.

Considered one of the most gifted British contributors to the picture book genre to have emerged in the last decade, Browne is acclaimed for creating often unconventional works in which he characteristically uses bright, symbolic pictures filled with surrealistic details and humorous visual puns to illustrate serious themes about personal relationships and social conventions. He is perhaps best known for *Gorilla* (1983), the fantasy adventure of a lonely girl who is infatuated with gorillas and asks her often absent father to give her one for her birthday. When he presents her with a toy, Hannah dreams that it turns into a real gorilla which, after putting on her father's clothes, takes her to a variety of interesting places before they return home; the next morning, Hannah's father offers to take her to the zoo. Usually considered a work which explores the archetypal emotions of childhood in an especially affecting manner, *Gorilla* won both the Kate Greenaway Medal and the Kurt Maschler Award in 1983 as well as being named a *Boston Globe-Horn Book* honor book in 1986. Two of Browne's other popular titles, *Willy the Wimp* (1985) and *Willy the Champ* (1985), continue his fascination with simian characters. In these works, which present young readers with the concept that our real natures cannot be hidden, Browne humorously depicts the adventures of a skinny chimp who builds up his body and heroically saves his girlfriend from danger without changing his unassuming personality. A former graphic designer and medical artist who has been influenced by surrealistic painters such as Magritte, Browne invests his watercolor illustrations with bold, rich colors, clear outlines which are often set against white backgrounds, and subjects which mix realism with fantastic, sometimes macabre, detail, a quality which has brought the artist some controversy. His version of *Hansel and Gretel* (1981), for example, has received a variety of commentary due to the fact that, rather than representing the tale as a period piece, Browne sets his illustrations in the present day and uses them to reflect the young child's subconscious. *Hansel and Gretel* was awarded a Kate Greenaway Medal commendation in 1982 and the International Board on Books for Young People (IBBY) Award for illustration for Great Britain in 1984. Browne has also illustrated several works by other authors in a style which incorporates some of the motifs he uses in his own books. He shared the Deutscher Jugendliteratur Preis in 1985 with author Annalena McAfee for *The Visitors Who Came to Stay* (1984), and has also illustrated a well-received version of Lewis Carroll's *Alice's Adventures in Wonderland* (1988).

(See also *Something about the Author,* Vols. 44, 45 and *Contemporary Authors,* Vols. 97-100.)

AUTHOR'S COMMENTARY

[The following excerpt is from an interview by Chris Powling.]

Art for Anthony Browne is perfectly *normal*—even if one of its crucial functions is to help us renew the way we see the

world. The freshness of his own vision, and his highly skilled craftsmanship, has already won him both the Kate Greenaway Medal and the Kurt Maschler Award. It's also brought him a delightful seventeenth-century house, one of the historic buildings of Kent, and a job he freely admits he can't believe he's being paid for. 'I'd do it for nothing if I had to.'

Yet, like many other illustrators, he came to children's books almost by accident. 'I couldn't make enough to live on as the designer of greetings cards and it was a toss-up between children's books and women's magazine illustration.' He'd already worked in advertising and as a medical illustrator, along with two short-lived attempts at becoming a teacher. His first try at a picture-book, moreover, was 'the wrong size, the wrong shape, the wrong number of pages and basically just derivative.' Luckily, though, Julia MacRae was amongst the first publishers he showed it to and she spotted at once that there were also one or two things he was getting right. He still speaks warmly of her encouragement and good advice and it's to her that **Piggybook,** a front-runner for many of this year's prizes, is dedicated.

Despite this roundabout route, Anthony Browne's arrival as one of the most original and accomplished of our picture-book artists seems to have been destined from the start. As a child in the fifties, growing up in the Yorkshire village of

Hipperholme, near Halifax, he was more conscious of comics and annuals than books. But he drew endlessly. 'Battles, as much as anything, I used to fill the page with lots and lots of battles—and lots of little figures with plenty of what would now be called surrealistic jokes. Things like a disembodied head with a speech-bubble coming out saying "Aaargh!" In those days I'd use arrows to point at something that was going on in the background and write a label in case I hadn't drawn it clearly enough—such as "An Invisible Man", that kind of thing.'

Even though he always knew 'Art was my best subject,' his passage through grammar school wasn't easy. Partly this was due to the low status it had in the academic pecking-order, a familiar enough circumstance, and partly to his Art teacher, 'a classic wide-brush man whose own work in oils was as far removed as it could possibly be from me with my sharp little pencil.' He passed O-level Art a year early but came bottom in the exam. Having been thwarted in his attempt to take Art, English and Biology at A-level, a combination which would have been very handy for his future employment, he transferred after a year to Leeds Art School.

It was there, embarked on a three-year course in graphic design, that the unthinkable happened. 'My father died. It was a great shock to me, an incredible shock. This God-like figure I thought would live forever, who I never dreamed would not be there, was suddenly gone. He was a frustrated artist, I suppose, born at the wrong time. From what I can gather his parents always strongly advised him against doing anything artistic because it was unreliable and you couldn't make a living out of it. Plus being much more difficult to go to art college in those days without grants. So he never actually found out what he wanted to do . . . but always, in his spare time, he drew—usually for us, my elder brother Michael and me. He didn't paint pictures and put them in frames and hold exhibitions and stuff, but he used to spend a lot of time with us as children drawing, and playing drawing games.' Is Anthony Browne to some extent fulfilling his father's unfulfilled ambition, then? 'It's not something I think about but I suppose in a way, yes. If he'd been given the opportunities I had, I'm pretty sure he'd have done something very similar . . .'

His father's sudden death affected him greatly. 'It took me a long time to get over it. As well as the surrealist painters, I was much impressed by Francis Bacon and for ages had this morbid death thing. I was always painting the insides of people showing on the outside, for instance—adolescent stuff, I know.' Perhaps, but perfect preparation for his subsequent job as a medical illustrator, the official recorder of the intricate goings-on in the operating theatre of a large hospital. But even this wasn't sufficient exorcism. Later, in the 'high-pressure, very difficult, very boring, incredibly well paid world of advertising, I still found it very difficult to paint anything happy . . . I remember I once had to draw this family having a nice time inside a caravan. And I couldn't! Whatever I did it looked as if something ominous was about to happen, or as if they'd just had a row or were about to stab somebody . . . I just couldn't paint a happy picture.'

The cure, amazingly enough, turned out to be greetings cards. He was taken on by Gordon Fraser who 'taught me how to do happy designs. Eventually I was able to do happy teddy-bears and happy cats. He was always very good to me.' Not least of the Fraser kindnesses, as it turned out, was his suggestion of a second string to the Browne bow to offset the precariousness of the card market. Why didn't he take up

magazine illustration, perhaps? Or children's books? Hence Julia MacRae and, in due course, *Through the Magic Mirror.*

He's very critical of the book now, 'In a way it was a fake book. It started the wrong way round. It began with images and was linked with words afterwards. They should both come together ideally.' Nevertheless it's been reprinted twice since 1976 and established the Browne hallmarks from the outset: the careful use of colour, the bold draughtsmanship, the gloriously inventive surreal humour. These were developed further in the books that followed—*A Walk in the Park, Bear Hunt, Look What I've Got, Hansel and Gretel, Bear Goes to Town*—all getting increasing critical attention as the distinctive Anthony Browne vision of things established itself. Then, in 1983, came those prizes for *Gorilla,* his classic account of a small girl's birthday gift which becomes so much more than a gift.

As with all his books, he's not sure how *Gorilla* came about. 'My audience, I suppose, is always me as a child—the book I'd have liked to have seen as a child. I don't ever really think "will seven-year-old children in 1987 like this book?" In some unconscious way I tune in to the child I was. I've heard Maurice Sendak say similar things and that's the only awareness of my audience I have . . . I suppose some vague part of me is aware of what the book is about but I shrink from making the process too self-conscious. It's why I'm a little wary even of talking about it in case I become pretentious or pompous. The books do come naturally. At any particular time I've always got three or four ideas which aren't quite fully formed in my head. It's a question of waiting for one of them to come to the surface. I'd find it very difficult to do a book to order—to do a commissioned book, for instance.'

Hence his preference for providing both the words and the pictures himself. (pp. 16-17)

[Growing] from within is, quite literally, vital to his approach which is why he firmly denies any propagandist intention behind books of his like *Willy the Wimp, Willy the Champ* and *Piggybook.* 'I couldn't do an "issues" book if I tried,' he says. Indeed, critics with a special care for such matters have taken several of his books to task. His updating of *Hansel and Gretel,* which he set in the 1950s, made one reviewer ask 'Where are the Social Services?' and he still recalls wryly the letter he received from a multi-racial educational group in Bedfordshire which accused *Willy the Wimp* of 'racism, sexism . . . and *transvestism*'. 'Till then it had never crossed my mind that because gorillas have got darker faces than chimpanzees, therefore the gorillas are black and Willy's white. As for the sexism, I'd concede they have a point in that the only female character in the book is negative, a secondary character. But how does this fit in with the charge that Milly, Willy's girlfriend, is just a dressed-up male anyway?' The ambiguous ending to *Piggybook* (see the car numberplate in that final spread) has also provoked objections yet it's as much a deliberate joke as the uncanny resemblance between Mrs Piggott, in the book, and his wife Jane, in real life. No one, least of all himself, is exempt from the Anthony Browne humour. (p. 17)

Anthony Browne and Chris Powling, in an interview in Books for Keeps, *No. 44, May, 1987, pp. 16-17.*

Sam walked on, out of the town, toward the woods.

From Look What I've Got!, *written and illustrated by Anthony Browne.*

GENERAL COMMENTARY

ELAINE MOSS

Anthony Browne uses the juxtaposition of the improbable in his pictures to jolt the reader into wide-eyed attention. Most of his books are visually hilarious but their underlying messages about values and personal relationships are serious. The surreal quality in his work has echoes of Magritte. Verbal and visual delights abound in [*A Walk in the Park*]. I looked at it dozens of times, alone and with children, but only this minute did I notice that the entrance to the park (one pillar bower-hatted, the other adorned with a cricket ball) has only one half gate. . . A great treat, this walk in the park.

Snooty Jeremy is given one expensive gift after another [in *Look What I've Got!*]: a football he can't control, a bike he can't ride sensibly, sweets that make him sick. But can he make Sam envious? No, because Sam has inner resources, imagination, soul. Surreal details in the pictures (a washing line with X-, Y-, and Z-front pants, jeans with feet still in them and socks doing a balancing act) make this a book with riches for the astute unhurried observer.

The decision to include an illustrated fairy tale [*Hansel and Gretel*] in this list was not taken lightly; picture-book treatment of fairy tales is for the very young as a rule. Hansel and Gretel as a story, however, is a terrifying tale of paternal weakness, (step-) maternal perfidy: it begs many questions, all of which are explored and brought horrendously close by Anthony Browne's bold determination to illustrate with modern rather than time-distanced paintings. Father is a woodcutter

in faded jeans and patched duffel coat; but his wife in her high boots, leopard-spotted coat and scarlet lipstick has clearly spent money on herself that should have bought food for Hansel and Gretel . . . Each picture tells its own story to the perceptive reader.

'One day Bear went to town,' says Anthony Browne innocently [in *Bear Goes to Town*]. He did indeed! Bear goes to town on those of us who wear leopard skin, eat beef, allow experiments on animals in order to test cosmetics. (pp. 11-13)

[In *Gorilla,*] Hannah's father is always too busy to talk to her; her mother (we must presume from the empty frame on father's desk) has left home. Hannah becomes besotted with gorillas: books about them, pictures of King Kong, her own drawings. Will father take her to see the gorillas in the zoo as her birthday treat? . . . Sad, lyrical, full of jokes and messages for those with their eyes open, this book ends in a mood of rare content. . . .

[In *Willy the Wimp* an] unusually light-hearted Browne takes a hilarious sideswipe at body culture. What happens, he asks, if the diffident personality survives inside the new muscle-rippling skin? Willy the Wimp, who 'wouldn't hurt a fly', takes a course of aerobics and finds out. (p. 13)

Elaine Moss, in a review of "A Walk in the Park" and others, in her Picture Books for Young People, 9-13, *second edition, The Thimble Press, 1985, pp. 11-13.*

JOHN ROWE TOWNSEND

The rising new name of the early eighties was that of Anthony Browne. He had published in 1977 *A Walk in the Park,* a neat and witty picture story in which children and dogs fraternize happily but the class-divided adults who have taken them to the park have nothing to say to each other. The bonus of the book is to be found in its incidental, surrealist details: the topiary figure that exactly resembles the lady passing it; the gentleman walking his pig; the hippo in the fountain.

The book that made Browne's name was *Gorilla.* Its story is simple. Hannah longs to see a gorilla, but Father hasn't time to take her to the zoo or anywhere else. She asks for a gorilla for her birthday, but only gets a toy one, which she doesn't think much of. In the night a 'real', full-sized gorilla appears, puts on Father's hat and coat, and takes her on a glorious adventure. . . . The book's attraction is the visiting gorilla himself: large, kind, reassuring, a person—indeed, a father—but with just a hint of pathos.

In *Willy the Wimp* the weedy little chimp who apologizes to everybody, even when it isn't his fault, takes a course of body-building, becomes muscular and walks tall—but at the end collides with a lamp-post, and apologizes to it. Willy, of course, is endearingly human. Anthony Browne makes effective use of clear, bright outlines, often against blank white backgrounds that give a cut-out effect. He is an able, witty artist, but I suspect that he owes some of his primacy to the primates. (p. 324)

John Rowe Townsend, "Picture Books in Bloom: British," in his Written for Children: An Outline of English-Language Children's Literature, *third revised edition, J. B. Lippincott, 1987, pp. 317-25.*

THROUGH THE MAGIC MIRROR (1976)

Toby's journey through the looking glass, which he enters in a moment of boredom at home, exposes him to a number of wonders; but they are all just passing sights, ticked off in a manner that could reduce the wildest dreams to an uninspired silly session. "An invisible man passed by" (you see only his clothes, hat, and briefcase), an oversized dog leads a man on a leash, mice chase a cat, choirboys float in the sky and at last the animals emerge from a zoo billboard and chase Toby . . . till he steps back through the mirror, and home for supper. Through all the derivative surreal scenes Toby is merely a bemused observer of gratuitous dislocation; he's relieved to be home again, but otherwise not affected. And if he's not, who will be?

A review of "Through the Magic Mirror," in Kirkus Reviews, *Vol. XLV, No. 2, January 15, 1977, p. 42.*

Let's go way out. There's a touch of the surreal and Harlin Quist in Anthony Browne's *Through the Magic Mirror.* Out of boredom Tony steps through a mirror and into a world where the sun is an orange, dogs take men for a walk, the sky is dark with flying choirboys and zoo animals move off billboards. A strange world indeed, but one that children will want to visit only once in these pages that serve mainly—the text being so thin—as a showcase for Mr. Browne's bold, pictorial style. (p.42)

George A. Woods, "Pleasures for the Eye," in The New York Times Book Review, *May 1, 1977, pp. 28, 42.*

A WALK IN THE PARK (1977)

[*A Walk in the Park*] is a straightforward account of working-class Smudge and her father taking their dog for a walk in the park where they meet middle-class Charles, his mother and their dog. Or rather, the children and the dogs meet while the parents ignore each other (spot the moral, dear reader). The children and the dogs play together happily until it's time to go home. The bright pictures in this book are pleasant enough, despite some surrealist detail that may bewilder literal-minded under-fives ("Mummy, mummy, why is that man taking a pig for a walk?" "Shut up, dear, and admire the clever artist.") Where the book falls down, I think, is in the treatment of the children. Anthony Browne has been so intent to avoid traditional sex stereotypes that he has made Smudge and Charles completely faceless and characterless creatures with the same length of hair and the same costume of trousers and jerseys. Perhaps we're not supposed to care which is which, even though Charles is described as being more timid on the swings than Smudge. I find it interesting, though, that it should be Charles who gives Smudge a flower at the end, and not the other way round. Gentlemen, however androgynous, still make the advances, it seems. (pp. 165-66)

Lance Salway, in a review of "A Walk in the Park," in Signal, *No. 24, September, 1977, pp. 165-66.*

A Walk in the Park is [a] very clever book. The idea, and the words in which it is expressed, could hardly be bettered. Two parties visit the park; Mr. Smith from his scruffy house with his tough daughter and his mongrel dog, Mrs. Smythe from her detached villa with pedigree son and dog. In the park the dogs soon bridge the social gap. The children take a little longer. The adults remain divided by the length of a park bench

and by generations of social conditioning. I wish Mr. Browne had left it at that. He has insisted on filling the pictures with irrelevant jokes: the park gates are decorated with Roman head, apple and chamber pot, one of the trees is a human leg, a respectable citizen takes his pig for a walk, while Tarzan swoops through the trees, and so on. The drawings are certainly funny and will set the kids chuckling, but they are at odds with the admirable central theme. (p.273)

M. Crouch, in a review of "A Walk in the Park," in The Junior Bookshelf, *Vol. 41, No. 5, October, 1977, pp. 272-73.*

In my last "Letter" I talked of the artist who presently dominates a new wave of English picture-book making, Raymond Briggs; Shirley Hughes now joins the rank of this new wave of artists. Charles Keeping has always been in the forefront; indeed, he was for a long time a lone figure in this now strong movement. In his two stories about the girl Shirley, John Burningham recently produced work of great interest, which refreshes the narrative forms open to the picture book. Nicholas Brennan . . . gave promise in *Olaf's Incredible Machine,* a promise I still think he will fulfill one day. And Janet Ahlberg . . . combines humor and inventiveness with an increasingly impressive technique. All these artists share an awareness of and a liking for both the popular and studio art of our time, an ability to translate these into picture-book and child-appealing images, and a high degree of technical skill. In other words, they are craftsmen who are socially and artistically in touch with the growing points of the world in which they—and more important, children—live.

There is one more name I'd like to add to my list: Anthony Browne. Browne's *A Walk in the Park* was one of our most vital children's books of 1977. . . . In some ways Browne's first book, *Through the Magic Mirror,* published a year earlier, is even more important because it firmly announces in an uncompromising way that Browne intends to bring into children's books some of the twentieth-century art which has often been thought too difficult for children to understand. Browne's work is representational in a manner that reminds me of Hockney, and although he tells a story, it is one that might have been illustrated by a Surrealist. Outside England this is not altogether exceptional. Some French and German picture books, for instance, try similar modes. But the English are a visually conservative lot, and to attempt such work here is not far short of artistic self-destruction, because the work won't be bought.

A Walk in the Park, however, has a more controlled narrative and a surface appeal. By which I mean stick-in-the-muds could easily think of it as a funny little story with some jokey pictures. Two adults—a suburbanite lady and a working-class man—take their children and their dogs for a walk in the park. During the walk, first the dogs and then the children get together, play, and enjoy themselves. The adults never do; they remain deliberately aloof, even when they are sitting on the same park bench. The story is about social class (an undying English preoccupation). But far more important, the story is also about different languages and the different uses of language. The language of words, the language of pictures, the language of visually symbolic relationships—the juxtaposition of disparate images that, taken together, make unexpected meanings—and, above all, of course, the language of narrative.

In one double-page spread, for instance, the dogs play among the trees, watched by parents and children. And among the trees we see a cosy woman pushing a pram out of which pokes the head of a very large dog. Robin Hood fires arrows at a target. A city gent, bowler-hatted, walks a tomato on a lead. A huge woodpecker looks askance, its beak pierced right through a tree trunk. And another tree is shaped like a human leg and ends in a human foot. Each detail, seemingly arbitrary, actually carries significance for one of the book's themes: language, social class, the nature of childhood, and the spiking of socially hindering conventions which are not only out-of-date but injuriously silly. We are being asked to think about and to look at all those subjects, and we are being asked to do so in linguistic and pictorial codes children can, with a little help from one another as much as from adults, probe and puzzle out for themselves. As with all modern forms of literature, the reader is being asked to contribute as much to the book as the author gave to it. (pp. 212-14)

> Aidan Chambers, "Hughes in Flight," in The Horn Book Magazine, *Vol. LVI, No. 2, April, 1980, pp. 211-14.*

BEAR HUNT (1979)

Very far from artless is Anthony Browne's **Bear Hunt.** In this book, art is everywhere, from the bright, buttonhole-stitched and rather archly sophisticated backgrounds to Bear's own pencilled hand which draws the means of his escape from every trap laid by the two stupid white hunters who stalk him through his preposterous jungle. The idea is clever and Bear, a portly teddy in a red-spotted bow, walks away with endearing placidity from each new peril but, for all its ingenuity and rich colouring, there is a coldness at the heart of this book. The element of delight . . . is absent here.

> Anne Carter, "Profit and Pleasure," in The Times Literary Supplement, *No. 4004, December 14, 1979, p. 129.*

This story is told with a minimum of words. In contrast to the simple text, the illustrations are bold, fanciful, and elaborate. This picture book lends itself well to several language arts activities. Young children could practice oral language skills as they describe and react to all the fascinating details in the illustrations. The book's simple text makes it an "easy reader" that provides beginning readers with an opportunity to enjoy independent work.

> A review of "Bear Hunt," in The Reading Teacher, *Vol. 34, No. 4, January, 1981, p. 479.*

Bear Hunt is the most successful and best integrated of the picture books [reviewed in this essay]. Bold black text under full page illustrations can be read easily by the beginning reader. However, picture and text tell the story together and demand that the reader pay close attention to both elements. Challenging but rewarding. . . . The sharp illustrations, simple scenes on the surface, are complex and clearly differentiate between the hunting and the drawing scenes. Hunting scenes are done in deep greens, blues, reds and lighter yellows. In the drawing scenes, the bear's pencil makes black line drawings on a white background providing a very visible contrast between scenes of danger and escape. Magic lies within the hunting scenes. A teacup, an egg, a glove become flowers. Lips, shoes, and fishes are leaves. Bear, hunters and a rescuing rhinoceros are drawn with character and humor. (p.39)

From Hansel and Gretel, *written by the Brothers Grimm. Illustrated by Anthony Browne.*

> Brenda Watson, "The Bear Facts and Fictions," in The World of Children's Books, *Vol. VI, 1981, pp. 37-40.*

LOOK WHAT I'VE GOT! (1980)

In fantasy form, **Look What I've Got** shows how to come to terms with the child who boasts that he possesses all the things other children could want. On Sam's walk through the town to the country, Jeremy appears and reappears with luxurious possessions which merely lead him into various troubles from which Sam silently rescues him (without thanks). Sam, no longer listening, finds treasures of a different sort hidden in the woods. But the story is incidental to the marvellous inventiveness of the illustrations. The clean bold colours depict a splendid mixture of realism and fantastic detail. On closer examination, such delights as a cow behind a house window, a bra with three cups on a most extraordinary clothes-line or a man with a fish on a lead provide perpetual surprises, which children will love.

> A review of "Look What I've Got," in The Junior Bookshelf, *Vol. 44, No. 4, August, 1980, p. 167.*

Anthony Browne has been praised, deservedly, for all his books, and when Jeremy says to Sam **Look What I've Got!** it pays the reader to look not only at what he has got but more closely at everything on the page. The normal child and adult eye is conditioned to see what it expects to see but Anthony Browne provides the eye with things that are not seen unless looked for. I have held open pages of his books in front of groups of teachers and, separately, groups of children and there are usually only one or two in each group who see, at first look, what is not normal on the page. Here is another Browne book to be used and enjoyed for both the minimal word content and the challenge to visual perception, by ages three to adult.

> *Margaret R. Marshall, in a review of "Look What I've Got," in* British Book News, *Autumn, 1980, p. 13.*

The odd touches within the smoothly colorful Magritte-like paintings are reminiscent of a Harlin Quist book, but the surreal art, with its absurd visual wit, makes very real the minimal text that details a familiar childhood situation. Sam's low-key triumph and the "hey, look at this!" appeal of the pictures make this a quirky winner for young readers and listeners close enough to catch the fun.

> *Nancy Palmer, in a review of "Look What I've Got," in* School Library Journal, *Vol. 28, No. 1, September, 1981, p. 104.*

HANSEL AND GRETEL (1981)

Perhaps because I find Hansel and Gretel terrifying I preferred Antonella Bollinger-Savelli's folksy but bold interpretation [*Grimm's Hansel and Gretel*] to Anthony Browne's grim modern dress version. It seems odd that the tale of a father, abandoning his offspring in connivance with his second wife should be thought suitable for children. But Hansel and Gretel is also a story of youthful quick-wittedness and bravery and it is sufficiently preposterous for a child to see that it belongs to the realm of fantasy. What then do we make of this contemporary stepmother's squalid dressing table with lipsticks, talcum powder and cigarette ends lovingly depicted by Anthony Browne? Is her taste for fake furs and stiletto heels the cause of the family's poverty? Why have the Social Services let them slip through the net? I really cannot envisage buying any child this book.

> *Tanya Harrod, "Illustrating Atmosphere," in* The Times Literary Supplement, *No. 4103, November 20, 1981, p. 1360.*

[Anthony Browne] is, in my view, one of our younger artists for children most worth watching and valuing. His ***Hansel and Gretel*** is no historical or vaguely fanciful vision. This woodcutter's family has television; their stepmother goes to bed in her hair curlers and probably takes sleeping pills (the bottle on top of the TV set). Theirs isn't the romantic poverty that people seem to have lived in, according to most illustrated folk tales, in the folk-tale past—but the virulent, neurotic-making form of modern Western deprivation. But, of course, it is all a metaphor of love, anyway, and clues are everywhere in Browne's pictures, helping us to see that the story may be as much an interior dream-worked experience going on inside the children as it is anything happening in external reality—just as *Where the Wild Things Are* is a dream-worked experience for Max.

So much detail and no space to tell you about it. So all I can say is that partly what excites me is the way Browne incorporates into all his work a representational style which manipulates symbolic images wittily and with strong emotional effect. Till now I've felt he was still a little tentative in this, still searching out his way. But ***Hansel and Gretel*** is not so much

searching as finding-and-making with a confidence and maturity one has been waiting for him to display.

With his books, children can always dive straight in and enjoy the game of "I Spy," picking out the visual jokes, the oddities, the apparent weirdnesses hidden in tiny details. But what some teachers who work carefully with his books discover is that the I Spy gaming doesn't stop on the surface. It grows into—actually is led by the artist's skill into—deep questioning. Why? the children ask when they have looked and game-played long enough. And the answers they find are spiral in nature. Each leads further and further into the story, into the thematic and life-questioning features that lie hidden beneath the narrative surface. In critical jargon, Browne's images resonate.

This ***Hansel and Gretel*** is made out of framed and reflecting images: mirrors, of course, but also windows and doors, trees, and domestic furniture. Even the book's pictures themselves are formally framed full-page, full-color pictures on the right; and on the left is the text, also framed, and set above it a framed vignette, like a close-up, of some small detail from a part of the story not illustrated in the main pictures but which carries an important meaning-directing clue.

Take just one recurrent image: a black triangle like a witch's hat. In the third double spread, when the stepmother has put the children to bed, that ominous triangle is seen as a church steeple in a picture hanging on the bedroom wall, as the gap between the inadequate curtains drawn across the window, as the shape of a mouse-hole in the wainscot, as the shadow of an object not visible on the chest of drawers, and as an object only half-seen on the top of the wardrobe—and that just might be a witch's hat itself. Put like this the idea seems overworked, too dominant. But because Browne's pictures are so carefully organized, so apparently straightforward and representationally realistic, you have to look quite a lot before finding orchestrations of this kind. In fact, his style is studied artifice with the quality of still life rather than of movement (just the opposite of Keeping), and it takes a lot of its cues from the surreal artists like Magritte. (pp. 706-08)

> *Aidan Chambers, "Making Them New," in* The Horn Book Magazine, *Vol. LVII, No. 6, December, 1981, pp. 703-08.*

When we first see Hansel and Gretel they are sitting with their father in a shabby living room; the wallpaper is peeling but the TV hasn't been hocked yet, and the stepmother, sitting apart, is watching it. The contemporary setting and slightly surreal style, far from striking an incongruous note, underscore the timelessness of this tale and the presence of the macabre in the everyday. A clutter of fancy cosmetics and the flashy clothes flaunted by the stepmother in the midst of the family's poverty suggest her sinister selfishness. A motif of dark parallel lines, like prison bars, recurs ominously throughout, and the resemblance between the stepmother and the witch is unmistakable. The translation is colloquial but faithful, preserving the white bird and white duck, for instance, who lead the children into and out of the forest, as well as the traditional tag that closes the story (given its own vignette). A useful contrast to prettified versions like Susan Jeffers'.

> *Patricia Dooley, in a review of "Hansel and Gretel," in* School Library Journal, *Vol. 28, No. 10, August, 1982, p. 98.*

Hansel and Gretel gives us two versions of the folk tale. The text supplies the one we know, and the illustrations reveal the one which, upon hearing the story, we may feel. (p. 123)

[Folk and fairy stories] may be experienced both with the conscious and the unconscious mind: while they entertain the former, they carry important messages to the latter. Although the stories' deepest meanings will vary not only from person to person but at various stages of each person's life, they deal with the process of human growth, from earliest dependency through to the ability to relate positively to the other sex, and the integration of opposing elements of oneself. They tell of darkest fears (desertion and death) and of brightest hopes (fulfilment and love).

If one accepts this aspect of the folk tale, the illustration of Anthony Browne's book acquires particular significance. The story is the expression of the psychic processes of the unconscious, and deals with the emotions that children experience when they are about five or six years old, about the age of Hansel and Gretel. Anthony Browne's interpretive pictures put into visual language the nature of these emotions. His book clearly does not belong to the conventional illustrated folk- and fairy-tale genre. It is a story which one could read to a young child, but also a story which may be felt and understood through the illustrations at a different level. It is well worth studying the book to see just how the artist's series of beautifully composed pictures—balanced in form, tone and colour, rich in imagery and symbolism—heighten the meaning of the written text. This combination of aesthetic and emotional values is the mark of a fine illustrator.

The most obviously unconventional element is Anthony Browne's decision to illustrate the old folk tale in contemporary dress, for the modern details are in themselves disturbing to an adult reader. Page after page we are shown carefully painted likenesses of everyday objects which contrast violently with expectations of what folk-tale illustrations should be like. (This may not be so startling for a child, who will usually not have preconceived notions and who will identify with the children in the story.) The modern urban-style brick house is not the kind of building we associate with 'the edge of the forest'. But in conjunction with the modern interiors and contemporary clothes it is probably quite close to the world as experienced by many children today. The Guinness bottle, the television set, the stained ironing board, the mirror above the mantelpiece; and the pills put the location more firmly in the Black Country or Forest Gate than in real country or fairy-tale forest.

The next unconventional element is characteristic of Anthony Browne. His earlier picture books invite close, leisurely, and repeated readings; he has always spiced his pictures with the kind of details children enjoy looking at and with surrealist jokes and visual puns. In *Hansel and Gretel* the jokes may be missing, but we are lured into the pictures just as cunningly by detail as the children are lured into the house by food. Gretel's dolly has a dress of the same material as Gretel's, talcum powder comes in an economy-size tin of a well-known brand, Hansel wears odd socks and an elastic belt with a snake buckle, and we can see the stitching on jeans and coat pockets. Continued close looking will raise questions about significant shapes and forms.

In one of his earlier picture books, *Through the Magic Mirror,* Anthony Browne sends his central character into a surrealistic world by use of the looking-glass device. In *Hansel and Gretel* he sends his readers to a different level of consciousness by the use of a film maker's technique. In the first full plate, the living room, a long shot of a mirror is shown, over the mantelpiece on the far wall. In the second full plate a dressing table is placed in the foreground, its relatively large swing mirror reflecting the bedroom in front of it. Here the artist starts playing with space in a very strange way indeed. The reflected room space in the mirror is where the reader would be 'standing'. This arrangement is repeated in the next full plate, where an even larger mirror occupies much of the picture surface, almost at the front picture plane. This time we 'stand' in front of the close-up of a wardrobe mirror, and again we see the reflection of the room that would be behind us. In reality we would see ourselves; in the book it is what we do not see that reminds us that the space we occupy is in the inner consciousness and not in the world of physical reality. We are inside the emotional event, not the woodcutter's cottage. The three mirrors have taken us in.

Anthony Browne now starts to signal the dual role which the stepmother will assume by the introduction of several triangular shadows, like the shape of a witch's hat, the largest of which is formed behind the stepmother herself. He also gives the stepmother a facial mole. Her features, much aged, and the mole appear as the witch's face later in the book.

Building upon an element already present in the story, the part played by birds, the artist introduces more of them in his illustrations and exploits an associated idea: cages. The first cage appears on the title page. It provides an excellent pointer for an interpretation of the story, for birds and cages of all kinds are what the story is about. It will not take a child long to notice that Hansel has a pet dove, that the birds' eating of the children's breadcrumbs prevents them from returning home the second time they are taken into the forest, that a beautiful white bird guides Hansel and Gretel to the gingerbread house, and that yet another white bird, a duck, carries them back across a great stretch of water when they are ready to return home. Nor would it take anyone long to associate the caged bird on the title page with the passive figures of Hansel and Gretel pictured in the living room, on the first full plate, seen with the back of a dining chair forming a strong pattern of bars in the foreground.

With continuing ingenuity Anthony Browne impresses the pattern of bars upon his pages and his reader. The bar motif is carried in the bedheads, the back-door grille, four immense looming trees which back the woodcutter's cottage, the constantly changing forms which the forest tree trunks assume, a small change to Eleanor Quarrie's text which allows Hansel to be shown imprisoned in a cage rather than in a stall, and a high proportion of compositions that stress vertical patternings and vertical emphases.

Adults, used to giving symbolic meanings to images in literature and art, will have little difficulty with interpretation; children will respond unconsciously, at an emotional level. The bird, then, may be seen as the symbol for the children's development and progression, and the cage as a metaphor for regression, inaction, and passive dependence. Birds point the children through the story and through their symbolic journey. The nature of that journey is the necessity for every child to relinquish his infantile dependency wishes and to achieve a satisfactory independent existence. In order to achieve this the child has to face his fears about death and separation, a thing which he cannot do by clinging desperately to his parents. If he attempts to cling on, he will have to be forced out, and naturally he will see this as a cruel occurrence, especially as it is his parents who will be doing the pushing.

As well as objects, Anthony Browne uses colour and pattern to carry symbolic meaning. Small areas and accents of intense red colour generally are significant. The stepmother has clearly defined red lips, owns red shoes, and the witch fastens her blouse with a red brooch. The forest floor is strewn with redcap toadstools, as is the path to the gingerbread house. Hansel's red ball, which makes a brilliant splash of colour in the first full plate, appears again in the last full plate, where it has rolled behind the door and lies, drained of all colour, in the shadow. The context in which the colour appears gives it meaning. The scarlet ball, symbol of early childhood, will not be what the Hansel who returns from the journey will need any more.

Pattern works in at least two ways—symbolically and structurally. Examples of the former may be seen in the first view we have of the family. Hansel, Gretel, her dolly, and the woodcutter are linked visually by their striped clothing. Later, when the family sets off into the forest, the stepmother leads the way in her imitation leopard-fur coat. Its dotted pattern is echoed in the redcap toadstools—a mock mother, in her mock fur coat, amidst the mock food? Later the pattern and colour of the coat recur as cake on the roof of the gingerbread house.

Structurally, Anthony Browne's almost obsessive delight in pattern, which is apparent in all his books, tends to destroy material reality. It is true that it is possible to count the blades in a tuft of grass, the pits in the bond of the brickwork in which the house is built, the grain on the floorboards, the texture of the tree bark. But the effect of this is not to create a naturalistic world, because the eye does not see the natural world in this way. He also uses a simplified frontal perspective which flattens the pictorial space; almost all the three-dimensional structures are drawn parallel to the picture plane, so that they can be 'read' as a flat repeating pattern. We cannot penetrate the picture plane. Thus Anthony Browne is creating a series of symbolic objects and, most of the time, is not interested in creating believable atmospheric space for either his characters or his readers to inhabit. By such devices the pictures help the reader to focus on the meaning behind the objects, which reveal not material reality but inner reality. This is how the folk tales themselves work, for though they are unreal and a child would not believe the events happened in fact, we know that they are not untrue; the inner experiences expressed through the events are familiar to us all.

In the midst of the patterning and rich detailing it is noticeable that the faces of the children are relatively unworked. Their features are small and only lightly defined, their appearance is typical rather than unique. Perhaps the artist

From Gorilla, *written and illustrated by Anthony Browne.*

wishes to help children who read his book to identify with Hansel and Gretel, by leaving their faces as ciphers. Hansel, with his spectacles, leads the development initially and may be seen as representing the more conscious, intellectual aspect of the soul, while Gretel represents the feeling aspect; as they co-operate with each other, they may be seen as the harmonious relationship of the anima-animus. Probably the most beautiful and aesthetically satisfying illustration in the whole book is a masterly little painting of the children lying side by side in their beds, drawing comfort from each other.

The last full plate—the children's return to the woodcutter—exemplifies the range of Anthony Browne's strengths. The viewpoint is from inside the dark house, looking towards the open back door. On the threshold stands the woodcutter, seen from behind. Of his children, clasped against his body, we see only Hansel's right arm and two small sections of his trousers, a bit of Gretel's head, her left arm, some of her coat and a section of her left leg. The parent and the children make one interlocking form, giving and receiving; it is male, female, child and parent. Their bodies cast one strong integrated stable shadow. The fact that there are no faces visible makes the image both memorable and universal. The children return from their symbolic journey, which is represented as infinite white space, and radiance flows into the dark room from outside, shimmering down the door frame. The bars of the back door cannot be seen, only the smooth surface of the plate glass, on which shines a Magritte-like blue sky, with drifting cloud reflection.

In Anthony Browne's last view of the family it is the parent who dominates the picture. The child is father to the man, and the integrated self can only come about through the necessary, inevitable and often painful journey away from childhood dependency. How the father, formerly weak and perfidious, can now be seen as comforting and loving is only an apparent contradiction. It is how the children see him that is important. Earlier they had projected their anxieties upon him; now, though they return to the same home, they have a different attitude to it and to him. They will not feel pushed out again, lost in the forest or seeking the gingerbread house. Those fears have been mastered. (pp. 123-27)

Without question, Anthony Browne's pictures supply a piece of visual storytelling, a psychological commentary, which interprets the folk tale in a positive way. The story of Hansel and Gretel deals with secret thoughts, fears and feelings which the artist's extraordinary mode of illustrating has given recognizable form. This is the nature of the expansion that takes place between the text and the pictures. (p. 128)

Anthony Browne provides no ancillary decoration, no visual relief from the text. His is a penetration of the tale. It is natural for us to wish to protect children from the dark side of man's nature, but to deny its existence or to trivialize it is dishonest. It is, after all, not unnatural to have powerfully contradictory feelings about others within the family; parents cannot always be good, brave, and unselfish; and even if they were, their actions would not always be interpreted by children as such. Although our popular culture keeps on playing Happy Families and shows us advertisements where laughing dads presumably come packaged along with the electronic games, and mothers stay twenty-seven for ever, with never a cross word, children know that real families are not like that. We should not be asking them to measure their feelings against this shallow kind of fantasy. Anthony Browne's visual interpretation of *Hansel and Gretel* offers children a

chance to recognize the nature of their deeper and truer feelings. (pp. 128-29)

Jane Doonan, "Talking Pictures: A New Look at 'Hansel and Gretel'," in Signal, *No. 42, September, 1983, pp. 123-31.*

BEAR GOES TO TOWN (1982)

Pure white, composed, toy-stiff, the hero of *Bear Hunt,* escaping trudging feet, meets a friendly cat and rescues him, together with other imprisoned domestic animals, from sinister black guards. The pencil he carries provides a logical line of drawing-magic, which is shown in pictures whose naturalistic style is superbly organised and expanded in static, framed scenes of striking design and composition; the atmosphere of mystery comes from a brilliant deployment of a series of apparently ordinary objects.

Margery Fisher, in a review of "Bear Goes to Town," in Growing Point, *Vol. 21, No. 4, November, 1982, p. 3990.*

Bear Goes to Town is a shock picture book on the anti-vivisection theme. To the casual glance it may look frolicsome for Bear is a jaunty character—but it becomes quickly clear that callous cruelty is Browne's target and it is not a pretty one. Bear and Cat pass a butcher's shop (the butcher's head is a piece of meat, there's an old leather boot next to the chops); suddenly Cat gets pounced on by a sinister black-garbed official and driven to a nameless place where cow, pig, hen, sheep, dog have preceded him. Bear (who has a magic pencil) draws himself a ladder and saw, frees the animals—except sheep who elect to stay safely in danger—from the ante-room to the lab, tricks the pursuing guards. This is a life and death adventure, its point sharpened by the innocence (except for the guards) of the characters, all charmers one usually meets in nursery tales.

Elaine Moss, "Moral Themes," in The Times Literary Supplement, *No. 4156, November 26, 1982, p. 1305.*

I like Bear. He is, in Whitman's words, 'so placid and so self-contained'. Bear, let me remind you, has a magic pencil, and when he gets in a tight corner he draws his way out. So, in this harsh urban world, he uses his pencil to excellent effect, and so saves his friend Cat and other harmless animals from a dreadful fate. All this with a quiet competence and without malice. The drawing is immaculate, so clean and precise and full of the detail which anchors the fantasy to the real world. Flawless. (pp. 218-19)

M. Crouch, in a review of "Bear Goes to Town," in The Junior Bookshelf, *Vol. 46, No. 6, December, 1982, pp. 218-19.*

GORILLA (1983)

Hannah seems the victim of a broken marriage. Father, solitary, always tired, lives for work; Hannah, solitary too, lives for gorillas, whom she reads about, draws, and watches on TV. She asks for one for her birthday, but when she finds her present in the middle of the night, it is a toy one. In her sleep, it turns into a huge gorilla who dons her father's hat and coat and takes her to the zoo (marvellous studies, here, of ape and monkey faces). Then they visit a gorilla cinema (Gorilla Batman), a restaurant, and finally join a dance on the lawn. And next day, father offers to take her to the zoo. The text is economical; it is the design which needs careful 'reading'. Subtly it supports Hannah's loneliness, in the bright corner of a dark empty room, in the middle of a huge brass bedstead, separate from her father—or close at last on her birthday. The detail (for instance of the happenings in the bedroom) will yield more each time to the reader—it is brilliantly worked out. (pp. 152-53)

A review of "Gorilla," in The Junior Bookshelf, *Vol. 47, No. 4, August, 1983, p. 152-53.*

The sparse text explains nothing but the most basic of the story line; it is the expansive illustrations that fill in all of the details of the story, from gorilla-decorated lampshades, to the gorillas Hannah draws, to the film in which Super Gorilla flies over a gorilla Statue of Liberty, to a romantic gorilla waltz by moonlight. In shading and in well-planned details, the expressive illustrations also convey a sense of Hannah's loneliness—her father reading the morning paper in a stark kitchen, Hannah watching television in a darkened, bare room. And then, after Hannah's fantasy adventure ends, Hannah (and young listeners) find that Hannah's father is indeed not the cold, uncaring man that he seemed, but rather a loving, attentive father. An exuberant story of a lonely little girl and a winsome ape.

Trev Jones, in a review of "Gorilla," in School Library Journal, *Vol. 32, No. 1, September, 1985, p. 113.*

Gorilla. The word may conjure images of wildness. Contrary to such preconceptions, Anthony Browne's new book, *Gorilla,* is a gentle story. . . . The words tell a simple story. But as in most picture books, the words tell only part of the story, the pictures do the rest.

And indeed, the finely crafted pictures by Mr. Browne, executed with impressive skill, enlarge and amplify the story. It is the pictures that make the story real and tangible. It is the pictures that show Hannah's loneliness. At breakfast, we see Father, with his sickly complexion, absorbed in his newspaper, across the table from Hannah yet so far away. The author convinces us that he knows and feels what he is telling through the illustrations. He even manages to express compassion and plead emotion on behalf of the caged primates at the zoo. Mr. Browne has approached his story with seriousness and sensitivity, yet had fun with humorous details.

Some details, however, while enriching the book, create problems. The sharply detailed wrinkles on the orangutan's and chimpanzee's faces seem excessive. Gorilla's face at the foot of Hannah's bed is more intimidating than the story calls for. Also, backgrounds occasionally distract from the subject matter, as in the picture of Father going to work. Poor man, in addition to his other worries, he must contend with serious competition, visually speaking, from the brick wall that looms behind him. Fewer or softened details might have eased the reading of the pictures. But these drawbacks pale when compared with the overall pleasure this tender and moving story gives.

Uri Shulevitz, "Gorilla My Dreams," in The New York Times Book Review, *November 10, 1985, p. 44.*

This highly symbolic story comes to life through Browne's unique full-color pictures. The stark shapes and unusual perspectives depict Hannah's loneliness and isolation. In contrast, the warmth between Hannah and her gorilla is shown by their friendly entwining and close eye contact. Particularly moving are the pictures of the zoo's caged primates, whose intelligence shines out through the bars. Although the abrupt transformation of Hannah's father is not truly justified by the preceding events, readers will feel a warm glow knowing the two have gotten together.

Ilene Cooper, in a review of "Gorilla," in Booklist, *Vol. 82, No. 10, January 15, 1986, p. 754.*

Hannah is an imaginative little girl who breaks the Freudian mold: never having seen a live gorilla, she nevertheless is infatuated by gorillas. She draws them, reads about them, has her lamp shade decorated with them; even the reproductions of the "Mona Lisa" and "Whistler's Mother" hanging on the walls are gorillas. But she also has a dad who can't find any time for her. So when he finally buys her a toy gorilla for her birthday, she fantasizes that he becomes a gorilla and takes her to the zoo, a movie, and dancing. On her birthday morning Hannah's dream becomes reality when her dad invites her to go to the zoo with him. The gutsy meaning of this profoundly simple story, told directly with refreshingly few words is to be found in the illustrations. With alternating small and opposing full pages—framed pictures on stark white paper—the book shows Browne's enjoyment of the visual patterns in our lives. He uses wallpaper, rugs, wood grains, brick walls, and furniture frames to satisfy our eyes' craving for aesthetic playthings while the actors get on with the adventures. In the first large illustration Hannah sits in the totally blue and white and black kitchen facing a father dressed in blue, white, and black reading a black-and-white newspaper. Her blue-and-white cereal box is decorated with a monkey. Later on, sitting in the corner of an empty room with only a TV on the floor, Hannah stares emotionless at the illuminated tube. Projected light creates a tiny colorful garden from the grotesque and menacing black shapes that cover the wall; the TV seems to trap her in its force field. There are humorous touches for the eager reader to catch and laugh at, including the details on the cover. But the portraits of the apes at the zoo are accurate renderings that communicate the proper melancholy of all caged animals. Despite the fantasy, Browne has created a picture book that explores real emotions with a beautifully realized child protagonist. Using his artistic skills, he's fashioned the visual metaphors that help us transcend superficial meanings and feel the power of the more archetypical emotions that bind children to parents and people to the other animals.

Kenneth Marantz, in a review of "Gorilla," in The Horn Book Magazine, *Vol. LXII, No. 1, January-February, 1986, p. 46.*

WILLY THE WIMP (1985)

Willy was considerate, gentle and endlessly forbearing. But the roughnecks in the streets had no time for his Ivy League smile, so he trained to be a toughie. He rescued Milly from a fate worse than death but then reverted to type—that is, back to being gentle, kind and courteous. This is one of the many books that set out to imitate Maurice Sendak's sophisticated messages. What both writers and publishers tend to forget is that Sendak is an original, who manages to portray through his illustrations the power of his extraordinary imagination, visual and otherwise. Even so, Sendak cannot get

From Piggybook, *written and illustrated by Anthony Browne.*

away from the fact that when he produces picture books like *Ida* they are quite unsuitable for children, even though they are masterpieces. *Willy the Wimp* tries to raise the idea that we cannot camouflage our natures. True, but children want straightforward stories and should be given them. They have lifetimes ahead for reflecting on the nature of human behaviour.

A review of "Willy the Wimp," in The Economist,
Vol. 293, No. 7370, December 1, 1984, p. 110.

To spoof the body-building mania, Browne gives us sheepish, stoop-shouldered, weakling chimpanzee Willy. . . . Called a wimp by "the suburan gorilla gang" (this British suburb, be advised, is a concrete wasteland), Willy sets out to build himself up—through a regimen of exercises, jogging, dieting (only bananas), aerobic dancing, boxing, and weight-lifting that, for a skinny little chimp, is pretty funny. (Not that Willy looks any funnier than the gorilla-bruisers he measures himself against.) Willy does finally develop a spectacular physique, and a self-confident stride. The suburban gorillas bothering girl-chimp Millie flee at his approach, and she calls him her hero. But when Willy is priding himself on his new stature, he walks smack into a lamp post—and, wimp-like, apologizes. To an extent, then, the book is a comic strip with a single haw-haw punch line. It also works, though, as a timely laugh at body-over-mind.

A review of "Willy the Wimp," in Kirkus Reviews,
*Juvenile Issue, Vol. LIII, Nos. 1-5, March 1, 1985,
p. J2.*

While the humorous illustrations are of fine quality in their cartoon design and bright color, there is some confusion in perception. In the last picture, Willy appears as a skinny

wimp. While the message is that Willy has not changed inside despite his physical changes, children may be misled and confused. It is worth noting that the book shows that Willy's changes take a lot of effort and that they happen gradually. However, the suggestion that making oneself bigger and stronger is an effective way to deal with one's environment is questionable. Also, the depiction of the only female character as a victim who needs rescuing by a big male is unfortunate. The book tells an amusing story, but picture books tell children something about themselves, and the point here is neither healthy nor constructive. (pp. 68, 70)

Jody Risacher, in a review of "Willy the Wimp," in
School Library Journal, *Vol. 31, No. 9, May, 1985,
pp. 68-70.*

Once a wimp, always a wimp, is the sly message of a hilarious picture book. . . .

[The] antics are pictured in glossy, precise illustrations, showing the ingenuous Willie at first limp and listless and finally muscular and flashing a triumphant grin. One of the most comical of the full-color illustrations depicts a slender, apprehensive Willie exercising his puny biceps between two condescending, muscle-bound gorillas. Very funny, the book will probably appeal more to aspiring athletes or wimps of junior-high age than to a young picture-book audience. (pp. 299-300)

*Ann A. Flowers, in a review of "Willy the Wimp,"
in* The Horn Book Magazine, *Vol. LXI, No. 3, May-
June, 1985, pp. 299-300.*

WILLY THE CHAMP (1985)

This is a delightful illustrated book with witty, brilliantly coloured pictures and an undemanding single line (or two) of text to every page. Willy is an unsuccessful, rather refined and intellectual chimp, well differentiated from the mass of huge and hearty chimps who laugh at him. It is, however, they who run away from the horrific Buster Nose and Willy who defeats him; I can see this winning manoeuvre being demonstrated in playgroups. It is a good book for reading aloud to groups as the pictures are large-scale, and with a little imagination the children could impersonate the simple-minded crowd on their racing bikes or posturing at the pool. Feminists may, however, dislike the silent and subordinate role for Willy's girlfriend Millie in her middle-aged-mother's outfit and the Marilyn Monroe look-alike chimp with her skirt billowing up over a drain.

Celia Gibbs, in a review of "Willy the Champ," in
British Book News, *March, 1986, p. 12.*

Anthony Browne, guru of gorilla buffs, follows *Willy the Wimp* with another witty tale of the chimp that wins in the end. Willy, keen on reading, music and walking in the park, is a flop at football, cycling and swimming. A chance encounter with Buster Nose, as massive and vicious a bully chimp as ever donned a studded jacket, switches from terror to triumph: Willy is the champ.

The illustrations in a riot of sparkling colour have an astonishing range: from brilliant red football shirts to the sombre threatening blacks of Buster Nose; from the pathetic Willy cowering against a wall and a group of he-chimp swimmers revelling in Willy's discomfort to a grinning cinema audience and a trio of determined racing cyclists. Details, too, are etched with convincing precision: the texture of skin, a handlebar basket, above all, the changing faces of Willy and his friends.

G. Bott, in a review of "Willy the Champ," in The Junior Bookshelf, *Vol. 50, No. 4, August, 1986, p. 139.*

Browne effectively uses his full-color palette of emphatic colors for emphatic situations and portrays Willy's innate equilibrium with constant, realistic hues all the way to his accidental, blushing triumph. There's play on pop culture, with muscle-bound pool-lurkers decked in gold and a flashy dancer in red high heels. Although the book's story line is simple, its visual sophistication makes it most accessible to older picture book readers, who will relate to Willy's self-contained success. This is a *Champ* for reading aloud in small groups or independently.

Carolyn Noah, in a review of "Willy the Champ," in School Library Journal, *Vol. 32, No. 10, August, 1986, p. 79.*

PIGGYBOOK (1986)

At first glance, a routine cautionary tale about Mrs. Piggott, who, weary of doing all the housework for her two sons and husband in addition to her other job, leaves home till they're ready to reform. But since Browne's imagination is never routine, *Piggybook* offers delightful surprises, both visual and verbal.

All three males order Mom about as they hurry off to their "very important" job and schools. Mouths greedily open, they well deserve Mom's succinct farewell missive: "You are pigs." Whereupon the three become pink pigs, and in trying to care for themselves create the sort of mess expected in a sty. Moreover, everything around them—doorknob, clock, teapot, even the family dog and the moon and trees seen through the window—is transformed by the pig motif which has been unobtrusively introduced from the first page, slyly hidden, for example, as Dad's shadow. Mom comes back looking serene and sweet. Thereafter, everyone shares tasks; they even look happier.

Spare use of carefully selected detail, crisply rendered, and witty characterization of the miscreants and their unwilling drudge, make this another on Browne's growing list of picture books that comment on the human condition with perception and originality.

A review of "Piggybook," in Kirkus Reviews, *Vol. LIV, No. 16, August 15, 1986, p. 1288.*

A wickedly feminist tale if there ever was one. . . . The feminist theme would bludgeon the plot were it not for the exceedingly clever illustrations: even before the porcine evolution of the males, there are hints of piggery everywhere—in the father's lapel carnation, the boys' upturned noses, a piggy bank, a light switch. After the transformation, pigs turn up everywhere, including on the wallpaper (which was formerly a rose design). Browne also uses a sly before-and-after technique in his portrayal of Mrs. Piggott, who starts out as a drab, shadowy figure, face averted, while the males are brightly drawn in full light and full-face. After the victory for women's rights, however, Mrs. P. is drawn in an equal style. In terms of cleverness and style, this one brings home the bacon.

Kathleen Brachmann, in a review of "Piggybook," in School Library Journal, *Vol. 33, No. 2, October, 1986, p. 157.*

In *Piggybook,* Anthony Browne attacks male chauvinism, and makes a case for the equal distribution of chores and the flexibility of male and female roles. His contemporary theme is perched boldly on the timeless framework of transgression, suffering, repentance, forgiveness and re-birth. . . . Mum's eventual return signals a new order: father and sons discover the positive pleasures of homecare while she enjoys herself mending the car—pigs might fly. Both funny and disturbing, Browne achieves a fine balance between the humour of the fantastic imagery and the seriousness of his message.

Jane Doonan, "The Pictured World," in The Times Literary Supplement, *No. 4365, November 28, 1986, p. 1345.*

John (Anthony) Ciardi

1916-1986

American poet.

An internationally acclaimed poet, essayist, critic, translator, teacher, and lecturer for adults, Ciardi is well regarded in the field of children's literature for his several collections of poems for readers in the early and middle grades. Ciardi created verses which mix often bizarre nonsense, ebullient wordplay, varied rhythms, and occasionally caustic satire with lyrical poetry which is thought to reflect the feelings and emotions of childhood with sensitivity. As with much of his poetry for adults, Ciardi's family and family life were important to his books for children as regards both inspiration and content. For example, in *I Met a Man* (1961), Ciardi used a controlled list of words provided by his publishers to create a book which he designed to be the first one his daughter would read to herself; in *The Monster Den* (1966), he playfully describes domestic life with his three youngsters as akin to living with savages. Ciardi wrote many of his poems from the point of view of a narrator who appears to be lecturing children on how to behave but who actually believes that these directives—and the adults who make them—are often laughable. He believed that children enjoy both poetry and learning and that they are not afraid of unfamiliar words. Consequently, his poems are often intellectually challenging. Some observers object to Ciardi's poetry on the grounds that it is too sophisticated for children and that its humor is too broad. However, most critics recognize Ciardi as a poet whose wit, candor, facility with language, and understanding of children help introduce young audiences to poetry in an entertaining and satisfying fashion. Poet and critic X. J. Kennedy has written of Ciardi: "Practically singlehandedly, he changed the whole character of American poetry for children, and made it possible for many writers to take the stuff seriously." Ciardi won the National Council of Teachers of English Award for Excellence in Poetry for Children in 1982.

(See also *Contemporary Literary Criticism,* Vols. 10, 40, 44, 46; *Something about the Author,* Vols. 1, 46; *Contemporary Authors,* Vols. 5-8, rev. ed., Vol. 118 [obituary]; *Contemporary Authors New Revision Series,* Vol. 5; *Contemporary Authors Autobiography Series,* Vol. 2; *Dictionary of Literary Biography,* Vol. 5: *American Poets Since World War II;* and *Dictionary of Literary Biography Yearbook: 1986.*)

AUTHOR'S COMMENTARY

I became a parent in about the same confused way as the rest of the human race since Adam and Eve, and, having so bewildered myself, I began writing poems for my three sweet savages because I am a poet and because poetry turned out to be a good way of playing with them.

Heaven knows, I have little enough theory of parenthood. As a rule of thumb, I am guessing that parents can get away with almost anything if they will spend a little time playing with their cubs. It's even all right to obey them the rest of the time. Or to make them obey you. Or to get just plain surly when that's the running mood.

We're pretty much permissive around my house—at least the kids aren't too strict with me. And they are generous enough to sit more or less patiently while Daddy reads his newest poems.

The fact is, they are now 9, 8, and 6½ and are practicing being blasé about it all. No matter: Every once in a while they trap themselves by quoting back to me something I wrote, and then I know they were listening after all. And I know—even better—that they remembered.

But even if they didn't care and didn't remember, I should go on writing children's poems. I did in fact begin writing these poems for them, but pretty soon I discovered I was writing very much for the child in me.

I accepted that discovery happily, for I am planning to have my childhood last a lot longer than theirs. At least it has so far. They are in a tremendous hurry to grow up: I have no such compulsion upon me.

I want only to live long enough to see the child in them catch up with them again in their own adulthood. I'll hope what they remember of my poems will keep that child not far under the surface as they go thru the stiff proprieties of adolescence and their own precociousness.

Meanwhile, I'll go on writing for myself and for any other children that will join me, whatever their age.

*John Ciardi, "Writing Poems for the 'Child in Me',"
in* Chicago Sunday Tribune Magazine of Books,
November 12, 1961, p. 4.

GENERAL COMMENTARY

PATRICK J. GROFF

John Ciardi has been on occasion a professor of English, the author of several books of poems for adults, a lecturer-at-large, a literary critic, the director of creative writing workshops, and one of the authors of a programed textbook on poetry (how to learn poetry in easily understood, discrete steps).

As a literary critic, he is widely known for the severity of his censure of mediocre poetry. . . . As poetry editor of *Saturday Review* for more than seven years he has been ruthless in his condemnations of what he sees as bad poetry. He tells, not without self-congratulation, of his ultimatum to the editor of that journal upon being offered the poetry editorship: two hundred or more poems previously accepted for publication would have to be returned—if he were to accept the position. That he got his editorship under these terms speaks of his reputation as a literary figure.

From these rather exalted heights of literary eminence Ciardi entered the field of children's literature. In the years 1959-1962 he wrote five books of poetry for children: *The Reason for the Pelican, Scrappy the Pup, The Man Who Sang the Sillies,* and *You Read to Me, I'll Read to You,* and *I Met a Man* [Critic's note: For brevity referred to as **RP, SP, MWSS, YRM, IRY** and **IMM.**] Obviously, Ciardi has accomplishments in both adult and children's poetry.

What is more, he has expressed with no uncertain conviction what poetry should be. Seldom, if ever, have students of children's poetry had, first, a complete description by a practicing critic of what a poem should be, followed by several books of his children's poetry. In the same year Ciardi's first volume of poems for children appeared he published *How Does a Poem Mean?* With this coincidence there became possible a unique opportunity: to see if a poet's work is what he says it should be. With the guidebook *How Does a Poem Mean?* and his books of children's poetry in hand, the rare occasion is found to examine a poet's assumptions about poetry through an observation of his practices.

In *How Does a Poem Mean?* Ciardi says writing poetry is first "tossing words into the air and catching them," having a good time by indulging in a self-delighting play with language. But, secondly, if this is to be a poetic experience, these words, he says, are then discovered to be "the very stuff of life," to be more far-reaching than their first appearance would suggest. The poem consequently becomes "a living experience, that deepens every man's sense of life," that makes him "more alert to life, surer of his own emotions, wiser." This seems a well-stated belief that, primarily, poems should have an attractive playfulness, and an immediate appeal, an ease of apparent meaning, and an evident understatement. But they should also have a profundity, a purpose not immediately discoverable, which is often seen as ambivalence or a refusal to be specific. These qualities should lead to a poem's enduring appeal, reading by reading, year after year. Too, the good poem should deflate pompous, overserious morality or

social pretense, the pictures a society has of itself, and directly satirize the habit of saying directly that something *is* something, Ciardi contends.

By holding this two-part definition of poetry in mind while reading Ciardi's poetry for children one is quickly struck by the emphasis he gives to its first part. Actual facts are of least consequence, Ciardi demonstrates. As seen in *How Does a Poem Mean?,* he takes as his prototype for children's poetry the nursery rhyme "Hey diddle diddle, / The cat and the fiddle," and Lewis Carroll's "Jabberwocky": " 'Twas brillig, and the slithy toves. . . ." This is evidence for Ciardi's belief that ". . . it may reasonably serve the purposes of good reading to pretend that there are no facts in [a] poem." Moreover, he insists that "to stress facts in poetry is often the quickest way to lose sight of the poem."

This belief is put on display in *The Reason for the Pelican,* where meaningless gamboling with words abounds. . . . (pp. 153-54)

On other occasions this juggling of words becomes recognizable ideas. These are inflated carefully into ultimate ridiculousness, however **(RP)**. Understandable are "Seven sharp propellor [*sic*] blades / Boring through a cloud," while far below are "Seven little oysters / Digging just offshore. . . ." Whimsey takes over as the blades

> Fly apart and fall
> On seven silver bubbles,
> Shattering them all.
>
> Blow another bubble,
> Place your bets.
> Ready oysters?
> Here come the jets.

Sometimes nothing is left but mysterious bafflement, as in **"Say Yes to the Music, or Else" (MWSS)**:

> Say *yes* to the music when it tickles
> And when you come to wash your toes,
> You'll never find them changed to pickles.
> That's the way the music goes.

Elsewhere the metaphors are so remote as to be unintelligible to the audience for whom they are supposedly intended. One of the things to think about before being born is to **(YRM,IRY)**:

> Study the immigration laws.
>   Don't just go barging gaily in.
> For it would give your parents pause
> If you were born an alien.

Other unorthodox offerings are found in his easy-to-read book of poems, *I Met a Man,* meant for the very youngest reader, Ciardi says. Here he tells of a "man that [*sic*] was trying to whittle a ship from a stick." Having no success "he threw it away and cut his throat." A well-meaning child slaps a fly off his father's nose so the parent can go on sleeping. When he is spanked, the child complains, and the father explains:

> "For trying to help, I have to thank you.
>   But for that smack on the nose, I'll spank
>   you!"

In this exhibition of the morbid and a contempt for so-called healthy personal relationships Ciardi seems to be looking sidelong to another audience: the adults to whom his sophistication and cleverness would appeal. "Look at the limits I dare to go!" he cries out, confident of adult attention.

As seen in these examples, to Ciardi poems do not have to be dignified, important, or understandable. His poems for children, therefore, are full of made-up, curious words, pointless or illogical rhymes, strained metaphors, improbable situations, and of difficulties in knowing who is speaking. He is often as cryptic as was Minnie in **"The Journey"** (**YRM,IRY**):

> She gave me directions that made no sense.
> I came to where I was not.
> I passed through a gate built in no fence
> To a house without a lot.

Furthermore, he believes that one should welcome into poems in general "the rush of every sort of experience." Partially this is because he writes "in the happy conviction that children [are] small savages with a glad flair for violence. . . ." Consequently, few prohibitions are put on the content of his poems. He freely fills them with situations seldom, if ever, found in children's poetry so far: death from suicide and killing, threats of child abandonment, repeated references to corporal punishment (both earned and unjustified), bizarre people (headless ones who talk, for example), hurtful gossip, talk of guilt feelings, fear of animals, disrespect for parents, children referred to as monsters, and so forth. Often this is intended as humor. As such, it is grisly.

A poet must be judged by his best, nevertheless, and Ciardi, as he wishes to, moves away from simple silliness toward the second prerequisite of good children's poetry, that it intensify the child's sense of life. This is sometimes done with inventive metaphors. . . . (pp. 155-56)

From Ciardi's knowledge of the mechanics of poetry as exhibited in *How Does a Poem Mean?* one would predict he could make good rhymes. Unfortunately for all poets, the rhyming vocabulary of English is relatively small when compared to foreign languages. There is an added handicap to good rhyming in children's poetry. The child's poet can choose freely from all the words available only at the risk of confusing and ultimately losing his audience. And yet, he, and not the rhyme scheme, should decide what is to be said. Ciardi rhymes well in spite of these natural obstacles. Although there are notable exceptions ("Some bears are fierce, and most grow fiercer / When any one bites off their ears, sir." [**YRM,IRY**]), generally his poems have words that fall into place naturally, much as if the needs of the rhyme were not there to restrict his choice. When tricky rhyme sequences are used, they appear to be contrived devices and not accidentally forced upon the poet. Of false rhymes, remarkably I found but one: see . . . indefinitely. Happily, the rhymes are usually muscular with the call for bodily action and involvement that comes with a masculine strength.

Words are the remaining details critical to a poem's distinctiveness. As we have seen, Ciardi not only believes but demonstrates that while feeling, suggestions, and images arise from words they should run free of them. Words, he explains, are only surfacing materials that cover over a poem's inner life. He gives explicit criteria for their choice, nevertheless. They should be surprising, that is, take the reader aback until he realizes their "rightness." Mechanically speaking, they should be made up of a higher ratio of verbs than adjectives,

and of "evidence" adjectives (a blonde girl) rather than "judgment" adjectives (a bad girl).

That Ciardi's words run free of coherence has been amply described above. That the words in his poems are surprising, there likewise can be little doubt. They are far from always "surprisingly right," however. "Sillies" may be what at times exasperated parents and teachers think children are. Is this what children think of themselves? Is a string of rather precious quotations of an apparently precocious child (**"Prattle," RP**) significant enough for other children that they will want to read them? Don't say "It's me," one poem demands. If you do, "Then hide your face. / You're in disgrace." Will anyone ever convince children that popular usage is disgraceful? There are many occasions of commendable choice of words, on the other hand. The words in *Scrappy the Pup* to describe a hen house becoming increasingly aware of a marauding fox are precisely right:

> First a very soft stirring-around of the quiet,
> Then a cluck—then a cackle—and then a whole
> riot!

As well, a consistent follow-through is made by Ciardi with his other requirements for words. The ratio of his verbs to adjectives runs higher even than the two to one he calls for in *How Does a Poem Mean?* "Judgment" adjectives are carefully avoided. He gets no closer to these than to give the Pelican a "splendid" beak, or to conclude the Heron is "crotchety."

The transformation from an adult to a children's poet must be full of hazards for any poet. Ciardi makes several serious mistakes that by and large preclude this transposition for him. First, the content of his poems is too naturalistic and sophisticated for children. Ciardi seems to want to add to the circle of violence and mistrust that now surrounds the modern child. It is apparent that he keeps his pledge to write for "yowling small savages," as he refers to children, and to give them their "natural food." This is all very upsetting, however, since poetry traditionally has been written not to cater to the most primitive or devilish feelings and sensations that can be mustered up, but rather to act as an antidote for the vulgar, the brutal, and the petty. Ciardi dismisses such criticism as a predictable outcry of offended Puritanism from overprotective "Militant Virtues."

In addition, Ciardi's poetry for children is often somber, obscure, and full of uncommon figures of speech, dialogues from unknown sources, and grim if not "sick" humor. His repeated reassurances in his *Saturday Review* column that his own family circle enjoys such fare run counter to other evidence from thoughtful evaluations of children's interests and of their capacities for understanding. He has not been able to forget the adults through whom most of his poems reach children.

Most damaging of all, Ciardi apparently believes that his set of rules for poetry should apply to that written for adults but not for children—because children as savages cannot appreciate the sensitive, the beautiful, or the moving. Actually, some of his best efforts are word games in which the child is led to discover a missing word—didactic exercises that are far removed from poetry. There is little chance, therefore, that many of his verses can meet the second requirement of poetry, that it give to the reader a new sureness of himself, a deepened perspective of his world, or a wiser reason with which to make important judgments. (pp. 156-58)

Patrick J. Groff, "The Transformation of a Poet: John Ciardi," in The Horn Book Magazine, *Vol. XL, No. 2, April, 1964, pp. 153-58.*

CHARLOTTE S. HUCK

Many of Ciardi's poems are enjoyed by boys and girls with enough sophistication to appreciate their tongue-in-cheek humor. His poems about imaginary animals, such as the "Shiverous Shreek" or the "Saginsack," are well liked. One fourth grade's favorite was about the disastrous custard made by **"Some Cook,"** while all children enjoy **"Mummy Slept Late and Daddy Fixed Breakfast."** In *The Reason for the Pelican,* there are some fine lyrical poems, including **"There Once Was an Owl," "The River Is a Piece of Sky,"** and **"Rain Sizes."** *Fast and Slow* contains the somewhat cynical title poem about a slow old crow who knows much more than the fast young one who can fly circles around him, but doesn't know where to go. The irony of **"Being Too Right To Be Polite"** may be lost on children but not on adults. Other poems in this book are very amusing and clever. Humorous poetry characterizes his other books. . . . Sophisticated Victorian illustrations by Edward Gorey complement Ciardi's spoof on today's parent-child relations. (p. 351)

Charlotte S. Huck, "Poetry," in her Children's Literature in the Elementary School, *third edition, updated, Holt, Rinehart and Winston, 1979, pp. 304-87.*

NORINE ODLAND

There is magic in the poetry John Ciardi has written for children. He uses words with whimsical agility. Humor in his poems allows a child to reach for new ways to view ordinary things and places in the world. In a few lines, a Ciardi poem can move a listener from one mood to another; the words tell the reader how the poem should be read.

Poet, critic, translator, teacher—all were among his accomplishments when John Ciardi began to write poems to amuse and please his daughter, Myra, and later his sons Benn and Jonnel. His observations of the success of the poems, not only for enjoyment but also for expanding language, encouraged the poet to write and publish poetry for children. (p. 872)

Absurdity is an element of humor to which children respond with applause. In *The Reason for the Pelican,* the absurd shape of the pelican is justified in the poem Ciardi chose to introduce a collection of verses which allow children to enjoy the bizarre and the ridiculous. The alliteration in the poem **"Rain Sized"** is so effective that children say they can feel the drops as well as hear them fall. **"How to Tell the Top of a Hill"** suggests to the reader or listener a solution which demands imagination reaching up and out, a solution far different from answers which are expected in a workbook exercise.

That John Ciardi was influenced by his children in his books of poetry, especially his early work, can be seen in the progression from an appeal to younger listeners to poems for older readers. An early book, *Scrappy the Pup* is, in children's way of describing it, a story poem. "Curly'cue ocean of blue" and "sound like sixty-six apes with their tails in the fan" provide vivid images for young children who are far from caring about identifying metaphors but relish the effect of those Ciardi has given them. The predictable ending makes children chant "read it again" so they can see how they were right in their predicting. (pp. 872, 874)

Ciardi, age two, with his mother Concetta DiBenedictis Ciardi.

In 1961, in the midst of a flurry of interest in controlling the vocabulary used in stories for children, John Ciardi wrote and published a book of poems, *I Met a Man.* The probable contention was that the words used in the poems were those of first-grade difficulty. No doubt the attention given to the book and the poems in it was influenced by the fact that it came from an established poet and critic, but not all the attention was positive by any means. The poems were not all gentle and sweet. One even conjured an image of bugs in sinks while another related the disaster which befell the discouraged whittler. Objections to the bugs in sinks were not heeded; the concern about the whittler was answered by adding two lines for those with a low imagination quotient. When the poems reached children there was no doubt about their success. Children responded to the total effect of the lyrical poems. The images have a base in children's experiences and then go on to new adventures in imaginative ways. Words are used and combined in gymnastic fashion. From *I Met a Man,* the poem **"The Man in the Onion Bed"** is an example of words and shapes of the poem giving clues to the pace for reading. There is a surprise ending in almost every poem, a requisite for the child who listens and immediately asks to hear the poem again in order to enjoy knowing what is coming. Riddles and puzzles are a part of the fun in some of the poems, e.g., **"Have You Met This Man?",** the one who has no house but stays in bed and turns out to be Mr. Clam. The recording of *I Met a Man* by John Ciardi is one to which children listen, entranced, and object strenuously if they are allowed to hear fewer than all of the poems. (p. 874)

It is easy to laugh with the characters [in *The Man Who Sang the Sillies*], for they seem to enjoy their predicaments. Some of the poems are long, others use just four lines to convey an image such as that in **"Warning"** which challenges the wisdom of diving into a whirlpool.

Descriptions of children as marshmallow sweet, or in his words, angelfluff, are not found in work by John Ciardi. The naturally grumpy child and the one who falls apart and pouts can be found in *You Know Who* along with those who giggle and grin and are happy to be here. Exaggeration, hyperbole, and playing with words and ideas make poems which reflect real feelings children recognize. Many of the poems are built on the premise of a question and the reader is allowed wide range when interpreting the answer.

In *You Read to Me, I'll Read to You,* the poems alternate between those with an easy vocabulary and those with words which reach beyond the limits of beginning vocabulary. Unlike the vocabulary, the humor and the sense of understanding feelings of children are not limited. **"Mommy Slept Late and Daddy Fixed Breakfast"** has proven its appeal by being chosen by children as their favorite in studies of children's poetry choices. The full-page drawing by [Edward] Gorey depicting Daddy and the waffles adds to the imaginative powers of the words. . . . There is great variety in the poems in this book, some wistful and wise, others boisterous and exuberant.

There is playful taking of sides between adults and children in *The Monster Den.* Nonsense prevails most of the time, but in good proportion. There is an occasional strand of real humor, of reflection on human behavior. Three children are introduced, each with a poem, before the monstering begins. Imaginative, lyrical, with no hint of condescension, the poems are accentuated with [Edward Gorey's] stark and strident drawings.

There is variety in topic and form in the poems in *Someone Could Win a Polar Bear.* Whimsey is the predominant accomplishment whether it comes with real or fanciful subjects. The poems demand a certain amount of sophistication from the reader and listener. **"The Rover,"** with a direction to be recited loud and with gestures, uses alliteration which young children devour for the over-all sound of it; older readers enjoy the more complicated finesse with words and meanings.

The title page for *Fast and Slow* suggests that these are "poems for advanced children and beginning parents." Satire in literature for children is often referred to as gentle, but that modifier is not appropriate in many of these poems. **"On Being Too Right to Be Polite"** is sharp but not cruel. **"When Happy Little Children Play"** is another satirical piece, one which exemplifies Ciardi's belief in those feelings. A poem about sharks, a subject which both children and Ciardi seem to like, contrasts danger and safety, and does it all with humor. The pun is lyrically developed in **"Bear With Me and You May Learn."** There is quick change of pace from one poem to the next. Pre-reading by an adult will assure greater verve when reading aloud to children. (pp. 874-75)

> *Norine Odland, "Profile: John Ciardi," in Language Arts, Vol. 59, No. 8, November-December, 1982, pp. 872-76.*

JON C. STOTT

Ciardi has criticized much children's poetry, saying that it seems to have been created with "a sponge dipped in warm milk and sprinkled with sugar." Not surprisingly, his own children's poetry is much different. Remembering his own youth, he notes that childhood is noisy, boisterous, and violent, and he tries to incorporate these qualities in his own poems, adding to them a sense of humor.

Although a few of Ciardi's poems are written from the point of view of a child, the narrator is generally an adult who seems to be lecturing children on the proper methods of behavior, but who understands his listeners' feeling that such rules and the adults who impose them are often foolish.

Ciardi's nonsense poems make excellent reading for families who sometimes think they are the only ones to quarrel and experience chaos. A book like *Fast and Slow* is a humorous way to introduce concepts to preschoolers. (pp. 76-7)

> *Jon C. Stott, "John Ciardi," in his Children's Literature from A to Z: A Guide for Parents and Teachers, McGraw-Hill Book Company, 1984, pp. 76-7.*

ZENA SUTHERLAND AND MAY HILL ARBUTHNOT

Much of [John Ciardi's] poetry for both adults and children has a brisk candor. In his poetry for children, though, the humor and nonsense soften a forthrightness that is sometimes tart. Many of his poems are satirical comments on the reprehensible behavior of children, a vein most appreciated by the sophisticated reader. However, the topics he develops are usually fresh and original, as, for example, **"How to Tell the Top of a Hill," "The River Is a Piece of the Sky," "The Reason for the Pelican."** And when he chooses a familiar subject like **"Halloween,"** he treats it freshly, so that it is unlike any other Halloween poem ever written—dramatic and weird, and a brain-tickler for the oldest and best readers. (p. 315)

> *Zena Sutherland and May Hill Arbuthnot, "The Range of Poets for Children," in their Children and Books, seventh edition, Scott, Foresman and Company, 1986, pp. 297-320.*

THE REASON FOR THE PELICAN (1959)

A warm and deserved welcome to this distinctive piece of publishing! These engaging poems . . . have qualities to catch the young reader or listener—their ebullient made-up words, facile rhymes, dashing rhythms, and humor. "I think the Python might like it / If someone who knows could decide / When he wriggles along through the jungle / Which end is getting the ride." Some will like best the charming, lyrical **"Rain Sizes."** The drawings in ink line [by Madeleine Gekiere] are sophisticated abstractions; some with an eccentric grotesqueness suggesting Lear are as right for this new fun as are Lear's for his nonsense, to which some of this is akin.

> *Virginia Haviland, in a review of "The Reason for the Pelican," in The Horn Book Magazine, Vol. XXXV, No. 5, October, 1959, p. 390.*

Here is a book of most superior nonsense poems with witty line drawings that illustrate them quite perfectly. Some, like the title poem, are amusing comments on odd animals . . . ; others introduce oddities Edward Lear would appreciate, the Bugle-Billed Bazoo, "the Brobinyak with dragon eyes," "the Saginsack with radio horns and aerials for ears" and Lucifer Leverett Lightinbug; while a few are about puzzling things in life like the sizes of raindrops, time, age, and dreams (of an army horse and an army jeep). All are written with zest and skilled craftsmanship. Their simplicity will delight the youngest children, their subtlety draw many a chuckle from their elders. There are no age limits up or down to clever nonsense. It's a matter, as John Ciardi put it himself in his dedication, of those "with an imagination that tickles."

> Margaret Sherwood Libby, "The Joy of Poetry, That Begins in Delight and Ends in Wisdom," in New York Herald Tribune Book Review, November 1, 1959, p. 2.

As a skilled professional, Mr. Ciardi is even more wary of the moralistic and sentimental in **The Reason for the Pelican** than he is in his several books of poems for adults. In this collection, nature is crazy, wild, gone. . . . The Brobinyak has teeth "about banana size" and is a very curious beast indeed, while the Saginsack has Radio Horns and Aerials for ears. I had the impression our children understood these animals, though there are moments when Mr. Ciardi's irrepressible facility leaves the children behind and starts addressing itself to Father. But that's really all right with Father; no poetry is good for children that isn't equally good for their elders.

> Walker Gibson, "Some Like the Tinkle of the Rhyme, Some Can Leave It Alone," in The New York Times Book Review, November 1, 1959, pp. 2, 44.

SCRAPPY, THE PUP (1960)

Very little *happens* in this rhymed story of a sleepy watchdog. Children who enjoy dogs, and doggerel, may like the book, but adults may be disappointed to see Mr. Ciardi's talents spent in such negligible fashion.

> A review of "Scrappy the Pup," in The Saturday Review, New York, Vol. XLIII, No. 42, October 15, 1960, p. 31.

A watchdog who can't wake up—except at mealtime—plays the title role in John Ciardi's little joke in rhyme. Scrappy, who "was never as tee-total twice-around happy / As when he was sleeping as sound as a log," sleeps through a raid on the chicken house, through lightning, thunder and rain, and it is only when his weary master is finally dropping off to sleep that Scrappy comes to—to howl for food. Compared to the ebullient nonsense of Mr. Ciardi's **The Reason for the Pelican,** this is very mild stuff. The verses are brisk, but there are only a few lines, such as the refrains, "In a rolly-blue curly-cue ocean of sleep" and "In a feather-snow, ferny-snow absence of sound" which are memorable. Much of the comedy is carried by Jane Miller's pictures. . . .

> Ellen Lewis Buell, "He Slept Through," in The New York Times Book Review, October 30, 1960, p. 46.

Narrative verse of the nursery sort is skillfully handled by John Ciardi, who has also written excellent nonsense in **The Reason for the Pelican.** Here a picture book is made of a tale he spins about Scrappy the pup. . . . Small children and many others will appreciate his master's exasperation when neither a fox in the hen roost, nor a wild storm, arouses him, although he will bark if any harm comes to the dish on which his precious food is placed. A sympathetic little verse made even more endearing by Jane Miller's black and white scratch-board drawings. . . .

> Margaret Sherwood Libby, in a review of "Scrappy

> the Pup," in Lively Arts and Book Review, November 20, 1960, p. 40.

I MET A MAN (1961)

When poet John Ciardi went in for nonsense verse, it was with a serious purpose and for a particular pleasure—namely, to write the first book which his first-grade daughter would read all by herself. Using two basic elementary word lists as his foundation, Mr. Ciardi has skillfully led the child a little beyond the scope of these lists, but always keeping in the area of familiar vocabulary. The result is a true achievement, not only in the realm of learning-to-read, but also in the realm of poetry and fun.

> S. B. B., "Rhyme Time," in The Christian Science Monitor, May 11, 1961, p. 2B.

We have poetry in this book, whether you define a poem as Robert Frost does—something that "begins in delight and ends in wisdom" or as "an invention: such invention as by producing something unexpected, surprises and delights," as wise old Dr. Johnson somewhat ponderously says.

Designed "for a special pleasure" because the author wished to write the first book his daughter should read herself, it captures interest immediately by short funny verses, using only the simplest words such as a six-year-old would recognise. Then having engaged her attention (and ours), he continues with rhyming riddles, echo rhymes (a superb one is **"I Met a Man Down in a Well"**) and word games, using unfamiliar words now and then, but always in such a way that they can be easily guessed from the context. Thus, though he is frankly helping his small daughter and other six-year-olds to learn, he avoids the stifling effect of controlled-vocabulary writing. Most Doctors of Education who edit such books live in terror lest a word not on the "lists" prove a lion to gobble up the helpless reader or at least paralyse him with fear. A poet knows better. He knows that "poetry and learning are both fun and children are full of an enormous relish for both."

One important thing about this book is its joyousness, the lilt of the verses, the infectiously gay rhymes which one is impelled to call out just as one taps one's foot to certain rhythms. Another is the intellectual challenge. It will take a clever six-year-old to work it all out, but there are more of them than stuffy grownups think, and who cares if a bit of help is needed? We admit that we were so enchanted with the book that we made excuses to try it out on groups of older children, one group of ten-year-olds and several of thirteen-year-olds, that age when one is insulted by being offered anything childish. They loved it, the brighter children delighting in it most, admiring the cleverness of the witty, picturesque twists to the rhyming and laughing at Robert Osborn's tan and black crayon sketches in exactly the right mood. We hope they'll let the six-year-olds in their families discover its joys and challenges for themselves.

> A review of "I Met a Man," in Lively Arts and Book Review, May 14, 1961, p. 3.

John Ciardi has undertaken that unusual tour de force for a professional poet—composing poems whose vocabulary is restricted more or less to the word lists of the first grader. One has to add "more or less," for he has allowed himself some leeway in order, he says, to lead the child "to recognize new words without outside help." This is commendable, and Mr.

Ciardi surely made the right choice, though one may suspect that the choice was made partly to afford the poet himself a little extra resource in constructing these verses.

They are on the whole sharp, amusing, and unsentimental poems that should be not only largely readable but also entertaining for a bright first-grader. Variations on the theme of "I met a man who . . ." did this or that provide plenty of opportunity for strange and amusing experience. . . . The book lacks the sophisticated zaniness of the author's earlier *The Reason for the Pelican,* and may therefore be a little less attractive to parents. But that may be just the point: here is a witty book for the beginning reader that he is actually expected to read for himself, with a minimum of assistance from the old folks.

> *Walker Gibson, "Poetic Variations," in* The New York Times Book Review, *July 16, 1961, p. 16.*

THE MAN WHO SANG THE SILLIES (1961)

Bedtime in John Ciardi's family must be a truly exciting time, and his "minnows" lively. Children will love the rhythm and implications of:

> Yes, The Sillies are the sweetest that
> I know.
> They're a nuisance, they're a bother.
> They're an everlasting noise.
> Sillies act like one another.
> Sillies act like girls and boys.
> Sillies think it's necessary
> Not to like what they are fed.
> They are very very very
> Hard to put to bed.

Refreshing after reading a good deal of doggerel to find different rhythms, in a book that is really a poet's playtime.

> *Alice Dalgliesh, in a review of "The Man Who Sang the Sillies," in* Saturday Review, *Vol. XLIV, No. 43, October 28, 1961, p. 36. The excerpts of John Ciardi's work used here were originally published in his* The Man Who Sang the Sillies, *J. B. Lippincott Company, 1961.*

Look to your laurels, Mr. Edward Lear! There's a Ciardi close behind you. *The Reason for the Pelican* was a cause for rejoicing in circles where the Jumblies, the Jabberwocks, Dongs and such are popular; so was *I Met a Man.* Now they have more wonderful musical nonsense verse excellently embellished with suitable gaiety and foolishness by Edward Gorey. A poet's skill, a lively wit, rollicking humor and a vivid awareness of the charm and cussedness of children are everywhere evident. Mr. Ciardi's "children are fit as sharks and crocodiles," and before you leave them and "douse the light" be sure you have "screwed their heads on tight," and also try to stop and think "have you washed their ears with ink?" Of course "they have titters up their sleeves . . . and they're always losing shoes, but they're very, very, very easy to amuse." Who wouldn't be if offered these verses? We love the thought of looking for "a bobble bird in a bangle thicket," of "a pun with a quibbedy ring" and of a "stick in the mud like Clarence Fud" who couldn't "say yes to music when it tickles" and "whose toes turned into ten dill pickles." Above all we love "The Stranger in the Pumpkin" who is shocked and exclaims that "it's all dark inside your head. What a dullard you must be! Without a light how can you see?". . . .

> *"Balladry and Rollicking Nonsense," in* Books, *New York, November 12, 1961, p. 4.*

Children will skip quite lightly to the tunes of John Ciardi's *The Man Who Sang The Sillies*. The language herein is easy riding, and as abandoned, as outrageous as are the authors's amazing flights of fancy. The titles are box office draws: **"As I Was Picking a Bobble-Bud," "The Most of Being a Boy Is Noise," "Margaret Nash Got Wet But I Don't Know How," "Lobster Music,"** and **"Say Yes to the Music, Or Else."** Edward Gorey's illustrations point up the dear madness of the poems.

> *Gwendolyn Brooks, "Inspired Arrangements of Words in Many Moods," in* Chicago Sunday Tribune Magazine of Books, *November 12, 1961, p. 4.*

John Ciardi's verse for children is so good that self-conscious adults can read it aloud without pain. Excellent in itself, it has a special quality that makes me love it this side of chauvinistic idolatry—it is American clear through. Ciardi is relaxed, in control, not faking; there is no hint of winnie-the-poohery. He is a grown man addressing his juniors, willing to entertain them. He is comical in a way that makes children grin and quickly appropriate his nonsensical jugglery. A local poll shows **"The Man in the Woods"** which is spooky rather than funny, to be the favorite.

> *Marie Ponsot, in a review of "The Man Who Sang the Sillies," in* Poetry, *Vol. CI, No. 3, December, 1962, p. 208.*

YOU READ TO ME, I'LL READ TO YOU (1962)

This is an experiment and, like all such, we shall need to await results to discover how the formula works. It involves verses using a first-grade vocabulary for the child to read, alternating with those for the parent or teacher to read to the child.

Although there is more variety here than in some verses written in a limited vocabulary, there is a certain unevenness in quality, and a number of them seem derivative. Small children, however, will enjoy in particular the Halloween verse, **"What Night Would It be,"** and **"My House Jack."**

> *Alexandra Reid Sanford, in a review of "You Read to Me. I'll Read to You," in* Saturday Review, *Vol. XLV, No. 45, November 10, 1962, p. 47.*

John Ciardi is quite definitely on the side of the angels. He believes in avoiding restrictions for children. Not only does he believe this but he actively sets about eliminating them. Cleverly in *I Met a Man,* he added to a restricted vocabulary new words that could be guessed and so made a children's game of outwitting the learned elders who were holding them back. Now, in his newest book of poetry, he goes even further by putting easy-to-read poems side by side with more difficult ones. The easy ones are printed in black for the child to read aloud, the more difficult ones in blue for the grown-up to read, and all are humorous and gay with zestful rhythms . . . It is hard to pick a favorite from the first (an easy one) about studying at close quarters the teeth of sharks (live sharks) to the first poem (an easy one) about which the man in the moon, after boasting of the times when he shines asks "when do *you* shine if you shine at all?" But we liked especially the nonsense poem, **"The Journey,"** the one about Chang

McTang McQuarter, a very mixed-up cat, and the poems describing a night that could be no other than Halloween.

> *Margaret Sherwood Libby, in a review of "You Read to Me, I'll Read to You," in* Books, *New York, November 11, 1962, p. 3.*

The title of John Ciardi's new book of poems for children indicates one of its inviting features: printed in black and blue ink alternately, the poems in black are for the child to read to you, while the ones in blue you read to the child. This, in itself, makes reading cooperative fun. The lines are of two, three or four feet, a meter that suits the child, and all speed along to accomplish their missions with faultless rhyme, alliteration and repetition. Every single poem and drawing [the illustrations are by Edward Gorey] is superior. . . . A perfect book for parent *and* child. (p. 3)

> *William Turner Levy, "Voices That Know How to Say It in Verse," in* The New York Times Book Review, *November 11, 1962, pp. 3, 61.*

According to the jacket, every other poem in this collection is written in a basic first-grade vocabulary so that the child and parent can read to each other alternately. If so, the basic first-grade vocabulary has fortunately burst the shackles of the usual primer, for one is entirely unaware of rigid limits here. The "you read to me" poems are printed in black, those that "I'll read to you," in blue; but which is "you," the child or adult? And after all, who cares? Blacks and blues are all fun to read and reread, aloud or to oneself. As always, Ciardi plays expertly with sounds, rhythms, and ridiculous ideas. Titles such as **"About the Teeth of Sharks," "Arvin Marvin Lillisbee Fitch,"** and **"How the Frightful Child Grew Better,"** suggest the kind of wonderful nonsense that fills this gay book.

> *Margaret Warren Brown, in a review of "You Read to Me, I'll Read to You," in* The Horn Book Magazine, *Vol. XXXIX, No. 1, February, 1963, p. 70.*

JOHN J. PLENTY AND FIDDLER DAN: A NEW FABLE OF THE GRASSHOPPER AND THE ANT (1963)

Apparently that ant never learns. Here he is again, in this rhymed retelling of the grasshopper-and-ant fable, still working hard and hoarding food through the winter while his sister makes beautiful music with a frivolous grasshopper (relax; they are married). Mr. Ciardi's considerable talent is evident here; the verse is often quite lovely (though sometimes not), but his skill is wasted in this unnecessary book. The moral is good too, but Aesop said it better.

> *Ellen Rudin, in a review of "John J. Plenty and Fiddler Dan," in* School Library Journal, *Vol. 10, No. 1, September, 1963, p. 104.*

[*John J. Plenty and Fiddler Dan* is] a long poem that fiddles gaily away in lilting rhythms. . . . [John Ciardi's] ant, provident John J. Plenty, is as industrious and hard-working as La Fontaine's. He works madly all summer collecting aphid butter, moth hams, flower fuzz and salad weeds and scorns his sister for marrying Fiddler Dan, the grasshopper. When winter comes, however, this new version carries the tale to a finer denouement than the old . . .

We are inclined to agree with the blurb on the book jacket, only making a slight change to "Poets' children, fiddlers and

grasshoppers will rejoice . . . and ants will do well to heed its lesson" (the blurb says "poets, children, fiddlers," etc.). The reason we cannot include all children is that sadly enough there are ant children as well as grasshopper children and the verse and its fine and unusual illustrations by Madeleine Gekiere . . . are strictly for grasshoppers, young and old.

> *Margaret Sherwood Libby, "When the Trees Became Torches," in* Book Week—The Sunday Herald Tribune, *September 29, 1963, p. 20.*

"A new fable of the grasshopper and the ant," told with fresh poetic interpretation and produced with elegance of illustration and design. . . . When the overzealous, hoarding John J. wobbles out of winter nearly starved from needless rationing, the moral is sung in new poetic terms. Children, who love to listen to tales told in verse, will delight in this version of the classic fable. It not only satisfies as a story-in-meter-and-rhyme but is genuinely good poetry.

> *Virginia Haviland, in a review of "John J. Plenty and Fiddler Dan," in* The Horn Book Magazine, *Vol. XXXIX, No. 5, October, 1963, p. 502.*

YOU KNOW WHO (1964)

Ciardi the cautionary rhymster rather than Ciardi the creative poet was at work with the 27 verses here. While there is humor in the verse-stories, most of them end with a very parental punch line: **"Calling All Cowboys"** ends "But tell him I said there's a price on his head, / And I'm out to get him. He's wanted—for bed!" None of these verses rises to the heights of humor or imagery that some of those found in **Reason for the Pelican** and **Man Who Sang the Sillies** achieve, nor are they easy reading in the **I Met a Man** style.

> *Barbara S. Moody, in a review of "You Know Who," in* School Library Journal, *Vol. 11, No. 2, October, 1964, p. 202.*

John Ciardi, who is aware, as most parents are, of just how beastly and ghastly children can be and says so rather often, is offering some variations on the theme in **You Know Who**. . . . In some 27 verses, some quite effective and lively, he refers to some one he knows (and "you know who") who is a sleepy head in the morning, unwilling to go to bed at night, noisy, and "runs in and out of the house too much." There is iron as well as irony in his tone as he pokes fun at the conceited and the laggard child and a paternal bossiness when he commands, "sit up when you sit down," that shows the seriousness behind the fun. (p. 30)

> *"Trips through Xanadu," in* Book Week—The Sunday Herald Tribune, *November 1, 1964, pp. 30, 38.*

As an admirer of Ciardi's wacky machine-made animals in previous volumes, I find this one a little tame, though pleasing. . . . It's interesting that in these poems addressed to children, and in Mr. Cole's selection [*Beastly Boys and Ghastly Girls*] too, the parent, in the great war of the generations, usually wins. In both cases we are dealing with light verse where society's teetering applecart is not to be upset. Furthermore Daddy usually gets the last word because—why not?—Daddy is the author. "Did you do as I said? . . . Good, go to bed!" As in his past verse for children, Mr. Ciardi is painstakingly simple in vocabulary, and admirably unsentimental in attitude. Children appreciate both these qualities.

The Ciardi family, 1956: Judith, holding Benn; Myra; Ciardi, holding John L.

Walker Gibson, " 'We Come to Know a Poem by Some Act of the Heart and Mind'," in The New York Times Book Review, *November 1, 1964, p. 57.*

THE KING WHO SAVED HIMSELF FROM BEING SAVED (1965)

John Ciardi's name is well-known, so is his poetic style, which has its enthusiastic supporters and its foes. This is a minor epic about a peaceable kingdom plagued by a too conscientious knight determined to prove himself a hero. The satirical legend has been overworked; this one doesn't offer much fresh humor. For our taste, the verses seem clumsy, the frequent use of parenthetical phrases and interjections make them awkward to follow and difficult to recite. Edward Gorey's characteristic pen and ink drawings do, however, add a sense of Gothic wit.

A review of "The King Who Saved Himself from Being Saved," in Kirkus Reviews, *Vol. XXXIII, No. 17, September 1, 1965, p. 900.*

The King Who Saved Himself From Being Saved is a satire on a knight who would a derring-do. Edward Gorey's crisp pen-and-ink drawings are, as always, a delight, but in this case Mr. Ciardi hasn't given him much action or variety to draw. . . .

Knight wants to slay Giant; King shoots him out of Kingdom

with a cannon. Mr. Ciardi's rhymes are adroit, and the book is a pleasure for adults; but kiddies of five and six *want* to believe in the derring-do of knights and heroes in far-away kingdoms. I don't think they'll appreciate disenchantment. (p. 33)

William Cole, "A Reptile in Residence," in Book Week—The Sunday Herald Tribune, *November 21, 1965, pp. 28, 33.*

This attractive little book. . . . has been received with mixed feelings, for it pokes fun at two sacred cows of the children's book field, the knight and fairy tales in general. It is more of an adult than a children's book, though some children may find humor in the story of a knight who was always trying to save someone and was finally eliminated (through non-peaceful means) by a king who wished to run a peaceful kingdom.

We *have* had too many books lately about knights slaying dragons, etc. Children are not so preoccupied with these clanking heroes as people seem to think.

Alice Dalgiesh, in a review of "The King Who Saved Himself from Being Saved," in Saturday Review, *Vol. XLVIII, No. 50, December 11, 1965, p. 45.*

THE MONSTER DEN: OR LOOK WHAT HAPPENED AT MY HOUSE—AND TO IT (1966)

John Ciardi has collected a group of poems he wrote for and

about his own three children into *The Monster Den* . . . [These] poems are not Ciardi at his top form. Some of them are overly sentimental—always a pitfall when dealing with one's own offspring. But the Victorian figures by Edward Gorey are elegant and droll: the girl looks like a baby Edith Sitwell, and the boys are presented as perfect little demons. It would be instructive to know what real-life Myra, Benn and John L. think about being so publicized. (pp. 6, 67)

> *Eve Merriam, "The Light and the Slight," in* The New York Times Book Review, *November 6, 1966, pp. 6, 67.*

Mr. Ciardi's *The Monster Den* has some lively, amusing stanzas, but as nonsense it is less successful on the whole than his earlier collection, *The Man Who Sang the Sillies.* The trouble is that Mr. Ciardi is writing about his own children, and a merry muddle of monsters they are when they are allowed to come alive in their own right, but at times the parents get in the way.

> *William Jay Smith, "Leaps and Falls," in* Book Week—New York Herald Tribune, *November 13, 1966, p. 14.*

This collection of nonsense verse may be about children but is surely not for them. John Ciardi's bizarre and, occasionally, humorous rhymes place the home as the monster den and the three children as monsters. . . . Edward Gorey's drawings, though quite appropriate to the text, do little to lessen one's disappointment in the whole "monstrous" idea.

> *Barbara S. Miller, in a review of "The Monster Den or Look What Happened at My House—And to It," in* School Library Journal, *Vol. 13, No. 6, February, 1967, p. 63.*

SOMEONE COULD WIN A POLAR BEAR (1970)

Carried away on wings of sing-song, the poet says less than he might if he weren't—like this duz (*I mean 'duz,' as he 'sez'* ((*he means 'says'* (((*he plays with parentheses too*)))))). Which is one way of showing how visual . . . and tiresome . . . his schemes are: sounds that double-talk to the ear pun on paper symbolically—if you read between the iambs without stopping at the first caesura. But as the "Rules" insist in the second of the 22 irking ironies: "If you get it right, right off the bat, / That ends it right away. / What's left to do when you've done that? / You've wasted the whole day! // Then everything's proper, do you see? / . . . *Don't be right till it's time to be.*" Some lines are more abstruse than others ("The Whispering Hearsay lives its life / In far-off Wild Conjecture"), some poems flimsier, less well-crafted; most are self-indulgences in verbal gymnastics, toned down only by the inky poker-faced cartoons [by Edward Gorey]. An invitation to de-puzzle: "If I go / Around in circles for an hour or so // Will someone think and tell me what to do? / Now don't be hasty: think your answer through. / Someone could win a Polar Bear.—Maybe you!" Maybe, with patience and a predilection.

> *A review of "Someone Could Win a Polar Bear," in* Kirkus Reviews, *Vol. XXXVIII, No. 16, August 15, 1970, p. 877.*

John Ciardi, who has written both pretentious and pleasing poetry for children, has come up this season with a collection of poems that are very much on the pleasing side of his ledger:

warm, witty and irreverent giggles of poems. With Edward Gorey's illustrations to compound the giggles, no laugher can lose, or want to miss *Someone Could Win a Polar Bear.*

> *A review of "Someone Could Win a Polar Bear," in* Publishers Weekly, *Vol. 198, No. 7, August 17, 1970, p. 50.*

This collection by the noted poet lacks the immediate appeal of his *You Read to Me, I'll Read to You,* but it grows on one after several readings. Though the poems tend to stretch the imagination to the point of incredulity, there is a fine sense of nonsense which holds the book together. Several selections such as **"The Blabberhead"**: "The Blabberhead is blubbery, / His face is full of shurbbery. / His neck is long and rubbery."; "About Moose *or* To hairy cows, the hairy bull Is handsomer than horrible"; and **"The Hairy-Nosed Preposterous"** are bound to be embraced enthusiastically, at once. Several others need to be read and reread, mulled over and chewed upon. But that, after all, is one of the joys of poetry. Good for all Ciardi fans or anyone who thinks poetry is important.

> *Barbara Gibson, in a review of "Someone Could Win a Polar Bear," in* School Library Journal, *Vol. 17, No. 5, January, 1971, p. 48.*

FAST AND SLOW: POEMS FOR ADVANCED CHILDREN AND BEGINNING PARENTS (1975)

About halfway through this collection of 34 rhymes Ciardi goes on for seven stanzas about **"The Man Who Had Shoes"** (but didn't wear them, preferring to keep them at home "under the bed with my wife" while he went about barefoot)—all, it seems, for the sake of the concluding pun: "For if I only wear them in / I cannot wear them out." There are several other "men who . . ." here—many of them celebrated at greater length and to less apparent purpose—so that after getting through a few of them you are unlikely to care what happens to the fat fireman on a ladder . . . or the man from Delaware who took his pig to market but couldn't find a parking space . . . or **"Tough Captain Spud and his First Mate, Spade"** who trade in Yo-Yo strings and bottle caps . . . not to mention that polka-dotted bear pursued by the sheriff because he's coloring the whole world wrong. A lot of the other rhymes are insults or coy threats (about a boa constrictor or "your" cousin a gorilla) addressed to "you"—with no hints as to why "you" should sit still and take them. Of the 34, a few of these are mildly amusing, more seem only to have amused their creator, and in others even he seems weary—probably from trying so hard to be funny.

> *A review of "Fast and Slow," in* Kirkus Reviews, *Vol. XLIII, No. 7, April 1, 1975, p. 378.*

Ciardi greets you like one of those wise; kindly uncles often met in books and all too seldom in real life. Not the sort to play house with you under the dining room table, it's true, but any poet who can convince you he has seen a polka-dotted yellow and blue bear with green whiskers and red ears in eastern Arkansas is worth your attention. And he answers your questions the way you always hope your teacher will. . . .

> *Nancy Willard, in a review of "Fast and Slow," in* The New York Times Book Review, *May 4, 1975, p. 24.*

Here is pure nonsense, wacky narratives, clever word plays, and ingenious rhymes which have a serious point. The collection covers a multitude of subjects, from Noah in his ark bewailing how much hay he must pitch for the elephant, to a cautionary verse on **"The Shark,"** to **"On Going to Hohokus,"** which includes all the strange names of towns in New Jersey. One selection, humorous but on a vital subject, is a love ballad in a very polluted world: "It was down by the Dirty River / That flows to the Sticky Sea / I gave my heart to my Bonnie / And she gave hers to me. / . . . It was high in the Garbage Mountains / In Saint Snivens by the Scent, / I married my darling Bonnie / And we built our Oxygen Tent." Ciardi's light verse is always witty and well-constructed and this book is no exception—it's a jumping, varied collection which lends itself well to reading aloud.

> *June Cater, in a review of "Fast and Slow: Poems for Advanced Children and Beginning Parents," in* School Library Journal, *Vol. 22, No. 3, November, 1975, p. 72.*

DOODLE SOUP (1985)

Ciardi offers a mix of narrative poems, poetic jokes, arrant nonsense, and a bit of word play. Almost every selection is funny, and many are barbed or caustic. Most children find Ciardi's tartness invigorating; most adults find his writing deceptively casual, intrinsically sophisticated.

> *A review of "Doodle Soup," in* Bulletin of the Center for Children's Books, *Vol. 39, No. 2, October, 1985, p. 24.*

That Ciardi loves language and delights in its subtleties and richness is clear in his new collection of poetry for children. Consistently well-written, the light verse is rousing and witty, and fairly insists on being read aloud. But perhaps the tenor of the collection can best be shown through excerpts: need, for example, **"A Lesson in Manners"**? "You should never be bad till you've been fed." Or insight into success? "There was a fine swimmer named Jack / Who swam ten miles out—and nine back! / (What more can I tell you? That boy had style, / But in the end, he missed—by a mile.)" . . . Children will especially appreciate the mischievous surprises and naughty anecdotes as well as the author's keen perceptions about what will delight them. [Merle] Nacht's pen-and-ink outlines, some with washes in shades of gray, are zany and expressive and totally in keeping with the spirit of the collection. Young or once-young, most readers will find this encounter with poetry irresistible.

> *Lee Bock, in a review of "Doodle Soup," in* School Library Journal, *Vol. 32, No. 5, January, 1986, p. 65.*

One swallow of ***Doodle Soup*** should be sufficient to send any reader back for a second taste. With a rather pleasing recklessness the award-winning poet skips from subject to subject so that the thirty-eight jouncing verses, most of them humorous and many nonsensical, offer a variety of subjects. . . . The poems, their wit extended by the simple lines of ink-and-wash illustrations, also read aloud well.

> *Karen Jameyson, in a review of "Doodle Soup," in* The Horn Book Magazine, *Vol. LXII, No. 2, March-April, 1986, p. 214.*

W(illiam) J(esse) Corbett

1938-

English author of fiction and short stories.

Corbett is best known as the creator of the Pentecost trilogy—*The Song of Pentecost* (1982), *Pentecost and the Chosen One* (1984), and *Pentecost of Lickey Top* (1987), epic adventures which blend suspense, humor, and philosophy to tell how a group of displaced harvest mice embark on a dangerous journey to find a new home and later surmount more obstacles in their attempt to keep it safe. In the first story, a brave young mouse named Pentecost, who leads his friends to the safe haven of Lickey Top, is killed heroically in battle; in the subsequent books, a second small mouse is chosen to become the new Pentecost. Corbett invests his works, which celebrate life, friendship, and forgiveness while representing such unpleasant aspects of the human condition as betrayal, revenge, and death, with strong Christian and allegorical elements. He creates a variety of animal characters whose natures are both noble and ignoble, and draws parallels between humanity and the qualities of his protagonists. Although he is occasionally criticized for overwriting, Corbett is usually praised for his originality and skill with characterization. He is also the author of a book of animal fables, *The End of the Tale* (1985). Corbett received the Whitbread Award in 1982 for *The Song of Pentecost*.

(See also *Something about the Author,* Vols. 44, 50.)

THE SONG OF PENTECOST (1982)

It's obviously not on—ten years after *Watership Down,* a tale of harvest mice, dislodged by human overspill, embarking on a perilous journey to pastures new. And yet it's not only on—it's gloriously on. W. J. Corbett has written a book, his first, that I suspect will make many children, and a large number of furtive adults, happy for a long time to come.

The Song of Pentecost begins with a snake, who has lost his father, and then loses the family pond to a scoundrel claiming to be a cousin and to have had oral promise of the reversion. The witness is a lying frog. The dispossessed recovers almost at once from his innocent condition, and vows to track the frog down. This can be done only with the help of the harvest mice: who will capture the frog, and guard him on the long journey back to the pond, in return for the snake's help in establishing them on Lickey Top. An owl is master there, but the snake promises that the bird is moved by amazingly kindly feelings towards mice. That is a lie. The story, in a tremendous way, is about liars, and rogues of every kind, who are shamelessly vile, or momentarily moved to immense sorts of repentance. The frog, for example, is suddenly swept away by the excitement of telling the truth: when the present adventure is over, he vows, he'll "travel widely about the world, unmasking lies and deceits".

Each character is given great comic particularity. . . . Mr. Corbett's inventions are close, constantly, to facetiousness and whimsy, and almost never slip into either.

When his mice have to cross a river astraddle the snake, who

is desperately holding his breath, the outrageous comedy is not incompatible with a great deal of excitement. The dialogue is memorable, especially in the field of insult and in the enthusiastic assertion of abominable ambitions: as with the insect who looks forward to "going down in history as the most despicable traitor of all time". There are touching moments, in which some tendency to sentimentality (of Kenneth Grahame's kind) is usually held in check: and in the middle of all that comic crispness, Mr Corbett can invest a character—the young and earnest leader of the mice, for example—with a curiously fresh, and touching, heroic quality. He is verbally enjoyable: "My snout is sealed", says Pentecost, and after awkward experiment the mice allow the frog "to frogmarch himself".

The final scene is too long, and contains gratuitous tragedy. But this is a story that gives instant pleasure, and would be a delight to read aloud. And despite the echoing nature of the territory it treads, it is essentially unlike any other story I've read.

Edward Blishen, *"Liars and Rogues,"* in The Times Literary Supplement, *No. 4156, November 26, 1982, p. 1302.*

[*The Song of Pentecost* is] a credible and compelling animal fantasy which can be read as adventure or as allegory. Many of the characters suggest familiar personalities, yet each character is true to animal nature, if not always to animal behavior. And while there are echoes of other stories, from *Pilgrim's Progress* to *Watership Down,* the total effect is a unique celebration of life and love suggested by the name "Pentecost," conferred on each generation of leaders. A remarkable first novel . . . . (p. 451)

> *Mary M. Burns, in a review of "The Song of Pentecost," in* The Horn Book Magazine, *Vol. LIX, No. 4, August, 1983, pp. 450-51.*

Corbett's first novel is a warm, wryly humorous, exciting tale of adventure. . . . The warmth is clearly shown by the allegiance of the mice to all of the creatures they encounter; the humor is best exemplified in a hilarious scene in which a senior woodpecker attempts to teach his trade to the young ones, who cannot hear him for the din of wood pecking; and the excitement is everywhere as unscrupulous animals deceive the innocent and natural obstacles hinder the animals' quest. Corbett offers a glorious celebration of life and of the natural order while acknowledging the reality of death. Although many of the characters have attributes which are not at all admirable, they are tempered by an undercurrent of Christianity. The theme of the young, the small, the innocent and the odd leading the others is a reassuring one. Pen-and-ink illustrations [by Martin Ursell] are lifeless and lackluster, but they cannot destroy the impact nor dampen the enjoyment of this well-told tale. (pp. 63-4)

> *David Gale, in a review of "The Song of Pentecost," in* School Library Journal, *Vol. 29, No. 10, August, 1983, pp. 63-4.*

All of [*The Song of Pentecost*] is so delightful that I will simply tell anyone interested in fine children's literature to drop everything and head for the bookstore. As for me, when my children return from summer camp, I am heading for the family reading chair, and, with at least two of them snuggled around me, I am sharing *The Song of Pentecost* with the ones with whom this delight should be shared. For everyone still young enough to love tales of magical animals who take terrible journeys in forests both deep and fancifully innocent.

> *Susan H. Harper, in a review of "The Song of Pentecost," in* Science Fiction & Fantasy Book Review, *No. 19, November, 1983, p. 47.*

PENTECOST AND THE CHOSEN ONE   (1984)

A prophecy from a greedy old hedgehog sends the second Pentecost, now leader of the mouse community on Lickey Top, to overcome his self-doubts and find the Chosen One with whom he is destined, it seems, to destroy a tyrant; but before this can happen there are dangers to face, from the sinister ruler Zero in Gas Alley, Blackshadow the lurking cat and even from a pop-group of waterrats delighted to add Pentecost's alto to their band; and events are complicated by the plots of the 'extremely rare, seven-legged, orange-backed cockle-snookle', a decidedly mixed-up insect (added, oddly, to a group of real animals). The author's ironic, direct prose in narrative is muffled by the pseudo-philosophical dialogue, verbose and inelegant, in which the characters debate their situation, their hang-ups and their ambitions. Part-satire of a vaguely political kind, part-adventure, the book suffers from over-writing and from a grandiose theme which neither comic character-drawing nor inventive scenes can really support.

> *Margery Fisher, in a review of "Pentecost and the Chosen One," in* Growing Point, *Vol. 23, No. 4, November, 1984, p. 4353.*

[*Pentecost and the Chosen One*] is an intriguing fantasy sure to please readers of all ages.

There is much to commend *Pentecost and the Chosen One.* Comparisons with *Watership Down* are perhaps inevitable, but Corbett's novel is suffused with a sense of humor which makes it distinct. Profound themes—friendship and betrayal, forgiveness and revenge, free will and destiny—are woven into the fabric of the story, but in such a manner that the story remains pre-eminent. "Peopled" with a cast of fully developed, memorable characters, *Pentecost and the Chosen One* is a beautifully written, suspenseful moral comedy. Pentecost at the end of the novel remarks to Fox that the title of a poem they hope to write "does hint at a certain warmth." I echo Pentecost's sentiment in regard to this exceptional new fantasy.

> *Randy M. Brough, in a review of "Pentecost and the Chosen One," in* Voice of Youth Advocates, *Vol. 10, No. 3, August-September, 1987, p. 128.*

The pacing, situations, and dialogue mark this sequel to *The Song of Pentecost* as very much a product of the twentieth century, although its length recalls the leisurely style of nineteenth-century animal fantasies. While it builds logically upon its predecessor, the book stands quite firmly on its own; the focus on a young, inexperienced protagonist makes it seem introspective and immediate. The result is a fascinating, readable mix of suspense with comedy, the profound with the absurd, philosophy with derring-do. . . . So convincing is the author's conception that the story takes on the flavor of a swashbuckling epic, despite the diminutive size of the heroes. There are wonderfully rich vignettes featuring minor characters—the blues-singing water rats, the hypochondriac owl, the interfering Cockle Snorkle bug. Original in concept and a wonderful read-aloud, the book is one of those rare fantasies that defies any attempt at classification by age. (pp. 62-3)

> *Mary M. Burns, in a review of "Pentecost and the Chosen One," in* The Horn Book Magazine, *Vol. LXIV, No. 1, January-February, 1988, pp. 62-3.*

THE END OF THE TALE   (1985)

W. J. Corbett's short stories in **The End of the Tale** have a similar cheerful nastiness to them. The creatures in them show the redder side of nature's tooth and claw. Jason the hare spends all his time dashing through the wolf-infested wood carrying notes from his neurotic mother to his Grandma, hoping he won't get hugged to death by a wolf; he does. Two monkeys invent a new pastime they call 'war'. A rotten weasel develops Hitlerian tendencies. The stories are written with a mordant wit. . . . (p. 26)

> *Naseem Khan, "Yukky Dip," in* New Statesman, *Vol. 110, No. 2850, November 8, 1985, pp. 26-7.*

W. J. Corbett made a formidable reputation with his two *Pentecost* books. He has now written a set of fables for our time, more wordy than Thurber's and—although [illustrator]

Tony Ross is tough and amusing—lacking the inimitable accompanying drawings by that master. In all sixteen tales the animal world shows in its distorting mirror some aspects of the human scene. They are shrewd and entertaining, but not, it seems to me, likely to attract young readers. The terms of reference are essentially adult.

> *M. Crouch, in a review of "The End of the Tale,"*
> *in* The Junior Bookshelf, *Vol. 49, No. 6, December,*
> *1985, p. 274.*

PENTECOST OF LICKEY TOP   (1987)

W J Corbett won a prize for his first book ***The Song of Pentecost*** and has written two sequels. What began as an irritating uncertainty of tone in the original book has hardened into horribly mannered prose which deliberately jangles registers and is as full of false notes as a beginner's violin practice. Every page has forced infelicities such as "my second beef is much more serious" or "never once did a fit of the titters threaten to overwhelm me". But the effect is cumulative; isolated examples fail to do it justice. The plot construction is as arbitrary as the argot. For some reason the author has it in for otters and one of them is the villain. Nobility is reserved, as before, to the mice—which is what Pentecost is—and occasionally the fox.

It makes you long for the literary equivalent of an olive or a piece of good bread to clean your palate.

> *Mary Hoffman, "Artless Animals," in* The Times
> Educational Supplement, *No. 3736, February 5,*
> *1988, p. 57.*

The fortunes and misfortunes of contrasting characters keep the action rolling; witty dialogue supplies not only humour but also a firm indication of individual personalities. The inhabitants of Lickey Top form a community of distinct creatures, from evil and smug Cockle-snorkle and aloof Owl to overbearing Otter and misguided Uncle Mouse, from bold and bothered Pentecost and impulsive lame mouse to impetuous fox cub and badger who isn't a badger.

It is a rich and colourful story, depending for its dynamic on ingenious twists and turns of plot and an emotional involvement in the menace that hangs over the Lickey Top colony—full marks for originality, perspective and entertainment.

> *G. Bott, in a review of "Pentecost of Lickey Top," in*
> The Junior Bookshelf, *Vol. 52, No. 2, April, 1988,*
> *p. 100.*

Norma Klein (Fleissner)

1938-1989

American author of fiction and picture books.

Considered one of the most controversial authors of realistic fiction for middle grade to high school readers, Klein is well known for creating works which concentrate on the growing independence and maturation of teenagers while demonstrating her trademark characteristics of colloquial dialogue, humor, and an emphasis on characterization. Centering on the interrelationships of her characters, she depicts the close associations teenagers share with their friends and peers as well as the awakening of young people to sexuality and to the complexities of life. Many of Klein's protagonists are bright, articulate, and liberal upper-class Manhattanites being raised by parents who bear the same characteristics. Within the milieu of her fiction, Klein represents a variety of contemporary nontraditional family situations: for example, the characters in her works often live with single parents, stepparents, or homosexual parents. The young adults in Klein's books face crises related to divorce, suicide, euthanasia, and similar challenges for which they are required to demonstrate adaptability and courage. Using male narrators almost as often as female and often adopting a first-person point of view, Klein is lauded consistently for accurately portraying the perceptions and emotions of young adults of both sexes. In Klein's fiction for adults, coming-of-age is also a thematic concern; several of these books, published as adult novels because of their explicitness, draw a significant young adult audience. In addition to her books for older readers, Klein also wrote several picture books and works for children in early elementary school.

Klein has been simultaneously praised and denounced for her portrayal of lifestyles some critics consider to be vastly dissimilar to those of most of her readers; however, her immense popularity seems to indicate that she addresses the universal concerns of many teenagers regardless of their backgrounds. In addition to her portrayals of alternative situations, Klein's works reflect her unconventional attitude toward premarital sex, abortion, and other sensitive issues. As a result, she has faced disapproval from teachers, librarians, parents, and critics. Many of these observers assert that her books should be banned, maintaining that such topics, along with the use of profanity, make the stories unsuitable for the middle-grade readers who comprise Klein's largest audience. Other observers believe that she avoids the opportunity to handle volatile subject matter with depth and complexity, choosing instead to take a relaxed, nonchalant stance. Although some of Klein's detractors contend that the resolutions in her books come too quickly and that she gives her readers inaccurate or incomplete information concerning such crucial topics as birth control and AIDS, her proponents are quick to note the relevance of her books in their treatment of blended families and liberal morality, and they cite her wide readership as a testament to her skill at reaching young people coping with contemporary society. Klein is often praised as an observant author who successfully depicted believable, fallible adult characters and convincing young adults in works distin-

guished by their frankness, empathy, vitality, and lack of condescension.

(See also *CLR,* Vol. 2; *Contemporary Literary Criticism,* Vol. 30; *Something about the Author,* Vol. 7; *Something about the Author Autobiography Series,* Vol. 1; *Contemporary Authors,* Vols. 41-44, rev. ed.; and *Contemporary Authors New Revision Series,* Vol. 15.)

AUTHOR'S COMMENTARY

[The following excerpt is from a speech originally delivered on September 28, 1986.]

When I was [a teenager] . . . , or slightly younger, my favorite writer was Maud Hart Lovelace, who wrote a long series of charming books about Betsy, a would-be writer, and her two friends, Tacy and Tib, growing up in turn-of-the-century Minnesota. Like the Little House in the Big Woods series, I still believe that there was genuine charm and appeal in these books. I read them all aloud to my daughters; I still reread them with pleasure. But I remember even then, when I was in my early teens, wondering with a kind of anxious despair: why isn't my life like this? I felt cheated, angry, bewildered. If these books had been science fiction or fantasy, I doubt I would have had those feelings. But these were realistic novels, and it was precisely for those realistic touches that I loved them. For instance, Betsy's desire to be a writer was taken seriously, both by her as a character and by her creator. She wrote throughout childhood and adolescence; she began sending her short stories to magazines while in high school. When she finally married her high school boyfriend, Joe, they used some of their housekeeping money so that Betsy could continue with her writing. Whether Lovelace would have consciously called herself a feminist I don't know, but there was certainly a feminist message in these books, one of the things that elevated them above the Rosamund du Jardin romance stuff that was circulating at the same time.

What was missing, then, from these books that made me feel as I did, and laid the groundwork for my later delight when I discovered writers who probed more deeply into human existence? Betsy's parents adored each other; so did Tacy's and Tib's. It wasn't just that there was no divorce, there was no seeming need for divorce. In this small town no one had parents who even argued or whose relationship was a source of any kind of concern to their children. Child abuse did not exist: parents from whatever background treated their children with respect and kindness. There was romance, but no sex. When Joe finally gives Betsy a kiss at the end of the eighth volume of the series, I think all of Lovelace's readers almost fainted. This was not, however, a come-on. In future volumes they got married and went on a honeymoon, but nothing ever happened beyond that first kiss. The most erotic detail, which stayed in my mind for years, was that Betsy once thought how nice Joe looked in his pajamas. (Thank God she didn't have any thoughts about what he looked like without them!) Few characters ever died, and if they did, they went straight to heaven. There was no illness of the kind that led to horrible physical suffering or the decline of the body. Grandparents didn't exist, so one didn't even need to focus on the elderly, and there were also no horrible accidents befalling any of Betsy's classmates.

In an article by Mark West, an English professor writing on censorship, there is an illuminating passage about why adults and children often tend to like different children's books. "Some adults," he states, "enjoy children's literature because it allows them to escape the complexities of adult life and relive the perceived pleasures of childhood. . . . Children, on the other hand, are anxious to grow up and like books that help explain the mysterious worlds of adolescence and adulthood." I think West's phrase, "the perceived pleasures of childhood" is as significant as the one about "escape the complexities of adult life." Adults know the horrors and are pretending, or trying to pretend, they don't exist. They like children's books that help them pretend. Hence, the enormous number of deceitful, rosy little books that are churned forth every year, win awards, and try to inveigle children in this same desire to escape. With some children this succeeds. With others, like myself, it created only a sense of rage and confusion at a growing awareness of how much of life was left out of books. I didn't know why, but I knew it bothered me.

For ardent readers, and most future writers are such from an early age, the discovery of a favorite writer is like falling in love. You remember the moment it happened, you remember what you were wearing, you remember the room you were in. So it was that—after years of reading Maud Hart Lovelace and progressing to a slightly more grown-up writer with a similar world view, Rumer Godden, many of whose novels

ended with rich old ladies leaving beautiful mansions in the country (complete with devoted scone-baking servants) to penniless but lovable heroines, I read my first short story by Anton Chekhov. I was in high school and I was baby-sitting. I wasn't reading this volume of stories for school; I can't remember exactly what made me pick it up, although we had many books at home, and I was allowed to read whatever I wanted. I remember the story, though, because I've read it dozens of times since. It was called "The Name Day Party." It was about a young woman, Olga Mihalovna, who is in her last months of pregnancy. She's at odds with her husband because he has become involved in a minor lawsuit that he refuses to talk to her about; she goes into a jealous rage when she hears him discussing it with a pretty young neighbor. During the course of the story Olga and her husband give a daylong party that, to her, with her growing physical exhaustion and bad temper, seems endless. Finally, as the guests leave, she bursts out with the anger she has been repressing all day; they have a major quarrel. Torn by emotion she goes into labor unexpectedly and too soon. She is given some form of anesthetic, but when she awakes up, she discovers her baby has been born dead. The last paragraph of the story is as follows:

> But nothing mattered to Olga Mihalovna now, there was a mistiness in her brain from the chloroform, an emptiness in her soul. . . . The dull indifference to life which had overcome her when the two doctors were performing the operation still had possession of her.

That was the end of the story. No reassuring conversation between husband and wife about how they would try to have another baby, no reassurance by the author that their marriage would last, no cheerful adages about "but I'm young, and I still have much to live for." Nothing but that final, quietly piercing line of despair and unadorned grief. Why then, as a teenager did I put down that story with a sense of incredible excitement and exultation, a conscious feeling: *from now on everything will be different.* I think if I can be allowed to speak for myself then, that what I was feeling was that it's okay to write about feelings and emotions and terrible events without prettying them up, that writers who dare to do this will give courage and joy to other people. Probably, with the egoism of a sixteen-year-old, I thought *I want to be one of those writers.*

Critics so often say to me that kids are too young to understand some of the topics I write about. Yet I think of myself and that Chekhov story. He was Russian, male, writing in the nineteenth century. His main character was not a teenager. She was married, as I had never been, pregnant as I had never been. One could find few connecting links between that woman and her experiences and my life as a New York teenager living at home with my parents. But the human truth of that story made all that totally irrelevant. I entered into and shared the feelings of that woman more deeply than I had been able to enter into the ebullient lives of all the teenagers I'd been reading about for years. That, I hope, is what literature does—not just taking the particular details of what we have actually experienced but the underlying emotions that may extend fathoms into the future. I had been condescended to again and again as a young reader. Most of the books for young people I read now are still doing the same thing. All I can say in defense of my own books is that I am trying, if nothing else, not to do that. (pp. 161-62)

[There is another] writer who, apart from Chekhov, was the great discovery of my own adolescence: D. H. Lawrence. Many writers that one loves as a teenager pale upon rereading when one is middle-aged. Lawrence doesn't for me, just as Chekhov doesn't. In Lawrence I think what struck me most was his open, intense lyrical exploration of sexuality. In the books I had read until that point sex was a taboo. It still is today, in 1986, in about 99 percent of young adult fiction. There may, as in the Betsy books, be a kiss. That's it. We're still caught in those movies of the forties where the couples embrace and the screen goes black or pans to the crashing surf. What does that imply to the millions of young people whose sexual feelings at this age are probably more intense than they will ever be again? That beyond a light romantic kiss, sexual feelings—to say nothing of, horror of horrors, sexual behavior—are shameful, ugly. Let's pretend it's not there, and maybe it will go away. (pp. 162-63)

But by writing about it [D. H. Lawrence] was saying "accept and rejoice in this aspect of human nature, examine it in all its complexity. Don't pull down a black curtain the moment two characters feel attracted to each other. Describe what they are feeling and thinking and doing." As with Chekhov, reading D. H. Lawrence made me, although I was a virgin, realize part of what made most of young adult fiction so distorted and so bland. He made me able to look ahead to adult life with some sense of possible excitement, not just bewilderment and humiliation. When I write about sexual feelings among my young protagonists, I'm trying to give them the awareness that what they are feeling is what human beings have felt for centuries, what their parents and grandparents felt. What is shameful in life is concealment and distortion and evasion, not truth.

The last writer who had a major influence on me as a teenager was Salinger. Later I came to appreciate his stories, but in the fifties, I remember my brother (who was a year and a half younger) and me reading sections from *Catcher in the Rye* aloud and literally breaking down in helpless laughter. I remember our response to one of the early scenes in the book in which the hero, expelled from boarding school, goes to see one of his professors who hands him back his final exam. What amazed us was that an author could use real language, colloquial language, in a book. Here were our friends, here were unidealized young people, doing badly in school, cursing, at odds with the world, described in the very words we would have used to describe them. And this was in a book; it was literature. Today Salinger is a classic, so one would think that some of the things he taught us would have become accepted in the world of teenage literature—for one, just the realization that a novel told in colloquial language can be just as "literary" as one told in fancy, stiff, enigmatic prose. Not so, alas. Critics still cling to the idea that the more accessible and down-to-earth a book is, the less "good" it must be for the reader. If it goes down like bad medicine, with difficulty and pain, then it's "literature."

When I look at these three writers who were to influence me in their very different ways, I see that what they represented were different elements that are crucial in my own work: a desire to probe the darker side of human existence (Chekhov); an honest approach to sexuality (Lawrence); humor and a colloquial style (Salinger). . . .

I am stressing my own tastes as a high school reader because, as I see it, the main readership of young adult novels is ten-to-fourteen-year-olds. By high school, most readers have either turned to adult fiction or stopped reading altogether. . . . It seems to me, therefore, senseless to spend a lot of time arguing or debating what is fit material for teenagers to read in high school when all of the questionable themes are written about in the adult novels they turn to at this age. Usually these adult novels go into the same material in much greater depth. But I still would have liked there to be, as I still feel there is not, a large body of excellent, probing literary material written with the same complexity as adult literature but in which the main characters are teenagers. We are still force-feeding teenagers literary pablum, as though they were babies, and are then surprised when they turn from books altogether as being too dull or too limited. Let's stretch their minds and imaginations as they deserve to be stretched. (p. 163)

If I am trying to say anything in this speech, it is that I am trying to write the books I would have liked to read when I was a teenager. My teenage years were neither less nor more difficult than those of my daughters or most teenagers today. My parents never got divorced, so I had a "stable home." On the other hand, they frequently quarreled terribly and, like all teenagers, I lacked the detachment to see this as their particular problem. I thought it was the way marriage was, and it scared me about the future. I was unpopular with boys. I had no psychic powers that enabled me to see my future husband looming into view when I was twenty-one. The pain of being a wallflower was not relieved in any way by reading books like *Seventeenth Summer,* or others of its ilk, where the heroine's main problem is how far to go or to which of the two adorable suitors for her hand she should give herself. I found my sexual feelings disturbing, and I never discovered, in the novels I read, heroines who shared any of these perfectly common emotions. If we admit that being a teenager at any time of history is, by some definition, terrible, then let us have books that acknowledge this, books that deal with some of these terrible problems without sugar coating and lies and evasion. Young people will be grateful for these books. They need them. (p. 164)

Norma Klein, "Books to Help Kids Deal with Difficult Times, I," in School Media Quarterly, *Vol. 15, No. 3, Spring, 1987, pp. 161-64.*

GENERAL COMMENTARY

JOHN GARVEY

[A woman I know] once asked her students to read Judy Blume's *Forever,* a book for older adolescents about a first love affair. The boy and girl, Katherine and Michael, have a pet name for Michael's penis: they call it Ralph. My friend asked her class the names of the novel's main characters, and no one could remember. But they all remembered Ralph. He was separate from the main characters, in his inarticulate way, just like their relationship. The message of *Forever* is that sexual relationships come and go, and what matters is how you relate to the things that happen to you. This relating should be done with maturity and understanding and responsibility, seasoned with the bittersweet knowledge that love affairs may end, but *you* have to go on whatever happens, so be careful (and don't get pregnant).

Relationships mean a lot in these books. They frequently seem, like Ralph, to have lives independent of the characters who are supposed to be having the relationships. Relationships are a form of heavy weather, and people participate in them, sometimes endure them.

At her best Judy Blume is a kind of training bra for Ann Beattie; at her worst she reads like Woody Allen without the humor. *Forever* features a grandmother who sends Katherine the following letter:

> I hear you and Michael are officially *going together.* Thought these might come in handy. And remember, if you ever need to talk, I'm available. I don't judge. I just advise. Love, Grandma.

This grandma is nothing like mine, who found the Andrews sisters risqué. This grandma sent Katherine

> a whole bunch of pamphlets from Planned Parenthood on birth control, abortion, and venereal disease. At first I was angry. Grandma is jumping to conclusions again, I thought. But then I sat down and started to read. It turned out she had sent me a lot of valuable information. . . .

An ideology is on the prowl here, meaning well every inch of the way. This preachiness can also be found in Norma Klein's books. Her *Mom, the Wolf Man, and Me* is about a child who lives with her unmarried mother, and the novel deals with the way the little girl manages to accept and like her mother's lover. Naturally the child has few problems; the main obstacles have to do with hung-up adults. In Klein's *It's Not What You Expect* a couple of kids help to raise money for a needed abortion, and at the end of the novel Mom confesses that she herself had an abortion, before it was legal, and she is very glad that the times are changing. (pp. 392-93)

These books say next to nothing about choice and commitment, but they are full of feelings and the right attitudes towards feelings, and the tricks chance can play on children who would rather their parents stay together than get divorced. The main work of these books is teaching children to cope. There is something dismal about teaching children to cope, where in previous generations books for children encouraged a larger imagining, a thrill at the size of the universe they might encounter. In these books there is at best a small satisfaction: you learn to line up with the Right Attitudes. . . .

It is important for adolescents to understand that feelings which are demanding and confusing are also quite normal; and if parents and schools won't tell their children about sex, better they should learn from Judy Blume than not learn at all. But more than information is being delivered here; a point of view is being urged on kids. The assumptions which saturate these books are the assumptions of upper-middle-class white liberals. They seem so self-evidently right to the authors that I am sure they don't see what an orthodoxy they have accepted. No doubt they think of their attitudes as simply true, and of more traditional attitudes as reactionary or unenlightened. The same point of view is shared by many of the educators who have pushed "values clarification" in the schools: people can find their own values, they assume, as if values were innate things. You go through your feelings and reactions—it is like looking for lice—until you find your values; they are in there somewhere, covered over with hang-ups and insensitivities.

An orthodoxy which does not admit that it is an orthodoxy is hard to deal with. Many of the opponents of liberal orthodoxy are themselves an unattractive lot. There are fundamentalists who want to censor school texts, move them to the right, and get Biblical creation taught in science classes. I would rather my children learn about Darwin in science class, and I don't want them to believe that America should "return to God," because this is idolatry: America was never God's chosen nation. But the fundamentalists have perceived one thing clearly: there is a new orthodoxy. It is being pushed in some schools, on television, and in a lot of children's literature. A few school boards have tried to make this fundamentalist objection to certain texts and library books look like the inquisitors versus us non-judgmental professionals, but frequently that isn't the case at all. The problem is that here one orthodoxy confronts another. (p. 393)

> *John Garvey, "The Voice of Blume," in* Commonweal, *Vol. CVII, No. 13, July 4, 1980, pp. 392-93.*

ZENA SUTHERLAND AND MAY HILL ARBUTHNOT

While Norma Klein has written for several age levels, her greatest impact is in stories for younger adolescents. . . .

Many of Klein's stories are about single-parent homes, divorce, remarriage, and the adaptability required of children. . . .

Klein is a thoughtful connoisseur of real people and sets down her observations skillfully for us. Her children are not divorced from adult problems and relationships, but live closely, in their urban existences, with real and surrogate parents, who are inevitably frank and open about their emotions. Only occasional older people—grandmothers, baby-sitters—ever suggest that different values might be held by other adults.

> *Zena Sutherland and May Hill Arbuthnot, in a review of "Mom, the Wolf Man, and Me," and "It's Not What You Expect," in their* Children and Books, *seventh edition, Scott, Foresman and Company, 1986, p. 336.*

SUNSHINE (1974)

Katherine Haydon married at 16. Three years later, she had divorced her husband, borne his daughter alone, and settled down to a warm, contented relationship with Sam, a struggling musician. Leg pains led her to medical treatment, a diagnosis of cancer and, finally, the realization that she was dying. This all happened to a young woman named Jacquelyn Helton who kept a journal for the little daughter she adored who would never know her mother. The novel is based on Helton's journal, and Klein has treated it with the sensitivity and respect it deserves. This is no *Love Story* with a scarcely ruffled heroine passing gracefully from the scene. It is full of pain, ugliness, and people who behave selfishly and badly as often as nobly. The book is unbearably poignant and very touching—someday young Jennifer Helton will read it with pride.

> *Barbara Nelson, in a review of "Sunshine," in* Library Journal, *Vol. 99, No. 16, September 15, 1974, p. 2176.*

If in their reading, reluctant readers are looking for an emotional experience, then they want the highs and the lows to be packed tight against each other. They haven't much patience with the long drawn out in-betweens. They want struggles where the odds are great and everything is super-sized.

One such struggle, with which most teenagers are now familiar, is the story of Jacquelyn M. Helton, the young mother who learns at eighteen that she has fatal bone cancer. Norma Klein's novel *Sunshine* is based on the television movie suggested by Helton's journals. Readers, reluctant and enthusiastic, who wept over the movie and watched the resulting TV special, will want to read this touching and unavoidably moving novel. The first person narrative is written in the honest and occasionally introspective style which permits identification with the brave young woman as she struggles to keep alive her hopes and dreams. (p. 93)

> *Alleen Pace Nilsen, Karen B. Tyler, and Linda Kozarek, "Reluctantly Yours, Books to Tempt the Hesitant," in* English Journal, *Vol. 65, No. 5, May, 1976, pp. 90-3.*

Girls have been reading this story avidly for the past eight years; it continues to be popular and universally admired. With a lower reading level than might have been expected this can surely be considered for your poorer readers. Even though the book is longer than high/lows generally are, the very short chapters and sentences are ideal for those students with short attention spans and the very moving story will retain interest.

> *Dorothy B. Bickley, in a review of "Sunshine," in* The High/Low Report, *Vol. 4, No. 7, March, 1983, p. 5.*

DINOSAUR'S HOUSEWARMING PARTY (1974)

Dinosaur enjoys the spaciousness of a penthouse apartment after leaving his cramped space in Greenwich Village; his best friends, Octopus and Worm, who have helped him unpack, decide to give Dinosaur a surprise housewarming party. Each brings a gift, each gift is described, they all have a good time. There's always some appeal in animals and in parties, and the illustrations [by James Marshall] are humorous, but the story has no focus. It's adequately written but this isn't Klein's metier.

> *Zena Sutherland, in a review of "Dinosaur's Housewarming Party," in* Bulletin of the Center for Children's Books, *Vol. 28, No. 9, May, 1975, p. 149.*

THE SUNSHINE YEARS (1975)

Before children's books caught up with the sophistication of children, one might have recommended this sequel to *Sunshine* for a YA audience. In the shortest of vignettes this continues the story of Sam, 26, a frequently unemployed Vancouver musician, a widower who has adopted his dead wife's five-year-old daughter. Sam loses out on one potential wife after another; Jill's natural father appears and buys her a doll house; a social worker comes to check out Sam's off-beat situation and Sam foolishly tries to con her. There's an attempt at hipness here, but it all has the self-conscious ring of sex instruction at a grade-school level.

> *A review of "The Sunshine Years," in* Publishers Weekly, *Vol. 208, No. 12, September 22, 1975, p. 133.*

A sequel to *Sunshine,* this book is composed of nine sequential episodes based on the TV series. . . . Though it's contemporary and fast reading, the use of profanity is questionable, as is the inconsistency of Sam's sexual code when he has affairs with sexually liberated Nora and ambitious Montana Smith (a girl) while Jill is asleep upstairs yet stutters with embarrassment when Jill matter-of-factly and innocently tells it like it is between him and Montana using terms Sam has obviously employed to explain sex to her.

> *Margaret Strickland, in a review of "The Sunshine Years," in* School Library Journal, *Vol. 22, No. 8, April, 1976, p. 90.*

HIDING (1976)

Separated from her brother and sister by an age barrier and denied normal family intimacy by parents who live apart most of the year, Krii Halliday chooses ballet training in London rather than college, hoping her shyly sensitive, emotionally insecure nature will be masked by her foreignness. Early on she meets Jonathan, an older part-time designer for the ballet school, whose easygoing, perceptive charm appeals to her longing for a close personal attachment and leads her into a casual sexual intimacy—accepted without question by her liberal parents, but with mixed feelings by Krii herself, whose constrained emotional background makes her unable to view sexual relationships in clear perspective. Jonathan, angered and frustrated by Krii's lack of self-esteem and refusal to make a full commitment to him, cruelly forces her to confront herself—which she finally does while hiding in her parents' attic. Though occasionally flawed by inconsistencies in plot development and cloudy, sometimes over-complicated character motivations, Klein's introspective rendering, written from Krii's own point of view, is an unusual portrait—more sophisticated in tone and mature in subject than most junior novels.

> *A review of "Hiding," in* Booklist, *Vol. 73, No. 5, November 1, 1976, p. 402.*

The book is well-titled, for hiding is the central idea in the plot and the key to the character of the heroine. Eighteen-year-old Krii Halliday has been an introvert all her life. . . . She says that "from the time I could say my alphabet, I knew perfectly well that the world would have no trouble whatever functioning without *me.*" Realizing that she is too small to become a first-class ballet dancer and depressed by Jonathan's marriage, she returns home and impulsively hides for a week in the attic of her parents' house. Somewhat unconvincingly, the author uses this brief respite to give her the courage to return to the world, enter college, and fight her constant impulse to hide herself away. Her quiet, introspective personality, her cool observation, and her secretiveness seem real; and although her struggles to escape from herself are rather touching, they can be almost as irritating to the reader as they were to Jonathan. (pp. 629-30)

> *Ann A. Flowers, in a review of "Hiding," in* The Horn Book Magazine, *Vol. LII, No. 6, December, 1976, pp. 629-30.*

IT'S OK IF YOU DON'T LOVE ME (1977)

The summer before her senior year, Jody meets Lyle, whose staid Midwest background differs completely from her liberal New York upbringing as the daughter of a twice-divorced mother who is currently living with a psychology professor. On the pill and sexually primed by her first love affair, Jody is eager to have a sexual relationship with Lyle, but he is hesitant; for one thing, he is still a virgin, and, for another, he feels that love should go along with sex. Eventually they begin a relationship that is both loving and sexual until Jody, who still has a long way to go toward maturity, decides to prove herself to her first boyfriend by sleeping with him again—an episode that temporarily disrupts her relationship with Lyle. Although sex is not Jody's only concern, it tends to dominate her thoughts and life. Characterizations and Jody's personal interactions—not only with Lyle but with her mother, brother, father, stepfather, and her mother's current lover—are convincing; dialogue is sharp; and the story, which contains a ready mixture of humor and poignancy, is sexually explicit but not exploitive. Jody's first-person narrative is for a more mature audience than Klein's earlier books, including the recent *Hiding.*

> *A review of "It's OK If You Don't Love Me," in* Booklist, *Vol. 73, No. 16, April 15, 1977, p. 1258.*

Like the heroine of Blume's *Forever,* 17-year-old Jody enjoys sex and takes informed precautions to avoid pregnancy. . . . Jody spends a lot of time analyzing her actions in an annoyingly flip way, a trait she comes by naturally since her twice-divorced mother discusses having her tubes tied as if she were deciding to have her shoes shined. Conversations between characters are very frank, often including a smattering of four-letter words, but Klein is disappointingly blasé in dealing with the real decisions young high school age women must make about the opposite sex.

> *Carol Schene, in a review of "It's OK If You Don't Love Me," in* School Library Journal, *Vol. 23, No. 9, May, 1977, p. 83.*

Norma Klein has a nice sense of what teen-agers today might be feeling about themselves, each other, their bodies and minds, their friends and parents. Her novel of an orphaned young Midwestern WASP, who meets a more sophisticated Jewish girl in New York with an assortment of father-figures courtesy of a mixed-up but non-malevolent mother, is low-key, credible, frank and gutsy.

In a narrative just over 200 pages, the author manages to write in an open, intelligent manner about such potentially ticklish subjects as contraception, pregnancy, racial, religious and regional prejudice, mother-daughter jealousy, divorced parents and even parent-child conflict over choice of colleges. Despite all this, you never have the sense that you are getting an informational handbook dressed up as a novel.

Best of all, Norma Klein avoids the darkest and most dangerous pitfall of an adult writing a dramatic story about adolescents: She is never condescending. One ends the book liking not only the teen-age characters but also the author who had the empathy, understanding and talent to create them.

> *Dan Wakefield, "Firepersons and Other Characters," in* The New York Times Book Review, *May 1, 1977, p. 10.*

TOMBOY (1978)

Eleven-year-old Antonia narrates this dreadful book in a slow self-conscious monotone. The events are strung together in an unfocused plot that fails to differentiate between the mundane and the significant (the death of an elderly neighbor has the same impact as having a friend sleep over). The characters, stick figures draped with details of fashionably hip, modern urban living, lack emotion and fail to show any convincing growth or self discovery. Into this uninvolving tale, Klein has injected a number of conversations that seem to be included simply to raise eyebrows. The discussions of diaper changes (Dad cares for the baby while Mom supports the family), seeing parents naked in bed, sex, puberty and menstruation are provocative but they do not bring this condescending story to life.

> *Christine McDonnell, in a review of "Tomboy," in* School Library Journal, *Vol. 25, No. 1, September, 1978, p. 140.*

Ten-year-old Antonia narrates some chatty episodes of surefire interest to similar-age readers. . . . Through it all runs the theme of sex-role development: male, female, and just plain human. Klein's style is so smooth and friendly, echoing exactly kids' own speech and thought patterns, that they won't mind some skimping on plot and character, especially for the same sound family that appeared in *Confessions of an Only Child.*

> *Betsy Hearne, in a review of "Tomboy," in* Booklist, *Vol. 75, No. 4, October 15, 1978, p. 382.*

This is less structured than the first book, more an exploration of a stage of childhood than a development of a conflict situation, although Toe does gain some perspectives on one's sex role. Still, it's realistic and candid, reflecting many typical concerns and interests of the ten-year-old, and it has humor, especially in the dialogue. Unfortunately, the type-face and leading make it a bit hard on the eyes. (pp. 100-01)

> *Zena Sutherland, in a review of "Tomboy," in* Bulletin of the Center for Children's Books, *Vol. 32, No. 6, February, 1979, pp. 100-01.*

LOVE IS ONE OF THE CHOICES (1978)

In this crisp contemporary novel, Klein contrasts the lives of two high school seniors who are best friends: Maggie, a brilliant science prodigy and ardent feminist, and Caroline, a quiet, self-contained beauty. With minimal plot and maximal dialogue, the author brings the girls through their respective sexual awakenings and to new realization of their inner—and outer—selves. Klein's characters are reactions against stereotypes: a father who cooks and a mother who doesn't, a boy who loves *Alice in Wonderland,* and lots of people over forty who admit to having and enjoying sex. The book moves right along, with many very funny conversations. But the world she has created is a rarefied one, in which everyone is brilliant and/or sophisticated, and there is always time to talk. It's fun to visit, but does anyone really live there?

> *Joyce Smothers, in a review of "Love Is One of the Choices," in* Library Journal, *Vol. 103, No. 20, November 15, 1978, p. 2351.*

Although they move in the world of exclusive private schools, liberal attitudes, and the cliché-ridden comfort of their middle-class Manhattan milieu, the characters in Klein's latest are not her usual teenage Beautiful People—brash, brilliant, and self-assured. High school seniors Maggie and Caroline are uncertain, vulnerable best friends struggling to establish their emotional and intellectual identities. . . . An improvement over Klein's superficial treatment of the same theme in her *It's OK If You Don't Love Me,* this sexually explicit look at the often confusing choices confronting young women today is sure of a widespread audience—the same one that responded to Judy Blume's *Forever* (1975).

> *K. Sue Hurwitz, in a review of "Love Is One of the Choices," in* School Library Journal, *Vol. 25, No. 4, December, 1978, p. 72.*

A pleasant surprise from an author whose recent work has been disappointing. . . . Ever since **Mom, the Wolfman, and Me,** we have been hoping for another book from [Klein] that takes a look at modern manners with compassion and wit. **Love Is One of the Choices** is that book—but much, much more. No junior novel, this, but a fully articulated and insightful double love story. The contrast between fiercely independent Maggie and artistic and dreamy Caroline is accentuated by the men they choose for first lovers. . . . Both young women struggle, but in different ways, to keep their own identities in the face of the temptation to surrender to emotional security.

A source of tension for the reader is that each appears to have chosen the man that would be right for the other. In the end the characters explore this perception and then set it aside. The story has a wealth of funny or poignant moments that hang in the memory: the friendly intellectual sparring between Maggie and her psychiatrist father, fragile Caroline's terror at a quarrel with Justin, Maggie and Todd's cheerful and matter-of-fact first bedding. Here is a love story that we can give to YA's without apology.

> *Patty Campbell, in a review of "Love Is One of the Choices," in* Wilson Library Bulletin, *Vol. 53, No. 8, April, 1979, p. 579.*

VISITING PAMELA (1979)

Carrie is afraid to go to Pamela's house to play, but she loves to have company in the secure surroundings of home. Her first visit to Pamela's results in a fast phone call to Mama, with tearful pleas to be picked up and taken home. But, by the time Mama arrives, Carrie is having fun. Though the black-and-white illustrations [by Kay Chorao] are gorgeous, they do not redeem the story. The reasons for Carrie's fears are not clear, nor are the reasons for the sudden change of heart. This is a disappointment.

> *Arlene Stolzer Sandner, in a review of "Visiting Pamela," in* Children's Book Review Service, *Vol. 7, No. 10, May, 1979, p. 92.*

This is a very contemporary story, speaking to the fears of children (seeing Pamela's pesty brother, Carrie worries that her mother might "get fat" and have a baby—enough theme for an entire book, here slipped in as a throw-away line), and done well enough to merit consideration.

> *Reva Pitch Margolis, in a review of "Visiting Pamela," in* School Library Journal, *Vol. 25, No. 9, May, 1979, p. 53.*

"The first time is the worst," Mommy says on the way home; but true as that may be, we still haven't seen Carrie stand up to grabby Pamela (part of her hesitancy about visiting) or solved the problem of a threatening dog. Still, in environs like New York where children aren't in and out of each others' houses, this may serve as a preview of the worst that isn't all that bad. . . . (p. 514)

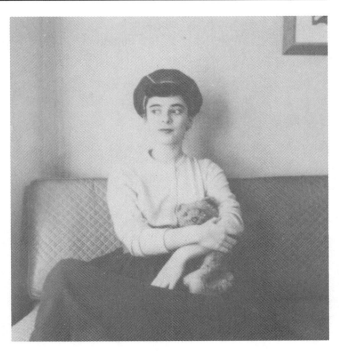

Klein as a high school student.

> *A review of "Visiting Pamela," in* Kirkus Reviews, *Vol. XLVII, No. 9, May 1, 1979, pp. 513-14.*

FRENCH POSTCARDS (1979)

Teenagers are the principals in this tale of Americans spending their junior year of college in Paris, and teenagers will probably be its most appreciative readers. In the foreground are four students preoccupied with their individual visions of love and strategies for finding it. Voluptuous Melanie trots in a number of Parisian men, Naïve Joel is swept off his feet by a perky clerk who sells him paper clips. Alex is obsessed by fantasies of Madame Tessier, their teacher. Laura, faithful for months to her beau in the States, attempts to bridge the Atlantic with postcards. Hearts break, then mend: all involved seem to mature a bit in the process. Although the plot suffers from lack of action, the story offers an entertaining insight into the traumas and triumphs of young love. Once again, Klein proves that this is a subject she handles deftly.

> *A review of "French Postcards," in* Publishers Weekly, *Vol. 216, No. 9, August 27, 1979, p. 383.*

That peculiar American rite-of-passage, the junior year abroad, becomes a travesty in this clumsy and insensitive "screenplay novelization." It purports to chronicle the activities of four young American students during a year of study in Paris, but the backdrop might as well be Hoboken, or the moon, for all the attention given to developing a sense of locale. The so-called students carry adolescent self-absorption to a ludicrous extreme, concerning themselves solely with not missing any opportunity to "do it" with some of the natives (they also do not have to worry about birth control, pregnancy, or VD). The characters, both American and European, are unencumbered by personalities, depth, or much in the way of feelings (with the exception of sexual desire). Unfortunately, the forthcoming movie and Klein's name on the cover of the paperback are sure to bring demands for this very poorly written title filled with vulgar language. (pp. 96-7)

Paula J. Todisco, in a review of "French Postcards," in School Library Journal, *Vol. 26, No. 3, November, 1979, pp. 96-7.*

A HONEY OF A CHIMP (1980)

Klein's writing is proficient and her main character, Emily, is a sturdy presence, thanks to an easy-flowing first-person narrative. The story—of Emily and her family's taking on a pygmy chimp and then finding a home for it when Emily's mother becomes pregnant—is wobbly, its effectiveness a function of technical skill rather than inherent soundness; the book is cloudy on animal care and treatment issues. "If she's too much bother, we'll bring her back," says Emily's mother. Certainly Olivia, the baby chimp, receives loving care in Emily's house, but she comes from a dealer in exotic pets (his business "looks kind of dingy," parrots there are "awfully mangy looking") and is, in fact, discarded by Emily's family in something less than a year because of the problems she poses. That her new home will be the progressive San Diego Zoo is a happy ending that dodges the issue of whether Olivia should have been a pet at all. The book flows well, and Klein readers will consume it easily, but it raises questions that merit group discussion.

Denise M. Wilms, in a review of "A Honey of a Chimp," in Booklist, *Vol. 76, No. 17, May 1, 1980, p. 1294.*

[This book is] a change from the usual giving-up-a-pet story, and it has some strengths and some weaknesses. Weaknesses: the improbability, even given money in the family, that Emmy, her parents, her uncle, and her baby sister would all fly out from one coast to another to see a pet and take Emmy's cello along. Strengths: the easy writing style, the natural dialogue, the casual incorporation of—and acceptance of—the fact that Emmy's uncle is gay. The chimp is an appealing subject, and the advent of the new baby is treated with nice balance: Emmy is a bit miffed but gets over it; some adults may object to the fact that, piqued by the fact that her mother is pregnant, Emmy discusses with her best friend the fact that she has walked in on her parents' love-making, and that the two girls discuss marital sex. (pp. 216-17)

Zena Sutherland, in a review of "A Honey of a Chimp," in Bulletin of the Center for Children's Books, *Vol. 33, No. 11, July-August, 1980, pp. 216-17.*

[Emily's] grandmother had polio as a young woman and since then has been obliged to use a wheelchair. She has managed to cope with her disability extraordinarily well . . . . (p. 274)

Emily's grandparent is treated as a talented, interesting, active woman who has had to adjust to the consequences of a disabling illness. . . . In addition to the central story line, Klein interweaves a number of side issues—a homosexual uncle who questions his lifestyle, a young friend of Emily's who has learned of her mother's affair, Emily's mother's miscarriages and yearnings for another child, children's discussions of the propriety of parents having intercourse—topics that are not standard fare in novels for schoolchildren. The author treats her attractive characters with wit and compassion, is sympathetic to the confusions and needs of preteenagers, and presents a believable, upbeat picture of the adjustments a pragmatic family might make to impairment. (pp. 274-75)

Barbara Baskin and Karen H. Harris, in a review of "A Honey of a Chimp," in their More Notes from a Different Drummer: A Guide to Juvenile Fiction Portraying the Disabled, *R. R. Bowker, 1984, pp. 273-75.*

BREAKING UP (1980)

The flyleaf on this novel asserts that it "accurately portrays family life," "love and commitment," etc. etc. Don't believe it.

The son and daughter of divorced parents go out to California from New York to spend the summer with their father and his new wife. The tale is told as a first-person narrative by the fifteen year old girl named Ali. There is not enough trauma to make a story out of the fact that the two are from a broken home, so add the spice of a best friend, named Marcie, the jealous sister of Ali's boyfriend, Ethan, (with the suggestion of an unnatural relationship), Marcie and Ethan being the offspring of a kooky mother who plays around. Throw in the "uplifting" conclusion in a discussion by two fifteen year old girls that it would probably be better if Marcie's mother got an abortion; then add a recital by Ali's brother of his indiscretions with his girlfriend, while her parents are away, and his naive explanation that his allnight stays are undetected by his father and stepmother because he comes home early in the morning before they are up. This is not enough? Add, then, the fact that Ali's own mother is gay, and her father wishes to go public in court with this information in order to gain custody of the children. In the finale of this "accurately portrayed family life," we have Ali in bed with her boyfriend in the room next to that of her mother and friend.

If love is no longer synonymous with honor, compassion, sacrifice . . . and family life is no longer the bastion of tender moral concerns and spiritual concepts . . . then this book is a winner. There is nothing quite as tragic as a losing winner.

Claire M. Dyson, in a review of "Breaking Up," in Best Sellers, *Vol. 40, No. 8, November, 1980, p. 301.*

An assertive, healthy lesbian parent is featured in Norma Klein's novel, one of the few books for teenagers which presents homosexuality as an acceptable alternative lifestyle. . . .

Throughout the novel, Ali becomes clearer about her own sexuality as well. . . . Such issues as jealousy, sexual relationships, divorce, pregnancy, abortion and love are explored realistically and matter-of-factly.

I have several criticisms of the book. Although the usual stereotypes of lesbians (masculine, man-hating, unsatisfied women) are contradicted, not enough information is provided about Cynthia and Peggy's relationship. Ali and her mother have a moving discussion about Cynthia's lifestyle, but it does not tell the reader much about her mother's daily life, personality or beliefs.

In addition, the negative comments about the lesbian lifestyle from Ali's father are left uncontradicted, even when Ali decides to return to New York. Readers could conclude that Harold's biased opinions are valid.

Furthermore, homosexuality is not presented as an option for teenagers in this book, though there is clearly a character (Ali's best friend Gretchen) who does not fit into heterosexual roles. Gretchen is very attached to Ali and does not have an interest in boys, yet the reader is left with the impression that she will grow up lonely and unfulfilled.

Characterization is occasionally stilted. Harold's new wife Eileen is a neurotic, self-indulgent hypochondriac, and this is blamed solely on her "unhappy childhood." Ali's relationship with Ethan happens too quickly, and the reader doesn't get a sense of what attracts them to each other and what thoughts they might have as they deal with their deepening sexual involvement.

Incorrect birth control information is presented in the last pages of the novel, when Ethan produces a three-year-old condom from his wallet before he and Ali make love for their first time. According to Planned Parenthood, a condom can become defective if kept for more than three months!

Despite my reservations, it is enlightening to see a novel which deals with lesbianism in a positive way and credits teenagers with the ability to make decisions for themselves and to feel deeply for each other.

> *Jay Meryl, in a review of "Breaking Up," in* Interracial Books for Children Bulletin, *Vol. 12, No. 3, April-May, 1981, p. 19.*

Klein manipulates her characters, and the situations seem a bit "set-up." The father's relationship with his second wife is traditional, over-protective, and generally negative. Mom and friend Peggy, for as much as we see of them, create a positive, egalitarian and supportive environment which seems less subtle than it needs to be. Also, Ethan and Ali become so physically magnetized after very few words that it is too contrived. The story, told in first person moves along clumsily at first, and simplistically, but is indicative of Ali's thought processes.

The anti-climax comes when Dad decides it would be ok when Ali decides to live with Mom and Peggy afterall. Throughout the book we are led to believe that he will go to court and file for custody.

Aside from all that, the story moves along and will engage those Klein fans and others who will be drawn by the cover or blurb. Not up to *Mom, the Wolf Man, and Me,* but an adequate read.

> *Sheila Pearsons, in a review of "Breaking Up," in* Voice of Youth Advocates, *Vol. 4, No. 2, June, 1981, p. 28.*

DOMESTIC ARRANGEMENTS (1981)

Are you ready for this? A 14-year-old girl is discovered having intercourse with her boyfriend in the family bathroom at four in the morning. This doesn't upset her mother in the least. Shortly afterward, the same girl attends, with her father, an exhibit of close-ups showing male sex organs. Later, she and her sister catch both parents in extramarital affairs. And that's only the beginning. Klein has never been one to make life easy for librarians, and this new piece of startling

"realism" is guaranteed to dredge up the latent conservatism in our most liberal adult readers. Young adults will like the book: it's funny, fast-moving, and full of teenage wish-fulfillment (the heroine stars in a Brooke Shields-type movie role, is interviewed for *People* magazine, receives a diaphragm for Christmas). But one has to look pretty hard to find redeeming social value here. (pp. 470-71)

> *Joyce Smothers, in a review of "Domestic Arrangements," in* Library Journal, *Vol. 106, No. 4, February 15, 1981, pp. 470-71.*

Klein would have done better to write this for a soap opera script rather than a story for YAs. Although the jacket copy refers to Tatiana's family as being a "recognizable family facing a recognizable dilemma—how to respond to their daughter's first affair," the characters and situations described are far from typical, or so we would hope.

The greatest frustration in reading this book is the seeming lack of concrete values toward sexuality and life in general presented by the parents of two teenage daughters, Tatiana and Cordelia. The sophistication level of the mother, Samantha, is indistinguishable from that of her daughters. For example, when 14 year old Tatiana asks if her boyfriend can sleep overnight with her, Mom replies, "sure, for how long?" with little concern. The daughters model Samantha's tendency to flirt, cajole, and manipulate Neil, the father. Neil is a noncommittal character. When Tatiana asks her father for a diaphragm for a Christmas present (her 16 year old sister had received one the year before) Dad's response is, "I don't feel comfortable with the idea, you're fourteen sweetheart. That's still extremely young." As a reader this was quite disturbing; after all Dad has been very much aware of Tatiana's intimate relationship with her boyfriend for several months.

We question the audience Norma Klein directed this book toward. The messages and values presented throughout make us feel this book is inappropriate for school library consideration.

> *Deborah Hollander, in a review of "Domestic Arrangements," in* Voice of Youth Advocates, *Vol. 4, No. 4, October, 1981, p. 34.*

ROBBIE AND THE LEAP YEAR BLUES (1981)

Joint custody has never been this funny! Eleven-year-old Robbie's divorced parents live in the same Manhattan apartment house, so once a week Robbie packs his knapsack and moves into the opposite side of the building. When his mother and father cross signals one weekend, Robbie ends up spending two days with Mom's divorced boyfriend, Paul, and his daughters. Paul picks Robbie up at the apartment Robbie's dad shares with Jill, an aspiring clown who is "between jobs," and it's love at first sight. As the adults juggle their emotional commitments, Robbie and cohort Thor share their feelings and insights about girls, relationships and marriage. Klein skillfully weaves many subplots—two love triangles and Robbie's changing feelings toward Paul's daughters and toward Eve, the girl he "marries" during leap year. The dialogue, especially between Paul's 12-year-old daughter and Robbie and between Paul and Jill, is flawless. Absorbing, fast-moving, full of life.

> *Symme J. Benoff, in a review of "Robbie and the*

Leap Year Blues," in School Library Journal, *Vol. 28, No. 2, October, 1981, p. 143.*

Although the plot here is unfortunately nonexistent, Klein does her usual competent job of handling innuendos of dialogue among characters coping with Ping-Pong relationships. . . . [A] noncommittal ending portrays two sets of parents bidding their camp-bound sons good-bye, with a sentence indicating that no one could tell which are divorced. More to the point is the difficulty in distinguishing adults from children; though these characters care about each other, they seem permanently arrested at a confused state of development.

> *Betsy Hearne, in a review of "Robbie and the Leap Year Blues," in* Booklist, *Vol. 78, No. 7, December 1, 1981, p. 499.*

The dialogue is natural and childlike, and the story is told in the first person in a quiet, matter-of-fact tone. In contrast to the many novels about children who are unsure of the love of their divorced parents, the book reveals the thoughts and actions of a boy who has a strong relationship with both parents, as he begins to apprehend the complexity of being an adult.

> *Karen M. Klockner, in a review of "Robbie and the Leap Year Blues," in* The Horn Book Magazine, *Vol. LVIII, No. 2, April, 1982, p. 165.*

THE QUEEN OF THE WHAT IFS (1982)

Hit harder than her brother or sister by their parents' separation, 14-year-old Robin, Klein's narrator, is even more disturbed by her father's affair with another woman, and shares her concerns with her levelheaded brother, whose calming influence helps Robin keep her emotions in check. Personal concerns about sex and romance surface to complicate her life further, but they take a clear second place to worries about her family. The portrait of the liberal, slightly offbeat Jewish family (here including a tennis-playing grandma with a live-in boyfriend), almost a hallmark of Klein's writing, is once again evoked, and the author demonstrates a sure feel for natural, realistic dialogue. But her fans will miss the force and energy of some of her previous books and find her characters, though quite likable, curiously insubstantial. Diverting, if one of Klein's less effective junior novels.

> *Stephanie Zvirin, in a review of "The Queen of What Ifs," in* Booklist, *Vol. 78, No. 20, June 15, 1982, p. 1364.*

Near the end Mom talks about the value of love in terms other than sexual, but one statement cannot erase the opposite message developed throughout the book. Klein does not present a realistic picture of life. Instead she exploits teenage girls' natural interest in sex. There are careless mistakes: Mom is said to have attended two different colleges; Robin says she gives two cello lessons a week but describes three pupils; her friend Terry tours France but returns instead from Rome. Klein's fans may have no objections to *The Queen* . . . , but librarians may prefer more thoughtful and careful writing.

> *Marsha Hartos, in a review of "The Queen of What Ifs," in* School Library Journal, *Vol. 29, No. 8,*

April, 1983, p. 125.

BEGINNER'S LOVE (1983)

Beginner's Love is hardly for beginners. And yet, what adult would bother reading a slow moving book about two 17 year olds just for a little sex? On the other hand, some teens would read a poorly written book, with shallow characters, minimal plot and insipid dialogue, just for a little sex. But in this case, they'd probably skim "for the good parts." Shy Joel has trouble meetings G-I-R-L-S. At a movie (*Endless Love,* of course) he and his best friend pick up Leda and Danielle, two hip New York girls. The affair between Leda and Joel is off and running. Joel tells the story in first person "stream of ramble." The dialogue is written in Valley Girl talk ("Like, you know . . . ," followed by some long-winded and tiresome thought). Every other sentence alludes to sex whether it's necessary or not. The book ends with Leda and Joel splitting up after her abortion. The depth of dialogue, feeling and emotion is embarrassingly shallow. This makes *Forever* seem like Pulitzer Prize material.

> *Lois A. Strell, in a review of "Beginner's Love," in* School Library Journal, *Vol. 30, No. 2, October, 1983, p. 180.*

Never one to shy away from the topic of sex (see **It's OK If You Don't Love Me**), Norma Klein's latest work addresses the intricacies of initial romantic and sexual rumblings. (p. 203)

Klein's novel is both explicit and thought-provoking. Joel's musings on sex and the relationship in general ring true, and the book contains a number of interesting minor characters. Only Leda's characterization is questionable, with her analogy between forgetting to brush her teeth sometimes and forgetting to insert her diaphragm sometimes being particularly inane for a supposedly intelligent young woman. Klein's explicitness and the somewhat casual abortion should insure controversy in some areas. Subject matter and readability, however, should insure popularity. . . . (pp. 203-04)

> *Kevin Kenny, in a review of "Beginner's Love," in* Voice of Youth Advocates, *Vol. 6, No. 4, October, 1983, pp. 203-04.*

In this typical teen novel, the main theme is the attitudes of high school-age youth toward sexual experience. A second theme is that of relationships: those between young people and their parents, spouse to spouse, brother to brother, and between partners in a sexual relationship.

In this book, Joel and Leda embark on a sexual relationship after several dates. The story, told from Joel's point of view, does not just relate sexual episodes, however. It deals with feelings and attitudes which stem from this kind of friendship. The feelings ring true and, in this regard, the author has done a good job of writing.

The reasons why this story is a typical teen novel are that it contains obscene words, deals with awakening sexual attitudes, and has a pregnancy-abortion dilemma. The scenes between Joel and Leda, alone at home while family members are out of town, are quite graphic.

Young people who never tire of reading the same story over and over will probably enjoy this book. It has little to recommend it as a good book, however.

Jane G. MacDonald, in a review of "Beginner's Love," in The Book Report, *Vol. 2, No. 4, January-February, 1984, p. 35.*

BIZOU (1983)

Bizou is a French child born of a black American woman, Tranquility, who went to model in Paris and married a well-known photographer. After his death she stayed because the French, according to Tranquility, are much more tolerant on racial matters. Bizou, then, is quite cosmopolitan as she embarks on an American vacation with her mother. But then her mother disappears, leaving Bizou in the charge of Nicholas, a just-met fellow traveler who is about to start med school. He is decent enough to aid Bizou in a search for Tranquility, whose trail is dim, for she has refused to speak to Bizou about who her family is and why she cut contact with them. Nicholas and Bizou's tracking brings them some answers about herself and her mother, plus the discovery of some family she never knew she had. The story moves easily, and Bizou's dilemma is one that holds interest. Klein's development is a bit pat: Nicholas is a little too good to be true. Also, there is the occasional obscenity and almost obligatory portrayal of unconventional lifestyles that one expects from Klein. However, she is a practiced hand at keeping readers afloat. Never deep and sometimes irritating, this is nevertheless very readable and full of popular appeal.

Denise M. Wilms, in a review of "Bizou," in Booklist, *Vol. 80, No. 4, October 15, 1983, p. 360.*

Klein's popular fast pace will attract readers unconcerned with her bland style, shallow characterization and an astoundingly unrealistic plot. She uses the problems of racism and child abandonment to make her story relevant, but fails to deal with them in any significant manner.

Anne Connor, in a review of "Bizou," in School Library Journal, *Vol. 30, No. 3, November, 1983, p. 94.*

The author's ear for dialogue remains true in the new novel, and her characters are engaging people. What happens to them, however, strains belief; and the development continually interferes with our growing absorption with the characters. . . . Bizou's feelings of betrayal ring true, as do her reactions generally, although readers may find cloying her confidences to the reader about her boyfriends. Her response to the superficial aspects of American culture provides an interesting perspective. The intricacy of personal relationships is believably presented; love is a complicating, rather than resolving, component. The ingredients of the novel have been assembled with sureness, but the outcome is disappointing.

Charlotte W. Draper, in a review of "Bizou," in The Horn Book Magazine, *Vol. LX, No. 1, February, 1984, p. 62.*

BARYSHNIKOV'S NUTCRACKER (1983)

Baryshnikov's Nutcracker is based on the American Ballet Theatre's production. The story is told in the first person by Clara, a 14-year-old child who yearns to be a woman. She breaks the spell that turns the Nutcracker into a handsome prince; travels to his kingdom and reluctantly returns home at the behest of her Uncle Drosselmeyer who warns, "You must finish childhood, dear Clara." The full-color photographs of the ABT production do capture the magic of the tale but they are almost swamped by the sentimental and detailed text. Warren Chappell's *Nutcracker* (1958) is still a superior introduction to the ballet and music, but readers (and fans) may enjoy having this contemporary version in book form.

Amy Kellman, in a review of "Baryshnikov's Nutcracker," in School Library Journal, *Vol. 30, No. 6, February, 1984, p. 72.*

ANGEL FACE (1984)

Yet another saga of a New York teen, this is mixed with a hodgepodge of most of the topics currently in vogue, each touched upon, but none really dealt with. Main character Jason, pet-named Angel Face because of his angelic appearance, is intelligent but not much of an achiever. He's heavily into dope; is preoccupied with sex, though he never gets past heavy petting, and is not above stealing, an act for which there is little remorse and no recriminations. His mom, unable to deal with her divorce, slams her car into an embankment and kills herself. Dad's "sex life started at age 45, in any real sense of the word"; brother Ty lives with his girlfriend at her parents' house; sister Andrea, a law student, is having an affair with a married man; sister Erin is an anorexic; black best friend Otis is sleeping with old-country Italian Marcella, who had an abortion last year, and on, and on . . . , Klein hits them all, even jokes about the frigidity of Jewish girls. But what is the point? What could have been an insightful treatment of some all-too common traumas is instead a melange of hip that comes off as insipid.

Denise L. Moll, in a review of "Angel Face," in School Library Journal, *Vol. 30, No. 9, May, 1984, p. 90.*

One of the paradoxes of childhood today is that adolescence goes on and on, and coincidentally children, in the midst of this endless adolescence, must often take on the emotional responsibility for parents whose lives have fallen apart.

So it is in Norma Klein's new novel with Jason Lieberman, called Angel Face by his mother because of his blond curls when he was small. . . .

Jason is a thoughtful boy, identifiable in the annals of sensitive teen-agers with a gentle but irreverent sense of humor, a clear eye for recording the passage of family events, a healthy, unsatiated lust and a tendency to dull the edges of life with marijuana. He loves his mother. And he should. Fay is one of Norma Klein's fine characters—wonderful and terribly sad, a woman for whom one-line jokes are the only defense against a life she can't put in order. After his father leaves, Jason has all he can handle with Fay. What he wants, however, is his own love affair, and when he finds it with his classmate Vicky, he becomes less satisfactory as a companion to his mother, which leads to disaster.

There are fine scenes in **Angel Face,** equal to any of the best scenes in Miss Klein's lively, engaging books—poignant, full of energy and humor, a slide-show view of Jason's life as a teen-ager. Her characters have a kind of courage and wit, a sense of the slender line between laughing and crying. They are resilient, ready to fight.

Angel Face is a serious book about the complicated relationship between a boy seeking his own romance and a mother who needs him to compensate for the desolation of her failed romance. The difficulty is that in the end Jason and his story are shortchanged. The story slips away from the real consequences of a tender and impossible relationship between Jason and his mother in which he cannot, of course, save her from herself and becomes too slight, less than its promise and intention. There is more to be said than Miss Klein has written. Her voice is strong as always but the real story between a mother and son is profound and should make us wonder more than we do.

> Susan Richards Shreve, in a review of "Angel Face," in The New York Times Book Review, *June 17, 1984, p. 24.*

Each of these books [*Angel Face, Here's Looking at You Kid* by Jane Breskin Zalben, and *Three Friends* by Myron Levoy] focusses on a young man's struggle to define himself, and each involves his quest for love and friendship. Each deals candidly with some real issues—suicide, divorce, sexual relationships, conflict with parents, peer pressure, the dilemmas of finding the "Right Girl." . . .

My ninth grade female friend, after burrowing through these three novels, said, "Adults think they know what goes on in a teenager's mind. But these stories don't seem real to me. They try to be real, but they're not."

My issues are different. I am bored with YA novels that focus on a boy's experience growing up, while girls, though presented as more assertive of late, are still basically accessories to a male's happiness. I am distressed by novels like Norma Klein's, which rather explicitly deal with sexual intercourse, but omit any information about birth control. I am depressed when I repeatedly see female characters who demonstrate that girls with brains can't be beautiful or totally sane, or that girls with good looks can't be intelligent. (All three books imply this!) And still, the control in relationships is maintained by boys, though these males seem to be more sensitive than those in earlier teenage novels.

I don't want to be entirely negative. These novels are reasonably well written and rather interesting; the issues facing the protagonists are contemporary, and families are not presented as "happily ever after" units. However, I'd like to see some YA novels with strong, assertive young women; situations that raise contemporary problems but present realistic solutions; and choices about women that go beyond "the brains or the body?" I'd also like to see novels with diverse economic settings, and with characters that reflect our pluralistic society.

> Jan M. Goodman, in a review of "Angel Face," in Interracial Books for Children Bulletin, *Vol. 15, No. 7-8, October-December, 1984, p. 33.*

SNAPSHOTS (1984)

Sean's friend Marc Campbell thinks his eight-year-old sister Tiffany would be a great model à la Brooke Shields. To convince his father of that fact, he enlists Sean to help him shoot some pictures of her with Mr. Campbell's expensive camera. Tiffany poses in her bathing suit (it's a hot summer day) and the boys await the day when the pictures come back from the lab. What happens instead is that the lab turns the pictures

over to the DA's office as possible child pornography, and the boys and their parents are subjected to an investigation and all its inherent emotional trauma before being cleared. The story is not an exposition of the child pornography racket, although something of its nature does come out in the story. Rather, the focus is on the thoughts and emotions of the boys themselves, particularly Sean, who does not get along well with his father. Klein takes pains to present him as an entirely normal young boy whose worries over his short size, what to do about girls, and how to handle his father are typical of anyone his age. The milieu is upper-middle-class Manhattan, an atmosphere that allows at least one arguably gratuitous scene––an overheard street conversation sporting the words "f —— me"—to seem less like provocation than casual scene setting. Klein's writing skills work to unfold the story smoothly, and she is deft at capturing the textures of the social strata in which her characters move. She's taken a very topical subject and turned it into an acceptable story that considers the ramifications of the boys' innocent but thoughtless behavior. A likely pick for popular reading.

> Denise M. Wilms, in a review of "Snapshots," in Booklist, *Vol. 81, No. 5, November 1, 1984, p. 369.*

[With] the click of a camera's shutter, Sean's perceptions of himself and his family are altered. Sean's conservative father plays out his own emotional insecurity in his suspicion of his son's intent, haranguing him all the way to an interview with the D.A., where gradually his loyalties become clear. Sean, who tells the story in relaxed first person, is solid and self-directed. He has a lot to handle: he has chosen to have a bar mitzvah, although his family is non-practicing, and he is struggling to establish his first romance. Nonetheless, he responds convincingly to the added burden of fear and guilt. Around him, a credible cast of family and friends react realistically to his crisis. In particular, his relationship with Joanie, his girlfriend, is drawn with sensitivity. If there are problems, they are that Klein uses a brief smattering of street language that adds nothing to the plot, and that *Snapshots* is overloaded with types: arch-conservative father, feminist sister, blind parent, female rabbi. However, the types avoid stereotype and the plot carries their weight. At book's end, the repercussions of a rather humdrum event fade. But Sean's maturity and the declared love and respect of his father remain. In *Snapshots,* Klein blends the themes of social responsibility, adolescent growth and father-son tension to achieve a portrait with vitality and significance. (pp. 90-1)

> Carolyn Noah, in a review of "Snapshots," in School Library Journal, *Vol. 31, No. 4, December, 1984, pp. 90-1.*

The chief plot thread is interesting although it's handled rather heavily; otherwise the writing is very good: smooth, well-paced, convincing as the voice of a bright young adolescent. The book is given color by minor plot threads, including Sean's first substantial relationship with a girl and his militant sister's successful campaign to have the bar mitzvah conducted by a female rabbi.

> Zena Sutherland, in a review of "Snapshots," in Bulletin of the Center for Children's Books, *Vol. 38, No. 6, February, 1985, p. 110.*

GIVE AND TAKE (1985)

Midwestern high-school senior Spence is smart, athletic,

good-natured, and very handsome. Because he wants to help people, he becomes a sperm-bank donor. But in the summer before college, he meets Audrey, two years older, divorced, sexually experienced, and relaxed, and he learns about making a "real woman happy." Meanwhile, he's pursued by his ex-classmate Taffy, whose unwanted pregnancy has trapped her in a teenage marriage. This is very much a formula coming-of-age novel, as Spence learns moral lessons about life and death and caring, and about not asking too much of himself. But he is a likable hero, well-meaning and confused, and Klein honestly depicts the difficulty and the ambivalence as well as the pleasure of sexual relationships.

> *Hazel Rochman, in a review of "Give and Take," in Booklist, Vol. 81, No. 20, June 15, 1985, p. 1436.*

Klein packs a wallop. The many stresses that confront [Spence] are portrayed honestly and realistically. It made me go back in my own mind to re-live the uncertainty of college and the death of a parent. The sexual scenes are not graphic, they are delicately handled. There is much to grapple with here, but it is worth it.

> *Annette Hizny-Fisher, in a review of "Give and Take," in Best Sellers, Vol. 45, No. 6, September, 1985, p. 239.*

There is so much going on in Klein's latest novel—at least 7 subplots involving 13 or more characters—that all of them must be treated superficially. That there are more than just "broken hearts" to worry about in adult relationships could be considered the primary theme of *Give and Take*. . . . In short, Klein attempts to people her book with many interesting characters and ends up overloading readers. Yet the book moves quickly, the dialogue flows naturally, and all the action keeps readers turning the pages. The sex is similar in quantity and quality to *It's Okay If You Don't Love Me* (1977).

> *Fran Wolfe, in a review of "Give and Take," in School Library Journal, Vol. 32, No. 1, September, 1985, p. 146.*

THE CHEERLEADER (1985)

Ninth grader Evan Siegal, who tells the story, is a really nice boy, friendly and helpful and willing to risk teasing if the cause is right—and it seems to him the cause is indeed right when a classroom discussion focuses on the fact that nobody ever spurs the girls' teams on with cheers as they do the boys'. Evan is derided by most of the other boys when he and his buddy offer to be cheerleaders; after they are so successful that girls ask for their autographs, Evan and his friend Karim are besieged by offers from other boys who want to join them. This isn't totally believable (Karim's father is a Saudi Arabian millionaire and his mother an American fashion designer who makes the boys fabulous outfits in rockstar style) but it's totally enjoyable in a book that has, in addition to its nonsexist message, good friendship values and peer relationships.

> *A review of "The Cheerleader," in Bulletin of the Center for Children's Books, Vol. 39, No. 1, September, 1985, p. 11.*

Klein's new book is ostensibly about two boys who become cheerleaders to support the girls' sports teams, but a lot of other issues such as puppy love, and the effects of divorce enter in as well. Evan Siegal—sensitive, innovative, warm—is the kind of guy most girls wish for, but he seems too good to be true. . . . It's a pleasant change to see a first-person novel written from a boy's perspective. This one, so light it could float, has wit and a certain style that buoys the appeal.

> *Ilene Cooper, in a review of "The Cheerleader," in Booklist, Vol. 82, No. 3, October 1, 1985, p. 263.*

Several factors make this a good novel for young people. The concerns of the characters are real and believable. Responses and emotions fit the situations. Even more important, the characters and their relationships ring true, especially within the two main families. The romantic reticence of Evan's older brother Gary and the infatuation of Rachel's younger sister when Evan becomes a school celebrity are pleasant diversions. Young readers will put down *The Cheerleader* feeling good about themselves and life in general. (p. 399)

> *James A. Phillips, in a review of "The Cheerleader," in Best Sellers, Vol. 45, No. 10, January, 1986, pp. 398-99.*

FAMILY SECRETS (1985)

Family friends since childhood, Leslie and Peter become lovers in their senior year in high school. But their relationship is strained when their respective parents divorce and Peter's father marries Leslie's mother. In alternating first-person narratives, the young people describe the difficulties of their relationships with their families and their fluctuating feelings for each other. Harvard-bound Peter loves Leslie but finds it hard to show it. Shy and overweight, he has always been rejected by his shallow father. Leslie finds Peter "solid and round and comfortable and gentle"; but, as he holds back from her in the first troubled months after the divorce, she sometimes sees him as sloppy and condescending. A demanding emotional part in the school play helps her with her confused feelings, as she comes to see that her stepfather's flirtatious manner toward her—the only role he knows with women—is contributing to her strain with her mother. As always with Klein, there is frank talk about sex and relationships; in fact, the earnest discussions of personal fulfillment are sometimes tedious, especially the angst of the parents. But no easy solutions are offered to Peter's and Leslie's problems of independence, love, and identity; and this is a welcome exploration of some of the complex undercurrents beneath the romantic stereotypes.

> *Hazel Rochman, in a review of "Family Secrets," in Booklist, Vol. 82, No. 3, October 1, 1985, p. 216.*

Chapters are told alternately by Leslie and Peter, giving depth and immediacy to the personalities and problems of two adolescents who are vulnerable, confused, and angry but who grope their way to a deeper affection and more permanent relationship from which both gain security. Although at times slow-moving, the story is strong in the sharpness of its characterization, the candor of its observations, and the smoothness of its writing style, notable for the fidelity of its dialogue.

> *A review of "Family Secrets," in Bulletin of the Center for Children's Books, Vol. 39, No. 3, November, 1985, p. 50.*

In an attempt to present two first-person points of view the author alternates the perspective for each chapter. This style is not entirely to my taste. It requires a small but significant adjustment at the beginning of each chapter which disrupts the flow and continuity of the story line. On the plus side, it does achieve the author's goal.

This book is most successful in its presentation of realistically ambivalent feelings between the various couples and an honest look at modern family dynamics. The two principal characters may not treat each other especially well but they are individuals with a sense of self-worth.

With the exception of Peter, whose relationship with his father has no discernible positive dimension, all the relationships between parent and child, and siblings and friends, explore both the positive and negative aspects of maturing relationships. Indeed, the extreme ambivalence revealed in the feelings of the young lovers for each other is a good example of the heightened intensity of post-adolescent feelings. In many respects this ambivalence mirrors the adult relationship portrayed in the book. The difference is that the adults are less willing to "let it all hang out."

The author is adept at drawing out the nuances of family relationships. Jealousy and covert sexual play are among the factors explored. How one adjusts to the artificial designation of roles in a re-assembled family is a dilemma a great number of young people may identify with. The mature youthful readership for whom the book is intended may also identify with the feelings of sexual awareness, remorse, stupidity, loyalty, inferiority, specialness, and being cheated and loved that Peter and Leslie experience. But I wonder if they will find the resolutions to the various interpersonal conflicts is morally unappetizing as I did.

> *Jeanne Windle Friedrichs, in a review of "Family Secrets," in* Best Sellers, *Vol. 46, No. 3, June, 1986, p. 116.*

GOING BACKWARDS (1986)

Charles Goldberg has a lot going for him—yet he feels like a loser. He's talented enough to attend a special high school, but he sees himself as fat, socially inept, undirected, and with no hope of getting a girlfriend. To top things off, his grandmother, who has Alzheimer's Disease, has moved in. As her behavior grows increasingly bizarre, Charles tries to cope with his low self-esteem and to help his father with the agonizing question of his grandmother. Before they place her in a nursing home, though, she dies. Despite his father's extreme reaction, Charles thinks things are looking up. He goes off to college, falls in love for the first time—and then his father dies. But by then Charles truly has matured: he is able to cope with the death and to help his family as well.

The underlying theme of death in this powerful but occasionally uneven story is woven deftly into Charles' story without weighing it down. However, three pages from the end, when it's revealed that Dr. Goldberg had given his mother an overdose of sleeping pills, the moral question of euthanasia is glossed over, lessening the impact of the startling revelation. Still, the strength here is in the intriguing, skillfully drawn characters—a most appealing one being the housekeeper, pivotal to Charles' emotional growth.

A moving, humorous, and triumphant story of a boy surviving adolescence.

> *A review of "Going Backwards," in* Kirkus Reviews, *Vol. LIV, No. 19, October 1, 1986, p. 1517.*

Klein dispels several stereotypes about Jews, Koreans, blacks, the role of women, anorexic girls, everyday life in New York City, and the sex life of middle aged and older adults. Some items in this well written, realistic novel which merit discussion are Charles' sexual experiences, Mr. Goldberg (a pathologist) giving Charles Valium or Dalmane to help him sleep, Charles and his father drinking together, funeral customs which might seem oversimplified or irreverent to some readers, and euthanasia. The book in its simplicity and honesty reminds us all of the adolescent traumas we each faced growing up; universal, timeless revelations which young people still struggle to cope with today.

> *Clara Hoover, in a review of "Going Backwards," in* Voice of Youth Advocates, *Vol. 9, No. 6, February, 1987, p. 285.*

A character in Richard Graber's new novel, *Doc*, says "Alzheimer's is more than a sexy diagnosis-of-the-year.". . .

Though both [Klein and Graber] have done a competent job of documenting the clinical symptoms of the disease, Norma Klein has written the far superior novel. She understands perfectly how to re-create the life of a family—its habits, colors and flavors, the sound of its talk. Her unusual method is to set up a houseful of interesting people and then apply the heat to see how they and their relationships melt and shift in the pressure cooker. Here it works superbly. . . .

Though the novels vividly portray the effect of the disease on teen-age grandchildren, other more troubling aspects have been overlooked. Both families are headed by wealthy physicians for whom the cost of custodial care is not a serious financial burden. And the six to eight excruciating years of Alzheimer's usual duration are truncated in both books by manipulated deaths. . . .

Going Backwards sidesteps the question of the morality of euthanasia, a theme not appropriate here, but anticipates recent genetic discoveries concerning Alzheimer's when Charles says, "I hope they find a cure before we're that age."

> *Patty Campbell, in a review of "Going Backwards," in* The New York Times Book Review, *March 15, 1987, p. 29.*

OLDER MEN (1987)

In *Older Men*, Klein confronts her own intense adolescent relationship with her psychiatrist father through the guise of the story of sixteen-year-old Elise and her adoring Daddy. But it is important to remember that this is exorcism, not autobiography. Unlike Klein, who only realized the obsessive nature of their tie long after her father's death, Elise, in the end, reluctantly comes to understand how to free herself.

But the price is high. Since childhood she has reveled in the exclusive attentions of her charming, zany father—his lavish compliments and gifts, their Saturday excursions full of impulsive adventure, his witty conversation over expensive dinners. A respected cardiologist at a large hospital, Dr. Nate Dintenfass turns the full power of his charm on his daughter and she, flattered and bewitched, finds her identity in his eyes. "I am valued," she thinks. Both of them are too sophisticated

The Klein family, 1984: husband Erwin, daughters Katie and Jen, and Klein.

for there to be any question of physical incest, but his psychological power over her is seduction, nevertheless.

Nate brings none of this charm to bear on his wispy and neurotic wife, June, and life with this difficult man has undermined her mental health. One night she wanders into Elise's room, dazed and disoriented, and spills out her resentment and jealousy. Nate is outraged and immediately has her committed to a mental hospital. . . .

At her summer job in a Village bookstore, Elise encounters bohemian Kara, the daughter of Nate's first wife, and becomes friends with her and her brother Tim. Elise is shocked to discover that Kara, too, was their father's darling until she showed signs of independence. (p. 51)

Tim (who has also spent time in a mental hospital) and Kara urge Elise to stand up to Nate to free her mother. She tries half-heartedly, but always falls back into the comforting haven of his approval. When the two of them go away for the usual family vacation in Maine, she feels as if she has abandoned her mother, but says nothing to disturb the surface tranquillity of their days on the beach. One evening Tim and Kara appear, much to Nate's outrage, and that night Elise and Tim make love in tingling apprehension of discovery by him. Elise remembers Kara's advice: "Every time you defy him, you'll bleed and feel pain, but you'll grow a little." Her resolve is strengthened, and when June escapes from the hospital Elise is at last able to confront her father and to prevent him from returning her mother to captivity.

Later in the fall, at college, she contemplates her new freedom and her lackluster continuing affair with Tim. "Will all my choices in men be in relation to my father," she wonders, "the connection between us no less strong despite my seeming to have broken away?"

The bare bones of the plot are insufficient to show the thematic richness of the novel. Dark Freudian implications are layered thickly, mental illness is explored as a form of sexist oppression, feminism becomes the rebellion of Electra. There is even an impassioned set piece on the falseness of the teenage romance novel. Yet, in spite of all this weight the story moves swiftly; the dialogue is witty; the characters, especially Nate, are complex and clearly drawn. This is Klein at her best—the most characteristic and the most moving and substantial work she has written yet. (pp. 51-2)

Patty Campbell, in a review of "Older Men," in Wilson Library Bulletin, *Vol. 61, No. 9, May, 1987, pp. 51-2.*

Klein attempts to endorse trendy values through Elise's experiences: casual "first sex" in an amusement park with a boy she's just met; awe of her "cool" stepsister, who gives her marijuana; and a casual sexual relationship with her stepbrother. But incest is a serious issue. By using overdrawn, stereotypical characters and melodramatic situations, Klein exploits its sensual appeal instead of giving it the serious exploration it merits—something that, as a compelling storyteller, she might have achieved. (p. 721)

A review of "Older Men," in Kirkus Reviews, *Vol. LV, No. 8, May 1, 1987, pp. 720-21.*

Elise's sexual experiences, first with a stranger and later with Tim, are described in some detail, with only a passing, ambiguous reference to birth control and no mention of the possibility of contracting AIDS; this seems irresponsible. Klein creates a strong sense of place, but her characters never fully occupy the vivid landscape. They are hollow types that fall into three categories: manipulators, the manipulated and the once manipulated, now embittered. Elise's break with her father shows a transformation in attitude that is both incredible and unmotivated.

A review of "Older Men," in Publishers Weekly, *Vol. 231, No. 21, May 29, 1987, p. 80.*

MY LIFE AS A BODY (1987)

Intelligent, shy Augie, a senior in high school, is fairly certain that romance will never play a part in her life. When she reluctantly agrees to tutor Sam, the new boy at school, she never dreams that they will fall in love. Sam is confined to a wheelchair and may be permanently brain damaged as the result of a car accident. As they work together, Augie and Sam establish a tentative friendship; after Sam's brain functions return to normal, he and Augie become sexually involved. Their relationship continues through the rest of their senior year, and then falls apart during their first year away from one another at college. Fortunately, Sam's disability is never the sole focus of this novel: if anything, greater emphasis is placed on Augie's growing acceptance of her own sexuality. Klein has avoided the pitfalls of didactic problem novels and instead has sensitively depicted the coming of age of two unusual characters. A literate, very readable and sexually explicit account of the complex social lives of privileged New York City teenagers.

A review of "My Life as a Body," in Publishers Weekly, *Vol. 232, No. 14, September 25, 1987, p. 112.*

The real problem with this novel about the sexual life of a 17-year-old intellectually and artistically gifted teen is not its modestly titillating sexual explicitness, its cultural stereotyping, or the fact that the protagonist sleeps first with a handicapped boy and later with one of her college professors; it is that the novel (and the sex in it) is ultimately so passionless.

While it's clear that Sam and Augie love each other, there seems little ecstasy in their love, and even less in Augie's discovery of her sexuality. And her college affair is so civilized and detached, it's practically sexless. By the end, Augie seems merely to be a survivor in an age when teens know how to have sex but cannot experience joy.

A review of "My Life as a Body," in Kirkus Reviews, *Vol. VI, No. 21, November 1, 1987, p. 1576.*

The story's theme is based on a question raised in Sam's and Augie's English class at the very beginning of the novel: What does Virginia Woolf mean by "telling the truth about my own experiences as a body"? In Augie's and Sam's relationship, logical minds and sexual bodies are often at odds, and their bodies are much more forgiving than their minds. Despite his new disability, Sam is sexually more at home with his body; Augie is much more hesitant. Sam's physical condition, in fact, makes him seem to her to be "neuterized" and therefore safe, just as later her college friend Gordon, a homosexual, is safe. The lives and loves of Gordon and of Augie's lesbian friend Claudia provide other looks at the same mind/body question.

Augie and Sam are not typical teenagers. They are brighter and more sophisticated than most, but because of Klein's excellent character development they are authentic. Stereotypes (e.g., kids in California are sexually precocious) and coincidences (e.g., the professor that Augie eventually becomes involved with is the ex-husband of the woman who becomes Claudia's lover) mar an otherwise thought-provoking and highly discussible book.

The attitude toward sex portrayed by Klein is generally liberal, but sex is neither accidental nor without emotional consequences. This is, in fact, a very serious look at the sexual decision-making and growth of real individuals. (p. 26)

Judith A. Sheriff, in a review of "My Life as a Body," in Voice of Youth Advocates, *Vol. 11, No. 1, April, 1988, pp. 25-6.*

NOW THAT I KNOW (1988)

As she did in **Breaking Up,** Klein here looks at the problem of having a homosexual parent, in this case, a father. Nina, thirteen, is a "J. C. K." (joint custody kid) who spends half the week with each parent. Her mother is bitter and lonely; her father somewhat better off, spending a lot of time with best friend Greg. That Dad and Greg are lovers will be sooner apparent to readers than to Nina, who finds out on her birthday that Greg is moving into her father's apartment. Smoothly, if with little depth, this tells of Nina's fears—of becoming second in her father's heart, of his getting AIDS—and her eventual (and too abrupt) adjustment to the situation. While not sexually explicit, this is familiar Klein mood and milieu—an Upper West Side populated by kids much smarter than their parents. Along the way, Klein tosses out a couple of bits of sexual information so incomplete as to constitute misinformation: friend Dara sees a TV special on teen pregnancy and says "Did you know there's only one day every month someone can get pregnant? Maybe even less. Maybe just twelve hours," and, at another point, Dad tells Nina that she doesn't have to worry about his getting AIDS because he's only slept with Mom and Greg, which fails to take Greg's sexual history into account. (pp. 158-59)

Roger Sutton, in a review of "Now That I Know," in Bulletin of the Center for Children's Books, *Vol. 41, No. 8, April, 1988, pp. 158-59.*

Klein's trendy story is fleshed out with strongly contrasted characters: Nina's father and his lover are comfortably monogamous "straight" gays, and her mother is a trifle hard to get along with and still shell-shocked over the divorce (at the story's beginning she still does not know that her ex-husband is gay). For contrast, there is Nina's friend Dara, who absolutely hates her divorced father, and Dara's mother, who has had more boyfriends than she can count. The subject of AIDS naturally comes up, though the story is no forum for AIDS information; in fact, the assertion of Nina's father that he is safe from the disease because of his monogamous lifestyle is misleading—what about his lover's past history? Klein is a smooth writer, and her dialogue (including several profanities) rings true to Nina's New York milieu. The positive portrayal of a gay parent is a definite plus; and although the subject matter here is inherently sensational, Klein tells her story in understandable terms and without exploitation. This will have a good deal of popular appeal, giving its message of understanding all the more import.

> *Denise M. Wilms, in a review of "Now That I Know," in* Booklist, *Vol. 84, No. 15, April 1, 1988, p. 1350.*

This is a highly charged situation, yet readers are never drawn emotionally into the story. Nina's reaction to discovering that she has a gay parent is more intellectual than emotional. She verbalizes, but she isn't convincing in her reactions. There is no strong feeling from Nina, no likely adolescent concern for what others might think. Nina grapples more with the fear that she'll be displaced in her father's affections than with his sexual preference, and she never sorts out whether her temporary avoidance of her father is because he is gay or because she is jealous of this relationship. Unusual for a YA novel, the adult characters are given more dimension here, while the teenagers remain somewhat flat. Nina's mother is cynical but vulnerable, disappointed with her life; her father is an honest and caring man, comfortable with what he has discovered about himself, but fearful of losing his daughter's love. A sensitive subject is handled too matter-of-factly here to be convincing.

> *Deborah Locke, in a review of "Now That I Know," in* School Library Journal, *Vol. 35, No. 9, June-July, 1988, p. 117.*

Hugh Lofting

1886-1947

English author and illustrator of fiction and poetry.

Regarded as one of the most original as well as one of the most controversial writers of children's literature, Lofting is best known as the creator of Doctor Dolittle, a courageous and compassionate nineteenth-century physician who gives up his practice in order to learn the language of animals and to attend exclusively to them. Lofting wrote twelve books about Doctor Dolittle which take him from his country home in Puddleby-on-the-Marsh to a variety of exotic and exciting places, including the moon. Dolittle's kindly nature leads him into a series of dramatic, often dangerous adventures from which he is rescued both by his ingenuity and by the animals and humans he has helped. Usually considered highly inventive works which successfully blend fantasy and accurate scientific facts in narratives filled with adventure and humor, the *Dolittle* series is acclaimed both for its literary and philosophical attributes. An engineer, architect, prospector, and surveyor who traveled extensively before settling in the United States, Lofting began the stories of Doctor Dolittle as letters to his children from the trenches of France, where he served in the British army during World War I and became outraged with the poor treatment received by the horses and other animals used in the war. This impassioned belief in decency and respect for the rights of others, no matter who or what they are, underscores the *Dolittle* series and is reflected in the character of the doctor, who is considered one of the most endearing and enduring figures in juvenile literature. Written in a prosaic yet lively style and illustrated with black and white pictures and color plates which are often considered more delightful than the stories for their expressiveness and charm, the *Dolittle* books become increasingly serious as the series continues, reflecting Lofting's preoccupation with war and less optimistic attitude toward the actions and attitudes of humanity. However, the works are usually regarded as superior nonsense as well as especially effective promotions of world peace and understanding.

The *Dolittle* books feature a variety of anthropomorphic animals credited with being true to their animal natures despite their human qualities. Lofting's human characters are fewer in number, but it is their presentation that brings Lofting the most controversy. Although Lofting sympathetically describes Tommy Stubbins, Dolittle's nine-year-old assistant and the narrator of the series, and faithful companion Matthew Muggs, an ex-burglar, several observers have complained about the author's treatment of his African characters, notably Prince Bumpo, a comical figure who tries unsuccessfully to become white, and the author's inclusion of racially questionable epithets, storylines, and illustrations. The public opposition against the *Dolittle* books was so fierce that the series was allowed to go out of print in the early 1970s; the books remained blacklisted until 1988 when revised editions, which deleted the objectionable content, were printed. Accused of being a racist and a white supremacist, Lofting is also considered an accurate reflector of the intellectual and social attitudes of his period who never intended to malign blacks in his works. The *Dolittle* series is most often ac-

claimed for providing young readers with wise and unsentimental examples of tolerance, generosity, kindness, consideration, and other values in stories which are never condescending and always entertaining. In addition to his books about Doctor Dolittle, Lofting created two stories for younger children about Mrs. Tubbs and her human and animal friends; a humorous cautionary tale in verse; a book of poetry; and a fantasy for middle-graders which combines the supernatural with the historical. *The Voyages of Doctor Dolittle* won the Newbery Medal in 1923 and *The Story of Doctor Dolittle* was given the Lewis Carroll Shelf Award in 1958.

(See also *Something about the Author,* Vol. 15 and *Contemporary Authors,* Vol. 109.)

AUTHOR'S COMMENTARY

It was during the Great War, and my children at home wanted letters from me—and they wanted them with illustrations rather than without. There seemed very little of interest to write to youngsters from the front; the news was either too horrible or too dull. And it was all censored. One thing, however, that kept forcing itself more and more on my attention was the very considerable part the animals were playing in the World War and that as time went on they, too, seemed to become Fatalists.

Oftentimes you would see a cat stalking along the ruins thru-out a heavy bombardment, in a town that had been shelled more than once before in that same cat's recollection. She was taking her chances with the rest of us. And the horses, too, learned to accept resignedly and unperturbed the falling of high explosives in their immediate neighborhood. But their fate was different from the men's. However seriously a soldier was wounded, his life was not despaired of; all the resources of a surgery highly developed by the war were brought to his aid. A seriously wounded horse was put out by a timely bullet.

This did not seem quite fair. If we made the animals take the same chances as we did ourselves, why did we not give them similar attention when wounded? But obviously to develop a horse-surgery as good as that of our Casualty Clearing Stations would necessitate a knowledge of horse language.

That was the beginning of the idea: an eccentric country physician with a bent for natural history and a great love of pets, who finally decides to give up his human practice for the more difficult, more sincere and, for him, more attractive therapy of the animal kingdom. He is challenged by the difficulty of the work—for obviously it requires a much cleverer brain to become a good animal doctor (who must first acquire all animal languages and physiologies) than it does to take care of the mere human hypochondriac.

This was a new plot for my narrative letter for the children. It delighted them and at my wife's suggestion, I decided to put the letters in book form for other boys and girls.

I would like to make it quite clear that I make no claims to be an authority on writing or illustrating for children. The fact that I have been successful merely means that I can write and illustrate in my own way. Whereas, I have always maintained that there is no end to the variety of ways there should be. This would indicate that no one is a real authority, which I think is probably true.

There has always been a tendency to classify children almost as a distinct species. For many years it was a constant source of shock for me to find my writings amongst "Latest Juveniles" or "Leading Juveniles" or some such category.

It does not bother me any more now, but I still do feel that there should be a category of "Seniles" to offset the epithet.

There are two points which I wish to bring out as of primary importance in writing for children.

First, the writing must be entertaining and nothing may be allowed to interfere with or sacrifice that entertainment. There is never any excuse for "putting over" a preachment under the guise of entertainment. The main trouble with children's books is that many writers and many publishers feel that because they are catering to young minds that pretty much anything will do. They don't admit that, of course, but it's true just the same.

Another trouble with the average writing for children is that authors always seem to think they must "write down" to them. I have found that the intelligent children (and I'm afraid that the intelligent children are the only kind I am interested in) resent nothing so much as being written down to or talked down to. Which, of course, is very natural. We

adults resent also, if we think a superior intellect is patronizing us. What the intelligent child likes is being "written up" to. He wants promotion; he wants to get into the adult world; he wants progress; and I have always maintained and always will maintain that there is no idea too subtle, no picture too difficult to be conveyed to a child's mind, if the author will but find the proper language to put it in.

Another thing I have always maintained is that there should be just as many kinds of stories and books for children as there are kinds of stories and books for grown-ups. . . . It is really pathetic that the majority of writers for children feel that the only material children are interested in is pussy-cats and puppy-dogs. When really there is nothing in the whole wide world that they are not interested in.

This is proved by the fact that, when ever a book is a real success for children, it is also a success and an enjoyment for grown-ups. If writers would only get away from this classifying of children as a separate species, we would get very much better books for the younger generation. For who shall say where the dividing line lies, that separates the child from the adult? Practically all children want to be grown up and practically all grown-ups want to be children, and God help us, the adults, when we have no vestige of childhood in our hearts. (pp. 237-39)

Hugh Lofting, in an excerpt in The Junior Book of Authors: An Introduction to the Lives of Writers and Illustrators for Younger Readers from Lewis Carroll and Louisa Alcott to the Present Day, *edited by Stanley J. Kunitz and Howard Haycraft, The H. W. Wilson Company, 1934, pp. 237-39.*

GENERAL COMMENTARY

CHARLES C. BALDWIN

Palmer Cox is dead, but—such is the irony of an author's life—the tiny creatures of his fancy, inherited from Scottish and German folklore, live on in ever new editions of the Brownie books. Palmer Cox is dead and Kipling bowed down under the weight of the white man's fallen prestige. There remains then only Hugh Lofting among the chance visitants from that never-never country that was the home of Peter Pan and the goal of Barrie.

There remains Hugh Lofting.

In my first uncritical enthusiasm I hailed his four volumes as the best four in all the boiling of books sent me for review. Such pictures, I said; and such captions; and (every once in a while) such superlative nonsense. It was Edward Lear with a dash of Eugene Field—Oliver Herford, married and raising a family—Belloc with no axe to grind. Yet I was not mad enough, even, then, to follow in Hugh Walpole's phrases and say it was *Alice,* the immortal, ever-young, ever-wise *Alice;* but it was good—good of its kind, most good and better than most.

And why not as good as *Alice?*

Because, in the first place, few men can write as Lewis Carroll wrote. Take the *Jabberwocky,* and think of Mr. Lofting attempting anything like it. Or like the *Hunting of the Snark.* Or those gravely serious lines that tell of the old man sitting on the gate, the old man who fired the brooks and mumbled to himself.

There is rhythm to Lewis Carroll's prose as there was rhythm to his verse; and purpose to his books as there is style.

And Carroll was more than a story-teller—he was a great critic of life and of literature. His parodies are exact. They touch the dross in Robert Southey and Isaac Watts—who wrote that drivel about "the voice of the sluggard"—they improve with laughter the solemn platitudes of fools.

Lofting writes facilely of impossible adventures. He does not deal, as Carroll did, in exact images. A good half of his fancy has no counterpart in real life. Should he get his characters into some inescapable dilemma he need merely invent their way out. He does not have to abide by any rules or speak in anything but abstractions.

And so his books lack form; and already I am tired of them. They seem shipshod, written on and on simply because their author has a contract with the newspapers. There was only so much of Alice as there is only so much of Falstaff or Hamlet or you or me. There is a limit even to *Doctor Dolittle,* but Hugh Lofting doesn't know it. He believes the Doctor capable of a thousand incarnations. That's the way with enthusiasts and bores—they never know when a subject is exhausted.

Perhaps my weariness is a reaction from the too great expectations I felt on first opening Mr. Lofting's books. Mr. Lofting is so clever a draughtsman, so frugal and careful, I was certain that he knew that one line too many can spoil a fine picture.

Besides I am not referring to *The Story of Doctor Dolittle,* his first book, but to its endless sequels. In the first book he really creates a character in the quaint and placid little medico who, for want of other patients, takes to waiting upon the animals and from his parrot learns their language, going later on a journey to Africa to stem an epidemic that has broken out among the monkeys.

However, I must protest against Hugh Walpole's introduction—"Here is the first real children's classic since Alice"—for here is a very poor second to the *Just So Stories.* Say what you will (and I'll join you) against his politics, Kipling knows English. There are no such phrases in *Doctor Dolittle* as occur in every line of the *Just So Stories.* Nor are there any adventures to compare with the adventures of Mr. Henry Albert Bivvens, A. B., the mariner with his infinite-resource-and-sagacity. Or any occasions that can make us forget how the camel got his hump. Or any such curious souls, O Best Beloved, as the bulgy-nosed elephant's child.

But most, of course, with me, it is a matter of plain writing, hard down-right writing, common sense writing, every day writing; and there isn't a chance in the world of Mr. Lofting's ever touching, with simple words and few—

> Unless I go to Rio
> These wonders to behold—
> Roll down—roll down to Rio—
> Roll really down to Rio!
> Oh, I'd love to roll to Rio
> Some day before I'm old!

Or, in the exaggerated beauties of a familiar prose—

> Once upon a time, on an uninhabited island on the shores of the Red Sea, there lived a Parsee from whose hat the rays of the sun were reflected in more-than-oriental splendor. . . .

Mr. Lofting hasn't got it in him, that's all—any more than Doctor Dolittle has in him the hearty resignation of G. K. Chesterton's Noah—"I don't care where the water goes so long as it doesn't get into the wine." If we are looking for that sort of exuberance, just that quality of artistic restraint and humorous aptness, this side the Atlantic, we must look to Don Marquis for it—and in prose to Ring Lardner.

Yet it is after all, I presume, a matter of taste. There are those who refer to Charlie Chaplin as common and those who think they can silence Darwin with votes in the Georgia State assembly. But if there be more children to read *Doctor Dolittle* than read the *Just So Stories,* it simply bears out my contention that children are no wiser than their parents. (pp. 342-45)

Charles C. Baldwin, "Hugh Lofting," in his The Men Who Make Our Novels, *revised edition, Dodd, Mead and Company, 1924, pp. 342-47.*

JEAN F. HALBERT

Oh, yes, Hugh Lofting has caught the imagination of his readers; and his books make enthralling reading for both young and old. Doctor Dolittle is an impossible man, with impossible linguistic abilities, and still more impossible adventures. But in spite of the extravagant fantasy we are convinced that the author is not "trying it on us." In fact, we *insist* he is not "pulling our leg." We have succumbed to his charm—aye, his genius. Lofting believes in his characters, and we believe in the Author.

But we would have you know this is not mere blind trust in the magician's wand—there are reason and legitimate power behind it, for Lofting's books may be analysed after the manner of literary criticism. As a children's author, Lofting stands high in merit. Wasn't he awarded the Newbery Prize in 1922 for just one of the *Dolittle* books? He writes for children (but, praise be, there's no age limit!); he does not speak at them or down to them; he identifies himself with them, and yet remains the omniscient, mature author. He is serious, terribly serious, about this Doctor Dolittle, with his tall hat and small bag and sick animals. He must know his characters well—they are so very real; not just how they look, but how they feel, their conceits, their humour, and their separate characteristics. These animals, although they speak, act perfectly according to their species, besides, in addition, performing human tasks. They are not "just animals." They are individual personalities perfectly combining their animal attributes with the corresponding human traits in their household offices. Dab-Dab is indeed a shrewish, meticulous, fussy housekeeper if ever there was one, but withal—a duck, and she has feathers, and she waddles! Gub-Gub, author of the *Art of Eating,* is still a pig—albeit, a conceited one.

Is there no bottom at all to Hugh Lofting's repertoire of animals and their expressive names? Could he have found inspiration while prospecting in Canada, or engineering in West Africa, or when having to do with railways in Cuba and Havana; or would experience with the Irish Guards in Flanders or work with the British Ministry of Information in New York open up his wonder world? He might have thought his great thoughts while fishing or mountain climbing or skiing—or, if he wasn't bunkered too often, while golfing. But he is the father of a son and a daughter. Perhaps there lies the answer!

The Pushmi-pullyu, the Wiff Waff, the Jabizri beetle, Pippinella, Jamaro Bumblelily, the giant moth—these and their company—what poetry of sound!

His "humans," though prosaic, are imprinted in your mind. There they are—Tommy Stubbins, Matthew Muggins the cat's meat man, Joe the mussel man, Luke the hermit, Bumpo the black prince, Blossom the showman, and Doctor Dolittle catching cold with one ear under water trying to learn shell fish language! Of course, you know Puddleby—it may be in the West of England to you and in the East to me—but it is real.

Hugh Lofting is a king of story tellers. The material he puts into each of these **Dolittle** books is astounding. Ten volumes, mostly of 320 pages each and overflowing with stories, happy, sad, exciting, amusing, reminiscent. The countries visited are not confined to the known earth; his subject matter is very varied. Plant lore, archaeology, geology, entomology; there may be much truth hidden in these extravagant tales and descriptions.

Nor does the author put too great a strain on the reader's powers of imagination; he supplies drawings, genius in line. We'll be in no doubt when we meet the Singing Trees or the Moon Man.

Humour, beauty of thought and diction, and fantasy are positive qualities of this animal saga. Suppress a chuckle, if you can, when you recall Dab-Dab saying of negro Bumpo's white face and black body: "Serve him right if he does turn black again! I hope it's a dark black!" There is beauty in the thought of the swallows assembling for the return to England and winging John Dolittle's ship to safety. Sheer fantasy indeed, Jip scenting direction and smelling across the ocean, "tar, Spanish onions, kerosene oil, wet raincoats, crushed laurel leaves, rubber burning, lace curtains being washed—no, my mistake, lace curtains hanging out to dry, and foxes—hundreds of 'em—cubs."

The popularity of the **Dolittle Books** overshadows Hugh Lofting's other writings. **The Story of Mrs. Tubbs, Porridge Poetry,** and **Noisy Nora,** are for the very young, yet **Porridge Poetry** would be ambitious for a youngster who wasn't blessed with a long slippery tongue to get round such words as "lollipopinjay." But the alliterative rhyme and glorious jingle and the inspired drawings more than make up for hard words. **Mrs. Tubbs** is a useful peg on which to hang some more animal tales, while **Noisy Nora**—who chewed with her mouth open—is a delightful journey of this naughty girl from the table to the stable, the cowshed, pig-sty, barn and open field, before she learns her lesson of table manners.

As for the **Twilight of Magic**—here is a tale—of children and magic, stone-built castles, and dream knights, superstition and witchcraft, exciting adventure and beautiful fantasy. Is it a straightforward fairy tale—or is it an historical pen-picture of mediaeval times—and of their changing spirit?

Can Hugh Lofting, author, be catalogued and pigeonholed? Can the wind be restrained? (pp. 13-15)

> Jean F. Halbert, "Hugh Lofting—An Appreciation," in The Junior Bookshelf, Vol. 1, No. 1, November, 1936, pp. 12-15.

E. H. COLWELL

To the average child the name of Hugh Lofting means the **Dolittle** books, for it is as the creator of the immortal and lov-

able Doctor Dolittle that Hugh Lofting will be remembered. (p. 149)

It seems that an appreciation of Hugh Lofting inevitably becomes an appreciation of Doctor Dolittle, for it is round the quaint figure of this modest, genial little man that all nine **Dolittle** books revolve. Doctor Dolittle lived in Puddleby-on-the-Marsh with his circle of animal friends, Dab-dab the Duck, Polynesia the Parrot, Jip the Dog, Too-too the Owl, Gub-gub the Pig, Chee-chee the Monkey and Whitey the Mouse. Each of these animals is typical of his kind but each has individuality, each remains an animal in his habits and reactions. We only understand what the animals say because the Doctor and Tommy Stubbins interpret for us. The only human characters of any importance are Matthew Mugg the Cats' Meat Man, ex-burglar and faithful friend of the unconventional Doctor, and Tommy Stubbins who becomes the Doctor's assistant at the early age of ten. Tommy Stubbins is Doctor Dolittle's "Boswell" and it is he who writes about his master's voyages and keeps a record of his scientific experiments.

Doctor Dolittle is a remarkable man, a scientist who spends his life in careful experiments and research. He lived in 1839 when there was still much to discover and he takes his discoveries so seriously that we must too. His interests lead him far afield into many dangers which make excellent material for exciting stories. Whatever the danger, the little man remains calm, and however awkward the situation he always retains his top hat and little bag. He is a born reformer and speaks out fearlessly whatever the danger to himself. "Why don't you have windows in your prisons, you black-faced ruffian," he says hotly—scarcely the best way to placate his jailor! He is unworldly and incurably generous, so that to acquire any money is merely an excuse for spending it on some helpless animal. . . . His great sense of duty and unselfishness calls forth the affection of his friends, human and animal, who unite to protect him from the results of his own kindness. Doctor Dolittle is certainly Hugh Lofting's masterpiece, and because we cannot but believe in him we accept the animals who surround him also.

Mr. Lofting's style is lively and full of interest and humour. He is a born story-teller. Not only are the books as a whole interesting, but each tale within them, however short and unimportant, is well told. Always sufficient detail is introduced to make the story, however incredible our reason tells us it is, appear quite possible. The imaginative child accepts such stories, the literal child is persuaded by their verisimilitude.

To hold a child's attention an author must have a sense of the dramatic. This Hugh Lofting certainly possessed. Think, for instance, of the Doctor pursued by yelling savages and with a chasm before him. Here is a situation with possibilities and the author makes the most of them by providing a Bridge of Apes across which the Doctor walks complete with hat and bag. Or do you remember the lighthouse story in **Doctor Dolittle's Post Office?** The lamp in the lighthouse is out, the keeper is lying unconscious, the Doctor is in pitch darkness in unfamiliar surroundings and can't find the matches, and a ship is driving "full steam ahead" on to the rocks. A situation the suspense of which would delight any child.

Hugh Lofting's sense of atmosphere is good also. He can give a real feeling of eeriness. Tommy Stubbins and the animals, having seen the Doctor's signals from the Moon, await his return in tense silence. The moonlit garden is deserted and a

Illustration originally from The Story of Doctor Dolittle, *reproduced from* Doctor Dolittle: A Treasury, *written and illustrated by Hugh Lofting.*

strange humming can be heard far above in the sky. It grows louder and louder into a booming roar that seems to fill the air and, suddenly, a great shape passes between the watchers and the Moon. Then—all sound ceases and there is a dead silence. What is going to happen? The spellbound child is ready for anything.

For sheer fun and absurdity the ***Dolittle*** books are hard to equal. The child chuckles as he reads the funny names—Bumpo of Jolliginki or the Latin name of the Wiff-waff, "Hippocampus pippitopitus" or Bumpo's English learnt at Oxford where the algebra hurt his head and the shoes his feet. And what fun to see a horse wear spectacles and a dog choosing boots not to *wear* but to *chew*. Can you imagine anything more comic than to see the fat little Doctor, in his showy Matador clothes, doing hand-springs on the bull's horns while his buttons fly in all directions with the strain? Of course the author's illustrations help the fun, for they express so admirably the character of the Doctor and his friends. The little chunky figures with their rotundities are just right, and even in the moon landscapes Mr. Lofting manages to convey a sense of eeriness with a few simple lines.

What an inventive mind the author has. Why have *we* never thought of allowing animals to run the circus themselves, or having an Opera in which all the chief parts are taken by birds and the orchestra is a sewing machine, a cobbler's last, a chain and a razor strop? It would be an excellent idea, too, to use the migrating birds as postmen, and a Zoo in which

the locks of the cages were on the *inside* so that the animals need not look at humans if they didn't want to, seems only fair.

Finally, and most important of all, Hugh Lofting has a respect for children and never writes down to them. He is not afraid to introduce long words and scientific facts into Doctor Dolittle's conversation, and he does not hesitate to express some of his own philosophy of life. "We have no balancing or real protection of life," says the Doctor, "With us it is, and always has been, 'dog eat dog.' Fighting, fighting all the time." And at last when he has returned from the Moon and seen what he considers to be a more rational world with a prospect of eternal life, he says sadly, "We are always rushing, afraid we won't have time enough to do all the things we want to before we die . . . But if we never grow old? What then? Always young. All the time we want for everything . . . That's the thing I'm working for—to bring everlasting life down to the earth. To bring back Peace to Mankind, so that we shall never have to worry again—about time."

So we have our last glimpse of him, the little reading lamp throwing a soft light upon his serious, kindly face, as he tries to set the world to rights. We may not believe in the Doctor's panacea for our restless world, but there could have been no more fitting end for this story, and we can understand why Hugh Lofting made this his last book.

Doctor Dolittle has already been a valued friend for twenty-five years. It will be for the children's librarians to see that future generations of children are introduced to him. I like to think that there will always be children to enjoy his adventures, chuckle over his absurdities and learn from him something of the spirit of kindliness and unselfishness that permeates these unpretentious books. (pp. 150-54)

> *E. H. Colwell, "Hugh Lofting: An Appreciation," in* The Junior Bookshelf, *Vol. 11, No. 4, December, 1947, pp. 149-54.*

HELEN DEAN FISH

It seems quite suitable that the title of an article on Hugh Lofting's imaginative character, Doctor Dolittle, should follow the familiar formula of a biography of a great man of the real world. For Doctor Dolittle lives, as truly as any man whose portrait has been painted, and his "work" is, in its way, as important as that of any prelate or potentate.

That is, if one considers it important to create and make real for children a dream of complete understanding and complete helpfulness between men and animals. Hugh Lofting was possessed by a great ideal of world peace and understanding, and deep in his characterization of Doctor Dolittle and in the Doctor's relations with his animal friends lies what Hugh Lofting had to say on this subject. It is a simple message and a very old one. It could transform this old world: *do to others (every other, man and beast) as you would like to have them do to you.*

Doctor Dolittle is beloved by children, whether they are conscious of the reason or not, because he can be depended upon to follow this golden rule. It is his kindness that continually leads him into adventures in which he meets danger and excitement. And he always comes out victorious because he is not only courageous but ingenious. Thereby he is the sort of hero with whom children will go through thick and thin.

Doctor Dolittle is a good man for children to know because he stands for kindliness, patience and reliability, mixed with delightful humor, energy and gaiety, a combination rarely met and hard to beat. (pp. 339-40)

The reception of *The Story of Doctor Dolittle* in 1920—on both sides of the Atlantic—is well known. The little doctor of the animals was instantaneously and universally beloved and the reason why his appeal continued, unabated, through volume after volume for the next thirteen years was because he possessed all the vitality, completeness and variety of a truly great human character. All that Doctor Dolittle does and says exerts charm for his young readers, just as a rare and beloved personal friend never fails to claim a child's allegiance and response. (p. 341)

Doctor Dolittle is everyone's friend and everyone's reading. There are Dolittle lovers all over the world . . . and Dolittle lovers everywhere understand certain things. They know, for instance, that every animal is an individual; they are likely to be a little more patient and politer than other people—especially to animals. And they share a dream of peace in all the world that may come some day if children will learn to practice Doctor Dolittle's particular brand of loving-kindness and friendliness.

Doctor Dolittle is an anchor to windward in a world increasingly difficult for children. He invites his reader into an imaginative world that is secure and delightful and that contrasts reassuringly with the confusion of a day spent in listening to the radio, seeing a movie or television, or "reading" the comics. Doctor Dolittle is always entertaining and exciting, but he is a person who gives a sense of dependability in a noisy and uncertain world. (p. 346)

> *Helen Dean Fish, "Doctor Dolittle: His Life and Work," in* The Horn Book Magazine, *Vol. XXIV, No. 5, September-October, 1948, pp. 339-46.*

DOROTHY C. SHENK

What accounts for the almost universal appeal of Lofting's famous Doctor? There are many factors which should be considered when answering such a question. For some, the animals, who retain their identity as animals, have a unique charm. Because you are in on the secret of understanding animal language, you are a part of the enthusiastic, and for the uninitiated, the out-of-the-ordinary behavior of these characters. Others become John Dolittle fans because the humor is inherent in the situations, many of which are everyday concerns dealt with in unorthodox ways. Maybe you became a convert through your love of adventure. There is never a dull moment, for one dilemma follows another across the pages of the *Dolittle* books. Possibly you delight in the beautiful, descriptive language which appeals to your senses as you see, hear, smell, and feel the events of which you are part. It could be that you are given a new status as you share in one problem-solving council after another where every one's ideas are given ear though they be as insignificant as an ant or a maggot or as important as an equal of the great Doctor. You have a stake in the results of the planning sessions and the solutions are often most bizarre but extraordinarily effective. It is not unlikely that the mysteries which Lofting includes in his plots, lead you from book to book causing you to suspend breathing for a moment now and again.

Throughout Lofting's books you are an insider sharing secrets and plans and possess sources of information unknown to the general run of commonplace folks. Undoubtedly, for many people, one of the chief appeals is in the style of writing which confirms experiences and extends these experiences into new, uncharted areas. Then, too, in most of the adventuring, the ethics please because right for a given solution seems right and wrong is clearly wrong. Problems get solved, those who harm others get rehabilitated or get corrective punishments, and helpful behavior or ideas win approval. Because of the unstinting help the charming, high-hatted Doctor gives to all species, he always has co-operating members of the animal kingdom who wish to show their gratitude for kindnesses done them or their fellows. (p. 202)

Many books in which animals talk like people have been considered sentimental. . . . Lofting's animals are plausible and do retain their identity. Even though Jip, the dog, helps keep house, you read of him sweeping the floor with a rag tied onto his tail for a broom. When information is needed to find a lost ship or a raft adrift at sea, fast flying birds take on the job of scouting. What is more sensible than that? (p. 203)

One source of amusement you get in reading Lofting is through your superior wisdom. How often have audiences been convulsed with laughter when they know an answer in a game like *Twenty Questions* while the panel gropes for information. Lofting keeps his readers informed and how they can laugh as a result! The rats leave the sinking ship and tell the Doctor how long it will stay afloat. The readers chortle while he filibusters with the pirates as the ship sinks. What anticipation there is when the Emir of Ellebubu tries to starve Doctor Dolittle into submission in *Doctor Dolittle's Post Office.* The Emir and his tribe do not know about the white mouse who gnawed the ropes from the Doctor's hands and is using a rat hole to bring food, water, and soap to him that he will remain shaved, well fed, and healthy. We, like the white mouse, can climb into John Dolittle's pocket and hold our hands over our mouths to keep from laughing aloud at the consternation in store for the outwitted Emir and his subjects.

There is humor, too, in the ludicrousness of some of the situations. When leaving for Africa, all of the homey details are taken care of—the water is turned off so the pipes won't freeze, the shutters are put on the house, the house is locked, the key is given into the safe keeping of an old horse in the stable, the packing is done, the ship is provisioned, *but no one thought of finding out the way to Africa.* What relief! A swallow knows the way.

Chuckle, you well might, at some of the simple deductions of the characters. Bumpo, an African prince, felt that Oxford was all right except that the shoes hurt his feet and the algebra his head. Gub-Gub, the pig, took one look at the beds on the ship and declared them to be nothing but shelves.

If you like to do things and have exciting adventures, Lofting provides them in plenty. Doctor Dolittle finds life full of problems to solve at home and abroad. . . . Always in caring for one problem, he is confronted with a series of related situations which must be cured or solved. No matter whether he is working on a money-making venture to finance his humanitarian projects or giving his last cent to rush to the aid of his loved ones, there is an atmosphere of danger and urgency in his enterprises. One moment, in *Doctor Dolittle's Circus,* he is riding in a coach with a seal dressed as a woman (she keeps slipping off the seat) and fearful of detection, and the next he is pursued by angry citizens who think he has thrown a woman into the sea. Always the animals and humans, for whom he has performed a kindness, rescue him.

Even though your fascination for Lofting's books lies in the exciting adventures and the humor, you cannot escape the beauty of the descriptive passages and the charm of the illustrations. You cannot help visualizing ships going seaward from a river port when you read of their "huge brown sails towering over the roofs of the town, moving onward slowly like gentle giants that walk among the houses without noise". The names are delightful. Spidermonkey Island, The Cat's Meat Man, the Bag-jagderags, Dab-Dab, Gub-Gub, Too-Too are but a few.

Lofting's unusual illustrations add to the distinctiveness of his books. They belong as exclusively to his characters as Tenniel's famous characterizations belong to *Alice in Wonderland.* Almost always you see the eccentric Doctor pictured as a short, chubby, frock-coated individual wearing a high hat. Often he is shown carrying his medicine bag. Most of the pictures are line drawings of the animals which serve to highlight some key idea of the chapter. (pp. 203-04)

The real sense of belonging you get as a Lofting reader is through your participation in the planning sessions and problem-solving councils. Everyone who has an idea is given a respectful ear. Often the exigencies of a situation bring help from the least expected source. This is possible because the conferees know the attributes of their tribes, colonies, and clans and the potentials of their flocking, swarming, and champion members. If outstandingly acute hearing is needed, someone will think of one of nature's creatures with unusual hearing; if vision is required, a bird is often chosen. Always the ones who offer opinions which have a chance of solving the situation are commended for their help.

When Long Arrow, the scientist, was lost somewhere on Spidermonkey Island, a bird of paradise, a parrot, and a beetle were the ones who had ideas and performed acts bringing about his rescue. How incongruous that such seemingly unimportant animals should aid humans in a crisis! (p. 204)

Naturally some of the plans relate to solving the many mysteries which are contained in the *Dolittle* books. Sometimes the suspense-arousing episode is settled in the next few pages, but those, like the one in *Doctor Dolittle's Zoo* regarding Moorsden Manor, are stirring and sustained for quite some time. This mystery started with the finding of a corner of a will on a piece of parchment in a mouse's nest. A fire in the cellar of Moorsden heightened the enigma since the owner was furious at Dolittle for breaking a window to put the fire out. Why should an owner become violent when his neighbors saved a valuable home from destruction?

Hugh Lofting does not preach, but the decisions the Doctor and his friends make are not vindictive. The pirates, who had been molesting ships at sea and had killed and stolen many times, were left shipless on a fertile island with instructions to raise seeds for the canaries. An idle, shiftless tribe called the Bag-jagderags were conquered, and the peace treaty required that they live peaceably and help the other tribe whenever a famine or disaster arose. Later the two tribes united under one king. (pp. 204-05)

The thoughtless vanity of the women who belonged to the tribe of Goo-Goos almost resulted in the extinction of the green-breasted martins. Plans were made to punish these wicked women although the method chosen was equally hard

on the men. . . . Wrongs got righted, and improvement in relationships usually accompanied the adjustments.

There are many evidences of thoughtfulness of others in the day-by-day dealings of the Doctor and his friends. Also, there is a pleasing flexibility in adjustment to the standards of living of others. Once in a while there are grumblings about foods which are different from the usual fare, but even this is only an occasional forgetting of good manners. If the food is served raw, you eat it that way. John Dolittle does. (p. 205)

The sailor who loaned Doctor Dolittle a boat to sail to Africa got two boats in return plus a rubber doll for his baby. Throughout the books you find exclamations like, "Are you all right?" "I'm so glad to see you." Amiability is a comfortable trait and generosity is not scoffed at.

Children cannot help approving of the man who invited the dripping Tommy Stubbins into his home and told him not to stop in the rain to wipe his boots on the mat. These same children will be pleased to find that when their beloved doctor visits Tommy's house, he wipes his feet carefully on the mat. Yes, they want their parents to approve of him just as Tommy wanted his parents to like his new friend. (p. 206)

All in all, the books written by Lofting which do not have Doctor Dolittle in them would not make him well known in the field of children's literature. The only contribution of two of them is in their presentation of human woes and shortcomings; gluttony, strife, disdain for the opinions of others, aches, and haughtiness. These are made sport of in flowery language.

Lofting's *Dolittle* books, however, give free play to all of the human emotions in a way which makes kindness, cooperation, considerateness, friendliness, politeness, compassion, and affection laudable characteristics. Sneakiness, stinginess, dishonesty, rudeness, disregard for the opinions of others, boasting, too high an opinion of one's self, meanness, and cruelty are shown to be obnoxious traits. While the characters one likes best have mostly desirable tendencies, they are not white-washed, and some evidences of prejudice, envy, and self-interest show up occasionally. (pp. 206-07)

Although John Dolittle lives in England, Lofting's birthplace, his adventures make him a cosmopolitan; hence children around the world find him equally delightful. Through Dolittle, Lofting extends your experiences to encompass the sea, the air, and the earth. In time you go back to pre-Noah days with the great turtles. Physical limitations do not hold you back because you can ride beneath the waters in the sea snail, be fed by the birds of the air, cross ravines and rivers through the courtesy of ape and crocodile bridges, and get information about anything, anywhere, at any time by asking members of the animal kingdom for help. While you read you have no doubts!

Children are respected by Hugh Lofting. At no time are they talked down to. His helper is truly his helper even though a child. His characters are mainly animals but they are true to their identity. Respect for the rights and ideas of others are shown regardless of the size, shape, or insignificance of the person or animal. Wrong is righted through ingenuity, and the wrongdoer is often made to see the error of his ways. Punishments are unique, tricks are harmless, and corrections are usually conclusively effected. Humor is not at the expense of others since the situations themselves induce the laughter.

Lofting had the enviable ability to create and express his creativity in such a way that the child finds confirmation of his own beliefs of right and wrong, the funny and the ridiculous, and the importance of the seemingly unimportant. His lovable, short, top-hatted, and shabby-bagged John Dolittle remains unhurried and even-tempered through the most unprecedented situations. Here is a safe person to stir the child's imagination, amuse him, entertain him, and make him alert to the world in which he lives. . . . The unparalleled Doctor Dolittle, with his large family of animal friends, will extend your experience for you; but no matter how he stretches your credulity, he never snaps it back at you. (pp. 207-08)

> *Dorothy C. Shenk, "Hugh Lofting, Creator of Dr. Dolittle," in* Elementary English, *Vol. XXXII, No. 4, April, 1955, pp. 201-08.*

MARCUS CROUCH

The Story of Doctor Dolittle is a creative work of nearly the highest order. *Doctor Dolittle* was a product of the war. Hugh Lofting, an Englishman who had gone to live in America in early manhood, returned home to join the Army in 1916. In the trenches he found little to enliven his letters to his children at home, but he became deeply interested in the part that animals, particularly horses, were playing in the war. It seemed unfair that, when they were wounded, their loyalty was repaid with a bullet. Why were there no horse surgeons? Presumably because no doctor could speak horse language. Out of this thought came story-letters about Doctor Dolittle of Puddleby-in-the-Marsh, who gave up his human practice to devote himself to animals and who taught himself even the language of fishes. It was one of the very few entirely original ideas in children's books. . . . [A] whole mythology was developed around Doctor Dolittle and, at any rate in the later books, a considerable demand was made on the reader's memory. It might be said that the *Doctor Dolittle* books are better in conception than in execution; the narrative is often slow, but the stories are illumined by so fine a blend of humour and humanitarianism that they have won generations of devotees in spite of their obvious defects. The intensely serious fun, the consistency, the fundamental sanity of these books, (for the fantasy lies only in the basic idea, not in the working-out) all make a direct and enduring appeal to children. (p. 47)

> *Marcus Crouch, "The Years Between," in his* Treasure Seekers and Borrowers: Children's Books in Britain 1900-1960, *The Library Association, 1962, pp. 38-54.*

JOHN COLEMAN

Coming to [Doctor Dolittle] as I do, late, a parent in the swinging or sanctimonious Sixties, I take leave to wonder whether the tremendous charm with which Hugh Lofting invested him and his exploits is going to be enough to keep his reputation alive among children. It's not merely the chancy aberrations from our social taste that concern me now: I'm thinking of the data that turn up in every other Sunday supplement about dolphins and monkeys, stranger than fiction and more awakening. Meanwhile, the shy pushmi-pullyu, the verbose fidgit-fish ('I was one of a family of two thousand five hundred and ten'), the 'One-act Plays for Penguins' Dolittle wrote when his *Post Office* was well under way, all this humour and invention is unlikely to go to waste for a few more years.

After all, Dolittle does a lot. He is about such arduous concepts as mercy, self sacrifice, courage and honesty. The Lofting drawings have their own appeal, somewhere along a line between Thurber and the Hergé of Tintin. Money is remedially scorned. Dolittle constantly goes broke and, in the charming non-Dolittle romance, *The Twilight of Magic,* all the stirring deeds stem from two kids worried about their father's debts. English literature, from E. Nesbit to Lawrence's short story, *The Rocking-Horse Winner,* has been fond of this inspiration in poverty. Here, at least, Lofting is likely to live.

> *John Coleman, "Supervet," in* New Statesman, *Vol. 73, No. 1889, May 26, 1967, p. 727.*

DIGBY B. WHITMAN

All great writers for children share certain qualities, but each must have at least one uniquely his own. One of the qualities Lofting shared with others is love of all living things, which is inseparable from love of life itself. Talking creatures appear in every fine imaginative work for children from Aesop to *The Hobbit*. His humor, and his great gift of direct, mouth-to-ear prose, are no more than Lofting's portion of elements omnipresent in good juvenile literature. The quality most peculiarly his own is the impression—and the manner in which it is conveyed—that he is only a spectator among the rest of the Dolittle audience.

In this, Lofting is *sui generis.* Never has a writer been so helpless, and hapless, in the hands of his characters. When one of them breaks into a speech, Lofting seems to stop writing and listen. Nobody could be more astonished when an interruption, a side-issue, takes the plot completely off its track. When the Doctor asks a thrush if all thrushes have always sung their Evening Song the same way, Lofting seems poised to record a yes or no answer and get on with the story. But what's this? "Oh, no," says the thrush. "In medieval times it was quite different. We ended on the major then, not the minor. Like this, Toodle-oo-too-tu! instead of *Toodle-du-du-tee-too!* About the 13th century a good many fine singers rebelled against several of the old musical rules, including the one forbidding consecutive fourths in the major scale and sevenths in the minor. That was around the time of Magna Charta. Everybody was rebelling against something then. They didn't allow accidentals in melodies before that, either. Now we just throw them in regardless. . . ."—and so on for pages, while Lofting listens bemused, his story forgotten, his pen fallen from his hand. . . .

As it was Dickens' greatest glory that he could never describe a gentleman it was Lofting's that he could never describe a dumb animal. The only mean or stupid creatures in his books, or in his world, are people.

> *Digby B. Whitman, "Doctor of the Year," in* Book World—Chicago Tribune, *November 5, 1967, p. 4.*

ISABELLE SUHL

[*The following excerpt is from an essay by a New York City librarian which was the first major reevaluation of a children's classic for its racist content by the Council on Interracial Books for Children. Prompting a debate of the merits of the* Dolittle *books throughout the United States and Europe, Suhl's essay is regarded as being a major force behind the discontinuation of active promotion of the series throughout most of the 1970s and 1980s.*]

This is the Year of Doctor Dolittle. Movie producers, book publishers, manufacturers, promoters and publicists, headed by Christopher Lofting, second son and sole literary heir of Hugh Lofting, are trying to turn the little Doctor into a new Davy Crockett. . . .

Who is the "real" Doctor Dolittle? And what manner of man is his creator, Hugh Lofting, who for more than forty years has been hailed as a genius and his books as "classics" by teachers, librarians and children's book reviewers? Rarely has a word of criticism of him or his books been heard. As a result of careful examination of four of the most popular of these books, I charge that the "real" Doctor Dolittle is in essence the personification of the Great White Father Nobly Bearing the White Man's Burden and that his creator was a white racist and chauvinist, guilty of almost every prejudice known to modern white Western man, especially to an Englishman growing up in the last years of the Victorian age, when the British Empire was at its zenith. These attitudes permeate the books I read and are reflected in the plots and actions of the stories, in the characterizations of both animals and people as well as in the language that the characters use. Editing out a few racial epithets will not, in my view, make the books less chauvinistic.

Consider the situation in *The Voyages of Doctor Dolittle*. . . . In this story Doctor Dolittle, accompanied by Prince Bumpo, ten-year-old Tommy Stubbins, Polynesia the

From The Voyages of Doctor Dolittle, *written and illustrated by Hugh Lofting.*

parrot, Chee-Chee the monkey and Jip the dog, arrives on Spidermonkey Island off the coast of Brazil in search of the "Red Indian" Long Arrow, the world's greatest naturalist. On his first day on the island, Doctor Dolittle rescues Long Arrow and a group of Indians entombed in a cave and brings fire to the heretofore fireless Indians of Popsipetel. This makes him so popular that he is constantly followed about by crowds of admirers. "After his fire-making feat, this child-like people expected him to be continually doing magic." He continues to solve problem after problem for the Indians. In consequence of his good deeds they ask the "Mighty One" to become "not merely the Chief of the Popsipetels . . . but to be . . . the King of the whole of Spidermonkey Island." Reluctantly he accepts, and with elaborate and fitting ceremony he is crowned King Jong.

He becomes, of course, the hardest-working, most democratic king in all history and brings his new subjects many of the blessings of white civilization—proper sewerage, garbage collection, a pure water-supply system, etc. He locates iron and copper mines and shows the Indians how to use metal. He holds court in the morning to settle all kinds of disputes, teaches to thousands in the afternoon and visits sick patients in the evening. The Doctor would like to go home, but the tradition of noblesse oblige hinders him. (p. 1)

His animal friends have different ideas. Polynesia the parrot "had grown very tired of the Indians and she made no secret of it. 'The very idea,' she said . . . 'the idea of the famous John Dolittle spending his valuable life waiting on these greasy natives!—Why, it's preposterous!' " When Polynesia gets an idea, she acts on it. In a matter of a few days she works out all the details of their departure, comes up with all the answers to the Doctor's objections and even succeeds in getting Long Arrow to urge the Doctor to leave. With that the Doctor gives in. Laying his crown on the beach where his "poor children" will find it and know he has gone, he heads back for England to carry on his "proper work" of taking care of the animals of the world. (p. 5)

The most famous of all Lofting's African characters is Prince Bumpo. He is at the same time his most outrageous creation, but apparently he was dear to the author's heart because he is one of the few human characters to appear in several books. . . .

It is in *The Story of Doctor Dolittle* that the objectionable episode about turning Prince Bumpo white occurs. Briefly, for anyone who is not familiar with it, the story is this. Doctor Dolittle and his animal friends are on their way home after curing the sick monkeys of Africa when they are captured for the second time by the King of the Jolliginki, Prince Bumpo's father. Polynesia the parrot slips out of prison, sees Bumpo in the garden reading fairy tales and overhears him say, "If I were only a *white* prince!" She tells Bumpo that a famous wizard, John Dolittle, is in his father's prison. "Go to him, brave Bumpo, secretly . . . and behold, thou shalt be made the whitest prince that ever won fair lady!" Then she rushes back to the Doctor and convinces him that if they are to succeed in escaping prison he must fulfill her promise, no matter what tricks are necessary to do it. Bumpo arrives as planned and begs the Doctor to turn him white so that he can return to The Sleeping Beauty who spurned him because he was black. The Doctor concocts a mixture of liquids which turns the Prince's face white. In gratitude, Prince Bumpo lets them out of prison and gives them a ship in which to sail away.

This summary merely suggests the objectionable nature of the episode. It must be read in full to understand the depths of Lofting's racism. Every line is replete with insults and ridicule. Of course, this is not the only racist incident in the book. There are many others. The treatment of Bumpo's parents, the king and queen, is as bad as any described earlier. It is impossible for Lofting to depict Africans, be they kings, princes or ordinary people, with dignity and genuine human qualities. The thought obviously never crossed his mind. To him they are only vehicles for so-called humor. . . .

If the characterization of Bumpo is bad in *The Story of Doctor Dolittle,* I maintain that it is worse in *The Voyages.* Even defenders of Hugh Lofting have had to denounce the racism of the white prince episode, but I have yet to see or hear any serious criticism of *The Voyages.* This book is, apparently, sacrosanct because it is a Newbery Award winner. I would like, therefore, to turn now to the treatment of Bumpo in this book.

Early in the story, Polynesia the parrot returns to Doctor Dolittle's household after an absence of five years in Africa. One of the first questions the Doctor asks her is about Bumpo. Polynesia informs him that Bumpo is now in England, studying at Oxford University. The Doctor is naturally surprised. Polynesia adds, "He was scared to death to come . . . . He thought he was going to be eaten by white cannibals or something. You know what those niggers are—that ignorant!" [This quotation is taken from page 36 of the official Lippincott edition. The copy I used was the 35th impression, bought in 1965 for a branch of the New York Public Library. In the paperback edition published by Dell in November, 1967, the word "nigger" has been changed to "native."] Polynesia continues her insulting explanation of why Bumpo came to England. Then the Doctor asks, "And The Sleeping Beauty?—did he ever find her?"

" 'Well, he brought back something which he *said* was The Sleeping Beauty. Myself, I think it was an albino nigeress. . . . ' [See note above.]

'And tell me, did he remain white?'

'Only for about three months,' said the parrot. '. . . It was just as well. He was so conspicuous in his bathing-suit the way he was, with his face white and the rest of him black.' "

I must interject one comment here. Polynesia speaks in this insulting way about Bumpo and also directly to his face on many occasions in all the books in which they are together, and never does the "good, kind" Doctor object or reprove her for even her bad manners, to say nothing of her degrading attitude.

Shortly after this conversation, the Doctor decides to go on the voyage to Spidermonkey Island, described earlier. He is looking for the right person to be the third member of his crew. One day when he was on the ship preparing for the journey, a visitor appears on the gangplank. He "was a most extraordinary-looking black man." He was dressed in a fashionable frock coat with an enormous bright red cravat. On his head was a straw hat with a gay band; and over this he held a large green umbrella. He was very smart in every respect except his feet. He wore no shoes or socks." Who is this apparition of sartorial splendor? Why, of course, none other than "Bumpo Kahboo-boo, Crown Prince of Jolliginki"! (In both name and attire, does he not call to mind that other Lippincott "classic" *Little Black Sambo?*) He has come to offer

himself as the much needed third crewman. When the Doctor asks what will happen to his studies and his university career, he replies that he had intended to take a three-month "absconsion" anyway and that by sailing with the Doctor he will not be neglecting his "edification" since the Doctor is a man of "great studiosity." So the Doctor agrees to take him along.

From this point on, both in *The Voyages* and *Doctor Dolittle's Zoo,* Bumpo speaks only in malapropisms—once more, the ridiculous African trying to be white, this one by unsuccessfully imitating the speech pattern of a cultured, educated Englishman.

On first glance the interracial nature of the crew might be construed as a positive contribution to race relations, but the opposite is true. Once the voyage is underway, Bumpo, African prince and Oxford scholar, is consigned to the stereotyped role of cook for the rest of the crew. Despite his age and college training, he is, at best, only on a par with ten-year-old Stubbins, the other crewman. On Spidermonkey Island, both of them help with the teaching of the Indians, but just at "simple arithmetic and easy things like that." Only the Doctor can teach the advanced subjects.

In his characterization of Bumpo, Lofting has missed few of the colonial Englishman's views of the "savage" nature of Africans. In tense, dangerous situations Bumpo is seen as a man of great brawn, little brain and brute violence. He is ready to resort to murder to save his friends. . . . There is even one suggestion of cannibalism as a solution to a problem. Polynesia worries that they have no money with which to replace the salt beef the stowaway ate. " 'Would it not be good political economy,' Bumpo whispered back, 'if we salted the able seaman and ate him instead?' " Polynesia . . . reminds him that they are not in Jolliginki, and besides, "those things are not done on white men's ships."

Extravagant praise has been heaped on Lofting's illustrations. Many are, indeed, delightful, but in my estimation, all the drawings of Africans are as insulting and offensive as the text. They are nothing more than grotesque caricatures. In combination with the text, they serve no other purpose than to make children laugh at those silly, funny-looking black people. (pp. 6-7)

If good books can help combat racial prejudice, as many of us believe they can, then is it not also true that some books can and do promote and foster racial prejudice? Must we not then be as willing to combat such books as we are to promote the others, even if those books have been called "classics"?

This well may be the Year of Doctor Dolittle, but it is also the Year of the Riot Commission's report to the President, in which white racism was clearly and sharply charged with being the main cause of last summer's race riots. In the light of that report and of the earlier Supreme Court decision on desegregation of schools, which pointed out that making white children feel superior to black children was as damaging to white children as the reverse was true for black children, what justification can be found by anyone—and I ask this particularly of those adults who still defend Lofting—to perpetuate the racist *Dolittle* books? How many more generations of black children must be insulted by them and how many more white children allowed to be infected with their message of white superiority?

When will we ever learn? (p. 6)

Isabelle Suhl, "The 'Real' Doctor Dolittle," in In-terracial Books for Children, Vol. 2, Nos. 1 & 2, 1968, pp. 1, 5-6.

EDWARD BLISHEN

Lofting was, in a literary sense, a fortunate man. His first book was founded on an invention that is not merely ingenious (and one he had the gift to build on, for much of a writing lifetime) but that also enabled him to express what he wished to say about the world, without stint or dilution or camouflage, to the very audience to whom he thought it most worth saying.

The **Dolittle** books are a growth rather than a coolly planned series. They change in character and deepen as the author increases his grip on his original invention and ploughs into the books more and more of himself. When **The Story of Doctor Dolittle** appeared in 1920, . . . it was welcomed by Hugh Walpole as the first children's classic since *Alice in Wonderland;* and the American committee that three years later awarded Lofting the Newbery Medal for his second book echoed this comparison. But, as we can now judge who possess the sequence whole, the comparison was misleading. *Alice* (and *The Wind in the Willows,* which the Newbery judges also mentioned) are classics of, as it were, perfection and completeness: we know where they begin and end. The **Dolittle** stories form a classic of another kind: in their rambling amplitude, their very unevenness, they are like life itself, and children can live in them, in a most generous sense. Indeed, as anyone knows who has read them through, and especially in the company of children, they merge into one another, confusingly. As with life, their interest is of a kind difficult to exhaust; but it can also be exhausting. The books lean on one another, contain contradictions, and abound in miscellaneous material. The very period which they cover is in doubt. There is no possibility of making a rational pattern out of such dates as swim to the surface; they dart about from somewhere round the opening of the nineteenth century, when Jip, the dog, knew George Morland, the portrait painter (1763-1804), to a date vaguely indicated by the sparrow Cheapside's reference to 'them old Crimea War veterans'. (At that period, Jip was still alive, the oldest of dogs; but by then, by similar internal evidence, John Dolittle must have been well over a hundred.) This vagueness of time is part of the magic of the Dolittle world, and seems unlikely to have been due to carelessness. The sense of the Doctor as an immortal is established by the typical device of being at once precise and improbable in this matter of dates.

One sees what drew Hugh Walpole to **The Story;** that book launched the *idea* of Doctor Dolittle—of the eccentric small-town doctor who turned from human medicine to the welfare of animals and, on the grounds of the enchanting argument that no patient can be well-served by a doctor to whom he cannot speak, set to and learned the languages of animals. And this idea, as Marcus Crouch has observed, is one of the few really original ideas in children's fiction. In **The Story** there is already much of Lofting's quality. Here is his gift for curious invention that is always on the brink of whimsicality, but rarely drops into it. His imagination is at once extravagant and practical; and the practical quality in it turns the pushmi-pullyu, for example (the creature presented to the Doctor by the monkeys in gratitude for his treatment of their sickness), which might have been only a mildly funny fantasy animal, into something more. The pushmi-pullyu could have used both his heads for talking, but did not do so since that would have squandered his special advantage of eating and talking at one and the same time without impoliteness. At that single and typical stroke, the pushmi-pullyu is raised above whimsy and becomes a permanent delight in the memory, preserved by Lofting's very special practical wit. This was to be the character of so many of his inventions; they are preposterous, and yet Lofting presents them with such a reasonable air that fantasy seems as well-founded as any ordinary fact of the everyday world. Part of his special appeal to children is due to this element, indeed child-like, of the ridiculous notion soberly justified.

Yet **The Story** was, if not a false start, then one that set the tone for the series simply by showing Lofting what it should not be. In it, he is writing down for children, as he never did again: the turns of language have a cosy, simple quality that makes a reader constantly aware that he is not to take the story seriously. It is the language of the conscious tall story for children: carrying still, perhaps, the tone of the original oral tales told by Lofting to his son Colin. There is other evidence that Lofting has not yet established his grip on the opportunity offered to him by his invention of Doctor Dolittle. Flaws are found of an odd kind for a man whose lifelong obsession was the need for tolerance between living things. It may be that in the 1960s we are more sensitive to the colour question than even radicals of Lofting's order were in the 1920s, simply because its consequences are now on all our doorsteps; but such an explanation hardly covers his treatment of the episode in which the African Prince Bumpo pleads to have the hue of his face changed from black to white. This is so much at odds with the philosophy Lofting spent his life expressing that one suspects that the facetious elements in this first book, and in the tradition of story-telling that it subscribes to, led him astray. He had invented a set of sketchily comic Africans belonging to an order of comedy that rather easily leads to insensitive joking. Call a Prince, Bumpo; call his tribe the Jollijinki; and a writer is on his way to a perilously indiscriminate and patronising broadness of humour.

Interestingly, when Lofting changed course in the second book, and thereafter, he retained many of the elements of this facetious tradition of writing, but rarely let them lead him again so far from his fundamental purpose of promoting the idea of respect and tolerance between living things. He grasped, one suspects, the significance and use, for him, of those elements: which lay, as I shall argue in a moment, in their anti-romantic quality.

If he started off on several wrong feet in **The Story,** he also started off on several marvellously right ones. The Doctor himself was already keenly focused, though he, who was to be so richly and circumstantially documented, was there only in relatively thin outline, and certainly lacked many of the subtler qualities he was later to be given. (The Doctor ends the story in what, looking back, one sees to be a quite uncharacteristic posture, satisfied with riches; although already his scorn for money is established, and the fortune that he acquires at the end of **The Story** falls into his lap and is not sought. In all the later books, splendidly, money slips off his lap as fast as it lands there.) There is already the exhilarating sense, present in so many of the books, of a world in which long daring voyages are undertaken at the drop of a hat—each in spirit a fantastic magnification of any child's day of adventure and makebelieve in field or street, or by pond or stream, to be ended with tea back at home, as all the Dolittle stories were ended. The Doctor's animal household is almost complete, and Sarah Dolittle, his sister, so brusquely driven from it when she complains about having a crocodile in the bath, has already made that brief appearance that is to be alluded to so often throughout the series, in a manner that makes Sarah a kind of touchstone of stuffy respectability: on the few occasions when, later, the Doctor actually blunders into her and her parsonical husband, it is always when John Dolittle is behaving in a more than usually unconventional fashion.

But the books that followed *The Story* immediately and enormously extended the range of the Dolittle world. The change is, first, one of tone. This is not merely a matter of Tommy Stubbins taking over as narrator; there is also a total change of manner. The accent, as it were, of the jolly and amusing uncle talking down to an audience of children is replaced by one that, fundamentally, is that of the serious memoir. The sentences grow longer; the restricted vocabulary of the first book is forgotten. The whole intent now is to suggest the reality of this world, to have it taken seriously by taking it seriously. This means, paradoxically, no loss of gaiety, but an increase in it. The fun of *The Story* was the fun of a confessed joke; all the fun of the following books derives its special rich quality from the suggestion, to which young readers readily submit, that we are not really joking at all.

To my mind the biggest change, to which I have already alluded, lies in his sudden confident handling of the facetious elements in his writing. These are found, from the very beginning, in the conception of the Doctor himself. Clumsy, 'round as a bee', enormous-booted, he is an overgrown boy in the dress of a Victorian general practitioner. The idea of marriage fills him with horror, he giggles when he is kissed. All this is, in origin, a projection of a boy's taste, and a facetious one. So, too, are the names: Bumpo, Matthew Mugg, Tripsitinka, the Jollijinki. In *The Story,* such names contribute to the air the book has of the deliberate joke; but from then on, they play a much subtler part in the whole texture of the fantasy. They merge with the general underlying theme of the series: that the human thirst for romance and dignity is the cause of much disaster. When the Doctor is elected king of the Popsipetel people, in *The Voyages*, it is observed of him that he 'may not have been as dignified as many kings in history who were always running off and getting themselves into romantic situations'. Essentially, as one who is against war and fox-hunting and the romantic notions that accumulate around them, and as an opponent of riches and honours—as an obdurate non-conformist—Doctor Dolittle must be seen as a round, solid, sensible figure, without dash or conventional dignity. And the names, blunt as the Doctor's boots, are used to confirm the anti-romantic character of the tales and their meanings.

The five books that followed *The Story—The Voyages of Doctor Dolittle, Doctor Dolittle's Post Office, Doctor Dolittle's Circus, Doctor Dolittle's Zoo,* and *Doctor Dolittle's Caravan*—form the ebullient, happy centre of the series. They follow no chronological sequence, but move about breathlessly among the events of the Doctor's life; and indeed they bear all the marks of Lofting's headlong delight in his own invention and in the world of fantastic creation to which it gave him entrance. It all seems to have come to him so fast that in his writing he is sometimes ahead of himself, sometimes behind. The charming but thin air of the original joke has gone, and the arrival (in *The Voyages*) of Tommy Stub-

bins as narrator has given the Dolittle scene its new solidity. The invention of Stubbins was a beautiful stroke, for it not only enabled Lofting to tell the story from a boy's point of view (which carried the child reader, so to speak, into the story), but it added to the stature of Doctor Dolittle in young eyes by displaying the natural tact with which he himself approached children. Who could resist an adult who treated a boy of ten as a man, addressing him gravely as 'Stubbins'? Tommy is planted in the stories as the representative of many juvenile desires: not only to be so treated, but also, for example, to be seen off on a long voyage, as Stubbins is, by parents who behave well—that is, they do not make a scene. Now, with the reality of this world guaranteed by Stubbins' presence, Lofting can snatch out of the air those delicious imaginative audacities that, in *The Story,* merely seemed leg-pulls, but that henceforth will take on the colour of items from a scientific memoir. *The Voyages* is full of these. What made the island so inconveniently float? Because it was accidentally filled with air. How, then, for the sake of its inhabitants, to bring it to rest? Topple down a huge hanging stone, which will naturally pierce the air chamber and cause the island to settle to a carefully determined depth. How shall the imprisoned Long Arrow get a message to Doctor Dolittle? Of course, by tying an appeal for help to the leg of that rare Jabrizi beetle. Nothing would be more likely to catch the Doctor's eye. This happens; and Lofting follows the line of fantasy with patient attention until it leads him to Tommy Stubbins' pleasant comment: 'I had not realised before how hard it is for a human being to walk slowly enough to keep up with a beetle.' The whole tone is so unexcitable, so prosaic, that the stroke of imagination comes, time after time, as a marvellous surprise. Examples of this strange wedding of prosaic and poetic abound throughout the stories. A favourite with children is the journey home to Puddleby across the ocean floor in the great transparent snail (again in *The Voyages*). The discussion of this journey is so practical and hard-headed that the romantic oddity of it is immensely heightened.

But apart from these large ingenuities—such as the whole concept, at once breathtaking and down-to-earth, of the postal service conducted by birds in *Doctor Dolittle's Post Office*—there is an incessant flow of tiny curious detail to stir and delight a reader's imagination. Such details may be embodied in a phrase: as when that eloquent shellfish, the fidgit, begins its life story (listened to by the Doctor with his ear beneath the level of the water in the listening-tank): 'I was one of a family of two thousand five hundred and ten . . .' Or as when Gub-Gub, the pig, telling his story about the Cook Goblins, mentions the 'cocoa-skin clothes lines' they invented—'little toy clothes lines to hang the skin off your cocoa on, neatly. (You know what a nasty mess it makes draped over the rim of your cup.)' . . . Lofting's fertility, in the invention of such exquisite comic detail, never failed him, even after the early exuberance of the series had been left behind. It reaches its peak in the account of the Mooniversary Dinner in *Doctor Dolittle's Zoo*. . . . It is a beautiful example of that combination of detailed veracity and general fantasy so characteristic of Lofting at his best.

After the Dinner, the Doctor amazes Stubbins by being able to recognise individual faces among the thousands of rats and mice around him. And, of course—amid all the curious inventions in these five books, the humour which ranges from the most ruthless punning to some subtle dry stroke of wit, thrown away—amid the plain excitements of voyaging, and the domestic comedies of the Doctor's household—there is deepening, always, the portrait of the Doctor himself as a man of uncommon sense and compassion, a nonconformist who goes to jail more often surely than any other hero of children's fiction, and with a greater sense that the prisoner may have more dignity than his jailer: as a man 'not fond of rules', who hates frauds, and publicity-seekers: as someone who so despises honours that he would prefer a pound of tea to a knighthood: as an opponent of all cruelty, but especially that of ordinary zoos, circuses and pet shops. The overgrown boy is left behind, and is replaced by someone of increasing moral stature—a critic of things as they are who creates instant and complete trust in those who meet him. The most obstinate difficulties give way before him: with no knowledge of sailing or navigation, he has only to take the helm of a ship to be sure of reaching his destination. He grows all the time, so that even his bachelorhood, based at first on a boyish joke, becomes a condition of his utter seriousness as a scientist: such a man, wrapped up in the quest for knowledge, filling an infinity of notebooks, would have no time for normal domestic life. 'When ever,' children have asked, 'did he have time to be a great gardener, too, and a great flautist?' But no young devotee of Doctor Dolittle ever complained that there was no rational answer to such questions. The greatness of the Doctor, as a creation, is that he is at once highly rational, and is not the prisoner of petty reason.

Perhaps none of the books of this period displays better than *Doctor Dolittle's Circus* that breathless zest and fantastic inventiveness of Lofting's writing which, more than anything else, accounts for the spell that the stories lay upon children who take to them. (pp. 19-28)

Doctor Dolittle's Circus is, in my view, only by a rather special supercharge of high spirits and invention the best of these five books, which themselves form the happiest of all Lofting's writing. The stories that he wrote for the *Herald-Tribune* and that posthumously were collected as *The Green Canary* and *The Puddleby Adventures* belong to the same confident period. But from then onwards a shadow falls. We know from Lofting's son Christopher that he had wearied of Dolittle; he 'tried to get rid of him by sending him to the Moon'. The attempt begins with *Doctor Dolittle's Garden* . . . ; a scrappy book, at first taking up the theme of *Doctor Dolittle's Zoo,* then turning to the Doctor's attempts to understand insect languages, and ending with his decision to go to the Moon. He has tired of 'the smaller geography':

> "Abroad!" John Dolittle's voice sounded to my
> surprise almost contemptuous. "Stubbins," he said
> suddenly in a strange, intense voice, "if I could get
> to the Moon!"

His household is disturbed by the longings and dissatisfactions that have him in their thrall, and indeed the disturbance is felt by the reader. Mysteriously, the positive and determined John Dolittle has been replaced by an unhappy dreamer. It is clear enough that the change reflects a change in his creator. This was about the time of the sequence of tragedies in Lofting's own life—the death of his first wife, followed so soon by the death of his second. He had lived with John Dolittle for eight years and more, and had come, we must guess, to the end of the original impulse of delight that had carried him through all those books. But there seems also to have been a deepening of Lofting's pessimism about human affairs. 'The Moon,' says Polynesia, the parrot, 'is the only thing that would satisfy you—like a baby.' Little doubt that the Doctor's small taste for conventional human society re-

flected his maker's; to go to the Moon would be to escape that society even more thoroughly. Doctor Dolittle had at first held it against men that they sought riches and honours, were indifferent to the search for knowledge, were thoughtlessly cruel to animals. Now his criticism of the human scene grows more radical: the Dolittle of *The Story* is a long way from the Dolittle of the *Garden,* who says, neither simplifying the language nor softening the thought: 'It is the intuitive knowledge which we humans are so short on—especially the so-called civilised humans.'

The series had begun by way of revulsion from the inhumanity of the battlefield; and from the beginning it was possible to say that the *Dolittle* books were part of the anti-war literature that followed the Great War—a unique part of it, in being addressed to children. But the earlier stories were too exuberant to dwell with any bleakness on the tragedy of human wars. Now, in *Doctor Dolittle's Garden,* the theme breaks through in the wasp's story of his presence at a human battle:

> 'It seemed such a stupid waste. From one end of
> our beautiful valley armies would come with can-
> nons and horses and everything . . . Then . . .
> they would go away again, leaving hundreds of
> dead men and horses on the ground which smelt
> horribly for a few days . . .'

By a typical stroke of ironic comedy, the wasp inadvertently changes the outcome of the battle; but the story remains the darkest of all those that, dotted throughout the books, usually so charmingly and lightly record the experiences of animals, insects, birds. (These inset stories form much of the miscellaneous material in the *Dolittle* books: many of them show the curious fantastic explicitness of Lofting's imagination at its best.) It is true that, here and there throughout the earlier adventures, Lofting has provided a political background to his world, in terms of the revolutionary befriended by a rat (*Doctor Dolittle's Zoo*), the machinery riots and the burning of a castle by revolted workers reported by Pippinella in her story (*The Green Canary*). A vague, warm-hearted, even sentimental radicalism has appeared at such moments, supporting his more precise attacks on human frailty with a view of the political world that saw it in terms of callous rulers, persecuted protesters. But until now, all this has had its setting of enormous general gaiety. There is still, of course, gaiety in *Doctor Dolittle's Garden,* and there is gaiety until the end: but now Lofting's anguished view of the conduct of living things comes through nakedly:

> 'This eternal war between the species—men against
> rats; rats against cats; cats against dogs, etc., etc.,
> there is no end to it—must lead finally to some sort
> of tyranny . . . What I would like to see . . . would
> be a happy balance.'

The actual circumstances of the journey to the Moon, described in *Doctor Dolittle's Garden,* are treated with all of Lofting's lively ingenuity. The scene of the arrival of the great moth that has come to fetch the Doctor on his medical errand (he is needed to tend to the ailing Moon Man) is one not easily forgotten, either for its grotesque poetry or for the characteristic measures taken by John Dolittle to revive the exhausted creature. . . . [Though the detail retains the] imaginative quaintness that has become Dolittle's hallmark, the atmosphere is twilit: the full day of the earlier stories has gone. The Moon is a utopia that strengthens the Doctor's growing pessimism about life on earth. There, on the planet, there was no struggle between the animal and vegetable kingdoms: 'We found the whole system of life . . . a singularly peaceful business.' John Dolittle reflects sadly: 'With us it is, and always has been, "dog eats dog" '; and as he trudges about the mysterious surface of the Moon, there is something suddenly forlorn and desolate about the chubby, sensible little man, as described and illustrated. It is as if a character from comedy, though a thoughtful and altogether unusual character, had suddenly wandered into the atmosphere of tragedy. (pp. 29-33)

This, Christopher Lofting tells us, was to be Doctor Dolittle's Reichenbach Falls. Here he was to remain, ministering to the Moon Man and filling his everlasting notebooks, while his friends on earth waited for his return, hopefully, for ever. But the resurrection of his hero was demanded of Lofting, as it was of Conan Doyle. *Doctor Dolittle's Return* again has its typical excitements and imaginative audacities. What child (as I know from reading these books with many children) ever forgets the arrival of the Doctor on earth, grown enormous by moon chemistry, and being for a long time unable to enter his own house! There are still delightful jokes—jokes that are pure Lofting. . . . But John Dolittle has returned to earth more, not less, anxious about the future of life here. . . . For once, though he never loses their loyalty, he has exhausted the patience of his household. There is affection, but there is also something careworn, about his housekeeper Dab-dab's outcry against his perpetual concern for more and more minute living creatures: 'He'll have a Wardrobe for clothing Moths or a Bedroom for Bedbugs before you know where you are.' But the strongest sign that Lofting was now building into the stories his sense that his longing for peace, expressed through John Dolittle, had become rather dark and desperate and obsessive, lies perhaps in Polynesia's reaction to another of these speeches (so rarely long for Doctor Dolittle) that he makes on his return to earth. The Doctor says:

> '. . . You can all very well see, can't you? that when I found a world which was run along sensible lines, where no kind of life trod on the toes of any other kind of life, I began to wonder if something of those ideas could be brought home and started here.'

Polynesia's response is simply to swear, in Swedish. It is partly a joke—Polynesia has always been a sensible, as well as a polyglot, bird; but it also seems to embody a very real gesture of self-deprecation on Lofting's part.

It is not my suggestion that, with these later books, the heart has gone out of the *Dolittle* series. Far from it. There are shadows, now, over the Dolittle world, and what for so long was so bubbling and gay is now shot through with melancholy. This is part of the total experience that this remarkable series gives to its readers: for some children, it may be the most influential and memorable part. But the author's personal misfortunes, his poor health, the approach of the 1930s with the dying hope they brought of international sanity, made him feed into his stories an exhaustion that is expressed through the Doctor himself, and a concerned bewilderment which becomes, in these books that revolve round the journey to the Moon, the mood of the Doctor's little household. (pp. 33-5)

The final volume, *Doctor Dolittle and the Secret Lake*, . . . is a book that falls curiously into two halves. The first half is full of the familiar enchantments: the beginning in the Puddleby household, the decision to take yet another journey, the journey itself. The Doctor is still low-spirited; he has been working, with the moon seeds he brought back with him to earth, on the secret of everlasting life. As he explained to Stubbins, now his fully-trained secretary, 'the trouble with our world down here was *time*. People were in such a hurry. If, said he, Man knew he could live as long as he wanted, then he would stop all this crazy rushing around; this fear—which even he, the easygoing John Dolittle, had felt—would be taken from us . . . Yes, it was a great dream.' But now he has given up that dream—he is beaten. Polynesia is impatient. 'He's gone stale,' she says. 'He needs a change from this beastly English climate.' It is, in some senses, the familiar formula for starting a Dolittle adventure: boredom sets in, the whole household needs a change: someone, as if it had never happened before, wistfully suggests that they might go travelling; and, by the operation of a most satisfactory magic, at once the opportunity for adventure arises. In this case they hear that Mudface, the ancient turtle, has disappeared from the African lake that is his home. Long ago, in *Doctor Dolittle's Post Office,* the making of an island where Mudface might live had been one of the most memorable fantastic scenes in the series: the island was built by millions of birds dropping, first pebbles and gravel, and then sand, and finally grass and other seeds, into the lake. Now, in this new adventure, a rescue operation is called for, and is the more eagerly embarked on by the Doctor because Mudface is a survivor of the Flood; and that is a story that has still to be recorded in the notebooks.

The theme, then, is worthy of a last book. This will be John Dolittle's greatest scientific exploit; it will be led up to by an adventure of rescue; it will raise his spirits, never so low. And indeed, the old energy of invention is at work throughout the whole of this first half of the story. The comic interplay of character among his travelling companions was never more lively. . . . And Lofting has lost none of his power to create a sudden warm fantastic scene, which makes young readers shiver with delight at an imaginative opportunity seized; as when, on its arrival at Fantippo, the ship is boarded by so many visitors ('like ants on a jam-pot') that it nearly sinks. And from now on, until the rescue of Mudface, he keeps, as so often in the stories, a small throb of constant excitement going, with its climax in one of the very best of his big, heroic, preposterous scenes. Mudface, they discover, is buried at the bottom of the lake in the ruins of his island. The only way to rescue him is to call upon the crocodiles and get them to dig the turtle out. And they come in multitudes. . . . Then follows the rescue and—it is to be the climax of the whole series—the recording of Mudface's memories of the Flood.

No story, clearly, could have served Lofting's purpose better, at the end (and he must have felt that it was the end) of the series. He handles it typically—a mixture of the queerly practical and the imaginative—and gives the legend a twist of his own, Mudface and his wife saving the lives of two humans and so assuring for mankind another chance. The whole Dolittle saga is given an extra depth when Mudface discloses that Noah, too, was a speaker of animal languages; suddenly, at this point, we see the Doctor as a re-created Noah, and this comic myth is brushed by a greater one. Yet for a second time, it seems to me, the Dolittle magic proves defective. The first time was on the Moon when, for all the characteristic and endearing ingenuity of the narrative, the poetic elements in the story were at times in conflict with the essential nature of the *Dolittle* series, which is one of broad humour and even burlesque. And now, once again, Lofting takes his little com-

From The Story of Mrs. Tubbs, *written and illustrated by Hugh Lofting.*

pany into what is truly a world of poetry, and the honest prose he employs does not quite carry him through.

The point is a difficult one, and I am brought to it not only by my own readings of **The Secret Lake,** but also by the common response of children to the second half of it: which is to find it curiously dull. It seems to me that in fact the concept of the series, its hilarities, its deadpan exaggerations, prevent it from ever rising to the heights to which, in these last books, but especially in the second half of **The Secret Lake,** Lofting was trying to take it. The concept had been able to support so many of his underlying seriousnesses, and even in the three books concerned with the voyage to the Moon, swept through though they are with a growing despair about the future of life on earth, the solid, touching image of the Doctor had almost held its own. But when we come to the story of the Flood, even Mudface's name sets up a conflict between itself and the imaginative atmosphere of the story. The events of the Flood have, in many respects, the tone of a typical Dolittle adventure; they are full of blunt, characteristically inelegant detail. Even the impatient interjections of the Doctor's companions, as the old turtle slowly tells his tale, seem at odds with the tale itself—or rather, with the high legend lurking behind it.

All this is merely to say that, in my opinion, and by the high-

est standards I am able to apply, the second half of **The Secret Lake** is a failure. It is so because, in the last analysis, the **Dolittle** stories by their nature cannot deal with legendary material so reverberant with poetry. In a sense, from **The Garden** onwards Lofting had been trying to make the series carry graver implications than, for all its quality, it was made to carry. Yet, having said this, one must add that the failure is a noble one: perhaps nobody else has ever tried, through a literary conception constructed to amuse and delight children, to say as much as these last books were attempting to say. And for all the strain that is set up between the essential limitations of the series, and the vision the author was attempting to pour into it, no one—and certainly no child—is ever the worse for having seen the Moon through Doctor Dolittle's eyes, or having read or listened to Mudface's curious account of the Flood. By another critic it might well be maintained that the prosy nature of that account—its being turned, as it were, into a special sort of Dolittle adventure—is thoroughly justified, since there is nothing sacred about the legend and it cannot be anything but good to retell it in terms entertaining to children. I could not agree with this view—and largely because I have found that children are not entertained by the story as Lofting told it: but this is certainly arguable.

I have had to devote so much attention to the second half of

The Secret Lake because I believe that one of the most interesting qualities of the *Dolittle* series, to any critic, must be the way Lofting made it say so much, and built so high upon an idea that was basically a broadly comic and stubbornly anti-romantic one: it is therefore important for a critic to mark the point where, as he sees it, the building grew a little higher than its foundations could bear. But, as would be agreed by most of the children I know who have made their way through the whole series, the Doctor himself loses nothing by this failure of the final tale to reproduce the magic of so many of those that went before it. It is a long way from the giggling bachelor of *The Story;* but, perhaps because Lofting put so much of himself into the character, it is still the same Doctor Dolittle—the same preoccupied, sensible, compassionate man—who promises Mudface, when his story is told, that he will write it all down in a book. If he does that, says Mudface, 'maybe war may stop altogether'.

'The Doctor, silent, thought a moment before he answered.

> "Indeed, I hope so," he sighed at last. "At least I promise you the book shall be written and I will do my best to write it well. How many will take any notice of it: that is another matter. For men are deaf, mind you, Mudface—deaf when they do not wish to hear and to remember—and deafest of all when their close danger is ended with a short peace, and they *want* to believe that war will not come back."

'He sighed': and the sighing John Dolittle—the sighing Hugh Lofting—is part of the unique image we carry away from these books. But there is also a laughing John Dolittle, and of course a laughing Hugh Lofting; and it is with them that this last of the long, marvellous series comes to an end. (pp. 36-41)

I have said before in this study that Hugh Lofting was an original, and it seems to me quite the most important thing to say about him. His originality lies in none of his specific talents. His sense of comedy, punning and often facetious, or depending on a startling alliance of the preposterous and the practical, is not unique. The early books especially bear strong marks of their period, in a certain cosiness, a sense that adventures properly end with feasts of bread and butter and strawberry jam. Anyone making a collection of children's books that were redolent of the 1920s would be bound to choose the Dolittles. And yet Lofting's work stands alone, among writing for children, for one very important reason. It is not the only children's fiction that has behind it a conscious purpose that might, in the widest sense, be called political. But no one else has set out, quite as he did, to create a hero, and a notion of heroism, that is radical, pacifist and profoundly opposed to common ideas of conventional respectability. The rich fun of the *Dolittle* stories and their marvellous and enduring novelty tend to obscure from us their deeply nonconformist nature. There is no means of calculating the effect they have had on children who have read them. One can only guess with some confidence that, having once identified yourself with John Dolittle, you would thereafter find it more difficult to identify yourself with the world's anti-Dolittles; with those who are cruel, and not only to animals, and with those who seek after riches and honours.

The stories have from time to time been discussed as though they were primarily a part of that children's literature that is concerned with talking animals. Hugh Walpole looked at *The Story of Doctor Dolittle* in this light. It seems to me that,

though the essence of the stories may seem to be that they are about animals that talk, the books are really about human behaviour. It is not merely the author's remarkable powers of persuasion that make us forget, much of the time, that we are moving among animals. It is also that the conduct and talk of his creatures is so often made to reflect on the ways of men and women. One can carry this argument too far, and obviously part of the charm and delight of the *Dolittle* books lies in their feeling for animal identity; but surely in a wider sense we are in the atmosphere of a metaphor, and when our attention seems to be directed to some oddity of animal existence, it is really some oddity of human existence that is being illuminated. In a sense, Lofting used animals to underline the unsatisfactory nature of the human world. When he says that 'the animal sense of humour is far superior to the human', he is giving us a salutary dig. And Polynesia, when she remarks: 'I suppose if people ever learn to fly—like any common hedgesparrow—we shall never hear the end of it', is being used to make Lofting's young readers reflect on the absurdity of human pride and pretensions.

It is even possible to say that a healthy young reader ought, at some point, to quarrel with Doctor Dolittle, and with his desertion of the world of human medicine. Lofting said that the Doctor turned away from 'the mere human hypochondriac', and those humans who seek the help of medicine are, of course, not all hypochondriacs, by any means. At the roots of this unique fantasy lies a pessimism about the world of men that a child should detect and question. There can be little doubt that Lofting would have been delighted if they did so. His aim was always to be provocative.

For a long time Doctor Dolittle has been a special taste among children, if only because really to enter and inhabit his world requires some literary patience and endurance. The books have been translated into many languages, and today they seem on the brink of a new and wider life, appearing as paperbacks . . . and forming the basis of a film. It is difficult to compare them with other children's classics, since they are so much more diffuse—simply, so much longer, when put together. But if the appetite for series, when they first appeared, was largely confined to the literate households of the time, it is now a taste much more widely spread, and one hopes that the new chapter in their history will bring them an immense new audience.

One hopes this especially because the world is still racked with those hatreds that in his writing, and in his choosing to write for children, Lofting hoped to play a part in dispelling. His work will always be rewarding for that richly inventive playfulness that is the mark of it—for the pure fun and surprise that it offers its readers, largely but not all young ones. Yet it is never possible to forget, in enjoying the high spirits of this writing at its best, that it stands high above most other writing for children for having at its heart this profound concern for sane behaviour among living creatures. And it immeasurably strengthens rather than weakens this humaneness of purpose that Lofting so often expressed it in terms utterly suitable for his audience, gay and light: as when (one really should end on Lofting's own special note of comic seriousness) the Doctor restricts his conversation with the twenty-four hour greenfly on the grounds that, for him, a half an hour of talking is the equivalent of eighteen months of a human life. It is really in the accumulation of such small comic touches, so many of them expressing most lightly a most serious concern with gentleness and kindness, that the importance of Hugh Lofting's work for children lies. (pp. 54-7)

Edward Blishen, "The World of Doctor Dolittle" and "A Summing Up," in Three Bodley Head Monographs: "Hugh Lofting" by Edward Blishen, "Geoffrey Trease" by Margaret Meek, "J. M. Barrie" by Roger Lancelyn Green, The Bodley Head, 1968, pp. 19-41, 54-7.

ROSEMARY WELLS

[*The following excerpt is from a letter by Wells, a noted author and illustrator of picture books and stories for older readers, to the editor of* Interracial Books for Children *in response to Isabelle Suhl's essay "The 'Real' Doctor Dolittle."*]

I have just finished reading the critique of the **Doctor Dolittle** books in your summer issue of two years ago.

As a child I read all twelve **Dolittle** books with delight, over and over again, and as a writer and illustrator of children's books now, I have often called on the vague and delightful memories I have of Mr. Hugh Lofting's prose, his whimsy and his imagination; so I began the article skeptically, to say the least.

I believe that all white people, no matter how intense their egalitarianism, how genuine their liberal feelings, how much they hate bigotry in any form, find themselves irrationally prejudiced against Black people in some ways. Sometimes this feeling is kept dormant, but it creeps out occasionally in all of us. I've never been able to understand this in myself. Where did it come from?. . . .

The **Dolittle** Books were only a small part of it, but the important thing is that I had *forgotten* all the incidents you describe. The only proper analogy I can make about my feelings now, is to compare them to a patient in psychotherapy, at the moment when the doctor discovers some long repressed trauma, and the patient suddenly understands many things about his life since that time. I remember the **Dolittle** implications now, and I think I understand myself a little better too. Thank you for publishing Mrs. Suhl's evaluation.

I suggest you send copies to every children's book publisher and children's librarian in the country.

Rosemary Wells, "Dr. Dolittle Still," in Interracial Books for Children, Vol. II, No. 4, 1970, p. 2.

FRANK EYRE

After the slightly false start of **The Story of Doctor Dolittle** everything that happens (once the basic suspension of disbelief has been achieved) has the logicality and inevitability of truth. If a man *could* talk to animals, and had the saint-like simplicity, complete unselfishness and insatiable curiosity of Dolittle, this, the reader feels, is how it would all have happened. This is how children reason, and this, no doubt, is why children all over the world have taken Dolittle to their hearts. The best of the stories are the five in the middle—**The Voyages, Post Office, Circus, Zoo** and **Caravan.** Thereafter the author's preoccupation with the horrors of war and man's perpetual egotism and greed becomes more obtrusive. It never completely darkens the picture, but it introduces an element that can disturb and perplex children and leads them to ask, worriedly, 'Why is it that the animals are always so much nicer than the humans?'

If it is true that the greatest writers in any field have always

something of value to communicate, then Lofting must be one of the truly great writers for children, because his message of tolerance, generosity, and unselfish helpfulness to others shines through so clearly. (p. 66)

Frank Eyre, "The In-Between Books," in his British Children's Books in the Twentieth Century, revised edition, Longman Books, 1971, pp. 59-75.

JANE W. SHACKFORD

[What] can be done about the Newbery Award winning and still popular **The Voyages of Dr. Dolittle** with its anomaly of derogatory images in the midst of a basically moral tale? How should the teacher handle the ridicule implicit in the buffoon-like caricature of Bumpo, the African Prince, or the condescending implications of "The Song of the Terrible Three?" (pp. 180-81)

Unquestionably, the simplest solution is to remove the **Dolittle** books from the shelves. Given the recent Disney production and the paperback editions now widely available in bookstores and supermarkets, this is not so easily done. Nor, perhaps, should it be. There is, in truth, a clear message of consideration for all living things and a delightful grave nonsense in these tales that give them both a moral and a literary worth. (p. 181)

It is Lofting's portrayal of Bumpo as foolish, polygamous and implicitly cannibalistic that provokes the greatest quandary. (p. 185)

As irresponsible as Lofting's portrayal seems, we cannot ignore the humor in Bumpo's speech: "Me thinks I detect something of the finger of Destination in this" or "Cease, I feel I am about to weep from sediment". Here, both added perspective and literary insight may be gained through a shared search for other fictional characters who, with their humorous misuse of language, have been similarly used as a source of amusement. Mrs. Malaprop provides the classic model: "We will not anticipate the past" or "His physiognomy so grammatical." Amy in *Little Women,* Oswald Bastable in *The Wouldbegoods,* Mr. Pecksniff and Mrs. Gamp in Dickens's *Martin Chuzzlewit* and Sam and Tony Weller in *The Pickwick Papers* offer other possibilities. Archie Bunker with such witticisms as "the survival of the fattest" will already be a familiar figure.

Unfortunately, the potential effect of Lofting's portrayal of Bumpo is far from humorous and requires further inquiry in an effort to properly place Lofting's images. . . . That the **Dolittle** stories were based on Lofting's letters to his own children will be of interest. That the background of Dr. Dolittle's foreign travels are the places that Lofting visited during his career as a civil engineer (his work on the Lagoo Railway in West Africa, for example) is certainly relevant. Further, one must consider what influence nineteenth century British colonialism and its attendant attitudes toward the African people may have had on Lofting as an Englishman writing in the first quarter of the twentieth century. (pp. 185-86)

The opportunities for role playing as a part of fostering the moral and critical potential of a personal position in this approach to **Dr. Dolittle** seem quite clear. The questions and discussions that relate to such a position must, of course, be geared to the appropriate level. Again, it is not as simple as merely pointing out that a book or character portrayal is racist or sexist. It is the reasoning process, not merely the content of moral choices, that is essential if children's capacity for critical thinking is to continue to serve them in yet untried situations.

An alternative to censorship in dealing with literary images, classic or current, that conflict with today's social ideologies has been proposed. Though the goal of teaching children to think critically about ideas and issues is not new, its potential as a counter to censorship has clearly been neglected. Thus, in an effort to stimulate recognition of this potential it is further proposed that there is indeed a methodology of dialogue from which teachers may develop their own liberating procedures. However, in wishing that children's literature might become the object of moral reasoning, it is not intended that it become the focus of moral or social issues to the neglect of imaginative perception and literary quality. It is for these attributes that *Mary Poppins* and **Dr. Dolittle** must be saved from the censor. (p. 186)

> Jane W. Shackford, "Dealing with Dr. Dolittle: A New Approach to the '-isms'," in Language Arts, Vol. 55, No. 2, February, 1978, pp. 180-87.

JOHN ROWE TOWNSEND

Hugh Lofting has been accused of being 'a white racist and chauvinist'; and undoubtedly there are parts of the **Dolittle** books that are now found offensive. Prince Bumpo, who is black and begs the Doctor to turn him white, and King Koko, who is usually either sucking a lollipop or using one as a quizzing-glass, have become notorious. Today it is all too evident that Lofting, who was born in England although he spent most of his adult life in the United States, shared the insensitivity of many Englishmen of his day to whom all foreigners were funny and those of a different colour were doubly funny. Lofting's lapses illustrate the extreme difficulty of escaping accepted attitudes, for he was far from being a crude imperialist, and he once wrote:

> If we make children see that all races, given equal physical and mental chances for development, have about the same batting averages of good and bad, we shall have laid another very substantial foundation stone in the edifice of peace and internationalism.

It is sad that a writer with such excellent intentions should have got himself into such posthumous trouble. I hope that in time Lofting will be forgiven, for assuredly there was no malice in this worried, sincere, well-meaning man. It is a rare individual who can rise above the general insensitivities of his own day, and none of us can tell what unsuspected sins we may be found guilty of in fifty years' time. (pp. 147-49)

> John Rowe Townsend, "Fantasy between the Wars," in his Written for Children: An Outline of English-Language Children's Literature, third revised edition, J. B. Lippincott, 1987, pp. 143-57.

SELMA G. LANES

[This] is the summer of Doctor Dolittle's return. After being in disrepute in the United States (land of their first publication) since the early 1970's, and out of print for almost a decade, both **The Story of Doctor Dolittle** and **The Voyages of Doctor Dolittle** are available again in what the publisher calls a centenary edition to mark Lofting's birth, punctiliously altered to offend none but the most diehard of their former critics. **Story** and **Voyages** are the first of eight projected Dolittle adventures to be reissued.

Among the earliest and harshest of the doctor's detractors was the New York librarian Isabelle Suhl who, in a 1968 Bulletin of Interracial Books for Children, charged that "the 'real' Doctor Dolittle is in essence the personification of The Great White Father Nobly Bearing the White Man's Burden and that his creator was a white racist and chauvinist, guilty of almost every prejudice known to modern white Western man." In her view, "editing out a few racial epithets will not make the books less chauvinistic."

Fans of Doctor Dolittle and his domestic menagerie of talking animals . . . will not recognize their hero in this inflamed and politicized rhetoric. We remember his enthusiasm for discovery: how he stayed up all one night trying to learn the fish language of the silver fidgit. We recall, too, his kind concern for both animals and his fellow man: how he crossed the sea in a borrowed boat to save the monkeys of Africa from a dread disease; and how he persuaded a judge in Her Majesty's Court to let Bob, a dog, testify at his master's murder trial, thereby saving a life. In a tight spot, this eccentric man of science always came through. As his young assistant, Tommy Stubbins, put it in **Voyages:** "Just to be with him gave you a wonderful feeling of comfort and safety."

This said, his critics had grounds for dismay. The original **Dolittle** texts were marred by a sprinkling of gratuitous racial epithets. Almost all of these emanated from the doctor's short-tempered parrot Polynesia, known for her command of "the most dreadful seafaring swearwords you ever heard." That's simply a fact, not an excuse. But these blemishes were all removed in an undated 52d printing of **Story** from which I read to my two sons around 1970. A reference to "darkies" had been altered to "people," "work with niggers" had become "work hard," and several other unfortunate locutions had been rendered admirably innocuous. It speaks volumes about the racial obtuseness of earlier decades that no one seemed troubled by their appearance in highly regarded works for children. . . .

The centenary edition's new excisions and revisions are far more extensive. The present editors obviously hope to obliterate every emotionally tinted word. Thus, though much of **Story** takes place in Africa, we hear no reference to skin coloration. When Doctor Dolittle's party first lands, they are no longer met by "a black man" coming out of the woods. He is simply "a man." Likewise, where once the monkeys, grateful to Dr. Dolittle, shouted, "Let us give him the finest present a White Man ever had!" they now say, somewhat flatly, "Let us give him the finest present ever given."

Gone too is every illustration featuring a black character: no more broad caricatures of the King of the Jolliginki or his Queen Ermintrude; no more Crown Prince Bumpo. Two full-page pictures retained from earlier editions have had black figures expunged. The engaging Prince Bumpo, heir to the throne of the Jolliginki, has even been removed from a cameo appearance on **Story's**" title page. If this verbal and visual caution occasionally seems almost craven—an avoidance rather than a positive confrontation of problems—Lofting is no longer alive to deal with the blind spots of his own era.

The most extensive text deletion is entirely commendable: the excision from **Story** of the discomforting scene in which Doctor Dolittle reluctantly agrees to transform Prince Bumpo into a white prince so that the Sleeping Beauty, his favorite fairy-tale character, will agree to marry him. The removal of this most flagrant Dolittle liability has been so deftly managed as to leave no gap in the narrative.

Happily, none of this well-intended editorial tinkering has had the slightest effect on the tales' enduring charms. They still exude the same cheerful optimism about life's possibilities and the world's wonders awaiting the reader's discovery. Perhaps most important, the **Dolittle** books are enthusiastic about the joy of using one's mind. What more can we ask of children's books?

If the world were ruled by logic, then surely all this doggedly well-meaning effort would succeed, and soon Doctor Dolittle would be restored to respectability for a new generation of children. But should the whole effort come a cropper, Hugh Lofting, for one, would not be surprised. Writing with uncanny prescience in 1930 about a now forgotten book of his called **The Twilight of Magic,** he said: "Perhaps we do not realize that fiction reading for children is not the same in our children's generation as it was in our own. Life cannot stand still. What was black yesterday is white today. What was white yesterday is black tomorrow. We have no excuse for supposing that those books which were given to us as the ideal reading fare for children are the ideal reading fare for the children of today." Yet those of us who loved Doctor Dolittle as children cannot help but wish him well in this slightly tardy centenary appearance.

Selma G. Lanes, "Doctor Dolittle, Innocent Again," *in* The New York Times Book Review, *August 28, 1988, p. 20.*

THE STORY OF DOCTOR DOLITTLE, BEING THE HISTORY OF HIS PECULIAR LIFE AT HOME AND ASTONISHING ADVENTURES IN FOREIGN PARTS (1920; British edition as *Doctor Dolittle*)

[*The following excerpt is from an introduction by Hugh Walpole to the tenth printing of* The Story of Doctor Dolittle.]

There are some of us now reaching middle age who discover themselves to be lamenting the past in one respect if in none other, that there are no books written now for children comparable with those of thirty years ago. I say written *for* children because the new psychological business of writing *about* them as though they were small pills or hatched in some especially scientific method is extremely popular today. Writing for children rather than about them is very difficult as everybody who has tried it knows. It can only be done, I am convinced, by somebody having a great deal of the child in his own outlook and sensibilities. Such was the author of *The Little Duke* and *The Dove in the Eagle's Nest,* such the author of *A Flatiron for a Farthing,* and *The Story of a Short Life.* Such, above all, the author of *Alice in Wonderland.* Grownups imagine that they can do the trick by adopting baby language and talking down to their very critical audience. There never was a greater mistake. The imagination of the author

From Porridge Poetry, *written and illustrated by Hugh Lofting.*

must be a child's imagination and yet maturely consistent, so that the White Queen in *Alice,* for instance, is seen just as a child would see her, but she continues always herself through all her distressing adventures. (pp. vii-viii)

Geniuses are rare and, without being at all an undue praiser of times past, one can say without hesitation that until the appearance of Hugh Lofting, the successor of Miss Yonge, Mrs. Ewing, Mrs. Gatty and Lewis Carroll had not appeared. I remember the delight with which some six months ago I picked up the first *Dolittle* book. . . . One of Mr. Lofting's pictures was quite enough for me. The picture that I lighted upon when I first opened the book was the one of the monkeys making a chain with their arms across the gulf. Then I looked further and discovered Bumpo reading fairy stories to himself. And then looked again and there was a picture of John Dolittle's house.

But pictures are not enough although most authors draw so badly that if one of them happens to have the genius for line that Mr. Lofting shows there must be, one feels, something in his writing as well. There is. You cannot read the first paragraph of the book, which begins in the right way "Once upon a time" without knowing that Mr. Lofting believes in his story quite as much as he expects you to. That is the first essential for a story teller. Then you discover as you read on that he has the right eye for the right detail. What child-inquiring mind could resist this intriguing sentence to be found on the second page of the book:

> Besides the gold-fish in the pond at the bottom of his garden, he had rabbits in the pantry, white mice in his piano, a squirrel in the linen closet and a hedgehog in the cellar.

And then when you read a little further you will discover that the Doctor is not merely a peg on whom to hang exciting and various adventures but that he is himself a man of original and lively character. He is a very kindly, generous man, and anyone who has ever written stories will know that it is much more difficult to make kindly, generous characters interesting than unkindly and mean ones. But Dolittle is interesting. It is not only that he is quaint but that he is wise and knows what he is about. The reader, however young, who meets him gets very soon a sense that if he were in trouble, not necessarily medical, he would go to Dolittle and ask his advice about it. Dolittle seems to extend his hand from the page and grasp that of his reader, and I can see him going down the centuries a kind of Pied Piper with thousands of children at his heels. But not only is he a darling and alive and credible but his creator has also managed to invest everybody else in the book with the same kind of life.

Now this business of giving life to animals, making them talk and behave like human beings, is an extremely difficult one. Lewis Carroll absolutely conquered the difficulties, but I am not sure that anyone after him until Hugh Lofting has really managed the trick; even in such a masterpiece as *The Wind in the Willows* we are not quite convinced. John Dolittle's friends are convincing because their creator never forces them to desert their own characteristics. Polynesia, for instance, is natural from first to last. She really does care about the Doctor but she cares as a bird would care, having always some place to which she is going when her business with her friends is over. And when Mr. Lofting invents fantastic animals he gives them a kind of credible possibility which is extraordinarily convincing. It will be impossible for anyone who has read this book not to believe in the existence of the pushmi-pullyu, who would be credible enough even were there no drawing of it, but the picture on page 145 settles the matter of his truth once and for all.

In fact this book is a work of genius and, as always with works of genius, it is difficult to analyze the elements that have gone to make it. There is poetry here and fantasy and humor, a little pathos but, above all, a number of creations in whose existence everybody must believe whether they be children of four or old men of ninety or prosperous bankers of forty-five. I don't know how Mr. Lofting has done it; I don't suppose that he knows himself. There it is—the first real children's classic since *Alice.* (pp. viii-xii)

> *Hugh Walpole, in an introduction to* The Story of Doctor Dolittle *by Hugh Lofting, 1938. Reprint by J. B. Lippincott Co., 1956, pp. vii-xii.*

Since the days of Thackeray there has always been a great deal to be said for the author who is also his own illustrator. Especially is this true of children's books, where another artist might have difficulty in catching the freakish imagination of the author. . . . In *Dr. Dolittle,* by Hugh Lofting, it is difficult to decide which is the more attractive—the charming nonsense that he writes or the delightful pictures he reproduced. Children all over the world will love this book with its story of the quaint doctor who gave up looking after human beings to devote himself to animals.

> *A review of "Dr. Dolittle," in* The Bookman, London, *Vol. LXIII, No. 375, December, 1922, p. 138.*

Hugh Lofting's enduring tale, *The Story of Dr. Dolittle,* has made, if one can believe the publicity, "its triumphant entrance on the movie screens of the world." We are promised technicolor, an original musical score, a cast of thousands, and ulcers for its competitors in the annual "Oscar" race. It *is* a delightful film. The reviews and audience reaction agree that this movie will be one of the "block busters" of the 1968 cinema. The interest the film will produce will undoubtedly have what the industry calls "spin offs." Toys, clothes, games, coloring books, comic versions of the film, and books based on the film itself are already on the market. Another "spin off" will be a rush to the libraries and the book stores for copies of the original version of *The Story of Dr. Dolittle.*

Ordinarily teachers, librarians, and devotees of children's books would foster the idea of the original's being featured in libraries and schools to offer the comparison of the movie version with the book as it was written. This book, however, the seemingly charming story of an English country doctor who learns to speak the language of animals and who goes to Africa to cure the monkeys might be another case. Teachers and librarians who know *The Story of Dr. Dolittle,* as it was written, may well be concerned with the fact that the book has, if not overtones, a nakedly racist message to offer! A message that clearly states that being white is definitely an advantage over being black, and that Africans, at least those in this story, are stupid, unaware, and are present only to be taken advantage of. (p. 437)

Should we pull *The Story of Dr. Dolittle* off the shelves? Shall we cut out the sections dealing with the African royal family? Shall we mumble and make weak excuses when children question? Certainly not! Censorship is not the answer. It is suggested here that we meet this situation head on, and use it as an effective teaching device.

Lofting published *Dr. Dolittle* in 1920. It was written some time before. The cultural and social values of that day, in terms of inter-cultural, inter-racial understandings, were considerably different from those that are developing in our present era. *The Story of Dr. Dolittle* simply states those values that existed then. That time has elapsed, and man is learning to live with man, a hopeful sign of progress. The racial bias, so clear in Lofting's writing of this book, seems out of doing with the times. It is! With historical perspective the racial attitudes found in *Dr. Dolittle* do take on a more understandable position. *The Story of Dr. Dolittle* was written in another time and therefore, in a figurative sense, another place. What was true in that time and place has changed and will continue to change. This needs to be pointed out to children.

One of the great values of children's literature, is to help youngsters understand the dynamic, constantly changing environment that we call society. Many children's books are geared to enhance just that concept. Few sources of learning can combine both intellectual and emotional involvement with a concept as well as can good children's literature. The book lists are full of suggested books that promise to do just that.

The Story of Dr. Dolittle brings one of our societies most urgent issues to the front: racial prejudice. It does it with taste that is highly questionable. The portrayals are cruel and will get a reaction that may be destructive. One would wish that this were not true of the book, but the facts show us it is. This book is going to be featured because of the film, and *The Story of Dr. Dolittle* is going to bask in the enviable spot of "best sellerism." We, as teachers and librarians, are faced with the problem of just what to do with Dr. Dolittle.

Perhaps one valid approach among others would be to put the book in historical perspective and help children, with the aid of this book, to know that times and human behavior change. What a valuable lesson in human relations that would be! That this book written so many years ago talks about race issues as they existed then, perhaps should not be overlooked for that quality alone! Teachers of literature to adolescents and college students often use books as a vehicle to broaden understanding of social issues. Why not at the elementary level as well? Perhaps it would be valuable to offer Lofting's portrayal of the Negro with more contemporary fiction, and invite comparisons. The Snowy Day, Lions in the Way, The Empty Classroom, are just a few that can be used as a comparison. It seems that this approach, to what could be a negative experience, could make it a valuable, positive one.

The Story of Dr. Dolittle, despite this objectionable section, is one of the most popular and delightful tales in children's literature. It is the first book in a series that keeps children's librarians busy checking them in and out of the children's room. It should not be hidden away or censored.

The way in which the teacher, parent, or librarian handles the sections discussed in this article, can make the difference between an embarrassing, perhaps dangerous, experience and a vital, socially needed, literary experience. That choice is with us now. It demands serious thought. (pp. 439, 445)

> *Dewey W. Chambers, "How Now, Dr. Dolittle?" in* Elementary English, *Vol. XLV, No. 4, April, 1968, pp. 437-39, 445.*

Hugh Lofting makes it quite clear that white girls do not pre-

fer black men. . . . [When Doctor Dolittle expresses doubt to Prince Bumpo that the whiteness he has been given] will last, Dab-Dab says, "Serve him right, if he does turn black again! I hope it's a dark black." This type of comment shows Lofting's real attitudes, and it cannot be discounted. There is no reason for Dab-Dab's animosity toward Prince Bumpo—except that Bumpo is black. In keeping his part of the deal, Bumpo has shown himself an honorable man. (pp. 108-09)

> *Dorothy M. Broderick, "Black Is Not Beautiful," in her* Image of the Black in Children's Fiction, *R. R. Bowker Company, 1973, pp. 103-18.*

THE VOYAGES OF DOCTOR DOLITTLE (1922)

If you are threatened with fire, flood, or earthquake, save "Doctor Dolittle" at all cost. He made his appearance with characteristic modesty last year, in *The Story of Dr. Dolittle.* But this particular reviewer must have been blinded with too much reading of serial stories and caught never a glimpse of the kindly naturalist, till *The Voyages of Dr. Dolittle* appeared unheralded and the reviewer war-whooped with joy. The two books are one, each better than the other, depending on which you read last. In many a household between now and the coming holidays, the unprincipled adults will be chuckling over the book in secret, while the innocent child waits patiently for Christmas morning to make the acquaintance of Doctor Dolittle. For more than half a century, Alice has ruled supreme in Wonderland. How glad she must be to make room on her throne for the genial animal-doctor, a man after her own heart, and his remarkable household. Read the book. Join that valiant crew that sailed in the porpoise-driven ship, cheer for the Doctor-matador at the last bullfight at Monteverde, but come back to dwell in the little house at Puddleby-on-the-Marsh, "just in nice time for tea." Read the book, and then say if you know a better guardian for your child than the adorable animalinguist, John Dolittle, M.D.

> *Mabel H. B. Mussey, in a review of "The Voyages of Dr. Dolittle," in* The Nation, New York, *Vol. CXV, No. 2996, December 6, 1922, p. 620.*

"Do you wish a ticket to go away and come back," asks the poet gravely, "or do you wish a ticket to go away and never come back?"

Mr. Lofting has Dr. Dolittle go away and come back. Children who know the Animals' Own Doctor through the two books about him would not want him to buy a ticket to go away and never come back. In the book of *Voyages* Tommy Stubbins, a cobbler's son, tells of a journey with the doctor from their home, Puddleby-on-the-Marsh. This is a little town with a river running through it. Sailing ships may follow this river like a street. "When they got round the bend in the river and the water was hidden from view, you could still see their huge brown sails towering over the roofs of the town, moving onward slowly like some gentle giants that walked among the houses without noise." This mystery of sails and roofs is the kind of picture which the artist-author sees in his own way but must allow us to see in ours. I have heard an argument between two young readers about the color of those sails. Weren't they cinnamon sails, or something nearer red? In the same earnest fashion they have discussed the plumage of the parrot, Polynesia, and what things were seen under the sea through the transparent shell of the marvellous snail.

Mr. Lofting makes many delightful drawings for his books, but he will not always commit himself. He offers his inventions with a gentle humor and with the kindliness of Dr. Dolittle at his kindest. But he knows what to leave to his readers.

> *Gracie Hazard Conkling, in a review of "The Voyages of Doctor Dolittle," in* The Yale Review, *Vol. XIII, No. 2, January, 1923, p. 410.*

Not since Lewis Carroll continued Alice's Adventures in Wonderland through the Looking-Glass, has an author responded to an encore more successfully than Hugh Lofting in his second volume of the biography of Doctor Dolittle. The sterling qualities of the Kindly One, as the good doctor is dubbed by the discriminating Popsipetels, shine undimmed through the adventurous pages of the Voyages. The fresh and the familiar invest this happy sequel with a blended charm. Polynesia the parrot is here, with all her old flair for leadership; faithful Jip, with his gold collar and his capacity for meeting an emergency; Dab Dab, the perfect duck of a housekeeper, and the African prince, Bumpo, now matriculated at Oxford where he likes Cicero—"Yes, I think Cicero's fine—so simultaneous. By the way, they tell me his son is rowing for our college next year—charming fellow." And there are even more new friends than old: Long Arrow, and Jabrizi, the Beetle, all the Men of the Moving Land, and last but not least the Great Glass Sea-Snail.

In the earlier book, the doctor's humanitarian impulses are in the ascendant—the vaccination of monkeys may surely be called humanitarian by courtesy. In the *Voyages,* his preoccupations are linguistic and philological, and his methods of passionate research into the sources of the shellfish language are interpreted for us by his ardent disciple, Tommy Stubbins, the nine-and-one-half-year-old son of the Puddleby cobbler. With Tommy we study the meagre vocabulary of the rare and solitary Wiff-Waff, and the hybrid soliloquies of the Silver Fidgit who learned his English during an enforced sojourn in a public aquarium.

But the adventures of this twentieth-century descendant of Sir John Mandeville and Baron Munchausen are not all in research. If Darwin, on the Voyage of the Beagle, had discovered Spidermonkey Island and played the Promethean rôle to the fireless Popsipetels, who can say what the effect might have been upon his scientific temperament? For the central adventure, toward which the others mount, occurs, modern fashion, in the heart of Doctor Dolittle, where the scholar and the utopist-administrator come to grips, and he makes his great decision, laying the wooden crown of the Popsipetels upon the beach of Spidermonkey Island, to "tiptoe incognito" back to the comparative seclusion of Puddleby-on-the-Marsh. (pp. 337-38)

> *Florence Converse, " 'The Voyages of Doctor Dolittle', " in* Fact, Fancy and Opinion: Examples of Present-Day Writing, *edited by Robert M. Gay, The Atlantic Monthly Press, 1923, pp. 337-38.*

The story is filled with originality and humor. Dr. Dolittle is a genuinely kind and lovable character. The author's funny and fanciful illustrations keep the spirit of the story. In spite of its many merits, the book has been less praised in recent years because of the depiction of the African, Prince Bumpo.

After reading the initial description of him, the reader is certain the author intends to make him a buffoon: He "was dressed in a fashionable frock coat with an enormous red cravat. On his head was a straw hat with a gay band; and over this he held a large green umbrella. . . . He was very smart in every respect except his feet. He wore no shoes or sox." The idea of his being made into a clown is reinforced when one observes that his speech is filled with long words, frequently incorrectly used. However, one soon learns of Bumpo's worth. Dr. Dolittle is genuinely glad to see him and is in no way condescending. On the voyage, Bumpo is treated as an equal in every respect and proves to be very well endowed with both intelligence and common sense. Polynesia, who has a keen mind but a rather vulgar way of speaking, uses the term "Nigger" a time or two but she does not mean it derogatorily. She relies on Bumpo to help her carry out practical matters that the kindly, but improvident, doctor would never think of. Although it is not likely the author intended to malign blacks, it is well that the offensive terms have been deleted from recent printings. (pp. 16-17)

> *Marilyn Leathers Solt, "The Newbery Medal and Honor Books, 1922-1981," in* Newbery and Caldecott Medal and Honor Books: An Annotated Bibliography, *by Linda Kauffman Peterson and Marilyn Leathers Solt, G. K. Hall & Co., 1982, pp. 11-226.*

THE STORY OF MRS. TUBBS (1923)

Without apparent theory, moral purpose, or a desire to be instructive, Hugh Lofting has proceeded joyfully to the making of literature. In this third volume of the admirable Dr. Dolittle's adventures, and in *The Story of Mrs. Tubbs,* a shorter story for smaller children, he has added to that rare list of juvenilia which includes Alice and her companions. Like Alice, Dr. Dolittle's friends are animals, and such animals: Dab-Dab, the accomplished duck housekeeper; Gub-Gub, the appealingly greedy little pig, and Speedy the Skimmer, the swallow who almost succeeds in annihilating time and space. Their adventure this time is a bird post office on a house-boat just off the coast of Africa, where tea is served every afternoon with cucumber sandwiches on Sundays, and where care is taken to provide the very best pens to write with because, of course, post-office pens are usually so bad. The enterprise is uncommonly successful, as anyone might have foreseen; "the post-office safe could hardly hold all the money taken in and the overflow had to be put in a vase on the kitchen mantelpiece." The book is filled with excellent suggestions for householders: pincushions served with the fish, for example, to stick your fish bones in instead of having them spread along the edge of your plate, and a speaking tube which leads to the open-air outside, into which any conversation, imperative but hardly suitable for the table, can be spoken. A thoroughly delectable book, in short, and rendered more so by the illustrations, done by Mr. Lofting himself and as merry and gentle and wise as any child could wish. (pp. 560-61)

> *Dorothy Graffe, "Children and Gentle Beasts," in* The Nation, *New York, Vol. CXVII, No. 3045, November 14, 1923, pp. 560-61.*

I hope the children will like **The Story of Mrs. Tubbs** as much as one adult reader loved and liked it. It is a most delicious little book, telling how Mrs. Tubbs, aged a hundred years, lost her farm and was on the world with her three friends, the pig, the duck and the dog, and how these faithful and wise animals gave her back her farm and her warm fire-side. It is in the true vein of the great fairy-story tellers, of Perrault, Grimm and Hans Andersen. I hope thousands of children will read about Mrs. Tubbs and her dear Pink, Penk and Ponk, and that it may become a classic among the fairy tales. (pp. 145-46)

> Katharine Tynan, "A Christmas Bundle," in The Bookman, London, Vol. LXVII, No. 399, December, 1924, pp. 145-46.

Let me dispose rapidly of a minor Hugh Lofting, **The Story of Mrs. Tubbs,** charming no doubt, for the youngest, but un-worthy of what was to come later. Even his drawings are still tentative here. (p. 42)

> May Sarton, "For the Once and Future Child," in The New York Times Book Review, May 5, 1968, pp. 6, 42-3.

DOCTOR DOLITTLE'S CIRCUS   (1924)

Doctor Dolittle, whether in picture or story, has always been irresistible, and this year we think he is more so than ever. He certainly belies his name for he is always doing *much* for others. Now that he has gone in for the circus business, to-gether with his little party (Jip the dog, Dab-Dab the duck, Too-Too the owl, Gub-Gub the pig, the pushmi-pullyu, and the little white mouse, not forgetting the Cat's-meat Man), his kindly ministrations are as much in demand as ever. The difficulty in providing the varied diet of his family was not an easy one to overcome, but was as nothing compared to the obstacles in the way of assisting Sophie the seal to escape and join her heartbroken husband in the Bering Straits. His mar-vellous facility in animal language opens the way to much en-tertainment. Those who have met Doctor Dolittle before will hardly be likely to miss further news of him, and those who have not, should not on any account miss this delightful in-troduction. We hope he has many adventures ahead of him.

> A review of "Doctor Dolittle's Circus," in The Book-man, London, Vol. LXIX, No. 411, December, 1925, p. 152.

PORRIDGE POETRY: COOKED, ORNAMENTED, AND SERVED BY HUGH LOFTING   (1924)

A book of quaint and jolly rhymes and quainter and jollier pictures by Hugh Lofting is sure of a welcome from all admir-ers of the **Dolittle** Books. Whether he is telling us about the "Food-Hymn of the Cook-Goblins," "The Pirate of the Kitchen Sink," or "The Toffee Analyst," or any one of the numerous characters he introduces us to, Mr. Lofting is al-ways entertaining. . . . Children may find some of the words in certain of the verses rather long, but they are nice-sounding words with a rhythm about them that is certainly attractive.

> A review of "Porridge Poetry," in The Bookman, London, Vol. LXIX, No. 411, December, 1925, p. 190.

Four years after **The Story of Dr. Dolittle** the inventor of the charming doctor showed himself equally adept at creating nonsense verse. Hugh Lofting . . . is a master of word play, as is shown on many a page of this volume "cooked, orna-mented, and served up" by him. . . .

In his free and easy manner Hugh Lofting offers here some of the same gentle humor and telling understatement that one finds in his prose. Like Edward Lear, he takes the furniture, the dead wood of everyday life, and sends it off for a walk or a sail. . . .

Long out of print, this book should be reissued, omitting the verse and drawing **"Scallywag and Gollywog,"** which would give offense to many readers. (p. 9)

> Virginia Haviland and William Jay Smith, "Rhymes," in their Children & Poetry: A Selective, Annotated Bibliography, The Library of Congress, 1969, revised 1979, pp. 1-13.

DOCTOR DOLITTLE'S ZOO   (1925)

Hugh Lofting's tales about Dr. Dolittle have won a great vogue among young people wherever the English language is read. This is the fifth of the series, and with each one of the successive volumes the wonder has grown that he could keep up the pace he had set in the first and that invention, fancy, whimsical humor, incidents, evolving story, should continue to bubble forth from his pen with as much grace and charm and freshness as in the beginning. In this new tale Dr. Dolittle and his famous company return from their voyagings to the old house at Puddleby and there, with the help of Stubbins, Polynesia, Too Too, Dab-Dab and all the rest of them, the Doctor plans and creates a wonderful, a most wonderful Zoo. It is his conviction that a zoo should be an animal home, not an animal prison, and so in the big old garden he and his help-ers make the most marvelous and fascinating Animal King-dom, or Town, that anybody could possibly imagine. There is a Mouse and Rat Club at whose meetings are told breath-taking stories of experiences, dangers and hair-breadth es-capes which fill several chapters. There is a rapid succession of thrilling events in the Zoo which finally reach their climax in a great mystery. The utmost effort of Dr. Dolittle, aided by all the animals, and especially by Kling, the Detective Dog, is needed to solve this mystery, but they finally do it, and so bring about some wonderful good fortune for all the animals. The book's quaint fancies, lively narrative and inter-esting story will make it quite as much a favorite with young readers as its predecessors have been. The author has as great a gift for drawing as he has for story telling, and his many illustrations—there are eighty-eight in black and white and a frontispiece in colors—are remarkable for their economy and expressiveness of line.

> "New Books for Children Herald the Holiday Sea-son," in The New York Times Book Review, No-vember 8, 1925, p. 4.

DOCTOR DOLITTLE'S CARAVAN   (1926)

From the day I opened the pages of Hugh Lofting's first book and read how Doctor Dolittle kept white mice in his piano there could be no further doubt; here was a character to be cherished through thick and thin, and though the cherishing has proved a lengthier job than one expected—he is now in his sixth volume—it has been better rewarded than most sim-ilar forms of perseverance, and I admit to following the latest venture of that eminently sensible gentleman in his caravan, if with a less bounding step, at least with the same undimmed though slightly hypnotic interest that I first followed his ship.

To invent a fantastic story is fairly easy, but Hugh Lofting's is the masterful fantasy that wears the semblance of real life. He produces a serious chronicle of that particular sort of dullness which is more fascinating than adventure, a chronicle to which his pictures add the last touch of conviction. It is impossible while reading not to take him seriously. What is enjoyable in his characters is not so much their humor as their profound commonsense—a quality one always suspected animals of possessing but which no other writer has so fully revealed. And above all this admirable fooling he bears the banner of humanitarianism sanely and without sentimentality.

> *Margery Williams Bianco, in a review of "Doctor Dolittle's Caravan," in* The Saturday Review of Literature, *Vol. III, No. 15, November 6, 1926, p. 277.*

No one who has heard boys and girls talk about Doctor Dolittle and seen their shining, reminiscent eyes, can deny his extraordinary hold on their affections. The reasons for this are more interesting than the blemishes in his creator's work.

Mr. Lofting has a vigorous imagination and inexhaustible invention. There are dramatic, exciting moments in his books. Read in **Doctor Dolittle's Postoffice** the story of the ship that, when the lighthouse lamp went out, was saved from running on the reefs by the combined efforts of the doctor, the sea-gulls, Dab-Dab the duck, and the canary who knew where the matches were. It is a thrilling, even moving chapter. Boys and girls love the sense of fun in the books, and reading them they chuckle to themselves—a good sign. The bringing together of the animal world and the world of men is an idea perennially fascinating to children. Nowhere has it been done more simply and convincingly, with so unforced a note.

The staunch little figure of Doctor Dolittle himself is the embodiment of pure kindliness, a quality which philosophers say the world needs today more than any other single thing. The depths of his compassion are as unplumbable as his hatred of injustice and cruelty. Whether it is a seal longing to escape from her tank to rejoin her afflicted husband in Bering Straits, or just a simpleminded old horse needing glasses, the good little man will do his best. If this hero were merely good and kind he might pall on the reader. But he is happy-go-lucky, improvident, ready to embark on any cause no matter how desperate; he is even just a bit ridiculous—but captivatingly so, one of those disarming people. In Doctor Dolittle himself lies the answer to most of the criticism of Hugh Lofting's work.

In his sixth and latest book, **Doctor Dolittle's Caravan,** the charm of the earlier volumes is lacking. The author is not as happy in his bird characters as in his animals. There are many dull pages. . . . Mr. Lofting's style has throughout been pedestrian. The language has been more commonplace and colloquial than the characterizations call for, and there have been ultramodern touches, plays to the adult gallery, that have no place in books for children. If anyone has been able to make a dent in the theory of the critical high hats that books in series tend to become ever more and more attenuated in interest it is Hugh Lofting, for **Doctor Dolittle's Postoffice** and **Doctor Dolittle's Circus,** the third and fourth books of the set, are almost as entertaining as the first and best-loved, **Story of Doctor Dolittle.** He must have a care, however, for even the appealing little round medical gentleman from Puddleby-on-the-Marsh who gave up his practice to be-

come an animal doctor cannot withstand the assaults of too long an exploitation. (pp. 353-54)

> *Marcia Dalphin, "The Doctor Dolittle Books," in* The New Republic, *Vol. XLVIII, November 10, 1926, pp. 353-54.*

The story of the Doctor's Caravan and of how he stages a Birds' Opera in a London theatre with a yellow canary as the leading lady, is told with the same whimsical, sympathetic touch that distinguished all the former **Dolittle** books. Mr. Lofting is to be highly commended for the skilful way in which he turns the limelight on the "animal shops" where animals are offered for sale; Doctor Dolittle's abhorrence of the usual animal shop because of its stuffiness and dirtiness which causes all kinds of unnecessary suffering, and his indignation at the man who buys wild birds and puts them in cages will find a warm response in the hearts of all animal-lovers. They will follow with delight the good Doctor's adventure in the shop where the blackbirds are encaged. How the Doctor disguises himself and steals into the shop at night and opens all the cages so that the blackbirds can fly out makes a stirring episode. It is a delightful book, and the illustrations, by the author, are in keeping with the quaint and original atmosphere of the story.

> *A review of "Doctor Dolittle's Caravan," in* The Bookman, London, *Vol. LXXIII, No. 433, October, 1927, p. 90.*

DOCTOR DOLITTLE'S GARDEN (1927)

Hugh Lofting's accounts of Doctor Dolittle's wonderful adventures and achievements have already become classics in the world of juvenile reading and the fact that they are greatly enjoyed by older people also is proof of their quality. Although this is the sixth of the series it shows no lessening in the power and fertility of his invention and his ability to make

From Doctor Dolittle's Caravan, *written and illustrated by Hugh Lofting.*

the most outlandish and amazing incidents and adventures seem realistic.

A review of "Doctor Dolittle's Garden," in The New York Times Book Review, *November 13, 1927, p. 35.*

Although Doctor John Dolittle has now adventured for a number of years, the ink in his veins courses as merrily as ever, and he is as lovable as he was in his Post Office days, and pleasanter company than he was last year. In this, the latest section of his biography, *Doctor Dolittle's Garden,* Mr. Lofting recounts many of the stories told to the Doctor by his dog and animal friends, and also tells of his scheme for arranging a country house for house flies. Luckily this plan is interrupted by the arrival of a giant moth, who descends from the moon to Doctor Dolittle's garden. Mr. Lofting breaks off his narrative at the moment when the Doctor, with some of his friends, who have used the moth as an aeroplane, first arrive on the moon. It is a little unkind of him to leave his readers in such suspense, but at least they can make sure of more to come. Mr. Lofting is to be congratulated on having once more recaptured the spirit of his earlier books; this one is sure to delight even those who have recently grown a little tired of the Doctor.

A review of "Doctor Dolittle's Garden," in The Spectator, *Vol. 141, No. 5224, August 11, 1928, p. 193.*

Full of originality, quiet humour, sound common sense, and interesting information about animals and insects, [this] is an absorbing and exciting book that Doctor Dolittle's numberless friends and admirers will hail with joy. Mr. Hugh Lofting's *Dolittle* stories must have done a great deal of good in strengthening the bond of sympathy and understanding between human beings and the animal world. In the present story a delightful and fantastic note is introduced when Doctor Dolittle finds an enormous giant moth in his garden one night outside his window. The moth's "shoulders behind the head, which pressed close against the panes, towered up to a height of at least two stories." After enormous difficulties in understanding the moth's language the Doctor realises that the moth has come from the moon, and eventually he undertakes a perilous journey to the moon—and in the next *Dolittle* book we shall probably learn what the Doctor found there.

A review of "Dr. Dolittle's Garden," in The Bookman, *London, Vol. LXXV, No. 445, October, 1928, p. 93.*

DOCTOR DOLITTLE IN THE MOON (1928)

"Human attention is like butter; you can only spread it so thin and no thinner. If you try to spread it over too many things at once, you just don't remember them." These wise words which appear on one of the first pages of the eighth and latest of the famous *Dolittle* books very aptly characterize our impression of *Doctor Dolittle in the Moon.*

Doctor Dolittle has been running thin. The illustrations have suffered as much as the text has from overwork.

While it is true that children's interest in a favorite character is often stimulated by their own imagination far beyond the limits of grown-up tolerance (and this knowledge has led us to deal gently with Doctor Dolittle long after we had ceased to read his adventures with any personal pleasure), the day

of reckoning is bound to come. We are inclined to think Doctor Dolittle's Waterloo lies in the marshy home of The Vanity Lilies of the Moon.

As to life in the Moon and the Man in the Moon, children have always liked to speculate with an upward stretch of the imagination. But this is a life to which poets and scientists know the roads and the ropes. More convincing revelations, more fortifying food than Doctor Dolittle's dull and unassimilated note-books suggest is essential. Mr. Lofting is not yet equipped for such a flight as this and Doctor Dolittle is a pathetic travesty of himself. We hope he falls into one of the craters of the Moon.

Anne Carroll Moore, "Spreading It Thinner," in New York Herald Tribune Books, *October 14, 1928, p. 8.*

Hugh Lofting's ever fertile imagination has produced another Dr. Dolittle book, this time, *Dr. Dolittle in the Moon*. . . . Out of the veriest fantasy, Mr. Lofting weaves fascinating and even convincing stories, which must make little eyes pop and little hearts throb. There are no books quite like them, and they have the advantage of their author's distinctive illustrations.

A review of "Dr. Dolittle in the Moon," in The Catholic World, *Vol. CXXVII, No. 765, December, 1928, p. 379.*

We understand that *Doctor Dolittle* is the favorite younger person's fiction in England today. This is the eighth volume concerning him. His character, created in narrative and illustration by Hugh Lofting, has taken American children by storm. One volume of his adventures after another has followed up his initial success.

To the present reviewer this latest story of the famous doctor creaks somewhat and runs pretty thin. Most of the illustrations are more careless and uninteresting than former work. The various phenomena furnished by vegetable life upon the moon rather pall. In fact, we found the story somewhat tedious.

Probably the main run of children will not agree with us. Everything in the book is easy to follow, and the conversations of the characters are so serious concerning their predicament that the illusion, for children, will be quite definitely preserved. The average child has very little sense of humor, or it is of the most rudimentary kind. Far cleverer, more original work, with more artfully worked-out detail would probably go over its head. Doctor Dolittle and his secretary and animal friends land on the moon from the back of a giant moth. Accept that and you at once accept everything and enjoy their journey of discovery, concerning which no great feats of the imagination are accomplished. Hugh Lofting knows his audience, he makes his episodes simple enough to be readily grasped. To us the present work is quite insipid cambric tea. It lacks the richness of certain of his former inventions. But children are traditional, and once they have whole-heartedly accepted an author they will go on reading him for a long time. As a child we could only read one or two of the Henty books, for the story—aside from the setting—was too nearly the same in each case. Yet boys that we knew devoured tons of those volumes. For Hugh Lofting and Dr. Dolittle we may, however, with sincerity wish a new source of energy. It won't do to let his series simply run on initial impetus. Too much good work has gone into some of the earlier books. The present one seems a bit tired.

A review of "Doctor Dolittle in the Moon," in The Saturday Review of Literature, *Vol. V, No. 24, January 5, 1929, p. 578.*

NOISY NORA (1929)

Children will chuckle with delight over this amusing tale and parents will bless Mr. Lofting for investing a widespread bad habit with so much fun while achieving its correction.

"Noisy Nora," who lived on a farm, had shocking table manners. She never said "please" or "thank you" and she always "ate with both hands at once," but the worst thing she did was to chew with her mouth open. "This made a terrible noise. Some people said it sounded like a seal coming up for air; others that it reminded them of the sea breaking against the rocks on a stormy night; others said that if they shut their eyes they would think of a herd of cattle tramping home through the mud." This was how she came by the nickname, "Noisy Nora," Mr. Lofting tells us.

And to this very bad habit was added another, that of stubbornness. The tale of how Noisy Nora is cured unfolds to the surprise and delight of any child. First she is sent to eat in the kitchen, but the dairy maids refuse to eat with her; then she is sent to the stable to eat with the horses, to the cowshed to eat with the cows, to the pigpen to eat with the pigs, to the old barn from which even the rats drive her out, and last of all she is sent to Top Meadow where it is so still that she can hear herself eat and at last she hears what a dreadful noise she had been making. "Then and there Nora made up her mind never again to chew with her mouth open and always to think of others when she was at table."

The little pink book, a trifle bigger than a Beatrix Potter book, is charmingly designed and decorated. Children learning to read and write will be delighted with the clear printing of the hand lettering, which furnishes them incidentally with good copy for their own efforts in book making.

There is a genuine atmosphere of country life in this little book which a child will feel—the little animals, the ants, the grasshoppers, the butterflies and birds in the Top Meadow have the thrill of their own life and suggest the possibility of more tales from Mr. Lofting for little children.

Anne Carroll Moore, " 'An Almost True Story'," in New York Herald Tribune Books, *July 7, 1929, p. 8.*

Nora is quite the most horrible looking child ever pictured in a book. The illustration of her is repulsive. No wonder that even the pigs could not endure her table manners. The book is a little moral preachment in favor of good table manners, but is saved from being painful by Mr. Lofting's humor and the excessiveness of Nora's bad manners. (p. 5)

Mary Graham Bonner, "A Shelf for the Younger Reader," in The New York Times Book Review, *July 28, 1929, pp. 5, 17.*

THE TWILIGHT OF MAGIC (1930)

So long have the ***Doctor Dolittle*** books represented the essence of Hugh Lofting's spirit that his enthusiastic public may be startled to see this latest imaginative experiment. ***The Twilight of Magic*** differs in subject and style from those other robust excursions among the humorous animals of his fancy. Here Lofting is not wholly a Jolly-cum-pop: he is a poet. In the medieval atmosphere of a town not yet freed from superstition move the figures of Giles, a nine-year-old boy, and his sister, Anne. Childish concern for their father's financial troubles leads them to ask aid from the singular old applewoman, Agnes, who threw a red apple into their window and is known in the neighborhood as Shragga, the Witch. Their visit to her wee, tumbledown hut is followed by a walk to the sea garden and the discovery of the Whispering Shell, a highly important element in the tale. It is in this first half of the book that Mr. Lofting is gorgeously himself. The children's mysterious adventures, their quaintly stiff conversations, the descriptions of the town and its stock characters, Michael, the Blind Man, Luke the Lame Boy, Johannes, the Philosopher, and the kindly young King spring before us as naturally as any other high-colored children of his fertile mind. Even grown-ups will read these breath-taking scenes, which have the flavor of the Middle Ages, yet oddly enough could be part and parcel of modern life and Giles and Anne two of the little people of today.

Why does Giles have to grow up at the King's Court and eventually fall in love with that beauteous Countess Barbara betrothed to the King? That is indeed a conventional termination to a wonderful wild goose chase of a fantasy, and, while it completes the narrative, we rebel against it. Giles and Anne should always have remained children. The second part of the ***Twilight of Magic*** is not in any way ill done: it carries out the tradition of the ancient fairy tales. But the charm of Part I has cooled off as the sharp, crisp taste of a fresh ginger cooky becomes slightly flat when it is set too quickly by a window where a breeze is blowing. Possibly this is because Mr. Lofting is not yet an adept at this particular kind of fantastic yarn. Not that there are not whimsical touches in it that whet the appetite,—such as that of the elderly princess, Sophronia, who coveted the Whispering Shell, and Geoffrey, the Gypsy who raised the white roses for the King. . . .

[The] strength of Hugh Lofting consists in the fact that he can always produce a sense of cosy reality in the minds of his child readers, even though his atmosphere is of a fantastic weaving. [A witness to this fact is] the description of the house of Agnes, the Applewoman, alias Shragga, the Witch; and as usual the animals have a loved individuality. . . .

The jacket describes his book as "a story of the Middle Ages in England,"—and it is quite and utterly mistaken. There is no mention of England. Why should there be? This is a fairy tale for any country, smacking perhaps a little of the Middle Ages, but like a conscientious fairy tale not adhering to any age. It is Lois Lenski who has shown intense enough understanding of both the letter and spirit of the book to make it glow from end to end with her decorations. Without these much of the witch-like beauty of the piece would be lacking.

Laura Benét, in a review of "The Twilight of Magic," in The Saturday Review of Literature, *Vol. VII, No. 18, November 15, 1930, p. 344.*

The Twilight of Magic seeks to capture within the pages of a young folks' story the moment in history when men first began to suspect that laws rather than magic governed happenings which they could not understand. That is a difficult subject for any kind of story, let alone a story for junior readers. If any one now writing could handle it, Hugh Lofting might be reasonably adequate, but even he has fallen somewhere between fact and fancy. Of all the writers of the past that we recall at the moment, George MacDonald seems the only one who could perhaps have been equal to the subject. Nevertheless *The Twilight of Magic* is good reading, and it is entirely possible that Mr. Lofting thought his purpose best served by giving history a touch of the supernatural, and the supernatural an historical setting. . . .

[It is] a pleasant tale full of action, with considerable vitality in the characterization.

The other aspect of the book—suggested by its title, *The Twilight of Magic*—will bear analysis without losing any of its interest. The age in which Giles and Anne were living was frankly superstitious, but the two children, types of the youngest generation, were not especially superstitious. Generally speaking, they were disposed to find natural explanations for what might look like magic. They knew that Agnes was not a harmful witch as many supposed, but a kindly old woman. Agnes accomplished seemingly difficult things, but the children knew that her magic was only skill and knowledge. They had faith that she could help them, not because she was in league with powers of darkness, but because she was wise and kind. The children were friends, too, with Johannes the hermit, harmless Johannes who was brought before the magistrate simply because he studied alchemy. "Chemistry, or alchemy," said Johannes, "is something that people still connect with witchcraft. The schools will admit a few works on mathematics—but nothing new in mathematics. Some day perhaps they'll let books on chemistry into schools. But not now. No, we have to work like thieves behind closed doors lest we be called wizards for bringing forth anything new."

So candles were burning here and there in the twilight of magic. If young readers miss a little of the full significance of that, they can at any rate enjoy this story about medieval folk who seem like people you might meet on your own street.

"Lofting, for Older Children," in The Christian Science Monitor, *November 22, 1930, p. 13.*

I am sorry to discover that Mr. Hugh Lofting can be other than first rate; his new book I found distinctly on the dull side. The opening chapters bring no enthusiasm to life in the mind, none of the expected interest is awakened in what is to follow, the characters (human beings this time) display no individualities that matter, and the story flags.

Eileen Squire, in a review of "The Twilight of Magic," in The London Mercury, *Vol. XXV, No. 146, December, 1931, p. 224.*

DOCTOR DOLITTLE'S RETURN (1933)

Another fresh phase in Doctor Dolittle's amazing career and not a whit less refreshing than any of the others. Each member of his quaint family, from Dab-Dab, the housekeeper (duck) to Gub-Gub the pig, always in hot water, is as familiar and unforgettable to countless readers as the famous Doctor himself. He has been visiting the moon, and now we find the family anxiously awaiting the Smokesignal which is to announce his return. What fun to see him coming along riding on an enormous locust, and what a thrill to hear the surprising and mysterious tales he has to tell. Mr. Lofting's word and pen pictures are quite inimitable.

A review of "Doctor Dolittle's Return," in The Bookman, London, *Vol. LXXXV, No. 507, December, 1933, p. 363.*

From a child's point of view, a new *Dolittle* book is always an event in publishing circles. Even an exacting grown-up recognizes that while some are better than others, there is no reason to deprive a child of any. Hugh Lofting takes his responsibilities seriously; he always gives his world-audience the best he has at the time he is writing. This time he has plenty to give. It is decidedly an important *Dolittle.*

This may be partly because he has taken time to let the reservoir of his invention fill up. It must be two years at least since Dr. Dolittle took that journey to the Moon, from which only children were confident he would return. Meanwhile Gub-Gub the pig held the franchise with chapters from his work in progress, the "Encyclopedia of Food." But there seemed no good reason why the hero of Puddleby-on-the-Marsh should ever come back there. It must not be forgotten that he has a definite, convincing and intractable personality. He is grieved not only by the unfairness of men to animals and by their cruelty to each other, but to the prevalence of such relations of animals one to another. In the Moon he found a kingdom where the rule of tooth-and-claw had been trained clean out of creation. It seemed a suitable place to stay, especially as men there could get as far back to Methuselah as under Mr. Shaw. But because this is what men need, Dr. Dolittle had to come back with it. The children were right in expecting him.

The *Dolittle* stories were born in the trenches. They were letters to children, but they were also Hugh Lofting's personal escape from the intolerable wrongness of life. Probably nothing would so please him as the assurance that he had helped to train a generation in the unshakable conviction that there should be never another war. Because he is a born writer for children, this passionate conviction never gets to the propaganda point. But its presence in his own consciousness makes all the volumes of this series a continuous classic for children. Though in this volume Dr. Dolittle returns eighteen feet tall, he is still the little brother of all the world.

May Lamberton Becker, in a review of "Doctor Dolittle's Return," in New York Herald Tribune Books, *December 10, 1933, p. 9.*

TOMMY, TILLY, AND MRS. TUBBS (1936)

Mr. Lofting, it is hardly necessary to state, knows children. He understands their desire to be amused and just what it is that 6-to-8-year-olds find exquisitely humorous. In *Tommy, Tilly and Mrs. Tubbs,* which has already been ranked by one group of children as "even nicer than *The Tale of Mrs. Tubbs,* because it is funnier," he gives us another instance of that serious make-believe, that perfectly reasonable and matter-of-fact treatment of nonsense, which delights a youthful audience. Reading the text and looking at the amiably absurd drawings, it seems quite credible that poor Mrs. Tubbs's house should be swept flat by the wind, and that the faithful animals, Polly Ponk the Duck, Peter Punk the Dog and Patrick Pink the Pig, should console and protect their mistress. Not only that, for by good generalship and constructive planning and with the aid of Tilly, Queen of the Swallows, and

Tommy, King of the Water Rats, they establish Mrs. Tubbs in the roofed-over cellar, a home which will be safe forevermore against all wind and storm and rain and snow. . . .

[The] suspense of the tale carries the young reader on from page to page, so that this will be an excellent addition to the books for beginners in reading, while still younger children will listen entranced when it is read aloud.

> *Anne T. Eaton, in a review of "Tommy, Tilly and Mrs. Tubbs," in* The New York Times Book Review, *March 7, 1937, p. 6.*

DOCTOR DOLITTLE AND THE SECRET LAKE   (1948)

It has been twenty-eight years since the first of the **Doctor Dolittle** stories appeared, since when the good doctor has become so firmly entrenched in children's affections the world over that one tends to identify him with his creator. When Hugh Lofting died last year his books had been translated into twelve languages, so there will be many waiting to read this last odyssey of the funny little man of good-will whose understanding of animal talk and animal nature made him uniquely beloved.

Once again, accompanied by Tommy Stubbins and his animal family, he journeys to Africa, through strange fantastic regions to the Secret Lake where millions of crocodiles help him extricate his old friend, Mudface the turtle, from trouble. And Mudface, who had been an unwilling guest on Noah's Ark, rewards the doctor with his own unorthodox, dramatic version of the Flood and its aftermath. Occasionally we agree with Cheapside that Mudface is a bit long-winded, but his story of the start of a new civilization is highly exciting and holds overtones of significance in this post-war world. The doctor is as capable and gracious as ever, the animals as amusing, and the author's inventiveness as fascinating. Age did not wither Hugh Lofting's infinite variety.

> *Ellen Lewis Buell, in a review of "Doctor Dolittle and the Secret Lake," in* The New York Times Book Review, *October 3, 1948, p. 35.*

To find ourselves once more in the company of the good doctor, Tommy Stubbins, Polynesia the parrot, Dab-Dab the duck, Gub-Gub the pig, and all the rest gives us the cosy feeling of a rainy day, an open fire and the tea table beside it. . . .

Mudface is without doubt long-winded, but the incidents of his story click into place with a logical attention to detail that children will find satisfying. Dr. Dolittle himself displays the same unselfish friendliness, energy and pluck that have endeared him to child readers for so many years.

> *Anne Thaxter Eaton, "Let's Read in the Holidays!" in* The Christian Science Monitor, *December 21, 1948, p. 11.*

The old hand had not lost its cunning when this story was written. The animal doctor and his faithful assistant, Tommy Stubbins, are as simple and delightful as ever and the strange assortment of creatures which make up his household and friends remain admirably in character. . . .

It is a long story but easy to read. It never gets dull or pretentious or self-conscious. It never loses its feeling of spontaneity and Hugh Lofting's pictures are as good as ever. I see no reason why those who have read and enjoyed **The Story of Dr.**

Dolittle (a necessary preclude to the proper enjoyment of any other story of the animal doctor) should not greatly appreciate this new one.

> *Eleanor Graham, in a review of "Dr. Dolittle and the Secret Lake," in* The Junior Bookshelf, *Vol. 13, No. 3, October, 1949, p. 142.*

DOCTOR DOLITTLE AND THE GREEN CANARY   (1950)

Hugh Lofting was one of the rare few who wrote stories for younger children that could be called miniature novels. His series about the beloved John Dolittle introduced a veterinarian here in 1920, long before the passion for dogs, horses and "vets" swept America, and has been popular all over the world. With their solidly good prose, wealth of action and humor, and generosity of length, these books have helped to hold the fort for the more intelligent level of pleasure-reading. Now we have a second posthumous volume, the twelfth, whose place in the story chronology is third, coming after the **Voyages** which features the same heroine, the canary "Pippinella."

Pippinella is sympathetic to us, twenty-five years after her creation, because she shares in the rather hectic variety of lives which the modern world forces on every one's attention. Life in a castle, a coaching inn, a coal mine, a cathedral town, a ship's barber shop, a tropical island; life with a tramp, or as the darling of a regiment—in half the book, Pippinella recalls it all in her own words, while the doctor takes notes and his animal family express themselves appropriately.

The only kinds of life the little bird speaks of bitterly are her periods in a pet shop and with a miner's family. In all other circumstances, caged or free, she has joy enough, generally, to record her experience in songs the doctor uses as a basis for his bird opera.

With Pippinella's story brought up to date, the Dolittle fami-

From Doctor Dolittle and the Secret Lake, *written and illustrated by Hugh Lofting.*

ly becomes absorbed in helping her find her most beloved master, an ex-duke, author, social reformer, and quondam window washer. "The enemy," whose country he hoped to reform by his writings, has pursued him, tried to steal his manuscripts, shanghaied him, etc. After an exciting chase, with the help of the sparrow-gangs of London, he and his writings are saved. And all go off to Puddleby.

Pippinella will delight children because her life is full of adult excitement: industrial revolution, poverty and riches, meanness and compassion, all are kaleidoscoped into her bird's-eye report on the world. She seldom philosophizes, and her only way of showing judgment is in the giving or withholding of her song. Through her, Hugh Lofting has left a "message" or two, that the children will fully appreciate.

> *Louise S. Bechtel, "More Puddleby-on-Marsh," in* New York Herald Tribune Book Review, *November 12, 1950, p. 7.*

[*Doctor Dolittle and the Green Canary*] is worth waiting for.

Pippinella, the Green Canary, played an important part in *Doctor Dolittle's Caravan,* but her story is so complex, exciting and humorous that it deserves a whole book. Despite its length, the story never flags or loses its tension; and the mystery of the window cleaner will fascinate most readers as it did Gub Gub. I suppose this will be the last of the *Dolittle* books. It is a worthy end to a great series. Great humour, tenderness, humanity, sanity—all the rare qualities which went to make up the character of the Doctor are here. He is as funny, as lovable and as splendid as ever.

> *A review of "Doctor Dolittle and the Green Canary," in* The Junior Bookshelf, *Vol. 15, No. 5, November, 1951, p. 216.*

In the recently published *Dr. Dolittle and the Green Canary* [Lofting's] imaginative interpretation of the ways of birds and animals is as convincing as ever. This time Pippinella, the green canary, is in the centre of the picture, telling the doctor the sad story of her life—how the soldiers rescued her from the Marquis's castle when it was burned to the ground, how she was stolen by a tramp, bought by Auntie Rosie, then given to a strange window-cleaner who lived in a windmill. After his mysterious disappearance she escapes from her cage and flies oversea in search of him. She finds him, loses him again, and finally comes into the possession of Dr. Dolittle. It is a pity that for as much as two-thirds of the book the doctor is no more than a passive listener. But in the last section, when he takes up the search in person, he comes into his own. The pace is brisker, the adventures more exciting; the window-cleaner is found and the thief who stole his papers caught redhanded. Unfortunately the principal human character, the window-cleaner, is never wholly credible, and his mysterious activities are too vaguely accounted for. Apart from this the book is extremely readable. There are many flashes of ironic humour and delicious absurdity, keen observation, vivid imagery (the ship that Pippinella sights in the storm is "like a great grey horse mired and floundering in a field of grey mud")—all this, and more. As strongly as in any of the books the reader senses Lofting's deep humanity, his pity for the under-dog, his hatred of violence and cruelty. Where in this world shall the heart be at peace? In an old cathedral town, says Pippinella, where life is leisured and comfortable, and deep-voiced chiming bells roll out the hours. But for whoever has wings and is free to fly it shall be in some

tropical land far over the sea "where the blue and yellow macaws climb ropes of crimson orchids."

> *"John Dolittle, M. D.," in* The Times Literary Supplement, *No. 2599, November 23, 1951, p. vii.*

DOCTOR DOLITTLE'S PUDDLEBY ADVENTURES (1952)

Hugh Lofting knew children so well and his style is so good that the best of these stories, first published about 1925, sound as if written for children of 1952. Some of them were published in this paper. Here are speedy action, crime on land and sea, and the pleasantly adult attitude of the famous animal doctor. . . .

There are eight stories of varied length. Most Dolittle fans will like "The Sea Dog," "Dapple," "The Dog Ambulance," and "The Stunned Man," with its dog detective. They may not care so much for the latter half of the book, with the stories about birds, a maggot, and a lost boy at the London Zoo. For continued interest, the long story of *Doctor Dolittle and the Green Canary,* the other posthumous book, is far better.

This twelfth *Dolittle* book is announced as the last to come in a series begun as illustrated letters to Lofting's own children, written from the front in World War I. The old doctor is more real to many children now grown up than many a true historic character. He has become a folk figure whose influence will go on and on, bringing laughter and escape into fantasy that is always sturdily attached to the doctor's coat-tails. We suggest that homes owning none of the books should buy the first book first.

> *Louise S. Bechtel, in a review of "Doctor Dolittle's Puddleby Adventures," in* New York Herald Tribune Book Review, *November 9, 1952, p. 8.*

The first story in this, the twelfth and last of the *Dr. Dolittle* books, is a sea-adventure told to the dog inmates of the Home for Cross-bred Dogs in Dr. Dolittle's yard. For it Hugh Lofting had made some of the funniest, most appealing drawings of dogs that have appeared in any of his books. There are forty-one stories in all, and they are all good. Boys and girls both will appreciate the exciting tale of how Kling, the detective dog, solved a knotty problem and the strange story of the Green Breasted Martins. It is a grand book to have in the family, to read aloud and to share with friends. There is a generous number of illustrations, including one of Gub-Gub, the Pig, opposite page seventy-eight that is worth the price of the book.

> *Mary Gould Davis, in a review of "Doctor Dolittle's Puddleby Adventures," in* The Saturday Review, *New York, Vol. XXXV, No. 46, November 15, 1952, p. 51.*

The last scraps and unconsidered trifles of the Lofting imagination have been gathered together to make a book which is full of delights and touched with the sadness of all last things. As all who love Doctor Dolittle (and what right-minded person does not?) know, Lofting had lived so long with his creation that there was always more material than could be crammed into the stories, teeming as they do with life and action. Here, then, are some of the stories which could not be squeezed into the full-length books. They include a highly characteristic detective story, featuring Kling the dog detective, a hilarious fragment about Jip's attempt to establish a dog ambulance, and one of Lofting's finest conceptions, concerning the adventures of a maggot with the wanderlust. No posthumous publication could enhance the reputation of Hugh Lofting; this confirms the conviction that his was one of the most tender, humorous and inventive minds of our century. (pp. 181-82)

A review of "Doctor Dolittle's Puddleby Adventures," in The Junior Bookshelf, *Vol. 17, No. 4, October, 1953, pp. 181-82.*

DOCTOR DOLITTLE: A TREASURY (1967)

What are the virtues that have made Hugh Lofting's books nursery classics?

First, his sheer inventiveness. You can always rely on him to think of something new; it was fairly late in life that he thought of describing Noah's Flood through the recollections of Mudface the African turtle. And who else could have invented the pushmi-pullyu? Then, the circumstantial detail. Remember that neat parody of Swift in *Zoo,* when members of the Rat and Mouse Club purloined a miniature of the Doctor for the Committee Room? Remember Bumpo licking the flavoured gum from the stamps, in *Post Office?*

And then, the character drawing. How real those animals are—Gub Gub spending his money on out of season vegetables and a daily trotter-shine, Jip with his capacity for masculine scorn ('We shouldn't have started with that ridiculous pig. He always puts a hoodoo on everything'), Dab Dab the conscientious housekeeper with her appropriate passion for clean linen. People come off well too, especially that semi-grotesque couple Matthew Mugg and his wife Thedosia, and of course the lively lad Tommy Stubbins, whose ingenuous accounts of travel with the Doctor add a new dimension to the stories. Above all, the ironical expression of Lofting's humanitarian views makes the books sheer delight to adults reading aloud and provides something for intelligent youngsters to discover by degrees.

Hugh Lofting's sister-in-law has chosen extracts of varying length as an introduction to the Doctor for young readers. Here is almost the whole of *Voyages,* that superb South American rescue story. Here are the two best bits from *Cir-*

cus (more rescues, of Sophie the seal and the family of Nightshade the fox). Here is Speedy the Skimmer with his bird's-eye view of Columbus discovering America (from *Post Office*) and a few shorter pieces from *Story, Caravan, Green Canary, Secret Lake* and *Puddleby Adventures.* I greatly miss that West African Wooster, Bumpo Prince of Jolliginki, but perhaps Lofting's treatment could give offence to some in these days. I miss the sophisticated fun of the Canary Opera and the thrill of the Bridge of Apes. I don't miss the two Moon books, for here Lofting's imagination flagged a little. But whatever the *Treasury* has had to put aside, there is enough in it to launch children on the full stories. . . . Not only children will be tempted by these samples; there are no age-frontiers for books as good as these.

Postscript. Among twenty-four drawings not previously published, one of Jip drawing the Dog Ambulance runabout, and a representation of the Jabrizi beetle's picture-letter should particularly please Dolittle addicts. (pp. 1126-27)

Margery Fisher, in a review of "Dr. Dolittle: A Treasury," in Growing Point, *Vol. 7, No. 1, May, 1968, pp. 1126-27.*

[The publisher Jonathan Cape,] seeing that the film will not only give the great Doctor a new lease of life but also a most undesirable face-lift, have persuaded his creator's sister-in-law to put together a selection from eight of the twelve incomparable books. These are no substitute for the full canon, but an appetizing introduction for those yet to meet Doctor Dolittle in all his splendour and, perhaps still more, a bedside book for devotees.

Doctor Dolittle is one of the very few entirely memorable creations in twentieth-century fiction, and like most of the greatest fictional characters he is a good deal bigger than any of his books. Some of the stories—if one dare criticize—are rather on the long side; they have longueurs if not tedium. A "treasury" like this has the advantage therefore of giving us the essence of the great man and of his company. A lovely book.

A review of "Doctor Dolittle: A Treasury," in The Junior Bookshelf, *Vol. 32, No. 3, June, 1968, p. 167.*

Toshi Maruki

1912-

Japanese author and illustrator of picture books.

The following entry presents criticism of *Hiroshima No Pika.*

Maruki is the creator of the picture book *Hiroshima No Pika* (1982; British edition as *The Hiroshima Story),* a work which relates the story of seven-year-old Mii and her parents during and after the atomic explosion in Hiroshima, Japan on August 6, 1945. A well-known artist who collaborated with her husband, Iri, on a celebrated series of murals depicting Hiroshima and Nagasaki in the aftermath of nuclear bombing, Maruki is herself a witness to the effects of Hiroshima. She based her book on the story of a survivor who met the artist at an exhibition of her paintings in 1953. *Hiroshima No Pika* uses a simple third-person narrative and powerful, expressionistic illustrations to reenact one family's true-life experiences; by relating graphic, troubling details in a calm, even tone, Maruki gives the reader an intimate knowledge of the tragedy and destruction that resulted from the disaster. For this reason, some critics are uncertain as to the age group to which the book should be recommended. They see it as too disturbing for most children, especially in the event that young readers will see only the horror and despair without understanding the lesson with which Maruki underscores her work, that of avoiding such catastrophes in the future. However, most observers note that Maruki gives her readers an accurate picture of historical interest and personal import with *Hiroshima No Pika* in a manner which is both poignant and compelling. In 1983, *Hiroshima No Pika* received the Ehon Nippon Prize for the best Japanese picture book, the Jane Addams Children's Book Award, and the Mildred L. Batchelder Award.

AMY L. COHN

Toshi Maruki, a Japanese artist, transforms the bright, vibrant colors that characterize the opening scenes of family life into a dismal, muddy palette that captures the subsequent violence and destruction. Her figures are of a monumental proportion, designed with an exaggerated emphasis on lower extremities. This emphasis combines with her use of a heavy, definite line to anchor figures to page and event. They are weighed-down, unable to escape the apocalyptic scene. This surrealistic quality extends the imagination as it reflects the real horror of nuclear holocaust. Although the drama of this fictionalized account stems from event rather than narrative, this haunting—and ironically beautiful—interpretation of a subject of acute concern and decidedly current interest insures *Hiroshima No Pika* a place in every collection.

> *Amy L. Cohn, in a review of "Hiroshima No Pika,"* in School Library Journal, *Vol. 28, No. 10, August, 1982, p. 119.*

BETSY HEARNE

This is a painful picture book, one that parents will not want to buy for bedtime sharing. It is also an extremely important book that should be bought and discussed with children in homes, schools, and libraries.

Like most effective works of art, **Hiroshima No Pika** tells a story instead of preaching a sermon. . . . The writing shifts clearly between Mii's personal view and a background explanation of what happened generally. The balance of small examples—a swallow hopping by because its wings are too burnt to fly—with historical description of a city laid waste is perfectly maintained. The most outstanding feature of the book is selection; everything unnecessary has been relentlessly excluded.

The text tells only half the story. Full-page paintings involve the reader in a journey that is indescribable beyond a certain number of words. The artist has walked a fine line between literal and expressionistic presentation. There is enough realistic detail to see and feel what is happening, with enough distance of things simply suggested to keep children from being overwhelmed by horror—again, that masterful selection of particulars. Color and movement sustain what detail there is and expand the impact of Mii's limited vision. We feel the trauma through identification with one child, but hers is multiplied by a swirl of bodies flung all around. Most lines are horizontal, shapes of the dead or dying, those fleeing across the pages. A burning red rivets the attention among black, gray, or dark green masses, with an occasional flash of intense blue in remnants of tattered clothing from a tranquil past.

As I write this on August 6, 1982, I wish no child had reason to read such a book. Certainly the artist/author and editor wished there had been no reason to create or publish it. But the fact that the events happened and should never happen again makes this important to every child at some stage when he or she can understand and deal with it, whether at the age of eight, with guidance from an adult, or at the age of 12 during a study of documentaries from World War II. No other book for children, outside of Eleanor Coerr's gentle *Sadako and the Thousand Paper Cranes,* turns atomic destruction from an abstraction to immediate reality, a surprising fact considering the literary reminders of the Holocaust. Children who see daily television newsclips of mutilated bombing victims in Beirut still cannot possibly realize the scale of futuristic warfare.

No one in America has ever felt the bomb. Even those in rural Japan were not sympathetic to the suffering of the survivor whose story is told here. It is hard to describe, hard to believe, hard to listen to. It will be even harder to experience if we do not listen. Our children need to laugh, but they also need to cry over other people's fates and grow a concern for the fate of their own world. The flight of the swallow will be in their hands.

Betsy Hearne, in a review of, "Hiroshima No Pika,"
in Booklist, *Vol. 79, No. 3, October 1, 1982, p. 201.*

NATALIE BABBITT

Hiroshima No Pika, by every dictate of convention, is a picture book. It has a large, square format, full-color pictures that occupy at least half of every spread, and a brief, simply expressed text. There can be no mistaking its intended audience. Toshi Maruki, the Japanese author-illustrator, states in an afterword that she has "written this book for grandchildren everywhere." She is a prize-winning artist, and the text is eloquent. But I would not give this book to anyone under the age of 10; it is far too strong. Neither would I give it to anyone over the age of 10; it is far too incomplete.

The dropping of atomic bombs on Hiroshima and Nagasaki in 1945 marked the end of one—and the beginning of another—profoundly complex situation. Only for someone who has some grasp of that fact can it begin to be encapsulated. A young child will see in Mrs. Maruki's book only a nightmare of fire, nakedness and death. Not a cautionary tale wherein if one is good one can escape disaster, but a tale wherein there is no escape, no matter what one does. There is no lesson to be learned because no solution is suggested—there is only the nightmare. For an older child, the inevitable question would be, "How could it have happened?" But the author gives no answers. The war that led up to it is barely suggested. It seems a random event, like the eruption of a volcano—and this it decidedly was not.

Children must learn on an ascending scale, according to their capability for understanding. They cannot swallow in one gulp such a graphic tract against nuclear warfare and be thereby prepared to stand against a recurrence. Better to begin gently their exposure to the hard fact of man's inhumanity. We cannot forget Hiroshima, no matter how much we may want to. But its lessons cannot be learned only through exposure to the horror, which in the end may encourage avoidance. Its lessons lie rather in some understanding of the moral instability of humans, which should encourage us to confront our philosophical and political systems. A child is not yet capable of such understanding and such confrontation. You would not hang Picasso's *Guernica* in the nursery.

Natalie Babbitt, in a review of "Hiroshima No Pika," in The New York Times Book Review, *October 10, 1982, p. 24.*

HAMIDA BOSMAJIAN

In the last two decades the ironic mode—the depiction of the human condition as limited by realistic historical time and space—has made definite encroachments on children's literature, particularly in stories about familial or social trauma. Though reviewers often question if works about child abuse, family disintegration, sex, violence, drug addiction, and prejudice can still be called children's fiction, perceptive adults would agree that such works can both have therapeutic value for young victims and raise the consciousness of youngsters whose environment is stable. There is, however, another category of the ironic mode in young people's literature: literature about historical trauma.

The nightmare of history is de-creation by adults, a nightmare that always includes children, be they enslaved Africans, Nazi holocaust victims, or survivors of Hiroshima. Historical trauma is a collective inundation of a culture; it affects the life, not just of the individual or the small group, but of the entire social order, its past, present, and future. The reader of literature about such traumas can no longer comfortably apply us/them dichotomies, for this literature universalizes moral problems, choices, and consequences. The image of the child in such literature, as recalled by a survivor-witness, is often a devastating ethical challenge, for children have often been singled out to suffer special brutalities.

We are loathe to shape our collective sin and guilt through the genre of children's literature. Perhaps we fear that to depict the children within the nightmare of history will both taint our own image of innocence and deny young readers trust in the future we shape; for is not children's literature a seduction of children into our symbolic structures and values? Yet children have lived and do live in historical time and voice their concerns today about the next possible nightmare—global nuclear war.

Three works that confront the themes and horizons of historical trauma in children's literature are Paula Fox's *The Slave Dancer,* Hans Peter Richter's *Friedrich,* and Toshi Maruki's *Hiroshima No Pika.* . . . [The] three cardinal sins of Western civilization—the enslavement of Africans, anti-Semitism and the holocaust, and the atom bomb as apocalypse—affect the child characters in these stories, and . . . they might influence the young reader's reaction to our civilization's discontents, crimes, and guilts. I contend that if such literary works are shared within a context where youngsters can voice their concerns and where adults are ready to engage in dialogue rather than diatribe, rationalization, and assuagement, they cannot but be therapeutic. They define and thereby set limits to the anxieties of young readers.

In each narrative the main character is a victim-survivor. In *The Slave Dancer* and *Friedrich* the narrator writes a confession because he witnessed and participated in historical crimes. Seven-year-old Mii in *Hiroshima No Pika* is a portrait ostensibly intended for the pre-analytical reader. The

From Hiroshima No Pika, *written and illustrated by Toshi Maruki.*

impact of her story, told in the third person, comes through the great simplicity of the text and its powerful illustrations. (pp. 20-1)

[The] book's last sentence, spoken by Mii's mother, presents the ultimate choice: "It can't happen again . . . if no one drops the bomb." Maruki decided to create the picture book after she listened to the spontaneous testimony about Hiroshima by a woman who came to see her picture exhibition about the atomic bomb. Her story is about a mother and daughter whose emotions and reflections are indirectly expressed through textual and pictorial images that are appropriate for a pre-school book. Japanese readers are likely to respond quite differently from American readers, the latter's heritage being that of perpetrator of this historical nightmare. Furthermore, the last sentence is more likely to be interpreted positively by Japanese, who view human beings as basically good whereas our tradition defines us as fallen and out of tune with nature and, therefore, more likely to drop the bomb.

Maruki's evocation of the sudden intrusion of "Little Boy," on August 6, 1945, into the life of ordinary people creates neither the apocalyptic myths nor the survival fantasies Ira Cherms discusses in "Mythologies of Nuclear War." The bomb drops while the family breakfasts. Mii's mother resolutely leaps into the flames to rescue her husband, bandages him with her obi, and carries him on her back out of the house and toward the river. At the same time she is always concerned about Mii, as fire and water constantly threaten to engulf the family. Mii sees heaps of dead and wounded, but the image that remains most in her consciousness is that of "a swallow. Its wings were burned, and it couldn't fly. Hop . . . hop. . . . " The harbinger of spring has been denied and will forever become part of Mii's sorrow.

After reaching the relative safety of an island, Mii and her parents fall asleep for four days. When mother and daughter return to Hiroshima, they find "A burnt out wasteland stretched before them as far as the eye could see." In contrast

to the firestorm, distinct pieces of rubble fill the field of vision where mother and daughter stand in an aura of relatedness. But the book does not end with a consolation: Mii's father dies of radiation sickness, and radiation keeps Mii from further growth, a fierce parody of the small child's secret wish. Mii will always be her mother's little girl since that fateful August day. "Sometimes Mii complains that her head itches, and her mother parts her hair, sees something shiny, and pulls it out of her scalp with a pair of tweezers. It's a sliver of glass, imbedded when the bomb went off years ago, that has worked its way to the surface." Mother and daughter do not dwell on their trauma, but those splinters are a shockingly novel image of memories that cannot be repressed.

Annually, mother and daughter express their emotions and memories through a communal ritual as Mii, along with others, mourns the dead by setting lanterns adrift in the seven rivers of Hiroshima to float to the sea. She marks one lantern "father" and the other "swallow" as her mother watches sadly. Maruki's final picture expresses serenity as brightly clad mourners set afloat warm-colored lanterns with their flames contained, spiritual symbols without the threat of conflagration. This picture also complements the last sentence, in that fire must be contained, and that can only happen if no one drops the bomb. . . .

[*The Slave Dancer, Friedrich,* and **Hiroshima No Pika**] do not project survival fantasies onto the nightmare of history, for each survivor-victim receives lasting physical, moral, or psychological damage. Each of the three child characters is denied wholeness through the process of individuation. We, who live in the fearful symmetry of the world of experience, would like our children to sing songs of innocence, but it is difficult to delude children who have intimations of nuclear war. By breaking with the convictions of children's literature, these stories open spaces or blanks for the young readers' thoughts. Young readers will fill the blanks and appropriate the text in ways not necessarily acceptable to adults. Yet, the damage will not come from books, for these books impress order on historical chaos. Stories that we hear or read are stories that can be told. While on the outer limits of children's literature, these books, too, share the subversiveness of children's literature written by adults. Through them we communicate to the child our suffering, sins, and guilts. A child character is central in each, and bears much of the burden, as a young scapegoat whose consciousness and conscience is to awaken to what our civilization lacked. Do we still expect children to redeem us even after we dropped "Little Boy" on Hiroshima? (p. 22)

Hamida Bosmajian, "Nightmares of History—the Outer Limits of Children's Literature," in Children's Literature Association Quarterly, *Vol. 8, No. 4, Winter, 1983, pp. 20-2.*

RAYMOND BRIGGS

When producing a book about nuclear war the writer-illustrator has to make a choice between two approaches. Does he attempt a realistic portrayal of the horror, or does he made use of symbolism and understatement? The first approach may cause the reader to close the book in disgust and disbelief; the second may mean that the power of a nuclear explosion is not communicated. The symbolic approach may also mean that the Art becomes more noticeable than the Bomb. In the case of a picture book, realism may lead to the horror comic and symbolism to the fairy tale. . . .

Toshi Maruki in **The Hiroshima Story** uses symbolism and understatement. These are no horrific pictures; The horror is conveyed by the text: "2,000 times the blast power of the largest bomb ever before used in war . . . total destruction extending 3km in all directions . . . metal and stone melted . . . 260,000 people died . . . nearly forty years later people are still dying . . . there is no cure for them . . ." The impossibility of illustrating material such as this forces the author to work in a symbolic, non-representational manner.

This symbolism, together with the Oriental style, tends to distance the subject matter from the European reader. Despite the factual text, in the pictures we are close to the world of the fairy tale. Years after the explosion a mother uses tweezers to pluck splinters of glass from her daughter's head, but she does it with a stylized gesture of balletic grace. Also, apart from the first two pages, which show a street scene and trams, there is scarcely a single modern object in the book. This gives the work a timeless quality and a universality, but it also tends to make Hiroshima fade into a mythological past. It may suit the apocalyptic nature of the Bomb, but the tragedy of nuclear war is that something so primeval and elemental could occur while the Archers are on the radio and the milkman is whistling up the garden path.

Kazuo Ishiguro, author of *A Pale View of Hills,* has pointed out the pitfalls for reviewers of [a book such as this]. He felt that his own book may have been treated with undue respect because he was Japanese and furthermore, a Japanese from Nagasaki. Does the awesome importance of the subject confer importance on any book dealing seriously with it? Is a book written in such a worthy cause automatically worthy? Is the reviewer to be unaffected by the knowledge . . . that Toshi Maruki went into the city after the explosion to help the survivors? Is it even possible to remain unaffected by this knowledge?

The subject of nuclear war in pictorial form needs a Munch, a Bosch or a Goya. At the moment it seems to be beyond the power of art to communicate and beyond the ability of the mind to comprehend.

Raymond Briggs, "Art of the Bomb," in The Times Educational Supplement, *No. 3524, January 13, 1984, p. 37.*

Robert N(orman) Munsch

1945-

American-born Canadian author of picture books.

Munsch is one of Canada's most popular creators of works for younger children. Recognized as a highly competent storyteller, he has transferred this talent to his picture books, which reflect his characteristics of surprising, humorous plots, familiar wording, and cycles of repetition which prompt audience participation. Most of Munsch's works originate from oral stories, which he reworks for at least three years prior to publication. Thought to lend themselves effortlessly to read-aloud circumstances, the books are considered fresh, bright depictions of young children who are remarkably inventive in their struggles against both the adult world and fantastical opponents such as marauding mud puddles, giants, and dragons. After receiving a master's degree in preschool education, Munsch worked in a day-care center, where he found that his penchant for storytelling was well received by his preschool audience. When the children began to clamor for certain stories in his repetoire, he retold them repeatedly, and they evolved into the versions he would eventually publish. In 1979 Munsch sent his first completed stories *Mud Puddle* and *Millicent and the Wind* to various publishers. Although *Mud Puddle* was published the same year, a suitable illustrator was not found for *Millicent,* delaying its publication until 1984; critics have commented that Munsch's style changed with *Millicent,* not realizing its actual place chronologically in his oeuvre. Munsch sees his books as unadulterated entertainment, and the unabashed fun he offers young readers seems to prove that he has kept his goal firmly in mind.

(See also *Something about the Author,* Vols. 48, 50, and *Contemporary Authors,* Vol. 121.)

AUTHOR'S COMMENTARY

[*Mortimer*] was the first story I made up even though it was not the first to be published. Its structure grew out of the simple fact that three and four-year-olds do not like to be lectured at. As nursery school teachers soon find out, the best way to keep a group of them interested is to let them participate in some way. *Mortimer* is, in fact, half way between a story and a song. Like a lot of my stories, it spread by word of mouth and by the time it was published there were lots of daycares in Ontario using it as an oral story.

Mortimer went over so well that I continued to storytell whenever I worked with young children. I soon noticed that while I made up lots of stories, there were only a few that the children kept requesting to hear again and again. They were the good ones. For most of this time I was working in daycare centres or nursery schools and usually making up a new story every day. I figured out once that the stories the children kept requesting came to 2% of my total output.

When the children kept requesting a story, it went through rapid evolution in plot and structure as I told it day after day. Often a good story would start out with an idea that the children liked (getting jumped on by a mud puddle was one) which was not backed up by much of anything. As the story evolved, it developed the structure and style of presentation that made it into an interactive participation sequence with the children. The more the children yelled out predictable repetition elements or imitated sound effects and gestures, the more they stayed put.

Note that at this period of my life I did not think of stories as things in themselves, but rather as little machines that kept kids happy and occupied. They existed only in interaction with the audience, were not written down and did not even have titles. Children requested stories by content or else they asked by the names of the child in the story. The names were especially meaningful because I used the names of the children I was working with at the time. So, "Tell Shelly" referred to a particular story.

When I got a job at the University of Guelph laboratory nursery school, I suddenly found myself in an environment where people got raises and kept their jobs by publishing. The laboratory school director, Bruce Ryan, and his wife, Nancy (a children's librarian!), both urged me to do something about my stories. So I started writing them down. At first I made the mistake of attempting to change my stories into what I considered good writing. They were terrible. Finally I tried keeping the text as close as possible to the oral version and that worked.

I think it worked because children's books are read aloud. It so happened that the oral version read quite well as long as I stuck to the oral version. In fact, the written text tended to lead to the same type of interactive participation that children liked in the oral version.

For me, writing often consists in coming up with a good oral story and then dictating it to myself as I type. Getting a good oral story takes at least three years of telling. The basic plot settles quite soon but the vital word changes that make a participation story work come very slowly. Often it is a case of finding the exact words that the kids expect will come next. Here is an example of what I mean from a later story:

> That is the ugliest thing I have seen in my life. If you think that I am going to put on that ugly snowsuit, you are CRAZY.

This simple fragment is a storyteller's dream, a perfect sentence; because if I say it in a certain way an audience of young children will join in on the word "crazy" even though they have never heard the story before. Actually, they don't join in on the whole word. They join in on the "zy".

I rate choral response elements in stories according to how many times I have to say them before the kids *spontaneously* join in. Thus in the *Mud puddle* story "Mommy, mommy, mommy! A mud puddle jumped on me" has a rating of three because I have to say it at least three times before kids will join in on their own when they are hearing the story for the first time. "Crazy" in the above example has a rating of one half because the kids join in (sometimes) when I am only half of the way through the word. It is very difficult to come up with that kind of wording. The above example did not appear in the story until I had been telling it for two years.

I think that "crazy" works there because it is the exact word that kids expect based on context and delivery. If I were to say "strange" or "dumb as a lobotomized dodo" the kids would not join in.

Now the link between a text that tells well and a text that reads well is not self evident. It took me a while to figure out that the books that were selling best were often the ones that were best developed orally. Once I figured that out, my writing of my oral stories became a lot easier. Munsch the writer simply wrote what Munsch the storyteller dictated.

But some of my stories are not oral stories and one is half and half. The half and half one is *Jonathan cleaned up.* It was a little story fragment that I used to tell about a boy whose house got turned into a subway station. Ann Millyard and Rick Wilks, from Annick Press, heard me tell it at a Toronto bookstore. They decided to publish it so I wrote the story and added an ending. The first part of the story is a simple oral participation story. The whole city hall part is written text. The two parts are really quite different. That second part of *Jonathan* was my first bit of regular written English. The book sold and I decided to try it again.

Murmel, murmel, murmel isn't an oral story at all. This led to an interesting problem when school audiences requested the story. If there were too many kids (say 400) it didn't work to read the book, as most of the people could not see the pictures. So I ended up developing an oral version of the story that works for storytelling.

I wrote *Murmel* just after we adopted our first child and it was, for me, a statement about adoption. Now it is not a very clear statement about adoption. I hate clear statements because they only mean what they mean. Unclear statements have the nice effect of meaning whatever they mean to whomever they mean it to and if various meanings appeal to various groups then the book sells more. Unfortunately, the one group that *Murmel* sometimes does not appeal to is adoptive parents, who are the one group I had especially in mind. They get upset because the book is about rejection as well as acceptance.

While I am on the topic of adoption, *David's father* is about adoption. More specifically it is about interracial adoption and the group I wrote it for was my family because nobody else ever gets that out of it. This brings up the problem of multilevel meanings. *David's father* means a lot of different things to different people and to lots of people it is a funny story that does not mean anything at all.

One child wrote me and said, "I like *David's father* because my father is just like David's father only smaller." For this child, *David's father* functioned like a traditional giant story.

Is the child correct?

Yes, the child is correct; because I want my stories to mean different things to different people. I spend time getting them to do that. So the correct answer to, "What does a Munsch story mean?" is, "To whom?". If you are the reader then you are the arbiter of the meaning. I set it up that way. Besides, I have probably changed my mind several times about what the story meant since I wrote it down. So your own meaning is yours. You as the reader own the story. Have fun. (pp. 22-5)

> *Robert Munsch, "Whatever You Make of It," in Canadian Children's Literature, No. 43, 1986, pp. 22-5.*

GENERAL COMMENTARY

JOAN McGRATH

Robert Munsch is first and foremost a storyteller. To hear him recount one of his original tales is a rare treat, for he throws himself into his delivery with extraordinary vigour. Fortunately, he is as fascinating in print as in person. (p. 92)

Mud Puddle introduces Jule Ann, a resourceful young woman of romper-room age who is beset by one of childhood's bugbears: dirt. A menacing mud puddle lies in wait for Jule Ann; literally, for this puddle lurks in a tree, on a rooftop, and behind the dog house, with intent to jump all over her, filling eyes, nose and mouth with mud. Any child knows the weapon with which to fight dirt, and Jule Ann enlists the aid of "smelly orange soap" to deal the mud puddle a crushing blow. (Munsch has since remarked that he is amazed he didn't realize in time that it should, of course, have been "smelly YELLOW soap".) This slight, funny story is gloriously satisfactory in that Jule Ann triumphs through her own ingenuity. She suffers the ritual three misfortunes, the telling of which becomes a kind of refrain dealing with baths, clean clothes, and fresh starts; and the final episode is perfectly definitive. Good (Jule Ann plus soap) triumphs over Evil (dirt), and the young reader is able to gloat with a pleasure untinged by regret for a too-sympathetic villain. It is unfortunate that Jule Ann has been drawn [by illustrator Sami Suomalainen] in several extremely unattractive close-ups, though pleasingly enough in perspective.

Munsch's work is more appropriately illustrated in *The Paper Bag Princess* and *Jonathan Cleaned Up—Then He Heard A Sound,* both with Michael Martchenko. *Princess* is a tale of castles, dragons, and the liberated Princess Elizabeth. When disaster strikes, and she is left destitute, without a castle or a dress to her name, this sturdy young woman, jauntily clad in a paper bag, outsmarts the dragon who has caused the trouble, frees her captive fiancé Prince Ronald, and finding him not-so-charming, goes off to do whatever liberated princesses do. *Princess* has drawn fire for being sexist in its treatment of ungallant Prince Ronald. It seems a contradiction in terms to describe so wildly original a conception as stereotypical, and that, after all, is what sexism is; the perpetuation of stereotypical thinking. Nobody ever said that all girls, boys, or for that matter dragons or newts, must be portrayed as *admirable.*

[*Jonathan Cleaned Up*] is the tale of a phantom Toronto subway station that suddenly appears in a nice tidy living room, with disastrous effects. Young Jonathan is equal to the situation: a judicious bribe of blackberry jam soon has the offending station removed, and in the last panel the disorderly subway crowd is just beginning to spill into the mayor's office. This cheerfully unlikely story, like the other Munsch tales (it is a great temptation to call them Munschkins) are the stuff of which lasting childhood favourites are made. (pp. 92-3)

Joan McGrath, in a review of "The Paper Bag Princess" and others, in Canadian Children's Literature, *No. 26, 1982, pp. 92-3.*

IRMA McDONOUGH

Many of the ideas for Robert's stories come from his child audiences. They say, "Tell us a story about a dragon," and that's what he does, with the children adding details "in group composition." Telling a story is just that for Robert. He thinks that psychologizing does not produce a good story.

Small children know they are powerless in an adult world so they respond well to fantasies of child power. That is why *The Dark* and *The Mud Puddle* are so popular; Jule Ann ends up the winner in a combat with "the dark" and "the mud puddle," both of which hold terror for some small children. Their vicarious victories are satisfying experiences. Even Jonathan's influence on the computer-man in *Jonathan Cleaned Up* . . . tickles the little reader who can appreciate the ridiculous situation and accept the solution as logical. *The Paper Bag Princess* is by far the most powerful hero, however, for she defeats a dragon and turns the tables on Prince Ronald.

Robert's contract with Annick Press allows him to choose the illustrator of his stories. He chose Michael Martchenko because "his work was a little bit crazy," reflecting a good imagination that we see at work in Robert's two latest books.

Robert's work too is "a little bit crazy," reflecting a double jointed imagination that finds the simple but inevitable conclusion to his fantastic set pieces. They jiggle the sensibilities enough off centre that readers just have to laugh.

All of his stories started out being told to children and were honed into their final form through dozens of tellings. Robert is a teller first, then an author. He professes to a very theatrical style that even adults enjoy. "When you tell a story you

put emphasis on certain words and you use your whole body to express your ideas," he says. "I make all sorts of strange noises to illustrate my stories, and you lose all of that in the translation to book form." His success as a storyteller has led him to offer storytelling workshops for adults "willing to develop or discover their storytelling skills." Participants begin constructing stories right away, in pairs or in groups, and in the end they have a story to tell. (pp. 13-14)

Irma McDonough, "Profile: Robert Munsch," in In Review: Canadian Books for Young People, *Vol. 16, No. 1, February, 1982, pp. 13-14.*

ANN VANDERHOOF

When National Book Festival co-ordinators asked schools to name the writers they would most like to have visit their classrooms during the National Book Festival this year, the most frequent choice was not a figurehead of CanLit such as Margaret Atwood, Farley Mowat or Margaret Laurence. Instead, it was Guelph, Ontario story-teller and author Robert Munsch.

Watching him in action telling his favourite story, *Mud Puddle,* it is easy to see why: "Jule Ann threw a bar of soap right into the mud puddle's middle," he exclaims, arm whipping out to imitate the action, hair in disarray, brown eyes twinkling. We are sitting in his living-room, which is more like a children's library and playroom. "The mud puddle said, 'Awk, Yuck, Wackh!'" he continues in his best disgusted mud puddle voice. "It jumped over the fence and never came back." His listeners—six-year-old daughter Julie and two adult visitors—are captivated; each hopes the next story Munsch tells will be her personal favourite. . . .

Munsch has developed a group of loyal readers—adults as well as children—and his books are selling well. It is easy to understand why his stories, such as *The Paper Bag Princess,* have adult appeal. In a delicious twist on the traditional princess-marries-prince-and-they-live-happily-ever-after theme, Munsch's princess rescues her prince only to be told to come back when she looks like "a real princess". "Ronald," the princess replies, "your clothes are real pretty and your hair is all neat. You look like a real prince, but you are a bum." And they don't get married after all. . . .

[Munsch] is currently a head teacher at the Family Studies Laboratory Preschool of the University of Guelph and lectures in the Department of Family Studies there. It was the director of the pre-school and the chairman of his department who, after seeing Munsch in story-telling action, encouraged him to write his stories down. During the summer of 1978, Munsch mailed a selection of them to about seven publishers.

"I'll never forget the day they arrived," recalls Anne Millyard [of Annick Press]. "I read three of them, laughed and laughed and said to Rick [her co-publisher and partner Rick Wilks], 'He's a wild and woolly man and we have to publish him.'"

This wild and woolly man, who claims he's been referred to as "someone who makes a damn fool of himself and looks well doing it", describes himself as almost a recluse while growing up, completely caught up in his own fantasy life. For the "vital statistics", a photocopied sheet he distributes to teachers and librarians mentions curry as his favourite spice, tequila as his favourite drink and erratic as his mental state.

This delightful wit is reflected in his stories, which often defy convention or portray situations where children turn the tables on the establishment. In *Jonathan Cleaned Up,* for example, Jonathan delivers cases of blackberry jam to the little man inside the computer at City Hall in order to get a subway station moved from his living-room (it gets moved to the mayor's office). "I've been waiting for someone to point out that the moral of that story is when in trouble, bribe the appropriate law official," Munsch chuckles. But the reason he thumbs his nose at the existing power structure is that "kids like stories about conflicts with adults, stories that are fantasies of overcoming adult power, which you really don't do if you're a kid." One of his still unpublished stories—the favourite, he maintains, of the kindergarten to grade 2 set—is The Fart, in which Jule Ann finds a great big purple, green and yellow fart lying on her bed, and various adults inform her that it can't be so because good Canadian families don't have such things. "The kids go absolutely bananas," Munsch says. The parents? "Eighty per cent think it's really neat; the other 20% ask, 'How could you?' " He describes his stories as middle-of-the-road taboo. "Farts are perfect: you're not supposed to talk about them, but they're not very threatening. If you tell stories about sex, for example, young children find that too threatening." . . .

Munsch's three most recent books are illustrated by Michael Martchenko, a Toronto designer. . . .

Martchenko's whimsical drawings—his dopey-looking dragon with a polka-dot napkin tied round his scaly neck for his dinner of a castle in *The Paper Bag Princess,* for instance—are the perfect accompaniment to Munsch's inventive stories. Munsch's next two books, *Murmel Murmel Murmel* (about a little girl who finds a baby in a sandbox), scheduled for publication next fall, and *50° Below* (about a boy whose father sleepwalks and almost freezes to death), slated for next spring, will also be illustrated by Martchenko.

Munsch's stories don't spring from his head in final form. They evolve through the telling. "All I'm trying to do is keep the audience from leaving when I tell stories," he says. "That's my bottom line." The kids—and adults—serve as "word processors" or "editors". *The Paper Bag Princess,* for instance, started out as a traditional prince-saves-princess story until a mother griped about the "they lived happily ever after" style ending. So Munsch tried the present variation and it stuck (although originally Elizabeth also socked Prince Ronald in the nose, which was changed when the publisher thought librarians would find it, among other actions, too violent).

Munsch believes most people can make up their own stories. "It's a real ego trip, it's fun and it's worth trying," he says. "And you're modelling a creative process that Canadian kids very rarely get to see. Most students—even in universities—have no appreciation of literature as a human endeavour. It's library stuff to them. If a parent tells a story at bedtime, a child is learning something it's very hard to get elsewhere." . . .

However, when amateur parental story-tellers decide they want to be published children's authors, Munsch finds they are inclined to make several common errors. First of all, they assume that because their child loves the story, all children will. "That doesn't mean a thing," he says. "Your own children like you too much. They'll sit on your lap to have a telephone book read to them." Also, he finds that stories from novice children's writers are too wordy and too moralistic.

He does not try, however, to immerse himself in the work of other children's authors, either amateur or professional. "I'm afraid of losing whatever weird thing I have in my head that makes me different."

Ann Vanderhoof, "The Weird and Wonderful Whimsy of Robert Munsch," in Quill and Quire, Vol. 48, No. 5, May, 1982, p. 37.

JOAN McGRATH

Robert Munsch, ably assisted by illustrator Michael Martchenko, has in recent months added five new titles for children to his rapidly lengthening list. Production at this rapid-fire pace tends to result in uneven quality. One of the five titles is quite notably charming, three are par for the high-powered Munsch-Martchenko course, and one is . . . well, perhaps not the best thing they've ever done.

Worst first. *The boy in the drawer* is inventive and mildly humorous, but a less than successful fantasy when all is said. Child heroine Shelley finds her bedroom inexplicably littered with socks. Upon investigation, she discovers a boy (smaller than a bread box), reading a book in her sock drawer. He glances up in an unfriendly way and says "Please go away. You are bothering me." She does—he vanishes, she tidies the mess. End of episode.

Next she discovers him in her bed, watering a tomato plant, with soil, puddles and mess everywhere. Same rude brush-off; again the boy vanishes. Mummy knows nothing about it. Shelley tidies the mess. (How?) End of episode. Then the boy paints her window black. Shelley objects, he repeats his only remark. This time, however, Shelley retaliates by painting one of his ears black. The boy grows two inches (he is not a metric boy, we ascertain). Mother is cross at the mess, and Shelley spends hours cleaning up AGAIN.

At last, suppertime. In the kitchen, Shelley finds her father busy cooking, mother reading (they are a contemporary family); apparently they are unaware that water is rising above their ankles and over the unprotesting cat's head, until Shelley mentions the matter.

Shelley opens the bread box, inside which the boy is taking a bath. She turns the cold water on, hard. The boy screams, jumps out, grows two more inches. There he sits, in the middle of the kitchen table. What a situation. What to do? Then Shelley is inspired. She pats the boy; he shrinks. Father hugs him; he gets smaller. Mother gives him a kiss, and he disappears entirely. Everything is, as Shelley says, "definitely okay."

But what has happened here? Is the mysterious boy to be interpreted as being a personification of trouble, a gremlin who will grow if he meets retaliation, or shrink and disappear if treated cheerfully? If so, the story should have begun about two pages earlier, based upon a fit of temper or some other discernible cause, rather than with an irrational, unmotivated mess for the blameless child to restore to order. Youngsters may accept the story as purely fantastic fun, and merely be amused by the horrid little boy's bad behaviour; but the "read to me" crowd of six years and under, the obvious audience for this picture tale, generally prefer the course of fictional events to be reasonable rather than irrational and arbitrary, while older children, able to read for themselves, will not often choose stories about "small fry" younger than themselves, like Shelley. There are some nice touches in *The boy in the drawer,* such as the picture of Shelley curled up with a copy of *The paper bag princess;* but they are touches that will tickle the adult reader-aloud, rather than the read-to child.

Far more appealing, with all the charm of the earlier "Munschkins," is *Murmel murmel murmel.* Robin finds a large hole in her sandbox, with something deep inside that says "Murmel Murmel Murmel." She reaches in and yanks the intruder out—it's a baby. Robin is nonplussed—a rare state of mind for a Munsch child, but reasonable in that she is only five years old. She realizes that she can't take proper care of a baby, so she goes in search of somebody who can and will. . . . Robin is just about worn out. Then a burly truck driver comes by. "Excuse me, do you need a baby?" Robin asks. The driver is not exactly eager, until the baby says "Murmel, Murmel, Murmel." THAT the driver can't resist. They make a simple trade—he takes the baby, and leaves his huge truck for Robin. It's pure fun, and the baby's charming bubbly "Murmel Murmel Murmel" really does sound like that special moment just before an infant begins to talk and then to talk and talk and talk endlessly . . . Maybe Robin caught her truck driver in the very nick of time. Youngsters will enjoy the take-off of those poor creatures who resist the blandishments of the mystery baby, for they really are funny caricatures. *Murmel murmel murmel* is vintage Munsch.

The three remaining titles are rather slight, but will undoubtedly find friends among the younger set. In *Angela's airplane,* the intrepid little heroine whose father contrives to get himself lost in the airport, somehow finds herself aboard a plane and begins idly pushing buttons. Of course, the plane takes off, and in landing it, under instruction by radio, Angela manages to smash it into little pieces, though she herself "didn't even have a scratch." She promises her father she will never ever fly another plane, but she doesn't keep the promise; she grows up to become an airplane pilot. Silly stuff, but cheerful and satisfying to a lot of would-be pilots, half-pint size or less, of both sexes.

Mortimer is the noisiest little kid who ever upset an entire neighbourhood. He has been put to bed, but sings his refrain of "Bang-bang, rattle-ding-bang, goin' to make my noise all day. Bang-bang, rattle-ding-bang, goin' to make my noise all day!" over and over until his parents, his seventeen brothers and sisters, and even the police are unnerved and embroiled in great big fights. Mortimer, bored with waiting for yet another hapless victim to come upstairs and tell him to "Be quiet!," falls peacefully asleep, while turmoil rages below. Again, a silly little story with a catchy refrain, one that most people would prefer NOT to hear echoing from the nursery of an evening . . . Mortimer is of indiscernible age; he could be a big baby, or a small boy—but he's such a pest, even somewhat older kids will probably find him amusing.

Unusually for Munsch, *The fire station* has two leading roles, those of Michael and Sheila, both apparently five years old or thereabouts. Sheila is a born instigator. She drags half-willing Michael into the fire station, lures him up onto the truck, and during an alarm, the two children, undiscovered, are taken to a fire, become completely discoloured with chemical smoke, and return home in such a state that their various parents don't recognize them—much in the time-honoured *Harry the dirty dog* tradition. Michael's mother washes him for three days to get him clean: Sheila's father scrubs her for *five* days to remove all the traces. At story's end, Sheila and Michael are looking speculatively at a police

station . . . and Sheila is dragging at an unwilling Michael AGAIN.

Munsch's little people can be relied upon to be resourceful, determined to a fault, and self-sufficient at least up until the point where baths become imperative. The world they live in is non-sexist to an idealistic degree; Munsch's celebrated *Paper bag princess* is by way of becoming a cult-heroine for the skipping-rope set; and his stouthearted young Jonathan, who could take on a whole subway system and WIN, is not above lending a hand with the housework. Such are the messages Munsch's work delivers, but never in a "messagey" way. Fairness and equality of opportunity are simply the atmosphere, the world-view, within which his cheerful children operate. Munsch has "a talent to amuse," and that is what he does first and best. His are stories for the telling: they come easily to the tongue, and fall pleasantly upon the ear. He understands the childish love of the repeated phrase or nonsense word ("Murmel, Murmel, Murmel"); the magic sequence of events that eager little listeners can gleefully foresee, as when all the harried adults, one by one, try to quell noisy Mortimer and are defeated; the wild exaggeration of seventeen desperate diaper salesmen in hot pursuit of the lady with the baby carriage.

The proof of one's success when telling stories to young children comes when the audience clamours to have a favourite tale told again and again. Robert Munsch's light, bright, popular stories for and about lively, self-confident Canadian kids survive the "Read it again" test as easily as his kids survive dragons, plane wrecks and apoplectic parents. Or whatever new obstacle he invents with which to challenge them next time . . . (pp. 88-91)

> *Joan McGrath, "Munschkinland Revisited," in* Canadian Children's Literature, *No. 30, 1983, pp. 88-91.*

SARAH ELLIS

Canada's Robert Munsch is a writer whose work shows a mastery of the form of the picture book as a small dramatic script. His picture books work well with a single child or a beginning reader, but their great delight is discovered in reading them aloud to groups.

Munsch's stories are mainly of contemporary, urban, domestic life with a large dash of extravagant fantasy. They reflect a jaunty belief in the power of children. His protagonists, reminiscent of those of Marie Hall Ets, are strong, confident, and full of initiative.

[Munsch's] plots have a sense of conjuring up magic, of a rope trick where knotty complexities are solved with a single twist and pull.

The words of the stories are simple and rhythmical. They urge the reader to say them aloud. The stories are full of noises, exclamations, funny voices, and the childlike naughtiness of saying "belly button" or "underwear." Munsch makes fine use of a refrain—from the baths that Jule Ann suffers after each encounter with the mud puddle, "Her mother picked her up, took off all her clothes and dropped her into a tub of water. She scrubbed Jule Ann till she was red all over," to Mortimer's loud song in *Mortimer,* " 'Bang-bang, rattle-ding-bang, goin' to make my noise all day.' "

Full of contemporary references to computers and chewing gum, to snowsuits and cheeseburgers, these tales have, nonetheless, the satisfying inevitability of folklore. With Sendak or Briggs one enters a richly-created private mythology. Such stories make us look into ourselves. Munsch is working in a different tradition. In his books we enter the public world. His books are popular not just in the sense that many children know them but in the sense of dealing with the familiar, recognizable surface of shared child culture.

And like folklore the stories have a life of their own outside the picture-book format. Munsch's illustrators match his style in many ways: Sami Suomalainen in the Jule Ann stories captures the lively, casual quality of the books; Michael Martchenko in the later books adds a talent for cartoonlike detail and caricature. But in these books the illustrations serve more as a decorative supplement to the story than as an integral part of it.

The stories survive well in the various formats in which they are published. Annick Press, Munsch's publisher, is an innovative and very successful small press which has tried to bridge the gap between quality children's book publishing and mass-market books in a variety of interesting experiments. Munsch's books, for example, are published in standard hard-cover, paperback and, in some cases, in child-priced paperback miniatures called "Annikins." The traditionally-designed picture book would not survive this kind of treatment. *Peter Rabbit* is diminished in a larger format; *Choo Choo* could never be smaller. But Munsch's books have a folk-tale resilience and robustness.

Newer editions of his books also show slight alterations in the texts. Munsch is a well-known storyteller, and the changes he makes in performance are then incorporated into the books themselves. Two recordings by Munsch, **Munsch: Favourite Stories** and **Murmel, Murmel, Munsch: More Outrageous Stories** remind us that the written versions are really like scripts or even musical scores.

Millicent and the Wind, his newest book, suggests that Munsch might be moving toward a more classic picture-book style. The story is quieter and more introspective, centering on the loneliness of a girl who lives without friends on a mountain. It is a more ambitiously produced book with illustration and design by Suzanne Duranceau. The illustrations add depth of character and include a fully realized prairie and foothill landscape full of changing light.

The resolution of the problem—in which a lively looking child, complete with Sony Walkman, is imported by the wind as a friend for Millicent—seems like an incident from an earlier Munsch book, and it doesn't fit entirely into this new style. But Munsch is obviously working toward some new use of the seemingly limitless potential of the picture-book form. It will be interesting to see what he and Annick Press do next. (pp. 342-45)

> *Sarah Ellis, "News from the North," in* The Horn Book Magazine, *Vol. LXI, No. 3, May-June, 1985, pp. 342-45.*

THE DARK; MUD PUDDLE (1979)

Books for very young children must, in many ways, present the greatest challenge. It is so important that they be visually appealing, as well as fun to listen to. It is a real bonus when such books can also remain entertaining for the adults who may have to read them aloud dozens and dozens of times.

[Two] books from Annick Press satisfy these criteria. . . . **The Dark** and **Mud Puddle** are the first of a series of stories by Robert N. Munsch, who originally told them to the children in the day-care centre where he once worked. The heroine of both stories, Jule Ann, encounters rather threatening situations—first a monster, The Dark, that grows ever larger by swallowing shadows, then a mud puddle that attacks her whenever she steps outside. Jule Ann deals with these problems with great resourcefulness and humour. . . . (p. 12)

> *Mary Ainslie Smith, "Small Wonders," in* Books in Canada, *Vol. 8, No. 10, December, 1979, pp. 12-14.*

There is much one can read into [*Mud Puddle*]. We discern that mud is bad (not the child for soiling her new clothes) and that the problem can be solved by forcefully driving off the mud puddle with soap (not by wearing appropriate clothing). . . .

Although the germ of the story—a mud puddle jumping out at a child—is at once imaginative and true to life, the author's treatment of it does not ring true. Good fantasy must span two worlds and be true to each. This story does not quite make it.

> *Marcia Shannon, in a review of "Mud Puddle," in* In Review: Canadian Books for Young People, *Vol. 14, No. 1, February, 1980, p. 53.*

Munsch's **Mud Puddle** and **The Dark** grew out of storytelling sessions with pre-school children. . . . (p. 115)

Though adults examine children's books with an eye and an ear for literary and artistic merit, we must also assess the impact of the book's content on children at varying developmental levels: there must be a good "match" between picture book and listener. Munsch, in both titles, develops stories out of simple emotional concerns which occupy pre-schoolers. Three to five year olds are frequently overconcerned about food, eating, and the fear of being eaten, not to mention dirt with its deliciously manipulatable quality (and suggestion of feces) and adult-imposed taboos about getting dirty. Children are concerned about darkness, loss of security, and monsters. Munsch understands this. In each of his books he personifies one such concern. Once a problem is visible, it can, of course, be tackled. Our heroine, the irrepressible Jule Ann—a female behavior model of whom feminists will readily approve—goes out to play wearing clean new clothes.

> Unfortunately, there was a mud puddle hiding up in the apple tree. It saw Jule Ann and jumped right on her head. She got completely all over muddy.

Mother scrubs her clean, and mud puddle strikes again. Eventually, Jule Ann does a little active problem-solving—(involving the antithesis of mud) and sends mud puddle fleeing. In Munsch's second title, "a small dark" falls out of the cookie jar and frightens Jule Ann by eating all the shadows and by expanding in size. Eventually, the dark covers the entire yard and goes to sleep on the roof of the house. Jule Ann again finds her own solution. In demonstrating her self-confidence by resolving the conflicts herself she conveys to young children that it is possible to cope successfully with problems. Bettelheim argues that this adequate resolution of a conflict is absolutely necessary for young children. It reduces the tension set up by the story situation and leaves the child feeling satisfied and confident that she/he too can cope. In Munsch's stories, each solution has a nice logical predictable connection to the problem. The stories work, thus, as small intellectual puzzles, ideally suited to the emotional concerns of a pre-schooler. They are structurally perfect and emotionally powerful. (p. 116)

Overall, Munsch's books are super stories for small children and will become standards in the repertoire of quality Canadian books. . . . Sendak has remarked that creating picture books is like walking a tightrope because one slip in either the writing or the illustrations destroys the unity of the book. Munsch does not slip. (p. 119)

> *Carol Anne Wien, "Mud, Bubbles, and Dark for Early Childhood," in* Canadian Children's Literature, *Nos. 15 & 16, 1980, pp. 115-19.*

THE PAPER BAG PRINCESS (1980)

A picture book full of clichés about a Prince, a Princess and a dragon: of course, the dragon has fiery breath, carries off Prince Ronald to a cave, and then, of course, there is a rescue attempt by the Princess. The only variation in this predictable story is its "modern day" slant: the Princess does the rescuing instead of the Prince, and in the end there is no marriage because the Princess takes umbrage at the Prince declaring her physical appearance is ghastly instead of praising her successful rescue of him from the dragon. . . .

However, children usually like stories about dragons—even those predictable and full of clichés—and libraries may wish to purchase the book for its popular appeal. It is certainly an ephemeral book but it could be entertaining as a quick read at story-time.

> *Hope Bridgewater, in a review of "The Paper Bag Princess," in* In Review: Canadian Books for Young People, *Vol. 15, No. 2, April, 1981, p. 49.*

Robert Munsch strikes again with yet another tautly constructed story, more snappy language, and playful ideas. He takes the traditional St. George and the Dragon fairy-tale and inverts the roles to develop a super-competent, clever princess. With Munsch's usual economy of prose, the story begins

> When Elizabeth was a beautiful princess she lived in a castle and had expensive princess clothes. She was going to marry a prince named Ronald. . . .

[Elizabeth] challenges the dragon the requisite three times, as in all true fairy tales, and he obligingly demonstrates his abilities. . . . Eventually, he falls asleep in exhaustion, and Elizabeth claims Ronald. The ensuing dénouement is the really unique portion of the story—but also is its problem. Ronald reacts to his rescuer with distaste:

> ". . . you smell like ashes, your hair is all tangled, and you are wearing a dirty old paper bag . . ."

Elizabeth, correctly deducing Ronald's true worth, counters:

> "Your clothes are really pretty and your hair is all neat. You look like a prince, but you are a bum."
> They didn't get married after all.

Consider the impact this ending has on children in the target age group. Girls enjoy the story, delight in Elizabeth's ability to demonstrate courage and problem-solving skills, but express disappointment that Ronald turns out so badly. Feminists can well argue that it is not too early for girls to learn that the prince often does not match the princess's expectations. The conclusions that the princess's goal of marriage to

the prince is inappropriate can be understood in the context of the diverse roles for both males and females which our society increasingly supports. However, the impact of the story on small boys is quite different and problematic. My five-year-old could not bear to hear Ronald called a "bum" and instructed the reader, "Don't read that part; don't turn the page!" In checking children's books for sexism, we instruct student teachers to watch for impact of the story on the child's self-esteem. Calling Ronald a "bum" with no further resolution in the story has a negative impact on boys; thus, it is sexist. Munsch has neatly inverted the roles and explicitly derided males. Rather than deciding whether this is a necessary and useful resolution, or an unfortunate and somewhat ruthless one, I prefer to recognize it as a trouble spot. Left as is, the conclusion limits the audience for whom appropriateness of the story can be guaranteed. Alternatively, Ronald and Elizabeth's relationship can be discussed and resolved when reading to both sexes. (pp. 56-8)

> *Carol Anne Wien, "Problem-Solving Models for Children," in* Canadian Children's Literature, *No. 22, 1981, pp. 56-61.*

[Some] books count on a basic literacy among their young readers—not just the ability to decode letters, but an easy familiarity with the enduring literary forms of our culture. **The Paperbag Princess** . . . is a running gag that depends on the child recognizing the anachronisms, tricks, and discordancies that are slipped into the basic fairy tale. The prince and princess have modern names, Elizabeth and Ronald, and are shown in 1980s preppy style with tennis rackets and "expensive" clothes—a deliberately jarring word in the fairy tale context, since kings may have ordered costly clothes for their daughters, but nothing was ever expensive for them. The emancipated ending, in which Elizabeth carries the day without Ronald's help, is a twist on the familiar pattern. So basic is the fairy tale structure to our civilization, so ingrained is its accustomed tone and style, that there can hardly be a child in the country who doesn't get the joke. (pp. 84-5)

> *Michele Landsberg, "Liberating Laughter," in her* Reading for the Love of It: Best Books for Young Readers, *revised edition, Prentice Hall Press, 1987, pp. 77-98.*

JONATHAN CLEANED UP, THEN HE HEARD A SOUND: OR, BLACKBERRY SUBWAY JAM (1981)

Author Robert Munsch gets better and better. In **Jonathan Cleaned Up,** the title character is left in charge of the apartment with strict orders to keep it tidy. Unfortunately, his home has just been turned into a subway station, and every few minutes a train stops, hundreds of people get out and make a mess. When Jonathan tries to protest to the conductor, he is directed to City Hall. There, a patronizing mayor explains that the computer is never wrong. The problem belongs not to the city, but to Jonathan who has no business building a house in a subway station. Jonathan eventually manages to trade four cases of blackberry jam for a relocation of the station, which simultaneously eliminates the fear of future messes and wreaks delicious revenge on those who would brush off a small boy with a problem. The whole story is wonderfully entertaining.

> *Adele Ashby, in a review of "Jonathan Cleaned Up—Then He Heard a Sound: Or Blackberry Sub-*

way Jam," in Quill and Quire, *Vol. 47, No. 8, August, 1981, p. 29.*

One of my favourite Canadian children's authors is Robert N. Munsch. His books are fun to read, although I suspect that at least part of his humour has more meaning for adults than for children. *Jonathan Cleaned Up—Then He Heard a Sound* is his fourth book for young children. Munsch's heroines in previous stories, the Paper Bag Princess and Jule Ann in *The Dark* and *Mud Puddle,* exhibited a cheerful self-reliance and a practical approach to their problems. Jonathan in this new story carries on that tradition. When a mistake at City Hall turns his nice clean apartment into a subway station, he tracks down the source of the problem and finds a solution.

> *Mary Ainslie Smith, in a review of "Jonathan Cleaned Up—Then He Heard a Sound," in* Books in Canada, *Vol. 10, No. 8, October, 1981, p. 33.*

What would you do if the subway stop was located in your living room and everyone thundered through at regular intervals? Jonathan goes to City Hall to find the answer and discovers a little man behind the computer who hungers for blackberry jam. Having greased the wheels, that is, got the jam to the little man, Jonathan succeeds in diverting the subway trains.

The last drawing is a wonderful punch line, but the zany logic that is needed to lead up to it doesn't quite work, mainly, I think, because of the blackberry jam. Nevertheless the book is lively, and parents will be amused, especially those who live in Toronto.

The watercolours [by Michael Martchenko] are the best part, especially the in-jokes, like having a mayor who looks like Nathan Phillips who has a picture of the new City Hall on his wall. Jonathan goes to the old City Hall, and there is a wonderful drawing of him climbing the steps, complete with traffic and streetcar in the foreground. In fact, the book is typically Toronto, an affirmation of our growing local talent for writing and illustrating books for children.

Young children will enjoy having the story read to them; the quick pace and colloquial tone lends itself to home and school use. Youngsters just into competent reading for themselves will find the short length and good graphic design just right for success.

> *Ruth Marks, in a review of "Jonathan Cleaned Up—Then He Heard a Sound: Or Blackberry Subway Jam," in* In Review: Canadian Books for Young People, *Vol. 15, No. 5, October, 1981, pp. 46-7.*

THE BOY IN THE DRAWER (1982)

The Boy in the Drawer is a whimsical fantasy about an impish gnome who comes from nowhere to bedevil Shelley and her family. Like all little imps, this one thrives on generating an angry response from his victims. Indeed, this imp grows larger and larger with each angry encounter until Shelley and her family finally make him disappear with—what else—love. A pat, a hug, a kiss, and sayonara! It's a somewhat quizzical tale that lends itself to multiple interpretations and applications in everyday situations. And it's a co-operative book in the sense that the reader supplies the moral context for the story.

The Boy is a Munsch classic; the story is told with humour and economy of language. . . .

> *Anne Gilmore, in a review of "The Boy in the Drawer," in* Quill and Quire, *Vol. 48, No. 8, August, 1982, p. 28.*

In this story, Munsch's fifth for pre-schoolers, Shelley, a resourceful little girl in ponytails, finds a very small, very unpleasant boy in her dresser sock drawer. . . .

Perhaps the story contains a moral about the best way to control undesirable behaviour in children, but it is also a lot of fun, and I think that's more important by far.

> *Mary Ainslie Smith, in a review of "The Boy in the Drawer," in* Books in Canada, *Vol. 11, No. 7, August-September, 1982, p. 39.*

MURMEL, MURMEL, MURMEL (1982)

Robert Munsch . . . has been improving book by book, and his latest, *Murmel, Murmel, Murmel,* . . . is the best children's story of the year. For five-year-old Robin, the mystery of where babies come from is solved rather unexpectedly one day when she discovers a big hole in the middle of her sandbox. Strange murmel-murmel noises come out of it. She reaches way down and gives a big yank, and out pops a round-headed little pacifier-equipped infant with his arms stretched out, all ready to be hugged. Babies seem to expect that sort of thing. But babies are not Robin's cup of tea, so she sets out to see if she can find someone to love this one. Many people, she discovers, have a baby allergy: Munsch is brilliant at his 1982 update of the unwanted foundling story. And his happy ending is happy in a totally unexpected way. (p. 57)

> *Anne Collins, "Tales for the Computer Generation," in* Maclean's Magazine, *Vol. 95, No. 50, December 13, 1982, pp. 56-8.*

ANGELA'S AIRPLANE; THE FIRE STATION; MORTIMER (1983)

Small both in size and price, Munsch's books are large on entertainment, imagination, and (thanks to Michael Martchenko) visual appeal.

The magic and delight of the Munsch books lie in the author's quirky sense of humour, his effective use of hyperbole, and his presentation of children as active, independent, and in control of their lives. In addition, Munsch's stories are wonderfully realized and enhanced by Martchenko's illustrations. Rarely have story and artwork been so successfully married.

An excellent example of this marriage is *The Fire Station.* It employs all the classic elements of a Munsch tale: unexpected adventure arising from an everyday situation, the conquest of fear, and the glory of messiness.

While exploring a fire station, Michael and Sheila find themselves accidentally carried off in a fire truck to a real-life high-rise fire. There they become so covered in glorious multicoloured smoke stains that on their return home even their parents don't recognize them. It's a child's version of nirvana—to be dirty to the point of anonymity.

No gentle lullaby tale of a compliant sleepy child, **Mortimer** is a bedtime story with a difference. Mortimer, like many of Munsch's children, is in firm and unquestionable control as, in turn, his mother, father, policemen, and 17 brothers and sisters tell Mortimer to be quiet. Each time they leave his bedroom, Mortimer belts out a defiant song of wakefulness. . . .

The last, and perhaps least successful, of the trio, **Angela's Airplane,** tells the story of how during an ordinary trip to the airport, five-year-old Angela runs off with an airplane. Angela survives, the plane doesn't, and she promises never to fly another airplane again. It's a promise Angela doesn't keep, as she grows up to be an airplane pilot. The story's leap into the future is atypical of Munsch and destroys the child-centred focus of his best stories.

> *Anne Gilmore, in a review of "Angela's Airplane," "The Fire Station" and "Mortimer," in* Quill and Quire, *Vol. 49, No. 8, August, 1983, p. 34.*

DAVID'S FATHER (1983)

In this delightful story, a young girl, Julie, meets David, a new boy in her neighbourhood. David seems like a "regular sort of boy" so Julie begins to play with him. When Julie is invited to David's house for dinner, she discovers that David's father is not an ordinary man but a giant. David's father consumes enormous quantities of strange food while Julie and David have cheeseburgers and milkshakes.

Despite some understandable hesitation, Julie learns to appreciate knowing a giant. After all, David's father can stop traffic, get store owners' attention, and intimidate local bullies. He is also very kind.

David's Father touches on a fantasy children (and some adults) have: to find someone big, powerful, and kind to protect them from a harsh world. And it does it with great humour and charm.

> *Frieda Wishinsky, in a review of "David's Father," in* Quill and Quire, *Vol. 49, No. 11, November, 1983, p. 23.*

[When] David, the new neighbor's son, invites Julie to his house, she finds that her worst fears are confirmed: David's father is a giant. But when she finds out that he can also be a friend—helping with the shopping, scaring off mean kids and helping to bandage a scraped elbow, Julie discovers that she really doesn't have to be afraid of giants. Julie's dilemma is a peculiar one, but one which should be appreciated and enjoyed by young readers and listeners who will delight in this gargantuan character. The writing is awkward in places, and dialogue is not set in separate paragraphs, which makes the text difficult to read.

> *Joe Bearden, in a review of "David's Father," in* School Library Journal, *Vol. 30, No. 9, May, 1984, p. 68.*

The well-merited popularity of Robert Munsch would seem to stem both from his humorously sympathetic appreciation of children's concerns and also from the gift of nonsense—the accumulation of absurd details, patterns of increasingly outrageous sequences, climaxed by an apt reversal, non-sequitur or unexpected twist. **David's father** is in the vein of Munsch's earlier books such as **The paper bag princess** and **Jonathan cleaned up** . . . , with its comical exaggeration and absurd

fantasy again well complemented by the expressive vigour of Michael Martchenko's illustrations. . . . Author and illustrator play on the contrast between alarming appearance and benevolent reality, simultaneously having fun with the tall tale and indirectly reassuring the reader that big, scary-looking adults may be kind-hearted parents as well. (p. 126)

> *Gwyneth Evans, "Problems and Pleasures in Picture Book Form," in* Canadian Children's Literature, *Nos. 39 & 40, 1985, pp. 125-30.*

MILLICENT AND THE WIND (1984)

Visually delightful, this is a fantasy that librarians will want to share during story hour. Millicent, a glorious red-haired child, lives with her mother on a bright mountain top, a three day's walk from the valley and civilization. She has no friends except the wind that whimsically blows through the pages of the book, talking to her, playing tag with her and running among the trees and rocks and sunshine. The wind follows Millicent to the valley where she and her mother have gone for supplies and rescues her from a teasing boy. Upon returning to the mountain top, Millicent is lonely until the wind blows away and returns with a special friend for her. Sunny, warm, bright and detailed watercolor illustrations [by Suzanne Duranceau] complement a text that will make children smile.

> *Pamela K. Bomboy, in a review of "Millicent and the Wind," in* School Library Journal, *Vol. 32, No. 1, September, 1985, p. 122.*

Millicent and the wind extends the range of Robert Munsch's work into a different type of fantasy—more gentle, evocative and poetic than his previous books. The effect of this new mood in the text is intensified by the illustrations by Suzanne Duranceau which use a delicate line and highly detailed realism to evoke an atmosphere at once very earthy yet full of magical possibilities. (p. 127)

The text manages to be beautiful and funny at the same time, effectively blending the poetic and grand with the homely and colloquial. "I am the very wind of all the world. I blow when I wish and talk when I want to. The day is so quiet and the sunshine so yellow that I feel like talking right now." The rhythms and cadences of the text reflect Munsch's skill as a storyteller, while the understated, matter-of-fact approach works as well for this type of fantasy as it did for describing the escapades of his urban children. (p. 128)

> *Gwyneth Evans, "Problems and Pleasures in Picture Book Form," in* Canadian Children's Literature, *Nos. 39 & 40, 1985, pp. 125-30.*

THOMAS' SNOWSUIT (1985)

Here is the story of an adult/child confrontation with a difference. When Thomas's mother insists that he wear a new brown snowsuit that is not particularly to his liking, to school, Thomas refuses. Mother wins the battle that ensues, but the war carries on in the classroom, and Thomas is ultimately victorious over the representatives of educational authority. It is apparent, however, even to the uninitiated, that there are no real winners in this type of conflict and that given the proper incentive, children are quite capable of making appropriate decisions without adult coercion.

Munsch's unique sense of humour is superbly complemented by [Michael] Martchenko's illustrations. The text is quite simple, the action almost predictably repetitious, and the drawings delightfully sympathetic to the ludicrousness of the situation. The ending completes this little satire, being sufficiently tongue-in-cheek to satisfy adults and kids. Fans of Robert Munsch will not be disappointed by his latest book. (pp. 30-1)

> *Patricia Sentance, in a review of "Thomas' Snowsuit," in* CM: Canadian Materials for Schools and Libraries, *Vol. XIV, No. 1, January, 1986, pp. 30-1.*

Thomas never suffers any ill-consequences for his rude behavior; he looks on with a smirk as his mother, teacher and principal are made to look foolish. In the end the principal retires to Arizona "where nobody ever wears a snowsuit." Thomas comes off as a manipulating, rude little brat. Audiences may chuckle over the cartoon-like illustrations; they are bright and colorful, and do fit the story. However, this is one Canadian import that should be left north of the border.

> *Evelyn Homan, in a review of "Thomas' Snowsuit," in* School Library Journal, *Vol. 32, No. 8, April, 1986, p. 77.*

---

50 BELOW ZERO (1986)

[*50 Below Zero*] tells the story of a boy who discovers his father is a sleep-walker—and who becomes responsible for getting him safely back to bed. As with other Munsch books (whose roots are in stories the author has tested verbally on many young audiences), this tale relies heavily on repetition. It is a mark of the author's ability that, just as the repetition of a key phrase became a grating annoyance to this reader, the text suddenly changed. The story has a surprise ending (another trademark of Munsch stories), effectively shown by illustrator Michael Martchenko, whose talents again complement those of the author.

An interesting aside: while fathers went missing in those liberated children's stories of yore, so mothers seem superfluous here. Munsch includes a mother in his story, but she appears only at the end of the tale.

> *Bernie Goedhart, "Dads Stage Return in Family-Style Titles," in* Quill and Quire, *Vol. 52, No. 4, April, 1986, p. 26.*

This read-aloud or read-aloud picture book for preschoolers and older children contains a zany situation and humorous role reversals, all mirrored in colorful, lively illustrations. When young Jason's father sleepwalks, the child-hero comes to the rescue, proving to be more than the adult's equal. The book's repetitious style and musical cadences accompanied by humorous illustrations will be successful in a storytelling setting. As in many Munsch books a surprise ending will leave readers smiling.

> *Joan Weller, in a review of "50 Below Zero," in* Canadian Children's Literature, *No. 44, 1986, p. 95.*

What starts off as a humorous idea is run into the ground with repetition in the text so that even the humor of the final picture is lost in the stupidity of the story. The humorous illustrations are large and colorful with a page of text facing each one, but the story rates a zero. (pp. 148-49)

> *Nancy A. Gifford, in a review of "50 Below Zero,"*

in School Library Journal, *Vol. 33, No. 7, March, 1987, pp. 148-49.*

LOVE YOU FOREVER (1986)

This newest story by Robert Munsch differs from those in his previous books by using a quieter and more introspective approach. Munsch shows the love a mother has for her son from the time of his birth to adulthood.

The words in Munsch's stories are always simple, and this book is no exception. He has a keen ear for words and sounds that appeal to children, catch their attention, and can be exaggerated in the telling. In *Love You Forever,* Munsch uses the words "crazy" and "zoo" to that effect. The use of the word "crawl" is another example. Munsch has the mother crawl across the floor to her son's bed to see if he is asleep. We laugh at the image, but the use of these words adds an element of slapstick that conflicts with the theme.

Munsch uses the same sentence pattern throughout the story, using repetition of words to accentuate each stage of development. Repetition of a song is also used. The song is sung six times by the mother and twice by the son. Since no accompaniment has been included, storytellers will be able to compose a tune that will suit their own styles of storytelling. With the use of a song, Munsch plays on the sentiments of his listeners to provoke a reaction that he will no doubt receive. A good supply of kleenex tissues will be needed.

In trying to show the enduring nature of a parent's love and how that same love is transmitted from generation to generation, Munsch has to show the child from birth to adulthood. This time span causes problems. As the child grows older, he is still being rocked at night by his mother when he is asleep, a situation that becomes sillier as both mother and child grow older. Because much of the story centres on the child when he is older, it is also apparent that this is not a picture book for a younger audience, although the cover gives that impression.

Perhaps this story should not be in picture-book format. Some illustrations [by Sheila McCraw] emphasize the ridiculousness of the story. It is one thing to imagine a frail old mother rocking her big, tall son, but another to see it illustrated. The illustrator has also taken licence. Once the son has moved away from home, the illustrator shows an older woman climbing a ladder to the second floor of a house, opening a window, and, finally, rocking a grown man. This lacks credibility and, while reminiscent of Munsch's previous books, does not fit here.

Love You Forever is sentimentality at its worst. This is not a children's story, but one that will appeal to adults who have experienced a feeling of loss as their children grow older. Munsch should go back to what he does best. (pp. 78-9)

> *André Gagnon, in a review of "Love You Forever," in* CM: Canadian Materials for Schools and Libraries, *Vol. XV, No. 2, March, 1987, pp. 78-9.*

I HAVE TO GO! (1986)

The children to whom this book is dedicated may not thank their parent(s) when they are teenagers. The story is built on a situation that every parent has endured—when a child picks an inopportune time to say "I have to go pee." Munsch makes the most of repetition in his story-telling—Andrew waits till he's in the car, or in a snowsuit, or in bed—and [Michael] Martchenko's illustrations reveal how terribly satisfied Andrew is when he discombobulates the adult world with his urgent announcement. In fact, there's a ritualized power-struggle in this situation: the adults hover too insistently over him to get him to go to the bathroom *before* getting into cars, snowsuits, or bed. It's very comic in the inimitable Munsch style, which includes throw-away lines for parents like when the grandmother says "I never had these problems with *my* children."

Mary Rubio, in a review of "I Have to Go!" in Canadian Children's Literature, *No. 46, 1987, p. 108.*

A potty-trained child from three to five will enjoy the humor in this preschool vignette, but like a family photo album, this subject has limited appeal. This is an attractive, well-designed, sturdy package, but an ever-so-additional choice.

Anna Biagioni Hart, in a review of "I Have to Go!" in School Library Journal, *Vol. 34, No. 5, January, 1988, p. 68.*

MOIRA'S BIRTHDAY (1987)

Like other books by Robert Munsch, *Moira's Birthday* starts off with a bang. Moira wants to invite "Grade 1, grade 2, grade 3, grade 4, grade 5, grade 6 aaaaand kindergarten" to her birthday party. Her parents are opposed. "You can invite six kids," they say. But Moira, unable to resist her friends' pleas, invites them all. And so begins a parent's nightmare. How do you feed all those kids? Where do you put them? And what about the mess?

Her parents are frantic, but Moira is calm and undaunted. "Don't worry, I know what to do," she says. Her solution, unfortunately, creates as much havoc as the problem. But fi-nally, after a few chaotic hours, the kids have been fed and the party is over—at least for a while!

This story will strike a responsive chord in parents and children. Any parent who has hosted a screaming horde of hungry children will vividly recall the experience, while any child who has wanted to invite all his friends to a party will relish the possibility.

In his usual style, Munsch laces his story with sound effects, repetition, and exaggeration. Characters scream, yell, and look frazzled, while the action moves at a fast and furious pace. All this makes for a very noisy book, and therein lies a problem: the histrionics often overwhelm the story narrative. . . . *Moira's Birthday* is entertaining, especially when read aloud. The sound effects are fun—if somewhat predictable—and the story is one kids will relate to easily. But one does hope that future Munsch books will stress story and character above an all-too-familiar style. (pp. 6, 8)

Frieda Wishinsky, in a review of "Moira's Birthday," in Books for Young People, *Vol. 1, No. 6, December, 1987, pp. 6, 8.*

A PROMISE IS A PROMISE (1988)

[This] is a rather long tale for preschoolers. It's about the imaginary Qallupilluit, who grab children when they get too near the cracks in the sea ice. Allashua is caught by the Qallupilluit and makes a foolish promise to gain her freedom. Her family extricates her and her siblings from a difficult situation by tricking the Qallupilluit. As with most Munsch stories this one lends itself to dramatic reading, suspense, and fun, but begins to sound too formulaic upon subsequent readings.

Andrew Vaisius, "Play Scripts with Pictures," in Books in Canada, *Vol. 17, No. 6, August-September, 1988, p. 36.*

Dorothy Hinshaw Patent

1940-

American author and illustrator of nonfiction.

A prolific writer of informational books on the biological sciences for readers in the early elementary grades through high school, Patent is respected for providing her audience with fascinating introductions which accurately present complex topics in a style often commended for its clarity and spirit. Acclaimed for their comprehensiveness, objectivity, and lack of condescension, the works, which explain the characteristics or behavior of insects, fish, plants, reptiles, and mammals as well as consider such topics as evolution and bacteria, are often acknowledged as superior examples of their genre. Patent brings her background as a zoologist to her books, and is often celebrated for the authoritativeness of her knowledge, for her inclusion of current, often obscure information, and for honestly discussing issues, problems, and facts often avoided by other authors for the age groups she addresses. Praised as an especially fine writer whose direct, relaxed style and sensitive tone are appropriate both to her subjects and to her audience, Patent also provides black and white drawings for some of her books which, along with diagrams and photographs from a variety of sources, are considered to add greatly to the usefulness and appeal of her works. Although some observers disapprove of the technical content of her books and the informality of her approach, most admire Patent for consistently providing young people with works which are thorough, interesting, and stimulating. Several of Patent's titles have been named outstanding science trade books by the National Science Teachers Association. In 1986, Patent was presented with the Eva L. Gordon Award for her body of work.

(See also *Something about the Author,* Vol. 22, *Contemporary Authors,* Vols. 61-64, and *Contemporary Authors New Revision Series,* Vols. 9, 24.)

GENERAL COMMENTARY

ZENA SUTHERLAND AND MAY HILL ARBUTHNOT

Dorothy Patent has become established as an author whose books are distinguished for their combination of authoritative knowledge, detached and objective attitude, and an ability to write for the lay person with fluency and clarity. Like that exemplary writer for younger children, Millicent Selsam, she communicates a sense of wonder at the complexity and beauty of animal life by her zest for her subject rather than by comments on the marvelous intricacy of the natural order. (pp. 497-98)

Butterflies and Moths: How They Function is a text that is a model of broad coverage, good organization of material, and clarity in writing style. The book examines almost every aspect of lepidopterans, and discusses the way in which moths and butterflies, in their various stages, are considered pests or benefactors by people. . . . In all her books, Patent carefully distinguishes between fact and conjecture but makes it clear that conjecture and theory, even when erroneous, are part of the scientific method and can be built on to reach truth. (p. 498)

> *Zena Sutherland and May Hill Arbuthnot, "Informational Books," in their* Children and Books, *seventh edition, Scott, Foresman and Company, 1986, pp. 484-548.*

WEASELS, OTTERS, SKUNKS, AND THEIR FAMILY (1973)

There have been several recent children's books on individual members of the mustelid family but Patent's admirably thorough survey covers them all with ease and authority. The author . . . rejects the fictionalized life cycle formula for a concise, straightforward report on the habits, diet and distribution of each member as well as the common characteristics of this varied family which includes the fierce and cunning wolverine, the delightfully fun loving otter, and the rare black-footed ferret who lives with and on the endangered prairie dog. Patent's topics range from the history of the fur trade to the process of delayed implantation which accounts for the eight-to-twelve month gestation period that allows many mustelids to mate in summer and give birth in the spring. An implicit defense of these maligned predators is built into the explanation of their place in nature. . . .

> *A review of "Weasels, Otters, Skunks, and Their Family," in* Kirkus Reviews, *Vol. XVI, No. 23, December 1, 1973, p. 1312.*

Dorothy Hinshaw Patent has written a highly interesting, readable and informative book. . . . Her style of writing is relaxed and enjoyable, and she evidently has closely observed the weasel family. . . . A few advanced elementary students would thoroughly enjoy this book, and elementary teachers will find it a valuable resource. . . . The only problem with the book may be the author's acceptance and discussion of evolution as a fact—there are a few areas in the U.S. where objections may be raised to the author's handling of this currently controversial subject.

> *A review of "Weasels, Otters, Skunks and Their Family," in* Science Books: A Quarterly Review, *Vol. X, No. 1, May, 1974, p. 76.*

A fascinating and comprehensive account of the Mustelid family of carnivores. Well-organized and fast reading, **Weasels, Otters, Skunks and their Family** presents to readers the distinguishing characteristics of each species, their feeding habits, and natural habitat. The mechanism of evolution is clearly discussed in its relation to these animals. The ideas of evolution, adaptation, and predator-prey relationships are reinforced throughout the book. . . . The excellent sketches by Matthew Kalmenoff and the list of well-chosen suggested readings complement the sensitively written text.

> *Heddie Kent, in a review of "Weasels, Otters, Skunks and Their Family," in* Appraisal: Children's Science Books, *Vol. 7, No. 3, Fall, 1974, p. 33.*

MICROSCOPIC ANIMALS AND PLANTS (1974)

This is a practical guide to microscopy that tells both what to see and how to see it—beginning with finding specimens, making infusions, and preparing slides. Patent introduces a wide variety of subjects for investigation, including common bacteria, rotifers, worms, and small crustacea, and places somewhat less emphasis on popular textbook examples such as the amoeba. Many of the suggested projects—frog development, cryptobiosis—would require follow-up reading but this is a sound, logically structured beginning for anyone confronted by the bewildering variety in a drop of pond water. And though the vocabulary is quite technical, Patent maintains an informal, easy tone throughout.

> *A review of "Microscopic Plants and Animals," in* Kirkus Reviews, *Vol. XLII, No. 23, December 1, 1974, p. 1263.*

There is a wealth of practical hints on microscope techniques in this beginner's book. Some of the "pluses" cover certain pitfalls involved in laboratory work with microscopes and related equipment. Unfortunately, the diagrams are poor and sparse, and the text smacks of a "lab" manual more than a lucid, exciting entree to the world of the minuscule.

> *Douglas B. Sands, in a review of "Microscopic Animals and Plants," in* Appraisal: Children's Science Books, *Vol. 9, No. 1, Winter, 1976, p. 33.*

Many interesting simple plants and animals are described in great detail in this book, which is a beginner's guide to a world of creatures found only under a microscope. . . . An appendix includes experiments and projects, a list of supply houses, and an annotated bibliography for further study. Well organized and easy to read, the book has excellent illustrations and is easier than other books on similar subjects.

> *Selina Woods, in a review of "Microscopic Animals and Plants," in* Appraisal: Children's Science Books, *Vol. 9, No. 1, Winter, 1976, p. 33.*

FROGS, TOADS, SALAMANDERS, AND HOW THEY REPRODUCE (1975)

An exciting introduction, and not just because Patent explores some of the bizarre byways of amphibian reproduction—like the Surinam toads which hatch live from sacs carried on the mother's back, or the eternally immature axolotl salamander which will change into a "new" adult form, not found in nature, if given a dose of thyroid or pituitary extract. Patent has clearly given some thought as to how to make her material both easy and vivid—her step-by-step description of embryo development is simultaneously precise and suspenseful, and her discussion of how frogs mate anticipates the very questions readers might be curious about ("You may wonder how one slippery frog can hang onto another slippery frog in the water"). Not a collector's miscellany like the Zapplers' useful *Amphibians as Pets,* this gives us the gist of current research free from the spiritless textbook drone that too often is the price we pay.

> *A review of "Frogs, Toads, Salamanders, and How They Reproduce," in* Kirkus Reviews, *Vol. XLIII, No. 6, March 15, 1975, p. 314.*

[*Frogs, Toads, Salamanders, and How They Reproduce*] may not have the catchiest title of the season, but it is a solid nature book. . . . It can serve a number of needs. It is a good book on reproduction and a rich enough essay on amphibians to be helpful to the high school biology student. It really is a very good book for any youngster interested in nature. (There is enough gee-whiz material included to satisfy some adults.) It is above average in all respects as it traces the incredible lives of the creatures that arose from the fish and made all the rest of us possible. It has a small but useful bibliography and a good index. This really is a book to be recommended for the young naturalist.

> *Roger Caras, "Animal World," in* The New York Times Book Review, *May 4, 1975, p. 45.*

There are 2600 species of toads and frogs and 320 kinds of salamanders, and the majority of them are unique. It would appear an awesome job to sort out these very varied and unusual animals, but Dr. Patent has done it very well. The chapters define amphibians in general, the huge variety within the species, and the curious and divergent courtships, incubation, and metamorphosis processes by which these animals are perpetuated. From chapter 6 on, we are treated to the more unusual aspects of all of these. . . . In all, this book is completely absorbing.

> *Heddie Kent, in a review of "Frogs, Toads, Salamanders, and How They Reproduce," in* Appraisal: Children's Science Books, *Vol. 9, No. 1, Winter, 1976, p. 32.*

HOW INSECTS COMMUNICATE (1975)

Communications among members of class Insecta and between insects and other groups of animals have not been thoroughly understood, although insects are the largest group of animals on this planet, the most successful group of invertebrates and formidable competitors of humans for survival on this earth. The author has successfully explained various complicated ways of communication in representative groups of common social and nonsocial insects. Visual, chordotonal, chemical and behavioral mechanisms of communication are explained in the simplest way possible. A highly technical vocabulary has not been used, making it easier for an amateur naturalist or a beginning entomologist to understand the subject. . . . The last chapter on communication in spiders and crabs makes interesting reading for a person trying to understand instinct in animals. Interesting for general reading and useful to young readers with an awakening interest in living creatures.

> *N. N. Raghuvir, in a review of "How Insects Communicate," in* Science Books & Films, *Vol. XII, No. 1, May, 1976, p. 25.*

Young persons are fortunate to have available this very readable book on insect communications, a dynamic field that is fascinating scientists in many fields. Biologists, entomologists, chemists, physicists, behaviorists, and others are finding that a myriad of challenges lies within the complex methods insects use to generate and receive messages. Slowly, pieces of the puzzle are falling into place. In 11 brief, fast-moving chapters, the author has attempted to cover the essentials of communications, devoting the first 10 to insects and the 11th to spiders and scorpions. Considering the scattered sources, the levels of sophistication involved, and the magnitude of the literature available, the author has successfully integrated the material for both the young scientist and the advanced lay reader. . . .

In summary, the book is well worth the attention of the young biologist-chemist and by the lay person desiring an interesting, lucid, and generally accurate account of insect communications. Typographical errors are rare and conceptual descriptions appear to be correct with one notable exception. The "even spacing" in the bark beetle . . . illustration refers to mines that are bored by larvae, both male and female, rather than the vertical boring by female adults as the author infers.

> *John B. Simeone, in a review of "How Insects Communicate," in* Chemistry, *Vol. 51, No. 3, April, 1978, p. 26.*

PLANTS AND INSECTS TOGETHER (1976)

This charmingly unpretentious book would be valuable as collateral reading for any junior or senior high school course in biology, evolution or ecology. The intricacies of the relations between insects and plants as brought about by co-evolution are presented in a lucid and easy style without the flamboyance or mystical superlatives of some "nature" books. . . . Patent is well versed in the latest research in entomology, and she touches upon new developments such as arrestants, sex pheromones and juvenile hormone mimics. Her book would provide stimulus to the bright student, knowledge for the average student and entertainment for the professional biologist.

> *Roy. T. Cunningham, in a review of "Plants and Insects Together," in* Science Books & Films, *Vol. XII, No. 2, September, 1976, p. 82.*

Dr. Patent is a walking biological encyclopedia! Her thorough grounding in research is very evident in everything she writes. **Plants and Insects Together** describes insects in all their complexity, plant structure, pollinization (some of it quite bizarre!), adaptation, and sympathetic and/or antagonistic behavior of insects and plants. Such complicated subject matter written by someone so knowledgeable could very well have been a labored and boring work, but not this book! Matthew Kalmenoff's superb black-and-white drawings and Dr. Patent's skill at simplifying her material and choosing the most exciting examples to hold a young reader's interest have produced a most readable and fantastically interesting book.

> *Heddie Kent, in a review of "Plants and Insects Together," in* Appraisal: Children's Science Books, *Vol. 9, No. 3, Fall, 1976, p. 33.*

An informative, objective detailing of the relationship between plants and insects—how they help and harm each other and how some have adapted to each other (e.g., the yucca plant and yucca moth). Patent discusses pollination, parasites, and insectivorous plants and devotes one chapter to orchids and their special relationship to insects (one orchid camouflages itself as a female bee so the male will try to mate and thus pollinate it). The writing is clear but pedestrian; the explanatory black-and-white drawings and diagrams [by Matthew Kalmenoff] are well matched to the text although at times the captions are confusing. Still the only other title covering the relationship between plants and insects is Adler's *Insects and Plants* (John Day, 1962) which is for younger readers and is not as detailed.

> *Cynthia K. Richey, in a review of "Plants and Insects Together," in* School Library Journal, *Vol. 23, No. 6, February, 1977, p. 67.*

FISH AND HOW THEY REPRODUCE (1976)

Fish reproduction is a subject in which instructive, often bizarre exceptions tend to overwhelm the few easily generalized rules. Patent's uncondescending rigor and lucid writing once again open up many areas that might have seemed too technical for discussion at this level: embryo development; John Wourms' research into annual fish (a group specially adapted to survive dry spells in lakes and rivers); and the complex parenting behavior of cichlids, including one valuable aquarium species that secretes a "milk" to feed its young. Rather more specialized in appeal than previous volumes, but an excellent choice for the young scientist who can handle more challenging concepts.

> *A review of "Fish and How They Reproduce," in* Kirkus Reviews, *Vol. XLIV, No. 17, September 1, 1976, p. 978.*

Lest children think fish are simple creatures with fairly simple modes of behavior, the author describes in ten chapters the complexities of fish, concentrating mainly on their reproducing habits. This is obviously geared for the more sophisticated reader who already has some general information about fish but who wants more scientific know-how on embryo development within a special species, like the "annual" fish which have special capabilities for adapting to dry spells in rivers and lakes, or a unique species which secretes a liquid substance for feeding of its young, etc. Informative and fascinating for a knowledgeable embryo ichthyologist.

> *Virginia A. Tashjian, in a review of "Fish and How They Reproduce," in* Appraisal: Children's Science Books, *Vol. 10, No. 2, Spring, 1977, p. 40.*

Here is a good general description of kinds of fish and the breeding habits of odd and familiar types. The discussion of the evolution of the modern fish is interesting. . . . Two criticisms: Only general names such as bass, puffer, sea devil, rock fish and flashlight are used with the illustrations; the author might have found the *List of Common and Scientific Names of Fishes* (Bethesda, MD: American Fisheries Society [5410 Grosvenor Lane] 1970) a useful reference. Also, a helpful addition would have been a pronunciation guide to some of the terminology. Good drawings [by Matthew Kalmenoff] and a satisfactory index, glossary and suggested reading list are provided.

> *B. L. Gordon, in a review of "Fish and How They Reproduce," in* Science Books & Films, *Vol. XIII, No. 1, May, 1977, p. 44.*

EVOLUTION GOES ON EVERY DAY (1977)

As in her previous books on less complicated aspects of natural history, Patent combines a specialist's understanding of her subject with a talent for making it clear to beginners. Emphasizing that evolution is change, which continues to occur, she discusses such phenomena as natural selection, speciation, genetic drift, and coevolution; directs attention to species that seem to be in transition today; takes up flu viruses as "fine examples of evolution in action"; provides a brief, demystifying description of the DNA molecule and how it codes for individual traits; and ends with an assessment of human interference in evolution via pesticides and pollution, engineered breeding, and DNA research. Relevant examples are integrated throughout to clarify and vitalize the concepts, so that one is never bogged down by abstraction or bored with pedantic detail. Less technical and less specialized than Adler's introduction to cell chemistry in *How Life Began* (revised this year), this will find a niche of its own; whereas Klein's *Threads of Life* (1970) covers much of the same material in terms of historical discoveries, Patent's is a more direct and integrated overview. And unlike Gallant (*How Life Began,* 1975), who felt the need to defend the theory of evolution, Patent concentrates on explaining it.

> *A review of "Evolution Goes on Every Day," in* Kirkus Reviews, *Vol. XLV, No. 9, May 1, 1977, p. 496.*

The smooth style and clarity of expression found throughout this book allow fast and easy reading. There is a fine historical review. Excellent examples of various biological concepts are present everywhere. These features have produced a superior, even exciting, book on modern concepts of evolution for the junior and senior high school student and even for the general adult reader. There are no references, but their omission allows an uncluttered progression of thought while one is reading. Besides, the author carefully names those important scientists whose work has been highly influential in shaping the development of evolutionary doctrine. Their ideas are described sufficiently to give the reader a solid taste. The book's glossary is not necessary because its terms are adequately defined in the text and the index is quite thorough. Only three

typographical errors were discovered. The title is well chosen. The author wants us to understand that evolution is not just a thing of the past, but a living and vital part of today. There is coverage of a broad array of life forms with just enough attention to human life to keep readers aware that they, too, are part of the process. The notable deficiencies in the text are a weak section on parthenogenesis and failure to discuss the use of colchicine in manipulation of plant genetics. There are a few occasions where phraseology could mislead the unalert reader, but these are not serious.

> *David L. Zartman, in a review of "Evolution Goes on Every Day," in* Science Books & Films, *Vol. XIII, No. 4, March, 1978, p. 208.*

Updated views on speciation, including recently found examples of the process, and comprehensive coverage of advances in genetics make the book valuable and important. Though much of it deals with speciation, the author describes how DNA codes proteins and how human beings influence selection—for instance, in the development of bacteria with the use of antibiotics, in the domestication of wild animals and plants to bring out pleasing characteristics, and in the cultivation of plant strains which are resistant to disease. Human evolution, genetic engineering, and problems of evolution not yet fully understood are intelligently discussed at the end of the book. To write so comprehensively is an accomplishment, and it means that the material is necessarily compact and requires in places a second reading. The book is ideal for the interested reader who has had introductory genetics in high school biology, for it offers more detail than can a general text. Other capable readers, if persistent, could also read the book, and those who want to know about genetics today should be grateful to have it. (pp. 307-08)

> *Sarah Gagné, "Evolution," in* The Horn Book Magazine, *Vol. LIV, No. 3, June, 1978, pp. 307-08.*

REPTILES AND HOW THEY REPRODUCE (1977)

Continuing the survey so ably advanced in ***Frogs, Toads, Salamanders and How They Reproduce,*** Patent introduces reptiles via their evolutionary origin, describes their structure, senses, ectothermic nature, and signal systems as all of these relate to function, then briefly examines the common features of reptile reproduction before going on to the distinctive patterns of turtles, snakes, lizards, and crocodiles. Patent knows how to stimulate curiosity (why should some reptiles lay eggs while others bear live young?) before answering the questions; she is always clear and intelligent on "what [cited] experiments teach us"; she fills readers in on revolutionary new ideas and findings (endothermic dinosaurs, parental care in crocodiles); and her scientific authority and workmanlike approach don't rule out a passing recognition of the "rarely graceful" aspects of "turtle love" or a side look at such curious behavior as the male snakes' combat dance. Exemplary, as usual.

> *A review of "Reptiles and How They Reproduce," in* Kirkus Reviews, *Vol. XLV, No. 21, November 1, 1977, p. 1146.*

Zoologist strikes again! The direct and unpretentious writing has almost a conversational flow, describing the evolution of reptilian species, the characteristics of each, and the characteristics they have in common. Separate chapters then describe patterns of courting and mating, nest-building, and—

in some species—care of young, social organization, establishment of territorial rights or individual dominance. The careful drawings [by Matthew Kalmenoff] are well-placed and adequately labelled, and the writing is scientifically exemplary, using technical terms when necessary and otherwise avoiding them, distinguishing between fact and theory, communicating a sense of appreciation for the intricacies of life forms without becoming rhapsodical about them. . . . Patently superior.

> *Zena Sutherland, in a review of "Reptiles and How They Reproduce," in* Bulletin of the Center for Children's Books, *Vol. 31, No. 6, February, 1978, p. 99.*

After contrasting the structure and modes of life of reptiles and amphibians, Patent discusses the reptiles' diversity as a group composed of four living orders. She emphasizes evolutionary relationships, paying particular attention to hot-blooded dinosaurs and to likenesses and differences between reptiles and endothermic birds and mammals. Later chapters present mating habits, embryological development and parental care (or lack of care) in typical members of the various groups of reptiles. Many interesting and little-known facts are included, such as the remarkable birth process of the yucca lizard of the Mojave Desert. Unfortunately, a few corrections are in order: The amniotic cavity is stated as being outside the amnion instead of within it. The combat dance or dance of the adders is now recognized to be a precourtship ritual fight in males of certain species, although the text states that "the function of the 'combat dance' of some snakes is not yet understood." . . . Young people should find this book stimulating reading: the index, glossary and well-rounded bibliography make it a useful reference.

> *Marie M. Jenkins, in a review of "Reptiles and How They Reproduce," in* Science Books & Films, *Vol. XIV, No. 2, September, 1978, p. 114.*

BEETLES AND HOW THEY LIVE (with Paul C. Schroeder, 1978)

This extensive assortment of data on the physical characteristics and behavior of beetles is both fascinating and confusing. The authors present basic patterns and principles of feeding, flight, reproduction, habitat, luminescence and other chemical functions involved in communication, defense, and securing prey. There is a sketchy glossary, a reading list, a chapter on collecting and observing beetles, and a list of biological supply houses. Some technical terms are not adequately explained, and some basic questions are unaccountably ignored (e.g., just what differentiates scarab beetles from other families?). Well-chosen photographs from the files of scientists attractively illustrate the text, but a serious omission is the lack of diagrams of complex physical features such as mouth parts and respiratory mechanisms. Both Wilfred S. Bronsons's *Beetles* and Ross Hutchins' *Insects in Armor: the Beetle* are better introductions, but this will be wanted for serious insect fans.

> *Margaret Bush, in a review of "Beetles and How They Live," in* School Library Journal, *Vol. 25, No. 7, March, 1979, p. 150.*

I very much enjoyed reading *Beetles and How They Live* and felt that it was a well written and readily understandable general account of how the beetles as a group live their lives. The

book is a nice balance between general topics which are well illustrated with specific examples (such as feeding, reproduction and flight), and the unusual specific bioluminescence of fireflies or the life story of the dung beetle. Since the group of insects we call beetles is such a numerous and diverse one, this seems like the only logical way to proceed. The book has some added features worth noting. Although the photographs were of varied quality, they were well chosen to illustrate the subject matter. I like the fact that some cumbersome terms were not explained in the text, which necessitated that they be looked up in the short glossary provided. This is good training for any beginning student. There was a good portion of a chapter towards the end of the book which dealt with collecting techniques which I was sorry to see get as much attention. Although this has been a standard section of any insect book in past years, I feel that, as with other animal groups, we are realizing that we live in a finite world and that indiscriminate collecting (particularly with a group that is colorful and easily found) is no longer a valid activity for all. However, I was very pleased to read the section on observing which is a very valid activity, along with photography which I wish had been included. I have similar feelings about the list of biological supply houses, but think that since it was included, it should have been more complete.

> *Peter M. Stowe, in a review of "Beetles and How They Live," in* Appraisal: Children's Science Books, *Vol. 12, No. 2, Spring, 1979, p. 48.*

In *Beetles and How They Live,* the authors describe beetle anatomy, feeding habits, flight, reproduction, interactions with other animals, and the benefits and damages attributed to some beetles. Although a few pictures are included in each chapter, more photographs and diagrams would increase reader interest. For example, a simple diagram would supplement the description of the anatomy of flight muscles, and a series of photographs of a typical beetle's life cycle (egg, larva, pupa, adult) would be instructive. The last chapter contains descriptions of some easy, observational experiments and ways to begin collecting beetles. A diagram showing the proper method to pin a beetle would be helpful. Collecting equipment and biological supply houses are listed. Special topics on the desert beetles, aquatic beetles, dung beetles and fireflies add breadth, while descriptions of the chemistry of certain beetle behaviors add depth to the book. The glossary is beneficial, but should be expanded. A good choice for collateral reading, particularly for an introduction to biological sciences.

> *Cindy Arey Lewis, in a review of "Beetles and How They Live," in* Science Books & Films, *Vol. XV, No. 2, September, 1979, p. 90.*

ANIMAL AND PLANT MIMICRY (1978)

Mimicry—"when one living thing resembles another so closely that it is in some way mistaken for the other"—is described by Patent, who draws extensively on examples from nature to make her point. Emphasis is on butterflies such as the monarch and its look-alike viceroy in discussions of physical characteristics, evolutionary phases, and reasons why creatures "fool" each other. Aggressive mimicry—disguise as a means of attracting potential prey—is explored along with the tendencies for mimicry found in the worlds of fish, social insects, and plants. A final chapter considers the unsolved problems in this area of study and talks about scientists' diffi-

FRIAR
Amauris niavius

ADMIRAL
Hypolimnas dubius

FEMALE MOCKER SWALLOWTAIL
Papilio dardanus

MALE MOCKER SWALLOWTAIL
Papilio dardanus

The admiral at upper right mimics the friar butterfly, though it is of quite a different family. The female mocker swallowtail mimics the friar, and also butterflies of various other families. Some of these mocker females look like their own males, which have the "swallowtails" on their wings. Drawing by the author.

From Animal and Plant Mimicry, *written and illustrated by Dorothy Hinshaw Patent.*

culties in proving that it even exists. The detailed text, including references to experiments, is supplemented by black-and-white photographs (unfortunately none are in color) and drawings, making this a valuable reference source for top biology students.

> *Barbara Elleman, in a review of "Animal and Plant Mimicry," in* Booklist, *Vol. 75, No. 7, December 1, 1978, p. 618.*

An excellent documented approach to plant and animal mimicry. The author immediately discusses the importance of avoiding teleological interpretations that mimicry is a conscious effort on the part of the copier. She begins with a brief review of early work, moves into the types of mimicry, gives many clear, interesting examples, and then most importantly, suggests problems remaining and theories advanced. . . . This book should cause a young scientist to become fascinated by the present and future of this intriguing evolutionary science.

> *Mary M. Allen, in a review of "Animal and Plant Mimicry," in* Appraisal: Children's Science Books, *Vol. 12, No. 2, Spring, 1979, p. 47.*

One of the outstanding characteristics of this book is the wealth of examples. These include not only interesting items of information but also results of quite recent research. Vari-

ous kinds of mimicry are explained, early studies discussed, and a brief but adequate presentation of the role of evolution in these adaptations is made. Plants, not often thought of in this connection, are shown to depend on mimicry in a number of cases. Various examples of vertebrate mimicry are given, from young snakes luring prey with tail movements, to the possible mimicry of honey badgers by young cheetahs. Butterflies and social insects are overemphasized. Granted, they present a bewildering array of every type of mimicry but the endless and varied examples are soon overwhelming. Photographs enhance the text, together with several excellent drawings by the author. The book is well indexed, and a brief glossary is provided. A list of suggested readings includes both books and magazine articles where an interested reader can find further information. Mimicry is a difficult subject to explain simply, but the author's presentation shows that she has a clear and well-balanced command of the topic. (pp. 152-53)

> *A review of "Animal and Plant Mimicry," in* Science Books & Films, *Vol. XV, No. 3, December, 1979, pp. 152-53.*

THE WORLD OF WORMS (1978)

This small volume full of scientific names and vocabulary is a valuable technical book for research on all kinds of worms from tiny microscopic parasites to common earthworms and leeches. There is a wealth of information, some matter-of-fact and some serious and interesting, for the serious student, but it is not a book for the casual reader. The black and white photographs and drawings are adequate for identification but add little appeal to the simple, rather drab format. CIP, glossary, bibliography, and index are all included.

> *Sallie Hope Erhard, in a review of "The World of Worms," in* Appraisal: Children's Science Books, *Vol. 12, No. 1, Winter, 1979, p. 30.*

This is a disappointing book. In what I can only guess is an effort not to write down to kids, Dr. Patent has come up with an approach that completely avoids talking about any phase of this fascinating subject that would engross the reader. Planarians, for instance, are discussed in detail right off. Yet we have no idea where we might see one, or if. It's only much later in the back of the book that we learn that we can even collect them. But by that time any youngster will have lost interest. Facts are presented here as if for a scientific paper. Comparisons are made that subsume prior knowledge that very few nine to twelve year olds have. The author constantly states a fact as being "familiar." Familiar to whom? Terms are used and then only vaguely explained, processes and morphology are gone into when we haven't been given basic facts. And then there are the misleading statements, i.e. on page 5 "All animals need oxygen inside their bodies to live" and then on page 11 ". . . flukes can live and grow in the absence of oxygen." Where is the magic in this presentation? Furthermore, the drawings and photographs are dreary. (pp. 30-1)

> *Barbara Brenner, in a review of "The World of Worms," in* Appraisal: Children's Science Books, *Vol. 12, No. 1, Winter, 1979, pp. 30-1.*

This attempt to provide an easy-to-read treatment of a neglected group of animals is well intended, but it suffers from a number of problems. The author and publisher [Holiday House] are encouraged to consult with experts on each of the major groups of worms in order to correct errors (and prevent further ones) and to provide additional, fascinating data. For example, the largest nematode is not 4 feet long; one from the placenta of the sperm whale is 25 feet long and 1 inch in diameter. Additional illustrations would be helpful, too. Chapters include discussions on flatworms, roundworms or nematodes, earthworms, leeches, and other annelids and miscellaneous groups. Information on reproduction and a chapter on finding worms are included. . . . While the text is easy to read, inconsistencies in the use of terminology can cause confusion. The term "secondary host" is introduced and defined on one page, but then a more appropriate term, "intermediate host," is used thereafter. The use of some scanning electron microscope photomicrographs would add greatly to the book's appeal. In one very poor photograph of hookworms, a male tail is identified as a head. Subheadings such as "Endless Swimmers," "The Catworm," "The Sea Mouse," and "Inside the Worm" should catch the interest of junior high school science students.

> *J. Ralph Lichtenfels, in a review of "The World of Worms," in* Science Books & Films, *Vol. XIV, No. 4, March, 1979, p. 220.*

SIZES AND SHAPES IN NATURE—WHAT THEY MEAN (1979)

The concept of function determining form that helped to focus Patent's *The World of Worms* is central to this stimulating review, which considers different body systems in terms of the job to be done: getting here and there, delivering vital materials, and so on. Patent starts out with a look at the paramecium, which even within its one cell has specialized parts to perform the same basic functions that are handled by the more sophisticated systems investigated later. Early on, she goes into the importance of surface volume ratio, which then helps to answer such questions as "why do water animals get so much larger than land ones?"—and, later, to explain variations in animals' digestive tracts. Patent has a way of making a sense of phenomena in nature (citing, for example, the "good reasons" for male animals' coloration and females' drabness) and she disarms with questions kids might consider too dumb to ask: "How does water from the roots get all the way up to the top [of a 300-foot redwood tree] when the tree has no 'heart' to pump it up?" In her bibliography Patent cites a Stephen Jay Gould column on animal sizes and shapes, and her readers will be well prepared for Gould; adapting her own form to her more elementary function, she offers the same sort of intellectual pleasure.

> *A review of "Sizes and Shapes in Nature—What They Mean," in* Kirkus Reviews, *Vol. XLVII, No. 11, June 1, 1979, p. 644.*

Sizes and Shapes in Nature is no mere description of the legs of a walking stick or of an elephant's nose; it is a fascinating, comprehensive explanation of how structures which are vastly different are individually suited to various animals. Eight major needs of all organisms are described—reproduction, circulation, and ingestion, for example—and then plants and animals are examined to see how these needs are met. The text moves from the general to the specific, instead of the other way around, as is common in many science books. Respiration, for instance, is described as a type of circulatory system; a sensible explanation is given of why paramecia and earthworms need no respiratory system at all; why fish need surface capillaries in contact with water; and how frogs make partial use of internal capillaries next to moist air sacs (lungs). The author has done a masterful job on a book that should be made widely available. My only suggestion is that a few more illustrations would have been helpful. Included is a glossary, suggested reading, and an index.

> *Sarah Gagné, "Evolution," in* The Horn Book Magazine, *Vol. LV, No. 5, October, 1979, p. 556.*

Dr. Patent has answered countless numbers of questions about living things that children and young people have wondered about and has done so in a well-organized, carefully written book. The structure and function of both plant and animal life from the smallest one-celled organism to the largest are examined in detail. Adaptations to various environments are illustrated with examples of common animals. There is a glossary, bibliography of both books and magazine articles and a good index in this excellent resource book. (pp. 45-6)

> *Glen O. Blough, in a review of "Sizes and Shapes in Nature—What They Mean," in* Appraisal: Children's Science Books, *Vol. 13, No. 1, Winter, 1980, pp. 45-6.*

RACCOONS, COATIMUNDIS, AND THEIR FAMILY
(1979)

A plethora of books have been written on individual mammal families. At least three have appeared recently—one is on the deer family and one on pigs—and Dorothy Patent's book is the best of the three. The text rings with the authority of a person experienced with the technical literature and with some of the animals discussed. Four chapters deal with raccoons—their natural history and relationships with man. The habits of coatis, ringtails, and other New World family members are also well described, though the animals are of less general interest. Finally, the panda bear and the lesser panda are considered, and we learn of the pandas' still puzzling connection to the bear and the raccoon families. The last chapter indicates the problems of keeping raccoons and other procyonids as pets. The author has provided a list of suggested reading, and an index is appended.

> *Sarah Gagné, in a review of "Raccoons, Coatimundis, and Their Family," in* The Horn Book Magazine, *Vol. LVI, No. 1, February, 1980, p. 86.*

A detailed study of the origins, habits, and adaptability of raccoons as well as of their many cousins around the world. A chapter is devoted to stories of pet raccoons, and another points out the problems of keeping any procyonid as a pet. There is also a clear explanation of an ongoing argument: how should pandas be classified, as bears or raccoons? . . . The writing style is highly readable, despite the quantity of information given; a few lighthearted anecdotes break the serious scientific tone.

> *M. Dorcas Hand, in a review of "Raccoons, Coatimundis, and Their Family," in* School Library Journal, *Vol. 26, No. 6, February, 1980, p. 71.*

This is one of those sophisticated volumes which can teach a child more than either parent or teacher is likely to, since most adults know less about raccoons and their allies than children do to begin with. The depth and accuracy of the author, while keeping within the range of a child's understanding, is amazing. Any child reading the volume not only will learn quite a bit about raccoons and coatimundis but also will know that much remains unknown at the other end of the Procyonidae spectrum where the ringtails and olingos live. The kid will be able to explain to you what a procyonid is and why one should never try to keep one as a pet, despite their cuteness as juveniles. The reader also will be able to discuss intelligently the question of whether the giant and lesser pandas should be classified as bears, coons or whether the two species even belong together despite their common name of panda. It is a well-organized and informative book. (pp. 63-4)

> *Wayne Hanley, in a review of "Raccoons, Coatimundis, and Their Family," in* Appraisal: Children's Science Books, *Vol. 13, No. 2, Spring, 1980, pp. 63-4.*

BUTTERFLIES AND MOTHS: HOW THEY FUNCTION
(1979)

Butterflies and Moths is an all-you-ever-wanted-to-know type of book. By describing and contrasting the life cycles of the butterfly and moth, Patent dispels some of the common notions about lepidopterans. She begins by discussing the courtship and the mating dance of the adult lepidopteran, pointing out that the chief task of the adult is reproduction.

The author then traces the series of events that occur from the time an egg is laid through the maturation of the butterfly or moth. These sections include lively reading about the anatomy, physiology and ecology of the egg, pupae and adult stages of the lepidopteran. An added feature of this book is a delightful discussion of some rather exotic butterflies and moths. Patent also elaborates on how lepidopterans please and harm humans. This book is a valuable source of information for anyone who wants to know more about butterflies and moths.

> *Yolanda Scott George, in a review of "Butterflies and Moths: How They Function," in* Science Books & Films, *Vol. XV, No. 4, March, 1980, p. 214.*

Moths and butterflies may be relatively small, but what a huge amount of information can be learned about them! Their beauty and the remarkable fact of their metamorphosis are the familiar things we know, but in her book, Dr. Patent goes into the whys and hows of these, and the whole extraordinary life story of the insect group known as lepidopterans. She describes in great detail exactly what her book title says ". . . How They Function". The author's clear, instructive and very absorbing style makes all her books accessible to nearly every child, and the depth of this study—the whole concept of butterflies and moths in all its ramifications—makes this a work for junior high and up.

> *Heddie Kent, in a review of "Butterflies and Moths and How They Function," in* Appraisal: Children's Science Books, *Vol. 13, No. 2, Spring, 1980, p. 62.*

[**Butterflies and Moths**] is a very interesting book which contains a wealth of information stimulating to people twelve years old or more. It covers a great range of subject matter in a manner that generates a desire to look into her suggested readings. The one fault I find with her presentation is the use of the concept that insects, or any animal for that matter, are friends or enemies of man. For example, she refers to the cabbage moth as an enemy and the silkworm moth as a friend. Animals have many ecological relationships with other animals, man included, but they can hardly be considered friends or enemies. It is an idea that has no place in the understanding of relationships between animals and their environment. This book does introduce the reader to some fascinating insect ecology and points at some of the complex relationships between lepidopterans and the various parts of their environment. It also touches on some of the newer attempts to control certain species using hormones and natural controls pointing out the problems of using non-selective pesticides or habitat destruction. I was very pleased to find that Ms. Patent had refrained from a chapter on collecting so often found in other children's books about insects, and indeed she points out how this practice has reduced many species. I was also pleased that she used adult terminology backed up with a good usable glossary. Not only does it make the book very readable, but affords the opportunity for a young reader to have practice with more complex terminology. (pp. 62-3)

> *Peter Stowe, in a review of "Butterflies and Moths and How They Function," in* Appraisal: Children's Science Books, *Vol. 13, No. 2, Spring, 1980, pp. 62-3.*

BACTERIA: HOW THEY AFFECT OTHER LIVING THINGS (1980)

Dorothy Hinshaw Patent has had fifteen books published in the past several years, for which one can be grateful. She has an exceptional flair for making facts interesting and for giving a general overview. For these reasons I would recommend **Bacteria** for casual browsing and even for a college freshman before he or she tackles a dry textbook. Numerous three-dimensional photographs made through a scanning electron microscope are included—of special interest because they are not often seen. The author acknowledges it would be impossible to cover all important bacterial relationships, but she makes an admirable selection in the chapters on bacteria in plants, in insects, in the digestive tracts of various animals, and in human beings.

> *Sarah Gagné, in a review of "Bacteria: How They Affect Other Living Things," in* The Horn Book Magazine, *Vol. LVI, No. 3, June, 1980, p. 326.*

This is a small book with a 'gee whiz' approach to bacteria. Where else could you learn that the bedrock pressure of "growing gypsum crystals" formed by Thiobacillus damaged over 40 buildings in Pittsburgh; that the cow rumen bacteria produces 60-80 liters of gas per day; that Bdellovibrio "dashes forth" at "amazing speed" only to "crash into its prey at full tilt"; or that Portuguese fishermen used luminescent bacteria to enhance their bait. The information appears to be accurate if you are willing to allow for much simplification (e.g., "biologists succeed in coaxing bacteria to make human insulin"). The most serious content problem is the lack of perception demonstrated in the author's discussion of the implications of applied genetic engineering. Although the book has a glossary, an index and suggested readings, it lacks any phonetic aids, gives no references, and has barely adequate graphics. This book might be used to stimulate a student's interest in bacteria but it has little value as a reference for understanding bacteria.

> *Bruce Haggard, in a review of "Bacteria: How They Affect Other Living Things," in* Science Books & Films, *Vol. 16, No. 2, November-December, 1980, p. 92.*

An outstanding writer of science books for children, Dr. Patent once again adds another well-organized and well-written text to her already long list of excellent offerings. . . . Clearly outlined, well-formulated with good photographs, including a good glossary, bibliography, and index, this is a superior addition to the lore of bacteria.

> *Virginia A. Tashjian, in a review of "Bacteria: How They Affect Other Living Things," in* Appraisal: Science Books for Young People, *Vol. 14, No. 2, Spring, 1981, p. 31.*

BEARS OF THE WORLD (1980)

Patent discusses the seven bear species, and comments on some of the habits or habitats, or the reproductive and breeding patterns that apply to all species. In the succeeding chapters, she discusses the American (black) bear, the grizzly, the polar bear, and others, in more detail; these are followed by a chapter on hibernation; the two concluding chapters are "Bears and People," which describes bear legends or early explorers' encounters with bears, and "Living with Bears," in which Patent discusses research, conservation, and the treatment of bears by the public. . . . As always, Patent is authoritative, clear, and objective, and her writing style is nicely honed. A bibliography and an index are included.

> *Zena Sutherland, in a review of "Bears of the World," in* Bulletin of the Center for Children's Books, *Vol. 34, No. 1, September, 1980, p. 18.*

One's first reaction to this small book is likely to be negative, since the pictures are muddy and random browsing yields sentences and thoughts that seem "unscientific." If this initial prejudice is overcome, however, one is left with a very fine book that presents a good overview of the subject to a junior audience. The reader not only will get a description of bears but also will get a feel for how scientific research is conducted. Differences in scientific opinion on some of the topics are openly presented, and given the skepticism of the target age group, this may improve readers' reception of the text. Aspects of basic biology, taxonomy, behavior and physiology all receive attention.

> *John D. Buffington, in a review of "Bears of the World," in* Science Books & Films, *Vol. 16, No. 2, November-December, 1980, p. 78.*

THE LIVES OF SPIDERS (1980)

The Lives of Spiders stops short of serving as the one book needed for older readers. It comes close, however, for it describes in highly readable style the major groups of spiders, discusses anatomy and webs, and gives remarkable examples of particular spider habits. What it lacks is an attempt to relate everyday spiders to the reader. Surely a few common American spiders could have been photographed and described. Why discuss *Argiope* without explaining that this is the common large yellow-and-black garden spider? Nevertheless, the text is excellent as a collation of up-to-date information on the general biology of spiders and the habits of many species. Tarantism and American poisonous spiders are especially well researched. Some minor quibbles: An illustration of a *stabilimentum* and of barbed tarantula hairs is needed; the comparison of spider silk and steel should say that the author is comparing *threads* of each; the description of how a maze web is built is unclear; and the reference to the bolas spider as a "fat, lazy" one should have been modified. In spite of these caveats, the book is a useful source of information.

> *Sarah Gagné, in a review of "The Lives of Spiders," in* The Horn Book Magazine, *Vol. LVII, No. 1, February, 1981, p. 81.*

Not as attractive as Shuttlesworth's *The Story of Spiders* nor as authoritative as Kaston's *How To Know the Spiders,* Patent's book contains much fascinating information but would not be particularly useful as a reference. The author's drawings are good, though few; some photos are blurred, and one appears to be turned sideways. The text is marred by occasional lack of clarity, misspellings and pronouns with ambiguous antecedents. The 20-item glossary is hackwork without focus, but the index is generally reliable. All of these lapses detract from an otherwise readable, useful book.

> *George Gleason, in a review of "The Lives of Spiders," in* School Library Journal, *Vol. 27, No. 6, February, 1981, p. 77.*

If you are not too proud to read a book written with a mini-

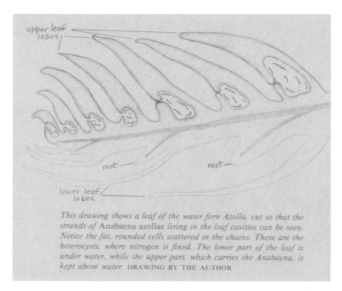

This drawing shows a leaf of the water fern Azolla, cut so that the strands of Anabaena azollae *living in the leaf cavities can be seen. Notice the fat, rounded cells scattered in the chains. These are the heterocysts, where nitrogen is fixed. The lower part of the leaf is under water, while the upper part, which carries the Anabaena, is kept above water.* DRAWING BY THE AUTHOR

From Bacteria: How They Affect Other Living Things, *written and illustrated by Dorothy Hinshaw Patent.*

mum of esoteric vocabulary, Patent's book will be an enjoyable introduction to the world of the ubiquitous spiders. While addressing her book to a high school audience, Patent has also done a remarkable job of retaining a high level of scholarship and breadth of coverage. She covers external morphology, the web-builders and the free-hunters, silk glands and web building, feeding and toxins, reproduction and communal living, spiders in superstition and myth. The excellent illustrations, all in black-and-white, are both pen-and-ink drawings and photographs. There are some fine scanning electron photomicrographs. There is a short glossary for the few technical terms used, an index, a bibliography, and for those aficionados who really care, the address of the American Tarantula Society.

> *Roy T. Cunningham, in a review of "The Lives of Spiders," in* Science Books & Films, *Vol. 17, No. 1, September-October, 1981, p. 21.*

HUNTERS AND THE HUNTED: SURVIVING IN THE ANIMAL WORLD (1981)

Though this shorter, less demanding introduction is more a sampling than a stimulating investigation like most of Patent's books, it nonetheless offers a clear, sharp, smartly organized view—made all the clearer and sharper by the excellent photos—of prey animals' defenses and predators' weapons and ploys for breaking through them. Describing each case succinctly, Patent leads easily from the aphids' waxy scales, and the secretions that win ants' protection for some honeydew aphids, to other animals' chemical defenses *against* ants; from lions' cooperative stalking to the "safety in numbers" of fish schools; from sea stars' remarkable assaults on shellfish to shrimps' persistent invasion of sea stars' tough outer shells. With due, if not new, defense of the predators' place in nature, a strong contender for survival.

> *A review of "Hunters and the Hunted: Surviving in the Animal World," in* Kirkus Reviews, *Vol. XLIX, No. 13, July 1, 1981, p. 804.*

Clear, readable, prose vignettes tell of hunters or prey, and the quality is sustained. The photographs of individual animals or groups admirably complement text passages. Three illustrations—one of a snake swallowing a toad, one of a lion dragging a gazelle and one of weaver ants tearing apart an ant of another species—might repel timid souls, but are necessary to the book and not sensational. It is interesting to read piecemeal or straight through; there is no technical vocabulary; and in a general collection this should be useful for years.

> *George Gleason, in a review of "Hunters and the Hunted: Surviving in the Animal World," in* School Library Journal, *Vol. 28, No. 2, October, 1981, p. 152.*

The most striking aspect of this informative book about predator/prey relationships is its superb black-and-white photographs, depicting both predators (like the snake gobbling up a toad, opposite the title page) and prey (like the inchworm on page fifteen, protecting itself against predators by camouflaging itself as a twig). The accompanying text, although not as exceptional as the illustrations, offers a comprehensive, easily understood and often fascinating account of how predators overcome or are outwitted by their prey.

The author also successfully explains the importance of this predator/prey relationship in maintaining the balance of nature, as well as how it relates to the food chain. Additionally, she emphasizes the concept that predators are also prey: toads hunt flies and are hunted by snakes; sea stars devour mussels and scallops and are in turn devoured by shrimp.

An index and a "Suggested Reading List" which includes both books and magazine articles add to the book's usefulness.

There are other books for approximately the same age group on approximately the same topic, including Alice L. Hopf's *Nature's Pretenders: Predators and Prey, and How Camouflage Works,* and Miriam Schlein's *Snake Fights, Rabbit Fights, and More: a Book About Animal Fighting.* However, even for those libraries that already have these titles, I would recommend **Hunters and the Hunted** for its reasonable price, its exceptional illustrations, and its deft and comprehensive coverage of one of the most important interactions among animals.

> *Lee Jeffers, in a review of "Hunters and the Hunted: Surviving in the Animal World," in* Appraisal: Science Books for Young People, *Vol. 15, No. 1, Winter, 1982, p. 52.*

HORSES AND THEIR WILD RELATIVES (1981)

Another of Patent's superior introductions. She begins with a description of the horse's body, comparing the eyes, teeth, and other features to humans' and emphasizing how horses are adapted to grass eating and designed for fast running over hard grassy plains. She shows how eohippus evolved to the present-day equus, describes feral horses' behavior in the wild, looks at different horses, zebras, and asses throughout the world, and ends with a look at equus' other relatives (tapir, rhinoceros) and where they fit in the evolutionary picture. The whole discussion gives an impression of pieces falling into place, with some pieces yet to be placed and others still missing; so that as usual readers come away with some understanding of the evolution of species as well as a good deal of information about horses.

> *A review of "Horses and Their Wild Relatives," in* Kirkus Reviews, *Vol. XLIX, No. 14, July 15, 1981, p. 875.*

Patent's book on the horse family is so absorbing that even riders who are not science-minded may be interested in it. How teeth, leg bones, hoofs, and body size could have evolved the characteristics of those of today's species of horses is a marvel. The first chapters discuss the evolution and distribution of the horse. A reader could acquire a sleuth-like interest in how some species evolved in one region, but their descendants now live in different regions. The book discusses the horses returned to a wild state—for instance, mustangs, the Camargue horses of France, the ponies of Assateague. Next, the author deals with the habits of various species of zebras and asses and with the "sad case of the quagga." Finally, we see the connection between the horse family and its nearest relations—tapirs, rhinos, and two extinct groups. Most of the information is well organized; Dorothy Patent could probably make interesting the life and ancestors of even a garden mole. (p. 559)

> *Sarah Gagné, in a review of "Horses and Their Wild Relatives," in* The Horn Book Magazine, *Vol. LVII, No. 5, October, 1981, pp. 558-59.*

In the eight chapters here, what makes horses so special is discussed, and how they came to be, their sociology, relatives (ancient and modern as well as wild horses, asses and zebras) is explained. Unfortunately, the information is more fantasy than fact. This reflected in the book's "suggested reading" section which is devoid of any scientific treatment of horses and suggests the superficial nature of the research done. There is obviously little familiarity with origins, evolution, domestication, or their consequences. Also, there seems to be a lack of understanding of the horse's systematics, anatomy, physiology, health, and disease. An indirect admission to this is made in Chapter 1, where it is said that "little is written about them" (horses). Therefore, there is little in this book that is not more adequately and accurately said in Lavine and Casey's popular *Wonders of the World of Horses* or more beautifully said in Mochi and Carter's *Hoofed Mammals of the World*—neither of which is listed in the suggested reading.

> *John D. Sink, in a review of "Horses and Their Wild Relatives," in* Science Books & Films, *Vol. 17, No. 2, November-December, 1981, p. 96.*

HORSES OF AMERICA (1981)

The second book on horses by the scientist and well-known author . . . discusses only breeds and types found in America: their histories, physical characteristics, and special abilities. Arabians, Morgans, Appaloosas, Thoroughbreds, and numerous others are described, as are such popular equine sports as rodeos, steeplechases, and polo. Striking photographs supplement the concise text, making a volume less detailed than some books on horses but one that is nevertheless a valuable and attractive reference work. With suggested reading, a glossary, and an index.

> *Karen Jameyson, in a review of "Horses of America," in* The Horn Book Magazine, *Vol. LVII, No. 6, December, 1981, p. 679.*

This book is an acceptable survey of popular horses found in the United States. Many interesting details about the characteristics and development of various breeds are included. The numerous black-and-white photographs are well chosen and include all horses mentioned in the text. However, some reservations prevent a higher rating. The style of writing is often awkward, and some sections are not well developed. Also, the index failed to direct me to the book's first use of the word "sclera." The information is accurate, and the many young people who love horses are likely to overlook these flaws.

> *Paul R. Boehlke, in a review of "Horses of America," in* Science Books & Films, *Vol. 17, No. 3, January-February, 1982, p. 163.*

The writer modestly omits her own **Horses and Their Wild Relatives** from the short bibliography. In this book she describes the evolution of horses, correctly identifying that they originated, and later died out, in America, and gives a brief history of their importance in the early West, their domestication, and present uses. American varieties of work, show, racing, and pleasure horses are discussed with a black-and-white photograph of most. Regrettably, some photographs are dark and details of physique and coloration are not clear. Color is sorely missed here to appreciate the hues and mixtures of grays, browns, and reds. The narrative is clear, interesting, and readable. There are many books on horses; however, this one is worthy since it focuses on breeds found in our nation, and young readers in their lifetime will have many opportunities to see most of the varieties described. Included are a table of contents and index. (p. 41)

> *James E. Palmer, in a review of "Horses of America," in* Appraisal: Science Books for Young People, *Vol. 15, No. 3, Fall, 1982, pp. 40-1.*

ARABIAN HORSES (1982)

Dorothy Patent has capitalized on her knowledge of horses to produce a third book, this one on the renowned Arabian breed. . . . Chapters here cover background information which any horse lover would want to pick up: on the breed's history and characteristics, foals, part-Arabian breeds, trail-riding contests, racing, horse shows, and on selecting one's own Arabian. Most pages are accompanied by excellent black-and-white photographs. These alone should allow an unknowledgeable reader to grasp the essence of the Arabian horse, and the text also helps. But for contrast, pictures of a few other breeds would aid the reader in verifying impressions. Included are lists of organizations and periodicals, an excellent glossary, and an index. (pp. 549-50)

> *Sarah Gagné, in a review of "Arabian Horses," in* The Horn Book Magazine, *Vol. LVIII, No. 5, October, 1982, pp. 549-50.*

[**Arabian Horses** is an] adulatory book. . . . The author drapes the Arabian in purple and gold, contrasts him with other horses in numerous ways and cites contributions Arab ancestors made to the Thoroughbred, Morab and POA breeds. Differences among Egyptian and Polish Arabian stock, color superstitions among Arabian people and Arabian success in endurance competition sustain interest. . . . [The] abundant information, lists of publications and organizations, glossary and index will please readers who admire the horse world's royalty from afar or who have to do book reports.

Pat Harrington, in a review of "Arabian Horses," in School Library Journal, *Vol. 29, No. 2, October, 1982, p. 154.*

Without using too much detail the author outlines the influence of many different breeds of horses. She also discusses the use of Arabians in racing and in the development of the Thoroughbred as a race horse with Arabian blood. . . . Patent's writing style is clear and especially adapted to grade-school readers. The author's points are made in a simple, straightforward manner. This book would be especially useful for young readers with a real or developing interest in horses.

R. C. Hammond, in a review of "Arabian Horses," in Science Books & Films, *Vol. 18, No. 4, March-April, 1983, p. 211.*

SPIDER MAGIC (1982)

[In **Spider Magic,** Patent] deals with a subject she has already covered. But the book on spiders is intended as an introduction for intermediate readers and is distinctly different from her previous one. The content is similar in scope to, but less detailed than, Dorothy Shuttlesworth's *The Story of Spiders.* Illustrations in the new book are magnified black-and-white photographs, a few of which are made with the scanning electron microscope and show minute anatomy in depth. I prefer photographs to drawings for their sense of reality; the reader marvels at the eyes and jaws of a wolf spider, a jumping spider eating another spider its own size, the inside of an egg sac, crab spiders that poison a bee before it can sting, and the tiny harmless mate of a black widow. But the colored drawings in Shuttlesworth's book are superior for identifying spider types by color and shape. In the photograph of a black widow in Patent's book it was necessary for clarity to draw lines pointing to the red hourglass, and the magnified photographs do not indicate actual length. Using these pictures, a novice out of doors would probably not recognize more than about half of the twelve spiders or spider groups. But the major purpose is to convey the interesting lives of spiders, which Patent does very well. In a world where so much science seems to be known, the last sentence may surprise the reader: "Even scientists still have a lot to learn about spiders." Index.

Sarah Gagné, in a review of "Spider Magic," in The Horn Book Magazine, *Vol. LVIII, No. 5, October, 1982, p. 550.*

In spite of the fact that there are numerous fine introductory books on spiders available for the seven-to-eleven year old, this one is worth purchasing if you can afford another and there is a demand.

Many basic questions about these common eight legged creatures are answered in the clear direct text with the help of a remarkable set of black-and-white photographs, many of which are clearly labelled. Microphotography brings out many details our eyes cannot see, and bold chapter headings organize the material well. Several especially interesting of the 30,000 known species of spiders are discussed, among them the crab spider that hides on flowers and feeds on bees, the ten inch tropical tarantula that can feed on birds and small snakes, and the water spider, that spends its whole life under water in an air bubble. Table of contents and index are included. A fine book, as we have come to expect from Dorothy Hinshaw Patent.

Diane Holzheimer, in a review of "Spider Magic," in Appraisal: Science Books for Young People, *Vol. 16, No. 1, Winter, 1983, p. 49.*

Just like other books by Dorothy Hinshaw Patent I have read, I very much enjoyed **Spider Magic** and found it not only scientifically accurate but easy to read. The book is written on a young child's level and, therefore, is somewhat general with a few interesting details introduced here and there. There is certainly enough detail to spark a child's interest and stimulate the search for more information. The text is beautifully illustrated with excellent microphotographs of spiders and parts of spiders.

The first few chapters are of general topics such as how spiders sense the world, use silk, how they eat, and how they grow. The chapters are then devoted to the different families of spiders such as crab spiders, wolf spiders, tarantulas, and cellar spiders. These chapters are short (80-120 words) and somewhat general but add some interesting information on these families. I found this book very interesting and worthwhile and suggest it to be a very valuable resource for the young person's library (pp. 49-50)

Peter Stowe, in a review of "Spider Magic," in Appraisal: Science Books for Young People, *Vol. 16, No. 1, Winter, 1983, pp. 49-50.*

A PICTURE BOOK OF COWS (1982)

For those who harbor a fancy for bovine quadrupeds, a new book by an author who specializes in science books for children offers much useful information and many photographs [by William Munoz]. The simple, readable text covers such topics as birth, the stages of growing up, the physical make-up of cows, and the differences between beef and dairy cattle. Text and illustrations are well-matched on the pages, but some of the photographs lack the sharp focus, the contrast of light and dark, and the variety of composition which we have come to expect in science books for children. The text, however, seems accurate and informative and discusses matters such as birth and castration with a matter-of-fact honesty which informs adequately, if briefly, but should not alarm young readers. Included where needed within the text is the pronunciation of unfamiliar words; a short index is appended.

Ethel R. Twichell, in a review of "A Picture Book of Cows," in The Horn Book Magazine, *Vol. LIX, No. 2, April, 1983, p. 185.*

It has only forty pages, but this book is packed with information about cows. . . . There is a section about beef cattle—the most popular breeds, their special feeding and care without, thank goodness, any details of their ultimate end. *A Calf is Born,* (Joanna Cole, Morrow '75) is a very good, similar book, but this **Picture Book of Cows** covers a broader field with added information.

Heddie Kent, in a review of "A Picture Book of Cows," in Appraisal: Science Books for Young People, *Vol. 16, No. 3, Fall, 1983, p. 52.*

Young children have a special fascination with cows . . . and they will find **A Picture Book of Cows** appealing. . . . The photographs are suitable for young children, but the information in the text is appropriate for older readers in the third through sixth grade. New words and terms, such as castration, homogenization, and pasteurization, are introduced and discussed. The more difficult words that are presented are phonetically spelled and placed in parentheses after the term. Teachers should be prepared to answer curious students' questions. Overall, *A Picture Book of Cows* is a good introduction to the life cycle and habits of one of our most important meat and dairy sources.

> Carol L. Reiner, in a review of "A Picture Book of Cows," in Science Books & Films, *Vol. 19, No. 2, November-December, 1983, p. 100.*

GERMS! (1983)

Many photographs, most of which have a high degree of magnification, are used to illustrate a text that is written in a succinct, direct style that neither depends on scientific terminology (although it is used, with discretion) nor oversimplifies. With calm authority, Patent describes what germs are, what they do, how they make people ill, and how antibiotics and antibodies combat the destructive effects of bacteria and viruses. A fine introduction to the subjects of germs, communicable illness, and immunization. An index gives access to a text that may also prove useful for slow older readers, since it is dignified in style and format. (pp. 215-16)

> Zena Sutherland, in a review of "Germs!" in Bulletin of the Center for Children's Books, *Vol. 36, No. 11, July-August, 1983, pp. 215-16.*

From the book children should get an excellent idea of what some disease organisms look like and how the body counteracts with its macrophages, antibodies, and T cells. Readers will also learn how man combats germs with shots and antibiotics and, in an interesting chapter, why different germs cause different symptoms. Tuberculosis bacteria, for example, require much oxygen and therefore live in the lungs. Because the book is intended for intermediate readers, it does not attempt to cover the subject completely. Hence, there is no list of common dangerous diseases; "new" diseases, such as Legionnaire's Disease, are not described (although a photograph of its bacteria is seen inside a macrophage); and the important fact that smallpox has been eradicated is unfortunately omitted. Nevertheless, photographs—particularly the three-dimensional scanning electron micrographs—make the book outstanding by offering visual images impossible only a few years ago. It is much easier to accept the existence of unfamiliar bodies such as T cells and macrophages when they are shown. Sometimes pictures are allowed to substitute entirely for "a thousand words": Through captions one learns of petri dishes and the electron microscope and how the effectiveness of an antibiotic can be measured. The author does not spare facts or scientific words, so the reader who makes an effort will learn a great deal. Other readers should gain at the very least some important concepts. With an index.

> Sarah Gagné, in a review of "Germs!" in The Horn Book Magazine, *Vol. LIX, No. 5, October, 1983, p. 606.*

This book is an interesting and effective effort to educate young children about infectious disease. There are few similar efforts that I know of directed at this age group—an age group filled with folklore about "germs." This book is not only a welcome addition to children's literature, but the ideas presented in it are focused and presented one at a time, thus avoiding confusion. The photographs are excellent in quality

including electron micrographs of bacteria, viruses, body-producing cells, and even a photomicrograph of the bacterium of Legionnaires' disease. By presenting accurate information about "germs," the book also promotes appropriate ideas about health and body maintenance and good attitudes toward disease prevention. I highly recommend it as a nice addition to elementary school libraries. (pp. 159-60)

> Margretta R. Seashore, in a review of "Germs!" in Science Books & Films, *Vol. 19, No. 3, January-February, 1984, pp. 159-60.*

WHERE THE BALD EAGLES GATHER (1984)

In Patent's typically creative and thoughtful presentation, the annual gathering of bald eagles in Glacier National Park provides entree to: 1) the problem of saving an endangered species from extinction; 2) the difficulty of following birds' movements, and how it's overcome; 3) the eagles' actual traits and habits; 4) the means of keeping up the salmon population on which they feed; 5) ongoing dangers to the eagles (including the notion of birds being "bad" or "good"). Children will be most interested in learning how the bald eagles are tracked—via tags or attached radio transmitters; in seeing how individual birds are trapped, examined, and tagged or radio-equipped at Glacier Park; and in learning, from the pinpoint photo-documentation, that they aren't hurt in the process. Patent is forthright and concrete about the present state of the bald eagle population, and today's threats (deforestation, poisons, feather-merchants, misguided ranchers); she also supplies a little national-bird lore. It's absorbing and, in the best sense, educational.

> A review of "Where the Bald Eagles Gather," in Kirkus Reviews, *Juvenile Issue, Vol. LII, No. 6-9, May 1, 1984, p. J46.*

A fine introduction to the national bird, this focuses upon those bald eagles that gather each fall for the salmon spawning in Montana's Glacier National Park. Starting from this point, Patent describes the eagles' feeding activities, their subsequent southward migration, and eventual return to Alaska and the Northwest Territories for breeding. The text is straightforwardly factual, well-organized, and fluent. As fascinating as the topic itself is, equally interesting is Patent's parallel discussion of how scientists gather information about the eagles; and her discussion of visual and electronic tagging is comprehensive.

> Zena Sutherland, in a review of "Where the Bald Eagles Gather," in Bulletin of the Center for Children's Books, *Vol. 37, No. 10, June, 1984, p. 190.*

Exceptional photographs [by William Munoz] set the mood for this informative book about our national bird. Young readers will be fascinated by the description of the methods of gathering information by the wildlife research project. Bird banding as well as the use of radio transmitters is described as the scientists study the habits and lifecycles of the birds. The text contains interesting well-organized information as well as a fine description of how scientists work.

> Glenn O. Blough, in a review of "Where the Bald Eagles Gather," in Appraisal: Science Books for Young People, *Vol. 17, No. 3, Fall, 1984, p. 36.*

FARM ANIMALS (1984)

Excellent black-and-white photographs [by William Munoz] and a clear and informative text introduce common farm animals. After a brief overview, the text is arranged in chapters dealing with animals by their function, e.g., "Meat Animals" includes beef cattle, pigs and sheep. The more popular breeds are described for each species. Young readers will learn much from this book, including the rapid growth rate of piglets, the origin of the domesticated turkey and the characteristics of the milk of various breeds of cows. . . . *Understanding Farm Animals* by Ruth Thompson contains much of the same information, but its busy format may hinder young readers. Patent's book is suitable for youngsters doing reports and attractive enough to entice browsers, who may pick up a new fact or two.

> *Barbara B. Murphy, in a review of "Farm Animals,"* in School Library Journal, *Vol. 31, No. 3, November, 1984, p. 127.*

Dorothy Hinshaw Patent's new book will be welcomed by teachers and youngsters as well, for it is an appealing, informational resource. . . .

The text has an enthusiastic tone and is well-written with plenty of interesting details.

Farm Animals is quite similar to a ten-year-old book by Elizabeth and Klaus Gemming called *Born in a Barn* which focuses on farm animals and their young. The text in Ms. Patent's book is better organized and more accessible, with more details about various breeds and somewhat more emphasis on the breeding and use of the farm animals. Librarians who can afford both books will find this new one a very worthwhile purchase. Table of contents and index included.

> *Diane Holzheimer, in a review of "Farm Animals,"* in Appraisal: Science Books for Young People, *Vol. 18, No. 2, Spring, 1985, p. 32.*

Farm Animals is a delightful picture book with all your favorites: cows, goats, pigs, sheep, horses, chickens, guinea hens, turkeys, waterfowl, even cats and dogs. The text is clearly written and accurate. [Mrs. Patent] includes many interesting details about the animals and gives a good sampling of representative breeds. . . .

The following statement about barn cats on page 68 might raise the eyebrows of some humane educators: "The cats mate, have their kittens, and grow up in the barn and around the barnyard, without ever going into the house." Throughout the paragraph the author gives the impression that barn cats are wild animals, that do not need to be neutered, spayed, or vaccinated. However, since there is a serious pet population and disease problem in the United States, farmers should be encouraged to care for their barn cats in the same manner as they care for their cows, sheep, horses, and turkeys.

Except for the section on barn cats, the author *does* encourage proper care of farm animals. She concludes her book by saying, "Besides benefitting our diet and easing our work, these animals provide companionship for us and for one another." I would recommend this book to all elementary school librarians.

> *Martha T. Kane, in a review of "Farm Animals," in* Appraisal: Science Books for Young People, *Vol. 18, No. 2, Spring, 1985, p. 32.*

Patent with Kiska, a gray wolf pup.

WHALES: GIANTS OF THE DEEP (1984)

Patent offers an attractive overview of whales that explains how they are specially suited to their underwater world and then looks at a number of individual whale species. . . . A section entitled "whale mysteries" touches on some of the many things we *don't* know about whales, while the problem of overhunting comes up for scrutiny in the final chapter. The book's design is attractive; and the illustrations (black-and-white photographs or old prints) are crisp and informative. A worthy introduction.

> *Denise M. Wilms, in a review of "Whales: Giants of the Deep," in* Booklist, *Vol. 81, No. 7, December 1, 1984, p. 527.*

Whales: Giants of the Deep is an exceptionally good book. . . . Photographs contribute largely to the excellence of the book. They were collected from many sources and contain much of the whale than just the tip of the back or fluke in the open sea. They show whales in action; whales recently killed or stranded; or parts of whales with baleen, teeth, and scars from barnacles or shark bites. Twelve species are depicted in photographs; a few others are sketched. . . . The author gives the current survival outlook for different species of whales, though experts can only guess about species that are seldom seen. In the five chapters of the book Patent covers general facts about whales, the common baleen whales, the common toothed whales, stranding, breathing, sonar, and a history of man's destruction of and recent efforts to save whales. The last topic is especially well handled. Dolphins and porpoises are given short shrift—since they are not whales in the common sense (although they are members of the larger whale group, the cetaceans). Inclusion of these animals would have made the book complete. (pp. 80-1)

> *Sarah S. Gagné, in a review of "Whales: Giants of the Deep," in* The Horn Book Magazine, *Vol. LXI, No. 1, January-February, 1985, pp. 80-1.*

Here is a whale of a book! It is well written, well illustrated, instructive, accurate, appealing, and provides excellent coverage of the topic. It explains clearly and logically "everything you wanted to know about whales" without getting bogged down in academic details, yet it does not skirt issues and problems. Two small technical slips of the pen over a 90-page span are not of sufficient importance to detract from the overall excellence of this interesting, packed-with-facts reference. **Whales** will delight middle- and intermediate-grade students and their teachers.

> *Sister Edna L. Demanche, in a review of "Whales: Giants of the Deep," in* Science Books & Films, *Vol. 21, No. 2, November-December, 1985, p. 101.*

THE SHEEP BOOK (1985)

In an attractive, complete, and clearly written look at domestic sheep, Patent has included information on the breeding and raising of sheep, the life of the flock, types and uses of wool, and the characteristics of seventeen breeds. . . . Since the book is written to be used easily by third-grade students, the author primarily uses short, simple sentences suitable for the younger readers who will be drawn to the book by its appearance. This book would be an especially good introduction for a child considering raising sheep as a project. Other available titles are not as accessible to younger elementary students.

> *Elizabeth S. Watson, in a review of "The Sheep Book," in* The Horn Book Magazine, *Vol. LXI, No. 5, September-October, 1985, p. 584.*

This is comprehensive, readable and interesting writing on domestic sheep. . . . Although the text is for general reading and reference there is good science here as relates to selection and breeding. Most, however, is on the kinds of sheep, family life, flock and range behavior, and the economics of the sheep industry. Good treatments are given on the growth, shearing, and processing of wool, ancestors of sheep, and the many varieties around the world. A delightful side topic is the use of dogs as guards and herders of sheep. The issue of humaneness is not identified but it is evident that the author is sensitive to this by the writing.

> *John R. Pancella, in a review of "The Sheep Book," in* Appraisal: Science Books for Young People, *Vol. 18, No. 4, Autumn, 1985, p. 32.*

Photographs [by William Munoz] that range from fuzzy to sharp illustrate a straightforward, clearly written text. . . . The text, which describes maternal care, the behavior of sheep, the dogs that guard or herd them, and the way wool is procured and processed, is as accurate and authoritative as are most books by Patent, a fairly prolific and very competent author/biologist.

> *A review of "The Sheep Book," in* Bulletin of the

Center for Children's Books, *Vol. 39, No. 2, October, 1985, p. 34.*

THOROUGHBRED HORSES (1985)

Dependably thorough and lucid in her writing, Patent here gives broad but fully detailed coverage to the topic of Thoroughbred horses. Her text includes a discussion of founding sires and blood lines; descriptions of breeding, training, and racing; Thoroughbreds used for participation in events or exhibitions other than racing; and other breeds that have been improved by introducing Thoroughbred strains. The writing style is crisp, and the book should prove interesting to the general reader as well as to addicted horse-lovers. A bibliography, glossary, and index are included; the book is profusely illustrated by photographs, many of which are action shots. (pp. 34-5)

> *A review of "Thoroughbred Horses," in* Bulletin of the Center for Children's Books, *Vol. 39, No. 2, October, 1985, pp. 34-5.*

Patent traces Thoroughbred history from uncertain ancestors of extinct types through the three known foundation stallions to today's celebrity sires and scientific breeding programs. . . . The abundance of new information will add depth to readers' knowledge and increase admiration for a glorious animal. Numerous full and half-page black-and-white photos, whose captions add facts about outstanding horses and jockeys, enhance the clear print and white space. The list of Triple Crown winners, glossary, bibliography and index add reference value. Easier to read than Wilding and Del Balso's *Triple Crown Winners*, **Thoroughbred Horses** is an excellent companion for the author's own **Arabian Horses.**

> *Pat Harrington, in a review of "Thoroughbred Horses," in* School Library Journal, *Vol. 32, No. 2, October, 1985, p. 186.*

[Patent's] account surveys history and breeding, training of racehourse, racing practices, and the several well known breeds (Morgan, Tennessee Walker, American Quarter Horse etc.) which have been strengthened by breeding with thoroughbreds. Well chosen photographs accompany the informative but also rather difficult and sometimes sketchy text. (Dressage, a less familiar style of showing trained horses, is a good example of skimpy explanation though the glossary definition at the end of the book offers a bit of clarification.) As the author has become quite prolific in books about horses, her competently developed writing seems also to be more utilitarian in tone, and some photographs are related in her various books. This is, however, a substantial introduction to a subject with undeniable appeal.

> *Margaret Bush, in a review of "Thoroughbred Horses," in* Appraisal: Science Books for Young People, *Vol. 19, No. 1, Winter, 1986, p. 30.*

QUARTER HORSES (1985)

The history of the popular American Quarter Horse, its migration across the United States, famous Quarter Horses, the uses of the Quarter Horse on a ranch or farm, Quarter Horse competitions and racing are described carefully and colorfully in chapters devoted to each of these topics. Short paragraphs, clear and sharp recent photographs as well as drawings [by William Munoz and others] make this a good choice for all libraries. Although the book will have the most appeal to readers in grades four to eight, it will be popular with junior and senior high reluctant readers because of the photographs, interesting subject matter and economical writing style. This book is less intimidating than *Quarter Horse* by Denhardt but cannot replace Miller's *Western Horse Behavior and Training.*

> Gayle W. Berge, in a review of "Quarter Horses," in School Library Journal, Vol. 32, No. 6, February, 1986, p. 88.

All you ever wanted to know about quarter horses and more! Everything from the history of the breeding of these horses for racing and for working cattle, through the life of the working quarter horse on western ranches, through shows, competitions and racing, to tips on buying a quarter horse— all are included in this book. Captioned black and white photographs abound to illustrate and expand upon the text. Thoroughly researched and well-written, this book will be enjoyed by a limited audience—that special, older child with a deep interest in horses or that student who is writing an in-depth specialty report. Index. Glossary. List of Associations and Publications dealing with this specific breed of horse. (pp. 53-4)

> Arlene Bernstein, in a review of "Quarter Horses," in Appraisal: Science Books for Young People, Vol. 19, No. 3, Summer, 1986, pp. 53-4.

Quarter Horses is equestrian education pure and simple. . . . For a youngster interested in horses this book will provide good reading and a wealth of information.

Photographs have been integrated into the book in a format that amplifies the narrative. Through the photographic record, the reader gains an insight into the versatility of this unique breed of horses.

Overall this is a crisp, interesting and well documented book. It gives an accurate portrayal of the world's most popular breed of horses. If the reader is sufficiently impressed, the last chapter tells how to select and buy a quarter horse of his/her very own!

> Harry O. Haakonsen, in a review of "Quarter Horses," in Appraisal: Science Books for Young People, Vol. 19, No. 3, Summer, 1986, p. 54.

THE QUEST FOR ARTIFICIAL INTELLIGENCE (1986)

A vigorous examination of the current state of research into the realm of artificial intelligence (AI) describes some truly amazing advances in computer technology now available. Using well-detailed examples, some with accompanying diagrams, Patent provides background on computer functions, introducing numerous terms that she further defines in an appended glossary. She continues with a wide-ranging consideration of the myriad difficulties involved in creating a computer that replicates the abilities of the mind to utilize language, sensory input, general knowledge, and common sense along with facts to solve problems. Moral and ethical considerations of AI are treated only peripherally, and readers unfamiliar with computers and terms will need to pay close attention to the text, but Patent has ably demonstrated that ma-

chines have a long way to go before they threaten human-kind. (p. 1202)

> Stephanie Zvirin, in a review of "The Quest for Artificial Intelligence," in Booklist, Vol. 82, No. 16, April 15, 1986, pp. 1201-02.

In some ways, the story of **The Quest for Artificial Intelligence** reminds one of the search for the Fountain of Youth which motivated the early Spanish explorers. Indeed, the analogy may not be at all farfetched, for it is really that which is discovered along the way to the goal that turns out to be more important and lastingly useful than that which inspired the search in the first place.

Dorothy Patent, with more than thirty books to her credit, mostly about animals, here turns to a study of the development of a process which some hope may allow computers to think like humans. The quest, as she describes it, involves a study of the human brain and mind and all the variables that affect how they function, in order to reproduce those functions in a supercomputer.

As Patent describes the search for a way to produce artificial intelligence, she recounts the various milestones in the process: the development of numerous machine and user languages based on the rules of logic, the creation of sophisticated game programs and expert systems, and the invention of robots. It is these particular accomplishments among others that have already proved the value of what the computer can do. Even if the computer scientists never actually create a machine that thinks exactly like a human (and many believe they never will), the results of their quest will continue to have lasting value for the improvement of our lives and the growth of knowledge.

Patent tells the AI story clearly and does not hesitate to explain complicated aspects of computer programming. The book is illustrated with photographs, diagrams, and cartoons. It contains a glossary, index, bibliography and a note on source material.

While this book is written for the teenaged reader, many adults could learn a great deal from reading it. It is a sober and well-reasoned account. (pp. 55-6)

> Rosalind von Au, in a review of "The Quest for Artificial Intelligence," in Appraisal: Science Books for Young People, Vol. 20, No. 1, Winter, 1987, pp. 55-6.

I'm impressed and respectful of any author who thinks that he or she can write about the concept of and research on artificial intelligence in a way that young readers will understand and enjoy. Yet, that's just what Dorothy Hinshaw Patent has done with this book. Ms. Patent has covered about every conceivable aspect of this (with all due respect to the younger generation) "awesome" topic. One can hardly imagine a more complex, more difficult subject for researchers themselves—let alone for the lay public—than understanding the operation of the human brain and finding ways to duplicate that process by means of machinery. Yet, Ms. Patent has apparently mastered the information and the skill to make the topic of artificial intelligence clear and understandable to her readers.

My only minor criticism is the author's rare tendency to step over the line of adolescent comprehensibility, as when she refers (page 150) to "an imaginary 'hypercube' in 14-

dimensional space". But that's a small complaint about a book that clearly succeeds by any other standard I can think of. Buy this book for your young readers!

> David E. Newton, in a review of "The Quest for Artificial Intelligence," in Appraisal: Science Books for Young People, Vol. 20, No. 1, Winter, 1987, p. 56.

MAGGIE: A SHEEP DOG (1986)

In *The Sheep Book,* Patent refers to several kinds of dogs that protect sheep, including the Hungarian Kuvasz, and goes on to distinguish them from other breeds that are trained to herd. Here she selects a particular guard dog, a Kuvasz named Maggie, and generates a text about the kinds of training it gets and work it does with the sheep. Black-and-white photographs on almost every page [by William Munoz] . . . prove the most lively focus of appeal. The text is disorganized and repetitive. Another problem is the very limited nature of the presentation; even a picture book at this level could have been much more interesting with the inclusion of other breeds or better yet, of the more varied role of the sheepherding dog, which is not even mentioned for those who don't know the difference between guard dogs and herders.

> A review of "Maggie: A Sheep Dog," in Bulletin of the Center for Children's Books, Vol. 39, No. 9, May, 1986, p. 176.

The text supplies captions for the appealing photos clearly portraying the unique relationship that develops between a guard dog and its charges. Simple enough for picture-book collections, the volume makes a nice addition to the growing number of information books for the very young.

> Elizabeth S. Watson, in a review of "Maggie: A Sheep Dog," in The Horn Book Magazine, Vol. LXII, No. 4, July-August, 1986, p. 467.

Maggie: A Sheep Dog is a clearly written story about a Hungarian Kuvasz. . . . The book's strengths are in the quality of the photographs and the clarity and simplicity of the story. Its weaknesses are in its rather excessively negative portrayal of the coyote as vicious predator. This book does, however, introduce the reader to a special kind of sheep dog, one that may be unfamiliar to most American audiences.

> Judy Diamond, in a review of "Maggie: A Sheep Dog," in Science Books & Films, Vol. 22, No. 2, November-December, 1986, p. 123.

DRAFT HORSES (1986)

In a clear writing style, Patent defines the five primary draft horse breeds, adding three other "draft animals"—the Norwegian Fjord Horse, the Austrian Hafflinger, and the mule. As well as covering the breeds' history and attributes, she also discusses care and uses of heavy horses in today's world. [William] Muñoz' black-and-white photos bring the horses to life, with most shots being informal poses of horses free in paddocks or tacked up in harness. This book is similar to Lavine and Casey's *Wonders of Draft Horses.* Both cover the same subject area for this age group. Lavine and Casey include more detail, with an emphasis on the historical background, while Patent concentrates on present-day uses of the horses. This new book may be more appealing to younger readers, with its simpler explanations and livelier text and photos. Knowledgeable readers may question a few minor slips—a horse's feet should be checked all year, not only in the springtime. Patent mentions a "female horse" and the horse's father and mother instead of the correct terms, mare, sire, and dam. These do not detract from the book's usefulness, either for recreational reading or information. (pp. 180-81)

> Charlene Strickland, in a review of "Draft Horses," in School Library Journal, Vol. 33, No. 2, October, 1986, pp. 180-81.

For city and country folk alike, this little primer is a revelation. Although it is printed in large type suitable for fourth to sixth graders and the text is pitched toward seventh to ninth graders, parents and horse lovers of all ages will learn that there is much more to the world of horses than racing or riding. Patent reminds us of what our grandfathers took for granted: draft horses, and mules, were a mainstay of our social economy and still are hard-working and dependable helpers. Most of us have heard of Percherons and Clydesdales, but this book informs the reader of the many other breeds of draft horses and of their origins, derivations, and specific traits. . . . The text generally flows smoothly, although there are some rough spots; for example, a simple line drawing of how a harness is put together would have been very useful.

> Martin W. Schein, in a review of "Draft Horses," in Science Books & Films, Vol. 22, No. 2, November-December, 1986, p. 123.

Belgians, Percherons, Clydesdales, Shires, and Suffolks are described and photographed in this outstanding book. The origins and traits of the various breeds are described. The many and varied uses for these beautiful animals are included and there is a section on their care. Actually, *Draft Horses* might be considered as two books, one the lucid, informative text, the other the especially clear, useful photographs by William Munoz.

> Glenn O. Blough, in a review of "Draft Horses," in Appraisal: Science Books for Young People, Vol. 20, No. 1, Winter, 1987, p. 55.

BUFFALO: THE AMERICAN BISON TODAY (1986)

D. H. Patent's *Buffalo: The American Bison Today* is a captivating account of the contemporary bison. Her portrayal of this imposing creature is forthright, realistic and creative. William Munoz' marvelous photos add greatly to describing the rutting rituals of summer, the population management in the fall, the bison's struggles for food in the winter and the birth and care of its newborn in the spring. This little book is action-packed, informative, and titillating to the curious, young and old.

> Jim B. Maland, in a review of "Buffalo: The American Bison Today," in Appraisal: Science Books for Young People, Vol. 20, No. 1, Winter, 1987, p. 54.

This delightful book will fit nicely in an elementary school library and be of great interest to young people who love animals. It is packed with facts about buffalo life, habitat, and interactions with other buffalo and with humans. Although it is aimed at youngsters, adults will also learn new facts. Black-and-white photographs of buffalo [by William Munoz] appear on nearly every page, and with the text cover buffalo life from birth to death, through all seasons. The book also describes how the Indians hunted and used the buffalo; the subsequent decline of the buffalo with overhunting and pioneer settlement; and the current status of the buffalo in Yellowstone and other reserves where it is protected and controlled. The book's final page includes sources for more information and a list of parks where buffalo can be viewed by visitors—a boon for anyone whose imagination has been stimulated by this great little book. (pp. 184-85)

> *Janan T. Eppig, in a review of "Buffalo: The American Bison Today," in* Science Books & Films, *Vol. 22, No. 3, January-February, 1987, pp. 184-85.*

ALL ABOUT WHALES (1987)

This does have, if not *all,* at least quite a bit of information about whales. It also features some first-class black-and-white photographs. There are also a few blurred shots, however, and some that are difficult to make out, as in the picture directing readers' attention to a blowhole "on the left side of the tip of the 'nose.' " Partly because of the abundant photographs and partly because of the frequent page headings, the organization seems somewhat fragmented. Students looking for facts, however, will find them accessible through this design format; the subject is a popular one for reports, and the overall combination of text and illustration is energetic.

> *Betsy Hearne, in a review of "All about Whales," in* Bulletin of the Center for Children's Books, *Vol. 40, No. 10, June, 1987, p. 193.*

Although the title is a misnomer, this attractive overview does provide a brief introduction to many aspects of whale physiology and behavior. Brief segments of text and a handsome selection of photographs describe the general physical characteristics of whales and then move on to the best known species of toothed and baleen whales. . . . The dark color and large mass of these animals cause some of the photographs to be a bit confusing, but the pictures are exceptionally well chosen, and some are quite intriguing—including a killer whale skeleton showing the finger bones, normally invisible, in the flippers. There is currently a dearth of good material in print on this appealing mammal, and this is informative and well structured if sometimes a bit sketchy. It complements more difficult and lengthy volumes such as the author's **Whales: Giants of the Deep** and Robert Gardner's *Whale Watchers' Guide.*

> *Margaret Bush, in a review of "All about Whales," in* School Library Journal, *Vol. 33, No. 10, June-July, 1987, p. 99.*

Inquisitive youngsters with a demonstrated interest in whales will find the answers to many of their questions as well as further fuel for their curiosity within the pages of this highly informative book.

Clear, concise prose is accompanied by a superb selection of nicely captioned photographs, each of which illustrates a particular anatomical feature or behavior of these amazing marine mammals.

Patent chooses to bypass completely the mythology and folklore surrounding whales in favor of a highly factual overview of current scientific knowledge in this area.

A particularly intriguing chapter deals with the diverse feed-

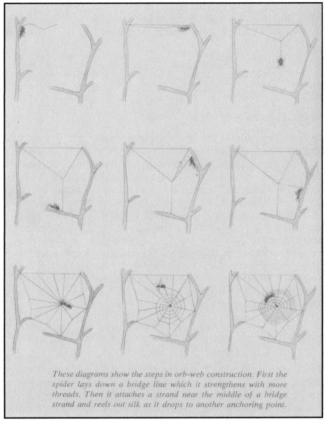

These diagrams show the steps in orb-web construction. First the spider lays down a bridge line which it strengthens with more threads. Then it attaches a strand near the middle of a bridge strand and reels out silk as it drops to another anchoring point.

From The Lives of Spiders, *written and illustrated by Dorothy Hinshaw Patent.*

ing techniques employed by whales. Pack hunting by killer whales, bubble feeding by humpbacks, and the as yet mysterious consumption of giant squid by sperm whales are all briefly explored.

One particular feature of this volume that commends it to me is the author's attention to how we know what we do about whales, and why some questions remain unanswered. Future marine biologists take note.

> *E. A. B., in a review of "All about Whales," in* Appraisal: Science Books for Young People, *Vol. 20, No. 4, Fall, 1987, p. 44.*

THE WAY OF THE GRIZZLY (1987)

A lucid, accurate rendering of the lifestyle of the grizzly bear. . . . Patent has been especially careful in explaining the bear's winter sleep, radically different from that of other hibernators. There is also a clear presentation of the problems arising when bear and human cross paths, and of the studies done to help preserve grizzlies outside a zoo. . . . This will certainly be useful to report writers, and it fills a gap. No other book for this age group covers the grizzly so competently and completely.

> *Patricia Manning, in a review of "The Way of the Grizzly," in* School Library Journal, *Vol. 33, No. 11, August, 1987, p. 87.*

Patent's readable discussion is divided into five chapters covering physical characteristics and comparison with other bear species, hibernation behavior, care of the young, American and Canadian research activities, and the complexities of the grizzly-human relationship. The author also proves to be a competent photographer, having contributed several pictures to the plentifully illustrated presentation. While the photographs by both Patent and [William] Muñoz differ considerably in quality of composition and clarity, the book is generally attractive. . . . The natural appeal of the subject also sustains visual interest. What reader could resist the pear-shaped twin and triplet cubs? The grizzled coats, distinctive faces and body shape, powerful claws, and, most especially, the massive size of this impressive animal are aptly conveyed in both photographs and text. Above all, this informative introduction provides a thought-provoking case for improving human respect and care of wildlife. (pp. 631-32)

> *Margaret A. Bush, in a review of "The Way of the Grizzly," in* The Horn Book Magazine, *Vol. LXIII, No. 5, September-October, 1987, pp. 631-32.*

The Way of the Grizzly is an intimate look into the life of perhaps the most feared bear in North America. . . . Relying on past studies by the Craighead brothers and recent studies by scientists with The Border Grizzly Project, Ms. Patent writes a highly accurate and up-to-date text. In addition, she gives a well-balanced treatment of the recent problems between grizzlies and people. Her basic view is that if we learn to manage the grizzly and its habitat more effectively, we can both minimize the danger to people and save this threatened species from extinction. This book will definitely help students to put the grizzly "horror stories" in their proper perspective.

The black-and-white photographs are of good quality and compliment the text beautifully. A reluctant reader could learn the basic facts by studying the pictures and reading the captions. (pp. 43-4)

> *Martha T. Kane, in a review of "The Way of the Grizzly," in* Appraisal: Science Books for Young People, *Vol. 20, No. 4, Fall, 1987, pp. 43-4.*

WHEAT: THE GOLDEN HARVEST (1987)

Photographs of excellent quality (some in color, and some in black-and-white) illustrate a text that is typical of Patent's writing: crisp style, logical organization, no padding. She describes the plant and its parts, explaining which parts are used for which food products; she discusses the different kinds of wheat, how wheat is grown and harvested, and how wheat products are processed into foods. A glossary and an index are appended.

> *Zena Sutherland, in a review of "Wheat: The Golden Harvest," in* Bulletin of the Center for Children's Books, *Vol. 41, No. 5, January, 1988, p. 97.*

This attractive reference on the growing, harvesting, and processing of wheat for elementary school children combines vivid information on food supply, nutrition, machine technology, and geography. Younger children would need to have it read to them while grade schoolers can tackle words like "noticeable" and "delicious" by themselves. Little boys will be particularly attracted to the clear color photographs of tractors, combines, and other agricultural machinery,

while city and suburb dwellers will get glimpses of what the "bread basket of the world" actually looks like. This is a good pictorial description of an important food source and exactly where it comes from.

> *Michele Bremer, in a review of "Wheat: The Golden Harvest," in* Science Books & Films, *Vol. 23, No. 3, January-February, 1988, p. 176.*

Patent begins this brief discussion of wheat by noting some of the uses of this most important food. The first chapter discusses the history of wheat, the three kinds, and their physical properties. Chapter two describes the growing of wheat in various parts of the country and explains the differences between spring and winter wheat. Chapters three and four deal with what happens to the wheat after it is harvested—storage, milling, and baking. The text is liberally illustrated with color and black-and-white photos [by William Munoz]. The captions add to the text's content. Some of the close-up photos of the growing wheat plants are misleading, as there are no points of reference to help determine the actual size of the plants pictured. The material is accurate and is presented in an adequate manner, but few of the photos were taken in major wheat producing areas of the country. The lack of people in any of the photos makes them appear lifeless and is unfortunate, particularly since people are a very important part of wheat production. Even with these minor shortcomings, this is still by far the best title available on this subject. Its attractive cover will help keep it from taking root on the shelf.

> *Eldon Younce, in a review of "Wheat: The Golden Harvest," in* School Library Journal, *Vol. 34, No. 6, February, 1988, p. 81.*

DOLPHINS AND PORPOISES (1987)

This is a well-organized, general introduction to a fascinating group of mammals. . . . The coverage is primarily natural history but with considerable input from knowledge gained from captive specimens. This latter source also provides most of the intelligence-testing studies and many interesting and amusing anecdotes (such as dolphins training people). Reliance on empirical data is stressed, and that is important given the anthropomorphic treatment often accorded these animals and the public's strong feelings about them in general. Also laudable is the use of metric equivalents for all English system measurements. Sixty-five good photographs (many excellent and only two blurred) effectively complement the well-written text. The book contains just five chapters, but each is clearly subdivided. A useful two-page index concludes the book. The only shortcomings include the absence of maps and color photographs. Also, while not necessary to the primary purpose of the book, some mention of the role of these animals in art, culture, or history would have been a nice touch. Overall, however, this is an excellent reference for young readers. (pp. 253-54)

> *Mark S. Rich, in a review of "Dolphins and Porpoises," in* Science Books & Films, *Vol. 23, No. 4, March-April, 1988, pp. 253-54.*

Dorothy Patent seems to do her best work in books such as this, which are suited to older readers and are substantial enough to allow her to range widely over facts, issues, and anecdotal materials. She has crafted a useful, readable volume which is both enjoyable and a good introduction to this popular group of animals. (p. 28)

Margaret Bush, in a review of "Dolphins and Porpoises," in Appraisal: Science Books for Young People, *Vol. 21, No. 2, Spring, 1988, pp. 27-8.*

Many books have been written on dolphins and porpoises but few have communicated these animals's spectrum of intelligence as effectively as Dorothy Patent's book. There were times while reading it when I was actually laughing out loud, such as when a bottle-nosed dolphin living in a tank adjacent to a killer whale habitually jumped into the whale's tank to play. To prevent this association, the keeper erected a high plywood fence. But the next morning, the dolphin was again frolicking with his friend. The killer whale had battered down the plywood enabling the bottle-nosed to jump into the whale tank.

This is a wonderful, clearly written book on all aspects of dolphin life presenting even in an unbiased manner both sides of the issue of capturing toothed whales.

B. G. H., in a review of "Dolphins and Porpoises," in Appraisal: Science Books for Young People, *Vol. 21, No. 2, Spring, 1988, p. 28.*

BABIES! (1988)

Illustrated with lots of informative color photographs of beautiful babies, this is an easy to read guide for younger children to the stages of infant development. Patent combines factual information ("Young babies are more interested in looking at patterns than in seeing solid colors") reassurance ("It may alarm you when the tiny body jerks with a hiccup but it doesn't bother the baby") and practical advice ("You have to be sure nothing dangerous can be reached from anywhere on the floor") in a smooth and simple text that will give older children a welcome sense of involvement with and responsibility for a new arrival.

Roger Sutton, in a review of "Babies!" in Bulletin of the Center for Children's Books, *Vol. 41, No. 8, April, 1988, p. 164.*

The development of an infant from birth to one year, illustrated with sharply reproduced color photographs. The baby's growth and acquisition of skills are clearly described; the impact of various stages on other family members is highlighted. The photos, from a variety of sources, are well chosen; just browsing through them is a pleasure. An excellent choice for parents to share with older siblings—and even children without a baby at home will enjoy learning about babies' growth.

A review of "Babies!" in Kirkus Reviews, *Vol. LVI, No. 7, April 1, 1988, p. 543.*

A developmental description of how babies grow from newborn to two years. The writing is dull, and the sentence structure is complex. Excellent full-color photographs of babies from several ethnic groups appear on every page; they will have more appeal for young children than the text and should inspire discussion between parent and child. Cole's *The New Baby at Your House* touches on the same material, but not in such detail, emphasizing, instead, the older sibling, while this book concentrates solely on the new baby. Both books, in concert, could be used to prepare a sibling for a new baby, and the mixed feelings attendant on the relationship.

Ann Scarpellino, in a review of "Babies!" in School Library Journal, *Vol. 34, No. 11, August, 1988, p. 91.*

Gary Paulsen

1939–

American author of fiction and nonfiction.

Although he writes successfully in a variety of genres, Paulsen is perhaps best known for creating powerful, evocative novels for young adults, often set in historical periods such as the 1950s. These works describe the coming of age of Paulsen's teenage protagonists through their relationships with nature and with sympathetic older adults, both relatives and friends. Set in the Midwest and western United States as well as in such areas as Mexico and the Canadian wilderness, the books characteristically feature young men, often nameless, who form bonds with adult males, several of whom have been affected by war. Through their relationships, these characters help each other to be physically or emotionally free. Implicit in several of Paulsen's stories is the physical survival of his protagonists, an attribute that causes his novels to be read as exciting, fast-paced adventures. However, he balances the characteristic action of his works by probing the thoughts and emotions of his characters as they move on inner journeys toward self-discovery. In addition, Paulsen invests his stories with strongly mystical elements, such as dreams, which play important roles in the maturation of his characters. Perhaps Paulsen's most well known novel is *Dogsong* (1984), which describes how an Eskimo teenager defines his identity through a vision quest he takes by dogsled through the Alaskan north. Throughout his fiction, Paulsen presents young readers with such themes as the celebration of nature and its influence on our lives, respect for individuality, acceptance of death, and the physical and mental destruction caused by war. Paulsen is also well known for his informational books on nature and sports. Describing the survival of moose, elk, buffalo, rabbits, mice, and other animals, his nature books blend fact and personal anecdote to create what are often considered unusual examples of their genre. Paulsen's sports books address such activities as basketball, hockey, boxing, hot air ballooning, auto racing, sailing, and hiking by including both descriptions of technique and humorous facts about the sport. Paulsen is generally regarded as an especially insightful writer whose books provide young readers with absorbing stories, thought-provoking themes, and unique information. *Dogsong* was named a Newbery Honor Book in 1985.

(See also *Something about the Author,* Vols. 22, 50, and *Contemporary Authors,* Vols. 73-76.)

AUTHOR'S COMMENTARY

[The following excerpt is from an interview by Maryann N. Weidt.]

Weidt: In *Something About the Author* (v.22), you say that you "believe in spiritual progress." Can you elaborate on that?

Paulsen: I have a spiritual belief which is really not explainable. I kind of live for a spiritual progress or perfection that has nothing to do with an organized religion. It is a personal

thing. If you grow one inch, it's better than going back a half an inch.

Weidt: Have you studied Eastern religions?

Paulsen: I've studied several. And I've studied the Bible, and I've studied American Indian beliefs. I went to several elders in the various tribes who were spiritual leaders and asked for advice. They were extremely helpful in guiding me. I don't think individuals have any strength on their own. I think they have to find strength from an outside spiritual source.

Weidt: Tell us about your family.

Paulsen: I have two grown children from a previous marriage, and a 15-year-old from my present marriage. I didn't get a chance to see the older ones grow up because of my own stupidity, and with the younger one, I have watched him grow, and it's really been neat. Now it's just amazing. He's better at many things than I am. I think he's probably smarter than me. And he has more savvy, more knowledge of people. He really tries to understand people, and he has a wonderful sense of humor. I've learned so much from him. You know, adults stink. We really do. We've polluted the earth. We've managed to probably destroy the human race. And kids haven't done that. In that sense, I think they are a lot smarter than we are. I kind of wish I weren't an adult.

Weidt: What does your youngest son want to do?

Paulsen: He draws a lot, and he paints. He plays a lot of *Dungeons and Dragons.* I would not wish a writing career on him. Writing is something that if you're cursed with, you do it.

Weidt: What was your own childhood like?

Paulsen: I was an Army brat. My Dad was a military man on General Patton's staff. I didn't see him until I was seven years old. He was fighting the war against Hitler. When I was 15, I started taking off. I'd go for a summer and hoe sugar beets, and during the school year I'd find things to do at night. For a while I set pins in a bowling alley. (pp. 129-30)

Weidt: Who are some of the women who have influenced your life?

Paulsen: My grandmother. During the war years, I lived with her. My mother worked in a munitions plant in Chicago, and she sent me back up to Northern Minnesota to live for seven years with my grandmother. And my mother, of course. And my aunts. I have several aunts who were very important in my life. I don't think there's any attempt on the part of men (writers) to understand what women are or the influence they have on our lives. Incidentally, my grandmother taught me how to crochet. When I was in battle or doing some of the other hard things in life, I found I had a tempering, a soft influence that I could use. It saved me many hours of agony. The male thing is to have an objective and go out and get it done. You can't stop. It's like the Iditarod, or combat, or all those stupid things that people do that are pointless. And when you try one of these things and you fail, and you do fail, you have this feminine influence to fall back on. You can lean back and say, all right, maybe the male side is crushed because I didn't make it, but I can also have compassion. I can try to understand my failure and I can try to learn from it.

Weidt: What questions do kids ask you when they write to you?

Paulsen: A lot of them are pretty basic: how long does it take to write a book. I'm interested in writing, how can I get into it. But now and then you hit a nerve, or they hit a nerve. At one of the talks I gave, I mentioned that my son doesn't like to read my work. The first time he told me that he couldn't read my work, it kind of hurt. We talk about it. But it's just that we're too close. A kid wrote and said, weren't you hurt that your son didn't want to read your work. I could see that nobody was listening to this kid. After *Winterkill* came out I got a lot of letters about drunk parents. Sometimes they'll tell me things they won't tell their parents.

Weidt: What was the first dogsled race you ever ran?

Paulsen: The (1200 mile) Iditarod. I don't like messing around. I like to start right at the top. . . .

Weidt: The dogs are extremely important to you and so is your writing. Is there a similarity between running dogs and writing?

Paulsen: If art works, it's just like running a team that works. You just let it go. If it doesn't work, you can't whip them and get them to go. If you have to whip dogs, you shouldn't have them. In a way, you follow them. You get what you want out of them, but you get it because they want it too.

Weidt: What do you read?

Paulsen: Hellman, Hemingway, Steinbeck. Melville a lot. I've read *Moby Dick* several times. But I didn't realize how incredible Melville was until I was older. I tend to read almost no contemporary authors. I don't know why. But recently I received two poems from an eighth grade girl, and I'm going to try and get them published. They are answers to a question in *Dogsong* which is not even asked, but which she felt.

Weidt: What's your next goal?

Paulsen: Just to write the stories. Just do the next story. (p. 130)

> *Maryann N. Weidt, "Gary Paulsen: A Sentry for Peace," in* Voice of Youth Advocates, *Vol. 9, Nos. 3 & 4, August-October, 1986, pp. 129-30.*

GENERAL COMMENTARY

BETSY HEARNE

Paulsen's strong writing gives these nature narratives [*The Grass Eaters* and *The Small Ones*] the punch they need to survive in the current surfeit of animal description books. From firsthand woods experience he mixes the reader a fresh blend of information and personal anecdotes that tell a lot about animal nature, both general and specific—rabbits, mice, and foxes in *The Small Ones* and moose, elk, deer, antelope, and buffalo in *The Grass Eaters.* There is no index, and the quantity of information is limited; but the quality is first-class, some scenes making an indelible impression of the central creature, presented neither clinically nor adoringly but respectfully and true to wild life.

> *Betsy Hearne, in a review of "The Grass Eaters" and "The Small Ones," in* Booklist, *Vol. 73, No. 3, October 1, 1976, p. 255.*

BOOKLIST

With their lightweight texts and catchy photographs [by Heinz Kluetmeier, ***Dribbling, Shooting, and Scoring—Sometimes*** and ***Hitting, Pitching, and Running—Maybe***] will work mainly as lures to more substantial reading fare. While some facts on technique are delivered on basketball and baseball, information plays a minor role in relation to the dominant purpose—pure entertainment. Stars appear in the action photos and the text is continually humorous, to the point of straining half the time. It's unusual that a basically attractive, if lean, book can easily be read and enjoyed by many poorly motivated older readers.

> *A review of "Dribbling, Shooting, and Scoring—Sometimes" and "Hitting, Pitching, and Running—Maybe," in* Booklist, *Vol. 73, No. 4, October 15, 1976, p. 328.*

ANDREW K. STEVENSON

Two mediocre mysteries [*The CB Radio Caper* and *The Curse of the Cobra*] in a new series geared for reluctant readers [Mallard Mystery Series]. In the *CB Radio Caper,* Malcolm "Mallard" Westerman, son of the police chief, and his friend Rick capture a kidnapper who uses a CB radio to extort money from his victims. In *The Curse of the Cobra,* the boys foil an insane villain who thinks he is a pharoah and is stealing Egyptian artifacts from a museum. Like the Alfred Hitchcock and the Three Investigators series by M. V. Carey, these stories have fast action in an easy reading style, but these pluses cannot cancel the unconvincing plots and thin characterization that, unfortunately, seem to be built into this type of series.

> *Andrew K. Stevenson, in a review of "The CB Radio Caper" and "The Curse of the Cobra," in* School Library Journal, *Vol. 24, No. 1, September, 1977, p. 134.*

MARTHA BARNES

[*Riding, Roping, and Bulldogging—Almost* and *Tackling, Running, and Kicking—Now and Again* present bits] of information about rodeo events and about football. . . . The commentary is too cute and overly concerned with pointing out the potential dangers of both sports. The vocabulary is not simple, and the text contains confusing, incomplete sentences. This is an attempt to jump on the high interest/low reading level bandwagon, but there are better titles, such as those in Marshall Burchard's Sports Star series, available for this age level [grades 3-4].

> *Martha Barnes, in a review of "Riding, Roping, and Bulldogging—Almost" and "Tackling, Running, and Kicking—Now and Again," in* School Library Journal, *Vol. 24, No. 8, April, 1978, p. 87.*

JOSEPH BEARDEN

Paulsen takes a tongue-in-cheek look at six sports—skiing, hot air ballooning, ice hockey, auto racing, boxing, and motorcycle racing—with strictly lightweight results [in *Downhill, Hotdogging, and Cross-Country—If the Snow Isn't Sticky; Facing Off, Checking, and Goaltending—Perhaps; Going Very Fast in a Circle—If You Don't Run Out of Gas; Launching, Floating High, and Landing—If Your Pilot Light Doesn't Go Out; Pummeling, Falling, and Getting Up—Sometimes; Track, Enduro, and Motocross—Unless You Fall Over*]. Page-by-page commentary often reads like insiders' humor, which on the surface appears harmless; but there are exceptions. For example, in *Launching, Floating High, and Landing—If Your Pilot Light Doesn't Go Out,* Paulsen states, "Getting airborne is more than half the battle. It's about like taking a kitchen stove into the backyard. Over the stove you jam a huge plastic garbage sack. Then you fire it and wait to go up." The inherent danger of such information, if followed literally by young readers, is not difficult to imagine. Not to be looked upon as reliable sources of information or instruction, the limited value of these books lies solely in their humor and in the color photographs [by Heinz Kluetmeier, Willis Wood, Melchoir DiGiacomo, Bob D'Olive, Joe DiMaggio, and others] which catch the equipment and action peculiar to each.

> *Joseph Bearden, in a review of "Downhill, Hotdogging, and Cross-Country—If the Snow Isn't Sticky" and others, in* School Library Journal, *Vol. 26, No. 1, September, 1979, p. 146.*

DAVID L. FAGLE

[The *Sports on the Light Side*] series addresses both the old and the new in sports, from boxing and skiing to modern hot-air ballooning. Each book in the series is devoted to a surrealistic report on the supposed "light side" of the sport. In the effort to appeal to very broad audiences, however, the tone becomes rather sarcastic and may encourage students to be smart alecks about the sporting experience. The titles indicate this rather brash approach, as in *Pummeling, Falling, and Getting Up—Sometimes* and *Launching, Floating High, and Landing—If Your Pilot Light Doesn't Go Out.* Other books cover car racing, motorcycling, skiing, and hockey.

On the Fry readability scale, books range from second grade (ballooning) to sixth grade (boxing). The vocabulary is sometimes coarse and colloquial. Curt phrases, used far too often in all the books, contribute to the uneven reading level.

The impressionistic, colorful illustrations are the best part of this series. Most of the books, however, do not have an appropriate sex balance—the action focus is overwhelmingly on males.

These books are not written for the faint-hearted—the illustrations are sometimes a bit too vivid and the script too lucid. Furthermore, the presentation is often trite. The negative attitude throughout the books does not recommend them as good learning tools. (pp. 123-24)

> *David L. Fagle, in a review of "Sports on the Light Side," in* Curriculum Review, *Vol. 19, No. 2, April, 1980, pp. 123-24.*

MR. TUCKET (1969)

A wild (i.e. unfocused, unfounded) Western that turns sanctimonious at the conclusion. Separated from his family and the Oregon-bound wagon train, fourteen-year-old Francis Alphonse Tucket is captured by brutish Indians, then helped to escape and in effect apprenticed by laconic trapper Jason Grimes (who can't stomach Francis or Alphonse and therefore calls him Mr. Tucket). Their beaver trapping carries some weight but their encounters with the celebrated Jim Bridger and with a cross section of Plains Indians amount to little more than a run-around (characteristically, when Grimes fires "an impossible sho" from "an impossible range" it is "impossible to tell" what he is doing). And then, without warning, Grimes, having killed the bad Indian, Braid, scalps him. . . . "He was of the prairie, the land, the mountains—and was, in a way, a kind of animal (like the Indians). It was not wrong—not for Jason Grimes. But for Francis Alphonse Tucket? For someone from a farm in Missouri? For someone with a family waiting in Oregon?" Unfortunate.

> *A review of "Mr. Tucket," in* Kirkus Reviews, *Vol. XXXVII, No. 15, August 1, 1969, p. 778.*

A cliché-ridden historical novel which takes place on the Oregon Trail in 1845. . . . The plot is obvious and contrived, characterization lacks depth, descriptive passages are unconvincing. Even avid Western fans will be disappointed.

> *Susan Stanton, in a review of "Mr. Tucket," in* School Library Journal, *Vol. 16, No. 4, December, 1969, p. 54.*

WINTERKILL (1976)

It's a measure of Paulsen's gut level effectiveness that one really does come to feel some affection for Duda, a corrupt cop who extorts graft from kids in the form of illegally taken fish, who spends most of his night shifts shooting rabbits and visiting his mistress, and who kills two unresisting bank robbers in cold blood. The narrator, a nameless kid virtually abandoned by his drunken parents, loves Duda for saving him from a maniacal foster father who tries to beat the sin out of him with a chain . . . and later for talking him out of marrying a fourteen-year-old classmate pregnant by another guy. Mostly, however, this kid has no one else to attach himself to, and the relationship that's meant to reveal a loving human being hidden behind a brutalized exterior is devalued because it's drawn solely in terms of the boy's weakness. By flirting with moral ambivalence to a degree uncommon at this level, Paulsen does shake up the reader's emotions. Ultimately Duda's brand of toughness is simply bathetic, but readers who can take the explicit violence and are mature enough not to mistake clever writing for profundity will want to make that judgment on their own.

> *A review of "Winterkill," in* Kirkus Reviews, *Vol. XLIV, No. 18, September 15, 1976, p. 1045.*

This is a downbeat tale of a semi-delinquent boy who is befriended by a cop. . . . The shocking conclusion in which Duda is shot to death by a disturbed youth is wholly in keeping with the characters Paulsen has so painstakingly created. Narrated convincingly by its young protagonist, this is reminiscent of Hinton's *The Outsiders* in its shattering portrayal of life on the wrong side of town.

> *Diane Haas, in a review of "Winterkill," in* School Library Journal, *Vol. 23, No. 3, November, 1976, p. 72.*

Without knowing from inside what a small town like Twin Forks, Minnesota, might really have been like in 1954, it is difficult to assess the credibility of **Winterkill.** Certainly the first-person narrative is plausible. This is the way one would expect a boy of thirteen to report on his unlikely friendship with Duda, a local cop whose hard-bitten exterior hides a surreptitious sympathy for the unhappy and the frustrated. . . . An ostentatious, sick violence runs through the book, in accounts of Duda's vicious attack on bank robbers after a car crash and his death at the hands of a minister's son on the run with a deer rifle. Underneath, an equally unpleasing strain of sentimentality informs Duda's intimate talks with the boy. This seems to me an unsuitably idealised portrait of a neurotic cop, a portrait which almost becomes a grotesque caricature. (pp. 3159-60)

> *Margery Fisher, in a review of "Winterkill," in* Growing Point, *Vol. 16, No. 3, September, 1977, pp. 3159-60.*

MARTIN LUTHER KING: THE MAN WHO CLIMBED THE MOUNTAIN (with Dan Theis, 1976)

After grabbing readers' attention with a dramatic account of King's assassination in which the killer is simply described several times as "the white man," the authors skillfully trace his personal, educational, philosophical, and professional development against the background of a repressive society. Despite the brief length and young-looking format, the treatment of King's principle of nonviolent protest, his successes and his failures, is quite substantive. The authors show only the positive side of King's personality and they assume most whites to be prejudiced, but this is still better than the other biography on this level, DeKay's *Meet Martin Luther King Jr.,* which is just as slanted but not as well written.

> *John F. Caviston, in a review of "Martin Luther King: The Man Who Climbed the Mountain," in* School Library Journal, *Vol. 23, No. 3, November, 1976, p. 61.*

The slightly melodramatic prose that describes King's activities just prior to his death gives way to more even-toned reportage of how he evolved into a leader in the civil rights movement. . . . Paulsen doesn't delve into recent disclosures involving FBI efforts to damage King's image at the time—such a postscript would have deepened the picture, but this is still an acceptable introduction to the man.

> *Denise M. Wilms, in a review of "Martin Luther King: The Man Who Climbed the Mountain," in* Booklist, *Vol. 73, No. 11, February 1, 1977, p. 837.*

HITTING, PITCHING, AND RUNNING—MAYBE (1976)

A wealth of color photographs highlights **Hitting, Pitching, and Running—Maybe** . . . , a high interest-low vocabulary book. The effort toward humor made by author Gary Paulsen is this title's saving grace.

> *A review of "Hitting, Pitching, and Running—Maybe," in* School Library Journal, *Vol. 23, No. 4, December, 1976, p. 70.*

THE GRASS-EATERS (1976)

Rather than writing a standard compendium of scientific facts about the grass-eaters (the author's term for members of the deer, moose, elk, and antelope families), Paulsen attempts to present them as "real animals": vivid, living creatures who have full and complex lives of their own. The three chapters are "The Giants" (moose—the most unpredictable of the grass-eaters), "The Deciding Time" (mating season), and "The New Time" (birthing season). The author's accounts of his own observations of and experience with these animals are brief but colorful, interesting, and above all, personal—something which should attract young readers; it could work with reluctant readers as well. They may share my regret at the book's brevity. Although the interior illustrations [by Kathy Goff], both drawings and photographs, are a disappointment after the cover painting, the general format is attractive; and with the subject and writing, makes this a good browsing item for larger nature collections. (pp. 40-1)

> *Daphne Ann Hamilton, in a review of "The Grass-eaters," in* Appraisal: Children's Science Books, *Vol. 10, No. 2, Spring, 1977, pp. 40-1.*

It is apparent from the first page that Paulsen loves the woods and has spent much time exploring, listening and watching. He may be accused of anthropomorphism, but in fact, his anecdotes portray animals not as extensions of people but as creatures who survive in a complex world and who are capable of more than mutely following instincts. More important is Paulsen's purpose in writing these books: "This book is an attempt . . . to show animals living in the woods as animals really *do* live in the woods . . . real animals. It is not a zoological study, nor yet another attempt to make an ecological statement. . . . This book, then is meant to take the animal out of his man-made 'eco-system' [and] likewise remove him from the 'cutesy' film industry, and put him back in the woods." By and large, Paulsen is successful in his goal. . . . His anecdotes are realistic, amusing and—most important for this age group—interesting. I would certainly recommend this book to future conservationists and naturalists—and to all children who love the woods.

Ann Seltz-Petrash, in a review of "The Grass-eaters," in Science Books & Films, *Vol. XIII, No. 2, September, 1977, p. 97.*

THE FOXMAN (1977)

A fair short story is expanded into this junior novel that is more tell than show, and a slogging, long way from the good opening to an improbable ending. Starting with a typical problem story (boozing parents, whose 15-year-old son is sent to live with his uncle in the upper Minnesota woods), readers lose sight of the parents entirely as the boy becomes his own man. He learns to work and hunt; discovers sex (nonexplicit); and becomes the friend of a hermit, the **Foxman.** Foxman asks the boy to burn his body in his shack after he dies; the boy complies and takes away a fox hide as a memento. That's it, folks. Characters are wooden, and most of what they do isn't lively enough to keep a body reading.

George Gleason, in a review of "The Foxman," in School Library Journal, *Vol. 23, No. 7, March, 1977, p. 153.*

Set during the Korean war, this [is a] combination wilderness/anti-war story . . . It's slickly written, with the North Woods dialect and descriptions of primitive subsistence farming to add some verisimilitude. But the boy's relationship with the old man seems stagey, and the Foxman himself only a mouthpiece.

A review of "The Foxman," in Kirkus Reviews, *Vol. XLV, No. 6, March 15, 1977, p. 291.*

In the area of the junior novel the pickings for boys are mighty slim, and so **The Foxman** is more than welcome. It is a real winner. . . .

Intimately narrated by the boy, the story offers deep insights into the relationships of the warm and loving characters created by Paulsen. The occasional allusions to sexual activity may offend some, but these are restrained and low key. The strong anti-war thread makes the book unique in literature for this age group [ages 13 and up].

Patricia A. Morgans, in a review of "The Foxman," in Best Sellers, *Vol. 37, No. 7, October, 1977, p. 204.*

THE SMALL ONES (1976)

The Small Ones is one of an unusual series of books about the behavior of animals in their natural habitat [*Real Animals* Series]. Paulsen does not describe animals either anthropomorphically or scientifically; rather he relates anecdotes, written in an informal, conservational style, that are based on his observations. The three chapters on wild rabbits, mice and foxes will appeal to the older child, and perhaps to adults who are fascinated by unusual animal behavior. For example, the fox is described as an intelligent animal with a sense of humor. According to Paulsen, foxes play practical jokes and then "laugh" (author's quotes) uproariously, making a "yakking" sound. The author's observation of a fox playing a trick on a prissy cat is bound to make every reader laugh.

Martha K. Piper, in a review of "The Small Ones," in Science Books & Films, *Vol. XIII, No. 2, September, 1977, p. 97.*

The Small Ones is a fanciful book about rabbits, mice, and foxes. Unfortunately the author spends a great portion of the book glorifying the small ones and contrasts their accomplishments with those of humans. According to the author, the mouse is about a million years ahead of man in architecture and engineering, having perfected the gothic arch and the vented rest room long before mankind. Furthermore, the author contends that the architectural accomplishments of mice put the beaver to shame. (Frankly, I doubt if the beaver gives a dam[n]!) Overall, the book is fun to read, but limited observations of animal behavior are blown out of proportion. The author's love affair with the small ones has led to the glorification of some fascinating creatures at the expense of objectivity in treating animal behavior. (p. 32)

Harry O. Haakonsen, in a review of "The Small Ones," in Appraisal: Children's Science Books, *Vol. 10, No. 3, Fall, 1977, pp. 31-2.*

As the author says, this book is neither an ecological plea nor a zoological study. Instead, in rather breezy style and with some very questionable statements ("Nobody really knows anything about wild rabbits"), he has written observations based on his own experiences as a naturalist about rabbits, mice, and foxes. The book is short—48 pages. . . . [The] anecdotes are unusual and delightful to read. The information is more for browsing or reading aloud than facts which a child needs for a report, but this does not lessen the attraction of the book. The description of rabbits playing fox-and-geese in the moonlight is just grand, and the description of a fox lying in wait for rabbits to come by, just to scare the daylights out of them by yapping suddenly as they pass him, is a priceless story! Aimed at ages ten to fifteen, it really could be enjoyed by any age. (pp. 31-2)

Heddie Kent, in a review of "The Small Ones," in Appraisal: Children's Science Books, *Vol. 10, No. 3, Fall, 1977, pp. 31-2.*

THE GOLDEN STICK (1977)

[Bart] is a new boy in school trying to make the first-string hockey team and to withstand the pressures of a home life with alcoholic, sometimes violent parents. . . . The mechanical plot seems to exist to teach the fundamentals of the game. Characterization (except for that of the brutal coach who taunts his players in order to win the Golden Stick award) is weak, and the format is off-putting with small, cramped print and pedestrian ink sketches [by Barb Ericksen].

Dan Barron, in a review of "The Golden Stick," in School Library Journal, *Vol. 24, No. 1, September, 1977, p. 148.*

TILTAWHIRL JOHN (1977)

Two episodes in the life of a runaway 15-year-old (nameless throughout) form the basis for this loosely constructed adventure set in the Dakotas and Wyoming. In the first, the boy hoes sugar beets with some Mexicans who have entered the U.S. illegally. Infuriated by the cruelty of Karl Elsner, the farm patrón who beats him and then tries to rape a young woman, the boy attacks Elsner with a hoe, flees and is picked up by three carnival performers: Wanda is a stripper, Billy decapitates chickens with his teeth, and John runs the tiltawhirl. Just as the boy comes to realize how vital it is to separate "carnie" life from "real" life, a man from John's past causes the two carefully delineated worlds to collide. With relief tempered by a few regrets, the young runaway decides to return to the security, responsibility, and boredom of home. The messages are clearly but not didactically spelled out, and the characters are a bit bizarre but well drawn (Tiltawhirl John seems too sketchily developed to receive title billing, however). The plot suffers not from the inclusion of harsh incidents (which are adroitly handled) but from a lack of cohesiveness: neither the two major nor the various minor threads mesh convincingly.

> *C. Nordhielm Wooldridge, in a review of "Tiltawhirl John," in* School Library Journal, *Vol. 24, No. 3, November, 1977, p. 75.*

"When you hoe beets you're alone, so alone you might as well be on another planet," and when you work a carnival, it's like being separate, detached, "from outer space"—and it's the runaway narrator's immersion in these other worlds that gives Paulsen's high-key, deep-think story a real punch. At sixteen, he's not ready to take up his uncle's offer of 80 flat North Dakota acres, not without a try for fame and fortune. The breakaway (said to resemble Paulsen's own) lands him first among brutalized wetbacks on a sugar-beet farm where nearly a month of dry beans and bread and short-handled hoeing "from can to can't" nets him—"I'll call it even," says the smirking *padrone*. On the road again after attacking the boss, he's picked up by carnies Tiltawhirl John (for the ride he operates), hard/soft wife Wanda, a stripper, and brother Billy, T-John's twin except for his shaved pate: he's the wild man who bites the heads off chickens. Billy's also the one who explains "the turkey world and the carny world," and—answering the boy's question—how it is that T-John can stand "all those turkeys seeing Wanda naked." But the glazed, bored, carny look that the boy learns—and his comfort at being one of the family—don't survive a fatal knife fight between T-John and Wanda's former lover that snaps the two worlds together. Home again farming, he won't forget, though, and neither will the reader. The acute observations outweigh the portentousness.

> *A review of "Tiltawhirl John," in* Kirkus Reviews, *Vol. XLVI, No. 1, January 1, 1978, p. 8.*

CAREERS IN AN AIRPORT　(1977)

[*Careers in an Airport* and Joy Schaleben-Lewis's *Careers in a Supermarket*] describe the responsibilities of workers . . . *in an Airport*—from sky cap and ticket agent to pilot and controller—and . . . *in a Supermarket*—from manager to meat cutter to checker and bagger. No information about educational requirements (except for the vague statement that some airline employees go to "special schools") nor differences in salary are given for any of the jobs and, although the language is nonsexist, the only females pictured in the uncaptioned photographs [by Roger Nye and Robert E. Lewis] are stewardesses, meat wrappers, and behind-the-counter types.

> *Carole Ridolfino, in a review of "Careers in an Airport," in* School Library Journal, *Vol. 24, No. 5, January, 1978, p. 90.*

THE GREEN RECRUIT　(with Ray Peekner, 1978)

The Green Recruit, an eight-foot-six-inch Besumi with all the skill and moves of the greatest basketball players who've ever lived. He is ostracized on Besumi because of his color, but he becomes an instant success on Earth. Any message the authors try to impart on racial prejudice fails but the fantasy element is more successful. The concept of traveling from New York to Chicago in five minutes and the way some potential muggers are treated in Central Park are particularly enjoyable.

> *A review of "The Green Recruit," in* School Library Journal, *Vol. 24, No. 9, May, 1978, p. 88.*

HIKING AND BACKPACKING　(with John Morris, 1978)

The authors' smooth informal style not only conveys much valuable information but also communicates their own love for the outdoors. Thoreau's admonition of "simplify-simplify" is readily apparent here in the advice given regarding choice of food, clothing, and equipment. (However, occasionally the attempt at simplification makes things too complicated, as in the advice for constructing one's own pack.) Much emphasis is placed on careful preplanning for all ventures into the wilderness. Facts are also included on first-aid, orienteering, coping with animals and reading animal tracks. In the interests of ecology, the section on massive wood gathering for a fire should be ignored.

> *Joan Hinkemeyer, in a review of "Hiking and Backpacking," in* School Library Journal, *Vol. 25, No. 3, November, 1978, p. 77.*

THE NIGHT THE WHITE DEER DIED　(1978)

Fifteen-year-old Janet lives a solitary life with her newly-divorced sculptor mother in a trendy artists' commune in New Mexico, until she meets a 53-year-old Indian, Peter Honcho, once a Pueblo governor but now a wino posing for tourists' photos in soiled Indian regalia. By day, Peter shows no interest in Janet; by night, transformed, he courts her in the manner of an Indian brave and she falls in love with the noble man he was. In the fantasy-dream setting of an Indian wedding, the two realize they are from different worlds, and Peter sends Janet back to hers while he prepares for his own "last battle." That night, Janet dreams the conclusion of her long-time recurring nightmare in which a white deer is shot by an Indian brave. The action is undercut by the strong feeling that everything is taking place only in the mind of lonely, pathetic Janet. In any case, the one-dimensional characters going through trite or contrived situations remove any importance from whatever meaning was intended.

> *Jack Edson, in a review of "The Night the White Deer Died," in* School Library Journal, *Vol. 25, No. 3, November, 1978, p. 77.*

A slight, heavy-breathing story that could be a parody of today's overwrought, under-thought fiction. To make it as brief as possible, 15-year-old Janet, who dreams each night of an Indian shooting an arrow at a deer (and then awakens), falls in love with 53-year-old wino Peter Honcho, who before he became the leading panhandler in Tres Pinos, was governor of the Indian pueblo. Because Janet cares, he cleans himself up—and the two enjoy a few moments of perfect harmony in the desert ("Janet thought this must be the way it was back when people lived in caves") before Peter stays behind to die. Then, of course, Janet has the dream again, the deer this time dies, and everything disappears . . . or perhaps it was all part of a "dream within a dream"? Who knows. Who cares.

> *A review of "The Night the White Deer Died," in* Kirkus Reviews, *Vol. XLVII, No. 5, March 1, 1979, p. 267.*

THE SPITBALL GANG (1980)

A series of bank robberies by a group of juveniles stir Stu and Greg, police who patrol the ghetto in Denver, into action. The tough cops (softened by a little emotion and humor), their rough language, and harsh descriptions of the scenes they encounter on the beat help to make this a very successful, nitty-gritty police detective story. Since a by-product of the realism is a few nasty words and a little romanticism of the macho ideal, it may not appeal to all, but the story will definitely be a success with Kojack fans. Stu and Greg eventually crack the case, and in the process, give the reader a real taste of the life and philosophy of a cop.

> *Arlene Stolzer Sandner, in a review of "The Spitball Gang," in* Children's Book Review Service, *Vol. 8, No. 14, August, 1980, p. 138.*

Will children have any interest in the thoughts of two police detectives puzzling over the corruption of youth? When two banks are knocked over in quick succession by an armed gang of nine- and ten-year-olds, a somewhat jaded pair of police stalwarts is set onto the case. Detective work is depicted in an antiromantic style, as the two protagonists endure boring routines and petty rivalries, an incompetent chief officer, and a vacuous TV reporter who dogs their heels. The police tend to assume that an adult is directing the robberies, but the final denouement leaves the two detectives in a state of appalled surprise. While the novel lacks the complexity of an adult mystery and resorts occasionally to clichés, young fans of detective fiction are likely to be intrigued by the glimpse of grown-up perspective on crime. (pp. 521-22)

> *Richard Ashford, in a review of "The Spitball Gang," in* The Horn Book Magazine, *Vol. LVI, No. 5, October, 1980, pp. 521-22.*

A child gang of nine year olds has been robbing banks in Denver, and it is up to likable police detectives Greg and Stu to solve the crimes. After discarding their original idea (midgets impersonating children), they start questioning Little League coaches and uncover an autocratic, anti-semitic coach as the instigator. Greg and Stu dig deeper and find that behind the coach is a gifted, handicapped (wheelchair from birth) 12 year old out to test his theories of behavior modification. In a soft-hearted, unexplained deviation from the law and order they supposedly enforce, the detective heroes let the boy go and have the coach take the blame. On the way to this act of kindness are homilies on the following: selfish, boorish reporters; upper-middle-class parents who defend their delinquent off-spring; and police bureaucrats who rise to the top without doing a thing while our heroes work like crazy to solve crimes. . . . The only spitballs coming from this book are aimed outside the thin plot at political and social targets, reflecting the prejudices of the author. They miss their mark (by far) and so, unfortunately, does this confused and shallow story.

> *Jack Forman, in a review of "The Spitball Gang,"*

> *in* School Library Journal, *Vol. 27, No. 2, October, 1980, p. 150.*

TV AND MOVIE ANIMALS (with Art Browne, Jr., 1980)

Paulsen and Browne discuss animals trained for acting careers, from such stars as Lassie and Cheetah to animals used as extras in television or movie features. In addition to details on filming, information on animal imprinting is presented in the clear, logically developed text, giving readers insight into how the animals in nature features and commercials can be filmed so closely. Although the photographs sometimes intrude upon the text, they add interest to the narrative.

> *Linda Ward Callaghan, in a review of "TV & Movie Animals," in* School Library Journal, *Vol. 27, No. 1, September, 1980, p. 77.*

SAILING: FROM JIBS TO JIBING (1981)

Though Paulsen is chatty and sometimes repetitive, he is inviting and encouraging as he simplifies and demystifies the art of sailing—his approach is commonsense, eschewing unnecessary knots and esoteric terminology. He helps the reader become familiar with a small sailing boat; explains interactions among boat, wind, and water as well as basic sailing maneuvers; gives solid advice on safety precautions and emergency procedures; and discusses equipment care, stowage, and repair. . . . A good starting place for the serious novice. A four-book bibliography, a glossary, and an index appended.

> *Sue-Ellen Beauregard, in a review of "Sailing: From Jibs to Jibing," in* Booklist, *Vol. 78, No. 6, November 15, 1981, p. 433.*

Gary Paulsen shares his mistakes (however embarrassing) in this introduction to the joy of sailing. ***Sailing: from Jibs to Jibing*** covers all the basics—getting a boat, learning to read the wind and water, basic techniques and simple repairs. There is a strong emphasis on safety (there are directions for practicing capsizing). The writing is clear, and the author's enthusiasm is evident. The occasional diagrams help explain some of the material, although more illustrations would be helpful. One irritation: in several places Paulsen indicates that more information on a subject will be provided in the last chapter, and the material simply isn't there. Gary Jobson's *How to Sail* has more diagrams and covers the same material. Robinson's *Better Sailing for Boys and Girls* is for a slightly younger audience and has good photos.

> *Elaine Fort Weischedel, in a review of "Sailing: From Jibs to Jibing," in* School Library Journal, *Vol. 28, No. 4, December, 1981, p. 86.*

A very basic book written in a readable, almost fatherly tone. The pluses are its simplicity, low reading level and careful explanation of fundamentals, including sailing, boat maintenance and safety, among other topics. Minuses are its cursory attention to sail repairs and certain other technical areas, as well as the occasional use of an unexplained nautical term. While ***Sailing*** . . . probably is not the basic book, it is not a bad buy, based on style and content, for this age group.

> *Delores Maminski, in a review of "Sailing: From Jibs to Jibing," in* Voice of Youth Advocates, *Vol.*

4, No. 6, February, 1982, p. 44.

DANCING CARL (1983)

Marsh tells the story of Carl, a middle-aged man, who appears in a small Minnesota town in 1958, the year he and Willy were 12. Carl takes control of the ice rinks, ruling them firmly. He also does strange, freestyle, mesmerizing dances on the ice to express his mood. When Marsh's war plane model sends Carl into a mad spell and a frightening dramatic revelation of his war experiences, the boys question his sanity. Then gentle Helen appears at the rink and Carl does everything in his power to show his feelings for her. He finally succeeds through a series of almost frenetic ice dances. The story has a heavy quality of reminiscence, which is reinforced by a fine capturing of place and time. While the low-key plot is well developed, the book's focus is on the character of Carl, and story is secondary. Readers will come away with a sense of having met an intriguing person, but many will find the story lacking in action.

> *Jane E. Gardner, in a review of "Dancing Carl," in* School Library Journal, *Vol. 29, No. 9, May, 1983, p. 84.*

In McKinley, Minnesota, the skating rinks were the life blood of the town each winter. In the late fifties Marsh and Willy were twelve, and Carl was king of the rinks. Maybe Carl was the drunken bum he looked like, or maybe he had escaped from a mental institution; but the town took care of its own and hired him as custodian of the rinks. A man of few words and intense strength, Carl went far beyond his duties; he helped small children with their skates and quietly separated a vicious hockey player from the game. In an attempt at friendly conversation, Marsh one night brought his model of a B-17, and Carl broke down with memories of his wartime experience in the plane, which burned and crashed, killing all the crew but him. Then Helen arrived in town and came to the rink. And Carl began to come out of his daze to court her in the only way he could: He danced. But perhaps it wasn't really dancing. " 'It's all movement—not a dance. Everything in life is a movement, a swirl, a spin.' " The townspeople hardly knew what to think, but they watched and knew he was a special person. "That winter Dancing Carl became everything at the rinks and taught us about living and being what we were and loving all mixed into the cold and ice-blue flat of the skating rinks." Filled with poetry and with life, the book is not only an insightful, beautifully written story for children but for readers of any age. (pp. 446-47)

> *Dorcas Hand, in a review of "Dancing Carl," in* The Horn Book Magazine, *Vol. LIX, No. 4, August, 1983, pp. 446-47.*

The author reveals through Marsh's eyes the flavor of a small town and its inhabitants. Descriptions and dialogue bring people and places to life; skillful foreshadowing keeps readers primed.

The book can serve as a stimulus for written expression: tell the story of Carl prior to 1958; what eventually happened to Carl and Helen? Compare with books such as *Onion John* and *Miss Maggie* for discussion of communities and respect for individuals. Identify literary techniques, i.e., use of dialogue, foreshadowing.

> *Inga Kromann-Kelly, in a review of "Dancing*

Carl," in Language Arts, *Vol. 61, No. 1, January, 1984, p. 68.*

POPCORN DAYS AND BUTTERMILK NIGHTS (1983)

It hurts to dismiss a novel like this. The writing is pleasantly poetic, although it wears on you after a time. The ideas it embodies are enriching. But the story is held together with too much honey and, like some of those great-looking treats from the dessert cart, it soon becomes difficult to swallow. The storyteller is Carley, a 14-year-old streetwise kid from Minneapolis. Often in trouble, he is sent to live with relatives many miles north in the farm country of Minnesota. There, working with his Uncle David in a blacksmith shop, the boy quickly learns a new, purposeful life and develops a strong bond with the older man. The setting is ideal and the characters attractive but everything is finally too perfect. Carley, introspective and wise, reasons like a well-educated adult. His reform comes too easily. His saintly uncle seems to speak only in pithy epigrams. Although the time is the 1940s, there is almost no mention of the war and we wonder why the family remains so poor when the Depression has ended and the father has more work then he can handle alone. To complete the picture, the author even throws in a pretty blond girl names Jenny, apparently so Carley will have someone to wax philosophical with on beautiful moonlit evenings. Alas, the novel reads too much like its title.

> *Robert Unsworth, in a review of "Popcorn Days & Buttermilk Nights," in* School Library Journal, *Vol. 30, No. 3, November, 1983, p. 96.*

This is filled with appreciation of rural life and has little good to say about city living; it stresses the work ethic and community life; it is adequately written but it is less about Carley than about David; it is weakened by some almost-rhapsodic passages about the smithy, and it is slight in structure, more nostalgia than narrative.

> *Zena Sutherland, in a review of "Popcorn Days and Buttermilk Nights," in* Bulletin of the Center for Children's Books, *Vol. 37, No. 4, December, 1983, p. 75.*

TRACKER (1984)

A simple, almost slight, story about tracking a deer through the Minnesota woods transcends the superficial through evocative writing and Paulsen's strongly felt convictions about death. John, 13, and his grandfather look forward to deer hunting each year—they love the woods, but they also need the meat for the long winter. This season, however, John is to go alone because his grandfather is dying of cancer. A doe, spotted near the barnyard a few days prior to opening of deer season, startles John with her unforgettable, piercing eyes. When he sees the animal again, it signals an omen that he feels is somehow attached to his grandfather's life—and death—and he determines to track the deer as far as it will go. Anyone who has gone hunting, tramped through the woods in winter, or feared the approaching death of a loved one can find a personal message in Paulsen's brief tale.

> *Denise M. Wilms, in a review of "Tracker," in* Booklist, *Vol. 80, No. 19, June 1, 1984, p. 1400.*

Powerfully written, the author explores with the reader the

inner-most frustrations, hurts, and fears of the young boy. It is an honest portrayal of grief. The sensitivity of this youngster also comes through in small imaginative poems expressing his feelings for beauty around him, even for his requisite chores.

A novel of similar concern is Monica Hughes' *Hunter in the Dark*. After learning that he has developed acute lymphocytic leukemia, sixteen-year-old Mike Rankin is determined to bring a dream to reality by hunting a white-tail deer. Readers will find much to compare between Mike and John.

> *Ronald A. Jobe, in a review of "Tracker," in* Language Arts, *Vol. 61, No. 5, September, 1984, p. 527.*

For the careful reader this title with its many layered meanings, its Haiku writing protagonist, its gentleness amidst the harshness of nature, of death, will be a special read. Those looking for a novel of hunting will need to look elsewhere. John's quest, the need to touch the deer—but not kill it, to assuage and conquer death, is poetry. Paulsen's earlier title *Dancing Carl* was chosen a 1983 YASD Best Book for Young Adults. *Tracker* deserves the same honor. (pp. 197-98)

> *Allan Cuseo, in a review of "Tracker," in* Voice of Youth Advocates, *Vol. 7, No. 4, October, 1984, pp. 197-98.*

DOGSONG (1985)

Once the 14-year-old protagonist's ability to survive in the frigid wasteland is accepted, readers may find themselves drawn into Paulsen's latest novel about a young man's crossover into adulthood. Eskimo youth Russel Susskit is hard put to accept the modernity of the world in which he is growing up and mourns the loss of the old ways of his people and the songs that proclaimed their existence. Following the tutelage of a village elder, he embarks on a dogsled journey northward, a pilgrimage of learning, testing, and self-discovery, during which dreams of a different, long-ago self blend with reality as he struggles to sustain himself, his team, and the young pregnant woman whom he rescues. Paulsen's mystical tone and blunt prose style are well suited to the spare landscape of his story, and his depictions of Russel's icebound existence add both authenticity and color to a slick rendition of the vision-quest plot, which incorporates human tragedy as well as promise.

> *Stephanie Zvirin, in a review of "Dogsong," in* Booklist, *Vol. 81, No. 15, April 1, 1985, p. 1114.*

Sadly, there is a conspiracy at work, to maim and kill the power of the imagination. Television, realistic films are the villains. But reading novels like this one can return the young to their inheritance. It should be an education for any adult to read this along with an interested child just to share in the joy of it all. . . .

There are thrilling episodes of Russel's learning of his song. We can feel the cold snow and ice upon his body. He discards use of snowmobiles or modern guns. It is a return to tribal lore which teaches him how to find food; even to reverence the dead animal which provides such. And mixed into the action is a dream which also teaches him to interpret life. There is poetic majesty in the descriptions without a touch of condescension to the young.

The acceptance of death by old Oogruk is a moving passage

as is the finding of Nancy, 14 years old and carrying the shame of her pregnancy into the wilds. The young survive through feats of skill and bravery which ought to allow anyone, but especially the young, to welcome a different kind of champion than presented in too many works of fiction today. The publisher suggests that this story is for 12 years and up. Amen to that.

> *Eugene J. Linehan, S. J., in a review of "Dogsong," in* Best Sellers, *Vol. 45, No. 4, July, 1985, p. 159.*

The author neither romanticizes the hardships of [the Eskimo] existence nor exaggerates the peculiarities of its customs; yet he succeeds in giving the brutal North a poetry of its own. If the merging of dream and real world is confusing from time to time, Russel's mental and physical stamina are never in doubt. How he will survive his return to village life is left unanswered. It is enough to have followed him through a moving and beautifully portrayed rite of passage. (p. 457)

> *Ethel R. Twichell, in a review of "Dogsong," in* The Horn Book Magazine, *Vol. LXI, No. 4, July-August, 1985, pp. 456-57.*

While the language of the book is lyrical, Paulsen recognizes the reality of Russel's world—the dirty smoke and the stinking yellow fur of the bear. He also recognizes the reality of killing to save lives, and of dreaming to save sanity, in the communion between present and past, life and death, reality and imagination, in this majestic exploration into the Alaskan wilderness by a master author who knows his subject well. *Dogsong* is a novel of survival that can be read on many levels and by different age groups. Its flowing language describing Russel's experiences make the book ideal for reading aloud to groups. (p. 321)

> *Nel Ward, in a review of "Dogsong," in* Voice of Youth Advocates, *Vol. 8, No. 5, December, 1985, pp. 321-22.*

SENTRIES (1986)

Part ode to the incredible luck of being alive, part cry of alarm, wholly a plea that life go on, Gary Paulsen's new book, *Sentries,* is strange, hard to pigeonhole. Unlike his *Dogsong,* . . . this collection of short fictions isn't exactly a novel. It has seven main characters, yet they don't know one another. Their paths don't cross, yet their stories produce a unified effect.

Sentries consists of four well-plotted stories told in 16 chapters set in peacetime, and four stark chapters, called "Battle Hymns," set during recent wars.

The peacetime chapters take place in several Western and Middle Western states. The four young people in them all make life-enhancing choices; whereas the three young men in wars have, by the author's definition, lost that privilege.

Sue Oldhorn, in Minnesota, chooses between the white world and her Ojibway heritage. David Garcia, a migrant worker from Chihuahua, casts his lot with his fellow beet harvesters; Laura Hayes, daughter of sheep ranchers, proves, while 3,000 lambs are born, that she's as much part of sheep ranching as if she'd been her parents' son. And Peter Shackleton—a contemporary version of John Lennon—breaks through to an astonishing new music.

The stories fall into a pattern: four segments each of Sue, David, Laura, Peter's stories, in that order, followed by a Battle Hymn. The interweaving conveys, better than philosophizing, the interconnections of life.

The first three Battle Hymns take place in Vietnam, over Germany in World War II and in Korea. Tim Johnson, a Marine rifleman; Richard Erickson, an Air Force gunner, and Ray Haus, an infantry soldier, act as war compels them to, and it wrecks their lives.

The final ominous Battle Hymn is merely two paragraphs. To quote or paraphrase would be a disservice. Yes, it's frightening. Yet so long as people still can choose to write, to read, and take to heart such books as this, so clear and brave, then surely there's hope for the future. Mr. Paulsen implicitly urges us to become "sentries," too.

> *Doris Orgel, in a review of "Sentries," in* The New York Times Book Review, *June 29, 1986, p. 30.*

Paulsen interweaves the developing stories of four teenagers with vignettes about veterans of three wars. The focus stories—a Native American girl denies the heritage that her grandfather tries to force upon her; an illegal alien looks for a better life as a migrant worker; a Montana farm girl tries to convince her father that the farm offers her the life that she wants; and a teenage rock star shuns the lure of drugs to hone his sound—are not completely satisfying as the protagonists are more archetypical than real. The self-contained war vignettes concern Lucky, who loves the fury of battle until his limbs are blown off in Vietnam; a farm boy fighting in World War II whose hopes and dreams are destroyed by the schrapnel that severs his spinal cord; and a sharpshooter, sent to Korea, who is destroyed by the terrible need to kill children who are assisting in the massacre of his unit. This emotionally charged story in particular is beautifully crafted and stunningly written. The final vignette focuses on a Bengal tiger and her cub as a flash starts World War III, and all of these lives are gone—not just the young men who fight for their country, but the young (and old) everywhere. Paulsen concentrates on depicting a generation struggling to realize its future, unaware of impending disaster, and he manages to involve readers despite the rigid, choppy format. The ending doesn't work within the structure of the book, but it does serve to emphasize the effects of nuclear war on innocents.

> *Anne Connor, in a review of "Sentries," in* School Library Journal, *Vol. 32, No. 10, August, 1986, p. 105.*

[Gary Paulsen] continues in literary excellence with this collectively powerful reminder of the formidable human waste nuclear war promises within the context of three previous damaging wars. In the vignettes of the *Sentries,* the reader sees all the beauty of human potential; the fusion, of the heart not the atom, of a modern Indian adolescent with the heritage her aging grandfather represents and the blending of the creative spirits of the rock composer, his black pianist mentor, and the audience which first hears his "new sound." The ongoing struggle of humanity for growth and accomplishment makes agonizing reading in light of the implications for loss, if that oft-predicted *Click* ever happens on earth. Highly recommended for all libraries and already nominated for YASD's 1986 Best Books list.

> *Evie Wilson, in a review of "Sentries," in* Voice of Youth Advocates, *Vol. 9, Nos. 3 & 4, August-October, 1986, p. 148.*

THE CROSSING (1987)

Returning to some of the themes of *Sentries,* Paulsen tells a harshly taut story, set in a Mexican border town, about two people who meet on the edge of oblivion.

Manny is an orphan who skitters along the border desperate to cross to the other side, if for no other reason than to escape the chicken hawks who prey on boys his age. Robert is a sergeant who crosses freely between Mexico and the US, but he is seeking another escape into the bottle, in carefully controlled drunks to obliterate memory of Vietnam. The two meet three times: once when Manny tries to pick Robert's pocket and is allowed to go free; once when, pulled together by inner compulsions they cannot identify, they spend a day in each other's company, if not together; and finally, on the border itself when the ultimate answer to their dilemmas presents itself, and, in his own way, each goes free.

Told from the point of view of both protagonists, the details of the story are familiar ones, and the style seems a bit too imitation-Hemingway. Paulsen, however, is skilled at pace, incident and characterization, and he uses these to pull the reader to the memorable—and powerful—last scene in which Robert's destruction is Manny's salvation. Graphic details and some harsh language make this a book for older children and teen-agers who will not want to put it down.

> *A review of "The Crossing," in* Kirkus Reviews, *Vol. LV, No. 13, July 15, 1987, p. 1074.*

Cut-throat editing would have made this a great short story. As a book, it is tedious and repetitious in places and several times the author is amateurishly obscure. The concept is interesting and will give middle class American kids something to think about.

> *Linda M. Classen, in a review of "The Crossing," in* Voice of Youth Advocates, *Vol. 10, No. 4, October, 1987, p. 206.*

In terse and understated prose the author brilliantly depicts Manny's appalling poverty and his matter-of-fact acceptance of life's inequities and builds a growing respect for the boy's pluck and lack of self-pity. Woven into Manny's story is that of Robert, a sergeant stationed at Fort Bliss, who is haunted by his war experiences and blunts those memories with alcohol. A strange relationship develops when Manny, caught while attempting to steal Robert's wallet, contrives to attach himself to the soldier and becomes his free-loading companion and guide to a bullfight. A profoundly moving conclusion finds Robert sacrificing himself in a death that powerfully recalls the slaughter he witnessed in the bull ring. . . . The author deserves high praise for his evocation of the smells and noise and heat of the Mexican setting and for his skillful portrayal of the young Mexican boy and the war-damaged Robert. Paulsen remains a detached observer, never lapsing into either judgment or sentimentality, and leaves Manny and Robert to act out their story with an affecting and convincing inevitability. (pp. 744-45)

> *Ethel R. Twichell, in a review of "The Crossing," in* The Horn Book Magazine, *Vol. LXIII, No. 6, No-*

vember-December, 1987, pp. 744-45.

HATCHET (1987)

A prototypical survival story: after an airplane crash, a 13-year-old city boy spends two months alone in the Canadian wilderness.

In transit between his divorcing parents, Brian is the plane's only passenger. After casually showing him how to steer, the pilot has a heart attack and dies. In a breathtaking sequence, Brian maneuvers the plane for hours while he tries to think what to do, at last crashing as gently and levelly as he can manage into a lake. The plane sinks; all he has left is a hatchet, attached to his belt. His injuries prove painful but not fundamental. In time, he builds a shelter, experiments with berries, finds turtle eggs, starts a fire, makes a bow and arrow to catch fish and birds, and makes peace with the larger wildlife. He also battles despair and emerges more patient, prepared to learn from his mistakes . . . His mixed feelings surprise him when the plane finally surfaces so that he can retrieve the survival pack; and then he's rescued.

Plausible, taut, this is a spellbinding account. Paulsen's staccato, repetitive style conveys Brian's stress; his combination of third-person narrative with Brian's interior monologue pulls the reader into the story. Brian's *angst* over a terrible secret—he's seen his mother with another man—is undeveloped and doesn't contribute much, except as one item from his previous life that he sees in better perspective, as a result of his experience. High interest, not hard to read. A winner. (pp. 1161-62)

A review of "Hatchet," in Kirkus Reviews, *Vol. LV, No. 15, August 1, 1987, pp. 1161-62.*

[*Hatchet*] deserves special attention. Written in terse, poetic prose, it is an adventure story in the best tradition, with each chapter moving from one climactic moment to the next. . . .

Gary Paulsen writes with the intensity and power of Robert Cormier, and the grace and style of Paula Fox—a winning combination of qualities. The book is as much an inward journey as a wilderness hike. In fact, protagonist Brian Robeson begins to see changes within himself as a kind of spiritual resurrection: "In measured time 47 days had passed since the crash. Forty-seven days, he thought, since he had died and been born as the new Brian." He begins to think in terms of "the new time," measures his days as "First Day," etc., eats "First Meat," as he evaluates his life in an almost primeval light.

Teachers will like this book for the richness of the text and the artfulness of the writing. Young adults will like it because it's such an engaging tale.

A minor flaw is the book's epilogue. In tidying up a lot of unanswered questions, it seems a bit too convenient, even tagged on. In fact, the way it is written, it could almost seem like an indication that this is a "true" story—which it isn't.

Stephen Fraser, "Exciting Tales of Challenge and Survival," in The Christian Science Monitor, *November 6, 1987, p. B5.*

This is a story of survival, and it has good pace, suspense, and convincing details of Brian's ingenuity and growing self-confidence. It is weakened by stylistic flaws (speaking of a coil of wire, "it sprung into a three foot long antenna") and by the melodramatic treatment of "The Secret," the fact that Brian had seen his mother, prior to the divorce, kiss a man whom she later "continued to see," as explained in an epilogue after Brian's rescue; but as a story of boy-against-nature, it's deftly conceived and developed.

A review of "Hatchet," in Bulletin of the Center for Children's Books, *Vol. 41, No. 4, December, 1987, p. 73.*

The novel chronicles in gritty detail Brian's mistakes, setbacks, and small triumphs as, with the help of the hatchet, he manages to survive the 54 days alone in the wilderness. Paulsen effectively shows readers how Brian learns patience—to watch, listen, and think before he acts—as he attempts to build a fire, to fish and hunt, and to make his home under a rock overhang safe and comfortable. An epilogue discussing the lasting effects of Brian's stay in the wilderness and his dim chance of survival had winter come upon him before rescue adds credibility to the story. Paulsen tells a fine adventure story, but the sub-plot concerning Brian's preoccupation with his parents' divorce seems a bit forced and detracts from the book. As he did in *Dogsong,* Paulsen emphasizes character growth through a careful balancing of specific details of survival with the protagonist's thoughts and emotions. (pp. 103-04)

Barbara Chatton, in a review of "Hatchet," in School Library Journal, *Vol. 34, No. 4, December, 1987, pp. 103-04.*

THE ISLAND (1988)

In contrast to Paulsen's other books about survival and perilous journeys (of the soul and otherwise), this one takes place almost entirely on a safe, tiny island in northern Wisconsin. Wil finds the island soon after his family has moved away from the city; his discovery begins in routine geographical investigation but soon becomes an intense (to him) inner journey to the sources of creativity. This novel is heavily thematic and unrelieved by action: while we are given to understand that Wil's meditative retreats and observations should be action enough, the narrative is static, and the insights banal and padded. "And after a time, after all of time, she nodded, because she had touched his temple and read about his grandmother and the herons and the loons and seen the paintings; she nodded and said she would help him, would help him, would help him." Paulsen seems more interested in expounding his rather sentimentally mystical ideas about art ("I am a painting,") than in telling a story. While Wil's essays about his grandmother, the heron, etc., sound like the author talking, each chapter begins with a long quote from Wil that demonstrates an entirely different voice, one with considerably more humor, genuine perception, and vivacity. These anecdotes reveal a Wil, and a Paulsen, that readers would like to meet.

A review of "The Island," in Bulletin of the Center for Children's Books, *Vol. 41, No. 9, May, 1988, p. 186.*

In his fiction for young people, Gary Paulsen has focused on the critical experience of a boy's coming-of-age. In novels such as *The Crossing, Dogsong* and *Hatchet,* Mr. Paulsen has imagined the initiation in the form of a fast-paced adventure story. The boy's self-discovery and maturation are achieved in a struggle for survival in a natural setting. Even though the boy's growth shows him to be more sensitive toward nature, other people and himself, there is a rather conventional macho ethos underlying the overall conception of plot, setting and action—and also the prose.

The Island is significantly different from these earlier books because it is essentially a meditative novel that subordinates, indeed practically stops, external action to concentrate on the reflections of a 14-year-old boy about the world around him and his relation to it. Islands, especially fictional ones, are magically suited by their isolation to reveal the potential hidden in all of us. Tom Sawyer liked to take his gang to Jackson's Island for the self-congratulatory fantasy he called "adventures"; in contrast, Huck Finn was so beset by real adventures, most of them terrifying, that he was content, when he got the chance, just to "laze around" on his raft and listen to the songbirds.

Mr. Paulsen's new book might well be subtitled *Zen and the Art of Boyhood.* Wil Neuton moves with his parents from Madison, Wis., to a small house in the north woods, miles from the nearest village, because of his father's work with the state highway department. He then discovers a lake with a single island in the middle of it . . .

The young boy, who was typically concerned with sports, grades, girls and competition in Madison, is suddenly transformed by the power of his secret place. He now spontaneously wants to learn about things for their own sake and senses that to understand something you have to become one with it. He practices meditation, then tai chi, which he develops from a Chinese form of martial exercise into interpretive dancing; he dances the heron's movements to know the heron—to become the heron. He draws and paints, and most of all he reflects on what he experiences and writes it down, in an effort to become it.

Each chapter is prefaced by a meditation from Wil's notebooks, and some chapters are separated by Wil's visions or interpretations of animals, people and objects in his life. These sections of the novel are reminiscent of the "Chautauqua" interludes in Robert Pirsig's *Zen and the Art of Motorcycle Maintenance,* explorations of the issues of subject, object and the nature of reality, as well as of the quality of human experience.

Even coming from a middle-aged philosophy professor like Mr. Pirsig, such thoughts are a bit much for many adult readers, and when they come from a 14-year-old there may not be much willing suspension of disbelief among the young-adult readers this book is intended for. Attention may turn to boredom or outright suspiciousness of the whole enterprise. It may well be that for young readers action is more powerful than symbol, the epic world more revelatory than the lyric. Nevertheless, Mr. Paulsen has evocatively presented the mysteriousness of the spiritual quest through the unconscious for wholeness and authenticity.

Later in the book, the social world of parents, bullies, reporters . . . and child psychologists finally arrives at the island. At first Wil resists them on principle. But he has been preparing himself to leave this special place because he has apprehended the fundamental truth that "all things change." Like Thoreau, another American sojourner in nature, Wil knows in his heart that he has other lives to lead and that his island world must ultimately include all others. Similarly, **The Island** seems to express and to represent Gary Paulsen's discovery that he has many other different kinds of books to write, a greater diversity of human experience to include.

Edwin J. Kenney, Jr., in a review of "The Island," in The New York Times Book Review, *Vol., No., May 22, 1988, p. 30.*

Once again Paulsen has shown his extraordinary ability to picture for the reader how man's comprehension of life can be transformed with the lessons of nature. With humor and psychological genius, Paulsen develops strong adolescent characters who lend new power to youth's plea to be allowed to apply individual skills in their risk-taking. There is much food for thought here for the adult reader as well, particularly in a powerful little chapter, "Bickerbits: an aid play to help understand and deal with adults." Admirably, Paulsen himself continues to be a risk-taker with format. **The Island's** chapters begin with anecdotes from Wil's wit and wisdom, and Wil's reflective stories and essays are interspersed throughout. Sounds fragmented, but this style serves to draw the reader into Wil's life, the anecdotes telling as much about his past pain as the immediate events on the island do about his present metamorphosis. Altogether an impressive and forceful work of reflective fiction. Must purchase for all school and public libraries. (p. 90)

Evie Wilson, in a review of "The Island," in Voice of Youth Advocates, *Vol. 11, No. 2, June, 1988, pp. 89-90.*

(Helen) Beatrix Potter (Heelis)

1866-1943

English author and illustrator of picture books and fiction.

The following entry emphasizes general criticism on Potter's career. It also includes a selection of reviews to supplement the general criticism.

One of the most beloved creators of books for children in the history of juvenile literature, Potter is renowned for bringing a new realism to the genre. In a striking departure from the animal fables predominant in her time, she invented an original world filled with characters who were clearly faithful to their animal natures yet human in their thoughts and actions. Her approximately twenty-five books for preschoolers and readers in the early elementary grades have set a standard by which subsequent picture books are measured as both art and literature. Her works characteristically reflect such features as animal protagonists who are devious but lovable, suspenseful plots, a warm domesticity depicted with many homey details, and human characters who are peripheral or nonexistent. Although she placed her books in peaceful natural and home settings, Potter wrote of a very realistic world of danger and death. While she does not avoid these topics, like her mention of the fact that Peter's father was made into a pie by the McGregors in her first story *The Tale of Peter Rabbit* (1902), Potter ends her books on a happy note. Her characters represent such childhood characteristics as mischievousness, foolhardy trust of strangers, and defiance of conventionalism while remaining true to their animal natures. Potter's acute awareness of both animal behavior and matters of interest to children have led to the astounding popularity of her books, which consistently sell hundreds of thousands of copies each year.

Possibly as an escape from the restrictions of her oppressive childhood, Potter penned works which emphasize imagination, humor, playfulness, and the security of a happy family. As a relief from the stifling atmosphere of her upper-class Victorian home, where she was taught by governesses and had no friends her age, she taught herself to capture the antics and idiosyncracies of the rabbits, mice, hedgehogs, and other animals that she brought into her nursery; she also sketched the scenery and wildlife of Scotland and England's Lake District, the sites of her family's summer vacations. Potter's first professional writing came as the result of a letter written in 1893 to the son of a former governess; in it, Potter described the adventures of a disobedient rabbit who suffers the consequences of his naughtiness. Years later, she decided to rework the story into a small book with black-and-white illustrations; failing to find a publisher, she published the book privately in 1901. A year later, Frederick Warne and Company accepted *The Tale of Peter Rabbit* after requesting that Potter do watercolor illustrations for the story. The successfulness of her books led Potter to free herself from her restrictive home life by purchasing farmland in the Lake District, and her works from 1905 to 1913 reflect her love of Hill Top Farm in Sawrey. In 1913, Potter married William Heelis, the solicitor who assisted her in the purchase of her land, and she turned to a life of sheep farming, which drastically reduced the quantity of her books. A dedicated writer whom some

critics consider one of the first to take children's books seriously, Potter followed every stage of the production of her works. She insisted that they be small enough for young children to hold comfortably, was emphatic about the placement of her texts to enhance suspense and to keep her readers turning the pages, and rewrote her prose and reworked her paintings repeatedly. Consequently, she produced texts which are considered masterpieces for their succinctness, clarity, and broad vocabulary, and watercolors which show countless details in both domestic settings and landscapes and, in their exactness and beauty, are thought to reflect a naturalist's observation and an artist's imagination. Through her insistence on quality and genius for recreating the busy world of small animals, Potter created enduring works which appeal to children for their freshness and lack of condescension. Potter won the Lewis Carroll Shelf Award posthumously in 1958 for *The Tale of Peter Rabbit* and in 1962 for *The Tailor of Gloucester*.

(See also *CLR,* Vol. 1; *Yesterday's Authors of Books for Children,* Vol. 1; and *Contemporary Authors,* Vol. 108.)

AUTHOR'S COMMENTARY

The question of "roots" interests me! I am a believer in

"breed"; I hold that a strongly marked personality can influence descendants for generations. . . . I am descended from generations of Lancashire yeomen and weavers; obstinate, hard headed, *matter of fact* folk. (There you find the downright matter-of-factness which imports an air of reality.) As far back as I can go, they were Puritans, Nonjurors, Nonconformists, Dissenters. . . . The most remarkable old "character" amongst my ancestors—old Abraham Crompton, who sprang from mid-Lancashire, bought land for pleasure in the Lake District, and his descendants seem to have drifted back at intervals ever since—though none of us own any of the land that belonged to old Abraham.

However—it was not the Lake District at all that inspired me to write children's books. I hope this shocking statement will not distress you kind Americans, who see Peter Rabbits under every Westmoreland bush. I am inclined to put it down to three things—mainly—(1) The aforesaid matter-of-fact ancestry, (2) The accidental circumstance of having spent a good deal of my childhood in the Highlands of Scotland, with a Highland nurse girl, and a firm belief in witches, fairies and the creed of the terrible John Calvin (the creed rubbed off, but the fairies remained). (3) A peculiarly precocious and tenacious memory. I have been laughed at for what I say I can remember; but it is admitted that I can remember quite plainly from one and two years old; not only facts, like learning to walk, but places and sentiments—the way things impressed a very young child.

Does not that go a long way towards explaining the little books? (pp. 69-70)

I think I write carefully because I enjoy my writing, and enjoy taking pains over it. I have always disliked writing to order; I write to please myself. (p. 71)

My usual way of writing is to scribble, and cut out, and write it again and again. The shorter and plainer the better. And read the Bible (*unrevised* version and Old Testament) if I feel my style wants chastening. There are many dialect words of the Bible and Shakespeare—and also the forcible direct language—still in use in the rural parts of Lancashire. (p. 72)

> *Beatrix Potter, " 'Roots' of the Peter Rabbit Tales,"*
> *in* The Horn Book Magazine, *Vol. V, No. 2, May,*
> *1929, pp. 69-72.*

GRAHAM GREENE

[The following excerpt is from an essay originally published in 1933.]

[In] 1904, with the publication of *Two Bad Mice,* Miss Potter opened the series of her great comedies. In this story of Tom Thumb and Hunca Munca and their wanton havoc of a doll's house, the unmistakable Potter style first appears.

It is an elusive style, difficult to analyse. It owes something to alliteration:

> Hunca Munca stood up in her chair and chopped
> at the ham with another lead knife.
>
> 'It's as hard as the hams at the cheesemonger's,'
> said Hunca Munca.

Something too it owes to the short paragraphs, which are fashioned with a delicate irony, not to complete a movement, but mutely to criticize the action by arresting it. The imperceptive pause allows the mind to take in the picture: the mice are stilled in their enraged attitudes for a moment, before the action sweeps forward:

> Then there was no end to the rage and disappointment of Tom Thumb and Hunca Munca. They broke up the pudding, the lobsters, the pears, and the oranges.
>
> As the fish would not come off the plate, they put it into the red-hot crinkly paper fire in the kitchen; but it would not burn either.

It is curious that Beatrix Potter's method of paragraphing has never been imitated.

The last quotation shows another element of her later style, her love of a precise catalogue, her creation of atmosphere with still-life. . . . The only indication in *Two Bad Mice* of a prentice hand is the sparsity of dialogue; her characters had not yet begun to utter those brief pregnant sentences, which have slipped, like proverbs, into common speech. Nothing in the early book equals Mr Jackson's, 'No teeth. No teeth. No teeth.'

In [1902 *The Tale of Peter Rabbit*] was published, closely followed by its sequel, *Benjamin Bunny.* In Peter and his cousin Benjamin Miss Potter created two epic personalities. The great characters of fiction are often paired: Quixote and Sancho, Pantagruel and Panurge, Pickwick and Weller, Benjamin and Peter. Peter was a neurotic, Benjamin worldly and imperturbable. . . . [Benjamin's] coolness and practicality are a foil to the nerves and clumsiness of his cousin. It was Benjamin who knew the way to enter a garden: 'It spoils people's clothes to squeeze under a gate; the proper way to get in is to climb down a pear tree.' It was Peter who fell down head first. (pp. 260-61)

At some time between 1907 and 1909 Miss Potter must have passed through an emotional ordeal which changed the character of her genius. It would be impertinent to inquire into the nature of the ordeal. Her case is curiously similar to that of Henry James. Something happened which shook their faith in appearances. From *The Portrait of a Lady* onwards, innocence deceived, the treachery of friends, became the theme of James's greatest stories. Mme Merle, Kate Croy, Mme de Vionnet, Charlotte Stant, these tortuous treacherous women are paralleled through the dark period of Miss Potter's art. 'A man can smile and smile and be a villain'—that, a little altered, was her recurrent message, expressed by her gallery of scoundrels: Mr Drake Puddle-Duck, the first and slightest, Mr Jackson, the least harmful with his passion for honey and his reiterated, 'No teeth. No teeth. No teeth', Samuel Whiskers, gross and brutal, and the 'gentleman with sandy whiskers' who may be identified with Mr Tod. With the publication of *Mr Tod* in 1912, Miss Potter's pessimism reached its climax. But for the nature of her audience *Mr Tod* would certainly have ended tragically. (pp. 262-63)

[No] charm softens the brutality of Mr. Tod and his enemy, the repulsive Tommy Brock. In her comedies Miss Potter had gracefully eliminated the emotions of love and death; it is the measure of her genius that when, in *The Tale of Mr Tod,* they broke the barrier, the form of her book, her ironic style, remained unshattered. When she could not keep death out she stretched her technique to include it. Benjamin and Peter had grown up and married, and Benjamin's babies were stolen by Brock; the immortal pair, one still neurotic, the other knowing and imperturbable, set off to the rescue, but the rescue, conducted in darkness, from a house, 'something between a cave, a prison, and a tumbledown pig-sty', compares grimly with an earlier rescue from Mr McGregor's sunny vegetable garden:

> The sun had set; an owl began to hoot in the wood. There were many unpleasant things lying about, that had much better have been buried; rabbit bones and skulls, and chicken's legs and other horrors. It was a shocking place and very dark.

But *Mr Tod,* for all the horror of its atmosphere, is indispensable. There are few fights in literature which can compare in excitement with the duel between Mr Tod and Tommy Brock. . . . *Mr Tod* marked the distance which Miss Potter had travelled since the ingenuous romanticism of *The Tailor of Gloucester.* The next year with *The Tale of Pigling Bland,* the period of the great near-tragedies came to an end. There was something of the same squalor, and the villain, Mr Thomas Piperson, was not less terrible than Mr Tod, but the book ended on a lyrical note, as Pigling Bland escaped with Pig-Wig:

> They ran, and they ran, and they ran down the hill, and across a short cut on level green turf at the bottom, between pebble-beds and rushes. They came to the river, they came to the bridge—they crossed it hand in hand—

It was the nearest Miss Potter had approached to a conventional love story. The last sentence seemed a promise that the cloud had lifted, that there was to be a return to the style of the earlier comedies. But *Pigling Bland* was published in 1913. Through the years of war the author was silent, and for many years after it was over, only a few books of rhyme appeared. These showed that Miss Potter had lost none of her skill as an artist, but left the great question of whither her genius was tending unanswered. Then, after seventeen years, at the end of 1930, *Little Pig Robinson* was published.

The scene was no longer Cumberland but Devonshire and the sea. The story, more than twice as long as *Mr Tod,* was diffuse and undramatic. The smooth smiling villain had disappeared and taken with him the pungent dialogue, the sharp detail, the light of common day. Miss Potter had not returned to the great comedies. She had gone on beyond the great near-tragedies to her *Tempest.* No tortured Lear nor strutting Antony could live on Prospero's island, among the sounds and sweet airs and cloudcapt towers. Miss Potter too had reached her island, the escape from tragedy, the final surrender of imagination to safe serene fancy:

> A steam of boiling water flowed down the silvery strand. The shore was covered with oysters. Acid-drops and sweets grew upon the trees. Yams, which are a sort of sweet potato, abounded ready cooked. The breadfruit tree grew iced cakes and muffins ready baked.

It was very satisfying for a pig Robinson, but in that rarefied air no bawdy Tommy Brock could creep to burrow, no Benjamin pursued his feud between the vegetable-frames, no Puddle-Duck could search in wide-eyed innocence for a 'convenient dry nesting-place'.

> NOTE. On the publication of this essay I received a somewhat acid letter from Miss Potter correcting certain details. *Little Pig Robinson,* although the last published of her books, was in fact the first

written. She denied that there had been any emotional disturbance at the time she was writing *Mr Tod:* she was suffering however from the after-effects of flu. In conclusion she deprecated sharply 'the Freudian school' of criticism.

(pp. 263-65)

Graham Greene, "Beatrix Potter," in Only Connect: Readings on Children's Literature, *Sheila Egoff, G. T. Stubbs, L. F. Ashley, eds., second edition, Oxford University Press, Canadian Branch, 1980, pp. 258-65.*

ELEANOR GRAHAM

Reading through a whole set of Beatrix Potters to-day, I have been struck with many things, but chiefly, perhaps, with the easy and sure contact she makes with the child. I had the feeling, though I may be quite wrong, that she had in mind the unspoilt children of the Lakeland villages when she wrote them. The domestic atmosphere is what you would have found thirty years ago (*Peter Rabbit* came out, I think, in 1902) in those grey stone cottages where the old-fashioned easy standards prevailed—easy because they were so clearly labelled *Right* and *Wrong, Must* and *Must not.*

The mother in these tales is always warm-hearted and even-tempered, the type who does not suffer from nerves or possess much imagination. She has no time for introspection and is never egoistic. Her love for her children never fails. It is part of her, so there is always a happy, *safe* ending. No food for nightmares. No suggestion of insecurity to disturb the equilibrium of the child. They are essentially happy family stories though in miniature, and I am sure that this atmosphere has contributed a great deal to their lasting success.

The appeal of the stories is effective because it touches a small child's own experience. Each, in terms of rabbits, kittens, or squirrels, deals with some little problem known to the young mind—but the author has a light hand. She exerts no moral pressure. In her simple tales, if punishment follows the lapse from goodness, it does so as simply and naturally as rain wets the grass—and just as the sun always comes out again to dry the ground, the unwavering, taken-for-granted affection of the mother is at hand to make everything right again. Moreover, the punishment is not as a rule dealt out from mother to child, but is the natural sequence of wrong-doing. Even a three-year-old, rightly brought up so far, will recognise the difference, and appreciate the simple lesson in cause and effect when Peter Rabbit deliberately and on purpose disobeys his mother, gets into terrible trouble, is sick and comes to the inevitable, inescapable nemesis of camomile tea!

It is also, I think, proof of their having been written for the robust country child that Beatrix Potter does not hesitate—as many of our critics to-day would have an author hesitate—to mention rabbit pie to rabbits or bacon to a pig!

I don't intend to involve myself in any arguing of morals on that score now—but the fact remains that the hardy child finds the idea of bacon from living pigs, more often than not, slightly funny and hardly ever frightening or tragic. Bacon is good. Rabbit pie is good. And if Peter Rabbit himself were caught and put in a pie, these children might not weep. Some tough grasp of real values keeps them steady. (pp. 172-73)

Each of her stories is exciting, an adventure with a plot, a climax and, as I said before, a happy ending. Many of them contain a simple lesson for those who care to look for it. *Peter*

Rabbit shows the wisdom of obedience, *Squirrel Nutkin* is in praise of industry and good manners. The moral of the *Tailor of Gloucester* is, I think, that one good turn deserves another.

There are familiar types of people portrayed in them, characters which village children will recognise very often out of their own experience—the super-particular housewife in the *Tale of Mrs. Tittlemouse*—(a most uncomfortable person where there are children); the cosiness of Mrs. Tiggywinkle in her little house entered by a door in *Cat Bells*—and her little habit of picking up dirty pinafores and handkerchiefs wherever she found them and whisking them into the wash-tub. (pp. 173-74)

It is interesting to discover the Lakeland background to the pictures in the Beatrix Potter books. Behind Jemima Puddle-duck and the others Miss Potter has painted, in her soft water-colours, the green valleys and the fells, the meadows, the loose stone dykes, the old grey farmhouses with their inviting kitchens and great gleaming stoves, the hooded carrier's cart, the great boulders, and the windswept trees. It is charming work, fresh and clean. Her little animals are genuine creatures, not sophisticated into neat little almost-boys and girls, in spite of their wearing clothes—which, by the way, are nearly always admitted to be a nuisance and an encumbrance to them. Peter is just such a rabbit as you might see in any wood, and not unlike the ones brought into cottage kitchens before the making of those succulent pies!

I suspect that the pernickety type of modern child-psychologist must have a struggle with herself over the Peter Rabbit books, for Miss Potter does not bind herself to stick strictly to natural history in its more difficult aspects. She does not feel obliged to reveal the murderous habits of father rabbits towards their young. On the contrary, she falsifies quite cheerfully, making, for example, Benjamin Bunny (after he had married and gone to live on the other side of the wood with his wife and children) behave like a human father. Yet she does not shrink from describing the very unpleasant characteristics of the fox and shows true country spirit in her disregard of Reynard's likely fate. (pp. 174-75)

Personally, there is not one of [Miss Potter's books] I should care to do without—except, possibly, *The Tale of Mr. Tod*—but then I am a town bird by circumstance if not by choice! I can best end this, I think, by a quotation from one of Miss Potter's own books:

> She has laid in a remarkable assortment of bargains. There is something to please everybody.
>
> (p. 175)

Eleanor Graham, "Beatrix Potter," in The Junior Bookshelf, *Vol. 3, No. 4, July, 1939, pp. 171-75.*

BERTHA MAHONY MILLER

No better fare will young parents find for their children than [the books of Beatrix Potter]. Fanciful and humorous though they are, they contribute to the understanding of little children and stimulate early and all unconsciously an interest in the child's own environment; for the characters, their joys, adventures and sorrows all center in their homes, the village and the country round about. They express, too, what is so common throughout folk literature, that old understanding among the so-called "dumb animals," their instinctive helpfulness and wisdom. (p. 231)

Beatrix Potter's books are picture story books, with the pic-

ture an integral part of the whole, and perfectly placed. There is a drawing in color reproduced from water colors for every page of text. However interesting to grown-ups backgrounds and details may be, each picture is thoroughly satisfying to the child for its close presentation of the story. *Peter Rabbit* and *Benjamin Bunny* are sometimes enjoyed by children as young as two. (p. 232)

These books are genuine classics because they have been written out of an environment known and loved, and to which they are true. They live for children because they are of those things which have given their author and illustrator infinite joy. There is a convincing matter-of-factness in their telling. Perhaps this is because so much in them is real. The places are real whether indoors or out. The furniture is real and always good. The cups and saucers, bowls, pitchers and plates are real, and lovely, too. The creatures are real. All have been passed through the imagination of Beatrix Potter in mysterious combination with things long remembered. Happily her imagination is thoroughly infused with humor. She has a genius, too, for knowing what will please very little children. The stories are not wishy-washy. There is plenty of nature and human nature in them and the salty commonsense that springs from the earth and life on a farm. (pp. 232-33)

For nearly forty years Beatrix Potter's little books have been providing youngest children with volumes charming on three counts—story, drawings and style of book. Like all genuine artists, she has spared no pains either in writing or drawing. Some years ago she wrote us that her usual way of working was to scribble, and cut out, and write it again and again. "And read the Bible (un-revised version and Old Testament)" if she felt her "style needed chastening." She also wrote then that many of the dialect words of the Bible and Shakespeare—and the forcible direct language—are still in use in the rural part of Lancashire. Her own books partake of these things. (p. 233)

Bertha Mahony Miller, "Beatrix Potter and Her Nursery Classics," in The Horn Book Magazine, *Vol. XVII, No. 3, May-June, 1941, pp. 230-38.*

WALTER DE LA MARE

[Beatrix Potter] was affronted rather than flattered when one of her devoted admirers and afterward greatly valued friend, who was the editor of The Horn Book, declared her little pictures comparable with Constable's. Contrariwise, she was intensely pleased when another critic remarked on the mastery of her prose. Absolute essence indeed it is, clean as a whistle, delicious to utter, and precise as a formula of Professor Einstein's . . .

[There] are three things which seem to me paramount in any account of Beatrix Potter, all of them rare. First, she not only had a true-blue and formidable character, she was also *a* Character. Such Beings are beyond all price in this rather stereotyped and grossly overpopulated world. Work, she was convinced, was man's earthly salvation. Next, whereas nearly all grown-ups are able to retrieve only the minutest recollections of their early childhood, she herself could recall clearly *being* 5. And how blessedly and triumphantly she proved it! And last, she possessed, as she herself declared, "the seeing eye." Habitually intense and intent was the use she made of it. It is of course not only a heaven-sent possession but also the grace, inspiration and joy of every poet that has ever walked this earth, and shared the stars.

Walter de la Mare, "Peter Rabbit, Beatrix Potter and Friends," in the New York Time Book Review, September 7, 1952, p. 30.

ALMA DEKSNIS

What is the enchantment of Beatrix Potter's books? The distinction of her work, a class of its own among children's books, rests on its consistently high quality; they are pieces of a real art. The notability of her work is based upon a naturalist's loving observation of animal life and on an imaginative understanding of its character. Her water-colors have the beauty and exactness one might find in some luxuriously produced books on natural history.

The author possesses the distinguished ability to create a special world and to fill it with original and believable characters. The fidelity to animal character is the very strength and vitality of her work. The life of her animal characters is so essential that the reader is freely convinced that the author believed in them herself. She possessed a high quality of deep imaginative persuasion that is necessary to any creator of character. It is a secret of a vital spark in **Tom Kitten** and all other pieces of art. The fidelity to animal character is the very power and vitality of her work. The animals are shrewdly personified and their stories, told throughout in human terms, are believable. Her books enlighten the nature of animals and human beings. Conveying truth by means of fantasy, enlarging our perception of life by poetic means, is one of the highest functions of art. Beatrix Potter conceived and loved the little animals that she drew and painted and interpreted the whole animal creation in human terms. Displayed in the trappings of their human counterparts, they reveal their true nature in an oblique way. For example, Jemima Puddle-Duck, lying first in the yard, then under the rhubarb leaves, and finally in desperation, in a wood-shed, raises the problem of frustrated maternity almost to the level of a farmyard tragedy. In the same way, Ginger the cat is a character of pure fantasy, but his cat nature is delicately underlined. Even the clothes in which her animals are so characteristically dressed contribute something to our imaginative understanding of their characters: Mrs. Tiggy-Winkle wears a print gown, petticoat, and an apron; Mr. Tod is dressed something like a dandy.

It is most noteworthy to mention that the animals appear without their clothes in the situations that stress and recall their true natures: Mrs. Tiggy-Winkle vanishing among the vegetables and shrubs; Jemima Puddle-Duck without her waggish bonnet when she has achieved the dignity of motherhood.

Beatrix Potter's real sense of animal beauty and her imaginative and truthful approach are the high qualities that exclude the grotesque element which mostly taints the nursery books about animal characters. The author creates humor by means of a delicate, ironical, and loving description in their characters and adventures without resorting to farce; she made her books like lyrics, out of emotional experience. She had a warm feeling toward the domestic details of north country farmhouse life and perpetuated it through her art. Her "domestic" books where life centers in the kitchen round the fire, are a delicate reflection of a simple life which had been continuing for generations. Her female animals are true to the north country, all good housewives: they do their baking, washing, etc.

The deeply felt beauty of the countryside is another point in

Facsimile of a letter that Potter wrote to five-year-old Noel Moore, the son of a close friend, on 2 September 1893 about the adventures of Peter Rabbit. Potter later turned this story into her first book for children.

Beatrix Potter's books which is hard to find in children's literature. The lakes, the fields, the stone walls are drawn with true feeling. The landscape of her books, suffused with innocence and happiness, are really in the north country and many of them can be identified. . . . (pp. 438-39)

Characteristic elements of Potter's work are natural beauty, a dewy freshness woven with sound humor. The author was deeply aware of the realities of nature, the earth and its seasons, of life and death. Her deepest source of emotional life and spiritual strength are never sentimentalized in any of her stories: Mr. Tod is a character of real terror not only to the innocent duck, but to all the small defenseless creatures of farmyard and wood; Johnny Town-Mouse, for all his instinct, lives in constant danger from the cat, and repeatedly takes shelter in the coal cellar.

Beatrix Potter was continuing, more or less consciously, the simple traditional style of the fairy tale. Instead of giants and monsters there are characters of little animals. Her stories point no moral. She believed that children are willing to be tormented with suspense, but not with unhappy endings: Tom Kitten can join his family, Jemima Puddle-Duck lives to raise her brood, Pigling and Pigwig escapes from being bacon and ham. (pp. 439-40)

Alma Deksnis, "Beatrix Potter," in Elementary English, *Vol. XXXV, No. 7, November, 1958, pp. 431-40.*

MARCUS CROUCH

[Beatrix Potter: A Monograph *was originally published in 1960.*]

Peter Rabbit has the charm of most first things, and one need not regret that a book which is often considered a little less than her best should have become the prototype of Beatrix Potter's work, giving its name to the whole series and entering, as few books have done, into the hearts and lives of innumerable people. It has great charm, economy and humour. The backgrounds are less developed than those of later books, and perhaps in consequence have suffered less through the deterioration of the plates in later reprints; but there are some delightful and subtle drawings, the robin finding Peter's shoe among the cabbages, the white cat by the goldfish pond, among others. What must have distinguished it among its contemporaries, apart from excellence of writing and drawing, was its consistency: it depicts throughout, a rabbit-sized world. (p. 181)

[**The Tailor of Gloucester**] is one of the author's finest [books], and exhibits if not her most characteristic at least her most accomplished drawing and evocative writing. The story is more compact in plot than most. It has an urban and an 'interior' setting. It is the only book in which a human plays a major part, and even here the tailor, poor man, is sick in bed for almost half the book. The text is longer than any other before **Little Pig Robinson.** Uncharacteristic perhaps, but Beatrix Potter certainly put her best into it. It was her favourite book, and many readers, myself among them, have found in it a richness, a poetical expression, a certain sadness even, which the rest of her work never touches. There are a few signs of artistic immaturity, perhaps. Children have sometimes been troubled because in places the exquisite pictures do not correspond, literally, with the accompanying text. But Beatrix Potter, and the finest of other English artists in this field, never equalled the lovely drawings of fabric and embroidery, of 'crockery and pipkins'. Her many visits to the Victoria and Albert Museum to study costume bore the richest fruit. (p. 183)

Although Beatrix Potter seems to have renewed her interest in squirrels during a visit to Long Melford in Suffolk, **Squirrel Nutkin** is a story of the Lake District and the topographical drawing of Derwentwater is the result of much preliminary work. Unfortunately a good deal of the charm of the drawing is lost in recent reprints. . . . Enough remains to make this one of the most colorful of all the books. The squirrels are consistently delightful, and the artist made the most of the opportunity they offer for design. . . . Another notable feature of **Squirrel Nutkin** is its use of shades of green; some of this gets lost in recent reprints but not all. The grey-green of the fir-cones with which Nutkin played ninepins is firmly contrasted with the greens of dock-leaf and nettle. Throughout the book there is a fine feeling for season; without any of the conventional russet leaves this is clearly autumn.

The Tale of Benjamin Bunny was written as a sequel to **Peter Rabbit** and appears to have been something of a chore. Margaret Lane quotes the author as writing that she was 'glad to get done with rabbits'. The book has little internal evidence of having been done with reluctance. It contains some very fine drawing, and the story has a sharp wry humour. (pp. 184-85)

The drawing of animals and plants is as good and detailed as one would expect. The text too is a model of economy. Benjamin, as hard and practical as his clogs, is neatly characterised in every word and line. With all the fun there is an earnest concern with ordinary things in this book almost more than any other. (p. 186)

Two Bad Mice is a book written and drawn to scale. . . . No human intrudes in this miniature world bounded by doll's house and mouse hole. The dumbness of the dolls—Lucinda showed a little emotion at seeing the havoc wrought in her house by the mice, but Jane only smiled—contrasts delightfully with the animation of the two mice. These are real animals, undoubtedly drawn from life. Of all the Peter Rabbit books this is perhaps the most immediately accessible to small children. Everything is within their experience but everything seen so clearly and with such a skill in interpretation that the book both confirms and extends the reader's experience. (p. 187)

There are two principal weaknesses in **The Tale of Mrs Tiggy-Winkle.** The plot is very thin, almost non-existent, and the concluding transformation of the homely 'very stout short person' into 'nothing but a Hedgehog' is clumsily contrived and difficult for small children to accept. An equally important disadvantage is the figure of Lucie. In *The Art of Beatrix Potter* there is a page of trial sketches of Lucie; a back view, several faces, feet and legs. They are evidence, if any were needed, that humans were beyond Beatrix Potter's range, and Lucie, who appears in sixteen of the twenty-seven plates, is just not well enough drawn. Everything else in the book is masterly. The mountain setting is most beautifully conveyed—even poor modern reprints have not lost all the magic of the view above Littletown—and Mrs Tiggy-Winkle's kitchen illustrates the artist's skill in creating atmosphere by a multitude of tiny details. As for the heroine, she is one of the nicest and most complete of all the animal characters; very definitely a craftswoman—not a laundress but 'an excellent clear-starcher'—and a kindly person taking pride in her work and an interest, critical but helpful, in her customers. A feature of the book, and one that children enjoy, is the link with the previous books. When Mrs Tiggy-Winkle complains that Mrs Rabbit's red handkerchief smells of onions, every reader of **Benjamin Bunny** knows why; and at the mention of Nutkin's 'red tail-coat with no tail' and 'a much-shrunk blue jacket belonging to Peter Rabbit' the listening children exchange knowing glances. (pp. 188-89)

Benjamin Bunny had been dedicated 'to the children of Sawrey', but **The Pie and the Patty-Pan** was the first book to be set in the village which was to be Beatrix Potter's home and the scene of many of her books. (p. 190)

The Pie and the Patty-Pan has some delightful drawing, particularly in colour, and is of considerable topographical interest. As a story for children it is a little less than perfect. The plot is excessively complex, and children, understandably, have difficulty in following its course. There is considerable charm in the social conversations but these are too long for very small readers. The blemishes are many; they are perhaps a small price to pay for many homely interior scenes and enchanting glimpses of the village and its surroundings.

The red boards of **Mr Jeremy Fisher** in 1906 enclosed what is one of the author's greatest *tours de force.* Once again, and perhaps more successfully than in any other book, she shows the scale of the world of small creatures. Mr Jeremy Fisher inhabits his own world, with his own delightfully water-logged house, his boat, his friends, his appetite. Everything is in scale. Then comes disaster. He is swallowed by a trout. The great creature, head to tail filling the picture diagonally, immediately brings home the smallness of Jeremy's world. All ends well, and the reader sees him, recovered and clothed again, entertaining his distinguished friends in the most urbane fashion. The memory remains however; Mr Jeremy Fisher is a very small great man.

The book—which like so many others originated in a picture-letter—has always been a particular favourite with children, for it contains so much that is dear to them. Mr Fisher's house, for example, is a child's dream house, the house where no one scolds. 'Mr Jeremy liked getting his feet wet; nobody ever scolded him, and he never caught a cold!' His fishing expedition is a child's joy, too, for all that it rained and the day nearly ended in tragedy. His boat, his tackle, everything is as a child would see it.

The drawing is very fine. Although the predominating tone is pale green there is no monotony, and the glimpses of rain-washed Lakeland—sadly faded though they are in present day reprints—are full of enchantment. Beatrix Potter had a sound instinct when and how to clothe her characters, and she is singularly happy here. Mr Fisher himself is Pickwickian. . . . How like frogs' legs his tight pantaloons are! He has a natural elegance which makes even sharper the loss of his galoshes (which the trout ate) and the damage to that macintosh which he was providentially wearing. His friends too, are masterly. Sir Isaac Newton, in tail coat, dress trousers (a little too long) and showy black and gold waist-coat, is the aristocrat gone to seed. Mr Alderman Ptolemy Tortoise has the imposing presence of the man of affairs. It comes as a shock to realise that, chain of office apart, he is naked!

Beatrix Potter felt for this book the affection of the creator for something quite original. After all those rabbits and mice, it had been a pleasant change to enter another world and to seek out the latent beauty and humour in very different creatures. (pp. 190-92)

Beatrix had bought Hill Top in 1905 and in a sense *Tom Kitten* was the fine first fruit of this venture, for Hill Top, and particularly its garden, is the scene of this most approachable story. Some of her plots have been criticised as complicated. Here is one that is crystal-clear and based moreover on a situation painfully familiar to most children. Mrs Tabitha Twitchit (who 'owned' Hill Top, cat-fashion, in reality) has invited fine company to tea, and washes and dresses her children so that they may do her credit. When they were ready she 'unwisely turned them out into the garden, to be out of the way . . .' How many mothers have regretted just such unwisdom?. . . It is inevitable that the kittens will spoil their clothes; where Beatrix Potter surprises us is by bringing in the Puddle-Ducks who dress themselves in the kittens' clothes. The denouement has the relentless inevitability of Greek tragedy!

There is fine observation not only in the lovely pictures but also in the writing. On the rare occasions that Beatrix uses description, it is sharply pointed. The ducks 'had very small eyes and looked surprised'. *Tom Kitten* is an example of how the animals put on character with their clothes. Look at Mr

Drake Puddle-Duck, anonymously ducklike, advancing on the clothes. In the next picture, having put them on (they fitted terribly), he has suddenly acquired individuality and an urbane manner. ' "It's a very fine morning!" said Mr Drake Puddle-Duck.' Tom, too, during his toilet is pure kitten. Dressed Kate Greenaway fashion he is Kitten-plus.

The garden scenes give enduring delight in this book. There are countless details for the small child to find for himself, of flower and tree and butterfly. (pp. 193-94)

The next book, *The Tale of Jemima Puddle-Duck,* appeared in 1908. Jemima Puddle-Duck was a real inhabitant of the Hill Top farmyard, and her Red-Riding-Hood-like adventure has the ring of truth. The story indeed starts in a completely naturalistic way with a farmyard scene including one of Beatrix Potter's unsuccessful attempts at drawing humans. Artistically many of the drawings are not completely satisfactory. (p. 194)

This is essentially an open-air story. The landscape drawing is of her best, particularly the scenes when Jemima sets off over the hill in search of a safe place, free of 'superfluous' hens, for her nest. In the second of these there is an enchanting glimpse of Esthwaite Water below. There are delicate clouds in the picture where Jemima tries to fly, but these like many other fine details, have all but vanished in recent editions. From her earliest years Beatrix had been an exact painter of flowers, and the foxgloves among which the gentleman in sandy whiskers appropriately has his home are among her finest of this kind.

If *Tom Kitten* and *Jemima Puddle-Duck* represent the outdoor life of Sawrey, *The Roly-Poly Pudding* shows the interior of Hill Top most successfully. (p. 195)

Like *The Pie and the Patty-Pan* it has a long text and is illustrated in line as well as in colour. The story is a complicated and slightly macabre one, but has nevertheless been a particular favourite with children. The theme is familiar to them—who has not taken evasive action when mother wants the children in a safe place?—and the climb up the chimney and the journey through the mouse-passages are a common fantasy. It is the house that gives unity to a story which becomes a little untidy in the telling. Children who enjoy the story know the house intimately; the elegant staircase, the kitchen range by which Tom made his rash ascent and where Mrs. Twitchit told the visitor her sad story, the roof with its sturdy towerlike chimney and enchanting view over the orchards, the nooks and crannies of Samuel Whiskers' domain. There is some very fine characteristic drawing in this book. Samuel Whiskers himself, fat and indolent as any Eastern potentate, sitting with hands across his vast belly, his scrawny spouse Anna Maria—how is it that they can be at once so rat-like, so sinister (in a human sense) and so likable? (p. 196)

Ginger and Pickles is a book of Sawrey; it contains moreover a roll-call of previous characters. Among the customers at Ginger and Pickles' shop are Peter Rabbit and Benjamin Bunny, Lucinda and Jane (of the Warne dolls' house), Samuel Whiskers and Anna Maria, Jeremy Fisher, Mrs Tiggy-Winkle, Squirrel Nutkin (who seems to be stealing from a sack of nuts left, unwisely, outside), Jemima Puddle-Duck, and sundry unnamed mice. Tom Kitten, Moppet and Mittens peer through the window, and their mother Mrs Tabitha Twitchit keeps the rival establishment in the village ('She did not give credit').

The real shop in Sawrey was kept by bedridden old Mr John Taylor, to whom the book is dedicated, and who is included in the story as Mr John Dormouse who 'stayed in bed, and would say nothing but "very sorry"; which is no way of carrying on a retail business'. Was it for his sake that the story was dragged out after the departure of Ginger and Pickles, to the detriment of the artistic unity? The truth is, I fancy, that Beatrix Potter was so much in love with her village that she found it difficult to end this story of her neighbours.

Apart from the untidy ending the story is a difficult one for children, who find the economics of shopkeeping as difficult as did Ginger and Pickles. Even with the author's explanations 'credit' is a difficult concept for small children, and what do they make of bills sent 'with compts'? The book is good fun and excellent in illustration, but with many readers it must be accounted a failure. (pp. 198-99)

The Tale of Mrs Tittlemouse is the story I remember most clearly from childhood, and I have always loved it dearly. It lacks the subtlety of the best of Beatrix Potter, and there are many with more exquisite pictures, but it has the virtue of simplicity and a positive quality of writing which makes it particularly memorable. Mrs Tittlemouse is the type of all distracted housewives who cannot make others live up to their standards, but she is a character as well as a type. The setting gives little opportunity for colourful and detailed drawing, and it is interesting to see how the artist varies her pictures within the same underground scene. The drawing of the various intruders, beetles, bees, ladybirds, butterflies, spiders, is precise and dramatic. As for Mr Jackson (toad, not frog) he is one of Beatrix Potter's happiest inventions. 'Tiddly, widdly, widdly, Mrs Tittlemouse!' haunted my childhood. They were perhaps the first truly poetic words I ever knew. (pp. 199-200)

The Tale of Mr Tod (1912) shows some deterioration in detail of the illustrations but the story is of the first quality. The book is longer than most and, like *The Pie and the Patty-Pan* and *The Roly-Poly Pudding,* is illustrated with many drawings in line as well as fifteen (sixteen including the elaborate cover-label) in colour. *Mr Tod* is a suspense story worked out in considerable detail and written with a conscious craftsmanship rare in Beatrix Potter. There is nothing elsewhere in her work comparable to the building up of tension as the two rabbits follow the trail of the kidnapping Tommy Brock, and the description of night falling outside the house is of almost nightmare quality. The fight at the climax of the story is splendidly done, subtly too, as it is seen entirely from the viewpoint of the rabbits who are reluctant witnesses of the epic struggle.

The length of the story, and its complexity, make it a book for children rather older than those who have enjoyed the simple excitement of *Peter Rabbit.* (pp. 200-01)

Much of the drawing in *Mr Tod* is not very good. There is little quality in the line drawings, and in the coloured plates one often looks in vain for the exquisite detail which makes each picture in the earlier books an adventure in discovery. There is some decline in the graphic delineation of character. Mr Tod and Mr Brock are portrayed admirably in words; the former lacks, in the drawings, that urbanity which gave style to the 'sandy-whiskered gentleman' in *Jemima Puddle-Duck.* The author maligns the badger—in nature it is Tommy Brock who suffers from Mr Tod's lack of personal hygiene—and she fails to capture his homely charms. This may be deliberate;

he is the villain of this piece. Perhaps the nicest touch in the story is the portrait of old Mr Bouncer, Benjamin Bunny's father, now 'stricken in years' and no longer a terror to cats and delinquent young relatives. The poor old rabbit, living in fear of his daughter-in-law's discipline—she takes away his pipe and rabbit-tobacco—and her retributive spring-cleaning, is almost painfully real. (p. 201)

In *The Tale of Pigling Bland* Beatrix was successful in one of the most difficult tasks which come a writer's way. She made an entirely good person interesting. Pigling's brothers and sisters (except Spot) are in one degree or another wicked or mischievous; Pigling is unfailing in courtesy and understanding. In him all piggy virtues are gathered. Responsible, brave, resourceful, it is good to think that at the end of the story he is on the way to fulfilling his ambition to 'have a little garden and grow potatoes'. Aunt Pettitoes is a memorable character, too. In her address to her departing sons she rises to lyrical and dramatic heights untouched in the Beatrix Potter stories since *The Tailor of Gloucester.*

' "Now Pigling Bland, son Pigling Bland, you must go to market. Take your brother Alexander by the hand. Mind your Sunday clothes, and remember to blow your nose . . . beware of traps, hen roosts, bacon and eggs; always walk upon your hind legs".'

This is a literary tale. The drawing is uneven in quality. At its best, in the picture of Aunt Pettitoes with her greedy litter, in the cover drawing of Pigling at the cross-roads, possibly in the drawing of Pigling eating his porridge by the fire, it is full of fun and character. It seldom has the feeling for landscape of the artist's best work. The writing is nearly as good as her best elsewhere, and the plot is handled with a nice feeling for its dramatic quality. 1913 marks the end of an important stage in Beatrix Potter's life. In *Pigling Bland* she says a tender, humorous farewell to her old life. (pp. 202-03)

The books produced during the years of [Beatrix Potter's] married life are for the most part based on earlier ideas or sketches. They are never without characteristic touches of humour or sharp observation; rarely do they enrich the reader with a new experience as almost all her earlier work had done.

Appley Dapply's Nursery Rhymes—a tiny book 5″ x 4¼″— came out in 1917. The first edition is undated. The companion volume, *Cecily Parsley's Nursery Rhymes,* appeared, again without a date, in 1922. They may conveniently be considered together. It seems clear that much, if not all, of the material of these little books belongs to a much earlier date. (p. 204)

If the two books of nursery rhymes are a heterogeneous collection they contain some of the artist's best drawing, particularly in *Cecily Parsley.* The two interiors of the Pen Inn have a homely charm, and Mistress Pussy's kitchen is as beautifully observed in its harmonious detail as the best pictures of Hill Top in *The Roly-Poly Pudding.* There are some delightful touches of original humour. Who else would have thought that 'my lady' into whose chamber goosey goosey gander intruded was a sow? . . .

Johnny Town-Mouse (published, undated, in 1918), whatever its actual date of composition, belongs in manner to an early period. The concern with detail, of materials or flowers, is as absorbed, and the invention of character is as strong. (p. 205)

One fault of the book, from a child's point of view, is the failure of the pictures to match exactly with the story. Children find it difficult to understand why Timmy Willie, while staying with Johnny Town-Mouse, is shown in two consecutive pictures enjoying life in the country.

Timmy Willie is an important addition to Beatrix Potter's gallery of portraits. He is a fully realised character, interesting in his own right and an excellent foil to the sharp-witted and sharp-worded Johnny. His final portrait, with sunshade and strawberry luncheon, is delightful. (pp. 205-06)

How good is *The Fairy Caravan?* It is enormously interesting to adult admirers for the light it sheds on the writer, her background, and her idea of what was worth writing. There are in it bits and pieces of several possibly good books in her usual manner. The book is as a whole untidy, ill-proportioned, often dull. The drawings are nearly all poor. She had told Warne's of failing sight in 1928 when she had done the delicate colour-work for *Peter Rabbit's Almanac.* This is sadly evident in *The Fairy Caravan,* where she is unable to do justice to her own invention in the characters of Tuppenny, Xarifa and Paddy Pig. Paddy is in essence one of her best ideas, and his sufferings at the hands of the nurse-manquée Mary Ellen, a 'fat tabby cat with . . . an unnecessary purry manner' are richly comic. Tuppenny, the guinea-pig whose hair responded only too well to Messrs Ratton and Scratch's elixir, and who made his first appearance very early in the Beatrix Potter story, might in other circumstances have been the hero of an excellent picture-story. After the first chapter he loses his way in *The Fairy Caravan.* (pp. 206-07)

Undoubtedly the book meant much to her—there was much of herself and her Lakeland life in it—and for that reason it must mean much to those who love her work and who treasure every hint of her personality, much as she treasured every feather from her beloved Charles the rooster's tail. It is nevertheless a sad book, as every work of fading genius must be sad.

The last book written and illustrated by Beatrix Potter was *The Tale of Little Pig Robinson,* published in 1930. . . .

Despite its present format, this book does not belong to the Peter Rabbit tradition, and perhaps for that reason it has been less enjoyed than some of the others. [Margaret] Lane calls it 'very dull'. This is unkind. There is much good in the book, if none of the author's best. The story is developed from a picture-letter . . . dated 1894. It is a long story, it must be admitted, far too long, and not well planned. A disproportionate amount of space is given to Robinson's walk to market. No doubt this is the part which the author liked best, but the story demands better construction than this. For the first and only time too, Beatrix Potter took one eye off nature and wrote the fanciful stuff which adults imagine that children like. When Robinson reaches his island he finds trees growing acid drops and sweets, and bread trees which grow 'iced cakes and muffins, ready baked'. The false note jars immediately.

Altogether, for all its length, this is a light-weight story. At its best it is something which the author had already done better. Robinson is no Pigling Bland, and his aunts, although their farewell speech is an echo of Aunt Pettitoes' lack the personality of their great prototype. The walk to market, however, is described with real feeling, and the story conveys something of the confused bustle of a country market. On the whole the illustrations are poor, the country scenes lacking in telling detail, and Mrs Flock, the keeper of the wool-shop, a shadow of Tenniel's drawing. One coloured picture alone reminds one of the halcyon days: Robinson in the High Street, a nice muddle of humans and animals among the shop-fronts behind him, and in the foreground a brilliant study of a cock and hen driving a trap. This has in it a rare touch of satirical comedy. (pp. 208-09)

Beatrix Potter's last gift to her American friends was a little story written in 1943 and first published in *Horn Book* in May 1944. This was *Wag-by-Wall,* a sentimental tale about an old countrywoman whose fortunes are retrieved at the last possible moment by the fall of an owlet down her chimney which reveals a stocking full of gold. There is not much intrinsic merit in the story, except perhaps in the observation, sharp as ever, of the behaviour of the cow and the owls.

The last published work of Beatrix Potter is *The Tale of the Faithful Dove,* a story written in 1907 and published by Warne's in America in 1956 with pleasant illustrations by an unnamed artist. It tells the story of Mr Tiddler, a Rye pigeon whose wife Amabella, avoiding the attack of a hawk, takes refuge in the chimney of a deserted house. Here she is befriended by a mouse and eventually rescued with her new-born son Tobias.

The story has some charm, particularly in the conversation between the trapped pigeon and her benefactors, a mouse of great gentility whose manners and costume are out of *The Tailor of Gloucester.* One is aware all the time, however, of the lack of the author's illustrations. With them the text could have been reduced by more than half and the story sharpened. (pp. 209-10)

From **The Tailor of Gloucester,** *written and illustrated by Beatrix Potter.*

From time to time there is a campaign against the dressed-up-animal school of children's books and those who have never read them denounce Beatrix Potter's books for their cosy, sentimental view of life. Peter Rabbit, they say, does millions of pounds' worth of damage to farm crops, Samuel Whiskers destroys and spreads disease, Mr Tod is a pest. Beatrix Potter knew all this better than most of her critics. She was a practical farmer for thirty years and a realist all her life. She knew what was the probable fate of Peter Rabbit, and for what reason Pigling Bland goes to market. 'Nature, though never consciously wicked, has always been ruthless', she said, and she always shows that unsentimental detachment which marks the true countryman. She likes her own creations, but she never leaves her readers seriously in doubt about them. Mr Samuel Whiskers is an attractive rogue, but the reader learns, without distress, that Moppet and Mittens make a good living out of rat-catching. They catch 'dozens and dozens of them'. Children too are ruthless. Hearing of Tom Kitten's plight in **The Roly-Poly Pudding** for the first time, Carol White [the daughter of Dorothy Neal White, who writes about the girl's reactions to literature in *About Books for Children,*] 'seemed to have no sentimental feelings about her hero's predicament at all'. There is nothing cosy about Beatrix Potter's world. She depicts accurately 'that pleasant unchanging world of realism and romance, which in our northern clime is stiffened by hard weather, a tough ancestry, and the strength that comes from the hills.'

It is that subtle mixture of 'realism and romance' which makes the world of her imagining so vivid and memorable. 'Here', says Dorothy White about her daughter's reaction to **Tom Kitten,** 'was a comprehensive universe' and it is the completeness and the consistency of her world that children unconsciously recognise and react to. Puzzling, sometimes frightening, things happen, but they happen within the framework of a known society. It is because the picture is so consistent and sharply realised that these stories become a part of the everyday life of those families in which they are shared between one generation and another. The stories are, in a fundamental sense, true; they are also equally basically good. The morality of Beatrix Potter is profound for all that is never stated. (pp. 215-16)

An otherwise excellent teacher said to me once, 'That Beatrix Potter's a terrible woman, don't you think?' I didn't, but I knew what he meant. The mannered style and in particular the fondness for fine polysyllabic words have distressed many well-meaning people; although I have never known them to distress a child. (It should be added that most children ought first to encounter these books with the help of an adult reader.) Beatrix Potter's style is as much a part of her art as her painting or her characters; all the elements in her books are inseparable. She used words which seemed the best for the purpose. A well-known modern writer has given her opinion that had she lived today Beatrix Potter would have had to rewrite the stories. What publisher would have dared to dictate to her? And one might as well try to rewrite an Elizabethan lyric! Beatrix might quote, with sufficient humility: 'What I have written I have written.' (pp. 216-17)

She never managed to draw humans, but in animal and flower drawing, in landscape and architecture she was a master. Her landscapes, for example 'Kirkcudbright Bay' in *The Art of Beatrix Potter,* are in the main stream of the English watercolour. She disliked critics who compared her with the great names of English painting, but in her miniature way that is

where she belongs. The most accessible of her originals (**The Tailor of Gloucester**) are in the Tate Gallery—where they face somewhat incongruously the splendidly erotic 'Königsmark' drawings of Rex Whistler. In them it is possible to study her strength and her limitations: the loving appreciation of fine old furniture, the texture of cloth and china, the kindly, shrewd drawings of animals, so true to their own natures even in fancy dress, the immature drawing (after Caldecott) of the tailor, the skilled selection of detail and of aspect.

Whatever pleasure there may be in examining the exquisite detail of these books, however, it is their total effect which matters. This results from a unique combination of observation, fine craftsmanship and a rich humane sense of values. The books 'have been written out of an environment known and loved, and to which they are true', says Mrs Miller, and it is in this fundamental truth that their essential virtue lies. Mrs Dorothy White writes, 'The Potter books . . . could compose a tiny child's library. If he read nothing else, he would have experienced in them the basic human types and the basic human emotions—but more than that, what tremendous fun he would have'. It was fun that Beatrix Potter sought to give; being herself, to fun she added, almost involuntary, truth and integrity. (p. 218)

Marcus Crouch, "Beatrix Potter," in Three Bodley Head Monographs: "Henry Treece" by Margery Fisher, "C. S. Lewis" by Roger Lancelyn Green, and "Beatrix Potter" by Marcus Crouch, The Bodley Head, 1969, pp. 162-224.*

MAURICE SENDAK

Not long ago I discussed children's books with some colleagues before an audience of intense, and deeply concerned, parents. From the outset, we on the panel made an effort to qualify our position as experts on children's literature; we all felt the distastefulness of being dubbed "experts." But these parents were full of complaints about the books being published for their children, and they seemed to feel that the members of the panel should agree with their complaints and do something about them.

Their concern, as it turned out, was due in a large measure to what they considered a lack of seriousness and proper attitudes on the part of the artists and writers now creating books for children; some other day I might have a few things to say about that complaint, but today I want to tell you about another one that was registered that evening. A gentleman in the audience raised his hand and with a voice full of righteous fervor declared that no one on the panel had as yet explained how a book as simple-minded and flat as **Peter Rabbit** deserved its prestigious reputation; worst of all, it seemed to him to be "neither fact nor even fancy"! To my horror there were some murmurs of approval and even applause. I was speechless with indignation, as any true, patriotic, Potterite would surely be in a similar situation. How does one answer such a sacrilege, besides the natural reply of, "Well, if you can't see!"? But apparently there are those who can't. What, after all, has **Peter Rabbit** to do with "the problems confronting our children in today's tangled world"?

It is true that **Peter Rabbit** cannot be used as a handbook for the care and feeding of rabbits, nor can it be defined simply as a fantasy. If poor **Peter Rabbit** doesn't fit into any of these departments, what is all the noise about? At least that is the question the gentleman in the audience seemed to be asking. The answer, of course, is "nothing," if one insists on breaking a work of art into bits and pieces for the empty satisfaction of putting it into some arbitrary pigeonhole, a pastime for the unimaginative and the Philistine alike.

We working artists on the panel made very plain the pointlessness of assigning this or that book to this or that pigeonhole. And that simply added to the confusion. (p. 345)

But I don't really mind being discredited for failing to care that *Peter Rabbit* is neither fish nor fowl, for being glad, in fact, that this work of the imagination defies pigeonholing. (p. 346)

Peter Rabbit, in its perfect tinyness, transcends all arbitrary categories. It is obviously no more a fact book about the habits of rabbits than it is a purely fantastical tale. It demonstrates that fantasy cannot be completely divorced from reality; that fantasy heightens, sometimes simplifies, and contributes new insights into that reality.

I would like to point to a few details that might help make my own feelings about it clear. I will refer, of course, to both words and pictures, for in this book there is no separating them. The art of imaginatively writing *and* illustrating picture books is, at its best, a subtle art, exemplified with rare excellence and understatement in Beatrix Potter's work.

First, this gentle book vividly communicates a sense of life, and this, I believe, is achieved through an imaginative synthesis of factual and fantastical components. Amazingly, Peter is both endearing little boy and expertly drawn rabbit. In one picture he stands most unrabbit-like, crying pitifully when there seems no way out of his dilemma. In another he bounds, leaving jacket and shoes behind, in a superb rabbit bound, most unboylike, proving what we already know from her published sketchbooks: that Beatrix Potter drew from careful observation of her subject. And how she could draw!—a gift not all illustrators are endowed with.

This book, so apparently simple, smooth, straightforward, is to my eye beautifully textured and deepened by the intimate, humorous observations that Beatrix Potter makes in her pictures. Each one, with a deft and always subtle touch, expands the meaning of the words. Take the birds, for example, that emotionally mirror the action. Flopsy, Mopsy, and Cottontail, the good little bunnies, are accompanied by two chipper, pecking birds whose busyness seems to represent the perfect, down-to-earth safety of those cautious three. On the other hand, the bird observing Peter on his dangerous mission has an air of still, sorrowful speculation. He represents, I imagine, the helplessness and concern we feel for Peter. He seems ancient and philosophic in his doomlike observation of Peter's shoe under the cabbage; I can almost see him shake his head. There is nothing chirpy about him; his movements are as quiet as the deadly atmosphere that hangs over Mr. McGregor's garden. But there is no mention of birds in the text until much later, when Peter, trapped in the gooseberry net, is implored by three sparrows "to exert himself." And what a brilliant threesome! There is such beauty in the drawing and it is so convincing, that their passionate outcry is almost audible—a miniature Greek chorus. Peter does exert himself, and escapes in the nick of time from Mr. McGregor's dreadful sieve; and the three sparrows, who surely could have flown off long before, have stopped with Peter up to the last moment, and all burst off to freedom together. They are apparently the same three who, near the end of the tale, anxiously watch Peter slip underneath the gate into the safety of the wood outside the garden; three birds who, in Peter's presence,

behave almost like guiding spirits. Around Flopsy, Mopsy, and Cottontail, there are merely realistic, garden-variety birds.

I admire tremendously the poetry of Miss Potter's art as she develops so personally and so beautifully, this fantastic, realistic, truthful story. There is Peter pathetically slumped against the locked door in the wall; and there is the old mouse, her mouth too full of a large pea to answer Peter's desperate inquiry as to the way to the gate and freedom. She can only shake her head at him, and he can only cry. This tiny scene has for me the exact quality of nightmare: the sense of being trapped and frightened and finding the rest of the world (in this case, an old mouse) too busy keeping itself alive to help save you.

And last, I recall my favorite scene of the white cat, that lovely creature so prettily painted in the sylvan setting of Mr. McGregor's garden. How fortunate her back is turned to Peter, who very wisely thinks "it best to go away without speaking to her; he had heard about cats from his cousin, little Benjamin Bunny." What a typical Beatrix Potter understatement! For me this picture marvelously blends opposing images: the sweet, surface charm of the delicate, watercolor garden dominated by a deceptively charming cat, who on closer observation turns out to be fearful in color; that is, its innocent whiteness becomes a dreadful *absence* of color. The taut, twitching tail and the murderous tension of muscle under the plump, firm exterior betray the true cat nature. The poor witless goldfish in the pond at its feet haven't a chance.

I have tried, and I hope without too much distortion, to suggest the kind of imaginative blend of fact and fantasy that, integrated and working together harmoniously, create for me the aliveness of *Peter Rabbit.* Fantasy, rooted in the living fact: here, the fact of family, of fun, of danger and fear; of the evanescence of life; and finally, of safety, of mother and love. Altogether the book possesses, on no matter how miniature a scale, a wonderful sense of life, and isn't that the ultimate value of any work of art? It transcends all petty theories and phoney categorizings. It is a standard that should be applied to every book for the young, and no book can claim the distinction of art without it. *Peter Rabbit,* for all its gentle tinyness, loudly proclaims that no story is worth the writing, no picture worth the making, if it is not a work of real imagination. It reminds us that genuine art, that is, art animated with the sense of life, adds to our own sense of life and actively helps us to a better understanding of this world and others—the others being perhaps our own inner worlds. (pp. 346-48)

Maurice Sendak, "The Aliveness of Peter Rabbit," in Wilson Library Bulletin, *Vol. 40, No. 4, December, 1965, pp. 345-48.*

RUMER GODDEN

[Isn't Beatrix Potter] too innocent for our modern world? Does the charm work on the children of 1966 as it worked on those of 1902?

The answer, I think, is evident. Most houses have one or two classics for children on their bookshelves: *Alice in Wonderland, Treasure Island, The Water Babies,* which are taken out, read and put back, often re-read. I should guess that few present the tattered appearance a Beatrix Potter book soon gets; her first editions are rare because her books are read until they are worn out. Children have taught themselves to read by them; they are learned by heart, and 3 or 4-year-olds pounce on the reader-aloud if one word is left out or changed. (p. 4)

As reader, listener, recital giver, broadcaster, teacher, aunt, mother, grandmother and godmother, I have never known Beatrix Potter to fail with a child who is a real child. Not all children are real children these days: they are so assailed by commercial products, comics, cheap books, television, and they live such an adult life, that some have become sophisticated into imitation grown-ups, which is sad, because "sophisticated" means alloyed, spoiled.

Writing about Beatrix Potter makes one examine the meanings of words because she was so exact in hers; when I spoke of her charm I did not mean her work was charming in the simple sense but in the sense of a spell; "charm," not "magic," because magic suggests whimsy which is far removed from her work. There is a quality in these books, something extra beyond the writing and painting itself, which makes them, as one perceptive critic wrote, "miniature classics of both art and literature, in fact the only real and outstanding classics for small children." This may seem an astonishing claim. There must, one thinks, be others. The "Winnie the Pooh" series? But A. A. Milne does not qualify for "both art and literature"—besides, for me, he always wrote with one eye on the grown-ups. Some other animal series? By comparison they all seem overdone. The claim is true: no one else has equaled Beatrix Potter.

To eyes and tastes that have been corrupted by the glossy slickness and marshmallow sweetness of the animated cartoon, the distorted illustrations and puerile texts of some of the so prevalent Beginning Books, this high rating will be difficult to understand. Such eyes, seeing the soft pastel of the Potter greens, grays and sepias, will dismiss her as "old-fashioned." One guesses they would have much the same reaction to a Constable, or a Samuel Palmer, artists with whom Beatrix Potter has been compared—though she said, "Absolute bosh. Utter nonsense," when told this.

Minds that think books for children should be told in a simple, limited vocabulary, will be puzzled too; Beatrix Potter used difficult words; "I am worn to a ravelling," says the Tailor of Gloucester, while the famous lettuces that were "soporific" occurs in *The Tale of the Flopsy Bunnies.* Her publishers wanted her to change "soporific" but Beatrix Potter was adamant; she knew that children revel in new words, long words, euphonious words. More puzzled are those people who think strong drama, life, birth, death, the harsh realities of life, should be kept out of children's reading, whereas Beatrix Potter could even be called a crime writer on her small scale; her thimbleful of suspense is real suspense. Other critics object that she isn't funny. As a matter of fact she is, but her humor, as Margaret Lane says in her biography, is "of a very ironical and loving kind." Small children, on the whole, are grave and like gravity; to make them laugh is not necessarily to capture their hearts.

"And she is sentimental," people will say. "Look at her names: Flopsy, Mopsy, Cottontail, Tittlemouse." This from a generation that accepts Dopey, Sleepy, Happy, Sneezy! Anyone who is truthful cannot be sentimental and Beatrix Potter's stories, however fantastical, are firmly founded on truth: a "tittle" is the smallest part of anything, a minute amount. What better name for a miniscule mouse? Flopsy is a wholly suitable name for a young rabbit whose ears do flop unless pricked erect by danger. Perhaps some of these critics,

as with many people brought up in our cities, have never seen a rabbit, and could not recognize one if they did—perhaps their idea of a rabbit is a blue or pink cartoon creature with exaggerated hind legs and whiskers and two outsize front teeth—whereas baby rabbits look exactly like the illustrations in *Peter Rabbit* or *Benjamin Bunny,* soft and endearing until picked up, when they show the surprising life and kick that are in the Beatrix Potter animals. The latter, no matter what their adventures, are real animals—not grotesques, as in most books that followed her.

She has such hundreds of imitators that it is difficult for us to realize that she was original, creating a whole new province of the animal world; through others, it has become not a world of animals but animal-humans doing human things with human thoughts. (pp. 4-5)

Beatrix Potter could never draw or paint anything from imagination—which is why, on a visit to Sawrey, so much springs to life; in Hill Top is the authentic cooking range with its ominous oven of the Roly Poly Pudding; the garden of Tom Kitten is there; the farmyard of Jemima Puddleduck. . . . Nor could Beatrix Potter draw humans; Mr. McGregor for instance is always in the far distance. One suspects she did not look at humans as deeply as she looked at animals; indeed it seems she saw people as animals rather than animals as people, a subtle distinction. "How amusing Aunt Harriet is," she writes in her journal. "More like a weasel than ever." The truth of her animals comes through their clothes and occupations. Under the prettiness of kittens and rabbits, of ducks and mice, is this reality that does not mince matters; Beatrix Potter knew that humans prey on animals, animals prey on one another and through all the books runs what Margaret Lane calls "a seam of toughness."

It is this that gives the best books their drama: Peter Rabbit's tenseness and uneasiness in Mr. McGregor's garden run all through *Benjamin Bunny;* the cat in *Johnny Town-Mouse* and *Two Bad Mice* stalks through the books. And is there a more sinister character in literature than the foxy Mr. Tod? How can anyone call Beatrix Potter sentimental who has read the passage in *The Tale of Mr. Tod,* in which Peter and Benjamin see through the window of Mr. Tod's house the preparations for that rabbit-pie dinner: "an immense empty pie-dish of blue willow pattern, a large carving knife and fork, and a chopper," while the oven door shook because of the struggles of the baby rabbits shut inside?

This all sounds horrifying yet Beatrix Potter is absolutely to be trusted; she always knew when to stop and knew too, that most children like to be harrowed as long as the story turns out well in the end, as hers invariably do. . . . (p. 5)

Perhaps the best of all Beatrix Potter books is *The Tailor of Gloucester.* Its spell is complete, a spell compounded of the old tailor's fever dream, the ancient city with its gables and cobbles and the moonlit Christmas Eve into which the legend of the animals talking at midnight comes like a peal of bells; the words are so skillful that the whole book has a rhythm of rustling and scampering, of tapping and little voices laughing, all light as mouse feet, maddening Simpkin the cat but coming to the old tailor's rescue. This is perhaps the most subtle children's book ever written, yet it is crystal clear. It is as exquisitely worked as the rare embroideries that Beatrix Potter studied in the Victoria and Albert Museum and painted into the Lord Mayor's waistcoat; the original water colors for *The Tailor of Gloucester* are so fine their full beauty cannot be seen without a magnifying glass.

Probably Beatrix Potter, as a perfectionist, was the first author and artist to treat children's books with the respect due to literature and art; to visit museums for them, research, study, consult, no detail being too small, no source too far. "The grammar does not seem right," she wrote anxiously of Mrs. Tiggy-winkle's song, to Norman Warne, her publisher—and Mrs. Tiggy-winkle was not to be just a washerwoman: "She exorcises spot or stain, like Lady Macbeth." Plainly her heart, mind and soul went into her books, the whole of her love, and it is significant that when, at 47, she married a lakeland solicitor and escaped from Bolton Gardens altogether, settling into a rich, fulfilled married and farmer's life, there were no more books of the old calibre.

The word "love" has crept in a great deal in this essay but perhaps it is the love that explains the potency of these small books; they were not written for money nor for fame—in fact, fame was the last thing Miss Potter courted or expected. They were not even written for love of children: though *Peter Rabbit* began as a letter to a little boy, there were few children in Beatrix Potter's life, and one guesses that on the surface she was a little stiff with them; "on the surface" because the inner Beatrix Potter knew exactly what they liked.

It was love of work itself, of little creatures and their animal natures, of their country background and of simple homelike things. Beatrix Potter loved flagged floors, scrubbed tables, a polished oven door, rag rugs; with her artist's eye for details, she delighted in the shape of a saucepan or a flat iron, a pattern of sprigged calico, the color of a pink and white pie dish. Children can share in this: hers was also the kind of love that is immensely reassuring to children, not sentimental but sensible, authoritative, knowledgeable, a love with wide open eyes; for 64 years, amply and spontaneously, children have given it back to her. (pp. 5, 45)

> Rumer Godden, "From Beatrix with Love," in The
> New York Times Book Review, *May 8, 1966, pp.*
> *4-5, 45.*

BETTINA HÜRLIMANN

What is the reason for the winning charm of [Beatrix Potter's] tiny books? There are many people who can recount witty or thrilling tales when they sit across the room from us, but fail completely in putting them down on paper just because they miss their live audience. With Beatrix Potter, however, one has the feeling that with every stroke of the pen or the paint-brush, with every word she writes, she sees her audience in front of her and translates for it her affection for the world of small animals. This is something which we find again and again—with *Alice in Wonderland,* with Hoffmann's books and with many others—it is a factor which is decisive in the creation of books for children. Nevertheless, it is a mistake to believe that mere contact with an audience is an automatic recipe for success—this is an error which has led to the printing of a vast deal of mediocre products. Other factors must also play their part. With the creator of *Peter Rabbit, Samuel Whiskers, Tom Kitten, Johnny Town-Mouse, Mrs. Tiggy-Winkle,* and all the rest, the other factor was above all her intimate knowledge of small animals. Even though Peter Rabbit wears a blue jacket with silver buttons, and Mrs. Tiggy-Winkle, the hedgehog, a starched apron, Beatrix Potter still knows what they look like underneath. And even though these animals may behave in a human fashion the artist knows all about their real lives. At the end of almost every one of these classic stories the animals end up without their disguise—ducks, hedgehogs, mice, rabbits, all of them. Peter Rabbit lies tired out and naked on the floor of his burrow, while his little coat and shoes serve Mr. McGregor as a scarecrow. He has become a small, helpless creature. And Mrs. Hedgehog, however human she may appear in her little underground kitchen busy with her flat-iron, is at the end of the book only a tiny, unclad, prickly beast disappearing from Lucy's sight up the hill.

In the final analysis it is the real animals which Beatrix Potter knows and loves and sets before children in a charming but very superficial disguise. There is nothing in this of the old symbolic animal fables. However old-fashioned she may be thought today, Beatrix Potter is very much of our own times and devoted to life in the real world. (p. 210)

> *Bettina Hürlimann, "Picture-Books in the Twentieth Century," in her* Three Centuries of Children's Books in Europe, *edited and translated by Brian W. Alderson, Oxford University Press, London, 1967, pp. 201-45.*

MARGARET LANE

Set in the midst of her long life, [Beatrix Potter's] charming creative period lasted for little more than ten years; at the end of that time her inner vision seemed to undergo a change, or her own life began to absorb her emotions, so that the magic evaporated. The writing of her stories had always been inseparable from their illustration; the flavour of the books is tasted equally and indistinguishably in pictures and text; and it is a curious fact that from the moment when her eyes began to fail and she lost her power of fine drawing, her stories lost their shape, their emotional concentration, and their poetry.

In those ten years or more, however, of exquisite achievement she had produced a series of little works impossible to imitate, and without any rival in the field of children's literature. By the end of her life, two generations of children had already been brought up on them, had their imaginations first stirred, their sense of beauty and humour first awakened by these fantasies of her own childhood transformed into works of art. . . . What is the secret of her excellence? Why are the Beatrix Potter books—some of them after sixty years of familiarity—still incomparably the favourites of the nursery, and as well known in their details to at least two generations of adults as traditional fairy tales?

The answer is that most satisfying of all possible answers—that they are good art. A high level of execution, founded partly on a naturalist's loving observation of animal life, partly on an imaginative awareness of its character, lifts her work into a class of its own among children's books. Her watercolours have the beauty and fidelity one might expect in some luxuriously produced set of volumes on natural history, and some of them (the illustrations of *Squirrel Nutkin* are a case in point) might almost be admired without remark in such a context; until some sly detail, faithful to squirrel character but not to squirrel habit, arrests the eye, and we find ourselves in a world where squirrels gather nuts into little sacks, play marbles with oak-apples on a level beech-stump, and cross the breadth of Derwentwater on rafts, using their tails for sails.

This fidelity to animal character is the very strength and sinew of her work. There is nothing grotesque or misleading,

From The Tale of Squirrel Nutkin, *written and illustrated by Beatrix Potter.*

however fabulous. All her little hedgerow, farmyard and wainscot animals are conceived with *imaginative* truth, and though they are shrewdly humanized, and their stories told throughout in human terms, there is, imaginatively speaking, not a word of falsehood. We close the books, knowing more about animal and human nature than we did before.

Conveying truth by means of fantasy, enlarging our perception of life by poetic means, is one of the highest functions of art, and it is not extravagant to say that in her small and special sphere Beatrix Potter performed it. She understood and loved the little animals that she drew and painted, and perceiving—perhaps even without being aware, for her response to imaginative stimulus was most innocent and direct—perceiving that invisible thread of sympathy which runs through the whole animal creation, including man, she interpreted her animals in human terms. Displayed in the trappings of their human counterparts, they reveal their own true natures by oblique methods, and we ever after know more about them from having observed their behaviour in significant disguise. (pp. 115-17)

Even the clothes in which her animals are so unerringly dressed contribute something, by however improbable a route, to our imaginative understanding of their characters. Mrs. Tiggy-Winkle wears a print gown, a striped petticoat and an apron—of course! one almost exclaims, what else would you expect?—Mr. Jeremy Fisher is dressed, apart from his mackintosh and galoshes, not unlike Mr. Pickwick, and the result is most suitable; and Mr. Tod, as one would predict of that vindictive and sandy-whiskered person, is something of a dandy. It is most interesting, too, to observe those situations in which the animals appear without their clothes: it is never done by accident, but always to stress and

as it were recall their true natures—Mrs. Tiggy-Winkle vanishing among the bracken at the end of the story; Jemima Puddle-Duck without her ridiculous bonnet and shawl when she has achieved the dignity of motherhood; most telling of all, the sandy-whiskered gentleman, unclothed, uncivilized, pure fox at last, turning over Jemima's eggs in the wood-shed.

Beatrix Potter's great sense of animal beauty, and the imaginative truthfulness of her approach, saved her from that element of the grotesque which infects nearly all nursery books about animal characters. (It is, of course, easier to caricature an animal than to draw it beautifully, which perhaps accounts for the great preponderance of ugliness and sham naïveté in children's books.) She knew it was quite unnecessary to distort animals and make them 'funny' in order to touch the imagination of a child. On the contrary, it was their very beauty, and the seriousness and reality of their little world, which had held her entranced through the long summer holidays of her own childhood, and which was the very basis of their appeal. There was humour enough, of a very delicate, ironical and loving description, in their characters and adventures, without resorting to comicality or any of the vulgar expedients by which children are nowadays amused on a commercial scale. (pp. 117-18)

One is not consciously aware of these things in childhood: response to the books is simple and direct, and it is not for many years that one realizes how very deeply they have sunk in, what a lasting little pattern they have imprinted at the back of the mind. Beatrix Potter's own emotional response to certain things in childhood has been most subtly and beautifully conveyed—the family lives that go on in burrows and holes, the natural detail of hedge and ditch and kitchen garden, the revelation of beauty and dewy freshness in the northern countryside, the homeliness of its farm kitchens, the cool smell of dairies, the fragrance of baking days—they are all now a part of our own vision. She has made her books, like lyrics, out of emotional experience, and it is this real feeling under the gentle playfulness of the fantasy that strikes so directly home. (pp. 118-19)

There is another element in Beatrix Potter's books which it is difficult to find elsewhere in children's literature: the deeply felt beauty of the countryside. The lakes, the fells, the stone walls and white-washed farms that she loved are drawn, on their modest scale, almost with the emotional feeling of a Constable: and the freshness and poetry of some of her little pictures (Mrs. Flopsy Bunny, for instance, coming hesitantly across the field and wondering 'where everybody was', or the squirrels fishing in the lake at evening and carrying their tribute of minnows through the wood) raises her to a humble but secure place in the British School. (p. 121)

Natural beauty; innocence; 'dewy freshness'; these are all elements of Beatrix Potter's work, but they are not the whole. Designed as it is for the very young, there is nevertheless nothing namby-pamby about it. It is completely free from any touch of sentimentality. An unstressed faintly ironical humour is alive on every page, and running below the surface of each narrative is a seam of something which can only be described as *toughness*. Beatrix Potter was deeply aware of the realities of nature; the earth and its seasons, the rhythms of sowing and harvest, of life and death, were her deepest source of emotional life and spiritual strength; and the laws of nature (especially those of pursuit and prey, with which the life of most wild animals is endlessly concerned) are nowhere softened or sentimentalized in any of her stories. Her rabbits tremble with good reason at the thought of Mrs. McGregor and her pie-dish, for that, after all, has been the end of their father. Mr. Tod is a figure of real terror, not only to innocent Jemima Puddle-Duck, who at first is too simple to realize what he is about, but to all the small defenceless creatures of farmyard and wood. (p. 124)

The pursuit and prey theme runs undisguised through many of the tales. Indeed, only from the purely 'domestic' stories— *Two Bad Mice, Mrs. Tiggy-Winkle, Mrs. Tittlemouse, Tom Kitten, The Pie and the Patty-Pan,* is it entirely absent. (p. 125)

In dwelling on this theme Beatrix Potter was following, more or less consciously, the simple traditional pattern of the fairy tale. Instead of giants and ogres and bad fairies, there are Mr. Tod and Samuel Whiskers to beware of. The results of too great innocence or rashness, in fairy tales or Beatrix Potter's stories, are much the same. The stories point no moral, unless it be that the helpless and the simple, if they are not very careful, may make a meal for somebody else; and *Jemima Puddle-Duck,* as she was fond of pointing out, is really *Little Red-Riding-Hood* re-told. Yet, though Tom Kitten is encased in suet crust and feels the rolling-pin, though the shadow of the pie-dish falls across the rabbits' lives, there are no tragedies. Children, as Beatrix Potter well understood, are willing to be harrowed with suspense, but not with unhappy endings; and our feelings are nowhere wantonly exacerbated. (p. 126)

The quality which most, in the last analysis, distinguishes Beatrix Potter among children's writers (and indeed distinguishes her in a much wider sphere) is her ability to create a special world and fill it with original characters who 'come alive'. 'It does not matter,' wrote Lord David Cecil in *Early Victorian Novelists,* 'that Dickens' world is not lifelike; it is alive'; and with Beatrix Potter, as with all artists who are genuinely creative, what really matters is the presence or absence of that vital spark. The life in her animal characters is so irrepressible that there are moments, even in reading her letters, when one is willingly convinced that she believed in them herself; that she *saw* the rat ever after as Samuel Whiskers, and the badger as Tommy Brock; and was more than half in earnest when she wrote 'Besides—*I* have seen that door into the back of the hill called Cat Bells—and besides *I* am very well acquainted with dear Mrs. Tiggy-Winkle!' She was able, at all events, in letters to children to give later news of her characters than had appeared in the books—a kindness which authors rarely perform for their readers, and which must, in a sense, have been the fruit of her imaginative conviction. (pp. 126-27)

[After] her death there was found among her papers a letter from Francis, her cousin Caroline Clark's little boy, the 'William Francis of Ulva' to whom, in 1912, *The Tale of Mr. Tod* had been dedicated.

> My dear Cousen B.,
>
> Thank you very much for the nice little book. Do you like Timmie Willie—I don't. I and my dog Jack are always killing him. We have great mouse hunts. One day we had a great hunting: one day I dug and dug till I got a mouse nest—and Jack swooled two mice like pills. We have Samule Whiskers all over the house: he ran over my hanktuhes in the landrey one day, and made them very dirty.

Complete belief in the reality of Samuel Whiskers, and in his presence in the laundry of a Highland house, is no special feat

in the imagination of a child. But to give Samuel Whiskers, in the first place, such compelling life, required a deep imaginative conviction in his inventor; and that quality, in common with all other first-rate and sincere artists, Beatrix Potter possessed, and to an eminent degree. 'No one,' wrote Dickens in the preface to *David Copperfield,* 'can ever believe this Narrative in the reading more than I believed it in the writing.' It is a condition of success with the novelist, as with any creator of character. It is the clue to the living pulse of Mr. Micawber; it is no less the secret of Tom Kitten. (p. 128)

> *Margaret Lane, in her* The Tale of Beatrix Potter: A Biography, *revised edition, Frederick Warne & Co. Ltd., 1968, 173 p.*

ELIZABETH NESBITT

It is difficult to capture the excellence and unique charm of Beatrix Potter's writing. The greatness of her books lies chiefly in a complete harmony of story expression and illustration. To analyze is to run the risk of shattering the totality of impression and of making commonplace the little world she created. If the plots of her stories were summarized, they might seem to be similar to many other shallow and footless stories written for little children. (p. 323)

Possibly the best way to attempt a critical evaluation is from the viewpoint of her contribution to literature for little children. The little books are perfect picture-story books, with complete harmony between picture and story, perfect placement of pictures, and detail in illustration which literally illustrates. It is difficult to contemplate what might have been had Beatrix Potter not had the twin talents of writing and drawing. There is, in her illustrations, an enhancement of the spirit of the story, its characters, its action, its humor, its pathos, set always against a background of unobtrusive beauty. From the beginning, any child can sense the mood of Peter Rabbit, as he stands with his back toward his mother and sisters, a stubborn, withdrawn look on his face. Many a child has wept over the pathos of the frightened little rabbit, with one foot over the other, one paw pressed against his mouth, the other against the locked door, under which "there was no room for a fat little rabbit to squeeze." And any child can chuckle sympathetically and with relief, over the Peter Rabbit, safe at home, but hiding under the bedcovers, only his ears showing, as his mother stands over him with a dose of camomile tea.

The manner in which she manages to humanize her animals, and still keep them animals, is mysterious and intriguing, and is the secret of that rare combination of reality and fantasy which gives her work so deeply genuine a quality and sets it apart from inferior works. With her, there is no caricature, no silly exaggeration, no vulgarity. Instead there is humor and pathos and a simple naturalness, which causes one to accept without question. Though they may be dressed in clothes, and performing human functions, her animals remain true to themselves and therefore convincing. Mrs. Tittlemouse, asleep in her chair, is the absolute exemplification of the exhausted and frustrated housewife, and still she remains mouse. The fidelity to detail of animal appearance and of scenes lends the pictures extraordinary authenticity and beauty—the woodland glade in *The Tale of Squirrel Nutkin,* with Nutkin, running just as squirrels do, the vista to be seen from the chimney of Tom Kitten's house, the lovely snowy street scenes in *The Tailor of Gloucester* are the finest art. Yet this background of beauty is never allowed to intrude upon the story quality of the pictures. Remaining background, it heightens the reality of the story, as do the lifelike interiors of cottages and farmhouses and shops—the fireplace in *The Roly-Poly Pudding* (1908), a replica of Beatrix Potter's own fireplace at Hill Top Farm, the cupboards and dressers, the old china. A child may sense, without conscious realization, the emotional quality such pictures contain, the pride, the serenity, and security imparted by loved, accustomed, prized possessions.

The stories themselves are swift-paced, action-full, chary of description. Always there is the comfortingly familiar, completely informing beginning, and the ear-appealing sounds of the proper names. (pp. 324-25)

Equally satisfying are the endings of the stories, with their finality and security, for while a small child wants suspense, he will not tolerate tragedy at the end.

The animals are little, appealing, familiar animals, living in a world of their own. Each animal lives in just the right kind of home for him. Mrs. Tittlemouse in a "mossy bank under a hedge"; the four little rabbits in a sandbank under the root of a very big fir tree; Mrs. Tiggy-winkle in a hill with a door that opened on a "nice clean kitchen with a flagged floor and wooden beams, just like any other farm kitchen"; Tom Kitten and his family in a real house, as befits a household pet. To the little child, whose instinct for personification is strong and who must necessarily interpret everything in terms of his own experience, it is entirely credible that animals should live so, and entirely acceptable that familiar surroundings and incidents of everyday life should be shared by animals. While Beatrix Potter does not hesitate to introduce hazard and danger and near tragedy, her books are permeated with a feeling of intimacy and coziness and of the pleasant life.

Her characters are uninvolved, one-type characters, consistently true in speech and deed to themselves. Mrs. Tittlemouse is a "most terribly tidy particular little mouse, always sweeping and dusting the soft sandy floors." Mrs. Tabitha Twitchit is an "anxious parent"; a wealth of characterization is in those two words. Peter Rabbit and Benjamin Bunny and Squirrel Nutkin are small rebels—set in contrast to their more docile and amenable companions. The events of the story develop naturally from the nature of the primary character.

Brief and toned-down for the little child as the books are, still there is no inanity, that frequent curse of writing for the very young. Common sense and shrewd humor give them strength; action and genuine adventure—even danger—give them suspense; sentiment without mawkishness gives them sincerity of emotional quality; the manner of their telling puts upon them the seal of imaginative truth. Beatrix Potter knew well that realism may be sound without being literal, and that truth goes beyond mere truth to fact.

In spite of the brevity of the stories, there is a plentitude of the right kind of detail, the kind of detail which is so eminently satisfying because it tells all and no more than one wants to know. It is concrete, specific, selective, and often imbued with an imaginative quality which gives vividness and a sudden sense of actuality. In Mrs. Tiggy-winkle's kitchen there is a "nice, hot singey smell," a phrase which produces an immediate sense impression so clear, so reminiscent as to transport the reader, or the hearer, immediately to the scene. (pp. 325-26)

Much of the beauty of *The Tailor of Gloucester* lies in its descriptive detail. "One bitter cold day near Christmas-time, the tailor began to make a coat (a coat of cherry-coloured corded silk embroidered with pansies and roses) and a cream-coloured satin waistcoat (trimmed with gauze and green worsted chenille). . . . There were twelve pieces for the coat and four pieces for the waistcoat; and there were pocket-flaps and cuffs and buttons, all in order. For the lining of the coat there was fine yellow taffeta, and for the buttonholes of the waistcoat there was cherry-coloured twist. . . . There were roses and pansies upon the facings of the coat; and the waistcoat was worked with poppies and corn-flowers."

Beatrix Potter's style is permanent and vital proof of the fact that literature for little children need not lack the stimulation of good, sound, and beautiful English prose. She herself has implied that she wrote and rewrote, tried out her writing with children, and then wrote again. But nowhere is there evidence of selfconsciousness or of writing down. There is the dignity of simplicity, the music of well-chosen words, the lilt of rhythm. (p. 326)

Pervading style and story is the feeling of deep love for the English countryside, not only for its physical beauty, but also for its spirit and tradition. So much is this aspect a part of the whole, so integrated is it with plot and style, that one may search almost in vain for descriptions of garden and hill and meadow. Only in *The Fairy Caravan* do such descriptions appear. Yet it is this quality of identification of story with a specific and real country which, as much as any other quality, places Beatrix Potter as a writer in the finest tradition of English prose.

The imaginative power that never degenerates into trivial fancy, the creativeness that never deteriorates into mere inventiveness, the ability to create plot and to infuse characters with life, the mastery of a simple and pure style, the knowledge of a small child's world—all these are hers. But there is something more elusive, less easy to define, which gives to her permanent distinction, and which, for more than fifty years, has called forth the warm response which small children lavish in such great measure upon books which are truly theirs. In all her writing, there is a convincingness, an effect of belief in her own story. In part, this is due to her almost matter-of-fact presentation, refreshing as a drink of cool water when contrasted with the preciousness, the over-elaboration and straining for effect characteristic of less able writers of fantasy. But there is something deeper and more significant here; underlining her stories are the eternal verities of life—love of home and countryside, the dignity of work, the decency of simple, average beings, the mingled humor and pathos of existence. It is the reflection of these imperishable truths which makes the tales of Beatrix Potter classics in miniature. (p. 327)

Elizabeth Nesbitt, "Classics in Miniature," in A Critical History of Children's Literature *by Cornelia Meigs and others, edited by Cornelia Meigs, revised edition, Macmillan Publishing Company, 1969, pp. 318-27.*

ALISON LURIE

Evidently there is something attractive to children about the very idea of animals, especially the sort we meet in Beatrix Potter's books: rabbits, mice, kittens, squirrels. For nearly 75 years young children have loved her books; they seem to feel comfortable with her characters, even akin to them somehow. And, after all, it is not so long since they too were inarticulate, instinctive small creatures, with simple animal needs and pleasures. They still know what it feels like to steal food when larger people's backs are turned, as Peter Rabbit does, or to playfully disorder an older child's dolls' house as the Two Bad Mice.

One special attraction of Beatrix Potter is that she portrays the world from a mouse's—or rabbit's—or small child's eye-view. The vantage point in her exquisite watercolors varies from a few inches to a few feet from the ground, like that of a toddler. And everything is in close-up: a cabbage leaf or a painted china cup or a spool of red thread are seen with the short-range clarity of focus which is physiologically possible for most of us only in early childhood.

Another attractive feature of these books, for a child, is that they do not attempt to point a moral. Peter loses his jacket and shoes in Mr. McGregor's garden, but a few books later he is back again looking for lettuce and onions with his cousin Benjamin Bunny, quite unrepentant. The author's sympathy and interest are evidently with Peter and Benjamin, and with the impertinent, reckless Squirrel Nutkin; and not with the other timid, good squirrels or with obedient, dull little Flopsy, Mopsy, and Cotton-tail. (p. 38)

> *Alison Lurie, "Beatrix Potter in Paper," in* The New York Times Book Review, *December 8, 1974, pp. 38-9.*

ALISON LURIE

When I first came across the Peter Rabbit books, I had no idea that Beatrix Potter was a grownup woman. Confusing her, I think, with the 8-year-old Beatrice whom (I had been told) a famous Italian writer once fell in love with on a bridge—a print illustrating this event belonged to my piano teacher—I thought of Beatrix Potter as a little girl. Certainly she was small enough to look at hollyhocks and tables and big dogs from below; or to see in the pattern of moss on an old stump the brilliant colors, fine close detail, and magic significance that only a child's eye can observe.

It was the illustrations that fascinated me; the stories, with their conventional nursery morality and air of breathless surprise at ordinary events, I did not care for—partly because I read just the early ones. It was only much later that I discovered the later tales of *Pigling Bland* and *Little Pig Robinson,* the two Potter heroes who manage to escape from the domestic scene into a wider and more exciting world, as she herself finally did.

> *Alison Lurie, in an excerpt in* The New York Times Book Review, *May 1, 1977, p. 25.*

JOHN UPDIKE

I read *Peter Rabbit* and its French translation *Pierre Lapin* to each of my four children in their season, but the book seems to have entered my pool of primal images at an earlier date; in some sense I have been gazing through those curious pickets at Mr. McGregor and then dodging his flowerpot since I was born. The beautiful softness of the drawings does not ultimately hide the earnestness of the adventure. The thrilling English text is even better in French, where Peter's sisters become the highly seductive (as I recall) "Flopsaut, Mopsaut, et Queue de Coton." This potent little book has made its influence felt in every burrow of our national life—

the Playboy dress code, the Hare Krishna movement, my own lapine novels, etc.

> *John Updike, in an excerpt in* The New York Times Book Review, *May 1, 1977, p. 25.*

WILLIAM STEIG

The work of Beatrix Potter first turned up in our house in 1917. My young brother, Arthur, the poet, then 3, knew *The Tale of Peter Rabbit* so well he could pretend he was reading it. A generation later my three children were enjoying Potter's books. There have always been a few around the house, sometimes made off with, sometimes replaced. Her simple stories and beautiful drawings are ideal fare for the very young. Their vision, their drama, their emotion seem to come out of a child's own innocent experience. In a strange way they are true to life. They remind me of haiku—nothing to them, yet so hard to do.

> *William Steig, in an excerpt in* The New York Times Book Review, *May 1, 1977, p. 38.*

P. L. TRAVERS

[Beatrix Potter] is one of the great archangels of literature. So much of my childhood—its deeps and terrors as well as its heights and joys—was locked up in her that when she died in 1943, I was amazed to learn that she had actually been alive. I could have gone and knelt at her gate and now it was too late. If one can bless an archangel then, indeed, she is blest.

> *P. L. Travers, in an excerpt in* The New York Times Book Review, *May 1, 1977, p. 38.*

ROGER SALE

People often say they love, or loved, this or that children's book, when in fact they don't, or didn't, but no one seems ever to be lying when they say they love [the books of Beatrix Potter. She] had a life that is hard to understand, but it is as clear as the water of mountain streams compared with the mystery of her achievement.

It has to do with smallness, one knows that, with the way Potter uses smallness to force concentration from her reader. The page is important, even the large amount of white blank space on many pages is important, because that too forces us to concentrate. But somehow these matters are difficult to speak of directly, so let me begin by quoting some sentences from a few of her major books, sentences that are clearly typical and distinctive enough even out of context. Then, as we go back and look at her life and her early work, we can keep in mind and ear the hard, bright, solemnly playful prose:

> Peter was most dreadfully frightened; he rushed all over the garden, for he had forgotten the way back to the gate.

> He lost one of his shoes among the cabbages, and the other shoe amongst the potatoes.
>
> **[*Peter Rabbit*]**

> As there was always no money, Ginger and Pickles were obliged to eat their own goods.

> Pickles ate biscuits and Ginger ate a dried haddock.

> They ate them by candle-light after the shop was closed.

[Ginger & Pickles]

Moppet and Mittens have grown up into very good rat-catchers.

They go out rat-catching in the village, and they find plenty of employment. They charge so much a dozen, and earn their living very comfortably.

[The Roly-Poly Pudding]

It is so apparently unremarkable, this writing, yet everyone who knows Potter knows that yes, that's it, the unmistakable Potter sound. It will take, however, many more words than are in one of her books to say how that prose came to be hers, as recognizable as Jane Austen or Dickens, and in its way every bit as good. In the process of discovering how she came to write as she did, we should also be able to learn about the kind of artist she is, and why smallness is so important to both the writing and the pictures. (pp. 127-28)

Beatrix Potter's journal, written between the ages of sixteen and thirty-one, could serve as a major exhibit in any demonstration of the ravages of the lives of the idle bourgeois late Victorian rich. Although it has no secrets to tell and never had to be hidden from anyone, Potter wrote it in a code she invented, not a particularly difficult or elaborate one, but a full written language nonetheless. The handwriting ranges from tiny to minuscule; there are sheets of six-inch by eight-inch paper that have 1,500 words on them. (p. 130)

After reading it, one is more inclined to think the code was designed not to hide anything but to give her something difficult to do. Since there is no reason to believe that any Potters ever laughed or enjoyed doing something together, we can see the journal as her fun, or relief. That she seldom wrote about anything personal probably means she had little personal to say; her feelings and desires were never consulted by others,

From The Tale of Benjamin Bunny, *written and illustrated by Beatrix Potter.*

so she seems to have suppressed or ignored them herself, and she does this so well, and so completely, that after a while one is not aware as one reads of any deep restraint being imposed. She does not know what life means, does not feel sorrow, and she is aware of the lack, but does not find it worth carrying on about. (pp. 132-33)

The one subject in the *Journal* where Potter always expresses her own taste and is never secondhand in her judgments is art, painting and drawing, her own and that of others. . . . (p. 133)

If Potter was lucky in anything, it was that the kind of art she wanted to do—copying, as she calls it—was work a young woman in her position could be encouraged to do. That her passion to copy was genuine is clear enough from "Why cannot one be content to look at it?" She drew out of boredom, she drew to escape bad times, but she also loved it. She stared, not as in a trance but with cleansing alertness, intensity, and impersonality, because the concentration could bring her out of herself and give her purposefulness. (p. 134)

[Her] earliest drawings of animals are, like those of insects and flowers, only careful work, but gradually she began to put these animals within a closed space—a garden, a doorway, a mousehole—and when she did, something began to happen. The enclosed space became the external equivalent of her own staring field of vision. Within it the care is still manifest, within it the less interesting parts of her landscapes could be pared away, but, most important, within it the faces of the animals begin to come to life, to be expressive, alert, amused or amusing, as though this rabbit, cat, or mouse were about to do something. Like Potter herself.

Given the confined nature of her life, given her tendency to write in tiny letters, given her desire to copy little things other people usually ignored, it is not surprising that enclosed spaces gave her the crucial assurance that within them she could be brash and full of pronouncements . . . The point is perfectly clear to anyone who goes through the indispensable *The Art of Beatrix Potter.* . . . [In the section called] "Animal Studies," in a woodmouse sent as a Christmas card when she was twenty, in a deer and fawn seen at the Zoological Gardens and done when she was twenty-five, one sees what was about to happen. Most noticeable are the limbs, drawn at rest but filled with potential energy, and the facial expressions just marked enough so we can imagine the same faces having other expressions than these.

There is no space at all in the drawing of the woodmouse, and the background for the doe and fawn is indifferently articulated. But in two other 1891 drawings, "The Rabbits' Potting Shed" and "The Mice in Their Storeroom," one sees the real thing, and so wonderfully done it is surprising that Potter did not recognize all she had discovered. The limbs that had been potentially capable of motion are now moving, the faces reveal thought and feeling, and from there it is only a small leap to showing animals doing human activities. The enclosed spaces seem to have had no effect on the animals, but they have helped Potter herself immensely, to imagine a scene, to suggest a drama, to lower the sky so all these are possible. The mice in their storeroom are doing nothing remarkable. One, facing us from a distance, is staring intently, while the other, nearer and with its back to us, is turning its head slightly to the left so we can see one eye focused, it seems, on the same spot the other mouse is looking at. If anything is happening for them to see, four bags, full of whatever it is mice store, hide it from us. It could be danger, or a companion coming through a mouse hole, but with such intent looks on the faces of the mice, it could not be a flyspeck or a mote in the sunlight. Something is going on. Get down low, cut out the farther space, note the haunches, ears, and eyes of mice, and everything comes to life. The drawing is funny, though the mice themselves are extremely serious. The meticulous care of the drawing keeps the scene looking realistic, free from caricature, so that the mice have become more like human beings as they have become more intensely mouselike. What is happening? The artist, master of the scene because herself free within the enclosed space, is thereby free to imagine, and when she does so she will begin to tell a story.

In 1893 Potter did a series of sketches for "Brer Rabbit and Brer Fox" and a sequence of six paintings for the rhyme "Three little mice sat down to spin," some of which, in revised and inferior form, were incorporated into *The Tailor of Gloucester* almost ten years later. Here the art is full-blown, because the story told in the rhyme enables each mouse to look somewhat different in each picture as the cat comes, tries to get in, and is thwarted. No longer studies of mice, but a mouse world. That the mice are spinning coats for gentlemen does not so much make them human as give them a great variety of things to be doing. The enclosing of the space allows us to imagine the domestic lives of mice as being like those of people, but what interests and amuses us most is the mouselike quality of these intense activities. Potter is still copying, but copying to put her own animals in her own world. She has discovered her métier, though her silence about all this in her *Journal* must suggest either that she did not think so, or was not sure of what she had done, or did not find it sufficiently different from what she had done in her head while staring at animals to be worth noting as a discovery.

There is nothing in the *Journal,* either, about a letter she wrote on September 4, 1893, to Noel Moore, the child of a former governess, the famous letter that begins:

> I don't know what to write to you, so I shall tell you a story about four little rabbits whose names were Flopsy, Mopsy, Cottontail, and Peter. They lived with their mother in a sand bank under the root of a big fir tree.

The story is only half as long as the *Peter Rabbit* published eight years later, and the drawings are crude indeed compared to the Brer Rabbit, Brer Fox, and three little mice she had done the same year. But it is a real story, and it ends, quite properly, with Flopsy, Mopsy, and Cottontail having bread, milk, and blackberries for supper. (pp. 135-37)

Peter's sisters get their berries, as why should they not, since they had gathered them, while Peter, put to bed with camomile tea, feels the consequences not just of his naughtiness but of his adventurousness and daring. Of course one would rather be Peter than his sisters, but that is no reason why they should not get their blackberries, just as Peter's silly courage is no reason why the world should suddenly be as he wants it to be. Mrs. Rabbit was right to warn her children about the garden, but of course we are glad Peter went, not because defiance is a virtue but because of all that Potter made him go through, wonderful but mostly miserable, while he was there.

The original letter only glimpsed this and offered Potter an outline when she returned to the story to take it seriously, which meant slowing the pace of the text, lengthening and thickening the story, working harder at the pictures so they were more interesting in themselves and commented on the text as well as illustrating it. With Jean de Brunhoff's elephants one feels a sense of the marvelous, so that one stares, relaxes, and asks for more. With Potter's animals one's role as a reader and watcher is much more active, and one feels a questioning, absorbed sense of the wonderful: Should rabbits wear jackets? Is Mr. McGregor a fool, or a bad gardener? Is Peter more a "true rabbit" when he eats green vegetables than his sisters are when they eat currant buns and blackberries? De Brunhoff's world is full, as large as a large page or pair of pages, so that to question it would be like questioning God; Potter's world is sharp, small, and it keeps changing on us ever so slightly, page-by-page, picture-by-picture, page-by-picture. As a result we leap, ask questions, feel content with our author because her demeanor is very knowing as well as very active: "He lost one of his shoes among the cabbages, and the other shoe amongst the potatoes." On the opposing page there is a picture of cabbages and a robin, and the precision of Potter's tone makes us want to know where the potatoes are, because we are as much inside Potter's knowingness as Peter is inside the garden. De Brunhoff invites us to look, and wonder, and be glad; Potter invites us to stare, and ask questions, and delight in never having answers enough.

Slight as it is, *Peter Rabbit* shows as much as anything Potter ever did what intentness could yield; a tossed-off cautionary tale is transformed into a story of sad adventure that has no moral but does have a complicated moral tone. It must have shown Potter herself all this too, because this time she followed up her success, exploited her discoveries. It must have mattered to her that the success was public and financial as well as artistic, and it brought her out slightly into the world, to talk things over with the Warnes, to put her profits in the bank. All this was too much like being in trade to suit her parents, but, if only for that very reason, it was what she needed. . . . [In 1905] she bought, entirely on her own, Hill Top Farm, Near Sawrey, in the Lake District. . . . She had a large enclosed space of her own now, though, and a whole slew of books followed, from *The Pie and the Patty-Pan* of 1905 to the climactic *Mr. Tod* eight years later. (pp. 141-42)

So much of what went into her books was a combination of old drawings and stories with new work and revisions that it is difficult to divide her books into periods. As we have noted, Potter was drawing almost as well as she ever did as early as 1893, and the writing as such does not get much better than *Peter Rabbit,* though it does get much fuller and much more daring. In the art of making a book where words and pictures play back and forth, with and against each other, *Peter Rabbit* shows her at close to her best. Nonetheless, the books that come after she bought Hill Top Farm are, on the whole, longer, richer, slightly darker, and better than those that come before, even though the pressure to keep new things in front of the public forced her to publish quite inferior books, often in the same year that she was also publishing one of her masterpieces. (pp. 142-43)

I would like to comment on those qualities in the Sawrey books that make them different from *Peter Rabbit* and that reveal her art at its densest and best.

The best of the Sawrey books are quite a bit longer than any of the early ones, and this means not only more pages, but more words per page, and some pages where there is no facing watercolor and only a line drawing for illustration. None of these facts represents an advantage in itself, and the relatively fewer illustrations per sentence and word seem a positive drawback. Even though Potter got to be very incisive with her line drawings, especially in building turns in extended sequences, the classic Potter book for many people remains the short text facing a watercolor. But there are many compensating gains. The world is fuller not just because the stories are longer, but because we have different kinds of animals having to live somehow, often in close quarters with each other, and we are asked to face the satisfying and nasty facts of life for those who live in barnyard and woodland, farmhouse and village. Satisfying and nasty—the terms consort very well with the young author of the *Journal,* but now her talents for relating the nasty and the satisfying found a subject she could stare at, ponder, play with. On a farm one kills one's pigs and ducks, and one tries to kill rats and mice and allies oneself with otherwise independent cats to do so. In a village slight nods of the head and small shifts in tone of voice reveal, to the practiced eye and ear, friendships and hatreds of many years standing. In the woods Peter Rabbit and Benjamin Bunny must learn to live, if they can, with foxes and badgers. In all these matters Potter found abundant material for her own careful, intent, complicating, and dispassionate genius. A question about manners can become, with nothing more than a turn of the page, a question about living and dying, and the variety of tones that can thus be evoked, still within small enclosed spaces, is greater, more amusing, and more somber than anything we find in the early books.

Potter always called her animals "rubbish," rabbits and mice and ducks and the like; they were not "serious" animals like sheep, dogs, and horses. When one visits Hill Top one is struck by how hard it must have been for her to keep "serious" animals out of her books, since sheep and dogs are everywhere, the basic work of the farm. Until she was married, though, and no longer an author, this work had to be left in the hands of others, which implies that she felt that she should not draw, or write about, the really serious matters. There was plenty to do with the "rubbish" animals, however, since even rats must live somehow, must they not, and how a rat is to live is not a trivial matter. That is to say, both Samuel Whiskers in *The Roly-Poly Pudding* and Peter Rabbit have adventures, but Peter's remain a naughty prank, while the struggle between cat and rat in a farmhouse is eternal and to that extent beyond moral questioning. This allows Potter a certain extravagance, whereby she can imagine whole families of cats and rats, each with their domestic problems, each therefore resembling human beings, and still never lose her sense that these animals are doing what comes instinctively to them. We find these instinctive activities in all the stories, of course—rabbits hunger for lettuce, squirrels hunt for nuts, mice are afraid of cats. But when, in *The Roly-Poly Pudding,* Potter gives us a family of cats and a family of rats, and makes them both long-time residents of a household, the instinctive desire of the cats to catch the rats implies an extended action, one which can also be played against the internal or domestic relations within each family. A story can then move in a number of directions without Potter's ever losing track of the fact that these are animals, doing what animals do. A mother worries for a lost child, a creature is annoyed when its privacy is invaded, a mate must trust another mate even when the other is essentially untrustworthy, and these are "human" events performed by cats and rats in ways that seem entirely "natural," so that when Potter leaps from one strand of her tale to another it simultaneously feels like an artistic feat of

some magnitude and a simple underlining of an essential fact of animal, and human, life. (pp. 143-45)

[Her last great book is] *Mr. Tod,* her story of the uplands, of the animal kingdom, of nature red in tooth and claw, of fierceness that wears a distinctly human face. The dates cannot be assigned with precision, but it would seem she wrote it after beginning the ordeal of her engagement with William Heelis and her separation from her parents. For most of its length *Mr. Tod* seems not so much to express that ordeal as to seek release from it, but then in the climactic battle we see something Potter could not have learned from staring at foxes and badgers, something she could often have observed by staring at people. Potter showed her own ability to be nasty as early as her *Journal,* but in *Mr. Tod* she seems to find such release in imagining the nastiness of others that she does not have to feel nasty herself, and her control is masterly throughout.

"I have made many books about well-behaved people," she begins, and "for a change I am going to make a story about two disagreeable people, called Tommy Brock and Mr. Tod." Since, of her previous seventeen books, no more than five could be said to be about "well-behaved people," we can only suspect how much she wanted a holiday from good manners and how much worse than usual were the characters she was about to consider. (p. 155)

We may recognize in this [book] . . . a use of the fastidious tone that might remind us of some of the dainty phrases in the *Alice* books; "not nice" is very much unlike Potter's usual prose, and calls attention to itself as a clear sign that what we are about here is perhaps a little more disagreeable than usual for the clear-eyed Potter:

> Now Tommy Brock did occasionally eat rabbit-pie;
> but it was only very little young ones occasionally,
> when other food was really scarce. He was friendly
> with old Mr. Bouncer; they agreed in disliking the
> wicked otters and Mr. Tod; they often talked over
> that painful subject.

The repetition of "occasionally" implies a restraint on Tommy Brock's part; yes, he does catch and eat and cook, apparently, young rabbits, but really, only now and then when wasps' nests are scarce. A fine fellow really, Tommy Brock, which slides us into Mr. Bouncer's view of him. It would never occur to us to say Jemima Puddle-Duck and the gentleman with sandy whiskers, a duck and a fox, made up an animal kingdom, nor would we say it about the cats and rats of *The Roly-Poly Pudding,* though they do make a very full house. Here, though, simply by triangulating fox and rabbit with badger, Potter suggests something almost that large and something so sinister that fastidious language may be called for. Look at Tommy Brock by himself and nothing could seem worse. Look at Tommy Brock looking at Mr. Tod and discussing "that painful subject" with old Mr. Bouncer, and our view of Tommy Brock shifts. Surely no one will mind the loss of an *occasional* young rabbit; they do breed fast, don't they? How strange some animals are, and all must live together somehow, and one way to do this is to try to overlook the fact that Tommy Brock has dirty clothes and eats one's grandchildren. One cannot afford to be too nice about these subjects. Fox and duck, thus, make a villain and a victim, while fox, rabbit, and badger make a whole world.

It has often been said that in her later books Beatrix Potter was no longer writing for young children, who, it is surmised, cannot take such complications of tone as I have been trying to describe. One might reply that Potter is never best understood as a writer for young children, but that is probably beside the point. These later books, *Mr. Tod* especially, are harsher, more disagreeable by far than *Peter Rabbit* or *The Tailor of Gloucester.* Indeed, in *Mr. Tod* Potter takes two of her early heroes, Peter Rabbit and Benjamin Bunny, and makes them into something like young readers who are here forced into a world that is too much for them, as though she now wanted to reveal what she had held back from her "many books about well-behaved people." She was, after all, now in her mid-forties and well versed in disagreeableness, her own and that of others. She might well have wanted to have done with that sort of restraint which had managed somehow to imprison her for so many years. Thus we are not, for a long time in *Mr. Tod,* inside an enclosed space, nor are we intently staring at anything. Potter is free, ranging up and down the woodland hillside, shifting her point of view widely and easily.

The passage most often cited to show the change in Potter's outlook comes almost halfway through *Mr. Tod,* when she is getting ready to move back one last time inside an enclosed space. One afternoon Mr. Bouncer is babysitting for his grandchildren. He lets Tommy Brock into the rabbit hole and lets himself be put to sleep by his own pipe smoke. When he wakes, Tommy and the Flopsy Bunnies are gone, and so Peter and Benjamin must set out up the hill to look for them. Knowing Tommy Brock, they know they will probably find him in one of Mr. Tod's houses, as indeed they do, at the top of Bull Banks. The bunnies are in the oven but still alive, and Tommy Brock is nowhere to be seen:

> The sun had set; an owl began to hoot in the wood. There were many unpleasant things lying about, that had much better have been buried; rabbit bones and skulls, and chickens' legs and other horrors. It was a shocking place, and very dark.

It is one of Potter's most brilliant moments. The setting sun and the owl give us atmospheric writing unknown elsewhere in Potter and cue us into a world that will, this time, move toward the "things" Potter had deliberately left vague hitherto. These things "had much better have been buried," which seems to pull us up short of specification, but then we are told: "rabbit bones and skulls, and chickens' legs and other horrors." Potter is, unquestionably and understandably, shocked. Foxes and badgers here are like adults, and what they do at night, after the sun sets and the owls begin to hoot, is best not discussed, or even discovered if possible.

The *most* sophisticated reader might see this simply as a verbal trick in which Potter giveth—look at these rabbit bones and skulls—and then taketh away—but they had much better have been buried, and it might seem even more of a trick since the taking away precedes the giving. The *least* sophisticated reader might see this as mere horror, and of course Potter's youngest readers are bound to include some of the least sophisticated. But the phrase "that had much better have been buried" is too resonant and too delicate to be either mere trick or mere horror. Potter does not say Mr. Tod should have buried these bones and skulls, though they are presumably his leavings. After all, he did not invite Peter and Benjamin here, and if they choose not to keep their usually discreet distance, they must take the consequences, surely. Nor can the rabbits whose bones these are care much, since they are dead no matter what. Potter's cry is not for any rabbits as

such, but for all those who remain among the living, especially rabbits. It is instinctive, unreasoning, though it will admit no theoretical justification, because no fastidiousness and no distance can keep us from finally acknowledging what foxes and badgers do to rabbits, or what people can and do do to all three. But like so many things we "must admit," we are happier admitting it from a distance, and this time Potter insists on taking all comfortable distance away from us.

We have come a long way from, and also not very far from, Peter Rabbit's father, who, we learn on the second page of Potter's first book, had an "accident" in Mr. McGregor's garden and was put into a pie. What happens to him is what might happen to his son, or what has happened to those distant cousins of his whose bones we are contemplating outside Mr. Tod's house. (pp. 156-59)

"There were many unpleasant things lying about, that had much better have been buried." That is the worst Potter can say of nature red in tooth and claw; its violence is ruthless but mainly rudely untidy, since it is hard enough to face young rabbits dying without also being forced to face their remains. Potter's is a human cry, since even sentient and talking rabbits like Peter and Benjamin are simply too scared to be outraged. It is an unreasonable cry, too, pathetic and weak in its human nicety in the face of the central fact of nature: all must live as they can, and all must die. It also expresses a limit, the farthest Potter will go in her contemplation of the disagreeable as seen in the lives of foxes, badgers, and rabbits. The story is only half over, but now we are to go back inside the enclosed space, and the horrors we will see there will bear a distinctively human face. To contemplate the disagreeable is, finally, to come back to people. (pp. 159-60)

Mr. Tod is a brilliant book, the climax of a brilliant career. No one should mind if it, or *Ginger & Pickles* or *The Roly-Poly Pudding,* too, never replaces other and earlier Potters in the hearts of most people, though it would be a shame if any of these late masterpieces were kept, for whatever specious reason, from anyone who is capable of attending to their great beauties. *Mr. Tod* cannot warm the heart, Lord knows, but such warming lies outside the scope of Beatrix Potter's work. . . . Potter's is a sterner beauty altogether. In almost every book she wrote she gave herself a task of such difficulty that even a small slip must seem like a glaring error, and when one writes that kind of book, where intelligence, intentness, and precision are crucial, one is not going to achieve, except very occasionally, warmth or compassion. In at least ten of these books Potter is nigh flawless in her difficult doing, and she emerges not just unscathed but triumphant, and cleansing.

A friend of mine once said, after comparing *Peter Rabbit* and *Mr. Tod,* that "disagreeableness as lovingly evoked as it is in *Mr. Tod* is the outer limit of unpleasant moral value, which makes the *Tod*-world nicely comfortable by comparison to, say, the world of Dr. Johnson's prayers and meditations." What I like best about that statement is that it properly suggests a limit to Beatrix Potter's achievement within a context entirely worthy of her. She was able to make smallness and enclosedness into literary and artistic virtues, as opposed to the moral virtue Kenneth Grahame made of these same qualities. The first, second, and third thing to do with Potter, unquestionably, is to say how wonderfully and memorably she animated and then filled her small worlds, and eventually one would want to go on to show how loose and baggy, how easy on themselves, she makes most other writers and artists seem.

But the world of Dr. Johnson's prayers and meditations, for one, was both more horrible and more profound than anything she could express. Having discovered what smallness could do for her, she could never open out from it farther than she did at the end, in **Mr. Tod.** Though on the whole her achievement seems much more considerable than Lewis Carroll's, he has moments in *Through the Looking-Glass* where his capacity for tears seems able to rebuke Potter for being so determinedly knowing.

But hers, after all, was another voyage, and its destination was not **Peter Rabbit** or **Mr. Tod** or any of the way stations in between, but William Heelis, and the quiet, purposeful, and fulfilling life she could have with him, and the sheep, and the land. We must be thankful it took her so long to arrive at her goal, but we must be glad, too, that after so much waiting and patient learning to live within enclosed spaces she could be free at last to find the work, silence, love—and perhaps the sorrow too—she had most wanted. (pp. 162-63)

Roger Sale, "Beatrix Potter," in his Fairy Tales and After: From Snow White to E. B. White, Cambridge, Mass.: Harvard University Press, 1978, pp. 127-64.

NICHOLAS TUCKER

The best story-books have always explored a whole range of interests and emotions, such as the tales of Beatrix Potter, which are still excellent examples of the type of fiction that so many younger children enjoy. Unlike books constantly searching for a surface realism, these stories have not dated whereas the fashions, milk-floats and telephones of *Topsy and Tim* will soon look antique, and in fact have already been changed in more up-to-date editions from 'frilly frocks and tartan knicker suits to anoraks and striped T-shirts'. But inhabited rabbit burrows and dressed up young animals belong to no particular time or place, and more importantly, Beatrix Potter writes about feelings and adventures that are part of every child's imagination—something that makes her an arresting as well as an entertaining writer for the young. Rather than try to discuss every writer who has appealed to children in this younger age-group and the possible reasons for their popularity, I shall focus particularly on Beatrix Potter's stories for all they can tell us in general terms about younger children's imaginative responses, and the ways in which an author can set about attempting to satisfy them. Not that Beatrix Potter's stories are always so successful: **The Tale of Little Pig Robinson** is untypically verbose, while an almost forgotten work, **The Fairy Caravan,** is nearly unreadable. Her best books, though, still show no signs of losing any of their appeal to children. Sales figures alone can only be a crude indicator of a book's popularity, since it is adults who make such purchases, but adults will not go on indefinitely buying books for younger readers which are meant to give pleasure but no longer do so. To this extent, Beatrix Potter's high sales over the last fifty years tell their own story.

However vivid an imagination a writer for young children may have, this must be expressed in a prose style that is simple, direct and memorable. In this respect, it is no accident that Beatrix Potter was always an admirer of and something of an expert on nursery rhymes, bringing out two mini-volumes of her own, **Appley Dapply's Nursery Rhymes** and **Cecily Parsley's Nursery Rhymes.** These collections mix some of her own rhymes along with other versions discovered by her in the British Museum library. In her stories, she often

quotes from old nursery rhymes; it is not fanciful to suggest that within her own writing she absorbed some of their smooth rhythms and direct vocabulary. When she finished a particular work, she would always keep at it, polishing the prose and cutting out redundant phrases. The very format of her books, with their small pages, each passage of text facing a picture, ensured that there were few words to spare in any story, and in the correspondence with her publishers there are many reminders of the care she took with her prose style. Sometimes this would show itself in her spotting a faulty rhythm. In **The Tale of Tom Kitten,** for example, she originally wrote a slightly clumsy sentence, 'There were very extraordinary noises during the whole of the tea-party somehow.' This was later changed to the superior, 'Somehow there were very extraordinary noises over-head; which disturbed the dignity and repose of the tea-party.'

'Dignity and repose' is not a phrase one would normally find in an infant's vocabulary, but Beatrix Potter knew what she was about. So long as the general context is clear, the odd expressive phrase, however unfamiliar, can always enliven an otherwise fairly basic vocabulary, which in any unrelieved form can soon become monotonous. . . . As she once wrote to her publishers, who were sometimes alarmed by her adventurous vocabulary, 'Children like a fine word occasionally', and so of course does a true author. . . . Elsewhere, she pushed her luck by the deliberate use of faulty grammar—something that might disturb pedants even now, when successful authors regularly receive worried correspondence about their supposed 'bad English', often regardless of its context. In her case, Beatrix Potter wanted to end **The Tale of Little Pig Robinson** with the lines, 'He grew fatter and fatter and more fatterer'. When her publishers demurred, she wrote back, 'Of course there is no such word; but it is expressive! If you don't like it, say "fatter and fatter and more fat"'. It requires three repeats to make a balanced ending'. Once again, she got her way.

Sometimes she stretches her love of occasional fine language to the limits of a young reader's tolerance. Her favourite work, **The Tailor of Gloucester,** strictly speaking needs to be read with the help of a specialist dictionary in order to understand or even pronounce technical terms like 'padusoy' (silk from Padua), 'lutestrings' (lustred or watered silk) and 'robins' (an old-fashioned term for trimmings). But as she writes in the text, 'Stuffs had strange names and were expensive in the days of the Tailor of Gloucester.' In fact, her fine illustrations give a good idea of such wealthy brocades, in contrast to the poverty of the tailor, and the effect would not be so vivid without the use of a few exotic, antique words. The same cannot be said about all her other obscurities, however, such as the references to 'seed-wiggs' in **The Tale of Ginger and Pickles,** along with one of her rare descents into baby-talk in the same story, where 'The handbills really were most "ticing".' Yet the sort of latitude Beatrix Potter felt able to take in her stories, combined with her professionalism when it came to scrutinising the result, is almost always a source of strength. (pp. 57-9)

[Although] many children's authors, when questioned, will maintain that they write primarily to please themselves and perhaps a few children in their circle too, this was particularly true of Beatrix Potter before she became famous. . . . She used to sketch her own pets to amuse and console herself long before she ever thought of publication, sometimes giving her much-loved animal models names like Hunca Munca and

Endpapers which appear in several of Potter's work. From The Tale of Benjamin Bunny, *written and illustrated by Beatrix Potter.*

Mrs Tiggy, later of course to be incorporated into her stories. Not surprisingly, this affection is also evident in the way she later illustrated her books, with the same animals lovingly depicted in all their various poses, set against a background where the sun always shines and colours merge gently into each other. Everything is neat, ordered and flourishing, adorned by flowers and set against a lyrical back-drop of mountains. This is nature at its most idyllic: a cosy and charming domestic setting. . . .

But it is not simply the prettiness and warmth of her stories that have always got through to children; there have also to be interesting, exciting adventures too, and here Beatrix Potter sometimes uses dark as well as lighter shades, also appealing to children but in a different way. (p. 60)

The appeal of this basic plot of pursuit and prey for young children is not hard to imagine. They too are simple and comparatively helpless; they too are aware of danger, and this is true whether children are neglected or as protected as it is possible to be. From early on, they all have some terrors that cannot be explained in any rational way, such as fear of the dark and all the natural or supernatural creatures that can be imagined to inhabit it. (pp. 60-1)

In many Beatrix Potter stories, the theme of danger gives both tension to the plot, and a sense of relief at the happy ending. There are no tragedies in her books, but a succession of very near escapes in a number of them. In most ways she was no sentimentalist, showing the cycle of predator and preyed upon with the 'gentle detachment' Graham Greene once

ironically but accurately ascribed to her. Yet she also recognised that her audience liked optimistic conclusions in its stories: once children had identified themselves with the animal heroes of her tales, it would be too harsh and depressing to show them coming to a sticky end. Instead, she sometimes pictures her characters living dangerously in a world which can be full of fearsome surprises. Although main characters survive, offstage personalities do not always fare so well. Peter Rabbit's father, no less, was baked in a pie for Mr McGregor, and other animals, from baby rats and mice to butterflies and grasshoppers (roasted with ladybird sauce) are also devoured at some stage in a story.

Other writers for children often gloss over these glimpses of a harsher reality in their adventure stories, but Beatrix Potter was not interested in this type of evasion. (p. 61)

Moments of fear have their place in stories for the young, however, so long as they are successfully contained by a plot that ends on a reassuring, consoling note. For young readers, the expression of some of their own nameless, common anxieties on the printed page may help render them more controllable, though as always not all children will react in the same way. For some, the fear evoked in the moment when, say, Peter Rabbit is caught in a net, or the sorrow conveyed by his sobs when he twice gives himself up for lost, may be altogether too strong to enable them to enjoy the story. (p. 62)

The fact remains, however, that humanised animals still tend to give authors more imaginative licence when it comes to placing them in various, sometimes extreme situations. While some young readers may still be equally upset over the fate of such animal characters, for other children, possibly brought up in the country, the killing of marauding rabbits or whatever may seem more of an everyday matter. But the popularity of Beatrix Potter's books, especially those about pursuit and the preyed upon, does suggest that this theme is of particular importance to small children, and that she deals with it in a way that her young readers generally seem to find acceptable. Not that she always writes about the fears that haunt children; some of her other stories are as tranquil as anyone could wish. But in nearly all of them she deals with issues of particular meaning to children, such as the relationship between parent and child, seen in many variations throughout her stories, or the constant way in which food is made to play an important part, even to the extent that heroes and heroines may sometimes be the intended main meal themselves.

In all her stories, in fact, Beatrix Potter describes a half-human, half-animal world, populated by partly-clothed animal characters who have courtesy titles and surnames, and visit each other exactly as humans do, but who also mix the gentilities of polite conversation with offhand references to a more savage state. This type of ambiguity enables her characters to flit between human and animal roles, according to the needs of the plot. Peter Rabbit, for example, is first established very much as an animal, surrounded by his family 'Underneath the roots of a very big fir-tree'. On the next few pages, however, everyone is given a more human shape, with Mrs Rabbit, in her voluminous dress and pinafore, helping to dress her children and then setting off through the wood 'to the baker's'. Peter himself, who like his mother walks on two legs, soon gets into trouble, and loses his shoes and his jacket—a crime whose seriousness will not be lost on young readers, still living in an atmosphere where domestic offences may always seem more significant than most others. Without his clothes, Peter returns to the animal state, running on four legs and twice evading attempts on his life.

Perhaps it would have been too frightening to show a humanised rabbit just about to have its back broken by Mr McGregor's enormous, nailed boot, however, and at that stage, readers may feel relieved to see Peter looking like an animal again. One of the constant themes of folk and fairy stories, also found in children's own nightmares, is the idea that there may be terrifying adult figures around with murderous intentions towards the young. There are various explanations for these fantasies; psychoanalysts, for example, may see them as an indirect reflection of a child's own aggression. As children get older, it is suggested, and beyond the age of immediate temper tantrums, they increasingly want to deny to themselves that they still have occasionally angry and even destructive feelings towards their loved ones when thwarted, and this they can attempt to do by projecting such feelings on to other, imaginary figures. In this way, children avoid the guilt and anxiety that can arise through awareness of their *own* capacity for destruction, at least in the imagination, towards those they are also dependent upon. But the adult figures who may best come to represent this projected hostility—from ogres to the rheumatic Mr McGregor—can still be fairly terrifying, and occasionally haunting characters in the imagination. In *The Tale of Peter Rabbit* the central situation—as we have seen—is made not quite so frightening for young readers through the use of characters who at the moment of greatest danger look more like animals than human beings. But despite the animal disguise, the plot here is still

near enough to some of children's most terrifying fantasies or nightmares in their own lives to make it of great, even sometimes compulsive interest for them; truly, a story that may be demanded over and over again.

Children can, of course, still identify with a character like Peter Rabbit when he is behaving more like a true animal, but perhaps with a different part of themselves. Peter as a humanised rabbit is no match for Mr McGregor, and young readers identifying with the diminutive, childlike figure suddenly confronting his enemy round the end of a cucumber frame, will quite justifiably shudder for his safety. Peter the rabbit, however, without his clothes—which at one stage almost fatally entangle him in a gooseberry net—is a more resilient quarry, scuttling away on all fours with all the speed of his kind. Here, Peter may represent for his young readers the toughness and freedom from constraint so commonly symbolised by wild animals in fiction. Children can identify their own fantasies of independence with the adventures of such characters, just as they can thoroughly enjoy the way that Peter makes a fool of his stern, adult enemy. Throughout Beatrix Potter's stories, in fact, her animals are allowed a licence not normally given to human characters—at least not without extra explanation or moralising. Her animal characters, for example, often steal, destroy, or invade each other's territory and even devour the young of other species. ('Yes, it is infested with rats', said Tabitha tearfully. 'I caught seven young ones out of one hole in the back kitchen, and we had them for dinner last Saturday.') This type of sentence does not make *The Tale of Samuel Whiskers* into a nursery equivalent of *Titus Andronicus;* cats *do* eat baby rats, after all, just as larger rats sometimes make away with kittens. But the way that very human-looking animals are still free to break various important human taboos makes stories about them especially interesting to children, themselves still prey to primitive fantasies in their own imagination.

There are many other advantages in using animal characters. Like children, they too are generally at the mercy of adult humans—another reason for identifying with them, especially those warm, furry animals that accept and sometimes return an infant's strong affections. They are also easy for everyone to identify with in other ways, since they transcend social class, skin colour and, to a certain extent, age. When they are introduced into a story, their existence can simply be stated, 'Once upon a time there were four little rabbits.' Beatrix Potter always took great care over the opening and concluding sentences in her stories. With animal characters, she could start off directly and end abruptly, without need for all the tying up of loose ends or other extra detail that audiences expect where human characters are involved (though fairy stories, for different reasons, can also get away with this type of brevity).

All Beatrix Potter's striking effects, however, are achieved in an atmosphere that conveys the assurance of the familiar, with stories usually set in the same rustic scenery, and characters who sometimes move from one book to another. Danger is often present, but not tragedy, meals of various sizes are enjoyed at regular intervals, and parents always care for their offspring, rewarding the obedient but never failing to punish the mischievous.

This type of predictability is echoed even in the physical shape of her books, so easy for young hands to hold and manipulate, and with their identical format, pictures on every page, and coloured end-papers showing other familiar and possibly favourite characters from different stories. All this can have a strong appeal to young readers, looking for order in their environment, including their early literature. But within these regularities, there is still variety to stop a child becoming bored. The tales range from the simple, almost monosyllabic *The Story of a Fierce Bad Rabbit,* to the extended prose of *The Tale of Samuel Whiskers,* and the plots vary from danger and suspense to descriptions of the blameless, uneventful life of Mrs Tiggywinkle.

Beatrix Potter is not the only writer to appeal to small children, but she is one of the best. In her books, she provides interest and excitement, and even in her illustrations there may still be hints for the wideawake of danger to come, such as pictures of the just visible trout nosing his way towards the unaware Jeremy Fisher, or Peter Rabbit's tell-tale ears sticking out of the watering-can where he is trying to hide from Mr McGregor. For older readers, there is also the gentle irony of these stories and the easy prose style; important for tales which are frequently read aloud. Within them, moralising, lengthy conversations, or detailed descriptions that hold up the development of a clear story line are always avoided. (pp. 62-5)

Nicholas Tucker, "Story and Picture-books (Ages 3-7)," in his The Child and the Book: A Psychological and Literary Exploration, *Cambridge University Press, 1981, pp. 46-66.*

RUTH K. MacDONALD

Of all her books *The Tale of Peter Rabbit* and its sequels are Potter's best-known and most successful. Spanning as they do her most active period of writing, a study of them shows the increasing complexities of her plots and characterizations, and increasing daring in her subject matter. The personalities range from a rabbit who is simply naughty to characters who are disagreeable and sinister. Though Peter and his cousin Benjamin remain paired as complementary versions of rabbit nature, they develop from carefree little rabbits to thoughtful adults capable of contemplation and cognition. To complement their growing depth of character, Potter added more complex villains to her other characters in the rabbit stories. While *Peter Rabbit,* her first book, is her best book for very young children, *Mr. Tod,* the last of the rabbit books, written nearly at the end of her writing career, is one of her most complex and successful in plot and tone.

Potter always felt particularly close to rabbits, having lived with them early on as pets and having observed them closely. The nature of her assessment of them is obvious from her journal: "Rabbits are creatures of warm volatile temperament but shallow and absurdly transparent. It is this naturalness, one touch of nature, that I find so delightful . . .". Given their shallowness as a species, Potter shows a remarkable ability to invest the rabbits with a variety of characters, all of whom are consistent with rabbit nature. Her success with rabbits is particularly evident in this skill in characterizing them, and her ability to body forth these different characters comes from her close observation of a variety of them.

The stories are all inspired at least in part by the Uncle Remus stories of Joel Chandler Harris. As early as 1893 Potter illustrated these stories, probably choosing them because she was looking for illustrating possibilities to pursue as a career and because the stories contained a rabbit as the major actor. But the African-American stories were particularly unsuited for translation to the setting of the lush English country garden. The characters, no matter how hard Potter tried to make them into Victorian gentlemen, resist any change from their basic natures as personified slaves and owners of the antebellum South.

The sole legacy of the Uncle Remus heritage occurs in two places. First, the fantasy of lavender, which the rabbits use as rabbit tobacco, was an idea that Potter found particularly engaging. It occurs first in her own private edition of *Peter Rabbit,* where she edited it out, later using it in characterizing old Mr. Bunny in *Benjamin Bunny.* Later still, in *Mr. Tod* old Mr. Bunny falls asleep from the drowsiness induced by his smoking and fails to guard his grandchildren adequately, setting off the complication in plot. The second legacy from Uncle Remus appears in the onomatopoeia Potter used to describe the sound that a rabbit makes when it is hopping. In *Uncle Remus* Br'er Rabbit moves "lippity-clippity, clippity-lippity." In *Peter Rabbit* Peter is described as making a similar sound as he hops: "lippity—lippity. . . ." Though Potter certainly knew the Harris stories, her characters, perhaps with the exception of Mr. Tod, are not modeled after Harris's. Whereas Br'er Rabbit is wily and wins by cunning, Peter and Benjamin succeed by ill-considered adventurousness and just plain luck. None of the rabbits is as motivated by vengeance as is Harris's rabbit. Though their world can be just as hard and unsympathetic as Br'er Rabbit's, the world that Potter creates for her rabbits is altogether a pleasanter, more abundant place. (pp. 23-4)

The popularity of *Peter Rabbit* has much to do with its timeless quality. The pictures and themes seem to be those of some past age, perhaps a pretechnological period, but no particular century. The enmity between humans and wild animals is a situation that has endured since the human race decided to take up farming. The outwitting of the large and powerful by the small and cunning is as old as David and Goliath, and is an archetype dear to the heart of any one who perceives that the world has victimized him. Children have always wanted to do what their parents have told them not to since Adam and Eve disobeyed. And parents have taken their misguided offspring back into the family ever since Genesis, when God gave His creatures the rest of His creation to live in. The archetypes upon which Potter modeled the exquisitely small story of the wayward rabbit are indeed large and timeless.

The illustrations also underscore the unspecified past intruding on the present that the text portrays. Mrs. Rabbit going forth on her shopping trip through the woods looks suspiciously like Little Red Riding-Hood, except that she has an umbrella. But the umbrella does not violate the sense of history in the picture as much as it underscores the sense of motherly anxiety. The lady rabbit is just cautious about the unexpected. Her anxiety about the possible excess of rain or sun from which the umbrella will protect her is a further extension of her anxiety about her children. The rabbit children wear out-of-style short cloaks or jackets of an unspecified past, but Peter wears blue, whereas his sisters wear deep pink, a sex differentiation by color handed down from the ancient Romans. And Peter's shoes are clogs or pumps, but not so fashionably portrayed that they are identifiable as anything but antique.

When Potter colored the pen-and-ink drawings of her private edition for Frederick Warne's edition, she had to do something about framing the backgrounds. Instead of having the pictures end at the edge of the paper, she chose to vignette them, that is, to enclose the colored pictures in an oval space of white, similar to an old-fashioned cameo or portrait photograph. This technique, too, lends to the pictures a sense of antiquity, of tastes formerly popular but no longer so. And the colors she used, almost translucent pastels, with a predominance of natural tones of green and brown, communicate a sense of fading from original brilliance and yet endurance in the dominance of the colors from nature in the rabbits and garden foliage.

Perhaps the major reason that *The Tale of Peter Rabbit* endures is the sense of the world that Potter created as ongoing, as permanent, uninterrupted by historical events or the intervening years. Rabbit and gardener continue to go about their business with no regard for the reader's visual intrusion into their fictionalized world. Any eye contact between reader and character is fleeting and of no purpose. Mr. McGregor returns to his gardening when he fails to catch Peter. Peter returns home and is nursed back to health, to raid and raze another day. The ending may be a closed one, but neither Peter's life nor Mr. McGregor's garden is irrevocably altered by the adventure, and modern technology and urbanization seem to have little influence on the relationships between gardeners and rabbits. Though publishing practices and popular tastes in children's literature change, yet the story of the rabbit and the farmer do not, except in bowdlerized and cheap reissues. The text and illustrations are reliable and enduring, and if the Easter Bunny is also named Peter, it is because his namesake is as perennial as he is. (pp. 32-3)

Beatrix Potter always maintained that the animals about which she wrote were "rubbish"—that is, not that they were worthless, but that they were expendable, not livestock or "working" animals. They were pets of one sort or another, and as such they could be carefully observed and studied without interrupting their purpose in life. In fact, these animals have no real purpose other than to survive and to give humans the pleasure and amusement of observing them. Potter's most felicitous and successful animal creations are her mice, who lend themselves easily to characterization and social behavior similar to humans. Though squirrels are near relatives of mice, Potter's imagination did not succeed with them very well, perhaps because squirrels are wild animals who do not live in close confines with human beings. Their intractability as pets made them less moldable in Potter's mind, and thus her two squirrel stories are some of her less satisfactory. (p. 54)

The Tailor of Gloucester is a very different work from *Peter Rabbit.* One suspects that those readers who had come to expect another rabbit adventure found *The Tailor* disappointing because the animals are involved in none of the drama of human-animal interaction. Although the mice in the story are in some peril from the tailor's cat, it seems unlikely that the cat will do anything more than worry them. The mice are not as daring as Peter; after all, they are supporters of the tailor, not his enemies.

The story is also a fairy tale, unlike *Peter Rabbit,* which more closely resembles a beast fable, and where the writer assumes a realistic, commonsense tone of narration. The events of the story presume an intimate, reciprocal relationship between humans and animals: Simpkin is more than a cat, he is nursemaid and companion. The mice are not verminous intruders, at least not to the tailor; they are the architects of the tailor's and Simpkin's ultimate good fortune. The story bears a resemblance to the Grimm brothers' "The Elves and the Shoe-

maker," in which a well-intentioned cobbler spends the last of his money on just enough leather for a pair of shoes. Because the man is good-hearted, elves come in the night and make the shoes for him. Their craftsmanship is so extraordinary that the shoes sell for a very good price, and the shoemaker has enough money to buy leather for more shoes, which he cuts out and which the elves finish for him.

Like many fairy tales, Potter's story presents a lesson to be learned. In both *The Tailor of Gloucester* and "The Elves and the Shoemaker" the artisan is good-hearted, thrifty, and skillful. Some magical force outside his own efforts rewards his virtues and changes his fortune for the better. The Christmas setting in *The Tailor* gives the tale a religious aura not found in any other Potter book. Likewise, in "The Elves and the Shoemaker" the cobbler says his prayers before he goes to sleep, leaving the impression that the cobbler is rewarded at least partly for his proper religious attitude and reliance on God. In neither story do the magical elements seem divinely inspired; neither mice nor elves leave messages of high import after they have done their work. But in each story the moral seems to be that hard work and generosity pay off, even if magic must intervene to effect the reward for those who deserve it.

It is easy to see why Beatrix Potter preferred *The Tailor of Gloucester* over her other books; both the story and the drawings permitted her to dwell on subjects for which she felt a particular affection. The fairy-tale genre was one that had appealed to her from childhood, though she seldom indulged herself in such tales in her books. The pictures of the mice show them posed in particularly playful attitudes, dressed in the antique clothing that had attracted her attention in the Victoria and Albert Museum. The detail of the china in the cupboard, of the mantlepiece before which the tailor warms and rests himself, of the old buildings and narrow passageways in the old city of Gloucester, were all subjects that Potter had found particularly fascinating and that she had sketched repeatedly over the years.

The human figure of the tailor, because he is seldom seen as the focal point of the illustrations, and because she did not pose him in full frontal view, did not give her the problems that she had in drawing humans such as Mr. McGregor in *Peter Rabbit.* The world of the mice, living in the walls of the old city, existing harmoniously among themselves with little interference from the humans who might otherwise have interrupted their lives, the exquisite delicacy of the embroidery on the garments she used as models, the elegant, antique finery of the mice when she draws them clothed, all required Potter to exercise extreme care and her ability to draw the exquisitely delicate details of her miniature fantasy world. The fact that the story is set in some remote past only heightened her pleasure in creating this world in her illustrations. (pp. 55-7)

Of all of Potter's books this one is the most romantic and fantastic. Though it shows none of the hardheaded realism of her other successful books, yet it still succeeds, partly because the animals are so carefully drawn and realized. Cats and mice were some of Potter's earliest pets, and mice in particular lend themselves to human clothing and postures. Though the fairy tales of Potter's retirement, especially *The Fairy Caravan,* are verbose and lacking in tension, such is not the case here. One suspects that Norman Warne's careful criticism kept the book from going in the same direction as *The Fairy Caravan* and that the illustrations, tapping as they do Potter's

From The Tale of Mr. Jeremy Fisher, *written and illustrated by Beatrix Potter.*

love of antiques and of fine detail, also kept her aware of her tendencies toward long, romantic descriptions. (pp. 66-7)

[*Squirrel Nutkin*] is at least partly a *pourquoi* story, one which explains the presence of an occasional short-tailed red squirrel, and the kinds of natural disasters occurring in a squirrel's life that might had led to such a mutilation without the loss of life. The story also explains what squirrels are saying when they chatter, and why squirrels chatter back and throw things on humans who presume to talk to them. In this way, the story becomes a sort of legend, with a feeling of folk-tale and tradition to it.

Nutkin is also the closest Beatrix Potter comes in her books to the kind of wildlife study typical in the books of Ernest Thompson Seton. Seton studied animal behaviors and habitats and wrote about them in order to contribute to a child's knowledge of natural history, but without attempting to personify the animal or tell a consistent story about him. Neither the squirrels nor the owl in this story wear clothes. The closest to human behavior they get is Old Brown's habit of using human utensils to eat his honey off a plate. In the main, the squirrels are squirrels, except for the opening fantasy about their sailing by using their tails. They do converse with Old Brown and walk single file, in uncharacteristically human orderliness. Nutkin is given to dancing on his hind legs. But Potter's animals here are at their least human, primarily because they live in their natural habitats and do not wear clothes. Nutkin's red tail holds the same kind of significance for him that Peter Rabbit's blue jacket does for the bunny. But Nutkin's tail is a defining part of his anatomy, and not an artificial covering, as is Peter's jacket. (p. 69)

Though Nutkin is a sympathetic character, the reader does not sympathize with him wholly, the way he does with Peter Rabbit. Nutkin shows bad manners and foolhardiness about the consequences of his lack of etiquette. The reader's ability to answer his riddles gives a further feeling of superiority. The harshness of the justice is mitigated by the fact that Nutkin is permitted to live and by the lack of ridicule from the other squirrels. But Potter's failure to imagine the squirrel as more thoroughly human, combined with her punitive justice, fail to draw upon her finer abilities in writing and make *Nutkin* one of her less successful stories.

The pictures suffer from what Potter feared would be the problem with *Peter Rabbit*—a prevalence of natural colors with insufficient contrast to keep them from becoming routine. In *Peter Rabbit* the pictures are rescued by the rabbits' clothing, especially the contrast of Peter's blue jacket with the rest of the natural setting. In *Nutkin* Potter had no such device to save the pictures from sameness. The squirrels are virtually identical, with little delineation of facial features among them and only Nutkin's high-stepping antics to set him apart from his kin. The story also has little to say about human beings in general and is pointed rather directly at naughty, intrusive children. Thus *Nutkin* does not draw on Potter's acute observations of human relations, but rather stoops rather didactically to talk to children. The reliance on the riddles, away from which Norman Warne gradually steered Potter, is still obvious here, and though Potter found pleasure in them, the reader gradually finds them tedious.

For all the wanton destruction in [*The Tale of Two Bad Mice*], it is one of Potter's most lighthearted creations. The atmosphere is due at least in part to the smallness of the mice and the dollhouse, and the miniature scale of the havoc they wreak, which makes their burglaries and vandalism more laughable than serious. The dolls, though pretty, are necessarily lifeless and hard to sympathize with. Their stiffness contrasts with the lithe, quick movements of the mice and the animals' ability to discover the truth about the dolls' lives: they are all show and no substance. The line about the dolls' foodstuffs, "They would not come off the plates, but they were extremely beautiful," shows the sole criterion by which the dolls and dollhouse can be evaluated: by their capacity to please the sight with their decoration and in their miniature scale. The opening description of Lucinda, who never requests any meals for Jane to cook, and Jane, who consequently never does any cooking, sounds so unnatural, even for dolls, that the animals' disgust with the lack of substance in the food mirrors the reader's lack of sympathy for the dolls.

That the mice steal what is useful for themselves seems a much more fitting use of the dollhouse furnishings. One can hardly feel sorry for the dolls, whose expressions are so frozen that they cannot express any horror when they return to the scene of the burglary. The lady mouse needs the cradle she steals for the many little mice she is raising at home, but Lucinda has no such offspring and no use for the cradle. The dress the mouse steals for herself makes her look charming, but it would not have had the same enchanting effect on the doll, who already looks as good as she can. The theft of the bolster, so that the mice can have their own feather bed, seems especially appropriate, since the dolls cannot recline comfortably or recognize comfort anyway. The mouse justifies her action to the reader because she has a good use for her theft. It is true that the mice do become greedy when they try to steal a bookcase and a birdcage, but they cannot fit either item into their hole. So they mitigate their acquisitiveness by leaving the superfluity behind.

Margaret Blount has noted that nearly all mouse stories involve comparison of the mice and their feats to the human giants who dominate their world. It may come as a surprise to the reader of *Two Bad Mice* that there is a little girl to whom the dollhouse belongs and that the little girl has a governess. But there have been hints of the human world throughout the book. The opening exterior view of the dollhouse facing the first page of text shows that the scene is not set outside. The wallpaper in the background and the carpet on which the dollhouse sits betray the presence of humans, as do the jumprope and badminton equipment surrounding the dollhouse. The human wallpaper may not be nearly so evident in the deteriorated plates used in currently available editions, but it is much more clearly detailed and telling in earlier issues. As Lucinda and Jane return from their outing, they are shown arriving on the scene in a doll carriage. Though the text does not mention a little girl at that time, the picture necessarily begs the question of who is pushing the carriage. When, on the next page, the existence of the dollhouse owner is introduced in the text, the reader who has already looked at the picture is not surprised.

The reader perceives that this little girl is just as imaginatively involved in the fantasy as the reader has been. Her solution to the mouse invasion is another layer of fantasy. If the dolls are not mature enough to care for themselves—and she has just shown her willingness to diminish them by treating them as her babies in the doll carriage—then she need simply impose another doll who will. But the efficacy of her solution is further brought into doubt when Potter presents a picture of the policeman doll, so ridiculously tall that he cannot see the mice on the floor, and so stiff and precariously balanced that he could not chase them anyway. Of course, the governess introduces a note of ominous reality. The only way to deal with mice is to trap them. But the governess, like most adults who cling to reality and will not see the capabilities of animals in fantasy, underestimates the cleverness of the mice in evading the human, bloodthirsty intrusion. They are smart enough to avoid the trap, and they pass this intelligence and wisdom on to their children. Thus, though Potter prematurely announces, "So that is the story of the two Bad Mice", she does so in an assumed adult, realistic voice, one not unlike, the reader suspects, the summary proclamation of the governess.

The story that proceeds after this announcement shows Potter's increasing willingness to defy the conventions of traditional storytelling. Though at the end of *Peter Rabbit* and *Benjamin Bunny* she slightly extends the story after the more obvious ending as the rabbits return home, she did not attach a lengthy coda to these stories to complicate them further. Rather, she introduced a simple denouement at the end of each to tie up loose ends. In *Two Bad Mice* Potter introduces loose ends that defy neat endings. The two mice subsequently atone for their misdeeds and are pronounced "not so very very naughty after all", even though one suspects the sincerity of their atonement. The sixpence that they give to the dolls to pay for their breakage is a crooked one, and thus not legal tender. And the lady mouse's cleaning must not be terribly taxing, given the dolls' inactivity. The sight of the two mice stuffing the Christmas stocking while the dolls sleep parallels the animals with Father Christmas, another fantasy creation. The lady mouse's cleaning forays "very early every morn-

ing—before anybody is awake" suggests two possibilities; either that she is not really cleaning at all, which is belied by the picture of her entering the house, capably wielding broom and dustpan; or that she is another creature of the night, like the sandman and the tooth fairy, which explains why dolls' houses are always so neat. Thus Potter defies the realistic ending and reasserts the fantasy by extending it.

The detail with which she drew the interior of the dollhouse and her mouse-eye perspective on the furnishings indicates the pleasure and persistence with which she pursued the accuracy of the drawings. She could not have clearly seen the staircase down which the mice proceed from an interior vantage point, given that there was no window in the dollhouse at that location for a photograph to be taken. Yet she could place herself imaginatively on the staircase and draw them in anatomically believable postures and in appropriate scale to the features of the house. Her pleasure in the many realistic details of the house, which had "real muslin curtains and a front door and a chimney" led her to strive for the inclusion of more and more miniature details in the pictures. At one point she wrote to Norman Warne about her pleasure in the pattern of the doll dishes included with the fake doll food: "The little dishes are so pretty I am wondering if I have made enough of them? Shall I squeeze in another dish?" And in the same letter she inquired about the color of the *Encyclopedia Britannica,* which she saw as one of the items the mice would not be able to fit in their hole. Fortunately, both the constraints of the book's format and the publisher's good advice kept her from overdoing the detail and surfeiting the viewer.

The success both of the dollhouse and of the book lies in the myriad details consistently miniaturized and copiously included. Potter further complicated the task for herself by using a small format, thus miniaturizing her pictures even more. The outlines surrounding the pictures make the details even smaller, both by the illusion of diminution that the frame creates and by limiting the picture to less than the whole page. Her continued fascination for dollhouses and miniatures is apparent from her collection of dolls, doll clothes, and a furnished dollhouse on display at Hill Top, collections to which she added even in her old age. Smallness for Potter was a lifetime obsession.

Part of her pleasure in telling the dollhouse story might have been the gentle mockery she was making of the domestic arrangements in her own home in Bolton Gardens. In another letter she wrote that the dollhouse was "the kind of house where one cannot sit down without upsetting something, I know the sort." Though she does not say so directly, the sterile stasis of the dolls' lives may have been modeled after the deadening sameness with which her parents conducted their lives. The Potters seemed unable to do anything for themselves, relying on servants to keep the house functioning. Those same servants wrought havoc by leaving the Potters' employment or when they failed to perform their duties exactly as the elder Potters wanted. This disruption must have seemed as devastating to the Potters as the mouse intrusion did to the dolls. The humans increasingly expected their daughter to oversee the servants and spare her parents the trouble of seeing to their own household affairs. Potter's obvious pleasure in the mice's high-spirited destruction, and her forgiveness of them in the end, may have been an imaginative release for her and a displacement of her own desire to disturb her parents' rigidity and complacency. In any case, Potter is clearly mocking the sterility of inactive lives surrounded by functionless decoration and having a good time while she is at it.

The reader wholeheartedly applauds Potter's final disposition of the bad mice, who are not really so bad. The open ending has the other merit of accurately describing the relationship between humans and mice. Both species coexist, side by side, in perpetuity, with only occasional intrusions of the mice upon the human realm, and with subsequent intervention of the humans into mouse society, with little effect. As long as the two species do not interfere with each other, the cold war continues, if interrupted only infrequently by admiring, appreciative, and loving glimpses of the small creatures by the larger ones.

Potter identified the book as one with particular appeal to girls, and one feels her own girlish pleasure at the miniatures and the indoor views of the dollhouse and mouse hole. Her success with mice is apparent here, due most likely to their diminutive, fastidious natures, and to their willingness to become pets and to be observed. Their miniature worlds only further added to her wonder and pleasure in the fantasy world she invents for them. (pp. 71-5)

Of all her animal creations Mrs. Tiggy-Winkle is one of Potter's most novel, for it is seldom that one sees in literature a personified hedgehog. Though animals of the unconventional, unpettable sort do occasionally appear in fairy tales and other children's stories, yet, with the exception of Kenneth Graham's riverbank characters, such animals are not usually well-developed or frequent actors in the stories. On the other hand, Mrs. Tiggy-Winkle is Potter's unique re-creation of the stodginess of a hedgehog into a fastidious washerwoman. The story is reminiscent of *Alice in Wonderland* in the dream-vision that Potter suggests to explain Lucie's visit to the hedgehog's home. But Mrs. Tiggy is created so consistently and convincingly as a country washerwoman that the reader hardly believes that Lucie, the little girl to whom Mrs. Tiggy appears, was only dreaming. (p. 88)

The story was written from Potter's own intimate familiarity with and affection for a pet hedgehog, acquired on one of the family vacations. The eyes of this particular pet engaged Potter's fancy, and there are many sketches of hedgehogs personified in Potter's early work, before she went on to become a published author-illustrator. Mrs. Tiggy's chattiness and competence derive from her model, a Kitty Macdonald, washerwoman to the Potter family during their summer vacations in Scotland from 1871 to 1882. Potter visited this woman several times after the family had decided to spend their holidays elsewhere, and was particularly struck by the woman's lively, active intelligence and phenomenal memory, even at the advanced age of eighty-four. The suitability of the hedgehog as personifier of the washerwoman arose out of their mutual rotundity and affection for the author. As a longtime friend and traveling companion of the author, Mrs. Tiggy presented herself as a likely candidate for a book of her own as early as 1901.

While Mrs. Tiggy's quizzical, perceptive eye and felicitous reincarnation as a washerwoman are part of the book's success, the drawings of Lucie are one of its chief failures. Potter had trouble drawing the little girl, not because the model was unwilling to pose, but because, once again, she was faced with her own inability to draw humans. The drawings of Lucie were further complicated by Potter's lack of attention to one significant detail: the color of Lucie's cloak, red in some of the original drawings, blue in others, and soft brown in her revisions. When she saw the first proofs of the pictures, she was indecisive about the red or blue, but both colors appeared too hot and vivid for Mrs. Tiggy's muted, pastel world. Both author and editor decided on brown for the final pictures. Potter drew and redrew Lucie's figure, both because of the editor's demand for better pictures, and because of the obvious need for consistency in the color of Lucie's cloak. Lucie's features were rubbed out and drawn again, sometimes even cut out and pasted in again on the original drawings as Potter worked through her revisions. As a result, the final pictures of Lucie are blurred, with none of the bold, sure line that Potter confidently used to draw Mrs. Tiggy. The little girl's postures were awkward and stiff and compare unfavorably to Mrs. Tiggy's deft, bustling activity in her kitchen. Potter tried recomposing some of the pictures to minimize her problems with the little girl's figure, exchanging Mrs. Tiggy's full back view for Lucie's, but nothing seems to have succeeded. Lucie in some pose or other, however minimized her presence might be in the picture, still had to appear.

The plot is also thin, with little of the complication evident in the earlier *Two Bad Mice* or later Sawrey books. It is Mrs. Tiggy's personality and lifestyle that hold the book together. Potter admitted to Norman Warne that she thought the book was another one for girls, like *Two Bad Mice,* and that girls would find the clothing particularly interesting. Like *Two Bad Mice, Mrs. Tiggy-Winkle* is also a story that revolves around a house, this time a hedgehog's burrow. Like most girls' books, the scene is primarily interior and the interests domestic. But there is a significant change from the mouse book to the hedgehog book in regard to domestic arrangements: Mrs. Tiggy is a countrywoman, and the detail of the stone floors, open hearth, and simple but comfortable bench before the fire, all show Potter's approval of the hedgehog's simple but cozy household. There is none of the ironic commentary about human housekeeping that the reader finds in *Two Bad Mice.* Instead, the reader finds total, loving approbation of the laundress, her home, and her pride in her business. One suspects that Potter found in Mrs. Tiggy many of the virtues she sought to pursue in her own life as a farmer and homeowner.

Though the scene is primarily interior, *Mrs. Tiggy-Winkle* gives the first glimpses of Potter's rural countryside, which she portrayed more fully as her Sawrey books progressed. There are a few wide vistas, showing the mountains which later connoted permanence and reliability for the author. There are stone fences, country pathways, and homes of natural, unadorned materials. *Mrs. Tiggy-Winkle* is the first of the books to celebrate this simple, unchanging way of life, and Potter's admiration for it is evident. (pp. 89-91)

[In *The Pie and the Patty-Pan*] Potter's focus in the story was as much on the picturesque beauty of the village as on the elaborate, if humorous, mannerliness of her neighbors. In a pattern that she was to repeat in later Sawrey books she lavished as much attention on the details of the floral profusion in the village and in her own garden as on the story itself. In fact, the story is a rather confusing one, and not one of her most popular, perhaps because it depends on a knowledge of old stoves used in open fireplaces and a series of inferences about the two pies that may be hard for very young children to figure out.

And yet the pictures are some of the most beautiful she ever drew, especially those of the many doorways and garden plots, with flowers typical of the various locales. The colors here are not the usual muted greens and browns that the viewer has come to expect of Potter, nor of the simple contrasts resulting from the colors of individual animals' clothing, with muted reds and blues chosen for their values of contrast. Rather, Potter used the whole range of bright colors, including oranges, violets, and bright yellows seldom seen in her other books. Even Ribby's carefully chosen lilac silk dress shows Potter's concern for color, and Duchess's luxurious black mane is unusually decorative for Potter's dogs.

The details of her house, including the oven with three doors, the top being decorative and unfunctional, as the narrative specifies, and the coronation teapot that Ribby proudly uses for this state occasion, are lovingly and minutely detailed. Potter even specifies that the hearthrug is made of rabbit pelts (in Potter's own house, the rug was of lambskin), and even the kinds of plants she had inside her house, which are all carefully and colorfully detailed, with much more brightness than in other Potter books. The large format that Warne used to issue the book originally, the captions under each picture, and the occasional lack of coordination between text and illustration, show her delight in the pictures, sometimes at the expense of the text. And yet her pride of ownership is evident, and one suspects that even if she had to observe manners as peculiar as those of Ribby and Duchess, yet Potter would have done so to make herself part of the village and establish herself as a hostess and accomplished homemaker.

Soon after she wrote to Noel Moore about Peter Rabbit's story in 1893, Potter wrote another picture letter to his younger brother Eric about the adventures of a frog who goes fishing. The scene was set on the River Tay near one of the Potters' Scottish vacation sites where Mr. Potter and his friends frequently fished. (pp. 95-6)

One cannot help but suspect that Potter modeled [the] gentlemanly activities [depicted in *The Tale of Mr. Jeremy Fisher*] after those of her father and his friends at his club. Their sole concern in life was how to occupy their leisure time, and the activities they invented to do so were pursued sometimes to the point of absurd obsession. They did little that was useful or needful, but yet they contrived to enjoy themselves. As Potter conceived of it, life on the edge of the pond was equally leisurely, though life-and-death concerns occasionally surfaced. . . . (p. 98)

In *Jeremy Fisher* Potter celebrated and preserved the leisurely lives and characters of her aquatic acquaintances in the country she was growing to love. As much as she found the lives of her father and his male acquaintances humorous and trivial, yet she valued their outdoor pursuits and the pleasure they found in nature, it would seem from her use of their sports in this book. She valued nature untouched by humans even more, as is clear from the careful observation she shows in her pictures. The story is not a particularly complicated one and was apparently written with few of her usually relentless revisions. Yet the pictures have a finished quality without this effort. They are truly remarkable in their coloring, dominated by the blue water and green marine growth. Her ability to show human society without also implying its damaging effects on flora and fauna further underscores the book's felicitous composition and success.

Tom Kitten is the first of Beatrix Potter's Sawrey books and introduces characters that she used in nearly all of the books about Sawrey that followed. Though one usually thinks of cats as pets, on a farm they are working animals and must earn their keep. Though they fall into the category of what Potter elsewhere called "serious" animals, yet they are also full of character and mischief. Tabitha Twitchit was a long-time feline resident of the farm at Hill Top, and an important ally in the perennial battle against the rats who threatened the conduct of businesslike farming. It is not surprising, then, to find her a focal character in three of Potter's books, and a peripheral character in one other. Her character here is a blend of Potter herself and someone who probably resembled Potter's mother, or perhaps some other proper Victorian matron.

Tom Kitten is a book about manners and how children react to them. . . . Let loose in the garden, the kittens do exactly what their mother has forbidden, first soiling their clothes and then losing them to a family of ducks, who retrieve them as the kittens gradually discard them. When their mother finds her offspring, her sense of social propriety is mortified, and she sends them upstairs to bed. She misrepresents to her guests that the children have the measles, while the guests in turn try to ignore the sounds of the kittens' romp in the bedroom. Meanwhile, the ducks wear the kittens' clothing while swimming and lose the garments at the bottom of the pond, where they look for them still. Thus, Potter explains in the fashion of the *pourquoi* fairy tale why ducks are so frequently seen with their heads in the water and their tails upright: they are looking for the clothes they have stolen from Tom Kitten and his sisters. (pp. 98-9)

Though one's sympathies tend to run with the kittens, as one might expect in children's literature, yet one senses that the author is not altogether condemning Tabitha for her attempts at propriety. Potter composed *Tom Kitten* just after she bought the farm at Hill Top, and her own pride at proper housekeeping and tasteful decoration is evident in the book. The new clock she had purchased for the main room of the farmhouse is prominently displayed with a proprietor's pride in the picture of Tabitha ushering her kittens upstairs to be washed and dressed. The flowered washbowl which the mother uses and the caned chair on which she stands the kittens to be washed are lovingly and carefully drawn. The profusely flowering garden to which the kittens are exiled is minutely observed in its artistically arranged species-specific blooms. One can feel Potter's approval of Tabitha's wish to provide her guests with an elegant occasion, and her wish to impress them.

But the reader also senses her criticism of such pretentious behavior and of the results of a social code that forces people, especially children, to be what they are not. The cadence of Tabitha's prohibition to the children as they are sent out into the garden strikes the reader as the production of one who heard many such orders peremptorily issued to her in her own childhood. The picture of the kittens' immediate distraction from and disregard for what their mother is saying is the sympathetic response of one whose own youthful reaction was to do as she pleased, in direct contradiction to parental orders. Potter herself wanted to make friends among the villagers at Sawrey; giving proper tea parties would have been one way to ingratiate herself. But, finally, her sympathies lie with the kittens, whose impulse is to have fun. Her dedication of the book "To All Pickles,—Especially to Those That Get Upon My Garden Wall" suggests her pleasure with animal pranks, which overrode almost any other consideration in her life. (p. 103)

The Roly-Poly Pudding seems to some readers ominous, with

From The Tale of Little Pig Robinson, *written and illustrated by Beatrix Potter.*

its foreshadowing of the difficulties Tom will encounter up the chimney signaling a growing tension over Tom's fate: "Now this is what had been happening to Tom Kitten, and it shows how very unwise it is to go up a chimney in a very old house, where a person does not know his way, and where there are enormous rats". Margaret Lane claims that it is the best of Potter's "great near-tragedies," a term originated by Graham Greene. Lane notes Potter's willingness to frighten her readers. It is true that there are a number of possibly fatal ends confronting Tom: incineration in the chimney if the newly started fire catches him, abandonment under the attic floorboards, where he is so tightly tied up that he can neither move nor call out for help, or cooking to death as the main course of the rats' dinner. The mutton bones that he finds in the chimney, where the rats are storing them, foreshadow Tom's own skeletal remains after his death. But the entire situation is so preposterous that Tom's dismal end seems unlikely. Samuel and Anna Maria are pictured as rats of substance, with plenty of girth and enough power to roll a rolling pin up the stairs to the attic. Yet it seems outrageous that they could actually frighten even a young kitten and tie him up. Samuel's portliness makes him an object of the reader's laughter. And his arguments with Anna Maria over the proper way to prepare a pudding hardly make him sinister. Though the story could be ghastly, yet from the beginning Potter creates an outlandish scene where, though the reader is clearly in the realm of fantasy, even so, common sense intervenes to mitigate any genuine threat. (p. 108)

The plenitude of pictures, both in color and in black and white, indicates Potter's willingness to spend time drawing and redrawing the interior of the house she loved so well. And her ability to draw the house from a cat's perspective shows her careful consideration of the house from all different angles, not just her own. Her drawing of Anna Maria's scurry along the floor in front of the dresser with the pretty plates indicates that if she did not get down on the floor herself to do the drawing, she was able to contemplate and observe what the room and the dresser would look like from the rat's perspective. Her drawings make the house look grand and spacious, in contrast to the small, cozy sense it has for humans. But from the point of view of cats, the house truly is large. And her two drawings that include the bannister and spindles on the stairway to the second floor imply her admiration for the carpentry and her affection for the claret-colored curtains which she hung in the window on the landing. Finally, her picture of the view of the countryside from the top of the chimney suggests that, in her rummaging about the house, and in the process of repair, she actually climbed on the roof herself to see what Tom Kitten sees. Her appreciation of the house not only extended to its small details, but also to its perspective from different points of view, literally, from the floor to the roof. (p. 109)

The book celebrates Potter's love, not only of the house, but of the way of life it represented for her, full of antiquity and order in her own house, with all of her special things exactly where she wanted them. For a woman who grew up in a house dominated solely by her parents and their wishes about arrangements, the owning of such a house must have been a great accomplishment. That the house should have included a population of rodents was a mere difficulty, and hardly an insurmountable one. Potter cherished the interruptions and impositions of that "Persecuted (But Irrepressible) Race," as she called the rats in her dedication so long as they did no real harm.

Jemima Puddle-Duck is Beatrix Potter's "poem about the farm," as Margaret Lane describes it. It is the first of her books set wholly and unequivocally at Hill Top Farm among the farm animals. It features as part of its panoramic background buildings and vistas specific to the farm and to the country around Near Sawrey. Those who visit Near Sawrey today will find little changed in the more than seventy years that have passed since the book was written. (p. 110)

Like Mrs. Rabbit in ***Peter Rabbit,*** Jemima Puddle-Duck is a character set in some not-too-distant but still remote past. Her shawl may have been typical dress for a farm lady of Potter's period, but the poke bonnet dates her as a resident of the past. The fox, never named as such, but always described as the gentleman "with the sandy coloured whiskers", wears a coat with a long tail. He cultivates manners so exquisitely proper that he, too, places himself in that uncertain past. As Potter pointed out, the story is a revision of the fairy tale "Little Red-Riding Hood" and thus properly belongs in a period "once upon a time," in any time but now.

Jemima is also modeled after a particularly quirky duck who lived on Potter's farm. She was known for trying to evade the farmer's wife and her children in their attempts to locate her eggs and take them away from her before she had a chance to mismanage their incubation. Mrs. Cannon, the wife of the tenant manager who ran Hill Top Farm in Potter's absence, was in the habit of confiscating the ducks' eggs and letting hens incubate them, ducks being, in her estimation, poor sitters and likely to abandon their eggs.

Though Jemima is rescued at the end, and there is something of a happy ending in the four new ducklings, still the story is one of Potter's more ominous. Jemima is such an innocent, so headstrong, that the reader doubts her judgment from the beginning. When she meets the gentleman, her inability to see through his invitation to sit on her eggs at his home further places her well-being in jeopardy and increases tension about the outcome. That the fox's home is placed among the fox-gloves is a sure sign to the reader that the gentleman is really no gentleman, but a fox. The gentleman is described as sitting on his tail, owing to the dampness, another ominous indicator of his real identity. (pp. 111-12)

The loss of the ducklings is sad for the duck as well as the reader, especially the child reader whose sympathies might naturally be expected to lie with the helpless egg-ducklings. It is likely, as Margaret Lane pointed out, that Potter felt obliged to end the story happily, for the sake of Ralph and Betsy Cannon, the children of her farm's manager and the people to whom the story was dedicated. Though she did not avoid horrific implications and grisly details it must have seemed unthinkable to let Jemima end as a bloody mess in the fox's lair, especially with children watching. Jemima is punished, but the harshness of the justice is mitigated to some degree by the fact that she is allowed one more chance to hatch a brood herself. (p. 113)

The story shows Potter at her finest in portraying the details of life at Hill Top and her love for the picturesque details of the village of Near Sawrey. But because of the archetypical model of the story—the helpless and naive beguiled but rescued from seeming self-destruction by the loyal and dependable—Potter manages to make this more than just a story of local color and interest. It is, as the dedication says, a "Farmyard Tale" with implications about self-preservation and shrewdness as admirable virtues. Graham Greene suggests that at this point in her life she suffered some kind of mental breakdown, given the ominous gloom he finds in the character of the sandy-whiskered gentleman. More likely she was simply coming to terms with life on the farm, where wild animals invade the domain of the domesticated ones and where death, if not always so threatening, was still part of the business of running a farm.

If *Jemima Puddle-Duck* is Beatrix Potter's story about farm-life in Sawrey and *The Roly-Poly Pudding* is her celebration of her farmhouse, then *Ginger and Pickles* is her celebration of village life, especially as it revolves around the main center of attraction and social life, the village store. The title of the book is not only the name of the establishment in Potter's fictionalized version of Near Sawrey, it is also the name of the two proprietors, a tomcat and a terrier, respectively. In this book Potter not only preserves in her fiction many of the people she has come to know in the village, she also portrays a new preoccupation that she found dominating her life since she had become a landowner and businesswoman: how to make a profit, and how to keep accounts. The book brings back many familiar characters from earlier Potter books as patrons of the store, at the same time that it introduces this new concern for bookkeeping and solvency while dealing with one's neighbors as clients. (p. 114)

The colored drawings for the book are much more vivid and varied in their tones than in other Potter stories, but perhaps this is because the animals here are not pursuing animal lives, with the exception of the mice, who are generally not shown wearing clothing as they follow their natural inclinations to raid the stores. Instead, these animals are behaving distinctly as humans, except when Ginger and Pickles admit their natural taste for some of the rabbit and mice customers. Shopping and shopkeeping are human pursuits, and so these animals are shown wearing human clothes. The colors of these clothes are all artificial, with no attempt to make the animals fit into nature by giving them clothing of natural browns and greens. Peter Rabbit's blue coat is definitely a man-made blue. Instead of wearing the more neutral black clogs of his own book, on the cover to *Ginger and Pickles* he wears red pumps. The walls of the shop are painted a brilliant green in contrast to the more muted, subtle tones that Potter used in other books in the woodland scenes. And the brick walls of the shop are fuchsia in color, as are the shawls of Jemima Puddle-Duck and Mrs. Tiggy-Winkle, and the tablecloths and chair in Ginger and Pickles' business office. Though fuchsia does occur in nature, it is not usual except in hybrid plants and a few wildflowers. Its prominence in this book points to Potter's design to record human village life through her animals, rather than to place her animals in a fantasy world that is parallel to the human realm. That the toy policeman-doll might summon a real policeman, and that Ginger and Pickles cast their accounts in pounds sterling indicates that this book describes human beings more than it does animals.

The book ends in one of Potter's most extended codas to any book. The story goes fully twenty pages beyond the closing of the shop by the cat and dog. Both animals find careers afterwards, and the shop changes hands. Their customers go on to several different provisioners, and suffer from these businesspersons' foibles, such as Sally Henny Penny's "Grand co-operative Jumble" and the unwillingness of the mice to follow the customary practice of taking back the unburnt ends of candles when their customers were finished with them. The dependence of any town on its shopkeepers, especially a small village where contact with the outside world was limited, is focal, for both patrons and proprietors. And for a small village the peculiarities of the shopkeepers would have been a subject of great interest and gossip. The lengthiness of the ending has much of the ungainly shapelessness of human gossip; it rambles on, and yet fittingly so, given the humanness of the story and its interest. Shopkeeping and all the accoutrements of a general store had long been thought appropriate materials for children, as seen in the many German toy books, with pop-up, fold-out pages full of the many products that such a general store would have. Yet here Potter gives her child readers a glimpse of what adults would also have found interesting about a store: the social life that revolves around it and the quirks of the residents of the village. (pp. 116-18)

As the last of the Sawrey books to be written during her period of phenomenal production, Beatrix Potter chose to write a love story. In keeping with the increasing complexity of her plots and the growing malignity of her villains, in *Pigling Bland* it is not natural, innate animosity of one species of animal for another that causes the conflict. Instead, it is man's use—and abuse—of farm livestock that sets the story's villainy in motion. Though the hero and heroine, both pigs, find happiness at the end, it is by evading the humans who threaten to make them into bacon that their happiness is finally realized. Though Potter herself denied that the happy couple is modeled after herself and her husband-to-be, she did admit that they took long walks along the same path that Pigling Bland and his girl-pig used. The comic ending of the dance and imminent marriage suggest that a similar escape into happily-ever-after was in store for her with marriage to William Heelis. (p. 120)

Unlike her other books, *Pigling Bland* was not extended past its real ending. In fact, the reader is pleasantly, if somewhat abruptly surprised by the ending, since the eventual fate of the two pigs is only implied in the closing couplets arranged as prose: "They came to the river, they came to the bridge—they crossed it hand in hand—then over the hills and far away she danced with Pigling Bland!" There is no description of their occupations in later life, as with Ginger and Pickles or Tom Kitten and sisters or Jemima Puddle-Duck. The book's end comes as a surprise because of the heightened tension in the lines preceding, underscored by the nearly breathless rhythm of the sentences. The tension is further drawn out because the two halves of the ending rhyme are separated by a turn of the page, and the fact that the rhyme is a rhyme at all is not clear until the "Pigling Bland" is made to rhyme with "hand in hand." The neat ending in couplet suggests a Shakespearean influence, as does the final dance, in its reassertion of cosmic order and continuance of life. The presence of the signpost, both in the frontispiece and in the final picture, suggests that the turning point is a clear, conscious decision to choose happiness and the farmer's way of life for Potter. The musical accompaniment by the rabbits signals a career come full circle, with the rabbits of the earlier books joining the pigs in a grand finale.

Potter's pictures for the story show her growing predilection for pen-and-ink sketches, and the felicity she felt resulted from quick sketching rather than laborious drawing. Certainly her drawings of the humans so prominent in this story was aided by this rapid method of composition, and by her good sense in focusing more on the animals in the story rather than on the humans. Her pictures of herself, at first just as a hand helping to dress the pigs for market, then in full frontal pose, are happily posed, in that she does not give her own figure facial detail, and the lack of eyes makes her presence less obtrusive. The presence of the hand is metaphorically suggestive, in that she is lending Aunt Pettitoes a hand in raising the litter, and in that she has a hand in deciding the piglets' fates. Warne's method of producing her books had changed, so that the colored pictures could not be placed anywhere in the book but only at designated intervals. Yet Potter was careful not to set what she considered too much text opposite the pictures, and carefully coordinated each picture opposite the appropriate text. This was the last time that she would take such care with a book, preparing more than a few colored drawings and creating a whole new story. (pp. 126-27)

Since the time of Aesop's fables, animals and stories about them have been assumed to be appropriate vehicles for moral messages. The transformation of the beast fable into the children's story was an easy leap, especially in the eighteenth century, when moral education became a primary goal. As rural landscape gave way to urban settings and the problems in the industrial revolution, the life of country and farm, including animal inhabitants, gradually became idealized. Thus, the nostalgia for childhood gradually incorporated idealization of farm and wild animals.

The environmental conservation movement beginning in the early twentieth century and the inculcation of its values among children added to the new interest in wildlife studies and animal stories for the young. Potter's books appeared at a time when animals and their lives were a ritual and requisite part of any young child's education. As Margaret Blount says, animal books are the kind that adults enjoy giving to children, regardless of whether children truly enjoy reading them.

Potter's books are particularly enjoyable for adults to read because of her subtle humor and lack of condescension, especially when the pictures comment ironically about the action and when the language is elegant. As Patricia Dooley has noted, when a parent can expect to read the same book over and over to please a child, anything the least bit interesting to the adult can be a welcome relief to the tedium. And as she further notes, the favorites of the adult rapidly become the favorites of the child. Especially in the mouse books, the detail of the pictures can supply new items of interest in repeated readings, another source of relief for the adult.

For the child, the pictures supply what Diana Klemin has called a "common visual heritage," showing how Western culture assumes that rabbit, mice, gardens, and country landscape should look. Picture books for the very young also introduce the child to the book itself and the conventions of reading. For example, children learn by experiences with books that books open with the binding to the left and continue chronologically from front to back. The pictures correspond in some way to the text on the same page or double-page spread. But though pictures and text may appear on the same page, the letters of the words are not part of the picture, even though the words may appear superimposed. The turning of pages indicates the passage of time. Pictures of the same characters appear and denote the same characters, not different ones, even though they may appear on different pages. All of these are conventions that children are not born with, but rather come to understand as they experience books, especially early picture books, including Potter's.

Because the Potter books are small, they do not adapt well to large storytelling situations, where many children might try to look at the same pictures at the same time. But their diminutive size does encourage an intimacy between adult reader and child listener, or between the child and the book. This experience of intimacy, between adult and child, and between the child and the easily handled book, encourages a comfortable, enjoying attitude toward reading, which was certainly in Potter's mind when she designed the small format. The relatively inexpensive price—as Potter said, all her young readers were "shilling" people—and the excellent quality of paper and binding even today, ensure a book that is both durable and important-feeling, the fine paper giving a sense of permanency and significance to the story and pleasure to the tactile aspects of the reading experience. One cannot overlook the relevance of the "feel" of a book in encouraging children to enjoy the reading. Books that smack of ephemerality and a trivial, "throw-away" experience may make for passing reading pleasure but give little sense of the dignity and durability of the joy of reading. Even the typeface may add to the reading experience. In Potter's case the type is a simple Roman style, but the added width of the downstrokes underscores the density and solidity of her blocks of text, while the small serifs lend a sense of elegance to her words. All of these features of her books tend to enhance their popularity. (pp. 130-32)

The books, *Peter Rabbit* especially, have been retold, re-illustrated, and otherwise violated by other authors and illustrators. Yet the originals endure, not to be overtaken by more modern updatings.

One of the reasons for this remarkable longevity is Potter's unwillingness to compromise the truth in order to shelter young readers. Though her endings are happy ones, they do not deny the existence of pain and death, and do not skirt the enmity between various animal species, or between the animals and human beings. Big animals eat little animals; humans eat all kinds of creatures. Adults sometimes use language that children do not quite understand, the meaning of which they can still derive from context. But though she does not deal with the more mature, bloody, grisly aspects of carnivore life, Potter faces it, admits it, and yet does not terrorize children with it. Her animals, especially the rabbits, glance fearfully out at the reader, as if admitting the frank terror with which human presence inspires them. As Blount says, the stories and pictures give credence to the idea that Potter is telling the truth, that the stories might really have happened, but never in the presence of human beings. Thus, the reader is invited into the fantasy with a sense that he is not being patronized, and that life is not being edited for his benefit and protection.

The animals are all small, and with the exception of the frogs, ducks, and insects, are all mammals, if not always furry and pettable, as with the hedgehogs and pigs. But their smallness makes them "rubbish" as Potter called them, all expendable animals, not those who work for a living, such as horses and sheepdogs. The smallness here is important; they are all smaller than children and thus inspire childlike mastery and patronage of their smallness. None of the animals is the equal of a child either in intelligence or size, and thus each can be admired by a child or sympathetic adult without being dealt with as a creature of equal or greater power or stature. The furry animals particularly invite sympathy because of the pleasure of petting them. But even Mrs. Tiggy and Pigling Bland have their charming, admirable qualities that make them pets rather than livestock. Jemima Puddle-Duck is the only central character who might be considered a "working" animal; but her unreliable nerves make her attempts at labor humorous, and she is too unsteady to be a producer of eggs and ducklings in the manner of a reliable farm duck. The piglets are surplus, and not yet large enough to be livestock; they are sent to market rather than being kept on the farm to be seriously businesslike. Thus their expendability and youthfulness makes them pets as well.

Potter's popularity has influenced her followers, but her influence is not as obvious among writers as it is among illustrators. Almost all rabbits in children's stories now look like Peter, and almost all landscapes are as expansively drawn and extensively colored. Though, as Margaret Blount points out, Potter's landscapes are of real places, yet for modern readers they are also idealized, for though the unspoiled Lake District still exists, it is not familiar to all readers, and most landscapes are somehow marred by the years intervening since Potter drew hers. The virgin territory that Potter recorded is almost unknown in technologically advanced cultures, as is the simple country life she preserved, especially in the Sawrey books. As in her work for the National Trust, one of Potter's greatest legacies is her preservation, both in the lands held in trust and in her books, of the way of life she came to live in that isolated part of England. This idealization of a landscape and a lifestyle now archaic, but also actually experienced, is part of the nostalgic, Anglophilic domain that predominates in illustrating for children.

Most of Potter's followers in the genre of the animal story are not really heirs to her legacy, for they follow the habits of Leslie Brooke and Thornton Burgess in giving animals clothing and personifying them without remaining true to animal nature. In many ways these animals are simply humans with animal heads on their shoulders, tricked out in elaborate but functionless human accessories. Though Marcus Crouch points to Alison Uttley and her Grey Rabbit books as direct heirs of Potter's animal techniques, yet these animals also do not wear their clothes as comfortably as do Peter Rabbit and kin. The heritage lies more clearly, as Crouch says, in the love of country life rather than in the actualization of animalness in Uttley's creations. As mentioned above, Potter is part of the trend in idealizing rural life as the perfect locale for childhood, but it is more the trend than Potter's direct influence that persists.

In the realm of bookmaking her influence is much clearer. Her format has been borrowed by a number of publishing houses for series of books, mostly of the inexpensive, easily reproduced sort. Some illustrators have tried re-illustrating Potter's books. But for an artist to take on the project of retelling a story where the illustrations are so well known that they are virtually identified as the story, where illustration and story are so familiar and intertwined as to be inseparable, the illustrator must have a whole new vision of the story, something new to say about it in his illustrations. That new vision must be clearly bodied forth in his illustrations so that the story really becomes his own. Few artists have tried and even fewer have succeeded in this task, and none have managed to do anything with Potter's books other than to disrupt and misinterpret the tales.

Potter's use of color and exquisite detail set a new standard in color illustration for children's books, and encouraged the use of more color and more careful drafting in pictures. Though it is difficult to single out any particular authors and illustrators who followed Potter as direct heirs, it is easy to see the greater attention to color, especially watercolor, and detail, and the increased number of serious artists who found children's books an appropriate medium for their professional efforts. Potter still maintains this standard for children's books and is not likely to be replaced or surpassed any time soon.

Potter's animals are all true to life, both as animals and as fictional characters. The reactions of her child readers kept Potter honest, both to child nature and to animal nature. The stories seem as if they might have happened. They do not beg questions to interrupt the feeling of internal consistency in the conception of the fantasy, the pursuit of the answers to which might have interrupted the suspension of disbelief that makes their fantasy possible. If one has not seen such animals, it is because they do not live in close, intimate quarter with human beings, or perhaps because one is not attentive enough. Only Potter could see what these animals were doing, and through her patient, carefully chronicled stories we come to know what J. R. R. Tolkien said is one of the most fervent wishes of humankind: to know what animals are actually saying. Potter's stories answer for the reader not only what animals are like, but also function as fairy tales do in telling us human beings what we are like. In her criticism of human manners and society Potter openly attacks human prejudice and presumption, and yet by using animals as her vehicles of criticism, she also shows the way to human improvement: be like animals, honest, straightforward, even violent, but always truthful and true to nature. (pp. 132-35)

Ruth K. MacDonald, in her Beatrix Potter, *Twayne Publishers, 1986, 148 p.*

MARGERY FISHER

An art critic once suggested that generations of artistic taste had been formed by Beatrix Potter's books. It is true that children brought up on them share certain responses to landscape painting as well as special attitudes to humanized animals in fiction. (p. 4)

Why has Beatrix Potter held her place unchallenged for the best part of a century? For one thing, because of her prose, her precisely selected words, elegant syntax, pace and tension, quiet humour. There is everything here to please a child and everything to impress adults; nobody who has ever read one of her stories to a small child can ignore the exactness, the luminous simplicity of her writing, the imagination that can see animals in terms of human action without distortion. The shorter tales can be understood by a two-year-old; the longer adventures of Mr Tod, Pig Robinson or Ginger and Pickles are best left for a year or two.

Then, her illustrations. A trained artist, observant and highly skilled in the tradition of English watercolour, she disciplined her vision to a format suitable for small hands and eyes. Her economy makes the pictures of all her successors seem cluttered and imprecise. She is equally at home depicting wide Lakeland landscapes such as Tom Kitten saw from a chimney stack or the close-up corners of the shop where mice helped the old Tailor of Gloucester to complete the Mayor's wedding garments. She can show us the neat, flickering movements of a mouse and the ponderous stateliness of Aunt Pettitoes in the pigsty, the elastic leaps of the frog Jeremy Fisher and the daintily fussy gestures of Mrs Ribby, the sociable cat. In her books the village of Sawrey and its environs come to life, and a whole set of animal characters parade for the delight of children, and of the child in all of us. (pp. 4-5)

Margery Fisher, "Beatrix Potter: 'The Tale of Peter Rabbit' (1902)," in her Margery Fisher Recommends Classics for Children & Young People, *Thimble Press, 1986, pp. 4-5.*

CHARLES FREY

The little books of Beatrix Potter, . . . provide at a glance all the aura of snugly domesticated pet-life that one could wish to associate with the grace and good will of their Edwardian progenitor some eighty years ago. In these books, things always turn out for the best; a pastel charm hangs over all. Kittens, ducks, and bunnies pass by in idylls of minor mishaps and major joys. Here life appears to be lightly dreamed in the mind of a comic Providence.

Still, without accepting the label of Lugubrious Analyzer, one might usefully note the extent to which an author-illustrator for young children, one such as Beatrix Potter, may mix her domesticating touch with a touch more nearly feral, finding almost mad energies in modern Edens. To get at a little of that mix between homiletic hominess and more savage celebrations will be my concern here. My main intention is to recognize and reverence the wider scope, the deeper fullness, the challenging maturity of an often-misinterpreted or taken-for-granted voice in children's literature.

Rabbits are often accepted by small children as comfortable familiars. Rabbits are easily domesticated, and Potter's drawings in *Peter Rabbit,* emphasizing the toddlerlike largeness

of heads and stomachs and switching from clothes to no clothes, continually suggest that crossing the line from natural rabbit to house rabbit and back may not be difficult. The frontispiece, which forecasts the ending of the story, immediately signals to the child viewer that sympathy as well as humor is directed at Peter. Snug in a very comfortable bed, he has enough spirit (even at the end of his ordeal) to resist his mother's dose of medicine. That we see only his ears and paws makes us laugh both at him and at his exasperated mother. Peter, then, is as much boy as rabbit. His sisters have rabbit names—Flopsy, Mopsy, and Cottontail—but he is different; he is "Peter," perhaps a more human creature than his sister rabbits. But what does it mean to be more human and a boy? Is that state of boy a naughty one? or nice? (pp. 105-06)

A young child listening to the story and looking at the pictures might easily become quite seriously wrapped up in the danger and excitement of Peter's flight. But Mr. McGregor's more violently intended ministrations in applying the sieve and his own foot to Peter are made to seem less violent by the composition of illustrations and wording of text. Peter looks rather sleek and graceful as he jumps away, and one notes his rabbity energy and his full form in contrast to the partially shown weapon of his enemy. In each drawing Potter scatters three things in an artful symmetry of flight, and the text assays internal rhymes that suggest providential control of the violence: "intended to *pop* upon the *top* of Peter"; "tried to *put* his *foot* upon Peter."

The action slows down and the text fills up as Peter enters a more reflective phase of his adventure, asking for help, becoming "puzzled," and learning quietly to avoid the danger of the cat. We see Peter watching the cat, then Peter watching Mr. McGregor, and then the three sparrows watching Peter exit under the gate. The last garden picture yields three blackbirds gazing inquisitively up at the "scare-crow" while another blackbird perches perkily on the cross piece. The incongruous scarecrow does not work, and we know why: the birds in the garden are the kind who can "implore" Peter to "exert" himself. Mr. McGregor's views of animal nature and intelligence are obviously crude and ignorant. But it's worth noting that Beatrix Potter's sophistication and delicacy of humor might be absorbed by young children only in subconscious and transmuted forms. In my experience, such children tend to take the story quite seriously and straightforwardly. Peter is in big trouble, and they know it. (p. 107)

The Tale of Peter Rabbit leaves us with a good many open questions concerning its intention and capacity to reassure child listeners and watchers that things work out for the best in a pretty fair world. Is it just coincidence that the protagonist of the tale is a boy and not a girl? Is Potter suggesting that it's more natural for boys to have such adventures? That for Peter it was more nearly fun than it would have been for his sisters? How near to fun is Peter's adventure in which he disobeys, overeats, is chased, becomes tangled in a net, gets soaked through, almost is stomped, is called a thief, cries, barely escapes, comes home exhausted, has to drink repellent medicine, and misses his sisters' desserts? The humorous touches of verbal humor and the restrained watercolors may mitigate a child's tendency to empathic misadventure, but surely a sense of fearful process can hardly be wholly repressed. Such boys as Peter, if not made of snails and puppy dogs' tails, are made in any case to seem out of control, out

An unfinished pen-and-ink drawing by Potter of Hill Top Farm in Near Sawrey.

of control over their own instincts and over the main elements in their environment.

Perhaps a last teasing question might be to ponder what part of Beatrix Potter is represented and active in Peter Rabbit? Would a social historian find food for thought in the Edwardian and Georgian false calms before the masculinist holocaust of World War I? Would a biographer wander into Potter's perhaps overprotected childhood replete with governess, home schooling, absorption in journals, art, and sympathy for pets and animals mistreated by alien fathers? Whatever one's conclusions, one would come back to **The Tale of Peter Rabbit** tolerably less inclined to view it as simply a cute little book of frothy incidents and happy ending. Peter, after all, is being chased by a creature who ate Peter's father and who would stomp Peter's life out with a hob-nailed boot. In the story, rabbits and children seem related to humans and grownups in a tangle of victimizing forces. That the beauty of the telling and the grace of the illustrations distance the reality of Peter's fear does not mean such fear vanishes completely for children experiencing the book. Where does the fear go? What, finally, does it signify?

In **The Tale of Squirrel Nutkin,** Beatrix Potter again sets up a challenge of a young male animal to the right of an older male to control who eats and is eaten in a semisacred space. Old Brown, the owl who controls the island to which the squirrels come for food-gathering, is not human as was Mr. McGregor, and Nutkin's affront does not involve thievery so much as a more direct assault upon Brown's exalted status. Brown, like a god, accepts offerings on his doorstep, seemingly in return for permitting the squirrels to gather food in his domain. But Nutkin refuses to participate either in the sacrifice or harvest. His principal intent is to tease Old Brown.

Just why he does that, we are never told. We may guess that Nutkin embodies urges deep in many of us to shuck the daily round of responsibility. But his irresponsibility merges with his frolicsome, dancing, riddling dare to expose the silent, menacing, pomposity of Old Brown who, like Mortality itself, seems to assume the right to dispense life and death to lower creatures but who can hardly claim to control the vast elements of wind and sun or the enigma of language in which one name is known through recourse to others. (pp. 107-09)

Potter's illustrations are wonderfully suggestive. Many are humorous in obvious and not so obvious ways. The squirrels use tools of rafts and oars and sacks and fishing poles. Old Brown at first seems just an owl with a crude tree-home. But as the story goes on and Nutkin loses more and more of his manners (as Peter Rabbit lost his clothes), the squirrels seem to revert more and more to merely animal nature whereas the house of Old Brown becomes more and more civilized. We even see him sitting in an elaborately carved chair eating honey with a spoon! Yet his fierce and Olympian silence consumes the most, consumes both the pertinent and impertinent offerings of the squirrels, the whole tale.

All of the squirrels other than Nutkin seem to be exponents of a ceremonial, in some ways religious and propitiatory, way of life. Though squirrels are herbivores, these squirrels are portrayed as catching sacrificial offerings of mice, moles, and minnows. Old Brown promptly eats their offerings (isn't that the third mouse's *tail* drooping out of Old Brown's mouth as Nutkin taunts him with the cherry riddle?), and he acts out the inscrutable ferocity of an ancient god. From this point of view, Nutkin might be viewed parodically as a kind of latter-day Promethean who champions the causes of poetry and pleasure as ends in themselves until made to suffer the consequences. Nutkin is plainly obsessed with Old Brown as himself the riddle of authority, a force that simply is itself, self-contained and betraying no use for words which always put one thing in terms of another.

The denouement is really quite terrific. The squirrels have worked in the fashion of Genesis for six days. They come on "Saturday," "for the last time," to give the great god Brown "a last parting present." Nutkin positively dances like a dervish in a flurry and fury of increasingly impertinent challenges to the Owl. All of Nutkin's *three* riddles tell Old Brown that the powers of authorities like him are helpless to deal with elemental problems such as mending eggs, driving sunbeams away, and turning the wind. Old Brown, in other words, is no God (his name, in fact, riddles over the word "owl" contained anagrammatically within it), so why should the squirrels kowtow to him? Or so one reading of Nutkin's challenge might go. And Nutkin is right. But neither is Nutkin an elemental force such as the wind is. When, in his hubris, Nutkin forgets that fact, makes "a whirring noise to sound like the *wind*," and jumps onto Old Brown, he makes sacrificially the point that his riddles have already made theoretically. Or, to put it another way, he feels impelled to test the truth of his thought. Living a "life of allegory," he forgets what a real owl can do to a real squirrel. And his punishment for that forgetting makes him shun the metaphysical round forever.

"This looks like the end of the story; but it isn't." Having edged close to a surprisingly violent dimension of her story, Potter eases up and gracefully dismisses Nutkin, practically with a suspended sentence, with a slap on the tail and some nonsense words. Readers are reinvited to think of the tale as a neat device for rehearsing some clever chestnuts of riddles for children by setting them in a narrative line. That a good deal more may have been at stake *need* detain no one.

Both *Peter Rabbit* and *Squirrel Nutkin* tell of boys who refuse to participate in the food-gathering work of their clan and who prefer to challenge authority through selfish and somewhat atavistic behavior. The stories *seem* to disapprove of this behavior. High diction phrases such as "excessively impertinent" suggest that the narrator's view is not from the child's eye but from the adult's. Yet the birds implore Peter to exert himself toward escape, and Nutkin's narrator appears self-consciously to intervene to release Nutkin from the Owl's deadly grip. Nutkin's riddles, moreover, give him a density of language that competes with the fancy vocabulary of grown-ups. Still, at the end, he is stripped of that language just as surely as Peter Rabbit is stripped of his blue coat and buttons. With part of our hearts we applaud, perhaps, the daring of the two lads; they follow their *process* to remarkable lengths of individuation. But, underneath, the tales are deeply cautionary: the expression of all that boyish energy and challenge rouses a violently retributive response from male power in the world. Life becomes a losing: no dessert, no more happy riddles. The stories bend us through the double bind of much trenchant narrative: yes, enjoy your adventure while you can, and push it to the farthest, but at the end be prepared to take your medicine, lose your tail, and have nothing left but a stamp of your foot to your impotent shouting: "cuck!"

Beatrix Potter specialized in ritual and semisublimated action of violent cast and fearful import. Her deft economy of narrative line, her set-piece, tableauxlike illustrations, and her zest for the most energetic issues of our desire and anger all took her, repeatedly, to the very jugular of myth and of archetypal dream. She epitomizes the still-underrated but manifest and even disturbing power of children's literature to speak to our keenest wishes and fears. Such literature might be compared to a shrouded dynamo or to a bejeweled Pandoran box. The energy it contains may be only half-noted or remembered by "groan-ups," but it can hardly be lost upon children who are in the very first process of shaping and being shaped by this passionate world. Such children's literature goes in deep. It stays there. Working. (pp. 109-11)

Charles Frey, "Victors and Victims in the Tales of 'Peter Rabbit' and 'Squirrel Nutkin'," in Children's literature in education, *Vol. 18, No. 2, Summer, 1987, pp. 105-11.*

CHARLES FREY AND JOHN GRIFFITH

Readers of **Peter Rabbit** have long noted Beatrix Potter's family-role stereotyping: The rabbit children live with their mother; the girls have rabbit names, the boy is Peter; the girls are good, the boy is naughty; the girls stay close to home, the boy has adventures; the girls gather food, Peter steals it. Peter's mischief is thus partly legislated from the outset by his position in the family. His trip to the garden is terrifying in one sense, but the tale is hardly cautionary. Though Peter loses his clothes, cries, almost gets trampled, comes home exhausted, and is made to drink medicinal tea, the child-reader is fascinated by and attracted to Peter rather than repelled by him. For one thing, Beatrix Potter's humor intervenes on Peter's behalf. Mr. McGregor is a comic antagonist who not only looks silly in his beard, specs, and old-fashioned cap but also calls out after a rabbit, "Stop thief!" We have time, after Peter becomes tangled in the gooseberry net, to consider the color, material, and newness of his jacket and buttons. The watering can "would have been a beautiful thing to hide in, if it had not had so much water in it." A mouse cannot answer Peter because of a pea in its mouth. Peter "thought it best" not to speak to the cat. Mr. McGregor's scarecrow is pictured as an absurd failure. The author is "sorry to say" that Peter was not very well. And so on. Child readers may not get all of the humor (such as the "accident" of Peter's father being put in a pie), but they can hardly miss sensing that Peter is in the hands of a comic providence who will make everything turn out all right. (p. 202)

Potter, like Grahame and Barrie, works in the direction of redomesticating children's literature in contradistinction to such authors as Lewis Carroll, Mark Twain, Robert Louis Stevenson, and Rudyard Kipling who pushed children's literature toward the more nearly savage and tragic. Rabbits and toy bears are accepted by small children as comfortable familiars. Rabbits are easily domesticated and Potter's drawings in **Peter Rabbit**—emphasizing the toddler-like largeness of heads and stomachs and switching from clothes to no clothes—continually suggest that crossing the line from natural rabbit to house rabbit is not difficult. The frontispiece, which forecasts the ending of the story, immediately signals to the child viewer that sympathy as well as humor is directed at Peter. Snug in a very comfortable bed, he has enough spirit (even at the end of his ordeal) to resist his mother's dose of medicine. That we see only his ears and paws makes us laugh both at him and at his exasperated mother. (p. 203)

The Tale of Squirrel Nutkin, the "tale of a tail," Potter's myth of origins as to why squirrels chatter rudely at us, is a good deal more ambitious and complicated than is **Peter**

Rabbit. The tale contains more riddles than Nutkin's rhymes contain: In what sense will it turn out to be a tale about a tail? (we don't find out until the end); why does Nutkin tell riddles?; why is he rude to Old Brown?; why doesn't he gather food?; is he challenging Old Brown's power to "own" the island in terms of controlling who eats and is eaten there?; is Nutkin a figure of fun or free will or pride?; is Old Brown a species of ravenous mortality whom Nutkin instinctively exposes as unable to put a broken egg to rights or drive a sunbeam from a kitchen or quiet the roaring in the wind?; is Nutkin reduced on the final page to an angry loss of language, of the power to control his tale? However we may look at the strange battle between over-voluble Nutkin and the silent, menacing Brown, Potter's arts of economy and suspense drive us on fascinated to the end. (p. 204)

Both *Peter Rabbit* and *Squirrel Nutkin* tell of boys who refuse to participate in the food-gathering work of their clan and who prefer to challenge authority through selfish and somewhat atavistic behavior. The stories seem to disapprove of this behavior. High diction phrases such as "excessively impertinent" suggest that the narrator's view is not from the child's eye but from the adult's. Yet the birds implore Peter to exert himself toward escape, and Nutkin's narrator appears self-consciously to intervene to release Nutkin from the Owl's deadly grip. Nutkin's riddles, moreover, give him a density of language that competes with the fancy vocabulary of grown-ups. Still, at the end, he is stripped of that language just as surely as Peter Rabbit is stripped of his blue coat and buttons. With part of our hearts we applaud, perhaps, the daring of the two lads; they follow their process to remarkable lengths of individuation. But, underneath, the tales are deeply cautionary: The expression of all that boyish energy and challenge rouses a violently retributive response from male power in the world. Life becomes a losing: no dessert, no more happy riddles. The stories bend us through the double bind of much trenchant narrative: Yes, enjoy your adventure while you can, and push it to the farthest, but at the end be prepared to take your medicine, lose your tail, and have nothing left but a stamp of your foot to your impotent shouting, "cuck!" (pp. 206-07)

Charles Frey and John Griffith, "Beatrix Potter," in their The Literary Heritage of Childhood: An Appraisal of Children's Classics in the Western Tradition, *Greenwood Press, 1987, pp. 201-08.*

Johanna (de Leeuw) Reiss

1932-

Dutch-born American author of autobiographical fiction.

Reiss has written two poignant autobiographical novels for middle-grade readers which tell of her experiences as a Jew in Holland both during and after World War II. *The Upstairs Room* (1972) recounts the nearly three years during which young Annie de Leeuw and her older sister Sini were hidden from by the Nazis by sympathetic Dutch Christians Johan Oosterveld and his family. An emotional story of deprivation, stifling seclusion, and agonizing boredom, *The Upstairs Room* is told in a matter-of-fact style which is highlighted by the vivid characterizations of the Oostervelds—heroic in their protection of Annie and her sister, yet displaying very human faults. In *The Journey Back* (1976), Reiss gives young readers an unusual account of her postwar experiences, beginning with the de Leeuw reunion and the family's subsequent readjustment and disillusionment. In both books, Reiss offers her audience an uplifting glimpse into the lives of people victimized by prejudice and saved by the humanitarian efforts of those who befriended them despite the danger to themselves. *The Upstairs Room* was chosen as a Newbery Honor Book in 1973; for the same work, Reiss was awarded the Buxtehuder Bulle in 1976 for creating an outstanding children's book promoting peace.

(See also *Something about the Author,* Vol. 18 and *Contemporary Authors,* Vols. 85-88.)

THE UPSTAIRS ROOM (1972)

I like *The Upstairs Room* by Johanna Reiss. She might have been Anne Frank's young—very young—friend. She was Dutch like her, Jewish like her, precocious like her. Her heroine Annie de Leeuw was 8 years old when, in 1940, the German tanks rolled into her town, Winterswijk. Decrees and injunctions followed. Jew hunts, racial measures, Jewish Star, deportations, general terror. Having found a haven with a kindly family of farmers, Annie goes through war, bewildered. She accepts her condition, but not herself; the suffering, but not the punishment. She remains a rebel to the end, hopeful to the end.

This admirable account is as important in every aspect as the one bequeathed to us by Anne Frank. Annie's ambivalent relationships with her father, her sister, the family that sheltered her, her discovery of concentration camp horror—we laugh with her and cry with her. With her we await D-Day and liberation, sharing her anxieties and her dreams. In the end, we are grateful to fate for having spared a child who can reminisce with neither hate nor bitterness but a kind of gentleness that leaves us with a lump in our throats. (p. 3)

> Elie Wiesel, "The Telling of the War," in The New York Times Book Review, *November 5, 1972, pp. 3, 22.*

Neither as wealthy nor farsighted as Judith Kerr's family who managed to leave Germany and to stay together (*When Hitler Stole Pink Rabbit,* Coward, 1972), the De Leeuws were forced to split up and hide in the homes of Nazi-hating countrymen. The youngest of three daughters, Annie, tells how she and her sister, Sini, hid for more than two years in the upstairs room of the peasant Oosterveld family—burly, capable Johan; his affectionate, nervous wife, Dientje; and Johan's crusty, sentimental mother, Opoe. Sini, in her late teens, worried about her looks and desperately missed dating. Pre-teen Annie talked to imaginary playmates—e.g., a window—and her legs began to atrophy from disuse. She gradually became so withdrawn and passive that even after liberation she cringed from contact with strangers. The sameness of the days was broken only by occasional false hopes, surprise Nazi searches, anti-Nazi conspiracies, and fights: Sini nagging an uncooperative Annie to exercise; Dientje being jealous of Sini; Opoe putting down Dientje's cooking and yelling at Annie for messing up a favorite cap. But the sisters knew they would be miserable if separated, and they and the Oostervelds grew to love each other dearly. Kerr's descriptions of place are more evocative but Reiss' book, written in a matter-of-fact, straightforward style, offers believable characterizations of unremarkable people who survived, if not thrived, and displayed an adaptability and generosity probably beyond their own expectations.

> Diane Gersoni-Stavn, in a review of "The Upstairs Room," in School Library Journal, *Vol. 19, No. 4, December, 1972, p. 62.*

Childhood memories of the Nazi reign of terror and of the war years in Europe have provided the background for a growing body of children's literature. For many readers, *The Diary of Anne Frank* remains the standard, other books being measured against its artless eloquence. Annie was about eight years old when Hitler's troops overran Holland and stripped the Jews of dignity, livelihood, freedom, and life. Annie's father chose for all of them the lesser agony of hiding rather than the certain horror of the concentration camps. Now nearly eleven, Annie, along with one of her grown sisters, must spend the next two and a half years living in secret on the second floor of a Dutch farmhouse. Without passion or heroics, she writes of their hosts, who emerge as stolid, courageous peasants, determined to keep the girls safe. Daily life in the hideaway is glimpsed through the understanding and the concerns of the child—the endless boredom, the long hours spent in bed, the longing for exercise and fresh air, the sisters' little quarrels, the undemanding generosity of their benefactors, and their hairbreadth escape when German soldiers move in and are quartered directly beneath their room. Although the story spans about five years, the style is curiously uniform throughout the book. And although matter-of-fact, understated writing often carries real impact, one wonders whether the short, choppy sentences and constantly repeated Americanisms like " '[b]oy, o boy' "—intended to add childlike verisimilitude and immediacy—would not have been more effective if some development were evident as the narrative progressed. (pp. 50-1)

> *Ethel L. Heins, in a review of "The Upstairs Room," in The Horn Book Magazine, Vol. XLIX, No. 1, February, 1973, pp. 50-1.*

THE JOURNEY BACK (1976)

It is springtime in Holland, 1945. People are planting marigolds. Under the German occupation they had been forbidden to do so. Orange was the color of the royal family.

Annie de Leeuw is free to go outside again after being hidden in one room of a farmhouse for nearly three years. She has just turned 13. Her legs are twisted and spindly from lack of use. Still, she radiates happiness as she walks through the streets of the tiny Dutch village of Usselo with Johan Oosterveld. The victory celebration goes on. The farmers shake their heads in amazement. That Johan is a real hero.

Johanna Reiss's first autobiography, *The Upstairs Room,* was a warm and sometimes eloquent testimonial to the courage of very ordinary people.

In *The Journey Back* Mrs. Reiss tries to capture the essence of the complex and difficult problems of her family—herself, two older sisters and her father—as they try to put their lives back together after the years of separation. Annie tries to tell us something important about how even in peacetime people have been torn apart, turned inward and prevented from communicating with each other. The trouble is that the author did not need 212 pages to do this. The message would have made a terrific last chapter in her first book. The story fails to engage the reader because it is difficult to identify with the heroine. We get a glimpse of Annie's wit when she describes her boorish new stepmother and a sense of her love for the Oostervelds. The true, deep emotions of Annie are hidden from view as her sisters desert her, her stepmother's sharp tongue criticizes and friendships fail to materialize. Annie needed to show us that she will no longer be a victim. The Annie de Leeuw here is a cardboard figure.

> *Bryna J. Fireside, in a review of "The Journey Back," in The New York Times Book Review, January 16, 1977, p. 10.*

Autobiography is an uneasy form of writing. The author with eyes for the effect of other people on herself may be as one-sided as the one so intensely preoccupied with self that she seems almost to be depicting a desert-island castaway. One way of surmounting this problem is to distance self through reminiscence, ordered and selected in the manner of fiction and integrating personal feeling carefully with external event. The story-form so successful in *The Upstairs Room* is repeated in its sequel, *The Journey Back.* . . . The feeling of claustrophobia in the first book, brilliantly sustained without sentiment or exaggeration, is evoked once more in the second, for Annie and Sini, in spite of rigorous seclusion, had enjoyed a warm, developing relationship with farmer Johan and his wife and the old grandmother, and now they find a different kind of restriction in the life they have returned to in Winterswijk. Scarcities of food and other essentials affect fourteen-year-old Annie less than the tiresome weakness of her legs and far worse than this is the fact that Rachel, oldest in the family, has shut herself off in religious obsession, while the stepmother who almost at once takes over the household, house-proud and socially exclusive, offers the girl discipline rather than affection. Hardly disposed to be taught to scorn the rough farming couple who saved her life, Annie is obliged all the same to conform to a new family pattern and her moods and trials are described with a discerning sharpness which emphasises a domestic and emotional aspect of war and its aftermath not often dealt with in books for the young. (p. 3135)

> *Margery Fisher, in a review of "The Journey Back," in Growing Point, Vol. 16, No. 2, July, 1977, pp. 3134-40.*

The circumstances are less dramatic than in *The Upstairs Room,* but the telling, again in short sentences, brief paragraphs, idiosyncratic but very easy to read, is even more assured. These are real people, not playing games or having adventures but coping with life as it came, in those hard days when peace had come and everyone was supposed to live happily ever after.

> *Ann Thwaite, "Occupational Terrors," in The Times Literary Supplement, No. 3931, July 15, 1977, p. 860.*

Joyce Carol Thomas
1938-

Black American author of fiction.

Thomas is the author of novels for young adults which celebrate the indomitability of the human spirit and the importance of community. Compared to such writers as Maya Angelou and Virginia Hamilton for the subject matter and lyricism of her writings, Thomas characteristically invests her works with mysticism and symbolism. Two of her stories, *Marked by Fire* (1982) and *Bright Shadow* (1983), trace the life of protagonist Abyssinia Jackson from her birth in a cotton field to her life as a young woman. Chosen at birth to become a healer and leader of her rural town, Abby survives trials of fire and water as well as personal violence—she is raped at the age of ten—and tragedies to family and friends as she comes of age. In *Bright Shadow,* Abby falls in love with fellow college student Carl Lee Jefferson, who loses his black father and discovers that he has a mother of Cherokee descent; the relationship of Carl and his father is also a focus of *The Golden Pasture* (1986), a story which predates the events of *Bright Shadow* by describing twelve-year-old Carl's experiences with a wild Appaloosa on his grandfather's ranch. Thomas continues her exploration of the lives of these characters in *Water Girl* (1986), which focuses on Abyssinia's teenage daughter, Amber Westbrook; discovering that her mother had given her up for adoption, Amber runs away and, after a mystical experience, realizes her affection for her adoptive home. In all of these works, Thomas presents strong and loving relationships between generations while reflecting her own experiences in Ponca City, Oklahoma, and Tracy, California, the settings for her books. With *Journey* (1988), Thomas moves in a new direction: blending elements of the folktale, the fantasy, and the horror story, *Journey* describes how Meggie, a black teenager blessed at birth by a tarantula, triumphs over evil with the aid of her spider friends and her boyfriend. Thomas, who is also a poet and playwright for adults, is often praised for her skill with characterization and dialogue and is usually considered an author whose works are powerful, evocative, and affirming. *Marked by Fire* received an American Book Award in 1983.

(See also *Contemporary Literary Criticism,* Vol. 35, *Something about the Author,* Vol. 40, *Something about the Author Autobiography Series,* Vol. 7, *Contemporary Authors,* Vols. 113, 116, and *Dictionary of Literary Biography,* Vol. 33: *Afro-American Fiction Writers after 1955.*)

MARKED BY FIRE (1982)

Reminiscent of Maya Angelou's *I Know Why the Caged Bird Sings* in its poetic language, its celebration of Black womanhood and its incident of a child protagonist temporarily struck dumb after being raped, this is a powerful representation of a Black rural Oklahoma community. The story—told in a series of brief concentrated vignettes—is mainly about the women, and it focuses on one special child among them, Abyssinia (Abby) Jackson: the ritual of her birth in the cottonfields with the women all participating in the pain and the joy; her growth as the gifted beautiful darling of the commu-

nity; the horror of her rape at age 10; her recovery and subsequent maturing. As she grows up, Abby learns—through her experiences with near drowning and with fire; through her dreams; and through her struggles with her alter ego, the mad Trembling Sally—that violence can lead to rebirth and to revelation; and that the fierceness of a tornado is as beautiful and necessary as Abby's own singing gift. The lack of a fast-paced narrative line and the mythical overtones may present obstacles to some readers, but many will be moved by the story of a girl who achieves recognition, not through individual career or relationship with a man, but as leader and healer of her community.

Hazel Rochman, in a review of "Marked by Fire," in School Library Journal, *Vol. 28, No. 7, March, 1982, p. 162.*

The title of this novel refers to a scar burned upon the face of Abyssinia Jackson on the day of her birth in 1951. The story is told through a calendar of events Abby shares with her parents and community members over the next 20 years. They work in cotton fields near Ponca City, Okla., where the author, Joyce Carol Thomas, grew up. Bootstrappers all, they face the trials of life with little complaint.

Abyssinia is a mischievous, happy child and an excellent student, and by the time she is 10 she reveals a fine singing voice. Owing to her skill as a storyteller and her services to the community, she is the pride of her friends and elders. But she loses her voice and bitterly questions her religious faith after being raped by a respected church member. . . .

The author thoughtfully records the child's grief, the sorrow of the rapist's wife and the frightened flight of the criminal after his release from prison. It takes time and another kind of suffering before Abyssinia begins to find her way back to the fullness of living. She sees Patience, her mother, who normally displays even more fortitude than her name suggests, ready at one point to commit murder.

Another unforgettable character, Mother Barker, is an important thread in the fabric of the story. A midwife and freethinker and spiritual adviser, she is the person who finally offers Abyssinia a goal in life. . . .

Some of the novel's in-the-nick-of-time rescues were difficult to believe. And I wondered if Mother Barker would have given that rather lengthy prayer while the tornado swooped toward the group huddled in the cotton field. Wouldn't she try to reach the Lord's ear a bit faster? But as the story progressed, I became engrossed, because Miss Thomas writes with admirable simplicity and finds a marvelous fairy tale quality in everyday happenings. Her people move through troubled times but never fail to celebrate sweeter days with church suppers and the joyous sound of gospel singers. Their unifying faith in God is the sturdy hub of the church wheel that encompasses the small congregation. . . .

Marked by Fire concerns human strength and frailty. It is a book about girls and women and the men in their lives. It tells of the best and worst times experienced by a small black community during a 20-year period. Joyce Carol Thomas's first novel is well worth reading.

Thomas, age thirteen, as featured in the Tracy Press *after winning the county spelling bee.*

Alice Childress, in a review of "Marked by Fire," in The New York Times Book Review, *April 18, 1982, p. 38.*

Joyce Carol Thomas captures the flavor of black folk life in Oklahoma. Those of us who associate Oklahoma with oil may be surprised by these characters of the 1960's who still toil in cotton fields whiling away the arduous hours by singing spirituals. The main character is Abyssinia Jackson, . . . who is marked by fire when her mother gives birth to her in a cotton field. This is the classical folk tale about the special child, marked at birth, set aside from all the others and destined to play a special role in the life of Ponca City, Oklahoma, an all black town. (p. 123)

Joyce Carol Thomas has set for herself a very challenging task. It is very difficult to create the atmosphere of a folk tale's never-never land in the contemporary reality of Oklahoma in the 1960's. One sees the heavy influence of Maya Angelou's *I Know Why the Caged Bird Sings,* whose imprimatur of Thomas's book is prominently displayed on both front and back covers. There are obvious influences from Jean Toomer's *Cane,* because of Thomas's use of very brief chapters, some of them only one and a half pages long, and her use of a full blown poetic style. Thomas' book works. (p. 124)

Wendell Wray, in a review of "Marked by Fire," in Best Sellers, *Vol. 42, No. 3, June, 1982, pp. 123-24.*

[Joyce Carol Thomas], best known as a Berkeley, California poet and playwright, has now emerged, with **Marked by Fire,** as a novelist deserving of all the recent critical acclaim this first novel has brought her way.

Marked by Fire is the story of Abyssinia Jackson, born in an Oklahoma cotton field in 1951, who "screamed her way into the world water on one side and fire on the other." While to many people this is the tale of the coming of age, intellectually and emotionally, of a young black woman whose birth was fortuitously witnessed by a collective of women folk who from that day and by that event became, in a sense, her godmothers, it is also the capturing in slow motion of a time and a place when environmental and social horrors were more out front, pouncing, and though complex not masked. In this is call for comparison with events today practically anywhere, rural or urban, Western or other areas where the idealistic spirit of bygone eras is designer cut and donned by ravishers who confuse capture and conviction. . . .

Thomas' poetic tone gives this work what scents give the roses already so pleasing in color. In fact often as not the lyrical here carries the reader beyond concern for fast action. Then too Thomas' short lived interest in playwrighting figures in her fine regard and control of dialogue. . . .

Struck dumb for a period following the rape, Abby regains herself in that company of women which this novel quite frankly is all about. Mother Barker, her mentor, is common sense and proverbial insight. The mad Trembling Sally—devil personified—is the most complex and fascinating of the townspeople. Even as she terrorizes the children with her antics, pursuing them with fire and poison, they yet pity her, knowing misfortune has made her that way. In this she serves Abby as that model not to follow. Trembling Sally is particularly beset with the notion of destroying Abby whom she regards as "just sly, that's all. Got the people fooled." But Abby, as does the author of this haunting tale, struggles free of adverse fate to find her voice and her place as mentor among women.

Dorothy Randall-Tsuruta, in a review of "Marked by Fire," in The Black Scholar, *Vol. 13, Nos. 4-5, Summer, 1982, p. 48.*

BRIGHT SHADOW (1983)

The sequel to Thomas's debut, **Marked by Fire,** reverberates with the lyricism that evoked unanimous critical praise. But readers need steely nerves to stick with the story of horrors visited upon young Abyssinia Jackson and her friends. [Her aunt] Serena's appalling death at the hands of a madman and the tragedy affecting Abby's lover, Carl Lee Jefferson, are crises the girl must surmount if she is to remain sane and hopeful. When Carl Lee disappears, Abby struggles through another time of despair, a battle to "believe in flowers," besieged by weeds. For those who can bear the assaults on their emotions, the novel is a remarkable second journey into the lives and times of the black western community.

A review of "Bright Shadow," in Publishers Weekly, *Vol. 224, No. 18, October 28, 1983, p. 70.*

In this sequel to **Marked By Fire** Abyssinia Jackson is attending college and falling in love with Carl Lee, though the latter displeases her father. Her quiet romance is interrupted by the psychotic murder of her Aunt Serena. Abyssinia, who has had some forebodings about Serena's new husband, is traumatized by her discovery of the mangled body. Her own faith, her parents' and Carl Lee's love and a mysterious cat sustain her through her grief, while her parents come to appreciate Carl Lee's support and concern. Meanwhile, Carl Lee loses his alcoholic father and discovers his Cherokee mother who has been lurking around town since her husband left her at the boy's birth. All this melodrama seems contrived in order to interrupt Abyssinia's romance. The world outside this rural black Oklahoma community never impinges on the characters, making the story seem even less credible. In contrast, Mildred Taylor's *Roll of Thunder, Hear My Cry,* which also focuses on a black family's strength in the face of brutality, seems firmly grounded in reality. But Thomas' story is readable and her sensuously descriptive passages celebrating the physical beauty of the black characters are a nice touch. Those who have read the first book may wish to follow Abyssinia's story despite its artificiality. (pp. 89-90)

Carolyn Caywood, in a review of "Bright Shadow," in School Library Journal, *Vol. 30, No. 5, January, 1984, pp. 89-90.*

[**Bright Shadow**] continues the story of the strong-willed, beautifully-developed character Abyssinia Jackson. . . .

Parts of Abby's life are reminiscent of Maya Angelou's, and Thomas' writing is every bit as eloquent as that found in Angelou's autobiography. Here's a love story that is really worth the reading time. It's also a pleasure to see such a quality book published as an original paperback. (p. 91)

Dick Abrahamson and Barbara Kiefer, "Books Worth Putting on Your Summer Reading List," in English Journal, *Vol. 73, No. 4, April, 1984, pp. 90-2.*

WATER GIRL (1986)

Thomas moves with good effect further into the realm of mysticism in the third book of a compelling saga that began with **Marked by Fire** and continued in **Bright Shadow.** Fifteen-year-old Amber Westbrook is the different one in her family—so intense that the books she reads plunge her into an emotion-laden, stridently expressed concern about inhumanity. But when she finds an old letter written to her parents before she was born, indicating that her natural mother is really her cousin Abyssinia, Amber, outraged and insulted, suffers the same pain she has felt for the persecuted blacks, Jews, Japanese Americans, and American Indians. With a full backpack, she slips away into the wilderness where, in searching for the meaning of her life, she has an experience comparable to an Indian vision quest. The story maintains a nice blend of the mundane and the stuff of legend, and, though the reader never knows why Abyssinia gave up her baby, in the long run it doesn't matter, for Amber comes to realize that "A mother is the one who loves you." Teens who liked the first two books won't be disappointed. (pp. 861-62)

Sally Estes, in a review of "Water Girl," in Booklist, *Vol. 82, No. 12, February 15, 1986, pp. 861-62.*

In essence, this paperback novel is about a black girl in a loving, cultured family who discovers she had been adopted, runs off for several days to brood about it, and comes home having realized that the place where she has been loved and nurtured all her life is home. This plot is padded by irrelevancies, gushy passages, stretched figures of speech, and interruptions (usually in flashback form) that slow the story at exactly the points at which action is crucial.

A review of "Water Girl," in Bulletin of the Center for Children's Books, *Vol. 39, No. 8, April, 1986, p. 160.*

A mood of intensity and anxiety is created by the terse style of writing. The plot is complicated by flashbacks which reveal Amber's character and symbolism which represents her thought processes. Fans of **Marked by Fire,** which relates the story of Amber's birth mother, will want to read this story of an adolescent search for identity.

Ruth Fitzgerald, in a review of "Water Girl," in School Library Journal, *Vol. 32, No. 8, April, 1986, p. 100.*

THE GOLDEN PASTURE (1986)

[**The Golden Pasture** is] a spirited, lyrical tale with a memorable cast of characters. Carl Lee, the son of a Cherokee mother (whom he has never known) and a black father, who is distant and unpredictable, has always felt closest to Gray Jefferson, his paternal grandfather, and often spends summers with him on his ranch, Golden Pasture. An ex-rodeo star, Gray is full of stories and has plenty of time for his grandson. The summer that Carl Lee is 12, Gray tells him he may enter the Boley rodeo if he's prepared. Carl Lee rescues an injured appaloosa and then surprises his grandfather by being able to ride the wild animal. The boy rides the horse in the rodeo, and on his day of triumph the past and the present come together in a stirring event that also reunites father and son. The end to Thomas's story may be no surprise, but readers will stay with her fast-paced tale. Thomas is a weaver

The Thomas family at a birthday party in 1983 "celebrating," Thomas writes, "the fruit of my family-raising years." From left, granddaughter Maria; son-in-law Herman; Thomas, holding granddaughter Crystal; son Roy; daughter Monica, with granddaughter Aresa.

of words, combining just the right ones to create a loving picture of three generations.

> *A review of "The Golden Pasture," in* Publishers Weekly, *Vol. 230, No. 4, July 25, 1986, p. 191.*

Thomas tells with poetic, pictorial simplicity the fable-like "growing up" story of Carlton Lee Jefferson, a 12-year-old boy of black and Cherokee heritage, and of his complex relationships with his black father and grandfather and a beautiful "raindrop" Appaloosa rodeo horse. The contemporary setting is the "Golden Pasture" ranch-land near Ponca City, Oklahoma; Thomas' love for this part of Oklahoma and empathy for her well-delineated characters emerge as she tells a story that has as its heart the idea that "we can't build a fence around our feelings or the people we love." . . . Some readers may feel that the apocalyptic-like climax of the book is somewhat contrived, but the story's tinges of realism and excellent characterization make the book a delight to read.

> *David A. Lindsey, in a review of "The Golden Pasture," in* School Library Journal, *Vol. 32, No. 10, August, 1986, p. 107.*

A symbolic coming of age by gentling a wild horse is at the heart of this story. . . .

Literal readers may be uncomfortable with the action's thunderbolt ending, but it's a good fit for the tone of the story, with its frequent echoes of the legendary and the traditional. The unusual, sometimes lyrical style and memorable characters raise this book well above the level of most conventional horse stories.

> *Janet Hickman, in a review of "The Golden Pasture," in* Language Arts, *Vol. 63, No. 7, November, 1986, p. 733.*

JOURNEY (1988)

This is a strained, disjointed mix of folktale, fantasy and horror. . . . From its opening scene—where in mythic tones the conversations between a wise tarantula and infant Meggie Alexander are recorded—to the closing scene of a spider's web triggering the lesson learned, this is supposed to be the classic search for inner and outer lives by an adolescent. In her inner world, Meggie has music and the faint recollection of a spider's wisdom; this has made her both the seeker and the object of the danger in her town. Young people are disappearing, and when one of Meggie's friends dies, she is determined to root out the evil and destroy it before it gets her.

With a small band of friends Meggie courts the kidnappers and is captured; the purpose behind the kidnapping the reader has known all along. Unfortunately, the grafting of fantasy and mystery onto a standard horror plot simply does not work and the variations in point of view are often confusing.

A review of "Journey," in Publishers Weekly, *Vol. 234, No. 11, September 9, 1988, p. 140.*

Thomas dramatically juxtaposes her story's horror with the joy of existence; and her appealing heroine, fast pace, and SF overtones will absorb readers. The book is distinguished by a lyrical style grounded in the black experience, with a strong resemblance to Virginia Hamilton's distinctive voice. Although there is nothing unusual in her plot, Thomas has neatly integrated into it a celebration of the value of black youth (especially teen-age males) and the message that fear is overcome when we "carry a light in our heart."

A review of "Journey," in Kirkus Reviews, *Vol. LVI, No. 18, September 15, 1988, p. 1410.*

This discordant mixture of fantasy and mystery is composed of too many elements that never blend successfully. The whimsy of the prologue is jarring when juxtaposed with the violence and bitterness of the ensuing chapters. The plot is absurdly illogical and fraught with inconsistencies and coincidence. Characterization is uneven: while Meggie is quite complex, others are caricatures of evil or mere sketches to supplement the cast. The language is artificial with a distorted syntax that becomes intrusive and confusing, and Thomas' imagery, which was so powerfully evocative and genuine in **Marked by Fire,** is overwrought and muddled here. A disappointment to fans of both genres.

Starr LaTronica, in a review of "Journey," in School Library Journal, *Vol. 35, No. 2, October, 1988, p. 165.*

CUMULATIVE INDEX TO AUTHORS

This index lists all author entries in *Children's Literature Review* and includes cross-references to them in other Gale sources. References in the index are identified as follows:

CA: *Contemporary Authors* (original series), Volumes 1-125
CANR: *Contemporary Authors New Revision Series,* Volumes 1-25
CAP: *Contemporary Authors Permanent Series,* Volumes 1-2
CA-R: *Contemporary Authors* (revised editions), Volumes 1-44
CDALB: *Concise Dictionary of American Literary Biography,* Volumes 1-3
CLC: *Contemporary Literary Criticism,* Volumes 1-52
CLR: *Children's Literature Review,* Volumes 1-19
DLB: *Dictionary of Literary Biography,* Volumes 1-78
DLB-DS: *Dictionary of Literary Biography Documentary Series,* Volumes 1-6
DLB-Y: *Dictionary of Literary Biography Yearbook,* Volumes 1980-1987
LC: *Literature Criticism from 1400 to 1800,* Volumes 1-10
NCLC: *Nineteenth-Century Literature Criticism,* Volumes 1-20
SAAS: *Somthing About the Author Autobiography Series,* Volumes 1-7
SATA: *Something about the Author,* Volumes 1-54
TCLC: *Twentieth-Century Literary Criticism,* Volumes 1-31
YABC: *Yesterday's Authors of Books for Children,* Volumes 1-2

Author Index

Author Index

Author Index

CUMULATIVE INDEX TO NATIONALITIES

Nationality Index

CUMULATIVE INDEX TO TITLES

Title Index

Title Index

Title Index

Title Index